Applied Behavior Analysis for Teachers

Tenth Edition

Applied Behavior Analysis for Teachers

Tenth Edition

PAUL A. ALBERTO
Georgia State University

ANNE C. TROUTMAN
University of Memphis

JUDAH B. AXE
Simmons University

Please contact https://support.pearson.com/getsupport/s with any queries on this content.

Cover Image: Oxygen/Moment/Getty Images

Microsoft and/or its respective suppliers make no representations about the suitability of the information contained in the documents and related graphics published as part of the services for any purpose. All such documents and related graphics are provided "as is" without warranty of any kind. Microsoft and/or its respective suppliers hereby disclaim all warranties and conditions with regard to this information, including all warranties and conditions of merchantability, whether express, implied or statutory, fitness for a particular purpose, title and non-infringement. In no event shall Microsoft and/or its respective suppliers be liable for any special, indirect or consequential damages or any damages whatsoever resulting from loss of use, data or profits, whether in an action of contract, negligence or other tortious action, arising out of or in connection with the use or performance of information available from the services.

The documents and related graphics contained herein could include technical inaccuracies or typographical errors. Changes are periodically added to the information herein. Microsoft and/or its respective suppliers may make improvements and/or changes in the product(s) and/or the program(s) described herein at any time. Partial screen shots may be viewed in full within the software version specified.

Microsoft® and Windows® are registered trademarks of the Microsoft Corporation in the U.S.A. and other countries. This book is not sponsored or endorsed by or affiliated with the Microsoft Corporation.

Copyright © 2022, 2018, 2015 by Pearson Education, Inc. All Rights Reserved. Manufactured in the United States of America. This publication is protected by copyright, and permission should be obtained from the publisher prior to any prohibited reproduction, storage in a retrieval system, or transmission in any form or by any means, electronic, mechanical, photocopying, recording, or otherwise. For information regarding permissions, request forms, and the appropriate contacts within the Pearson Education Global Rights and Permissions department, please visit www.pearsoned.com/permissions/.

Acknowledgments of third-party content appear on the appropriate page within the text.

PEARSON, ALWAYS LEARNING, and MYLAB are exclusive trademarks owned by Pearson Education, Inc. or its affiliates in the U.S. and/or other countries.

Unless otherwise indicated herein, any third-party trademarks, logos, or icons that may appear in this work are the property of their respective owners, and any references to third-party trademarks, logos, icons, or other trade dress are for demonstrative or descriptive purposes only. Such references are not intended to imply any sponsorship, endorsement, authorization, or promotion of Pearson's products by the owners of such marks, or any relationship between the owner and Pearson Education, Inc., or its affiliates, authors, licensees, or distributors.

Library of Congress Cataloging-in-Publication Data

Names: Alberto, Paul, author. | Troutman, Anne C., author. | Axe, Judah B., author.
Title: Applied behavior analysis for teachers / Paul A. Alberto, Anne C. Troutman, Judah B. Axe.
Description: Interactive tenth edition. | [Hoboken, New Jersey] : Pearson Education, Inc., [2021] | Includes bibliographical references and indexes. | Summary: "Why do people behave as they do? Why do some people behave in socially approved ways and others in a manner condemned or despised by society? Is it possible to predict what people are likely to do? What can be done to change behavior that is harmful to an individual or destructive to society? In an effort to answer questions like these, human beings have offered explanations ranging from possession by demons to abnormal quantities of chemicals in the brain. Suggested answers have been debated, written about, attacked, and defended for centuries and continue to be offered today. There are good reasons for continuing to investigate human behavior. Information about the development of certain behaviors in human beings may help parents and teachers find the best way of childrearing or teaching. If we know how people are likely to behave under certain conditions, we can decide whether to provide or avoid such conditions. Those of us who are teachers are particularly concerned with changing behavior; that is, in fact, our job. We want to teach our students to do some things and to stop doing others. To understand, predict, and change human behavior, we must first understand how human behavior works. We must answer as completely as possible the "why" questions asked above. Therefore, Alexander Pope's dictum that "the proper study of mankind is man" (perhaps rephrased to "the proper study of humanity is people") needs no other revision; it is as true in the 21st century as it was in the 18th"—Provided by publisher.
Identifiers: LCCN 2020057914 (print) | LCCN 2020057915 (ebook) | ISBN 9780135607558 (paperback) | ISBN 9780135606056 (ebook)
Subjects: LCSH: Behavior modification. | Students—Psychology. | Human behavior.
Classification: LCC LB1060.2 .A43 2021 (print) | LCC LB1060.2 (ebook) | DDC 370.15/28—dc23
LC record available at https://lccn.loc.gov/2020057914
LC ebook record available at https://lccn.loc.gov/2020057915

5 2022

ISBN 10:   0-13-560755-8
ISBN 13: 978-0-13-560755-8

Dedication

This book is dedicated to Dr. Bill Heward, teacher, mentor, colleague, and friend.

About the Author

Judah B. Axe, Ph.D., BCBA-D, LABA, received his M.A. and Ph.D. in Special Education and Applied Behavior Analysis from The Ohio State University. He is currently a Professor of Behavior Analysis, and a former Associate Professor of Special Education, at Simmons University in Boston, MA. He has published over 30 articles and chapters, mostly on his research with children with autism and related disabilities in the areas of verbal behavior, social skills, and challenging behavior. Dr. Axe has served on the editorial boards of five behavior analytic journals and has held leadership positions with the Association for Behavior Analysis International, the Berkshire Association for Behavior Analysis and Therapy, and the Cambridge Center for Behavioral Studies.

Paul A. Alberto After receiving his undergraduate degree from Hunter College in New York City he taught elementary aged students with intellectual disabilities in the south Bronx. While teaching he completed a master's degree in Special Education: mental retardation at Fordham University. He moved to Atlanta and completed his PhD in Special Education: Severe Disabilities at Georgia State University. His professional career in higher education has been at GSU in the Department of Educational Psychology and Special Education. He is the Dean and Regents' Professor in Intellectual Disabilities in the College of Education & Human Development.He is the director of GSU's Bureau for Students with Multiple and Severe Disabilities and the coordinator of the teacher education program in Multiple and Severe Disabilities.

Anne C. Troutman After receiving her undergraduate degree in elementary education from the University of Georgia in 1964 Anne taught elementary grades for 5 years. She completed her Master's Degree in special education from Georgia State University and taught students with behavior disorders in self-contained and resource settings and served as a crisis intervention specialist and special education supervisor. After receiving her Ph.D. from Georgia State in 1977 she taught graduate and undergraduate students in general and special education at The University of Memphis until her retirement in 2009.

Preface

We initially prepared *Applied Behavior Analysis for Teachers* because we wanted a technically sound, systematically organized, but readable and even enjoyable text for our own students. We want students to understand concepts of applied behavior analysis and know how to apply those concepts in classrooms and other settings. We believe, and our belief is supported by research, that applied behavior analysis is the most powerful teaching tool available.

We have not provided a cookbook with step-by-step directions for solving every possible problem an educator might encounter. That would be impossible. What makes working with children and young adults so much fun is that each one is different and no one procedure will be effective for all of them. We want our readers to be able to use the principles to create their own recipes for success. Successful application of the principles requires the full and active participation of a creative educator. Because we believe that applied behavior analysis is so powerful, we stress learning to use it appropriately and ethically. The text is organized in a manner that allows instructors to assign students a behavior-change project concurrently with class discussions and readings. The text progresses from identifying a target behavior to collecting and graphing data, selecting an experimental design, conducting a functional analysis, arranging consequences, arranging antecedents, and promoting the generalization of behavior change. We've tried to provide students with the basics of a teaching technology that will serve as a solid foundation for other methods courses.

New to This Edition

It is incredibly heartening to be updating this text for its 10th edition after the book has inspired the use of applied behavior analysis in classrooms for over 40 years. In this edition, we continued working to make the text readable and user-friendly, as well as including many examples we hope students will enjoy reading. Our examples describe students from preschool through young adulthood functioning at various levels of ability. We describe excellent teachers as well as poor ones. Many of our examples describe the kind of teachers we think we are and hope your students will be—good teachers who learn from their inevitable mistakes. While the basic principles of behavior have not changed over the last 40 years, the robustness of the applications of applied behavior analysis for providing meaningful improvements to the lives of students with and without disabilities has soared. Those advancements are captured in the updates made to this edition.

- **New References, Figures, and Tables.** This edition contains over 850 new references, with Chapters 4, 7, 8, 9, and 10 each containing over 100 new references. There are 21 new figures. Many of these (8) are new examples of single-subject design graphs in Chapter 6. Many (6) are examples of data collection sheets and apps for self-monitoring in Chapter 12. There are 8 new tables. Many of these (3) are applications of positive reinforcement in Chapter 8, including praise and group contingencies.

- **Advancements in Technology.** In this edition, we replaced examples of overhead projectors, dictionaries, file cabinets, and digital cameras, with smartboards, internet searches, digital files, smartphones, and apps. There are around 24 such changes with respect to technology. Many of these (12) are examples of devices and apps used for data collection (Chapter 4) and self-monitoring (Chapter 12).

- **Positive and Sensitive Language.** Some of the language and examples in previous editions reflected the culture of prior decades, which used language we now consider negative and biased. Some of the negativity was related to how others viewed behaviorism and applied behavior analysis. Although those negative opinions remain, we believe the culture is more accepting of behavioral approaches to education and other societal endeavors compared to past decades. We changed phrases such as "students with behavior problems" to "students who exhibit challenging behaviors." We removed references to "uninformed people" and "useless procedures." We removed examples of a teacher "tearing her hair out" and a person squirting a dog in the face with hot sauce. We removed reference to a student who was always late to class or never showed up. There are around 30 such updates in this edition that reflect more positivity and sensitivity to diversity, equity, and inclusion. Most of these (19) are in Chapters 2 and 13 as they discuss ethical considerations in applied behavior analysis.

- **Ethical Guidelines.** There were several expansions and updates to ethical considerations when using applied behavior analysis. Two major documents were discussed: the ethical code of the Behavior Analysis Certification Board® (Chapter 2) and the position statement on restraint and seclusion from the Association for Behavior Analysis International (Chapter 9). Ethical considerations were also discussed in terms of single-subject design (Chapter 6) and the need for training in conducting functional analyses (Chapter 7) and administering restraints (Chapter 9).

- **New Terminology.** To reflect updates in the literature on applied behavior analysis, there are around 20 new terms or modified definitions of terms. New terms include motivating operations (Chapters 1 and 7), whole-interval DRO and momentary DRO (Chapter 9), resurgence in FCT (Chapter 9), behavioral momentum theory (Chapter 9), video prompting (Chapter 10), and self-graphing (Chapter 12). Changes to terminology include changing "behavior modification" to "applied behavior analysis" (Chapters 2 and 13), "controlled presentation" to "trial-by-trial recording" (Chapter 4), "changing conditions design" to "multiple treatments design" (Chapter 6), "behavior" to "challenging behavior" (when appropriate; Chapter 7), "reinforcer sampling" to "preference assessment" (Chapter 8), "multiple stimulus presentation" to "multiple stimulus without replacement (MSWO) preference assessment" (Chapter 8), "decreasing assistance" to "most-to-least prompting" (Chapter 10), "increasing assistance" to "least-to-most prompting" (Chapter 10), and "self-recording" to "self-monitoring" (Chapter 12). Finally, there were clarifications and modifications to the definitions and descriptions of positive reinforcement (Chapter 1), negative reinforcement (Chapter 1), social validity (Chapters 2 and 6), extinction (Chapter 9), discriminative stimulus (Chapter 10), and generalization (Chapter 11).
- **Vignettes.** Throughout the text, vignettes involving Professor Grundy, his students, and colleagues have been updated to reflect changes in the field.

In addition, Chapters 8 and 9 contain seven instances of making stronger connections between explanations of concepts and vignettes. This helps exemplify the concepts in the vignettes and clarify the purposes of the vignettes.

Key Content Updates by Chapter

- **Chapter 3:** Put the components of behavioral objectives in more behavioral language and provided updated definitions of "on-task behavior."
- **Chapter 4:** Updated comparisons between measurement systems and methods of measuring interobserver agreement.
- **Chapters 5 and 6:** Emphasized "x-axis" and "y-axis" over "abscissa" and "ordinate" and updated the terminology and guidelines for determining experimental control with the alternating treatments design.
- **Chapter 7:** Expanded the description of the scatter plot, added guidelines for ABC data collection, updated the comparisons of functional behavior assessments and functional analyses of challenging behavior, expanded the descriptions of conditions in a function analysis, introduced a "multiple functions" category of function-based interventions, added the "check in/check out" and "daily report card" procedures of Positive Behavior Support (PBS), and updated examples of Schoolwide PBS.
- **Chapter 8:** Discussed the method of simply applying contingencies rather than first stating the contingencies, added preference assessment methods (pictorial, video, activity, free operant), updated guidelines on using token reinforcement, expanded on the Good Behavior Game, and introduced teaching at the "instruction level" versus the "frustration level."
- **Chapter 9:** Decreased examples of using punishment, added diagrams depicting differential reinforcement procedures, added information on legislation regarding physical restraint, added a table on how to implement extinction given different functions of challenging behavior, and cautioned against implementing extinction alone.
- **Chapter 11:** Updated the conceptualization of "train and hope," highlighted the importance of conditioning attention as a reinforcer, introduced the Verbal Behavior Milestones Assessment and Placement Program (VB-MAPP), and expanded on the examples and applications of lag schedules of reinforcement.
- **Chapter 12:** Added a flow chart of steps for implementing self-monitoring and emphasized the need to teach students how to self-manage.

These changes provide up-to-date, cutting-edge definitions and examples in applied behavior analysis to maximize the effectiveness of teachers in classrooms.

Pedagogical Features:

To facilitate learning, this edition includes **Discussion Questions** at the end of each chapter, **explanatory asides** that clarify key points or make inter-textual connections, and **vignettes** to provide opportunities to see concepts in action.

Discussion Questions

1. Write a short letter home to the parents or guardians of the students with whom you will be working this year. Describe your procedures (based on the principles of applied behavior analysis described in Chapter 1) without using any terminology likely to upset the parents.

2. One of your colleagues has cornered you in your classroom after school. She has heard that you are using "behavior modification" with your students and thinks that you are inhumane, coercive, and unethical. What will you say to her?

Guidelines for the use of aversive and exclusionary procedures will be provided in Chapter 9.

A belief that behavior is lawful does not imply that human beings are not free to choose what they will do.

Watch 'Em Like A . . .

Mr. Hawk was a teacher in a short-term rehabilitation class for 10- to 13-year-old students with serious behavior problems. His job was to get his students' academic skills as well as their behavior up to snuff and very quickly reintegrate them into general education classrooms. He provided behavioral consultation to the classroom teachers and continued help with academics as necessary. Some of his students remained with him full time for several months; others began attending some general education classes within a week. Mr. Hawk used a token reinforcement system (see the discussion beginning on page 219 about token reinforcers) and prided himself on finding unusual, but effective, activity reinforcers simply by listening to students, asking what they wanted to do, or watching what they chose to do when they had free time.

Some of his students, for example, used their points to spend 10 minutes sitting on Mr. Hawk's motorcycle, safely parked in the faculty parking lot with the ignition key in Mr. Hawk's pocket. Some students helped the building engineer empty trash; others played with games or toys in the classroom. One boy, who showed some characteristics of autism, preferred to straighten and reorganize various manipulatives and teaching materials; Mr. Hawk was going to be sorry to lose Richard.

One day Mr. Hawk got a new student. In an effort to give him some immediate academic success and to provide an opportunity for reinforcement, Mr. Hawk gave Aidan a math assignment on the computer. The format was colorful, highly interactive, and entertaining. Mr. Hawk chose a level that he knew would be fairly easy for the boy. After a few minutes, Aidan blurted out, "Wow, this is baaad!" whereupon the young man at the next computer leaned over toward him and said softly, "Careful, man, you let him find out you like something, next thing you know, you'll be earnin' it doin' something you don't like."

Burrhus Teaches the Professor

Professor Grundy was sitting on the sofa reading the newspaper. Burrhus padded into the room, lumbered over to Grundy, and stuck his huge head under the professor's arm between the professor and the paper. "Look, Minerva," said the professor, scratching Burrhus on the head, "he likes me. Good boy. Good boy. Aren't you a good boy?" He continued to scratch; Burrhus remained close to the professor, occasionally inserting his head and being petted and praised. Later that day the professor returned from the grocery store. Burrhus lumbered over, stuck his head between the professor and the grocery bag and precipitated the bag to the floor. "He didn't mean to," stated the professor. "He was just glad to see me. Weren't you boy?" he crooned, stepping over the broken eggs that Mrs. Grundy was cleaning up. "Want to go chase your ball?" After dinner Grundy retired to his study to complete work on an important manuscript. Burrhus accompanied him and settled in a place close to the professor's feet. All went well until Burrhus got up, inserted his head between the professor and the computer screen, drooled into the keyboard, and smeared the screen. Grundy leaped up and shouted, "Minerva, call this dog! He's driving me crazy! He's going to have to learn to leave me alone when I'm working."

"Oliver," said Mrs. Grundy tartly, "you have been reinforcing him with your attention for nudging you all day. Now you're complaining. Do you expect him to know you're working? I talked to Miss Oattis this morning. She's teaching a dog obedience class starting next week. I think the two of you need to go."

Pearson eText, Learning Management System (LMS)-Compatible Assessment Bank, and Other Instructor Resources

Pearson eText

The Pearson eText is a simple-to-use, mobile-optimized, personalized reading experience. It allows you to easily highlight, take notes, and review key vocabulary all in one place—even when offline. Seamlessly integrated videos and other rich media will engage you and give you access to the help you need, when you need it. To gain access or to sign in to your Pearson eText, visit: https://www.pearson.com/pearson-etext. Features include:

- **Video Examples** Each chapter includes *Video Examples* that illustrate principles or concepts aligned pedagogically with the chapter.
- **Interactive Glossary** All key terms in the eText are bolded and provide instant access to full glossary definitions, allowing you to quickly build your professional vocabulary as you are reading.

LMS-Compatible Assessment Bank

With this new edition, all assessment types—quizzes, application exercises, and chapter tests— are included in LMS-compatible banks for the following learning management systems: Blackboard (9780137322121), Canvas (9780137322169), D2L (9780137322176), and Moodle (9780137322152). These packaged files allow maximum flexibility to instructors when it comes to importing, assigning, and grading. Assessment types include:

- **Learning Outcome Quizzes** Each chapter learning outcome is the focus of a Learning Outcome Quiz that is available for instructors to assign through their Learning Management System. Learning outcomes identify chapter content that is most important for learners and serve as the organizational framework for each chapter. The higher-order, multiple choice questions in each quiz will measure your understanding of chapter content, guide the expectations for your learning, and inform the accountability and the applications of your new knowledge. When used in the LMS environment, these multiple choice questions are automatically graded and include feedback for the correct answer and for each distractor to help guide students' learning.
- **Application Exercises** Each chapter provides opportunities to apply what you have learned through Application Exercises. These exercises are usually short-answer format and can be based on Pearson eText Video Examples, written cases, or scenarios modeled by pedagogical text features. When used in the LMS environment, a model response written by experts is provided after you submit the exercise. This feedback helps guide your learning and can assist your instructor in grading.
- **Chapter Tests** Suggested test items are provided for each chapter and include questions in various formats: true/false, multiple choice, and short answer/essay. When used in the LMS environment, true/false and multiple choice questions are automatically graded, and model responses are provided for short answer and essay questions.

Instructor's Manual (9780135606230)

The Instructor's Manual is provided as a Word document and includes resources to assist professors in planning their course. If you do not use a Learning Management System, or if you prefer to administer assessments on paper, you can copy and paste items from the instructor's manual to create your own quizzes, assignments, or tests.

PowerPoint® Slides (9780135606100)

PowerPoint® slides are provided for each chapter and highlight key concepts and summarize the content of the text to make it more meaningful for students.

Note: All instructor resources—LMS-compatible assessment bank, instructor's manual, and PowerPoint slides are available for download at www.pearsonhighered.com. Use one of the following methods:

- From the main page, use the search function to look up the lead author (i.e., Alberto, Troutman, & Axe) or the title (i.e., Applied Behavior Analysis for Teachers). Select the desired search result, then access the "Resources" tab to view and download all available resources.
- From the main page, use the search function to look up the ISBN (provided above) of the specific instructor resource you would like to download. When the product page loads, access the "Downloadable Resources" tab.

Acknowledgments

We would like to thank all the people who helped us in the process of producing **Applied Behavior Analysis for Teachers, Tenth Edition**, including all the professionals at Pearson with whom we have worked. Thanks to Rebecca Fox-Gieg, Curtis Vickers, Janelle Rogers, Karthik Orukaimani, and Kevin Davis. Thank you to Sarah Frampton for preparing the online learning materials. Thank you to Ellie, Maren, and Nora Axe for your love and support. We appreciate the suggestions of those who have reviewed the text.

We continue to appreciate the users of the text. We often hear from people who first read the book as undergraduates and who now assign it to students in their own university classes. We are honored to be partners in the development of those who teach.

Brief Contents

1 Roots of Applied Behavior Analysis 1
2 Responsible Use of Applied Behavior Analysis Procedures 21
3 Preparing Behavioral Objectives 40
4 Procedures for Collecting Data 63
5 Graphing Data 101
6 Single-Subject Designs 118
7 Determining the Function of Behavior 164
8 Arranging Consequences That Increase Behavior 203
9 Arranging Consequences That Decrease Behavior 250
10 Differential Reinforcement: Antecedent Control and Shaping 289
11 Providing for Generalization of Behavior Change 325
12 Teaching Students to Manage Their Own Behavior 348
13 Putting It All Together 368

Glossary 388
References 392
Name Index 431
Subject Index 445

Contents

About the Author   vi
Preface   vii
Acknowledgments   xi

1   Roots of Applied Behavior Analysis   1

Learning Outcomes   1
Chapter Outline   1
The Usefulness of Explanations   2
     Biophysical Explanations   2
     Biochemical Explanations   3
     The Usefulness of Biophysical and Biochemical Explanations   4
Developmental Explanations   5
     Psychoanalytic Theory   6
     A Stage Theory of Cognitive Development   7
     The Usefulness of Developmental Explanations   7
Cognitive Explanations   8
     The Usefulness of Cognitive Explanations   9
Behavioral Explanations   10
     Positive Reinforcement   11
     Negative Reinforcement   11
     Punishment   11
     Extinction   12
     Antecedent Control   12
     Other Learning Principles   13
     The Task of the Behaviorist   14
     The Usefulness of Behavioral Explanations   14
Historical Development of Behaviorism   15
     Historical Precedents   16
     Psychological Antecedents   16
Summary   19 • Discussion Questions   20

2   Responsible Use of Applied Behavior Analysis Procedures   21

Learning Outcomes   21
Chapter Outline   21
Concerns About Applied Behavior Analysis   22
     Confusion with Other Procedures   23
     Reaction to Controversial Procedures   24
     Concerns About Coercion   25
Ethical Use of Applied Behavior Analysis Procedures   26
     Treatment by a Competent Behavior Analyst (Van Houten et al., 1988)   28
     Services Whose Overriding Goal is Personal Welfare (Van Houten et al., 1988)   29
     Behavioral Assessment and Ongoing Evaluation (Van Houten et al., 1988)   31
     A Therapeutic Environment (Van Houten et al., 1988)   31
     Programs That Teach Functional Skills (Van Houten et al., 1988)   33
     The Most Effective Treatment Procedures Available (Van Houten et al., 1988)   34
Accountability   35
Theory or Recipes?   38
Summary   39 • Discussion Questions   39

3   Preparing Behavioral Objectives   40

Learning Outcomes   40
Chapter Outline   40
Definition and Purpose   41
     Pinpointing Behavior   43
Educational Goals   44
     Establishing Goals   44
Components of a Behavioral Objective   46
     State the Learner   46
     State the Target Behavior   46
     State the Conditions of Intervention   49
     State Criteria for Acceptable Performance   50
Format for a Behavioral Objective   52
Expanding the Scope of the Basic Behavioral Objective   54
     Hierarchy of Response Competence   55
     Hierarchy of Levels of Learning   57
     Learning Levels for the Learner with Limitations   59
Behavioral Objectives and the IEP   60
Summary   62 • Discussion Questions   62

4   Procedures for Collecting Data   63

Learning Outcomes   63
Chapter Outline   63
A Rationale   64
Choosing a System   64
Anecdotal Reports   68
     Structuring an Anecdotal Report   69
Permanent Product Recording   71
Observational Recording Systems   73
     Event Recording   73
     Interval Recording and Time Sampling   81
Duration and Latency Recording   91
     Duration Recording   91
     Latency Recording   92

xiv Contents

How Can All This Be Done?	93	Application	146
Technology for Data Collection	94	Advantages and Disadvantages	147
Summary of Data Collection Systems	96	Multiple Treatments Design	147
Reliability	96	Implementation	148
Factors That May Affect Data Collection and Interobserver Agreement	98	Graphic Display	150
		Application	150
Summary 99 • Discussion Questions 99		Advantages and Disadvantages	153
		Evaluating Single-Subject Designs	154

5 Graphing Data 101

Learning Outcomes	101
Chapter Outline	101
The Simple Line Graph	102
Basic Elements of the Line Graph	102
Transferring Data to a Graph	104
Additional Graphing Conventions	113
Cumulative Graphs	114
Bar Graphs	115

Summary 117 • Discussion Questions 117

Analysis of Results	154
Visual Analysis of Graphs	155
Ethical Considerations with Single-Subject Design	158
Action Research and Single-Subject Design Tools	159
Components of Action Research	159
Single-Subject Design Parallels and Contributions	160
Example of an Action Research Study	160

Summary 161 • Discussion Questions 162

6 Single-Subject Designs 118

Learning Outcomes	118
Chapter Outline	118
Variables and Functional Relations	120
Basic Categories of Designs	120
Single-Subject Designs	122
Baseline Measures	122
Intervention Measures	124
Experimental Control	124
AB Design	125
Implementation	125
Graphic Display	125
Application	125
Advantages and Disadvantages	127
Reversal Design	127
Implementation	127
Graphic Display	129
Design Variations	129
Application	130
Advantages and a Disadvantage	131
Changing Criterion Design	131
Implementation	132
Graphic Display	133
Application	133
Advantage and Disadvantage	136
Multiple Baseline Design	136
Implementation	136
Graphic Display	138
Application	138
Advantages and Disadvantages	142
Alternating Treatments Design	143
Implementation	143
Graphic Display	144

7 Determining the Function of Behavior 164

Learning Outcomes	164
Chapter Outline	164
Behavior and Its Function	165
The Behavior Support Plan	170
Functional Behavior Assessment and Behavior Support Plan	173
Settings for Conducting Functional Analysis	185
Brief Functional Analysis	186
Positive Behavior Support	197

Summary 201 • Discussion Questions 201

8 Arranging Consequences That Increase Behavior 203

Learning Outcomes	203
Chapter Outline	203
Positive Reinforcement	205
Choosing Effective Reinforcers	206
Making Reinforcers Contingent	211
Making Reinforcement Immediate	211
Types of Reinforcers	211
Contracting	228
Variations in Administration of Reinforcers	231
Group Contingencies and Peer Mediation	235
Schedules of Reinforcement	237
Negative Reinforcement	243
Inadvertent Use	243
Appropriate Means of Escape	245
Using Negative Reinforcement for Instruction	246
Natural Reinforcement	247

Summary 248 • Discussion Questions 248

9 Arranging Consequences That Decrease Behavior — 250

Learning Outcomes — 250
Chapter Outline — 250
Procedural Alternatives for Behavior Reduction — 252
Level I: Reinforcement-Based Strategies — 253
    Differential Reinforcement of Lower Rates of Behavior — 253
    Differential Reinforcement of Other Behaviors — 255
    Differential Reinforcement of Alternative Behavior and Incompatible Behavior — 258
    Noncontingent Reinforcement — 261
Level II: Extinction — 264
    Delayed Reaction — 265
    Increased Rate — 266
    Controlling Attention — 266
    Extinction-Induced Aggression — 267
    Spontaneous Recovery — 268
    Imitation or Reinforcement by Others — 268
    Limited Generalizability — 269
    Sensory Extinction — 269
Punishment — 271
Level III: Removal of Desirable Stimuli — 271
    Response-Cost Procedures — 271
    Time-Out Procedures — 274
Level IV: Presentation of Aversive Stimuli — 277
    Types of Aversive Stimuli — 279
    Disadvantages of Aversive Stimuli — 282
Overcorrection — 284
    Restitutional Overcorrection — 284
    Positive-Practice Overcorrection — 284
Summary 286 • Discussion Questions 286

10 Differential Reinforcement: Antecedent Control and Shaping — 289

Learning Outcomes — 289
Chapter Outline — 289
Antecedent Influences on Behavior — 290
Differential Reinforcement for Stimulus Control — 292
Principles of Discrimination — 292
    Discrimination Training — 293
Prompts — 295
    Rules as Verbal Prompts — 295
    Instructions as Verbal Prompts — 296
    Hints as Verbal Prompts — 296
    Self-Operated Verbal Prompts — 296
    Visual Prompts — 297
    Modeling — 300
    Physical Guidance — 302
    Other Tactile Prompts — 303
Fading — 303
    Most-to-Least Prompting — 303
    Graduated Guidance — 305
    Time Delay — 305
    Least-to-Most Prompting — 307
    Effectiveness of Methods for Fading Prompts — 308
    Effective Prompting — 309
Teaching Complex Behaviors — 310
    Task Analysis — 310
    Chaining — 313
    How to Manage Teaching Chains — 317
Differential Reinforcement for Shaping — 318
Summary 324 • Discussion Questions 324

11 Providing for Generalization of Behavior Change — 325

Learning Outcomes — 325
Chapter Outline — 325
Generalization — 327
    Stimulus Generalization — 328
    Maintenance — 328
    Response Generalization — 329
Programming for Generalization — 329
    Train and Hope — 331
    Sequentially Modify — 332
    Introduce to Natural Maintaining Contingencies — 333
    Train Sufficient Exemplars — 336
    Train Loosely — 339
    Use Indiscriminable Contingencies — 341
    Program Common Stimuli — 342
    Mediate Generalization and Train to Generalize — 345
Summary 346 • Discussion Questions 347

12 Teaching Students to Manage Their Own Behavior — 348

Learning Outcomes — 348
Chapter Outline — 348
A Common Experience — 350
Preparing Students to Manage Their Own Behavior — 351
    Goal Setting — 352
    Self-Monitoring — 354
    Self-Evaluation — 357
    Self-Reinforcement — 359
    Self-Punishment — 360
    Self-Instruction — 360
Self-Management for Special Populations — 364

Self-Management for Learners with Severe
   Disabilities ... 364
Self-Management for Learners with Mild Disabilities ... 365
Self-Management for Students at Risk ... 367
Summary 367 • Discussion Questions 367

13 Putting It All Together ... 368

Learning Outcomes ... 368
Chapter Outline ... 368
Stimulus Control ... 368
   Physical Arrangement ... 369
   Time Structure ... 370
   Instructional Structure ... 371
   Verbal Structure ... 372
   Specificity ... 372
   Economy ... 372
   Consequences ... 373
   Rules and Procedures ... 373
   Teacher Characteristics ... 374
A Look into Learning Environments ... 374
   Remember Miss Harper? ... 374
   Ms. Mitchell's Self-Contained Class ... 376
   Ms. Washington's Resource Room ... 378
   Who Needs ABA? ... 380
   A Schoolwide Positive Behavior Support System ... 382
   Mr. Boyd's Math Classes ... 383
   Ms. Michaels Has It in the Bag ... 385
Summary 387 • Discussion Idea 387

Glossary 388

References 392

Name Index 431

Subject Index 445

Chapter 1
Roots of Applied Behavior Analysis

Learning Outcomes

1.1 Describe the limitations and potential usefulness of biophysical and biochemical explanations.

1.2 State what can be learned from developmental explanations.

1.3 Explain the limitations of cognitive explanations of behavior.

1.4 Describe the usefulness of behavioral explanations and define positive reinforcement, negative reinforcement, punishment, extinction, and antecedent control.

1.5 Describe the origins of a behavioral explanation for behavior.

CHAPTER OUTLINE

The Usefulness of Explanations
    Biophysical Explanations
    Biochemical Explanations
    The Usefulness of Biophysical and Biochemical Explanations

Developmental Explanations
    Psychoanalytic Theory
    A Stage Theory of Cognitive Development
    The Usefulness of Developmental Explanations

Cognitive Explanations
    The Usefulness of Cognitive Explanations

Behavioral Explanations
    Positive Reinforcement
    Negative Reinforcement
    Punishment
    Extinction
    Antecedent Control
    Other Learning Principles
    The Task of the Behaviorist
    The Usefulness of Behavioral Explanations

Historical Development of Behaviorism
    Historical Precedents
    Psychological Antecedents

Summary

Why do people behave as they do? Why do some people behave in socially approved ways and others in a manner condemned or despised by society? Is it possible to predict what people are likely to do? What can be done to change behavior that is harmful to an individual or destructive to society?

In an effort to answer questions like these, human beings have offered explanations ranging from possession by demons to abnormal quantities of chemicals in the brain. Suggested answers have been debated, written about, attacked, and defended for centuries and continue to be offered today. There are good reasons for continuing to investigate human behavior. Information about the development of certain behaviors in human beings may help parents and teachers find the best way of childrearing or teaching. If we know how people are likely to behave under certain conditions, we can decide whether to provide or avoid such conditions. Those of us who are teachers are particularly concerned with changing behavior; that is, in fact, our job. We want to teach our students to do some things and to stop doing others.

To understand, predict, and change human behavior, we must first understand how human behavior works. We must answer as completely as possible the "why" questions asked above. Therefore, Alexander Pope's dictum that "the proper study of mankind is man" (perhaps rephrased to "the proper study of humanity is people") needs no other revision; it is as true in the 21st century as it was in the 18th.

In this chapter we consider the requirements for meaningful and useful explanations of human behavior. We then describe several interpretations of human behavior that have influenced large numbers of practitioners, including teachers. The discussion traces the historical development of a way to understand and predict human behavior called **applied behavior analysis**.

The Usefulness of Explanations

Learning Outcome 1.1   Describe the limitations and potential usefulness of biophysical and biochemical explanations.

> A useful theory has inclusiveness, verifiability, predictive utility, and parsimony.

If a way of explaining behavior is to be useful for the practitioner, it must meet four requirements. First, it should be *inclusive*. It must account for a substantial quantity of behavior. An explanation has limited usefulness if it fails to account for the bulk of human behavior and thus makes prediction and systematic change of behavior impossible. Second, an explanation must be *verifiable*; that is, we should be able to test in some way that it does account for behavior. Third, the explanation should have *predictive utility*. It should provide reliable answers about what people are likely to do under certain circumstances, thereby giving the practitioner the opportunity to change behavior by changing conditions. Fourth, it should be *parsimonious*. A parsimonious explanation is the simplest one that will account for observed phenomena. Parsimony does not guarantee correctness (Mahoney, 1974) because the simplest explanation may not always be the correct one, but it prevents our being so imaginative as to lose touch with the reality of observed data. When the bathroom light fails to operate at 3 a.m., one should check the bulb before calling the electric company to report a blackout. There may be a blackout, but the parsimonious explanation is a burned-out bulb. In examining some of the theories developed to explain human behavior, we shall evaluate each explanation for its inclusiveness, verifiability, predictive utility, and parsimony.

Biophysical Explanations

> Some theorists contend that human behavior is controlled by physical influences.

Since physicians of ancient Greece first proposed that human behavior was the result of interactions among four bodily fluids or "humors"—blood, phlegm, yellow bile (choler), and black bile (melancholy)—theorists have searched for explanations

> ### Professor Grundy Traces the Cause
>
> Having observed an undergraduate student's behavior for some time, Professor Grundy noticed that the student was always looking down in his notebook and doodling. Grundy couldn't tell if DeWayne was paying attention or not and grew quite concerned. Because the professor was certain his dynamic, meaningful lectures were not related to this behavior, he decided to investigate the matter. He paid a visit to the high school attended by the student and located his 10th-grade English teacher, Ms. Marner. "Yes, DeWayne was always doodling in high school," said Ms. Marner. "He must have picked that up in middle school."
>
> Professor Grundy then went to visit the middle school. "You know," said the guidance counselor, "a lot of our kids do that. Their elementary school just doesn't curb that behavior in time." At the elementary school, Professor Grundy talked to the principal. "DeWayne was doing that since day one. I'm pretty sure his mom is an artist—he probably started it by watching her."
>
> Professor Grundy, sure that he would at last find the answer, went to talk to DeWayne's mother. "I'll tell you," said DeWayne's mother, "he takes after his father's side of the family. They're all a bunch of doodlers."

for human behavior within the physical structure of the body. Such theories have included those based on genetic or hereditary factors, those that emphasize biochemical influences, and those that suggest aberrant behavior is caused by some damage to the brain. The following anecdote indicates a belief in hereditary influences on behavior.

GENETIC AND HEREDITARY EFFECTS DeWayne's mother explained his doodling behavior by referring to hereditary influences. Could she have been right? The effects of heredity on human behavior, both typical and atypical, have been investigated extensively. There is little question that intellectual disabilities, resulting in significant deficits in a wide range of behaviors, is sometimes associated with chromosomal abnormalities or with the inheritance of recessive genes. Evidence indicates that other behavioral characteristics have some genetic or hereditary basis as well. It is generally accepted that persons with autism have abnormalities in brain development and neurochemistry and that there may be genetic factors related to this disorder (Malik et al., 2019; Woodbury-Smith & Scherer, 2018). Many emotional and behavior disorders, such as anxiety disorder, depression, schizophrenia, oppositional defiant disorder, and conduct disorder, appear to have some genetic origin (Burke & Romano-Verthelyi, 2018; Salvatore & Dick, 2018). Attention deficit disorder and attention deficit hyperactivity disorder also appear to be genetically related (Faraone & Larsson, 2019), as do some learning disabilities (Mazzocco et al., 2016; Petrill, 2014).

When DeWayne's mother explained her son's behavior to Professor Grundy, her claim that DeWayne takes after his father's family may have involved a degree of truth. It is possible that certain genetic characteristics may increase the probability of certain behavioral characteristics.

Biological Explanations
Pearson eText
Video Example 1.1
In this video, a speech and language pathologist explains how a nativist theory of language emphasizes the role of biology in behavior expression. Notice how the educator draws connections between the brain's functioning and a computer, with particular inputs and outputs. What are some limitations of this approach?

Biochemical Explanations

Some researchers have suggested that certain behaviors may result from excesses or deficiencies of various substances found in the body. These chemical substances are labeled differently from those hypothesized by the ancient Greeks but are often held responsible for similar disturbances of behavior.

Biochemical abnormalities have been found in some children with serious disturbances of behavior. Investigation of such factors, however, has established only that biochemical abnormalities exist, not that they cause the disorder. Other behavior disturbances characterized as hyperactivity, learning disability, or intellectual disability

Some children with disabilities show biochemical abnormalities.

> ### Professor Grundy Learns to Think in Circles
>
> Professor Grundy, as one of his instructional duties, visited student teachers. On his first trip to evaluate Ms. Harper in a primary resource room, he observed that one student, Ralph, wandered continuously about the room. Curious about such behavior, because the other students remained seated, Professor Grundy inquired, "Why is Ralph wandering around the room? Why doesn't he sit down like the others?" Ms. Harper was aghast at such ignorance on the part of a professor.
>
> "Why, Ralph is hyperactive, Professor Grundy. That's why he never stays in his seat."
>
> "Ah," replied the professor. "That's very interesting. How do you know he's hyperactive?"
>
> With barely concealed disdain, Ms. Harper hissed, "Professor, I know he's hyperactive because he won't stay in his seat."
>
> After observing the class for a few more minutes, he noticed Ms. Harper and the supervising teacher whispering and casting glances in his direction. Professor Grundy once again attracted Ms. Harper's attention. "What," he inquired politely, "causes Ralph's hyperactivity?"
>
> The disdain was no longer concealed. "Professor," answered Ms. Harper, "hyperactivity is caused by brain damage."
>
> "Indeed," responded the professor, "and you know he has brain damage because ..."
>
> "Of course I know he has brain damage, Professor. He's hyperactive, isn't he?"

have been linked to biophysical factors such as hypoglycemia, malnutrition, and allergic reactions. It is often suggested that biochemical or other physiological factors may, along with other influences, result in damage to the brain or central nervous system.

BRAIN DAMAGE The circular reasoning illustrated by Ms. Harper is, unfortunately, not uncommon. Many professionals explain a great deal of students' inappropriate behavior similarly. The notion that certain kinds of behavior result from brain damage has its roots in the work of Goldstein (1939), who studied soldiers having head injuries during World War I. He identified certain behavioral characteristics, including distractibility, perceptual confusion, and hyperactivity. Observing similar characteristics in some children with cognitive disabilities, some professionals concluded that the children must also be brain injured and that the brain injury was the cause of the behavior. This led to the identification of a hyperkinetic behavior syndrome (Strauss & Lehtinen, 1947), assumed to be the result of minimal brain dysfunction in persons who had no history of brain injury. This syndrome included such characteristics as hyperactivity, distractibility, impulsivity, short attention span, emotional lability (changeability), perceptual problems, and clumsiness. Large numbers of children with these characteristics are currently being diagnosed with attention deficit disorder (ADD) or attention deficit hyperactivity disorder (ADHD) (American Psychiatric Association, 2013), but there is little empirical support for using the possibility of brain injury to account for problem behavior in all children who show such behavioral characteristics.

> Hyperactivity is not necessarily caused by brain dysfunction.

Many children are presently being defined as "at risk" for the development of academic and social problems because of the effects of both influences before birth (such as parental malnutrition or substance abuse) and environmental factors. In recent years fetal alcohol syndrome, smoking by expectant mothers, illegal drug use by expectant mothers, and pediatric AIDS have apparently resulted in increased learning and behavioral problems in children (Chasnoff, Wells, Telford, Schmidt, & Messer, 2010; Scott-Goodwin et al., 2016; Phillips et al., 2016; Whittington et al., 2018). Although there are clear indications that these factors result in biochemical, central nervous system, and other physiological abnormalities, no specific behavioral deficit or excess has been directly attributed to any specific factor.

The Usefulness of Biophysical and Biochemical Explanations

The search for explanations of human behavior based on physiological factors has important implications. As a result of such research, the technology for preventing or lessening some serious problems has been developed. Perhaps the best-known example of such technology is the routine testing of all infants for phenylketonuria (PKU), a hereditary disorder of metabolism. Placing infants with PKU on special diets can prevent the intellectual disabilities formerly associated with this disorder (Berry, 1969). It is possible that future research may explain a good deal more human behavior on a biological or hereditary basis. Currently, however, only a small part of the vast quantity of human behavior can be explained in this way.

Some biophysical explanations are testable, meeting the second of our four requirements for usefulness. For example, scientists can definitely establish the existence of Down syndrome by observing chromosomes. Some metabolic or biochemical disorders can also be scientifically verified. Verification of such presumed causes of behavior as minimal brain dysfunction, however, is not dependable (Werry, 1986).

Even with evidence of the existence of some physiological disorder, it does not follow that any specific behavior is automatically a result of the disorder. For the teacher, explanations based on presumed physiological disorders have little predictive utility. To say that Rachel cannot walk, talk, or feed herself because she is developmentally delayed as a result of a chromosomal disorder tells us nothing about the conditions under which Rachel might learn to perform these behaviors. Ms. Harper's explanation of Ralph's failure to sit down on the basis of hyperactivity caused by brain damage does not provide any useful information about what might help Ralph learn to stay in his seat. To say that Harold cannot read because he is a child at risk is to put Harold at the greater risk of not learning because we have low expectations for him. Even apparently constitutional differences in temperament are so vulnerable to environmental influences (Chess & Thomas, 1984) that they provide only limited information about how a child is apt to behave under given conditions.

The final criterion, parsimony, is also frequently ignored when physical causes are postulated for student behaviors. Searching for such causes often distracts teachers from simpler, more immediate factors that may be controlling behaviors in the classroom. Perhaps the greatest danger of such explanations is that some teachers may use them as excuses not to teach: Rachel cannot feed herself because she is developmentally delayed, not because I have not taught her. Ralph will not sit down because he is brain damaged, not because I have poor classroom management skills. Irving cannot read because he has dyslexia, not because I have not figured out a way to teach him. Biophysical explanations may also cause teachers to have low expectations for some students. When this happens, teachers might not even try to teach things students are capable of learning. The accompanying chart summarizes the usefulness of biophysical theory.

The Usefulness of Biophysical Theory

	Good	Fair	Poor
Inclusiveness			✓
Verifiability		✓	
Predictive Utility			✓
Parsimony			✓

> ### A Freudian by the Garbage Can
>
> Upon returning to the university after observing student teachers, Professor Grundy prepared to return to work on his textbook manuscript, now at least 7 months behind schedule. To his horror, his carefully organized sources, notes, drafts, and revisions were no longer "arranged" on the floor of his office. Worse, his carefully organized sticky notes had been removed from the walls, door, windows, and computer. Professor Grundy ran frantically down the hall, loudly berating the custodial worker who had taken advantage of his absence to remove what he considered "that trash" from the room so that he could vacuum and dust.
>
> As Grundy pawed through the outside garbage can, a colleague offered sympathy. "That's what happens when an anal-expulsive personality conflicts with an anal-retentive." Grundy's regrettably loud and obscene response to this observation drew the additional comment, "Definite signs of regression to the oral-aggressive stage there, Grundy."

Developmental Explanations

Learning Outcome 1.2 State what can be learned from developmental explanations.

Observation of human beings confirms that many predictable patterns of development occur. Physical growth proceeds in a fairly consistent manner. Most children start walking, talking, and performing some social behaviors such as smiling in fairly predictable sequences and at generally predictable chronological ages (Gesell & Ilg, 1943). Some theorists have attempted to explain many aspects of human behavior—cognitive, social, emotional, and moral—based on fixed, innate developmental sequences. Their proposed explanations are meant to account for normal as well as "deviant" (other than the accepted or usual) human behavior. The following sections review two of the numerous developmental theories and examine their usefulness in terms of inclusiveness, verifiability, predictive utility, and parsimony.

Psychoanalytic Theory

Although many different explanations of human behavior have been described as psychoanalytic, all have their roots in theories of Sigmund Freud, who asserted that normal and aberrant human behavior may be understood and explained on the basis of progression through certain crucial stages, perhaps the most commonly accepted and most widely disseminated of his theories. The hypothetical stages include oral (dependent and aggressive), anal (expulsive and retentive), and phallic (when gender awareness occurs). These stages are believed to occur before the age of 6 and, if mastered, result in emergence into the latency stage, which represents a sort of rest stop until puberty, when the last stage, the genital stage, emerges.

This theory suggests that people who progress through the stages successfully become relatively normal adults. In Freud's view, problems arise when a person fixates (or becomes stuck) at a certain stage or when anxiety causes a regression to a previous stage. People who fixate at or regress to the oral-dependent stage may merely be extremely dependent, or they may seek to solve problems by oral means such as overeating, smoking, or alcohol or drug abuse. A person fixated at the oral-aggressive stage may be sarcastic or verbally abusive. Fixation at the anal-expulsive stage results in messiness and disorganization; at the anal-retentive stage, in compulsive orderliness.

A Stage Theory of Cognitive Development

Jean Piaget was a biologist and psychologist who proposed a stage theory of human development. Piaget's descriptions of the cognitive and moral development of children have had extensive impact among educators. Like Freud, Piaget theorized that certain forces, biologically determined, contribute to development (Piaget & Inhelder, 1969). The forces suggested by Piaget, however, are those enabling the organism to adapt to the environment—specifically, assimilation, the tendency to adapt the environment to enhance personal functioning, and accommodation, the tendency to change behavior to adapt to the environment. The process of maintaining a balance between these two forces is called equilibration. Equilibration facilitates growth; other factors that also do so are organic maturation, experience, and social interaction. Piaget's stages include sensory-motor (birth to 1 1/2 years), preoperational (1 1/2 to 7 years), concrete operations (7 to 11 years), and formal operations (12 years to adulthood).

The Usefulness of Developmental Explanations

Both developmental theories we have discussed are inclusive; they apparently explain a great deal of human behavior, cognitive and affective, normal and atypical. Verifiability, however, is another matter. Although Piagetian theorists have repeatedly demonstrated the existence of academic and pre-academic behaviors that appear to be age related in many children, attempts to verify psychoanalytic explanations have not been successful (Achenbach & Lewis, 1971). Considerable resistance to verifying theoretical constructs exists among those who accept the psychoanalytic explanation of human behavior (Schultz, 1969). Although it can be verified that many people act in certain ways at certain ages, this does not prove that the cause of such behavior is an underlying developmental stage or that failure to reach or pass such a stage causes inappropriate or maladaptive behavior. There is little evidence to verify that the order of such stages is invariant or that reaching or passing through earlier stages is necessary for functioning at higher levels.

The accompanying chart summarizes the usefulness of developmental theory.

The Usefulness of Developmental Theory			
	Good	Fair	Poor
Inclusiveness	✓		
Verifiability			✓
Predictive Utility		✓	
Parsimony			✓

Some developmental theories can predict what some human beings will do at certain ages. By their nature these theories offer general information about average persons. However, "a prediction about what the average individual will do is of no value in dealing with a particular individual" (Skinner, 1953, p. 19). Developmental theories provide limited information about what conditions predict an individual's behavior in specific circumstances. The practitioner who wishes to change behavior by changing conditions can expect little help from developmental theories. Developmental explanations of behavior are equally inadequate when judged by the criterion of parsimony. To say that a child has temper tantrums because he is fixated at the oral stage of development is seldom the simplest explanation available. Because of their lack of parsimony, developmental explanations may lead the

Piaget's Stages in Action
Pearson eText
Video Example 1.2
In this video, an educator presents tasks to children of varying ages to assess for some of Piaget's core developmental achievements. The performance of the students varies according to age, aligning with Piaget's stages based on ages. Consider the Usefulness Checklist as you watch and consider how this might apply to a student with a developmental delay. What are some limitations of this approach?

> **Professor Grundy Gains Insight**
>
> Having been thoroughly demoralized by his interaction with his student teacher, Professor Grundy decided to pay another surprise visit that afternoon. He was determined to avoid subjecting himself to further ridicule. He did not mention Ralph's hyperactivity but instead concentrated on observing Ms. Harper's teaching. Her lesson plan indicated that she was teaching math, but Professor Grundy was confused by the fact that her group was playing with small wooden blocks of various sizes. Ms. Harper sat at the table with the group but did not interact with the students.
>
> At the conclusion of the lesson, Professor Grundy approached Ms. Harper and asked her why she was not teaching basic addition and subtraction facts as she had planned.
>
> "Professor," stated Ms. Harper, "I conducted my lesson exactly as I had planned. The students were using the blocks to gain insight into the relationship among numbers. Perhaps you are not familiar with the constructivist approach, but everyone knows that true insight is vital to the learning process and that it is impossible to teach children; we can only facilitate their own inner construction of knowledge."

teacher to excuses as unproductive as those prompted by biophysical explanations. Teachers, particularly teachers of students with disabilities, cannot wait for a student to become developmentally ready for each learning task. An explanation that encourages teachers to take students from their current levels to subsequent levels is clearly more useful than a developmental explanation—at least from a practical point of view. We might expect Professor Grundy's developmental colleagues, for example, to explain Grundy's difficulty with the concept of hyperactivity on the basis of his failure to reach the level of formal operational thinking required to deal with hypothetical constructs. Might there be a more parsimonious, more useful explanation of his behavior? Professor Grundy continues to collect theories of behavior in the following episode.

Cognitive Explanations

Learning Outcome 1.3 Explain the limitations of cognitive explanations of behavior.

The educational theory espoused (in a somewhat exaggerated form, to be sure) by Ms. Harper is based on an explanation of human behavior and learning that combines elements of developmental theory, especially Piagetian, with a theory first described in Germany in the early part of the 20th century. The first major proponent of this explanation was Max Wertheimer (Hill, 1963), who was interested in people's perception of reality.

Wertheimer suggested it was the relationship among things perceived that was important rather than the things themselves. People, he suggested, tend to perceive things in an organized fashion, so that what is seen or heard is different from merely the parts that compose it. He labeled an organized perception of this type a *gestalt*, using a German word for which there is no exact English equivalent but that may be translated as "form," "pattern," or "configuration." English-speaking advocates of this view have retained the word *gestalt*, and we call this explanation Gestalt psychology. Those who have applied this explanation to education believe that learning depends on imposing one's own meaningful patterns and insights on information and that rote learning, even if it leads to correct solutions to problems, is less useful.

Gestalt psychology has had considerable influence on education. The best-known educator to espouse this approach to understanding behavior is Jerome

| Educators who espouse gestalt theory encourage "discovery learning."

Bruner (1960). What has come to be called the cognitive theory of education places an emphasis on rearranging thought patterns and gaining insight as a basis for learning new academic and social behaviors. The resulting teaching practices are called discovery learning. Learning is explained on the basis of insight, pattern rearrangement, and intuitive leaps. Teachers do not impart knowledge; they merely arrange the environment to facilitate discovery. Motivation is presumed to occur as a result of innate needs that are met when organization is imposed on objects or events in the arrangement. Motivation is thus intrinsic and need not be provided by the teacher. In its latest manifestation, cognitive theory applied to education has been termed *constructivism*. This approach holds that teachers cannot provide knowledge to students; students must construct their own knowledge in their own minds (Fosnot & Perry, 2005; Taber, 2019). "Rather than behaviours or skills as the goal of instruction, concept development and deep understanding are the foci" (Fosnot, 1996, p. 10).

The Usefulness of Cognitive Explanations

Cognitive theory explains a great deal of human behavior. Theorists can account for both intellectual and social behavior. Virtually all behavior can be explained as the result of imposing structure on unstructured environmental events or of perceiving the relative importance of such events. Thus, cognitive theory meets the criterion of inclusiveness.

The theory lacks verifiability, however. Because all of the processes are supposed to take place internally, there is no way to confirm their existence. Only the outcome is verifiable—the process is assumed.

The predictive utility of cognitive theory is also limited. In academic areas, the teacher who uses a discovery or constructivist approach has very little control over what students will discover or construct. Most advocates of this approach would insist that they do not want to predict outcomes of learning. Unfortunately, this unwillingness to control the outcome of the teaching–learning process has led to rather poor results. Educational practices based on a cognitive approach have been less successful than those emphasizing direct instruction (Engelmann & Carnine, 1982).

Addressing our final criterion, we must conclude that cognitive theory is not parsimonious. In neither intellectual nor social areas are the explanations necessary in understanding or predicting behavior.

The Usefulness of Cognitive Theory	Good	Fair	Poor
Inclusiveness	✓		
Verifiability			✓
Predictive Utility			✓
Parsimony			✓

Although all of the theories described so far provide information about human behavior, none of them meets all four of our criteria. The explanations we have provided are very general, and our conclusions about their usefulness should not be taken as an indication that they have no value. We simply believe they provide insufficient practical guidance for classroom teachers. After the following vignette, we shall describe a behavioral explanation of human behavior that we believe most nearly reaches the criteria of inclusiveness, verifiability, predictive utility, and parsimony.

Professor Grundy Takes Action

Professor Grundy had an absolutely rotten day. A number of the students in his 8 a.m. class had come in late, disrupting his lecture. He had been ridiculed by a student teacher; his precious manuscript had been retrieved from the dumpster in a sadly wrinkled and malodorous condition; his colleague had made repeated references to "anal-expulsive" and "oral-aggressive" tendencies during the day in spite of Grundy's protests.

After arriving at home and pouring himself a large drink for medicinal purposes, Grundy decided something must be done. He made several detailed plans and retired for the evening, confident he was on the right track. The next morning he arose, enthusiastically determined, in spite of a slight headache, to put his plans into action.

His first step was to arrive at his 8 a.m. class 5 minutes early—somewhat of a novelty because he usually arrived several minutes late. He spent the extra 5 minutes chatting affably with students and clarifying points from the previous day's lecture when asked to do so. At 8:00 sharp, he presented each of the five students present with an "on-time slip" worth 2 points on the next exam.

After the morning lecture, Professor Grundy proceeded to his office, where he affixed to the door a large sign reading "PLEASE DO NOT CLEAN THIS OFFICE TODAY." He then opened the window, wondering just what the biology department had deposited in the dumpster to cause so strong a smell. He spent an hour reorganizing his notes.

Next, Grundy once again visited Ms. Harper, this time suggesting that she would receive an unsatisfactory grade for student teaching unless she learned to control Ralph's behavior and to teach basic math facts. Her habitual expression of disdain changed to one of rapt attention. Professor Grundy had observed that Ralph, because he was too "hyperactive" to remain in his seat, spent the time while other students worked wandering from toy to toy in the free-time area of the classroom. He suggested that Ms. Harper allow Ralph to play with the toys only after remaining in his seat for a specified length of time: very short periods at first, gradually increasing in length. Grundy further suggested the student teacher make flash cards of basic addition and subtraction facts, allowing the students to play with the colored blocks after they had learned several combinations.

Returning happily to his office, the professor encountered his psychoanalytically oriented colleague, who once again jocularly repeated his insights into Grundy's character. Ignoring the comments, the professor began an animated conversation with the departmental office associate, praising the rapidity with which she was helping him reorganize his manuscript. She assured him it had first priority, because she couldn't wait to be rid of the stinking pages.

Within a short time, Professor Grundy felt that he had things under control. Most of the students enrolled in his 8 a.m. class were present and on time every morning, even though Grundy had begun to give "on-time slips" only occasionally. Ms. Harper had stopped sneering and started teaching. Ralph's wandering had decreased dramatically, and the math group had learned to add and subtract. Grundy continued to ignore his colleague's comments, which gradually ceased when no response was forthcoming, and his notes and drafts were rapidly being transformed into a freshly processed manuscript. The only negative outcome was a sharp note from campus security stating that the condition of his office constituted a fire hazard and that it must be cleaned immediately.

Constructivist Classroom
Pearson eText
Video Example 1.3
In this video, educators describe their constructivist classrooms and approach to learning. How do the educators draw a distinction between their approach and a "pour and store" approach to learning?

Behavioral Explanations

Learning Outcome 1.4 Describe the usefulness of behavioral explanations and define positive reinforcement, negative reinforcement, punishment, extinction, and antecedent control.

In the preceding vignette, Professor Grundy emerged as the behaviorist that he is. To solve some of his problems, he used techniques derived from yet another explanation of human behavior. The behavioral explanation suggests that rather than looking inside a person for the cause of a behavior, we look to the environment, usually the immediate environment, to explain behavior. This explanation states that human behavior, both adaptive and maladaptive, is learned. Learning occurs as a result of the consequences of behavior. To put it very simply, behavior that is followed by pleasant consequences tends to be repeated and thus learned. Behavior that is followed by unpleasant consequences tends not to be repeated and thus not learned. By assuming that his students, including DeWayne, came to class late, that the custodian cleaned, that the student teacher ridiculed, that Ralph wandered, and that his psychoanalytic colleague teased because they had learned to do so, Professor Grundy was able to teach them to do other things instead. In doing so, he applied several learning principles underlying the behaviorists' view of human behavior. The following sections introduce these principles, each of which will be discussed in detail in later chapters. A word of caution: in applied behavior analysis, these terms are used very differently than they are used in everyday language. Pay close attention to the technical definitions.

Positive Reinforcement

Positive reinforcement describes a functional relation between two environmental events: a **behavior** (any observable action) and a **consequence** (a result of that action). Positive reinforcement is demonstrated when a behavior is followed by a consequence that increases the behavior's future rate of occurrence.

Many human behaviors are learned as a result of positive reinforcement. Parents who praise their children for putting away toys may teach the children to be neat. This also works in unintended ways: parents who give their children candy to make them stop screaming in the grocery store may teach the children to scream. The cleaning behavior of Professor Grundy's custodian undoubtedly was learned and maintained through positive reinforcement, as was the wit of Grundy's psychoanalytic colleague. Grundy used positive reinforcement (on-time tickets, conversation, and time with toys) to increase his students' rate of coming to class on time and the amount of time Ralph stayed in his seat.

> Chapter 8 describes reinforcement in detail.

Negative Reinforcement

Negative reinforcement describes a relationship among events in which the rate of a behavior's occurrence increases when some (usually aversive or unpleasant) environmental condition is removed or reduced in intensity. (This may be different from the definition you previously learned.) Human beings learn many behaviors when acting in a certain way results in the termination of unpleasantness. Professor Grundy, for example, learned that opening windows results in the reduction of unpleasant odors in closed rooms. Similarly, the office associate reorganized his manuscript rapidly because when she finished, she could throw away the smelly papers.

Punishment

The word **punishment** also describes a relationship: a behavior is followed by a consequence that decreases the behavior's future rate of occurrence. An event is described as a **punisher** only if the rate of occurrence of the preceding behavior decreases. Behaviorists use the word *punishment* as a technical term to describe a specific relationship; confusion may arise because the same word is used in a nontechnical sense to describe unpleasant things done to people in an effort to change their behavior. To the behaviorist, punishment occurs only when the preceding behavior decreases. In the technical sense of the term, something is not necessarily punishment merely because

> Chapter 9 describes punishment and extinction in detail.

someone perceives the consequent event as unpleasant. A behaviorist can never say, "I punished him, but it didn't change his behavior," as do many parents and teachers. It is punishment, in the technical sense, only if the functional relation can be established. People could say that Professor Grundy's verbal threat to Ms. Harper, for example, was apparently a punisher: her ridiculing comments to him stopped. Of course, we wish he had used a more positive approach.

Extinction

When a previously reinforced behavior is no longer reinforced, its rate of occurrence decreases. This relationship is described as **extinction**. Recall from our vignette that when Grundy no longer reacted to his colleague's ridicule, the behavior stopped. For a behaviorist, all learning principles are defined on the basis of what actually happens, not what we think is happening. Grundy may have thought he was punishing his colleague by yelling or otherwise expressing his annoyance. In reality, the rate of the behavior increased when Grundy reacted in this way; the real relationship was that of positive reinforcement. The behavior stopped when the positive reinforcer was withdrawn.

Antecedent Control

Requirements that a functional assessment or analysis be performed for students with disabilities before changes in placement can be made (see Chapter 7 for a detailed discussion) have greatly increased interest in antecedent control. Teachers and researchers have come to rely much more frequently on examination of antecedent events and conditions, those occurring before the behavior, to determine what might be setting the stage for appropriate or challenging behaviors. There is also increased emphasis on manipulating antecedent conditions or events to manage and prevent challenging behavior.

> Stimulus control is the focus of Chapter 9.

An antecedent that occurs immediately before a behavior is called a discriminative stimulus and is said to "occasion" (to set the occasion for) a behavior. There is a functional relation, called **stimulus control**, between behavior and an **antecedent stimulus** rather than behavior and its consequences. Consequences must have been present during the development of the relation, but the antecedent condition or event now serves as a signal or cue for the behavior. In our vignette, the custodian's adherence to posted notices had apparently been reinforced in the past, so Professor Grundy's sign was effective even in the absence of a reinforcer or a punisher.

Another type of antecedent that affects behavior is **setting events**, which is similar to **motivating operations** (Chan, 2016; Iovanonne et al., 2017; Michael & Miguel, 2020; Nosik & Carr, 2015). These conditions or events may occur simultaneously with a discriminative stimulus or hours or even days before. They may occur in the same setting or in a completely different one. They influence behavior by temporarily changing the value or effectiveness of reinforcers. The simplest kinds of motivating operations are deprivation and satiation. A student who has just come in from the playground, sweating buckets from playing a hard game of kickball, is likely to be more responsive to a tall glass of water as a potential reinforcer than one who has just consumed a large glass of water in the air-conditioned cafeteria. Kazdin (2000) described three types of setting events: social, physiological, and environmental. Bailey, Wolery, and Sugai (1988) subdivided environmental setting events into instructional dimensions, physical dimensions, social dimensions, and environmental changes. These varieties of conditions and events may include variables as diverse as a noisy or uncomfortably warm classroom (environmental), the presence of a disliked staff member or peer (social), or a headache (physiological).

Bailey et al. (1988) included considerations about instructional materials that may not be age appropriate or gender appropriate. It may be that no reinforcer will (or indeed should) induce a teenager to touch, much less read, a colorfully illustrated book about a small doll. We believe that issues of students' ethnic or cultural heritage can also serve as setting events. Students are much more motivated to interact with materials that portray people like themselves (Fong et al., 2017; Sciuchetti, 2017). Attention to cultural diversity may enable teachers to provide reinforcers that are more meaningful and powerful and to avoid strategies that are ineffective or offensive. Strategies such as personalized contextual instruction (Voltz, 2003) that embed instruction into contexts of interest to students in a given setting may enhance the value of reinforcers. The Music Hath Charms anecdote describes a classroom using this approach.

Other Learning Principles

In addition to these major learning principles, Professor Grundy illustrated the use of several other influences on human behavior described by behaviorists. These influences include **modeling** and **shaping**. Modeling is the demonstration of behavior. The professor had been modeling inappropriate behavior—coming to class late—and his students had apparently been imitating that behavior. People learn many behaviors, both appropriate and inappropriate, by imitating a model. Infants learn to talk by imitating their caregivers; adults can learn to operate complex machinery by watching a demonstration.

Shaping uses the reinforcement of successive approximations to a desired behavior to teach new behavior. Grundy suggested that Ms. Harper use shaping to teach Ralph to stay in his seat. She was initially to reinforce sitting behavior when it occurred

Music Hath Charms

Ms. Garcia, a general education teacher, Mr. Walden, a special education teacher, and Ms. Nguyen, a paraprofessional, share the responsibility for an inclusive primary class of 25 students that they privately agree "gives new meaning to the term diversity." Their students range in age from 7 to 9. They teach 14 boys and 11 girls: 12 African-American students, 8 Hispanic students, and 4 Asian students. They have 7 children with learning disabilities, 4 children with behavior disorders, and 2 children who are intellectually gifted. And they have Yuri, a boy from Russia who has autism. What the children have in common is eligibility for free or reduced-price lunch and the fact that all of their teachers believe every one of them is capable of great things.

Things had been going well; the teachers used the standard curriculum and a combination of group and individual teaching. They used a simple point system with the class as a whole (the students could earn tangibles and activities for completing work and behaving appropriately) and implemented more complex positive behavior support plans with some children with more challenging behaviors. The students were making good academic progress but, as Mr. Walden stated at a meeting one afternoon, "Nobody seems real excited about school except us." The three teachers decided to implement an integrated unit approach that Ms. Garcia had learned about in a class she was taking at the local university and researched on the Internet and at the university library. The next morning Ms. Garcia explained the plan to the students, asking them to think about what they would like to study. The students seemed to think the teachers must be kidding and made several suggestions ranging from sports to dinosaurs, but most of the interest appeared to center around music. "Rap!" shouted several students. "Salsa!" suggested others. "All right," agreed Ms. Garcia, as Ms. Nguyen and Mr. Walden moved around praising students who were attending, "Let's make a list of what we already know about music and then a list of things we would like to know. Ms. Nguyen, would you help Yuri put the sticky notes with our ideas on the board?"

After almost an hour they had a good list to start out with and the teachers were startled to see that it was almost lunchtime. They were even more startled to realize that no one had given the students points all morning and that verbal praise and pats on the back had been enough.

for short periods of time and gradually increase the sitting time required for Ralph to earn the reinforcer. Many behaviors are taught by shaping. Parents may praise a young child effusively the first time she dresses herself, even if her blouse is on inside out and her shorts are on backward. Later she may earn a compliment only if her outfit is perfectly coordinated.

The Task of the Behaviorist

> If you can see it, hear it, feel it, or smell it, it's observable. If you can count it or measure it, it's quantifiable.

Behaviorists explain the development of both typical and atypical human behavior in terms of the principles just described. An important aspect of this approach is its emphasis on behavior. To qualify as a behavior, something must be *observable* and *quantifiable* (Baer, Wolf, & Risley, 1968). We must be able to see (or sometimes hear, feel, or even smell) the behavior. To make such direct observation meaningful, some way of measuring the behavior in quantitative terms (How much? How long? How often?) must be established. Behaviorists cannot reliably state that any of the relations described as learning principles exist unless these criteria are met.

Skinner (1953) suggested that behaviorists are less concerned with explaining behavior than with describing it. The emphasis, he states, is on which environmental factors increase, decrease, or maintain the rate of occurrence of specific behaviors. It is important to note that behaviorists do not deny the existence of physiological problems that may contribute to some behavioral problems. Nor do most behaviorists deny the effects of heredity (Mahoney, 1974) or even developmental stages (Ferster, Culbertson, & Boren, 1975). Their primary emphasis, however, is on present environmental conditions, both antecedent and consequent, maintaining behavior and on establishing and verifying functional relations between such conditions and behavior.

The Usefulness of Behavioral Explanations

One of the most common criticisms of the behavioral approach is that it leaves much of human behavior unexplained. Emphasis on observable behavior has led many to assume that behavioral principles can account for only simple motor responses. However, Skinner (1953, 1957, 1971) applied basic learning principles to explain a wide variety of complex human behavior, including language, education, economics, politics, and religious beliefs.

The fact that behavioral principles have not accounted for all aspects of human behavior should not lead to the assumption that they cannot. In the years since Skinner first identified the principles of behavior that developed into the discipline of applied behavior analysis, many aspects have been accounted for. Many phenomena have yet to be explained. "In the meantime—which may last forever—the best strategy is to isolate variables that influence important behavior and manipulate those variables to make life better" (Poling & Byrne, 1996, p. 79). Because behaviorists refuse to theorize about what they have not observed, explanation must await verification. Behaviorists are ready temporarily to sacrifice some degree of inclusiveness for verifiability.

Verifiability is the essence of the behavioral explanation. Other theorists posit a theory and attempt to verify it through experimental investigation. Behaviorists, on the other hand, investigate before formulating what may be described as generalizations rather than theories. That adult attention serves as a positive reinforcer for most children (Baer & Wolf, 1968; Harris, Johnston, Kelley, & Wolf, 1964) is an example of such a generalization. This statement was made only after repeated observations established a functional relation between children's behavior and adult attention. (Note that adult attention does not always function as a positive reinforcer.) The following chart summarizes the usefulness of behavioral theory.

The Usefulness of Behavioral Theory	Good	Fair	Poor
Inclusiveness		✓	
Verifiability	✓		
Predictive Utility	✓		
Parsimony	✓		

The focus of the behavioral approach is changing behavior. Predictive utility is an essential part of any behavioral explanation. Functional relations are established and generalizations are made precisely so that they can be used to change maladaptive or inappropriate behavior and increase appropriate behavior. Behaviorists are reinforced by changing behavior, not by discussing it. Unless it is possible to use generalizations to predict what people will do under certain conditions, behaviorists see little point in making the statements. An enormous body of evidence exists, representing the application of learning principles to human behavior. Such data make possible the prediction of behavior under a wide variety of conditions.

Behavioral explanations are parsimonious, satisfying our fourth criterion for usefulness. Describing behavior solely in terms of observable, verifiable, functional relations avoids the use of "explanatory fictions." Such fictions are defined only in terms of their effects, resulting in the circular reasoning we discussed earlier. Rather than invoking "hyperactivity"—an example of an explanatory fiction—to explain Ralph's out-of-seat behavior, Professor Grundy chose a behavioral approach to look at what happened before and after Ralph left his seat. In this way, behaviorism avoids explanations distant from observed behavior and its relationship to the environment. It is unacceptable to explain out-of-seat behavior by labeling the cause as hyperactivity or to explain messiness as fixation at or regression to the anal-expulsive stage of behavior. Neither explanation adds useful information about the problem, nor strategies to improve the behavior.

The assumption that behaviors are being maintained by current environmental conditions and that the behavior may be changed by changing the environment is not merely parsimonious, it is supremely optimistic. The teacher who concentrates on discovering and changing the environmental conditions maintaining students' inappropriate or maladaptive behavior does not give up on them because they have cultural differences, intellectual disabilities, brain damage, emotional disturbance, hyperactivity, or are at risk, or developmentally unready to learn; she teaches them. If students' behavior is described in terms of behavioral excesses (too much moving around) or deficits (too little reading) rather than in terms of explanatory fictions, the teacher can go about the business of teaching—decreasing behavioral excesses and overcoming behavioral deficits.

> "Explanatory fictions" explain nothing. Behaviorists explain behavior on the basis of observation, not imagination.

Historical Development of Behaviorism

Learning Outcome 1.5 Describe the origins of a behavioral explanation for behavior.

Behaviorism as a science has roots in philosophical and psychological traditions originating several centuries ago. The learning principles described earlier certainly existed before being formally defined. People's behavior has been influenced since

Who is B.F. Skinner?
Pearson eText
Video Example 1.4
In this video, B.F. Skinner's contributions to the study of psychology are briefly explained. What distinctions do you notice between behavior analysis and the other theories in this chapter?

https://www.youtube.com/watch?v=tqabCNrenZo

the beginning of civilization. In the following section, we will examine several historical descriptions of how people have used the relation between behavior and its consequences. Then we will trace the development of behaviorism as a formal way of explaining, predicting, and changing human behavior.

Historical Precedents

The arrangement of environmental conditions in order to influence behavior is by no means a recent invention. It is said that the ancient Romans put eels in the bottom of wine cups to decrease excessive drinking. Crossman (1975, p. 348) provided a historical example of the use of positive reinforcement:

> There is a fascinating history behind the pretzel. About 610 an imaginative Alpine monk formed the ends of dough, left over from the baking of bread, into baked strips folded into a looped twist so as to represent the folded arms of children in prayer. The tasty treat was offered to the children as they learned their prayers and thereby came to be called "pretiola"—Latin for "little reward." (From the back of a Country Club Foods pretzel bag, Salt Lake City.)

Benjamin Franklin demonstrated that adults' behavior could also be changed, using a rather different positive reinforcer (Skinner, 1969). When a ship's chaplain complained that few sailors attended prayers, Franklin suggested that the chaplain take charge of serving the sailors' daily ration of rum and deal it out only after the prayers. Attendance improved remarkably.

Parents and teachers have likewise applied the principles of learning in their efforts to teach children. "Clean up your plate and then you can have dessert," says the parent hoping for positive reinforcement. "When you finish your arithmetic, you may play a game," promises the teacher. Parents and teachers, whether they are aware of it or not, also use punishment: the child who runs into the street is scolded; the student who finishes his assignment quickly is given more work to do. All of us have heard "Just ignore him and he'll stop. He's only doing it for attention." If he does stop, we have an example of extinction. Of course, many parents and teachers extinguish appropriate behavior as well, paying no attention to children who are behaving nicely. Negative reinforcement is demonstrated in many homes every day: "You don't play outside until that room is clean." Teachers also use negative reinforcement when they require students, for example, to finish assignments before going to lunch or to recess. Kindergarten teachers who ask their charges to use their "inside voices" are trying to establish stimulus control. Whenever teachers show their students how to do something, they are modeling.

> Behavioral principles operate whether anyone is consciously using them.

It becomes apparent that a person does not need to know the names of the relationships involved to use them. Indeed, applying behavioral learning principles sounds a lot like common sense. If it is so simple, why must students take courses and read books? Why have such quantities of material been written and so much research conducted?

The answer is that it is inefficient to fail to arrange environmental conditions so that functional relations are established, or to allow such relations to be randomly established, or to assume that such relations have been established based only on common sense. This inefficiency has resulted in high levels of maladaptive behavior in schools and sometimes frighteningly low levels of academic and pre-academic learning. It is our aim in writing this book to help teachers become applied behavior analysts. The derivation and definition of the term *applied behavior analysis* will be discussed in the remaining sections of this chapter.

Psychological Antecedents

RESPONDENT CONDITIONING Most people are aware of the work of Ivan Pavlov, who observed that when a tone was sounded as dogs were fed, the dogs began to salivate when they heard the tone even when food was not present. (Anyone who feeds dogs can observe a similar phenomenon when the dogs arrive drooling when they hear the food pans being taken from the dishwasher.) Pavlov's precise observation and measurement have served as a model for experimental research to this day. His classic experiment involved pairing food powder (which elicits salivation, an automatic reflex) with a tone that would normally have no effect on dogs' salivation. The presentation of the tone preceded the presentation of the food powder; after repeated pairings, salivation occurred when only the tone was presented (Hill, 1970). The food powder was labeled the *unconditioned stimulus* (US); the tone, the *conditioned stimulus* (CS). Salivation is an unconditioned response to food powder and a conditioned response to the tone. The relationship may be represented as shown in the accompanying diagram. The process of pairing stimuli so that an unconditioned stimulus elicits a response is known as *Pavlovian, classical,* or *respondent conditioning*.

ASSOCIATIONISM Another influential experimenter whose research paralleled that of Pavlov was Edward Thorndike. Thorndike studied cats rather than dogs, and his primary interest was discovering associations between situations and responses (Thorndike, 1931). He formulated two laws that profoundly influenced the subsequent development of behavioral science. The Law of Effect (Thorndike, 1905) states that "any act which in a given situation produces satisfaction becomes associated with that situation, so that when the situation recurs the act is more likely than before to recur also" (p. 203). Second is the Law of Exercise, which states that a response made in a particular situation becomes associated with the situation. The relationship of the Law of Effect with the principle of positive reinforcement is obvious. The Law of Exercise is similarly related to the stimulus control principle discussed earlier.

BEHAVIORISM The term *behaviorism* was first used by John Watson (1914, 1919, 1925). Watson advocated the complete abolition of any datum in psychology that did not result from direct observation. He considered such concepts as mind, instinct, thought, and emotion both useless and superfluous. He denied the existence of instinct in human beings and reduced thought to subvocal speech, emotion to bodily responses. A Watsonian behaviorist of our acquaintance once responded to a question by saying, "I've changed my mind (you should excuse the expression)." The true Watsonian does not acknowledge the existence of any such entity as "mind."

> If we were all Watsonians, we couldn't say, "She hurt my feelings," "My mind wandered," or "Use your imagination."

Watson and Raynor (1920) conditioned a startle response in a baby, Albert, by pairing a white rat (CS) with a loud noise (US). Watson contended that all "emotional" responses such as fear were conditioned in similar ways. In an interestingly related procedure, Jones (1924) desensitized a 3-year-old child who showed a fear response to white rabbits and other white furry objects by pairing the child's favorite foods with the rabbit. This procedure was unfortunately not carried out with Albert, who moved away before his conditioned fear could be eliminated. Albert might have been scared of white rats all his life, which may have created a number of problems, including preventing his employment as a behavioral psychologist.

OPERANT CONDITIONING The learning principles described at the beginning of this section are those suggested by proponents of an *operant conditioning* model for explaining, predicting, and changing human behavior. The best-known operant conditioner was B. F. Skinner (1904–1988), who first distinguished operant from respondent conditioning.

> Operant behaviors are emitted voluntarily; respondent behaviors are elicited by stimuli.

Respondent conditioning, you will recall, deals with behaviors elicited by stimuli that precede them. Most such behaviors are reflexive; that is, they are not under voluntary control. Examples include sweating, blushing, and pupil dilation. Operant conditioning, on the other hand, deals with behaviors usually considered voluntary rather than reflexive. Examples include pulling, pushing, walking, talking, writing, and contorting—the types of behaviors important in schools. Operant conditioners are concerned primarily with the consequences of behavior and the establishment of functional relations between behavior and consequences. The behavioral view described earlier is that of operant conditioning, which will be the emphasis of the entire text.

Skinner's early work was with animals, primarily white rats. In this, he followed in the tradition of earlier behaviorists, to whom this particular animal was so important that one researcher (Tolman, 1932) dedicated a major book to Mus norvegious albinius, a strain of white rats. Bertrand Russell, the philosopher, is said to have suggested facetiously that the different emphases in European (primarily gestalt, introspective, and theorizing) and American (primarily behavioral, active, and observational) studies may have resulted from differences in the breeds of rats available. Whereas European rats sat around quietly waiting for insight, American rats were active go-getters, scurrying around their cages and providing lots of behaviors for psychologists to observe.

Skinner also worked with pigeons. He explained (1963) that, while in the military during World War II, he was assigned to a building whose windowsills were frequented by these birds. Because there was very little to do, he and his colleagues began to train the pigeons to perform various behaviors. This subsequently developed into a rather elaborate, successful, although ultimately abandoned before fully operational, project to train pigeons to deliver guided missiles to enemy vessels. The pigeons, of course, were limited to one delivery. Although "Project Pigeon" was a source of personal and professional frustration to Skinner, it is credited with moving his interest firmly and finally from the laboratory into applied settings (Capshew, 1993).

> Applied behavior analysis must deal with socially important, observable behaviors. Relationships between behaviors and interventions must be verified.

Early application of operant conditioning techniques to human beings was directed toward establishing that the principles governing animal behavior also govern human behavior. The use of these principles to change human behavior—initially called *behavior modification*—did not really emerge in nonlaboratory settings until the 1960s. One of the authors remembers being told in an experimental psychology course in 1961 that there was some indication operant conditioning could be applied to simple human behavior. As an example, the instructor laughingly described college students' conditioning their professor to lecture from one side of the room simply by looking interested only when he stood on that side. The instructor insisted, rather pompously, that it would not be possible to modify his behavior in this way, because he was aware of the technique. He was wrong; he was backed into one corner of the room by the end of the next lecture.

At that time, however—in spite of Skinner's (1953) theoretical application of operant conditioning techniques to complex human behavior and pioneer studies such as those of Ayllon and Michael (1959) and Birnbrauer, Bijou, Wolf, and Kidder (1965)—few people anticipated the enormous impact that the use of such principles would have on American psychology and education and other disciplines. The application of behavior modification in real-life settings had become so prevalent by 1968 that a new journal, the *Journal of Applied Behavior Analysis*, was founded to publish the results of research. In Volume 1, Number 1, of the journal, Baer, Wolf, and Risley

(1968) defined applied behavior analysis as the "process of applying sometimes tentative principles of behavior to the improvement of specific behaviors, and simultaneously evaluating whether or not any changes noted are indeed attributed to the process of application" (p. 91).

Baer and his colleagues (1968) suggested that for research to qualify as applied behavior analysis, it must change socially important behavior, chosen because it needs change, not because its study is convenient to the researcher. It must deal with observable and quantifiable behavior, objectively defined or defined in terms of examples; and clear evidence of a functional relation between the behavior to be changed and the experimenter's intervention must exist. In a more recent retrospective analysis of the progress of applied behavior analysis since 1968, the same authors (Baer, Wolf, & Risley, 1987) suggested that in spite of considerable opposition and in light of many failures of the procedures in real settings, applied behavior analysts should persevere. They stated, "current theory has worked far too well to be abandoned in the face of what are more parsimoniously seen as technological rather than theoretical failures" (p. 325). In other words, we still cannot always make what we know ought to work actually work, but that is a problem of implementation, not an indication of the inadequacy of applied behavior analysis as a discipline. Applied behavior analysis is more rigorously defined than behavior modification. In our earlier vignette, Professor Grundy apparently succeeded in modifying behavior, but he failed to meet the criterion of analysis—he had no way of knowing for sure whether his techniques changed behavior or whether the change was mere coincidence. Maintaining data about behavior change (or the lack of it) is a fundamental tenet of applied behavior analysis. It is required for many procedures necessary for students with disabilities, including functional analysis of behavior, discussed in Chapter 6, and Responsiveness to Intervention (RTI) (Bradley, Danielson, & Doolittle, 2007) used as part of the identification process for students with special needs. This book is designed to help teachers become applied behavior analysts, effective modifiers of behavior, and efficient analyzers of the principles of learning involved in all aspects of their students' performance.

Teachers who learn and practice the principles of applied behavior analysis can help their students master functional and academic skills in a systematic and efficient manner and can document their students' progress for parents and other professionals. They can manage behavior positively so that their focus remains on learning. They can teach students to get along with peers and adults and to make good choices. By providing learning environments that are safe, joyful, and successful, they can make enormous differences in students' lives.

Classical vs. Operant Conditioning
Pearson eText
Video Example 1.5
In this video, the key differences between operant and classical conditioning are reviewed. Operant conditioning is based on the application of reinforcement and punishment. What are some examples of operant conditioning that you have experienced?

https://www.youtube.com/watch?v=H6LEcM0E0io

Summary

We described a number of approaches to explaining human behavior. We evaluated these approaches in terms of their inclusiveness, verifiability, predictive utility, and parsimony. We also described an explanation of human behavior that appears to us to be the most useful—the behavioral explanation.

In tracing the history of the behavioral approach to human behavior, we emphasized the development of a science of applied behavior analysis. We discussed the necessity for concentrating on socially useful studies of human behavior and on careful observation of the establishment of functional relations. We also provided a rationale for learning and using the principles of applied behavior analysis and some examples of their use in various educational settings.

Discussion Questions

1. Mr. King is a consultant teacher for students with special needs in an elementary school. He is working with Ms. Lowe, a third-grade teacher, who wants Jaylon, one of her students, to stop wandering around the room and to finish, or at least attempt to finish, his assignments. When Mr. King suggests a program using stickers to reinforce Jaylon's appropriate behavior, Ms. Lowe states that the boy is ADHD and that nothing will help until his parents agree to put him on medication because ADHD is a medical problem. What should Mr. King say to Ms. Lowe?

2. Mr. King has suggested to Ms. Nakamura that she use stickers that can be traded for free time to help Maria, one of her kindergarten students who becomes easily frustrated and cries a lot when asked to work independently. Ms. Nakamura decides to give Maria a sticker whenever she works independently for several minutes and reports that she doesn't think Maria is crying as much and that the program seems to be working. She thanks Mr. King for his help. Is Ms. Nakamura practicing applied behavior analysis? Does it matter? Should Mr. King tell her?

Chapter 2
Responsible Use of Applied Behavior Analysis Procedures

 Learning Outcomes

2.1 Describe three factors that lead to concerns about the use of applied behavior analysis procedures.

2.2 List the criteria for verifying that procedures for behavior change are being ethically implemented.

2.3 Describe the effectiveness of providing accountability when using applied behavior analysis procedures.

2.4 State the justification for ensuring that professionals working with individuals with challenging behaviors understand the theoretical basis of the procedures that they implement.

CHAPTER OUTLINE

Concerns about Applied Behavior Analysis
    Confusion with Other Procedures
    Reaction to Controversial Procedures
    Concerns about Coercion

Ethical Use of Applied Behavior Analysis Procedures
    A Therapeutic Environment
    Services Whose Overriding Goal Is Personal Welfare
    Treatment by a Competent Behavior Analyst
    Programs that Teach Functional Skills
    Behavioral Assessment and Ongoing Evaluation

Accountability

Theory or Recipes?

Summary

This chapter addresses many of the issues raised by those who practice applied behavior analysis and those who disagree with its use. First, we will consider some of the concerns often expressed and some possible causes of these concerns. Then we will examine and respond to some of the specific criticisms of behavioral procedures, particularly as these methods are used in educational settings. We will suggest ethical guidelines for using procedures, Professor Grundy will answer some common questions asked by people new to applied behavior analysis, and we will submit reasons for thoroughly understanding procedures and principles.

Concerns about Applied Behavior Analysis

Learning Outcome 2.1 Describe three factors that lead to concerns about the use of applied behavior analysis procedures.

Resistance to the use of operant procedures to change behavior has come from several sources. The term *behavior modification*, which was historically used to describe such techniques, has caused some confusion. Because the word *modification* is synonymous with *change*, the term *behavior modification* has often been misused to refer to any procedure that has the potential to change behavior. This contamination of the term is one reason that we prefer the term **applied behavior analysis**.

Other objections to operant procedures have come from those who feel that any systematic effort to change behavior is coercive, and thus inhumane. Those who take this position often describe themselves as "humanists." Their objections are based on a rejection of a deterministic viewpoint and advocacy of free will and personal freedom. The intuitive appeal of these humanistic values makes humanists' rejection of behavioral procedures a formidable objection, although as we shall see, such objections frequently rely on a rather shaky logical foundation.

> Some people believe that changing behavior invariably infringes on personal freedom.

The very effectiveness of applied behavior analysis procedures is one source of much concern about this approach. It is ironic that many people are comfortable with ineffective techniques or with techniques whose effectiveness lacks verification. This is sometimes because those less-effective techniques are easier, faster, and less costly to implement, such as medication. Implementing assessments and procedures based on applied behavior analysis are more time consuming, and also quite effective.

The battle to bring about "the destruction of the behaviorist evil and the hegemony of the cognitive good" (Schnaitter, 1999, p. 209) reached its peak in the 1970s and 1980s, and the fervor of the criticisms is well characterized by Schnaitter's description. Applied behavior analysis was virtually ignored by researchers and teachers outside of special education during the 1980s (Axelrod, Moyer, & Berry, 1990), perhaps because its critics perceived that the battle had been won and "behaviorism" defeated. Two of us were in graduate school when the debate was in full swing and one of our fellow students was confronted with the statement "behaviorism is dead!" "What?" she replied, "Have they repealed the laws of behavior?" Applied behavior analysis again became the target for attack (Haberman, 1995; Kohn, 1993, 2018), even by some special educators (Pugach & Warger, 1996). Axelrod (1996) suggested several possible reasons for this:

- Behavioral approaches are too much work and provide too little reinforcement.
- Behaviorism contradicts the popular developmental views of education and psychology.
- Behavior analysis is a threat to the prevailing power structures in education and psychology.

- Positive reinforcement is a practice that often lacks social acceptability.
- Behavior analysis fails to glorify human beings as do other psychologies and philosophies. (pp. 248–253)

Anyone who has ever taught reading using a direct instruction approach (Engelmann et al., 1988; Fishley et al., 2017; Kamps et al., 2016; Kourea et al., 2018), derived from behavioral principles, can attest that it is a lot more work than, for example, providing students with a literacy-rich environment and waiting for literacy to emerge. Implementing behavior support plans is a lot harder than sending students to the principal's office and subsequently suspending or expelling them.

In addition to addressing Axelrod's (1996) concerns, we will discuss some other reasons why applied behavior analysis continues to be controversial.

Confusion with Other Procedures

Much of the public outcry against what is historically called *behavior modification* results from the use of this term to describe procedures that are totally unrelated to applied behavior analysis. Popular journalists (Holden, 1973; Mason, 1974; Wicker, 1974) and even behavior modification professionals (McConnell, 1970) caused incalculable harm to the image of applied behavior analysis during the years when its use with human beings was in its developmental phase by including unrelated treatment procedures under the heading of behavior modification. Hypnosis, psychosurgery, brain implants, drug therapy, and electroconvulsive shock treatment have all been lumped under this label. Such procedures undoubtedly change behavior, but they are not related to the systematic changing of behavior by application of behavioral principles. It would be equally logical and equally erroneous to list under the title of behavior modification the entire array of therapeutic interventions including "psychoanalysis, Gestalt therapy, primal screams, lectures, books, jobs and religion" (Goldiamond, 1975, p. 26). Although many criticisms of applied behavior analysis were reactions to its use many years ago, more recent publications have blamed behavioral procedures for everything from the failure of public education to teach large numbers of children to the destruction of the American work ethic (Haberman, 1995; Kohn, 2001, 2018).

One of us has heard several times, "Oh, you're a behaviorist – are you going to shock me?" This is such an unfortunate association given that the father of behaviorism, B. F. Skinner, was vehemently against the use of punishment and aversives (Skinner, 1953). He abhorred the use of corporal punishment in schools and in the military, and implored members of society to instead use positive reinforcement. Applied behavior analysis certainly does not include such treatments as electroconvulsive therapy or brain surgery; neither does it involve the use of drugs. The effective application of appropriate behavioral procedures often reduces the need for such drastic interventions. This was strongly demonstrated many years ago in studies using positive reinforcement as an alternative to medication for children labeled *hyperactive* (Ayllon, Layman, & Kandel, 1975) or as having *attention deficit disorder* (Rapport, Murphy, & Bailey, 1982). It is possible that behavior modification, in the proper sense of the term, will ultimately diminish the use of surgery, drugs, and other such behavior-change techniques. It is therefore particularly unfortunate that the improper use of the term has caused so much public hostility to a technology that is so potentially benign, and so potentially effective. Rather than *behavior modification,* we suggest teachers use the term *applied behavior analysis.*

Applied behavior analysis refers only to procedures derived from the experimental analysis of human behavior. Because of the negative connotations of *behavior modification,* administrative staff, fellow teachers, and other professionals may be as confused about how applied behavior analysts use these terms as parents and school board members. Some textbooks and other materials widely used in preservice teacher

Misconceptions about ABA
Pearson eText
Video Example 2.1
In this video, a speech and language pathologist shares her view of ABA. In what ways does her presentation of ABA align with and differ from this text? What misconceptions about ABA does she hold?

> Applied behavior analysis is not hypnosis, prefrontal lobotomy, brain implants, drug therapy, or shock treatment.

education programs may well contribute to this confusion. We must work to undo these negative associations and explain the many benefits of applied behavior analysis. The use of terminology has consistently caused problems for behaviorally oriented practitioners. It may be that it is not what behaviorists do that disturbs people but the way they refer to it. Teachers should be careful how they talk about procedures, even among themselves. Problems may arise because of the way programs are described, even when the programs themselves are appropriate.

Risley (1975) described a time-out procedure that was disallowed primarily because staff members referred to the free-standing structures built for short-term exclusion as "boxes" and to the procedure as "putting him (the resident) in the box." That the "boxes" were large, adequately lighted structures made no difference. The use of the wrong words resulted in withdrawal of approval for the program. Those of us who tend toward flippant labels would be especially wise to guard our tongues when discussing procedures with people who might misunderstand.

Carr (1996) suggested that we modify our language even more drastically when addressing the general public, including parents and educators who are not behavior analysts. He advocated using the language of ethics, focusing on values such as compassion, dignity, and honesty rather than the technical language of concepts and procedures. In other words, rather than saying that we use positive reinforcement to increase the future probability of behavior, we should say that we use it because "it is a humane procedure (compassion) that can help individuals lead better, more fulfilling lives (dignity), and we offer it sincerely (honesty) as feedback" (p. 266). This is certainly not an attempt at deception; we believe that most behavior analysts are honest, compassionate, and supportive of the dignity of every individual. Critchfield et al. (2017) further recommended using everyday language with non-behavior analysts to help disseminate the effective science and set of practices.

Reaction to Controversial Procedures

Not all misunderstanding or hostility has resulted from those outside the field. Both professionals and the public frequently reject procedures derived from the experimental analysis of behavior. Some parents and educators even reject the use of positive reinforcement, stating that students should be intrinsically motivated and that systematic positive reinforcement reduces intrinsic motivation (Balsam & Bondy, 1983; Deci, 2016; Kohn, 2001, 2006, 2018). There is actually very little evidence for this claim (Cameron, Banko, & Pierce, 2001). Cameron and Pierce (1994) examined 96 published studies and found that intrinsic motivation is more often increased than decreased when positive reinforcement is used (see also Cameron et al., 2005).

It is easier to understand people's rejection of procedures that cause pain or discomfort and the use of exclusion. Although these are only a few of the tools of the applied behavior analyst, their use has received a disproportionate share of attention from the press, the public, and the judiciary (Connolly, 2017; Stolz, 1977). It is sufficient to note that aversive or exclusionary procedures may create problems in two ways:

1. Their misuse is common and often described by users as behavior modification.
2. Their use, even when appropriate, causes more concern than other behavioral procedures.

> Guidelines for the use of aversive and exclusionary procedures will be provided in Chapter 9.

It is fully understandable that procedures causing pain or discomfort to any individual, but particularly one who is disabled, are reasons for concern. The controversy about aversive procedures will be discussed later in this chapter and at length in Chapter 9.

Concerns about Coercion

The notion that applied behavior analysis is inhumane rests on the assumption that each human being should be free to choose a personal course of behavior. It follows, for those who criticize behavioral procedures, that any systematic attempt to alter the behavior of another human being is coercive and thus inhumane.

This criticism of behavioral techniques is based on the philosophic concept of free will. Advocates of the assumption of free will tend to attribute human behavior to forces arising from within the individual, and thus not subject to prediction or control. This is an example of the glorification of human beings described by Axelrod (1996). In other words, people are different from animals in that they just do what they do because they decide to do it. A deterministic position, on the other hand, holds that even human behavior is **lawful behavior** (subject to prediction) and its causes can be identified in environmental events. A determinist recognizes systematic relationships among such events (Chiesa, 2003) and considers human behavior as part of the system. This contrasting view concludes that human behavior is subject to lawful prediction. People do things, or decide to do things, because of past events and present circumstances. It is important to distinguish between the use of the term *lawful*, in the sense of an orderly relationship between events, and any implication of authoritarian control. Many criticisms of applied behavior analysis are predicated on a misunderstanding of that simple concept (Dollard, Christensen, Colucci, & Epanchin, 1996; Nichols, 1992). *Lawful*, in the sense used here, refers to relationships among events that occur naturally, not to attempts to legislate human behavior.

> A belief that behavior is lawful does not imply that human beings are not free to choose what they will do.

Applied behavior analysts, by definition, are also determinists. Their position is predicated on solid evidence that "the assumption of **determinism** is both justified and essential in dealing with human behavior" (Craighead, Kazdin, & Mahoney, 1976, p. 172). This confirmation has come from a large body of psychological research, some but by no means all of it conducted by those who call themselves applied behavior analysts. The assumption of lawful relationships among events and behavior does not imply a rejection of human freedom. For the applied behavior analyst, "freedom is defined in terms of the number of options available to people and the right to exercise them" (Bandura, 1975, p. 865). It is unfortunate that because of "misunderstandings of Skinner's thought, it is believed that, somehow, behavior analysis has the power to remove the ability of the individual to choose alternative responses" (Newman, Reinecke, & Kurtz, 1996, p. 277). The goal of the behavior analyst is to increase, not decrease, such options or alternative responses and thus to increase the freedom of the individual. The high school student who repeatedly fails English is not free to attend college. The child who is afraid to interact with peers is not free to make friends. People who have severe behavioral deficits may have no options at all; they cannot move around, take care of their basic needs, or control their environment in any way. This emphasis on options or choices will be addressed later in this chapter and throughout the text. It is the cornerstone of providing appropriate educational services to every individual.

> Behaviorists define freedom in terms of a person's ability to make choices and to exercise options.

A crucial concept in understanding the deterministic position is that the relationship between behavior and the environment is reciprocal (Bandura, 1969; Craighead et al., 1976). Environmental events control behavior, but behavior inevitably alters the environment as well. This reciprocal relationship exists between people. The behavior modifier's behavior is changed by the actions of the subject of the modification. Thus, everyone influences and controls others' behavior. It is impossible to abandon control; we inevitably influence the behavior of other people (Bandura, 1975; Rogers & Skinner, 1956). For example, a child who seldom smiles is not very pleasant to be around, so teachers and other children may avoid him. If his teacher systematically reinforces his occasional happy facial expressions, the child will smile more. Because a smiling child is pleasant to be around and to interact with, he will himself become more reinforcing to others, including his teacher. She will then have more opportunities to reinforce smiling.

Seen in this context, behavioral technology is neither dehumanizing nor inhumane. When goals are **humane**, we must offer the most effective means available to reach them. In many cases, the proven effectiveness of applied behavior analysis procedures makes them the most humane choice.

Ethical Use of Applied Behavior Analysis Procedures

Learning Outcome 2.2 List the criteria for verifying that procedures for behavior change are being ethically implemented.

All teachers—whether or not they are also applied behavior analysts—are concerned with ethics. Before describing ways in which teachers can behave ethically, we will discuss the concept of ethics itself. A decision or action is ethical if it is right. That, of course, is a deceptively simple statement. The determination of what is right, according to whom it is right, and how we decide it is right has occupied philosophers and others since the days of Aristotle. Very simply stated, a teacher who is doing the right thing is behaving ethically. Doing the right thing, however, means far more than avoiding censure or even complying with a set of ethical guidelines or standards. Several associations, including the Council for Exceptional Children (2010) and the Behavior Analyst Certification Board (BACB, 2014; Bailey & Burch, 2016), provide such guidelines, and teachers and other professionals should certainly be familiar and comply with those applying to them. We, however, are not "more concerned that ... teachers follow the rules than that ... teachers become ethical beings" (Watras, 1986, p. 14). Simply because something is accepted practice does not ensure that it is right (Kitchener, 1980). People following rules (or obeying orders) have done some very wrong things over the centuries, and no set of rules can ever cover every eventuality. Teachers must be prepared to act ethically in the absence of guidelines and even when their actions are in conflict with guidelines or instructions.

The ways prospective teachers become ethical beings has been the subject of intense interest among teacher educators. A volume of the *Journal of Teacher Education* (1986) was almost entirely devoted to the issue. The consensus appears to be that discussing ethical dilemmas in a forum of other interested prospective and practicing professionals best develops ethical reasoning. Ethics should not be addressed in a single course but should permeate all courses (Pastrana et al., 2018). If ethical issues do not arise and are not discussed in your classes, we suggest you bring them up.

Although the primary reason to behave ethically is to act consistently with what one believes is right, there is another reason. Teachers must always be aware that other people are concerned with teachers' doing the right thing. Previous sections have acknowledged that people are especially apt to worry about ethics when behavioral techniques are used. Unless teachers take particular care to act ethically and to assure others that they do, they may find noneducators seeking and acquiring more and more control over what may and may not be done in classrooms.

Those who practice applied behavior analysis have agreed for many years that a number of factors must be considered when attempting to determine whether a proposed intervention is ethical. These include "community standards, laws, prevailing philosophies, individual freedom and responsibility of the clients through informed consent as well as the clients' attitudes and feelings" (Sulzer-Azaroff, Thaw, & Thomas, 1975). In the case of schoolchildren or residents of an institution,

---

Humanism
Pearson eText
Video Example 2.2
In this video, B.F. Skinner discusses his view on humanism. He articulates how a culture grows in strength, by investing in human potential. How does this philosophy relate to the mission of education?

https://www.youtube.com/watch?v=KKG—VDFcGs

Awareness of potential criticism may help avert interference from uninformed persons.

it is important to seek the opinions of the parents or guardians of the students to ask them how they feel about procedures being used or proposed for use with their children. It may seem strange for behaviorists to concern themselves with such subjective criteria as attitudes and feelings, but Wolf (1978) made a strong case for considering these factors. If participants do not like a program, he said, "They may avoid it, or run away, or complain loudly" (p. 206). Wolf suggested that social validity should be established for goals, procedures, and outcomes. **Social validity**, or consumer satisfaction, is simply the acceptability of a program or procedure to its consumers (Carter & Wheeler, 2019; Common & Lane, 2017). To assess the social validity of interventions, applied behavior analysts sometimes give questionnaires, interviews, and surveys to the parents and other teachers of the students. Even though applied behavior analysts do not typically use such subjective means of data collection due to cautions about their validity, "it is entirely possible that even quite invalid queries into social validity are better than no queries at all: Giving consumers any opportunity to express complaints and discontents that otherwise would go unnoticed may save at least some programs from fatal backlashes, at least if the offended consumer is moved enough by simply the existence of an otherwise inadequate social-validity assessment form to write in its margins or talk to the appliers" (Baer, Wolf, & Risley, 1987, p. 323).

There are several more objective means of assessing social validity. If teachers or other interventionists continue using an intervention and the students maintain their skills, this is an indication that the teachers accepted the use of the intervention (Kennedy, 2002). In addition to asking teachers and parents, applied behavior analysts may be interested if the students themselves find an intervention socially valid. A way to assess this is to expose a student to multiple interventions, such as functional communication training and extinction, and then letting the student choose one of those procedures for continued use (Hanley, 2010). Many, but not all, articles published about research using applied behavior analysis address the issue of social validity (Park & Blair, 2019; Snodgrass et al., 2018).

There is an interesting relationship between social validity and procedural integrity. Procedural integrity is the extent to which a teacher implements a procedure as it is written or described. When teachers have poor procedural integrity, the student's behavior change is minimal (Brand et al., 2019). When researchers or consultants ensure high procedural integrity through effective training, there are higher levels of social validity (Park & Blair, 2019). In other words, when teachers know how to implement an intervention correctly, they find the intervention acceptable. Conversely, when there is a high degree of social validity, there is a high degree of procedural integrity (Strohmeier et al., 2014). That is, if a teacher finds an intervention acceptable and doable, she is more likely to implement it correctly.

Teachers using behavioral procedures concern themselves with factors occurring outside of their classrooms. Goals, procedures, and outcomes must be acceptable to the consumers of education—students, parents, and the community. Stainback and Stainback (1984) suggested that increased attention be given to qualitative research methods that provide "more attention to the social and educational relevance of research efforts" (p. 406). Leko (2014) used qualitative research to assess the social validity of a direct instruction reading intervention with middle school teachers. Based on this work, Leko provided a more robust definition of social validity in terms of evaluating "(a) macro- and micro-goals; (b) procedures for planning, delivering, and assessing instruction; (c) intervention materials; and (d) outcomes related to instructional quality, stigmatization, and students' achievement, socio-emotional development, and engagement" (p. 284). Additionally, it is critically important for teachers and researchers to be attentive to the wide cultural diversity present in most communities and to select goals, procedures, and outcomes congruent with that diversity (Fong et al., 2016).

We hope we have convinced you that it is in your best interests to behave ethically. Although we acknowledged earlier that guidelines are necessarily incomplete, we believe it would be unethical not to provide some. It would be difficult to imagine an ethical position that did not focus on protecting students' rights. The Ethical Code of the Behavior Analyst Certification Board (BACB, 2014) contains 10 sections related to functions of behavior analysts in schools and other settings. We summarize five of these sections most pertinent to teachers using applied behavior analysis in schools: responsible conduct of behavior analysts, behavior analysts' responsibility to clients, assessing behavior, behavior analysts and behavior-change programs, and behavior analysts' ethical responsibility to colleagues.

In addition, a statement approved by the Executive Council of the Association for Behavior Analysis (ABA) from 1988 includes a list of individual rights that provides teachers with the basis for making ethical decisions about many issues. The statement begins: "We propose that individuals who are recipients or potential recipients of treatment designed to change their behavior have the right to (1) a therapeutic environment, (2) services whose overriding goal is personal welfare, (3) treatment by a competent behavior analyst, (4) programs that teach functional skills, (5) behavioral assessment and ongoing evaluation, and (6) the most effective treatment procedures available" (Van Houten et al., 1988, p. 111). We integrate some of these topics into the themes from the BACB and then address the remaining topics.

A Responsible and Competent Behavior Analyst

Responsible Conduct of Behavior Analysts (BACB, 2014)

Behavior analysts demonstrate responsibility when they are honest, follow through with commitments in a timely manner, and show respect to people from diverse backgrounds. They are ethical when they base their assessments and interventions on published research and continually engage in professional development to stay current on research. Behavior analysts must practice within their scope of competence. That is, if a new behavior analyst completed a supervised practicum in a classroom with students with autism and other developmental disabilities, she is qualified to work with students with autism but not necessarily with students who have bipolar disorder. Behavior analysts do not have multiple relationships, conflicts of interest, or exploitative relationships. This includes not having sexual relationships with clients or students and not giving or accepting gifts from clients or students. However, some argue that gift-giving should be allowed as it aligns with the values of certain cultures (Witts et al., 2018).

Treatment by a Competent Behavior Analyst (Van Houten et al., 1988)

These days, becoming a Board-Certified Behavior Analyst requires a great deal of training and experience. This is generally a minimum of a master's degree, seven courses in applied behavior analysis, 1500 hours of supervised practical experience, and passing a four-hour board exam. Not all teachers using applied behavior analysis will be board certified, but this gives an indication of the amount of training needed to be fully competent in using the concepts and procedures. Sometimes teachers attend a workshop on applied behavior analysis, and because some of the procedures seem simple, such as praising good behavior, they feel they can implement the procedures correctly in their classrooms. However, it is not possible to learn in a few days enough about applied behavior analysis to implement ethical, effective programs. Professionals providing professional development workshops to teachers sometimes think their workshop will change the teachers' practices; this has been shown to be false (Kirkpatrick et al., 2019). One of the authors attended a meeting many years ago during which she was asked to develop a packet for other faculty members that would enable them, after a few hours' reading, to include applied behavior analysis techniques in their methods courses and thus obviate the need for a separate class on behavior management. When she retorted that she had taken eight courses in applied behavior analysis and had been practicing the procedures for 17 years, and was still learning, the reaction was typically: "But ABA is so simple!"

A concerning outcome of this thinking is that people who do not adequately understand the concepts and procedures often misuse them. A common example is that teacher who attends the workshop, buys a bag of candy, and proceeds to hand out "reinforcement" indiscriminately. When this doesn't improve the students' behavior, the teacher may conclude that applied behavior analysis does not work. An unfortunate side effect is that the children treated in this manner may become *more* disruptive because the teacher provides it even when they being disruptive. Moreover, parents become upset because their children's teeth are decaying and their appetites are spoiled; the principal expresses annoyance because she receives numerous irate phone calls from those parents; other teachers become enraged because their students demand candy, too; and the escutcheon of applied behavior analysis suffers another blot.

The principles of applied behavior analysis are indeed easy to understand. Their effective implementation, however, is not so simple. In addition to a thorough understanding of the principles, acquired from qualified instructors, supervised practice is critical. This is particularly important for difficult procedures, such as shaping, functional analysis of challenging behavior, and transfer-of-stimulus-control techniques.

In contrast, what has been shown to work is direct training of teachers or other staff members to implement procedures based on applied behavior analysis. This commonly is in the form of *behavioral skills training*, which consists of providing instructions, modeling the procedures, role-playing, and providing feedback (Brock et al., 2017; Davenport et al., 2019; Fetherston & Sturmey, 2014; Hogan et al., 2015; Homlitas et al., 2014; Kirkpatrick et al., 2019; Sawyer et al., 2017; Smith & Higbee, 2020). This is also referred to as competency-based training, with the idea that training ends when the teacher or staff person has implemented a procedure with a high degree of accuracy (Reid, 2017).

> Implementing these procedures is not always as easy as it sounds.

> Good supervision includes training, observation, and evaluation.

Scope of Competence
Pearson eText
Video Example 2.3
In this video, a behavior analyst describes how to practice ethically by identifying areas of competence. How might these practices be useful for educators utilizing ABA procedures?

https://www.youtube.com/watch?v=5DP8Ifko7qA

Behavior Analysts' Responsibility to Clients and Consent

Behavior Analysts' Responsibility to Clients (BACB, 2014)

It is important to determine who is the "primary ultimate beneficiary of services" (p. 6)—usually the student—and maintain collegiality and communication with parents and other professionals involved. Behavior analysts should make clear to all involved their specific duty, such as providing direct teaching or consultation. The confidentiality of information and documentation about a student must be protected, and consent for video or audio recording of the student must be attained from parents. Finally, "clients have the right to effective treatment" (p. 8); that is, a behavior analyst must identify the best intervention for a client based on research and implement that intervention as much as needed to achieve a meaningful improvement.

Services Whose Overriding Goal is Personal Welfare (Van Houten et al., 1988)

It may seem obvious that the behaviors targeted for change should be those whose change will benefit the student. Nevertheless, accusations have been made that residential institutions (*Wyatt v. Stickney*, 1972) and schools (Winett & Winkler, 1972) use behavior-change programs primarily to reduce behaviors that disrupt the smooth functioning of the institution or school but are not detrimental to residents or students. Winett and Winkler examined articles detailing behavior-change programs in the

Journal of Applied Behavior Analysis from 1968 through 1970. They stated that the majority of the articles concerned the attempted suppression of talking, moving around, and such disruptive behaviors as whistling, laughing, and singing. Winett and Winkler concluded that the technology of applied behavior analysis was being used merely to establish "law and order" (p. 499) rather than to serve the best interests of students. Winett and Winkler's famous phrase is that too many programs were only teaching students to "be still, be quiet, be docile" (p. 499).

We have come a long way since the early 1970s, but even nowadays, teachers of students with severe disabilities sometimes emphasize goals related to sitting in a chair, reducing loud vocalizations, reducing stereotypic behavior, and putting hands in the "ready position." These goals are often cited as being prerequisites to learning academic, communicative, and social skills. However, public school teachers today are required to align teaching goals with state curriculum standards, even with students with severe disabilities (Saunders et al., 2017). Readiness, functional, and academic skills must all be balanced in curricula for students with severe disabilities. Even back in the early 1970s, although O'Leary (1972) agreed with Winett and Winkler (1972) that careful examination of goals is important, he disagreed with their conclusions. He cited numerous studies that demonstrated the researchers' concern with such behaviors as academic response rates, talking, prosocial interactions, and language and reading skills. O'Leary did agree with Winett and Winkler's call for "extensive community dialogues concerning those behaviors and values we wish to develop in our children" (p. 511). We must continue pushing this agenda forward.

> Applied behavior analysis procedures may be abused if students' rights and best interests are not considered.

For selected goals to be in the best interests of the students, they or their parents must voluntarily agree to the goals. Federal legislation, as well as the BACB (2014) and ethics codes of related disciplines, such as school psychology (Jacob et al., 2016), requires that parents or guardians consent to programs planned for their children with disabilities. Such a requirement is intended to ensure that participation in programs is voluntary. It is not necessary to acquire parental consent for all aspects of a teaching program, however. Martin (1975) suggested that widely accepted strategies for overall classroom management and student motivation do not require anyone's consent, even if the teacher decides to change from one strategy to another. Consent is required for procedures not yet widely accepted and for those applied only to individual students.

The consent that ensures voluntary participation in behavior-change programs must be both informed and voluntary (Rothstein, 1990). **Informed consent** is based on full understanding of the planned program. Informed consent does not occur unless parents or other advocates demonstrate that they comprehend all aspects of the program, including possible risks. If necessary, information must be provided in the native language of those involved. Educational services based on applied behavior analysis are occasionally delivered through teleconsultation, such as by using videoconferencing. Peterson et al. (2019) suggested three components of teleconsultation that require consent: providing the teleconsultation; video or audio recording the sessions; and consent for assessments, such as a functional behavior assessment.

Ethical Guidelines for Conducting Assessments

Assessing Behavior (BACB, 2014)

Behavior analysts must conduct assessments, such as a functional behavior assessment, before recommending or implementing interventions. They must obtain consent to conduct assessments. They must share the results of assessments in understandable ways. To evaluate and make decisions regarding interventions, behavior analysts must collect, graph, and share data.

Behavioral Assessment and Ongoing Evaluation (Van Houten et al., 1988)

Ethical teachers cannot and do not arbitrarily decide what to teach students to do or to stop doing. Goals and objectives for each student must be based on careful observation of what the student does under a variety of conditions. After goals are selected and programs implemented, the ethical teacher keeps track of how the program is going. It is insufficient to make statements like "I started using counters to help Ben with his math and he seems to be doing better." We want you to be able to say, "I observed that for 4 days Ben got only 2 to 3 of 10 one-digit addition problems right. I gave him 20 counters and showed him how to use them. He got 6 right that day, 7 yesterday, and 9 today. When he gets all 10 right for 3 days in a row, I'll go on to subtraction." We will teach you how to say that in "behaviorese" in Chapter 4, which covers using data collection to assess and evaluate the results of procedures.

> Information for goal setting comes from many sources: tests, records, observation, parents, teachers, and the students themselves.

Behavioral Strategies and Least Restrictive Environment

Behavior Analysts and Behavior-Change Programs (BACB, 2014)

Behavior analysts must base individualized interventions on behavior analytic principles. They must obtain consent before implementing or changing interventions and they may involve students in planning interventions. Behavior analysts set objectives for interventions, specify the needed settings, and set criteria for terminating services. Because the use of punishment procedures is controversial and can be dangerous, there are several ethical guidelines for their use. Because of the sensitive nature of these guidelines, we quote them here:

(a) Behavior analysts recommend reinforcement rather than punishment whenever possible.
(b) If punishment procedures are necessary, behavior analysts always include reinforcement procedures for alternative behavior in the behavior-change program.
(c) Before implementing punishment-based procedures, behavior analysts ensure that appropriate steps have been taken to implement reinforcement-based procedures unless the severity or dangerousness of the behavior necessitates immediate use of aversive procedures.
(d) Behavior analysts ensure that aversive procedures are accompanied by an increased level of training, supervision, and oversight. Behavior analysts must evaluate the effectiveness of aversive procedures in a timely manner and modify the behavior-change program if it is ineffective. Behavior analysts always include a plan to discontinue the use of aversive procedures when no longer needed. (p. 13)

Another way to state a major guideline regarding punishment is that punishment should be a "last resort" after documenting the ineffectiveness of procedures based on positive reinforcement. Similar to (a) above, behavior analysts use the least restrictive procedures; that is, procedures not more restrictive than are needed to accomplish desired behavior change. For example, time-out is more restrictive than functional communication training. Additionally, similar to the cautions with using punishment, behavior analysts must not use positive reinforcers that may be harmful to students' health. For example, decades ago, teachers or researchers used cigarettes as positive reinforcers for the newly learned skills of adults with disabilities; can you imagine doing that today?

A Therapeutic Environment (Van Houten et al., 1988)

The environment for students with disabilities must be the least restrictive environment for those individuals. The least restrictive environment is not necessarily the general education classroom or even a regular school for all students. It is that environment that "imposes the fewest restrictions necessary, while insuring individual safety and development. Freedom of individual movement and access to preferred activities, rather than type or location of placement, are the defining characteristics of a least restrictive environment" (Van Houten et al., 1988, p. 112).

Recently some educators have suggested that the only appropriate environment for any child, however severe the disability, is in a general education classroom, with peers of the same chronological age. Discussions of this practice, known as *full inclusion* (Guralnick et al., 2008; Kauffman et al., 2020; Zigmond et al., 2009), should certainly include the issue of whether it is possible to provide a safe, humane environment that is responsive to individual needs for every child with a disability in a general education classroom. Those who advocate full inclusion of students with disabilities argue that the effects, positive or negative, it will have on typical students or those with disabilities are not an issue. Separate classes for students with disabilities constitute segregation. Inclusion is a civil right and it is *unethical* to exclude any student (Stainton & Clare, 2012). Providing a safe environment is unarguably necessary. Doing so requires such simple and obvious, but too often neglected, steps as removing any potentially dangerous items or storing them so students do not have access to them. When a student stabs another student with the teacher's 4-inch pointed scissors, our first question is why, in a classroom where some students are known to have violent outbursts, the scissors were not locked away.

Students' safety outside the classroom must also be assured. Students with disabilities are especially vulnerable, for example, to verbal, physical, and sexual abuse from their peers. Such bullying, which has become a nationwide concern for all children, may be an even greater danger for these students (Maiano et al., 2016). Students' safety must be monitored in halls, restrooms, cafeterias, playgrounds, and buses. Peers are not the only ones who may abuse or neglect students, and regular schools and classrooms are not the only places where abuse or neglect can occur. Recently, in the city in which one of us lives, a student living in a residential treatment facility was left on a school bus overnight. His parents thought he was at the facility, and the staff at the facility assumed his parents had taken him home for a visit, as they sometimes did. Someone should have checked.

Providing a humane environment means more than refraining from neglecting or abusing students. Every human being has a right to be treated with dignity. "Minimally dignified treatment requires sanitation, cleanliness, comfort, and attempts at respectful communication and consent" (Schroeder, Oldenquist, & Rohahn, 1990, p. 105). This means, among many other things, not talking about students' problems in front of them, even if they are too young or too low functioning to understand. It means not having a student "do his thing" for visitors, even if his "thing" is funny. It also means not treating older students with disabilities like babies by, for example, changing their clothing in front of others. An attempt was made recently to introduce one of us to a 20-year-old man who was seated on a portable toilet shielded from the rest of the classroom by a screen. That was a violation of dignity both inhumane and unethical (Pennington et al., 2016; Turnbull, 2017).

An environment sensitive to individual needs provides each individual with a comfortable place or places to sit, interesting things to look at and do, and opportunities to engage in age-appropriate and functional activities. It allows students some choices about what they will do, when they will do it, and how they will do it. There has recently been an increasing emphasis on providing choices for individuals with disabilities (Kautz et al., 2018; Skerbetz & Kostewicz, 2015) as a strategy for increasing appropriate academic and social behaviors, but also as something to which everyone has a right. The right to make choices, particularly for children and for older persons with disabilities, must be balanced with the responsibility of their caretakers to help them make appropriate ones (Bannerman, Sheldon, Sherman, & Harchik, 1990). Of course, children will inevitably have to do things they do not want to do. These tasks should lead to positive reinforcement and a feeling of accomplishment. After all, adults often do things they dislike, but are glad they did them. For example, we, like Dorothy Parker, loathe writing but love having written.

Therapeutic Environment
Pearson eText
Video Example 2.4
In this video, an educator is working with several young students. Which features of a therapeutic environment do you notice in this setting? How does this educator emphasize reinforcement in her practices?

Additional Ethical Guidelines for Teachers

Behavior Analysts' Ethical Responsibility to Colleagues (BACB, 2014)

This final guideline we share from the BACB's Ethical Code is: "Behavior analysts promote an ethical culture in their work environments" (p. 15), and they hold colleagues accountable for violating ethical or legal guidelines with students or clients.

Teachers and applied behavior analysts, especially those working with students with disabilities, always function on a team, such as an Individualized Education Plan (IEP) team. Behavior analysts are required to model ethical behavior and defend their actions using the BACB ethical code, if needed. If behavior analysts observe colleagues breaking the ethical code, they must raise the infraction to the person, the supervisor, and possibly the BACB.

Programs that Teach Functional Skills (Van Houten et al., 1988)

Students need to learn skills that will enable them to function effectively in their environment. Teaching those skills should be the primary focus of every student's educational program. What skills are functional will be different for each student. It is functional for some students to learn algebra so they can learn geometry and trigonometry. It is functional for others to learn household skills so they can be contributing members of their families. In every case the choice of skills must be based on the assumption that "unless evidence clearly exists to the contrary, an individual is … capable of full participation in community life and [has] a right to such participation" (Van Houten et al., 1988, p. 113).

This assumption is a cornerstone for educators. It means, in our opinion, that it is unethical to believe that any young child, even if poor, at risk, or disabled, is not capable of learning academic and pre-academic skills. As a resource teacher and friend said, "I teach as if every one of my 6-year-olds will be going to Harvard." We believe equally strongly that it is unethical to waste the time of students for whom there is clear evidence that they are not capable of mastering traditional academics. An individual with a disability who can take care of her personal needs, help around the house, do simple shopping, entertain herself, behave appropriately in public, and perform routine tasks, including those related to paid employment, if possible, has functional skills. Such skills should be the focus of her education. It is of great importance that the particular environment in which an individual lives be considered when decisions about functional skills are made (Schroeder et al., 1990). The customs and values of a given community are as important as the resources available.

It is sometimes necessary to eliminate or reduce the rate of some student behaviors. A child who bites himself must be stopped from doing so. A student who hurts others cannot be allowed to continue. Students who are so disruptive that they cannot be maintained in a classroom must learn to stop running, screaming, or destroying property. Merely eliminating such behavior, however, is indefensible in the absence of a plan to develop constructive behavior. A student who just sits quietly doing nothing is not much better off than she was before intervention. Teachers must pay attention to developing behaviors in the student that will lead to improved learning or social interaction. Attention to functional assessment and analysis, as discussed in Chapter 7, will enable teachers to substitute appropriate behaviors for those that are disruptive or dangerous.

In some cases, inappropriate behavior may be decreased by reinforcing constructive behavior rather than by directly attempting to decrease destructive behavior. For example, increasing functional communication, self-control skills, and "life skills," such as tolerating the delay of reinforcement and being "friendly," may result in decreased inappropriate behavior (Luczynski & Hanley, 2013; Robison et al., 2020; Charlop-Christy et al., 2002). In general, for students who display any appropriate behavior at all, the teacher should try reinforcing such behavior and monitoring the effects of this procedure on the inappropriate behavior. Some students' repertoires of appropriate behavior are so limited and their performance of inappropriate behavior so continuous that there is little or no opportunity for a positive-reinforcement approach. In such cases, after a rigorous functional analysis, the teacher may first have to undertake elimination of the maladaptive behavior. This should be only a first step, however, and should never be undertaken without a detailed functional analysis (BACB, 2014). As soon as possible, the student must be taught to substitute constructive behaviors that lead to the acquisition of functional skills.

The Most Effective Treatment Procedures Available (Van Houten et al., 1988)

"Before behavior analysis, custodial care was often the best anyone could do. But that's not true anymore. Generally, a right to effective intervention now means a right to a behavioral intervention" (Malott et al., 1997, p. 414). We believe this statement, which the authors made about persons in residential treatment, has broad application. There is no excuse for programs, in schools or elsewhere, in which the goal is merely to keep students just quietly occupied or merely kept from harming themselves or others.

Many behavior analysts are amused when colleagues bring up the "new" requirement for "evidence-based treatment" or "evidence-based practice" and the difficulty of providing the evidence. We have been requiring it and providing the evidence for decades.

A primary consideration that guides professionals and parents in designing a program to change a student's behavior is the proven effectiveness of a technique in changing similar behaviors in similar students. The most ethical and responsible procedure to use in changing both academic (Heward, 2003) and social behavior is one that has been established as most effective (Travers, 2017). Throughout this text, we will discuss research related to changing specific behaviors and provide suggestions about effective procedures. Teachers who plan behavioral programs should also continually review current professional journals in order to keep abreast of new developments (Carr & Briggs, 2010). Many journals provide information on behavior-change procedures for use with students who have specific disabling conditions and with students in general education classes who display certain deficits or excesses (Gillis & Carr, 2014).

In some cases, it may not be possible, ethical, or legal to use a procedure that has been proven effective. Recent reports of abuse and misuse of restraint and seclusionary procedures in particular have led to numerous legislative and policy statements attempting to regulate or even forbid such procedures. Although there is no general agreement as to whether such procedures are ever necessary or appropriate, there is general agreement that training, oversight, and supervision are critical (Council for Children with Behavior Disorders, 2009; Luiselli et al., 2015; Ryan, Peterson, & Rosalski, 2007; Vollmer et al., 2011). Before using any aversive or exclusionary procedure, teachers should examine their employers' guidelines or regulations pertaining to such procedures, because rules may vary considerably. The unauthorized use of even short-term exclusion, a relatively mild but effective technique, may result in criticism or misunderstanding.

The use of aversive or seclusionary interventions should, in any event, be reserved for severely maladaptive behaviors that have not been modified successfully using positive means. Many behaviors targeted for deceleration may be eliminated using positive or nonaversive procedures that we will describe later in this text.

We discussed the movement toward inclusion of students with disabilities earlier in the context of safety, but it is also important to consider placement of students in

> Techniques for decreasing behavior will be described in Chapter 9.

terms of its effects or outcomes. Research on the outcomes of inclusion has focused on social effects (Carter et al., 2016; Fryxell & Kennedy, 1995), academic effects (Duchaine et al., 2018), and on-task behavior improvements (Reeves et al., 2013), which are often positive for all students (Agran et al., 2020; Barrett et al., 2020). Educational success of students with disabilities does not come from simple placement in a general education classroom; rather, teachers must use procedures to promote learning in inclusive classrooms (Brock & Carter, 2016; Lovelace et al., 2013; Obiakor et al., 2012), also termed "curricular inclusion" (Giangreco, 2020; p. 25). Some practices for promoting inclusion are cooperative learning, universal design for learning, and embedded instruction (Alquraini & Gut, 2012). Inclusion appears not to have deleterious effects on the academic performance of typical students (Stahmer & Carter, 2005) but there are indications that the academic performance of some students with disabilities may suffer in comparison with those served in more traditional special education placements, such as pull-out resource programs (Fuchs et al., 2015).

Accountability

Learning Outcome 2.3 Describe the effectiveness of providing accountability when using applied behavior analysis procedures.

Accountability implies publication of goals, procedures, and results so that they may be evaluated. Applied behavior analysis lends itself easily to such accountability. Goals are stated behaviorally, procedures described clearly, and results defined in terms of direct, functional relations between interventions and behaviors. It is impossible to conduct applied behavior analysis as described by Baer, Wolf, and Risley (1968) without being accountable. The entire process is visible, understandable, and open to evaluation. The result of such accountability is that parents, teachers, administrators, and the public can judge for themselves whether an approach is working or whether a change is needed.

Teachers should not view the requirement of accountability as negative or threatening. It is to a teacher's advantage to verify the effectiveness of his or her teaching. This approach enables teachers to monitor their own competence and to demonstrate this competence to others. It is much more impressive to face a supervisor at a yearly evaluation conference armed with charts and graphs showing increases in reading ability and decreases in disruptive behavior than it is to walk in with only vague statements about a pretty good year.

To whom are teachers accountable? In terms of ethical behavior, the answer is "to everyone." Teachers are accountable to their profession, the community, their administrative superiors, the parents of their students, those students, and themselves.

The teacher who follows the suggestions provided in this chapter should avoid many problems associated with the use of applied behavior analysis procedures in the classroom. Table 2.1 summarizes these suggestions. No amount of prevention can forestall all criticism; nor can a teacher avoid making mistakes. Systematic attention to the ethical standards in the ABA's statement, however, can minimize criticism and enable teachers to learn from mistakes rather than become discouraged by them.

Table 2.1 Suggestions for ethical use of applied behavior analysis

Assure competence of all staff members.
Choose appropriate goals.
Ensure voluntary participation.
Be accountable.

> Accountability is a major benefit of applied behavior analysis.

Effective and Accountable Practice
Pearson eText
Video Example 2.5
In this video, an educator meets with the parent of a student to discuss a student's program. What layers of accountability do you notice in this video? Does this parent appear satisfied with the services provided to her child?

Let's listen in on Professor Grundy, whose workshop discussion may address concerns you have. All of the questions the professor answers here are inevitably addressed to everyone who undertakes a career as an applied behavior analyst.

Professor Grundy Conducts a Workshop

The superintendent of schools in a large metropolitan area near the university asked Professor Grundy to conduct a 2-hour workshop on applied behavior analysis for elementary and secondary teachers. Although aware of the limitations of such short-term workshops (Kirkpatrick et al., 2019), Grundy concluded that if he confined himself to a description of basic learning principles, no harm would be done. On the appointed day, Grundy, dressed in his best tweed coat with leather elbow patches, stood before 700 teachers, and wondered how he got himself into this mess.

After a slow start, during which several teachers fell asleep and numerous others openly graded papers, Grundy hit his stride. He delivered a succinct, snappy talk full of humorous anecdotes and sprinkled with just enough first-name references to his friends, all "biggies" in applied behavior analysis and all totally unfamiliar to the teachers. As Grundy reached the conclusion of his presentation, glowing with satisfaction, he noticed to his horror that he was coming up about 45 minutes short of the amount of time agreed to in his contract. Over the thunderous applause (resulting at least partially from the fact that the teachers thought they were going to be released early), Grundy called faintly for questions. There was considerable rumbling and shifting about, but when the superintendent mounted the stage and glared fixedly at the audience, the hands began to go up. The nature of the questions made Grundy vow never to be caught short again, but he did his best to answer each.

Question: Isn't what you're suggesting bribery?

Answer: I'm glad you asked that question. [Grundy fumbles with his smartphone, thumbing the infernal thing, then begins reading.] According to the interweb, bribery is something given to pervert the judgment or corrupt the conduct of a person. In that sense, the use of the principles I have described is certainly not bribery. Teachers use the principles of learning to motivate their students to do things that will benefit them—things such as reading, math, and social skills.

A second definition is that a bribe is anything promised or given to induce a person to do something against his or her wishes. Some people might say that's exactly what I'm advocating. As a behaviorist, I have some difficulty with the word *wishes*, because I cannot see wishes but only actions. It appears to me that students have a free choice as to whether they will perform a behavior for which they know they will receive a reinforcer. My interpretation is that if Joanie, for example, chooses to perform the behavior, she has demonstrated her "wishes." The word *bribery* definitely implies something underhanded. I prefer to think of applied behavior analysis procedures as open, honest attempts to change students' behavior in a positive direction. Any other questions? If not . . .

Question: But shouldn't children be intrinsically motivated? Surely they don't have to be rewarded for learning. They should want to learn.

Answer: Madam, why are you here today? I'm sure that given the choice of spending the day at the mall or coming to an in-service session, your intrinsic motivation for learning might have wavered just a little. All of us here are being paid to be here; most adults, even those who enjoy their work enormously, would not continue to perform it in the absence of some very concrete application of the law of positive reinforcement. Why should we expect children to perform difficult tasks for less than we expect of ourselves?

Question: But won't our students expect rewards for everything they do?

Answer: Certainly. And why not? As your students become more successful, they will begin to respond to the reinforcers available in the natural environment—the same reinforcers that maintain the appropriate behavior of students who are already successful. Good students do not work without reinforcers. Their behavior is reinforced by good grades, by parental approval, and, yes, by the love of learning. When doing good work has been consistently reinforced, it eventually does become a secondary, or conditioned, reinforcer. We cannot, however, expect this to happen overnight with students who have had very little experience with success in learning tasks. Does that answer your questions? Thank . . .

Question: At our last in-service session, the speaker told us that using rewards will decrease intrinsic motivation.

Answer: That's a rather widespread notion nowadays (Kohn, 2018). Not everyone agrees, however, and many question the validity and interpretation of the studies cited as evidence for it (Pierce & Cameron, 2002; Slavin, 1991). There's so much evidence of the effectiveness of behavioral procedures that, in my opinion, it is unethical not to implement them.

Question: Doesn't this kind of behavior management just suppress the symptoms of serious emotional problems without getting at the root cause?

Answer: Oh, my. That's a very complicated question. Behaviorists don't accept the concept of emotional problems caused by some underlying root cause. We have found that if we deal with the problem behaviors, the roots just seem to die out. Human beings are not like weeds whose roots lurk under the surface of the ground waiting to send up shoots as soon as it rains.

Question: Yes, but everyone knows that if you suppress one symptom, a worse one will take its place. Doesn't that prove there are underlying problems?

Answer: No, sir, everyone does not know that. Human beings are no more like piston engines than like weeds. Just because one symptom "goes down," another one will not necessarily "pop up." My colleagues (Baer, 1971; Bandura, 1969; Rachman, 1963; Yates, 1970) have reported extensive research indicating that removal of so-called symptoms does not result in the development of new ones. As a matter of fact, when children's inappropriate behaviors are eliminated, they sometimes learn new, appropriate behaviors without being taught (Chadwick & Day, 1971; Rapp et al., 2004). Even if new maladaptive behaviors do occur—and they sometimes do (Balson, 1973; Schroeder & MacLean, 1987)—there is no evidence to show they are alternative symptoms of underlying deviance. Functional analysis generally indicates that those behaviors served a communicative function for the individual and that new behaviors are a continued attempt to communicate some need. If appropriate behaviors are taught that meet the same communicative purpose, the inappropriate ones will go away. Now if . . .

Question: Isn't what you're talking about based on the behavior of animals such as rats and monkeys? That's how you train a dog, for heaven's sake: Give him a treat when he does a cute trick and hit him with a rolled-up newspaper when he's bad. Isn't it unethical to treat our kids like animals?

Answer: Early research studying the laws of behavior was conducted with animals. This doesn't mean we control human beings as if they were nothing but white rats or pigeons, or even dogs. Such animal research provides only a basic foundation for studying behavior. Decades of research have applied those principles to humans—children and adults—in classrooms and other real-world settings to generate the types of strategies that can help your students. These procedures take into account the complexity of human behavior and the undeniable freedom of human beings to choose their course of action. What's unethical is not learning and applying all we can from whatever source.

Question: This stuff may work on those special education kids, but my students are smart. Won't they catch on?

Answer: Good heavens, of course they'll catch on. The laws of behavior operate for all of us. We can change behavior in youngsters with very severe disabilities, but it's a very complex process. With your students, you can shorten and simplify the procedure. You just tell them what the contingencies are. You don't have to wait for the students to learn from experience. Applied behavior analysis procedures work on everyone, even professors. Take punishment, for example. If I ever agree to do another workshop, it'll be a cold day in . . . Pardon me. Any more questions?

Question: But how can applied behavior analysis work with my kids? I don't care how much candy you gave them, they still couldn't read.

Answer: Applied behavior analysis is not just giving students candy. If your students do not respond verbally to the written word, then you must bring their responses under stimulus control. That's applied behavior analysis. If they have no vocal language, you shape it; that's applied behavior analysis. If they just sit there and do nothing, you get their attention. AND THAT'S APPLIED BEHAVIOR ANALYSIS! ARE THERE ANY MORE QUESTIONS?

Question: I think the whole thing sounds like too much work. It seems awfully tedious and time consuming. Is it really worth the trouble?

Answer: If ... it's ... not ... worth ... the ... trouble, ... don't ... do ... it. Behaviors that are serious enough to warrant more complicated procedures take up an enormous amount of your time. You don't use a complicated procedure to solve a simple problem. Try timing yourself with a stopwatch. How much time is this problem taking the way you're handling (or not handling) it now? Try applying systematic contingencies and keeping records. Then compare the amount of time you've spent. You might be surprised! Now, I really must ...

Question: I have only one student with really serious problems. If I use some systematic procedure with him, won't the others complain? What do I say to them?

Answer: The problem will not occur as often as you think. Most students know that a student who is not performing well needs extra help and are neither surprised nor disturbed when he gets it. Few students will even ask why that student is treated differently. If they do, I suggest you say to them, "In this class everyone gets what he or she needs. Harold needs a little extra help remembering to stay in his seat." If you consistently reinforce appropriate behavior for all your students, they will not resent it when a more systematic procedure is implemented for a student with special problems. If that's all, I ...

Question: Most of my students with problems can't learn much because they come from very bad home situations. There's just nothing you can do in such cases, is there?

Answer: Pigeons can learn to discriminate between environments and to perform the behaviors that will be reinforced in each. Are you implying your students are less capable than birds? Such an assumption is inhumane. Blaming poor learning or inappropriate behavior on factors beyond your control is simply a refusal to accept responsibility. Now coming to school with basic needs met, such as enough food and sleep, is critical. If you can have discussions with parents about that, that will likely serve you well. However, although you have little influence on your students' environment outside your classroom, you have an enormous influence on that classroom environment. It is your job to arrange it so your students learn as much as possible, both academically and socially. What do you think teaching is, anyway? Teach is a transitive verb. You're not teaching unless you're teaching somebody something.

Question: Have you ever taught school?

Answer: At this point Professor Grundy became incoherent and had to be helped from the podium by the superintendent. As he drove home, he realized he had made a number of mistakes, the first of which was agreeing to do the workshop. He had assumed that teachers expecting to receive concrete help with classroom management problems would be interested in a theoretical discussion of learning principles. He had also assumed that the teachers would immediately see the relationships between these principles and the behaviors of their students. Grundy realized it was unreasonable of him to expect this. He did decide, however, that he needed to include more practical applications in his courses on applied behavior analysis.

Misconceptions about ABA in the Classroom
Pearson eText
Video Example 2.6
In this video, an educator clarifies a common misconception that ABA can only be practiced by behavior analysts. How might behavior analysis and education work effectively together?

Theory or Recipes?

Learning Outcome 2.4 State the justification for ensuring that professionals working with individuals with challenging behaviors understand the theoretical basis of the procedures that they implement.

Professor Grundy was undoubtedly correct in his belief that the effective use of applied behavior analysis requires knowledge of the basic principles. Teachers often reject theory and seek immediate practical solutions to specific problems. It is human nature to hope that simply asking how to solve a specific problem will result in a specific answer applicable to all students in all situations. It was once suggested that we include an alphabetical list of behavior problems with a solution for each as an appendix to this text. Such a cookbook approach, however, has serious limitations. Although students supplied with cookbook methods may acquire competencies more quickly, the students who are required to spend more time on basic principles tend to show more competence in the long run (White, 1977). In other words, teachers must incorporate the "analysis" in applied behavior analysis (Schlinger, 2017). We will do our best with numerous examples throughout the text to help you solve many problems that teachers encounter, but what we really hope is that you will use our discussion of behavioral principles along with our examples to enhance your own ability to create solutions to whatever problems come your way.

Summary

This chapter described several objections to the use of applied behavior analysis techniques. These techniques have been criticized on the basis that they interfere with personal freedom and that they are inhumane. We have described our reasons for disagreeing with these objections. Properly used, applied behavior analysis procedures enhance personal freedom by increasing options. Applied behavior analysis procedures are humane because they are an effective tool for increasing options and teaching appropriate skills.

Applied behavior analysis procedures will be used ethically if the program includes a therapeutic environment, services whose overriding goal is personal welfare, treatment by a competent behavior analyst, programs that teach functional skills, behavioral assessment and ongoing evaluation, and the most effective treatment procedures available. Teachers who choose applied behavior analysis procedures and consider these factors know they are acting in the best interests of their students.

Discussion Questions

1. Write a short letter home to the parents or guardians of the students with whom you will be working this year. Describe your procedures (based on the principles of applied behavior analysis described in Chapter 1) without using any terminology likely to upset the parents.

2. One of your colleagues has cornered you in your classroom after school. She has heard that you are using "behavior modification" with your students and thinks that you are inhumane, coercive, and unethical. What will you say to her?

Chapter 3
Preparing Behavioral Objectives

Learning Outcomes

3.1 Identify the purpose for writing behavioral objectives.

3.2 Identify the process and components of writing educational goals.

3.3 Identify the components of behavioral objectives.

3.4 Identify ways to measure mastery based on a hierarchy of response competence.

3.5 Identify ways to measure mastery based on a hierarchy of levels of learning.

3.6 Identify ways to incorporate behavioral objectives in individualized education programs.

CHAPTER OUTLINE

Definition and Purpose
  Pinpointing Behavior

Educational Goals
  Establishing Goals

Components of a Behavioral Objective
  State the Learner
  State the Target Behavior
  State the Conditions of Intervention
  State Criteria for Acceptable Performance

Format for a Behavioral Objective

Expanding the Scope of the Basic Behavioral Objective
  Hierarchy of Response Competence
  Hierarchy of Levels of Learning
  Learning Levels for the Learner with Limitations

Behavioral Objectives and the IEP

Summary

In this chapter we will discuss the first step in carrying out a program for behavior change: defining the target behavior—the behavior to be changed. A target behavior may be selected because it addresses a behavioral deficit (such as too few math skills) or a behavioral excess (such as too much screaming). After the behavior to be changed has been identified, a written **behavioral objective** is prepared. A behavioral objective describes the behavior that should result from the instruction or intervention that is planned. It describes the intended outcomes of instruction, not the procedures for accomplishing those outcomes (Konrad et al., 2014).

A behavioral objective for a student who demonstrates a deficit in math skills would describe the level of math performance the student should reach. A behavioral objective for a student who screams excessively would describe an acceptable level of screaming. Anyone reading a behavioral objective should be able to understand exactly what a student is working to accomplish. Because behavioral objectives are such an integral part of planning for student behavior change, they are required as part of the individualized education program (IEP) for students with disabilities. We will also talk about the relationship between objectives and the IEP.

You will meet some teachers who are learning to use a behavioral approach in their teaching. Through them, you will encounter some of the difficulties of putting behavioral programs into effect. Consider the plight of Ms. Samuels, the resource teacher, in the vignette below.

> A behavioral objective is a statement that communicates a proposed change in behavior. It describes a level of performance and serves as a basis for evaluation.

Definition and Purpose

Learning Outcome 3.1 Identify the purpose for writing behavioral objectives.

The vignette below illustrates one of the most important reasons for writing behavioral objectives: to clarify the goals of a student's behavior-change program and thus to facilitate communication among people involved in the program. Because it is a written statement targeting a specific change in behavior, the objective serves as an agreement among school personnel, parents, and students about the academic or social learning for which school personnel are taking responsibility.

> Behavioral objectives improve communication.

An objective may also serve to inform students of what is expected. It is a statement of proposed student achievement and tells students what they will be learning or in what manner and to what degree their behavior is to change. Providing students with a statement of proposed learning outcomes enables them to match their performance with a standard of correct or expected performance. This allows for ongoing evaluation and provides informative feedback and reinforcement (Mazzotti, Test, & Wood, 2013).

A second reason for writing behavioral objectives is that a clearly stated target for instruction facilitates effective programming by the teacher and ancillary personnel. A clearly stated instructional target provides a basis for selecting

Are We Talking About the Same Thing?

Ms. Wilberforce, the third-grade teacher, was in a snit.

"That special ed consulting teacher," she complained to her friend, Ms. Folden, "is absolutely useless. I asked her two months ago to work on vowels with Martin and he still doesn't know the short sounds."

"You're absolutely right," agreed Ms. Folden. "I told her last September that Melissa Sue had a bad attitude. The longer the special ed teacher sees Melissa Sue, the worse it gets. All Melissa Sue does now is giggle when I correct her. It seems to me that we were better off without special ed teachers."

Meanwhile, Ms. Samuels, the special ed teacher, was complaining bitterly to her supervisor.

"Those general education teachers are so ungrateful. Just look at what I've done with Martin. He can name all the vowels when I ask him, and he even knows a little song about them. And Melissa Sue, who used to pout all the time, smiles and laughs so much now. I've done exactly what the teachers asked—why don't they appreciate it?"

A Matter of Opinion

Mr. Henderson, the teacher of a preschool class for students with developmental delays, hurried to the principal's office in a state of complete panic. The parents of Alvin, one of his students, had just threatened to remove the boy from school. They insisted Mr. Henderson was not teaching Alvin anything and was not making it possible for Alvin to spend more time with his general education kindergarten class. Mr. Henderson had agreed in August to work on toilet training with Alvin and felt the boy had made excellent progress. Alvin's parents, however, were upset because Alvin still had several accidents every week. They and the kindergarten teacher insisted that Mr. Henderson had not reached his stated goal.

"I have toilet trained Alvin," howled Mr. Henderson. "Wouldn't you consider only two or three accidents a week all right?"

---

appropriate materials and instructional strategies. Mager (1997) pointed out that "machinists and surgeons do not select tools until they know what they're intending to accomplish. Composers don't orchestrate scores until they know what effects they are trying to create" (p. 14). Clearly written behavioral objectives should prevent the classroom teacher from using materials simply because they are available or strategies simply because they are familiar. The selection of materials and teaching strategies is more likely to be appropriate if objectives are clearly defined.

There is yet another excellent reason for writing behavioral objectives. Consider Mr. Henderson in the vignette above.

> Behavioral objectives help evaluate progress.

Mr. Henderson's panic could have been prevented if a clearly written objective statement had come out of the August meeting. If a definition of *toilet trained* had been established at the beginning of the year, there would have been no question as to whether that objective had been achieved. Behavioral objectives provide for precise evaluation of instruction. When a teacher identifies a deficit or an excess in a student's behavioral repertoire, he has identified a discrepancy between current and expected levels of functioning. If the teacher states a performance criterion (the ultimate goal) and records ongoing progress toward this goal, both formative (ongoing) and summative (final) evaluation of intervention procedures become possible so that programs can be changed as necessary and plans made for the future. Ongoing evaluation and measurement enable the teacher, the student, or a third party to monitor progress continuously and to determine when goals have been reached. Continuous monitoring minimizes individual interpretations or prejudices in judgment when instructional procedures or a student's performances are evaluated.

Because behavioral objectives identify agreed-upon expectations that facilitate effective programming and effective communication among students, parents, teachers, and other professionals, they are used in a variety of situations. In general education they may be used by a teacher and student to set a goal for improving performance in long division or adding algebraic equations. They may be used between a therapist and a student to set targets for speech or physical therapy or between a student and the school psychologist to target a change in behavior. In the most formal and extensive use, behavioral objectives are an essential element of an IEP. When it is determined that students are eligible for special education services because a disability has been identified, students become eligible for a wide array of professional services to meet unique learning needs. In order to outline an educational plan and the services that will be provided a given student, an IEP is developed that sets out academic and behavioral/social goals for the student during the school year. As we will see, these goals are operationalized by writing behavior objectives.

Pinpointing Behavior

Before an objective can be written or a behavior-change program initiated, the target behavior must be described clearly. Referral information may often be vague and imprecise. To write effective objectives, the applied behavior analyst must refine broad generalizations into specific, observable, measurable behaviors. This process is frequently referred to as **pinpointing** behavior.

Pinpointing may be accomplished by asking a series of questions, usually including "Could you please tell me what he *does*?" or "What exactly do you want her to *do*?" For example, teachers often refer students to a behavior analyst because of "hyperactivity." The referring teacher and the applied behavior analyst must define this hyperactive behavior by describing exactly what is occurring. Is it that the student, like Ralph in Ms. Harper's class, wanders around the room? Does he tap his pencil on the desk? Does he weave back and forth in his chair?

Many categories of behavior may result in referrals and require pinpointing. Here are a few examples, with some questions that may help to refine the definition:

Sebastian can't do math: Is the problem that he does not have basic arithmetic computation skills, or that he cannot finish his problems within the time limit set, or that he refuses to attempt the problems?

Rebecca is always off task: Is the problem that she stares out the window, or that she talks to her neighbor, or that she scribbles in her book instead of looking at the chalkboard?

Robert is always disturbing others: Is he grabbing objects from someone, or talking to others during lessons, or hitting his neighbor, or knocking neighbors' books off the desk, or pulling someone's hair?

Desiree's lab projects are a mess: Is it that she cannot read the instructions in the lab manual, or that her handwriting is sloppy, or that she does not do the prescribed steps in the right order, or that she can do the experiments but cannot write the results coherently?

Teresa throws tantrums: Is she crying and sobbing, or is she throwing herself on the floor, or is she throwing objects around the room?

A teacher may ask a similar series of questions in describing more complex or abstract categories of behaviors. If the referring teacher said, "Carol doesn't use critical thinking skills," the applied behavior analyst would want to know if Carol

1. distinguishes between facts and opinions;
2. distinguishes between facts and inferences;
3. identifies cause–effect relationships;
4. identifies errors in reasoning;
5. distinguishes between relevant and irrelevant arguments;
6. distinguishes between warranted and unwarranted generalizations;
7. formulates valid conclusions from written material;
8. specifies assumptions needed to make conclusions true. (Gronlund, 1985, p. 14)

The behavior analyst may need to address other issues. If, for example, a student is out of his chair at inappropriate times, the teacher's concern may be either the number of times he gets out or the length of time he stays out. The student who gets up only once, but stays up all morning, is doing something quite different from the student who hops in and out of his seat every few minutes. Different intervention strategies and data collection techniques are needed. For complex behaviors such as temper tantrums, during which many discrete behaviors may occur simultaneously, it may be helpful to list the behaviors in some order of priority. They might be listed, for example, in order from least to most interference to the child or to the environment. After referral information has been refined so that target behaviors can be clearly described, **educational goals** and eventually behavioral objectives can be written.

Communicating Effectively
Pearson eText
Video Example 3.1
In this video, the IEP team discusses a student's strengths and weaknesses and develops a plan of action. How did clear communication play a role in this process?

Educational Goals

Learning Outcome 3.2 Identify the process and components of writing educational goals.

| Goals precede objectives.

Objectives should be derived from a set of educational goals that provide the framework for the academic year. These goals should evolve from an accumulation of evaluation information and should be correlated with curriculum planning. Goals define the anticipated academic and social development for which the school will take responsibility. During goal selection, educators estimate what proportion of the student's educational potential is to be developed within the next academic year. Thus, educational goals (long-term objectives) are statements of annual program intent, whereas behavior objectives (short-term or instructional objectives) are statements of actual instructional intent, usually for a three- to four-month period (quarterly) for individuals with more severe disabilities and for the length of time of the school's grading period for students with mild disabilities.

Establishing Goals

A multidisciplinary team is responsible for setting goals for students who are formally referred for special services. The team may include the student, the student's parents or guardians, representatives of general and special education, representatives of therapies that may be included in the student's educational program (e.g., speech–language, physical, occupational), and the school psychologist or counselor. When gathering data on which to base a student's educational program, the team will review the results of various evaluations to determine the student's current level of functioning. These data may include:

| Formal sources of information for goal setting.

1. *School psychology:* information from instruments that are primarily tests of intelligence, such as the Wechsler Intelligence Scale for Children–V (Wechsler, 2014), the Bayley Scales of Infant Development–III (Bayley, 2005), or the Kaufman Assessment Battery for Children, 2nd ed., NU (Kaufman & Kaufman, 2018); and tests that screen for behaviors of specific disabilities, such as the Childhood Autism Rating Scale, 2nd ed. (Schopler, Van Bourgondien, Wellman, & Love, 2010).
2. *Educational achievement:* information from instruments that test general academic achievement, such as the Wide Range Achievement Test–Revision 5 (Wilkinson, 2017), the *Woodcock-Johnson® IV Tests of Achievement* (Mather & Wendling, 2014), and the Brigance Comprehensive Inventory of Basic Skills II (Frency & Glascoe, 2010); or are specific to an academic area, such as the Key Math-3 Diagnostic Assessment (Connolly, 2008).
3. *Adaptive behavior:* information from instruments that rate the conceptual (e.g., language and academic skills), social, and practical skills (e.g., daily living skills) needed to function in one's everyday life in school, at home, and in the community, such as the Adaptive Behavior Scale, 3rd ed. (Harrison & Oakland, 2015), or the Vineland Adaptive Behavior Scales, 3re ed. (Vineland III; Sparrow, Cicchetti, & Saulnier, 2016).
4. *Therapeutic services:* results of speech–language pathology, physical therapy, and occupational therapy evaluations.
5. *Physical health:* results from neurological, pediatric, vision, and hearing screenings.

| Informal sources of information for goal setting.

In addition to these more formal sources, the goal-setting group should also consider parental desires and concerns. Recommendations from previous teachers are considered as well. The social and academic environmental demands of the present classroom, the home, the projected educational placement, or a projected work site should be examined. Based on this accumulated information, the committee proposes a set of educational goals for the student. An estimate of progress is then included in the long-term objectives prepared for the student's IEP.

For students who have not been identified as having special needs, formulating educational goals does not involve such an extensive accumulation of information.

Assessment may be limited to group achievement tests supplemented by informal teacher-made assessments. Goal setting also is constrained by the adopted curriculum. For example, each class of fourth graders in a given school district is usually expected to learn the same things. Under a standard curriculum, all students at a certain grade level are to be instructed in the natural resources of Peru, the excretory system of the earthworm, multiplication of fractions, and reading comprehension. The teacher's task is to translate these goals into reasonable objectives for each member of a particular class, some of whom may already know these things and some of whom lack the basic skills necessary to learn them. The teacher may write behavioral objectives for the class as a whole, giving consideration to the general characteristics of the group. In addition, if the teacher is to help a particular student who is having problems or to teach a reading group that is progressing slowly, that teacher may write additional behavioral objectives to prescribe a course of instruction that will facilitate learning.

Because educational goals are projected over long periods of time, they are written in broad terms. For practical application, however, they need to be written in terms that are observable and quantifiable. As you learned in Chapter 1, applied behavior analysts deal only with observable behaviors.

> Write goals in observable and quantifiable terms.

For students who do not have disabilities or who have mild disabilities, goals are needed only for each curriculum area. For very young students or those with severe disabilities, goals should be written in a number of domains of learning:

1. cognitive
2. communication
3. motor
4. social
5. self-help
6. vocational
7. maladaptive behavior

Hypothetical long-term goals for Aiden, a student with learning problems in math, and for Tanika, a student with severe disabilities, are as follows.

Aiden Will

Mathematics: Master basic computation facts at the first-grade level.
Social studies: Demonstrate knowledge of the functions of the three branches of the federal government.
Reading: Identify relevant parts of a story he has read.
Science: Demonstrate knowledge of the structure of the solar system.
Language arts: Increase the creative expression of his oral language.
Physical education: Increase his skills in team sports.

> Long-term educational goals for a student with mild disabilities.

Aiden's general education teacher will be responsible for setting all goals except the one in mathematics. Aiden may go to a part-time special education class (resource room) for mathematics, or an inclusion specialist may come to his classroom.

Compare Aiden's goals with Tanika's.

Tanika Will

Cognitive: Categorize objects according to their function.
Communication: Demonstrate increased receptive understanding of functional labels.
Motor: Develop gross motor capability of her upper extremities.
Social: Participate appropriately in group activities.
Vocational: Complete assembly tasks for a period of at least 1 hour.
Maladaptive behavior: Decrease out-of-seat behavior.
Self-help: Demonstrate the ability to dress independently.

> Long-term educational goals for a student with severe disabilities.

Teachers use these broad goals to create statements of instructional intent (behavioral objectives).

Behavioral objectives are not simply restatements of goals; they break goals into teachable components. Complex goals may generate many objectives. A goal that states a student will learn to play cooperatively with other children, for example, may require individual objectives identifying the need to share, to take turns, and to follow the rules of a game.

Components of a Behavioral Objective

Learning Outcome 3.3 **Identify the components of behavioral objectives.**

In order to communicate all the necessary information and provide a basis for evaluation, a complete behavioral objective should

1. state the learner;
2. state the target behavior;
3. state the conditions of intervention; and
4. state criteria for acceptable performance.

State the Learner

Behavioral objectives were initially designed to promote individualization of instruction (Gagne, 1985). To promote individualization, the teacher must re-identify the specific student or students for whom each objective is developed. Restatement reinforces the teacher's focus on the individual learner and communicates this focus to others. Thus, we include in a behavioral objective statements such as

| Use the student's name.

- John will ...
- The fourth graders will ...
- The participants in the training program will ...
- The members of the Rappers cooperative learning team will ...

State the Target Behavior

| State what the student will do.

After the team selects and defines deficient or excessive target behaviors, the teacher identifies exactly what the student will be doing when the desired change has been achieved. This statement spells out a precise response that is representative of the target behavior.

There are three basic purposes for including this component in the behavioral objective:

1. It ensures that the teacher is consistently observing the same behavior. The observation and recording of the occurrence or nonoccurrence of exactly the same behavior allows for an accurate and consistent reflection of the behavior in the data to be collected.
2. The statement of the target behavior allows for confirmation by a third party that the change observed by the teacher has actually occurred.
3. The precise definition of the target behavior facilitates continuity of instruction when people other than the teacher are involved.

To achieve these three purposes, the target behavior must be described so that its occurrence is verifiable. Precise description minimizes differing interpretations of the same behavior. A student's performance of a given behavior can best be verified when the teacher can see or hear the behavior or see or hear a direct product of the behavior. To attain this precision and clarity in an objective, the verb used to delineate the behavioral response should describe a behavior that is directly *observable, measurable*, and *repeatable*.

Though teachers of the gifted would like students to "discover" and art teachers would like students to "appreciate," objectives described in this manner are open to numerous interpretations. For example, it would be difficult for a third party to decide whether a student had performed the following behaviors:

- *recognize* the difference between big and little
- *understand* the value of coins
- *develop* an appreciation of Melville
- *remain* on task during group work
- *refrain* from aggression

The use of such vague terms leads to confusion and to disagreement about whether a behavior is occurring. Because any behavior can be described in a number of ways, everyone involved in a behavior-change project must agree upon a common description of the behavior. This description is the **operational definition** of the behavior. It is the definition under which everyone will operate when discussing, observing, counting, reporting, or consulting about this student's performance of this behavior, thus eliminating as much ambiguity as possible. The operational definition contains an agreed-upon description of observable and measurable characteristics of the motor performance of the behavior. These characteristics are clearly stated so that everyone can agree that the behavior has been or has not been performed.

A variety of approaches can be taken to define a behavior operationally. Table 3.1 presents examples of several ways to define on-task behavior. An operational definition usually contains a list of categories or specific examples of behaviors. Fairbanks, Sugai, Guardino, and Lathrop (2007) and Jessel, Ingvarsson, Whipple, and Kirk (2017) used short lists of categories of behaviors. Regan, Mastropieri, and Scruggs (2005) and Kranak, Alber-Morgan, and Sawyer (2017) used more extensive lists with examples. Within their definition, Regan et al. additionally defined a behavior with a negative example. Kemp and Carter's (2006) definition provides examples of when a student is actively on task and when passively on task. Callahan and Rademacher (1999) prepared a list for the observer and a list specifically for the student. For Brooks, Todd, Tofflemoyer, and Horner (2003), on-task behavior was a concern during individual seatwork and during group instruction. Therefore, an operational definition was written for both instructional formats. Cirelli, Sidener, Reeve, and Reeve (2016) and Thomas, DeBar, Vladescu, and Townsend (2020) included angle measurements.

Table 3.1 Operational definitions of on-task behavior

Fairbanks, Sugai, Guardino, and Lathrop (2007)	Orientation toward the task at hand, compliance with all directions, and working with appropriate materials.
Jessel, Ingvarsson, Whipple, and Kirk (2017)	"looking in the direction of the worksheet with the pencil in his hand, writing on the worksheet, or using the calculator on the iPad to solve the worksheet problems" (p. 249)
Regan, Mastropieri, and Scruggs (2005)	Student (a) is in designated area of room; (b) is manually engaged with appropriate materials; (c) is reading/writing the question/entry; (d) refrains from making derogatory comments about task/other; (e) asks relevant question(s) to adult; (f) maintains focus on appropriate task and/or the journaling tools, and (g) may appear in thought by intermittently and quietly looking away from material and not writing (engaged only with self).
Kranak, Alber-Morgan, and Sawyer (2017)	"looking at the teacher during teacher-led instruction, looking at and/or writing responses on a worksheet, answering questions on signal, answering questions correctly, and following teacher directions" (p. 455)
Kemp and Carter (2006)	Active on-task behavior is actively participating in the lesson by physically (a) looking at the teacher or material or task to which the teacher is referring (e.g., looking at a book being read, looking at a worksheet, looking at an activity being modeled by the teacher); and (b) looking at another student responding to the teacher (e.g., looking at the student answering the teacher's question).
Brooks, Todd, Tofflemoyer, and Horner (2003)	For individual seatwork: "Keeping eyes on work, keeping pencil in hand, and working on the assignment quietly." During group instruction: "keeping eyes on speaker, keeping hands free of materials, and following group directions."
Cirelli, Sidener, Reeve, and Reeve (2016)	"(a) visually attending to worksheet and/or appropriate materials (i.e., head orientation within approximately 45° of worksheet/materials) and (b) manipulating any work materials appropriately (i.e., as they were designed to be used)" (p. 288)
Thomas, DeBar, Vladescu, and Townsend (2020)	"physically oriented toward relevant material (i.e., face within 45° of the iPad®) or physically engaged in the target step or steps of the task analysis. On-task behavior also included complying with an instruction." (p. 42)

Operational definitions with multiple indicators may make it harder to count accurately the number of times a behavior occurs, making it difficult to know when the student has reached the criterion. One way to avoid this potential problem is to operationally define the outcome of a complex behavior. To measure on-task behavior, for example, the objective may indicate the number of math problems to be completed within a time limit. The student can accomplish this outcome only by remaining on task. (This difficulty is discussed further in Chapter 4.)

Aggression is an example of a general description of behavior that may be operationally defined both functionally, in terms of its consequences or outcomes, and topographically, in terms of the movements comprising the behavior (Barlow & Hersen, 1984). Outcomes of aggression are operationalized by Torelli et al. (2016; p. 166) as "forceful physical contact between Lucas, or an object controlled by Lucas, and another person," and by Winborn-Kemmerer et al. (2010) as property destruction. Aggression has been defined topographically as grabbing, pushing, pinching, scratching, shoving, poking, flicking, spitting, hitting, kicking, biting, pulling hair, head butting, throwing objects at the therapist, and attempts to aggress (e.g., raising hand above head toward the therapist; Fuhrman, Greer, Zangrillo, & Fisher, 2018; Hood, Rodriguez, Luczynski, & Fisher, 2019; McCord, Ringdahl, Meindl, & Wallace, 2019; Oropeza, Fritz, Nissen, Terrell, & Phillips, 2018; Slocum, Grauerholz-Fisher, Peters, & Vollmer, 2018). Providing specific examples of the target behavior increases clarity.

The need for an operational definition is reduced when more precise verbs are used in the objective. Increased precision also promotes more accurate recording of data. A precise behavioral description such as "will sort" rather than "will discriminate," "will circle" rather than "will identify," or "will state orally" rather than "will know" is less likely to be interpreted differently by different observers and reduces the need for repeated verbal or written clarification. Here are some more examples of precise behavioral descriptions:

- will point to the largest item in an array
- will verbally count the equivalent in dimes
- will write a translation of the prologue to *The Canterbury Tales*
- will look at his book or the speaker

One guide for selecting appropriate verbs has been offered by Deno and Jenkins (1967). Their classification of verbs is based on agreement of occurrence between independent classroom observers. They arrived at the three categories of verbs: *directly observable action verbs* (e.g., underline, write, point to, walk, read orally, state), *ambiguous action verbs* (e.g., inquire, acknowledge, check, group, convert, identify), and *not directly observable action verbs* (e.g., distinguish, recognize, infer, wonder, learn, discover, understand). The word, "identify," is often used when writing objectives for students. The problem is that when people are asked to demonstrate how to identify, they do several different behaviors, such as say, point to, and write. In most cases, it is better to use those more observable terms rather than "identify."

In order to evaluate a description of a target behavior, Morris (1976, p. 19) suggests using his IBSO (Is the Behavior Specific and Objective?) test questions:

1. Can you count the number of times the behavior occurs in, for example, a 15-minute period, a 1-hour period, or 1 day? Or, can you count the number of minutes it takes for the child to perform the behavior? That is, can you tell someone the behavior occurred X number of times or for X number of minutes today? (Your answer should be yes.)
2. Will a stranger know exactly what to look for when you tell him or her the target behavior you are planning to modify? That is, can you actually see the child performing the behavior when it occurs? (Your answer should be yes.)
3. Can you break down the target behavior into smaller components, each of which is more specific and observable than the original target behavior? (Your answer should be no.)

Pinpointing Behavior
Pearson eText
Video Example 3.2
In this video, an educator demonstrates pinpointing behaviors that may be interfering with Dylan's learning. What does she do to address these behaviors?

State the Conditions of Intervention

The third component of a behavioral objective is the statement of conditions. The statement of conditions lists antecedent stimuli, including instructions, materials, and setting. It may also include the types of assistance available to the students. These elements may be part of the natural environment in which the behavior is to be performed, or they may be provided by the teacher as part of a specific learning task. The statement of conditions helps assure that all aspects of the learning experience will be consistently reproduced.

> Conditions are antecedent stimuli related to the target behavior.

The teacher may set the occasion for an appropriate response using any or all of several categories of antecedent stimuli:

1. Verbal requests or instructions:
   Sam, point to the little car.
   Debbie, add these numbers.
   Jody, go back to your desk.

2. Written instructions or format:
   Diagram these sentences.
   Find the products.
   Draw a line from each word to its definition.

3. Demonstration:
   This is how you use litmus paper.
   This is how to operate ...

4. Materials to be used:
   A worksheet with 20 single-digit addition problems
   A tape recorder with the "play" button colored green and the "stop" button colored red

5. Environmental setting or timing:
   In the vocational workshop
   In the cafeteria
   On the playground
   During independent study period
   During transition between classes

6. Manner of assistance:
   Independently
   With the aid of a number line
   With partial physical assistance from the teacher
   Receiving only verbal prompts

The teacher must be sure that the verbal or visual cue planned does in fact provide an opportunity for the desired response by the student. That is, a teacher should deliver an unambiguous request or instruction to the student. The teacher who holds a flash card with the word *get* and says, "Give me a sentence for *get*," is likely to hear, "I for get my milk money" or "I for get my homework."

> Providing appropriate antecedent stimuli will be discussed in Chapter 10.

The materials described in the objective should ensure stimulus consistency for the learner and reduce the chance for inadvertent, subtle changes in the learning performance being requested. For example, presenting a red, a blue, and a green sock and asking the student to "point to red" is a less complex task than presenting a red car, a blue sock, and a green cup and making the same request. Giving the student a page with written instructions to fill in the blanks in sentences is less complex when a list of words that includes the answers is provided. Asking the student to write a story based on a picture is different from asking the student to write a story without a visual stimulus.

Ms. Samuels Teaches Long Division

Ms. Samuels was once again in trouble with a general education teacher. She and Mr. Watson, the sixth-grade math teacher, had agreed she would work on long division with a small group of students. Ms. Samuels had carefully checked to be sure the method she taught them to use was the same as Mr. Watson's. She made dozens of practice worksheets, and the students worked long-division problems until they could do them in their sleep.

Ms. Samuels was predictably horrified when Mr. Watson asked her if she ever planned to start working on division with the students. Investigation revealed that when they were working with the other sixth graders, they were expected to copy the problems from the math book to notebook paper; several of them made so many copying errors that they seldom got the correct answer. The conditions under which the task was to be performed were thus significantly different.

Conditions of the Intervention
Pearson eText
Video Example 3.3
In this video, an educator provides Vince several antecedent stimuli to support him in completing a sorting task (e.g., a sorting visual, picture cards, and vocal instructions). Consider if Vince is ready for more or less material support with this task.

The following are examples of condition statement formats:

- Given an array of materials containing ...
- Given a textbook containing 25 division problems with single-digit divisors ...
- Given the manual sign for "toilet" ...
- Given the use of a thesaurus and written instructions ...
- Given a pullover sweater and the verbal cue "Put on your sweater." ...
- Given a ditto sheet with 20 problems containing improper fractions having unlike denominators and the written instruction to "Find the products" ...
- Without the aid of ...

Careful statement of the conditions under which the behavior is to be performed may prevent problems like the one encountered by Ms. Samuels in the vignette above.

As part of a plan of instruction for students with learning problems, teachers may need to include extra support in the form of supplementary cues, such as a model of a completed long-division problem for the student to keep at his or her desk. It is important to include a description of such supplementary cues in the condition component of the behavioral objective to avoid misunderstandings. When the cue is no longer needed, the objective may be rewritten.

State Criteria for Acceptable Performance

Criterion statements set minimum performance standards.

In the criterion statement included in a behavioral objective, the teacher sets the standard for minimally acceptable performance. This statement indicates the level of performance the student will be able to achieve as a result of the intervention. The performance itself has been defined; the criterion sets the standard for evaluation. Throughout the intervention process, this criterion is used to measure the effectiveness of the intervention strategy selected to meet the behavioral objective.

The basic criterion statement for initial learning or **acquisition** indicates the *accuracy* of a response or the response's *frequency of occurrence*. Such statements are written in terms of the number of correct responses, the student's accuracy on trial presentations, the percentage of accurate responses, or some performance within an error of limitation. Here are some sample criterion statements:

17 out of 20 correct responses
label all 10 objects correctly
with 80% accuracy
on 80% of opportunities
20 problems must be answered correctly (100% accuracy)
4 out of 5 trials correct
on 5 consecutive trials
complete all steps in the toilet-training program independently

list all four of the main characters in a book report of no less than 250 words with no more than 5 errors in spelling
on each occasion

Two additional types of criteria may be included when time is a critical dimension of the behavior. *Duration* is a statement of the length of time the student performs the behavior. *Latency* is a statement of the length of time that elapses before the student begins performing the behavior.

> See Chapter 4 for an extended discussion of duration and latency.

- Criterion statements addressing duration:

  will complete within 1 hour
  for at least 20 minutes
  for no more than 1/2 hour
  will return within 10 minutes
  within 2 weeks

- Statements addressing latency:

  within 10 seconds after the flash card is presented
  within 1 minute after a verbal request

Certain types of content require particular criterion levels. When a student is acquiring basic skills on which other skills will be built, a criterion of 80% may not be high enough. For example, learning "almost all" of the multiplication facts may result in a student's going through life never knowing what 8 × 7 is. There are other skills as well that require 100% accuracy. Remembering to look both ways before crossing the street only 90% of the time may result in premature termination of the opportunity for future learning!

> Writing criterion statements in terms of percentage requires care. How many problems, for example, would a student have to solve correctly to satisfy a 90% criterion on a five-item math quiz?

For certain students, a disability may influence the force, direction, or duration of the criterion set by the teacher. For example, a student may not be able to hammer a nail all the way into a piece of wood; range-of-motion limitations may influence motor capability for reaching; hypotonic muscles (those with less-than-normal tone) may limit the duration of walking or sitting; or a muscular condition may limit the perfection of cursive handwriting.

When setting criteria for acceptable performance, teachers must be careful to set goals that are sufficiently ambitious, yet reasonable. Selection should be based on the nature of the content, the abilities of the students, and the learning opportunities to be provided. Criteria should provide for the development of a functional skill. There is no sense in teaching a student to play a game only so well that he gets beaten every time he plays or in teaching a student to do math problems only well enough to earn a high F in the general education classroom. There is evidence (Haas, Stickney, & Ysseldyke, 2016) that setting ambitious goals results in more learning, but teachers should not set unobtainable goals that will result in frustration for students.

In addition to considering the number or percentage correct and the accuracy of response, writers of behavioral objectives must also determine the number of times a student must meet a criterion to demonstrate mastery. For example, how often must Jane perform a behavior successfully on 8 out of 10 trials before the teacher will be convinced of mastery and allow her to move on to the next level of learning or to the next behavioral objective?

It may be inferred from an open-ended criterion statement that the first time a student reaches 85% accuracy, the skill will be considered "learned," or that from now until the end of the school year, the teacher will continually test and retest to substantiate the 85% accuracy. Either inference could be false. Therefore, a statement such as one of the following should be included in the behavioral objective to provide a point of closure and terminal review:

85% accuracy *for 4 consecutive sessions*
85% accuracy *for 3 out of 4 days*
on 8 out of 10 trials *for 3 consecutive teaching sessions*
will return within 10 minutes on *3 consecutive trips to the bathroom*

Format for a Behavioral Objective

Learning Outcome 3.4 Identify ways to measure mastery based on a hierarchy of response competence.

A management aid for the teacher in writing behavioral objectives is the adoption of a standard format. A consistent format helps the teacher include all the components necessary for communicating all intended information. No single format is necessarily superior to others; teachers should simply find one that is compatible with their writing style or with administrative policy. Here are two such formats.

Format 1

Conditions: Given 20 flash cards with preprimer sight words and the instruction "Read these words"
Student: Sam
Behavior: will read the words orally
Criterion: within 2 seconds for each word with 90% accuracy on 3 consecutive trials.

Format 2

Student: Marvin
Behavior: will write 20 fourth-grade spelling words in cursive handwriting
Conditions: from dictation by the resource teacher with no more than 2 errors for 3 consecutive weeks.

The following behavioral objectives may be derived from the educational goals previously set for students Aiden and Tanika.

Mathematics

Goal: Aiden will master basic computation facts at the first-grade level.
Objective: Given a worksheet of 20 single-digit addition problems in the form 6 + 2 and the written instruction "Find the sums," Aiden will complete all problems with 90% accuracy for 3 consecutive math sessions.

Social Studies

Goal: Aiden will demonstrate knowledge of the functions of the three branches of the federal government.
Objective: After reading pages 23–26 in the text *Our American Heritage*, Aiden will list the 10-step sequential process by which a bill becomes a law. This list will have no more than one error of sequence and one error of omission. This will be successfully accomplished on an in-class exercise and on the unit-end test.

Reading

Goal: Aiden will be able to identify relevant parts of a story he has read.
Objective: Given the short story "The Necklace," Aiden will write a minimum 200-word paper that (1) lists all the main characters and (2) lists the sequence of main events, with no more than two errors.

Science

Goal: Aiden will demonstrate knowledge of the structure of the solar system.
Objective: Given a map of the solar system, Aiden will label each planet in its proper position from the sun with 100% accuracy on 2 consecutive sessions.

Language Arts

Goal: Aiden will increase the creative expression of his oral language.

Objective: Given an array of photos of people, objects, and locations, Aiden will tell a 5-minute story to the class that makes use of a minimum of 7 items, on 3 out of 5 days.

Physical Education

Goal: Aiden will increase his skills in team sports.

Objective: Given a basketball, Aiden will throw the ball into the hoop from a distance of 10 feet in 8 out of 10 trials for 4 consecutive gym classes.

Recall from our earlier discussion that although Aiden has mild learning problems, Tanika has much more severe disabilities. Here are some objectives and corresponding goals for Tanika.

Cognitive

Goal: Tanika will be able to categorize objects according to their function.

Objective: Given 12 Peabody cards (4 foods, 4 clothing, 4 grooming aids), a sample stimulus card of each category, and the verbal cue "Where does this one go?," Tanika will place the cards on the appropriate category pile with 100% accuracy for 17 out of 20 trials.

Communication

Goal: Tanika will demonstrate increased receptive understanding of functional labels.

Objective: Given an array of 3 objects found in her snack-time environment (cup, spoon, fork) and the verbal cue "Pick up the ...," Tanika will hand the teacher the named object 9 out of 10 times for 4 consecutive snack times.

Motor

Goal: Tanika will develop gross motor capability of her upper extremities.

Objective: Given a soft rubber ball suspended from the ceiling and the verbal cue "Hit the ball," Tanika will hit the ball causing movement 10 out of 10 times for 5 consecutive days.

Social

Goal: Tanika will learn to participate appropriately in group activities.

Objective: When sitting with the teacher and two other students during story time, Tanika will make an appropriate motor or verbal response to each of the teacher's questions when called upon a minimum of 3 times in a 10-minute period for 5 consecutive days.

Self-Help

Goal: Tanika will demonstrate the ability to dress herself independently.

Objective: Given a pullover sweater with the back label color-cued red and the verbal cue "Put on your sweater," Tanika will successfully complete all steps of the task without physical assistance in 2 out of 3 trials for 4 consecutive days.

Vocational

Goal: Tanika will complete assembly tasks for a period of at least 1 hour.

Objective: Given the four parts of a plumbing "U" in sequential order, Tanika will assemble at a rate of one per 3 minutes without error during 3 vocational periods for 4 weeks.

Maladaptive Behavior

Goal: Tanika will decrease out-of-seat behavior.

Objective: In the period from 9:00 to 9:20 a.m. (functional academics), Tanika will remain in her seat, unless given permission by the teacher to leave, for 5 consecutive days.

Expanding the Scope of the Basic Behavioral Objective

Learning Outcome 3.5 Identify ways to measure mastery based on a hierarchy of levels of learning.

Once a student or group of students has acquired the behavior described in an objective, teachers may simply note that the objective has been mastered and move on to the next one in the sequence. This may be inappropriate unless the student can perform the behavior in circumstances different from the initial teaching environment. In order for the students to have functional behaviors, those that can be performed under different conditions, to different criteria, or in the absence of reinforcement contingencies, provision must be made to expand students' ability to use the behavior. Two possible perspectives on expanded use are

1. programming according to a hierarchy of response competence.
2. programming according to a hierarchy of levels of learning.

Professor Grundy's Class Writes Behavioral Objectives

It was the time of the semester for Professor Grundy's 8 o'clock class to learn about behavioral objectives. After presenting a carefully planned lecture (remarkably similar to the first part of this chapter), Grundy asked if there were any questions. Dawn Tompkins stopped filing her nails long enough to ask, with a deep sigh, "Yes, Professor, would you please tell me what a behavioral objective is, exactly?"

"I was under the impression, young lady, that I had done just that," replied Grundy. "Is anyone else confused?"

A chorus of muttering and rumbling ensued from which Grundy was able to extract clearly only two questions: "Is this covered in the book?" and "Will it be on the test?"

After once more presenting a drastically abbreviated description of the components of a behavioral objective, Grundy announced that each member of the class was to write a behavioral objective for the curriculum area of science and present it to him for checking before leaving class. This announcement, followed by a chorus of groans and considerable paper shuffling, also brought forth a flurry of hands:

"You mean list the components?"
"No," said Grundy. "Write an objective."
"You mean define a behavioral objective?"
"No," said Grundy. "Write one."
"But you never said anything about writing them."
"What," Grundy retorted, "did you think was the purpose of the lecture?"

After everyone who lacked these tools had been provided with paper and pencil, silence descended upon the class. DeWayne was the first one finished and proudly presented his objective to the professor:

To understand the importance of the digestive system.

"Well, DeWayne," said the professor, "that's a start, but do you not remember that a behavioral objective must talk about behavior? Remember the types of verbs I described . . ." When DeWayne continued to look blank, Grundy rifled through his briefcase and found his notes.

"Look here," the professor said. "Use a directly observable verb like these."

DeWayne returned some time later with his rewritten objective:

To label the parts of the digestive system.

"Good, DeWayne," sighed the professor. "That's a behavior, all right. Now, do you recall the components of a behavioral objective?" Once again, DeWayne looked blank. Grundy carefully wrote:

Conditions Student Behavior Criteria

across the long side of the ATM receipt DeWayne had evidently found in his wallet. DeWayne returned to his desk.

An hour and a half later, as Grundy was regretting ever having given this assignment, DeWayne returned again:

Given an unlabeled diagram of the human digestive system, fourth-grade students will label the major parts of the digestive system (mouth, esophagus, stomach, small intestine, large intestine) with no errors.

Grundy read DeWayne's objective with interest, because his own digestive system was beginning to be the major focus of his attention. "Excellent, DeWayne," said the professor. "I

(Continued)

suppose it's too late to get lunch in the cafeteria. Why didn't you do this in the first place?"

"Well, Professor," answered DeWayne, "I didn't really understand what you wanted. I'm still not sure I could do another one."

After getting some crackers from a vending machine, Grundy returned meditatively to his office. He found a piece of paper and began to write as he munched:

Given a worksheet listing appropriate verbs and the components of a behavioral objective, students enrolled in Education 411 will write five behavioral objectives including all components.

After musing for a few minutes, he added:

in less than half an hour.

"Perhaps," Grundy muttered to himself, "if I had been sure what I wanted and told the students at the front end, they would have had less trouble figuring it out."

Hierarchy of Response Competence

A measure of response accuracy (8 out of 10 correct, for example) is only one dimension for evaluating performance. It represents the acquisition level of response competence. At this level, we merely verify the presence of the ability to do something the student was not previously able to do and the ability to do it with some degree of accuracy. Moving to measures of competence in performance beyond accuracy, beyond this acquisition level, requires alterations or additions to the statements of criteria and conditions. Such alterations reflect a hierarchy of response competence. Once a child can perform the behavior, we are then concerned with fluency, or rate, of performance, as well as performance under conditions other than those imposed during the initial teaching process.

A response hierarchy should contain the minimum levels of acquisition, fluency, maintenance, and generalization.

As an example of the use of this hierarchy, let us assume John has reached the acquisition level on the following objective:

Given two quarters, two dimes, two nickels, and one penny and the verbal cue "John, give me your bus fare," he will hand the teacher coins equaling 75 cents in 8 out of 10 trials for 3 consecutive sessions.

Lauren has reached acquisition on this objective:

Given a worksheet with 20 division problems with two-digit dividends and single-digit divisors, Lauren will write the correct answer in the appropriate place on the radical with 90% accuracy for 4 consecutive days.

After John and Lauren have met these stated criteria for their performances, the teaching concern should turn to their **fluency** of performance, or the rate at which they perform the behavior. Fluency refers to the appropriateness of the rate at which the student is accurately performing this newly acquired response. In John's case, we know that he can select the appropriate coins to make 75 cents, but this does him little good if, when we take him to the bus, it takes him 5 minutes to do it. The bus driver cannot wait this long. In Lauren's case, we know she can now solve division problems, but it takes her so long that either we interrupt her when her reading group is scheduled or she misses part of her reading lesson so she can finish her problems.

In both instances, the students are demonstrating accurate performance at an inappropriate rate. Recognizing the necessity for an appropriate rate of performance, a teacher can indicate an acceptable fluency when the behavioral objective is written. This is accomplished by adding a time limit to the statement of criteria, as found in parentheses in the following objectives:

Given two quarters, two dimes, two nickels, and one penny and the verbal cue "John, give me your bus fare," he will hand the teacher coins equaling 75 cents (within 30 seconds) in 8 out of 10 trials for 3 consecutive sessions.

Given a worksheet with 20 division problems with two-digit dividends and single-digit divisors, Lauren will write the correct answer in the appropriate place on the radical (within 20 minutes) with 90% accuracy for 4 consecutive days.

For typical learners and those with mild disabilities, the rate is often included in the initial objective, thus combining acquisition and fluency in a single instructional procedure. Instructional attention is given to fluency because when a student's performance becomes fluent, the behavior is retained longer, persists during long periods of the task, is less affected by distractions, and is more likely to be available in new learning situations (Binder & Watkins, 2013; Burns, Ysseldyke, Nelson, & Kanive, 2015).

> Programming for maintenance will be discussed in Chapter 11.

It is not necessary to adjust the original behavioral objective to include the level of competence labeled **maintenance**. Maintenance is the ability to perform a response over time without reteaching. Maintenance-level competence is confirmed by using postchecks or probes, during which the teacher rechecks the skill to be sure the student can still do it. Maintenance may be promoted through building in the opportunity for overlearning trials and distributed practice. **Overlearning** refers to repeated practice after an objective has been initially accomplished. An optimum number of overlearning opportunities is approximately 50% of the number of trials required for acquisition of the behavior. If it takes John 10 teaching sessions to learn to tie his shoes, we should ideally provide 5 additional sessions for overlearning. *Distributed practice* is practice that is spread out over time (as opposed to *massed practice*, which is compressed in time). An example of massed practice familiar to college students is cramming for an exam. The material may be learned between 10 and 6 the night before the test, but most of it will be rapidly forgotten. If maintenance is desired, the preferable approach is studying for short periods every evening for several weeks before the exam, using distributed practice. Another means of providing for maintenance, alteration of schedules of reinforcement (Conine, Vollmer, & Bolivar, 2020; Skinner, 1968), will be discussed in Chapter 8.

> Distributed practice is a more efficient way of learning for long-term maintenance.

The level of response competence labeled **generalization** is of great importance in assuring that a behavior is functional. A student has a generalized response if he or she can perform—and adapt, if necessary—the behavior under conditions different from those in place during acquisition. A generalized response is one that also continues to occur after instruction has been terminated. A response may be generalized across at least four basic dimensions. The condition statement may be written to reflect the student's ability to perform the behavior in response to various verbal or written instructions, with various materials, for or with various persons, and in various environments (settings). The following examples illustrate this point.

Beyond Acquisition Goals
Pearson eText
Video Example 3.4
In this video, the degrees of accuracy and independence demonstrated by the student are consistent with the acquisition phase. The student also responds almost immediately, which demonstrates fluency. What other dimensions of response competence may be relevant to target?

Various Instructions

Given an array of coins and the verbal instruction, "Give me bus fare" ("Give me 75 cents," "Give me what you need for the bus") ...

Given a worksheet with 30 one-digit subtraction problems and the verbal (or written) instruction, "Find the difference" ("Solve these problems," "Write the answers to these problems") ...

Various Materials

Will write his name, address, phone number, and birth date in the appropriate blanks on at least three different job application forms ...

Will demonstrate the multiplicative principle of math using counting chips (a number line, paper and pencil) ...

Various Persons

Will use the sign for "toilet" as a signal of need to her teacher (parent) ...

Will comply with instructions from his math (English, social studies, science) teacher (mother, father, coach, piano teacher) ...

Various Settings

Will pull up her pants after toileting in the restroom in the special education class (in the restroom near the class she joins for art) ...

Will remain in his seat and complete assignments in math (English, social studies, science) class ...

Hierarchy of Levels of Learning

It may seem that writing behavioral objectives inevitably focuses teacher attention on concrete, simple forms of learning. Indeed, this has been one of the most frequent criticisms of a behavioral approach. It is not necessary, however, to confine behavioral objectives to lower levels of learning. Bloom (1956) has proposed hierarchies of learning in cognitive, affective, and psychomotor areas. These hierarchies classify possible learning outcomes in terms of increasingly abstract levels. They are helpful in writing objectives in behavioral terms because they suggest observable, measurable behaviors that may occur as the result of both simple and complex learning. The cognitive hierarchy, which will serve as our example, contains six levels of learning, as described below (Bloom, 1956).

Many behavioral objectives are written in terms of the knowledge level of the hierarchy—we simply want students to demonstrate they know or remember something we have taught them. Once the student has achieved mastery on the lowest of the six levels, the teacher can shift programming toward higher levels of learning by preparing subsequent objectives that alter the target behavior and criterion statements. As an aid in this process, Gronlund (1985) prepared a table (Table 3.2) that illustrates behavioral terms appropriate to describe target behaviors at each level of learning.

KNOWLEDGE Bloom (1956) defines learning at the knowledge level as the recall or recognition of information ranging from specific facts to complete theories. These memory functions are the only behavior to be demonstrated at this basic level of cognitive learning. The following acquisition objectives are examples written for students at this level:

After reading Biology for Your Understanding and completing the exercise in Chapter 2, Virginia will list the biological categories of the Linnaean system in their order of evolutional complexity without error during 2 class sessions and on a unit-end exam.

Given the symbols for the arithmetic processes of addition, subtraction, multiplication, and division, Danny will respond with 90% accuracy on a multiple-choice test of their labels and basic functions.

Given a list of Shakespearean plays, Deborah will underline the names of the tragedies with no more than one error.

COMPREHENSION Once the student has reached the performance criterion at the knowledge level, the teacher moves to the comprehension level, the understanding of meaning. The student may demonstrate comprehension by paraphrasing and providing examples.

Here are some sample objectives at this level:

Given the Linnaean system of biological classification, Virginia will provide a written description of an organism in each category. The description will include at least one factor that distinguishes the category from others.

Given a worksheet of 40 basic arithmetic examples requiring addition, subtraction, multiplication, and division, Danny will complete the sheet with 90% accuracy.

Table 3.2 Examples of general instructional objectives and behavioral terms for the cognitive domain of the taxonomy

Illustrative General Instructional Objectives	Illustrative Behavioral Terms for Stating Specific Learning Outcomes
Knows common terms	Defines, describes, identifies, labels, lists, matches, names, outlines, reproduces, selects, states
Knows specific facts	
Knows methods and procedures	
Knows basic concepts	
Knows principles	
Understands facts and principles	Converts, defends, distinguishes, estimates, explains, extends, generalizes, gives examples, infers, paraphrases, predicts, rewrites, summarizes
Interprets verbal material	
Interprets charts and graphs	
Translates verbal material to mathematical formulas	
Estimates future consequences implied in data	
Justifies methods and procedures	
Applies concepts and principles to new situations	Changes, computes, demonstrates, discovers, manipulates, modifies, operates, predicts, prepares, produces, relates, shows, solves, uses
Applies laws and theories to practical situations	
Solves mathematical problems	
Constructs charts and graphs	
Demonstrates correct usage of a method or procedure	
Recognizes unstated assumptions	Breaks down, diagrams, differentiates, discriminates, distinguishes, identifies, illustrates, infers, outlines, points out, relates, selects, separates, subdivides
Recognizes logical fallacies in reasoning	
Distinguishes between facts and inferences	
Evaluates the relevancy of data	
Analyzes the organizational structure of a work (art, music, writing)	
Writes a well-organized theme	Categorizes, combines, compiles, composes, creates, devises, designs, explains, generates, modifies, organizes, plans, rearranges, reconstructs, relates, reorganizes, revises, rewrites, summarizes, tells, writes
Gives a well-organized speech	
Writes a creative short story (or poem, or music)	
Proposes a plan for an experiment	
Integrates learning from different areas into a plan for solving a problem	
Formulates a new scheme for classifying objects (or events, or ideas)	
Judges the logical consistency of written material	Appraises, compares, concludes, contrasts, criticizes, describes, discriminates, explains, justifies, interprets, relates, summarizes, supports
Judges the adequacy with which conclusions are supported by data	
Judges the value of a work (art, music, writing) by use of internal criteria	
Judges the value of a work (art, music, writing) by use of external standards of excellence	

Note: From *How to Write and Use Instructional Objectives* (5th ed.), by Norman E. Gronlund, 1991, Upper Saddle River, NJ: Prentice Hall, Inc. Copyright © 1991. Reprinted by permission.

Given the metaphoric passage, "Oh that this too, too solid flesh would melt ..." from *Hamlet*, Deborah will write an essay describing the literal intent of the passage. The essay will be a minimum of 300 words.

APPLICATION Programming at Bloom's *application level* requires the student to use the method, concept, or theory in various concrete situations. Consider these objectives:

Given the names of five organisms and the Linnaean system, Virginia will place each in its proper category and write a list of rationales for placement. Each rationale will contain a minimum of two reasons for placement.

Given a set of 10 paragraphs that present problems requiring an arithmetic computation for solution, Danny will write the correct answer, showing all computations, with 100% accuracy.

After reading *Hamlet*, Deborah will be able to explain the parallels between Hamlet's ethical dilemma and the problem of abortion and to cite an additional current parallel example of her own choosing.

ANALYSIS *Analysis* is the ability to break down material into its constituent parts in order to identify these parts, discuss their interrelationship, and understand their organization as a whole. The following objectives are analytically oriented:

Given a list of five organisms, Virginia will use appropriate references in the library to investigate and report to the class the role of the organisms in either the food chain or in the ecological stability of their habitat.

Given a written statement of the associative property, Danny will be able to explain accurately to the class, using examples at the chalkboard, the property's relation to the basic additive and multiplicative functions.

After having read *Hamlet* or *Macbeth*, Deborah will guide the class in a discussion of the play's plot development. This discussion will be based upon a schematic representation of each scene that she will provide in written form.

SYNTHESIS At the cognitive level of *synthesis*, the student should demonstrate the ability to bring parts together, resulting in a different, original, or creative whole:

Given a list of reference texts, Virginia will write a 1,000-word summary explaining the biological classifications in Darwin's theory of evolution. The paper will be evaluated on the basis of accuracy, completeness, organization, and clarity.

Given the numerical systems of base 10 and base 2, Danny will orally demonstrate the use of the functions of addition, subtraction, multiplication, and division within each system.

Given the study of the Shakespearean tragedy *Macbeth*, Deborah will rewrite the end of the play in iambic pentameter, assuming that the murder of the king was unsuccessful.

EVALUATION The highest level of learning demonstrated in this hierarchy is *evaluation*. The student is asked to make a judgment of value:

Based on the principles of mutual exclusion, Virginia will devise a taxonomy for the classification of means of transportation and provide a justification for the categories created and their constituent parts.

Given a set of unknown values and a given arithmetic computational function, Danny will explain the probability of differing answers that may be correct.

Given plays by Shakespeare and Bacon, Deborah will state a preference for one and justify her preference in a 500-word essay based on some element(s) of style.

Bloom's Heirarchy In Action
Pearson eText
Video Example 3.5
In this video, consider how the activity may align with Bloom's (1956) hierarchy of learning.

Learning Levels for the Learner with Limitations

In most instances of planning for expanded instructional intent, we tend to focus on a hierarchy-of-response competence for learners with significant disabilities and a hierarchy of levels of learning for the typical or above-average learner. This dichotomy is not necessarily warranted simply by the level of the student's functioning. Consider

> Even learners with limitations can acquire higher-level cognitive skills.

the following examples of how we may write behavioral objectives for the limited learner in conjunction with levels of learning:

Knowledge:	Given a common coin and the verbal cue, "What is the name of this?," George will state the appropriate label on 18 out of 20 trials for 5 consecutive sessions.
Comprehension:	Given a common coin and the verbal cue "What is this worth?," George will count out the coin's equivalent in pennies and state something to the effect that "A dime is worth 10 pennies" on 8 out of 10 trials for each coin.
Application:	When presented with 10 pictures of food items, each with its cost written on it, George will count out coins equal to the amount written upon the verbal cue "Show me the amount" on 18 out of 20 trials.
Analysis:	When presented with pictures of items, each with its cost printed on it, a $1 bill, and a verbal cue such as "Can you buy a pencil and a newspaper?," George will respond correctly on 18 out of 20 trials.
Synthesis:	Given a $1 bill and the instruction to buy various priced items, George will simulate the buying exchange and decide whether he was given correct change without error on 10 trials.
Evaluation:	Given a $1 bill and a 5-mile ride from the workplace to his home, George will use the $1 for the bus ride rather than a candy bar.

Behavioral Objectives and the IEP

Learning Outcome 3.6 **Identify ways to incorporate behavioral objectives in individualized education programs.**

The development of educational goals (long-term objectives) and behavioral objectives (short-term objectives) for students in need of special education services was included as one of the mandates of the original Education for All Handicapped Children Act of 1975 (P.L. 94-142), and its current successor, the Individuals with Disabilities Education Improvement Act of 2004 (P.L. 108-446, IDEA). Among the results of this legislation have been the formalization of the planning aspects inherent in the writing of goals and objectives and the provision for active parental participation in the educational planning process. This planning process results in the development of an **individualized education program (IEP)**. The IEP has at its core the listing of the goals and objectives for the student's educational program for the year and how progress toward these goals will be measured (Hyatt & Filler, 2016). In addition to this core element, an IEP contains components or statements regarding transition planning and services, positive behavioral interventions and supports, participation in state and district assessments, extended-school-year services, participation in the general education curriculum (including necessary modifications), and interaction with students not identified as disabled. The federal rules and regulations include six elements as part of the IEP:

1. a statement of the student's present levels of educational performance, which may be assessed by standardized norm-referenced tests, classroom-based assessments, direct observation, and curriculum-based measures (Harmon et al., 2020)
2. a statement of measurable annual goals for students with mild disabilities or a statement of annual goals and short-term instructional objectives for students with significant disabilities
3. appropriate objective criteria and evaluation procedures and schedules for determining, on at least an annual basis, whether the short-term instructional objectives are being achieved

4. a statement of the specific special education and related services to be provided to the student
5. projected dates for initiation of services and the anticipated duration of the services
6. the extent to which the student will be able to participate in general education programs, and any modifications or accommodations necessary to enable that participation

> IDEA requires an IEP for every student with a disability.

These elements illustrate commonalities in the development of behavioral objectives and the development of the IEP. Both processes include the accumulation of data to determine the student's current levels of performance, the statement of appropriate goals, the development of behavioral objectives (short-term) for attaining the goals, and a data-based review of objective mastery.

Special education eligibility requires the existence of a disability based on the student's individual characteristics and current level of performance. Evidence of a disability is derived from data from individual intelligence tests, behavioral assessments, academic achievement, and reports of various ancillary professionals. As a result of educational initiatives and the 2004 reauthorization of the Individuals with Disabilities Education Improvement Act (P.L. 108-446), some states also require information gathered from a student's response to interventions implemented to address that student's learning or behavior difficulty. The framework for providing this information is referred to as RTI (Response to Intervention). RTI is used to assist in distinguishing between a learning difficulty that simply requires supplemental instruction and a disability requiring special education services. If a student is found to be eligible for special education services, RTI information helps individualize goals and programming.

A basic RTI model has three tiers. Tier 1 provides school, grade, and/or class-wide practices acknowledged as basic to good instruction and behavior management (e.g., additional practice opportunities, clearly stated rules for appropriate behavior, and increased opportunities for reinforcers and rewards). Tier 2 provides more targeted practices, such as small-group instruction for students having academic difficulty, and social skills training and self-management strategies. At each level, practices must be evidence-based (i.e., have a research basis substantiating effectiveness) and use a data-based method of progress monitoring. It is the data resulting from this monitoring that informs educational goals and the IEP. Tier 3 intervention is provided by special education and related professionals. Practices employed are highly individualized, provide intensive support, and are sustained over longer periods of time. When such intensive intervention is considered, it is part of what initiates an evaluation to determine if a disability is present and an IEP required (Fuchs, Fuchs, & Vaughn, 2014; Jenkins, Schiller, Blackorby, Thayer, & Tilly, 2013; Lindstrom, 2019).

Incorporating Data
Pearson eText
Video Example 3.6
In this video, an educator describes the systems of data collection and progress reporting they have integrated into their daily practice. Review which recommended practices she is describing.

The following recommendations will facilitate management of an IEP and monitoring of its constituent objectives:

1. Short-term objectives should be sequentially related to goal statements. Across a sequence of objectives, the teacher can systematically alter the elements of objectives. For example, aspects of the *conditions* (materials, setting, format, type or amount of assistance or accommodation provided to the student), the *response* (e.g., response mode; the cognitive or physical difficulty or complexity of the response required), and/or the *criterion* (e.g., the amount of response required in number or duration; rate; number or types of errors permitted) may be increased or altered as the teacher shapes the student's response to one that meets a standard set for performance or is more functional.
2. In the case of students with mild disabilities, the goals and short-term objectives should deal directly with the reason for their referral for special education services. "They need be written only for the special services necessary to meet the

child's needs arising from the disability, not for the child's total program, unless all areas are so affected" (Bateman & Linden, 1998, p. 43).

3. For students with moderate, severe, and profound disabilities, two or three short-term objectives per curriculum domain should be included in the IEP because in most cases all areas of the student's educational performance are affected by the disability.

4. New short-term objectives should not be added until maintenance has been achieved on current objectives and generalization instruction has begun.

5. Management of the IEP should be a continuous process. Teachers and administrators should not overlook the regulations stating that a review should be conducted "on at least an annual basis," not "only on an annual basis."

    a. The objectives for students with mild disabilities should be reviewed as soon as achievement has been verified to assess whether the original need for special education services still exists.

    b. Reasonable review dates should be set for objectives of students with moderate and severe disabilities. As objectives are met, the teacher should add new short-term objectives and notify the team members, including the parents, in writing, with full justification provided at the annual review. Such a procedure will foster the student's progress and prevent stagnation of instruction until the full team can be gathered.

6. Review dates should be set considering the need for instruction at higher levels of learning to promote full functional use of a skill.

> When Aiden's math skills are at grade level, he no longer has a disability.

> Tanika's objectives should be reviewed frequently so that she will make the maximum possible progress.

Summary

We described the process of writing behavioral objectives and the relationship between such objectives and the IEP required for students with disabilities. This process is an integral part of any program for behavior change, whether the program is directed toward academic or social behavior. A program for changing behavior is unlikely to be successful unless we are sure what constitutes success. Behavioral objectives facilitate communication, so that everyone knows the goal of instruction. They also provide for evaluation, so that everyone knows whether the goal has been reached.

Discussion Questions

1. Douglas and his teacher agreed that on the days he sat in his seat for the entire reading lesson he would be allowed to pick the teams for that day's volleyball game. At the end of the second day Douglas and his teacher had a disagreement as to whether having his feet on his desk was appropriate in-seat behavior.
   a. What are two ways in which "in-seat behavior" could be operationalized such that Douglas is very clear what it means to be in his seat?
   b. How would you write a criterion statement for an objective for Douglas's in-seat behavior?
   c. What should the teacher do if Douglas does meet the criterion for in-seat behavior but makes rude comments to Jenny during the lesson?

2. Replace each of the following vague verbs with one that is more specific:
   a. Mario will be able to discriminate between a few and a lot.
   b. Mario will be able to recall the major rivers of the United States.
   c. Mario will be able to identify the parts of a flower.
   d. Mario will be able to understand the results of global warming.
   e. Mario will know the 6 and 8 multiplication tables.
   f. Nikki will recognize the main characters of a story.
   g. Nikki will appreciate the differences among various cultures.
   h. Nikki will be competent in telling time.
   i. Nikki will appreciate the works of Monet.
   j. Nikki will learn to operate a calculator.

3. Most teachers are required to write objectives as part of lesson planning or in IEPs. Many teachers consider writing these objectives to be unnecessary paperwork. Does the time taken to write objectives improve instruction, or are those teachers right?

Chapter 4
Procedures for Collecting Data

 Learning Outcomes

4.1 Identify the seven dimensions of behavior.
4.2 Identify components of anecdotal reports.
4.3 Identify components of permanent product recording.
4.4 Identify the five observational recording systems and when to use each system.
4.5 Demonstrate how to calculate reliability for each of the five observational recording systems.
4.6 Identify factors that impact the accuracy and reliability of data collection.

CHAPTER OUTLINE

A Rationale

Choosing a System

Anecdotal Reports
    Structuring an Anecdotal Report

Permanent Product Recording

Observational Recording Systems
    Event Recording
    Interval Recording and Time Sampling

Duration and Latency Recording
    Duration Recording
    Latency Recording

How Can All This Be Done?
    Technology for Data Collection

Summary of Data Collection Systems

Reliability

Factors That May Affect Data Collection and Interobserver Agreement

Summary

Most teachers regard the kind of data collection procedures that we shall discuss in this chapter with the same enthusiasm they reserve for statistics. In some cases, their comments are thoroughly justified. Some of the systems we will review are not practical for everyday classroom use. Classroom teachers may never use some of the more complex systems. Understanding how these systems work, however, helps in understanding published research about applied behavior analysis. This chapter describes the most common data collection systems and shows how many of them can be adapted for classroom use.

A Rationale

Even after accepting the feasibility of data collection in the classroom, many teachers see little value in it. Beyond recording grades on tests, most teachers have traditionally kept very few records of their students' academic and social behaviors. There are, nevertheless, excellent reasons for teachers to collect classroom data.

First, observation and measurement make it possible to determine very accurately the effects of a particular instructional strategy or intervention. Precise observation and measurement of behavior enable teachers to determine the success or failure of their strategies. Second, the types of data collection procedures discussed in this chapter allow for ongoing (formative) as well as terminal (summative) evaluation of instruction or intervention. The data collected enable teachers to make decisions and alterations during the course of a program rather than waiting, perhaps for weeks or months, to see if it was ultimately successful. Such use of systematic formative evaluation significantly increases students' achievement, both statistically and practically (Fuchs, 2017; Graham, Hebert, & Harris, 2015). Finally, collecting and reporting effect-based data is the ultimate tool of accountability (Deno et al., 2009).

By writing behavioral objectives, teachers communicate their intent to change particular behaviors. They also state the criteria they will use to judge whether change procedures have been successful. In many classroom situations, the intervention's effect on the students' original level of performance would be evaluated by administering a pretest and posttest. However, the precision desired within a behavioral approach to instruction and in program evaluation necessitates additional data.

| Behavioral evaluation requires observation of students' current functioning and ongoing progress.

Behavioral evaluation has two requirements. The first is a detailed observation of a student's current functioning. This observation should reflect the conditions and description of the behavior stated in the objective. For example, a behavioral objective stating that students should solve 25 long-division problems in 30 minutes requires that the teacher determine how many long-division problems the students can already solve in 30 minutes. Second, evaluation of an instructional program must facilitate ongoing monitoring of the teaching and learning process and provide a system for terminal evaluation. Evaluation must be continuous so that programs can be adjusted as instruction progresses. As the students in our example receive instruction in long division, the teacher might record daily how many problems they solve in 30 minutes, thus providing continuous evaluation. The monitoring process can provide guidelines for continuing or changing instructional techniques and help avoid false assumptions about student progress. Such false assumptions are unfortunately very common, as illustrated by the vignette on the next page.

Choosing a System

Learning Outcome 4.1 Identify the seven dimensions of behavior.

The first step in the evaluation of ongoing measurement of behavior is the selection of a system of data collection. The characteristics of the system selected must be appropriate to the behavior being observed and to the kind of behavior change desired.

| Dimensions for observation of behavior.

Behavior may be measured and changed on a number of dimensions (Cooper, Heron, & Heward, 2020).

Ms. Waller Gets an App

Ms. Waller was ecstatic. After months of complaining that she had no materials to use to teach reading to her most challenging reading group, a colleague told her about an app for teaching reading. When she purchased and downloaded the app, the tutorial indicated the app could be programmed on multiple devices in a classroom. The tutorial also demonstrated the many impressive features that justified the hundreds of dollars invested.

"All you have to do," the tutorial assured her, "is put the students in front of the app. Everything else is taken care of ... you don't do a thing."

Ms. Waller briskly administered the pretest included with the app, scheduled each student for 15 minutes a day on a classroom device, and assumed that her worries were over.

At the end of the school year, Ms. Waller administered the posttest. Imagine her distress when, although several members of the group had made remarkable progress, some students had made none at all.

"I don't understand," she wailed. "The app was supposed to do everything. How was I supposed to know it wasn't working?"

"Perhaps," suggested her principal, kindly, as he wished her success in her new career in retail, "you should have checked before now."

---

1. *Frequency:* The frequency of behavior is simply the number of times a student engages in it.

    Brett got out of his seat 6 times in 30 minutes.

    Yao did 6 of 10 math problems during a timed trial.

    Marvin had 8 tantrums on Wednesday.

    Lois's hand was in her mouth 5 times during storytelling.

    When determining frequency of occurrence of a behavior, we count the number of times the behavior occurs within an observation period (for example, 10 seconds or a 40-minute science class). If we want to make comparisons of the frequency of a behavior across observation periods (e.g., from one lunch period to another), the observation periods should be of the same length.

    If a behavior can occur only a limited number of times, that information should be provided as part of the frequency data. Knowing that Yao solved 6 math problems correctly, for example, has little meaning unless we also know that there were 10 math problems in all. For some behaviors there is no maximum number. For example, there is no maximum number of times a student may call out or leave her seat during class.

2. *Rate:* The rate of behavior is frequency expressed in a ratio with time.

    Brett got out of his seat 0.2 times per minute.

    Yao did 0.6 math problems per minute during a 2-minute timed trial.

    Marvin had 1.3 tantrums per hour in a 6-hour school day.

    Lois put her hand in her mouth 0.5 times per minute during a 10-minute story time.

    If all the observation periods are the same length, one simply reports the number of occurrences and the length of the observation periods. Rate, however, is most often used to compare the occurrence of behavior among observation periods of different lengths. Converting frequency data to rate data enables us to compare data if we are unable to standardize observation periods or opportunities to respond. It makes it possible to compare data, for example, if observation periods are interrupted or if worksheets have different numbers of problems. Rate is calculated by dividing the number of times a behavior occurred by the length of the observation period. For example, if Brett got out of his seat 6 times during the 30-minute math lesson on Monday morning, his rate is 0.2 per minute (6 occurrences divided by 30 minutes). If he left his seat 8 times during a 40-minute social studies class with the fourth grade, his rate is still 0.2 per minute (8/40). The rate is the same across observation periods and, in this example, across settings.

3. *Duration:* The duration of a behavior is a measurement of how long a student engages in it.

   Brett was out of his seat for a total of 14 minutes.

   Brett was out of his seat an average of 3 minutes per instance.

   Yao worked on her math for 20 minutes.

   Marvin's tantrum lasted for 65 minutes.

   Lois had her hand in her mouth for 6 minutes.

   Duration is important when the concern is not the number of times Brett gets out of his seat, but how long he is out of his seat each time he gets up or how long he stays up during a given observation period. He may leave his seat only twice during a 40-minute lesson, but if he stays up for several minutes each time, that is a different problem from popping up and going right back down again. If we record the duration of Brett's out-of-seat behavior, we can state that he was out of his seat for a total of 8 minutes during the 30-minute class, or we can report the length of each instance, or we can compute the average amount of time he spent out of his seat during each instance.

4. *Latency:* A behavior's latency is the length of time between instructions to perform it and the occurrence of the behavior.

   After I told Brett to sit in his chair, it took him 50 seconds to sit down.

   After the teacher said, "Get to work," Yao stared into space for 5 minutes before she started her math.

   It took 20 minutes for Marvin to become quiet after I put him in time-out.

   After I told Lois to take her hand out of her mouth, it was 2 minutes before she did so.

   Latency is relevant when the concern is not how long it takes a student to do something, but how long it takes to begin to do it. For example, Yao may solve 60% of her math problems correctly within an acceptable amount of time once she *starts*, but it takes her 7 minutes to get started.

5. *Topography:* The topography of behavior is the "shape" of the behavior—what it looks like.

   Yao writes all the 4s backward on her math paper.

   Marvin screams, kicks his heels on the floor, and pulls his hair during a tantrum.

   Lois's hand sucking involves her putting her fingers in her mouth up to the knuckles.

   Topography describes a behavior's complexity or its motor components. A tantrum, for example, may involve many behaviors performed simultaneously. Some behaviors consist of a chain, or sequence, of individual responses that usually occur together.

6. *Force:* The force of a behavior is its intensity.

   Yao writes so heavily that she makes holes in her paper.

   Marvin screams so loudly that the teacher three doors down the hall can hear him.

   Lois's hand sucking is so intense that she has broken the skin on her thumb.

   Describing the intensity or force of a behavior often results in a qualitative measure that is hard to standardize. We are attempting to communicate how loud a scream is (usually without the use of an audiometer), how hard a child is banging a table, or how forcefully he is hitting himself or another child.

7. *Locus:* The locus of a behavior describes where it occurs, either in the environment or, for example, on the child or victim's body.

   Brett walks to the window and stares outside.

   Yao writes the answers to her math problems in the wrong spaces.

   Marvin hits his ears during a tantrum.

Lois sucks the fingers of her left hand.

Locus describes either the target of the behavior or where in the environment the behavior is taking place.

The decision to use a particular system of data collection is based partly on the dimension of behavior that is of concern and partly on convenience. Systems for collecting data can be classified into three general categories. The first is recording and analyzing written reports that ideally include a full record of behaviors emitted during an observation period. The second is the observation of tangible products resulting from a behavior. The third is recording a sample of the behavior as it occurs. These systems may be categorized as follows:

Analyzing written records:	Anecdotal reports
Observing tangible products:	Permanent product recording
Observing a sample of behavior:	Event recording
	Interval recording
	Time sampling
	Duration recording
	Latency recording

Dimensions of Behavior
Pearson eText
Video Example 4.1
In this video, a student is repeating, writing, then reading a sentence. Notice that there is a short latency to repeating the sentence, but a longer latency to writing it. The duration of the writing response is also moderately long, with several errors. Consider how you might prioritize the dimensions for a behavioral objective.

The Professor Effects a Rescue

As Professor Grundy was walking to his car, he observed a congregation of students, including DeWayne, gathered around something that was not visible to him. His curiosity aroused, he strolled over to the group. As he got closer, he observed the object of the students' interest, which was an extremely large white dog. The animal was panting, its head was drooping, and it appeared emaciated. Its coat was matted and filthy, and it was dragging about 3 feet of chain from a metal choke collar drawn tightly around its neck.

"Look, Professor," said DeWayne, "I think it's a white St. Bernard. Do you think it bites?"

"See here," said the professor firmly, "it is dangerous to approach strange dogs. Someone should call the campus police and tell them to alert the city animal control officers." The dog, apparently determining that the professor was the highest authority present, staggered over to him, rested his huge head against Grundy's leg, and gazed at him soulfully with large, brown eyes.

"On the other hand," said the professor, taking the end of the chain and gently tugging, "perhaps I'll just make a call myself." The professor returned to his department with the dog. As he passed the departmental secretary, she gasped with alarm and began, "Professor, you can't..."

Grundy took his stopwatch from his pocket, activated it, and handed it to her. "This won't take 5 minutes," he said. "Time the duration and see for yourself." The professor placed a call to a colleague at the veterinary school who, upon hearing Grundy's description of the animal and its condition, stated, "What you've got there is a Great Pyrenees. What's he doing? I can hardly hear you."

"What he is doing," replied the professor, "is scratching. The topography of the behavior is that he is using his left hind foot to scratch behind his left ear. His foot is moving at a rate of 75 movements per minute according to the second hand on my watch. The force is sufficient to scatter dog hair and various other debris over a 3-foot radius, and his foot is hitting the floor between every third to fourth scratch with sufficient force to be heard in the lobby. He has been scratching for 3 minutes now, and he began scratching within 15 seconds of entering my office."

> "Oh," said the veterinarian a little blankly, "probably fleas." (The professor looked furtively down the hall hoping the secretary couldn't hear.) "Why don't you bring him by the clinic and we'll check him out. It sounds like he's been on the road for a while. If he's healthy, we can see about getting in touch with a rescue society. They have a lot of trouble placing those big guys, though."
>
> As Grundy returned through the lobby, retrieving his stopwatch from the secretary and confirming the duration of his stay as 4 minutes, 34 seconds, the secretary said, "He's really a sweet bunny of a boy, isn't he?" The dog wagged his long, plumy tail weakly. "Look, Professor, I think the sweetie likes me."
>
> "His name," stated the professor firmly, "is Burrhus."

Anecdotal Reports

Learning Outcome 4.2 Identify components of anecdotal reports.

Anecdotal reports are written to provide as complete a description as possible of a student's behavior in a particular setting or during an instructional period. Anecdotal reports do not identify a predefined or operationalized target behavior. After recording and analyzing data, the observer expects to identify a specific behavior that needs changing. Anecdotal reports are useful primarily for analysis, not for evaluation.

Teachers, parents, and therapists frequently use an anecdotal system of data collection to describe some general disturbance that is taking place or a lack of academic progress. For example, it might be reported that "Sheila constantly disrupts the class and does not complete her own work" or "During therapy sessions, I cannot seem to get Sheila under control to do the needed speech remediation."

Reports such as these are common and should prompt the applied behavior analyst to pinpoint the behavior (see Chapter 3). Should the specific behavior continue to elude identification, the analyst must further isolate and identify a target behavior that may be the source of the complaint in the natural setting of the behaviors—such as at the dinner table or in the classroom during reading period—and attempt to write down everything that occurs.

This system of data collection produces a written description of nearly everything that occurred in a specific time period or setting. It results in a report written in everyday language, describing individuals and interactions, rather than isolated marks on a data sheet. Wright (1960) provided some guidelines for writing anecdotal reports:

| Guide to writing anecdotal records.

1. Before beginning to record anecdotal data, write down the setting as you initially see it, the individuals in the setting and their relationships, and the activity occurring as you are about to begin recording (for example, lunch, free play).
2. Include in your description everything the target student(s) says and does and to whom or to what.
3. Include in your description everything said and done to the target student(s) and by whom.
4. As you write, clearly differentiate fact (what is actually occurring) from your impressions or interpretations of cause or reaction.
5. Provide some temporal indications so you can judge the duration of particular responses or interactions.

One of the authors of this text still uses this procedure today. It can be useful to write the time for each observation in a left-hand column of the piece of paper.

Structuring an Anecdotal Report

After observations have been made, an anecdotal report must be analyzed to determine the behavior(s), if any, that should be the subject of a behavior-change program. The observations in this initial anecdotal format are difficult to separate into individual behaviors and relationships, so it is helpful to present the anecdotal data in a more schematic manner for review. Bijou, Peterson, and Ault (1968) employed a system for sequence analysis in which they redrafted an anecdotal report into a form that reflects a behavioral view of environmental interactions. By this system, the contents of the report are arranged into columns divided to indicate antecedent stimuli, specific responses, and consequent stimuli. This table format clearly represents the temporal relationship among individual behaviors, the antecedents that stimulate them, and the consequences that follow and maintain them (Borrero, England, Sarcia, & Woods, 2016; Martens et al., 2019).

The anecdotal report in Figure 4.1 was taken in an elementary classroom. It records a period of interaction between a student named Brian, his teacher, and the members of his reading group.

Using the approach suggested by Bijou and his colleagues, the beginning of this report could be transposed into columns as begun in Figure 4.2. The antecedents, behaviors, and consequences are numbered to indicate the time sequence. Note that transposing the report makes it apparent that in several instances, consequences of a given response can become the antecedents for a succeeding response.

Figure 4.1 Excerpt from an anecdotal report

9:40 a.m.: Brian is walking around the room, touching various things such as plants on the windowsill. Teacher says, "It's now time for reading group. Everybody bring your books to the round table. You too, Brian." Teacher goes to table. Brian continues to wander. Teacher, in louder voice, "I'm still waiting." She goes and puts her hand on his shoulder. Brian pulls his shoulder out from under her hand. She takes him by the hand to the group of four other students. Brian sits. Teacher says, "Open your books. Where is your book, Brian?" Brian says, "Back there." "Back where, Brian?" "In my desk." "Go get it." "I will read from her book." "No, Brian, please go get your own book" (about 15 seconds pass). "Now, Brian, we are all waiting for you." Brian says, "So wait, we have plenty of time." Teacher stands. Brian gets up, goes to his desk (where he sits). When first student, Larry, is finished reading, teacher says, "Brian, come back here. It's almost your turn to read." Brian comes back to the table. Carl is reading. Brian makes a noise with his nose. Karen, sitting to his left, giggles and says, "Yuk." Teacher tells Karen to stop talking. Brian makes nose noise again. Karen, "Oh, yuk, yuk." Teacher says, "Brian, I see you. Stop it. Do we all see Brian? That is no way to behave when we are learning." Brian drops his book, bends down to get it, his chair falls. Teacher tells him to "come sit next to me." Brian moves his chair and begins to hum quietly. Teacher stands, moves 3 feet away from table, and tells Brian to move his chair "over here away from the group." Back at table she says, "Do we all see Brian and what happens when you disturb the group?" Larry raises his hand. "Yes, Larry?" Larry says, "They don't get to read." Teacher says, "Yes, very good, Larry. Now let's read again: your turn, Mary." Mary starts reading. Brian is rocking in his chair, Karen looks and giggles. Brian continues to rock: his chair falls backward. Teacher reprimands him, takes him to front of room, and puts him in chair facing blackboard. Brian is singing. Larry yells, "Stop singing. You're disturbing me." Brian quiets down, begins drawing on blackboard (teacher is seated with her back to him). Brian intermittently sings loud enough to be heard. Twice teacher says, "Quiet down, Brian." Reading group ends (17 minutes later). Students are told to line up at the door. On the way out teacher tells Brian how good he was while separated from the group. "But tomorrow you will have to read first in group." 10:35 a.m.: Brian is sent to P.E. with classmates.

Questions for analyzing anecdotal information.

When the content of an anecdotal report has been arranged in a format that clearly presents the sequence of and the relationships among behavioral events, the source of the problem behavior may be determined. The following questions help in analysis:

1. What are the behaviors that can be described as *inappropriate*? The behavior analyst should be able to justify labeling the behaviors as inappropriate, given the setting and the activity taking place.
2. Is this behavior occurring frequently, or has a unique occurrence been identified?
3. Can reinforcement or punishment of the behavior be identified? Teachers, parents, other children, or some naturally occurring environment event may deliver consequences, intentionally or otherwise.
4. Is there a pattern to these consequences?
5. Can antecedents to the behavior(s) be identified?
6. Is there a pattern that can be identified for certain events or stimuli (antecedents) that consistently precedes the behavior's occurrence?
7. Are there recurrent chains of certain antecedents, behaviors, and consequences?
8. Given the identified inappropriate behavior(s) of the student and the patterns of antecedents and consequences, what behavior really needs to be modified, and who is engaging in the behavior (for example, the referred student, the teacher, or the parent)?

Anecdotal recording may easily be biased. When classroom teachers serve as observers, they may already have ideas about why a student is engaging in inappropriate behavior and may observe behavior more readily that agrees with those ideas. Any observer

Figure 4.2 Structure of an anecdotal report

Time	Antecedent	Behavior	Consequence
9:40 a.m.		1. Brian is walking around room.	
	2. Teacher: Time for group. . . . "You too, Brian." T moves to table.		
		3. B continues to walk	
			4. T: "I'm still waiting."
	5. T puts hand on B's shoulder.		
		6. B pulls shoulder.	
			7. T takes B's hand and leads him to table.
		8. B sits.	
	9. T: "Where is your book, B?"		
		10. B: "Back there."	
			11. T: "Back where?"
		12. B: "In my desk."	
			13. T: "Go get it."
		14. B: "I will read from her book."	

should be careful to record as much activity as possible without censoring or making value judgments about the importance or relevance of behaviors as they occur. While watching and making notes, the observer should not try to decide whether one behavior is a result of another, but rather should just record what behavior followed another. Observers should also be alert to avoid distractions. Full attention must be given to observing the behaviors of the target student no matter what (unless, of course, someone is in danger) else occurs. No one can simultaneously collect anecdotal data and instruct other students. This may be particularly difficult for a teacher who naturally feels responsible for everything going on even when others are conducting instruction while she is collecting data. When analyzing anecdotal data, one should also bear in mind that most students behave differently when they see they are being watched and notes are being taken. Observers must make every effort to be as inconspicuous as possible by avoiding making unnecessary noise, reacting, and making eye contact with students.

The use of anecdotal reports is not always practical for general education teachers. Special education teachers may be called upon to observe students who are having behavioral or academic difficulty or who are in the process of being referred for special education services. For such observation, skill in recording and analyzing anecdotal data is extremely valuable. Anecdotal reports can enable these teachers to determine what factors in the classroom are occasioning or maintaining appropriate and inappropriate behaviors. This information will serve as the basis for making decisions about possible changes in the classroom environment or in behavior-management strategies. Anecdotal observation may also be used as a first step in a longer process for dealing with persistent, highly disruptive, or seriously harmful behaviors. This process, known as functional assessment (see Chapter 6), requires detailed observation, analysis, and manipulation of objects and events in a student's environment to determine what is occasioning and maintaining the behaviors.

Permanent Product Recording

Learning Outcome 4.3 Identify components of permanent product recording.

Teachers have been using **permanent product recording** since the first time a teacher walked into a classroom. A teacher uses permanent product recording to grade a spelling test, verify the creation of a chemical emulsion, or count the number of cans a student has placed on a shelf. *Permanent products* are tangible items or environmental effects that result from a behavior. Permanent products are outcomes of behavior; thus, this method is sometimes called *outcome recording*. This type of recording is an *ex post facto* method of data collection.

> Permanent product recording is the easiest to use, but not all behaviors leave a permanent product.

To collect permanent product data, the teacher reviews the statement of the behavior as written in the behavioral objective and determines what constitutes an acceptable outcome of the behavior. For example, if the behavior is building a tower of blocks, the objective states whether the student is required to place one block on top of another or whether the blocks should be arranged in a certain color sequence. If the behavior is academic, conditions also are specified. For example, the objective may specify the number of spelling errors permitted in a written paragraph or the number of references required in a term paper. If the behavior is vocational, quality may be specified as well as the number of widgets to be assembled. In each case, the teacher reviews the operational definition of the behavior. After evaluating the products of the required behavior, the teacher simply notes how many of the products were produced and how many were acceptable according to the definition.

Because the concrete results of a behavior are being evaluated and recorded, the teacher does not have to observe the student directly engaged in the behavior. Convenience is the explanation for the frequent use of permanent product recording in the classroom: It causes minimal interference with a classroom schedule.

> Applications of permanent product recording.

The versatility of permanent product recording makes it useful in a variety of instructional programs and settings. In educational instruction, permanent product recording has been used to record data on academic tasks such as spelling accuracy; grammatical elements in writing, such as capitalization, complete sentences, and punctuation, number of words written, and elements in paragraphs; completion and accuracy of arithmetic problems; and performance on science, reading comprehension, and Greek history quizzes. It has also been used to record note taking during lectures and completion and accuracy of homework assignments. In vocational instruction, permanent product recording has been used to record outcomes of tasks such as pot scrubbing, racking dishes, and assembling doorknobs and object hangers (Boyle, 2013; Falkenberg & Barbetta, 2013; Grossi & Heward, 1998; Hansen & Wills, 2014; Jimenez, Lo, & Saunders, 2014; Konrad, Trela, & Test, 2006; Kourea, Konrad, & Kazolia, 2019; Lee & Singer-Dudek, 2012; Mason, Kubina, & Hoover, 2013; Schieltz et al., 2020; Stringfield, Luscre, & Gast, 2011; White, Houchins, Viel-Ruma, & Dever, 2014).

The main advantage of permanent product recording is the durability of the sample of behavior obtained. The permanent product is not apt to disappear before its occurrence can be recorded. In light of this, the teacher may keep an accurate file of the actual products of certain target behaviors (such as test papers) or a report of the products for further review or verification later.

Permanent product recording may include the use of audiofile, videotape, and digital recording systems. With recording equipment, teachers can make samples of specific transitory behaviors that would not ordinarily produce a permanent product. Samples of behavior in hectic settings such as play groups can be recorded and analyzed at leisure. Samples of behaviors from nonschool settings such as a student's home can be made by parents and brought to professionals for analysis. Individual and group samples of expressive language, for example, have been audiotaped (Garcia-Albea, Reeve, Reeve, & Brothers, 2014; Grieco et al., 2018) and videotaped (Duenas, Plavnick, & Maher, 2019; Ward & Shukla-Mehta, 2019). Samples of student performance in general and special education settings have been videotaped to allow collaboration among interdisciplinary team members to determine educational goals and intervention techniques (Losinski, Maag, Katsiyannis, & Ryan, 2015; Prykanowski, Martinez, Reichow, Conroy, & Huang, 2018). Recording audio and video files allows for data collection after the fact, just as grading a student's exam or composition after school does.

> Behavioral dimensions for which permanent product recording may be used.

What permanent products or outcomes might be observed for each of the behavioral dimensions discussed in the section on choosing a system of data collection?

Rate: number of written products of any academic behavior per unit of time

Duration or latency: unfortunately do not lend themselves to permanent product recording unless recording equipment is available

Topography: the correct formation of letters or numerals; following a pattern in such activities as pegboard designs, block building, or vocational assemblies

Force: too light, too heavy, or uneven pressure when writing or typing; holes kicked in a classroom wall by a student having a tantrum

This list of examples is by no means exhaustive. Because permanent product recording is relatively simple and convenient, teachers can be imaginative in defining behaviors in terms of their outcomes. We have known teachers who operationally defined

- *test anxiety* as the number of visible erasures on a test paper
- *sloppiness* as the number of pieces of scrap paper on the floor within 2 feet of a student's desk
- *hyperactivity* as the number of table tennis balls still balanced in the pencil tray of a student's desk

The following vignette examines one use of permanent product recording.

Using Permanent Products
Pearson eText
Video Example 4.2
In this video, the team discusses how technology can be incorporated to capture a student's communication attempts. Notice how the team considers the advantages of technology for developing collaboration.

Mr. Martin Observes Room Cleaning

Mr. Martin, while majoring in special education, was a night-shift assistant at a residential school for students with severe emotional and behavioral problems. One of his duties was to see that each bedroom was cleaned before bedtime. He decided to establish some system for reinforcing room cleaning but was uncertain about what he should measure. When he tried measuring and reinforcing the time students spent cleaning their rooms, he found that although there was a great deal of scurrying around, the rooms were still very messy.

Because the major problem appeared to be clothes, toys, and trash scattered on the floors, beds, and other furniture, he decided to use the number of such objects as his measure. Each evening before lights-out, he stood at the door of each bedroom with a clipboard containing a sheet of paper with each resident's name and a space for each day of the week. He rapidly counted the number of separate objects scattered in inappropriate places and entered the total in the space on his data sheet.

Observational Recording Systems

Learning Outcome 4.4 Identify the five observational recording systems and when to use each system.

Whereas the permanent product method of data collection records the outcome of a behavior, **observational recording systems** are used to record behavior samples as the behavior is actually occurring. A data collector may choose from several basic observational recording systems. Teachers who are interested in recording the number of times a behavior is occurring may select **event recording**. Those who want to find the proportion of a specified time period during which the behavior occurs may select **interval recording** or **time sampling**. **Duration recording** allows the teacher to determine the length of time the student spends performing some behavior. **Latency recording** measures the length of time it takes a student to start doing something. An illustration of the relationship between observational recording procedures and the components of a behavioral, stimulus-response sequence is shown in Figure 4.3.

Event Recording

Event recording is a frequently used observational recording procedure because it most directly and accurately reflects the number of times a behavior occurs. When using event recording, the observer makes a notation every time the student engages in the target behavior. Tallying these notations gives an exact record of how often the behavior occurred. A count of the target behavior is made during a specified

> Event recording provides an exact count of how many times a behavior occurs.

Figure 4.3 Observational data collection systems as related to the basic behavioral paradigm

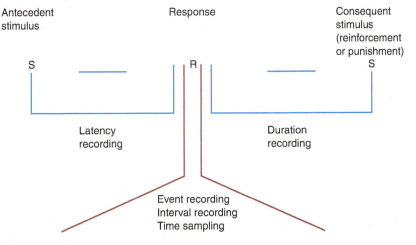

observation period—for example, during a reading period or during lunch. Recording how often the behavior occurs within a given time period documents its frequency. If the lengths of the observation periods are constant, the observer may simply report the number of times the behavior occurred (frequency), or the observer may report the rate, the number of times it occurred per minute or hour during that period. Rate may also be reported if the observation periods vary in length. Another strategy is to standardize the length of the observation period—for example, by taking data for just the first 20 minutes of the period each day.

Event recording is usually the method of choice when the objective is to increase or decrease the number of times a student engages in a certain behavior. Event recording may be used to record an increase in an appropriate social behavior, such as counting the number of times a student shares a toy with a classmate. It may be used to record an increase in an academic response (counting the number of correctly defined science vocabulary words) or a decrease in an inappropriate behavior (counting the number of times a student curses during physical education class). Because the teacher attempts to record the exact number of times the behavior occurs, event recording must be used with behaviors that are discrete. **Discrete behaviors** have an obvious, or agreed upon, beginning and end. The observer can make an accurate frequency count because he or she can clearly judge when one occurrence ends and the next begins. Event recording has been used for counting and recording behaviors in a range of content areas, including *academics*: reading, reading fluency, sight word fluency, writing, spelling, vocabulary skills, multiplication, and division; *communication*: requesting, labeling pictures, speech, manual signs, microswitch presses, and communication with peers using a speech-generating device; *self-help*: eating nonpreferred foods and walking; *social skills*: listening, social gaze, social initiations, empathic responding, turn taking with peers, complimenting, and perspective taking; *leisure skills*: playing songs and videos using a microswitch. Event recording has also been used to count instances of inappropriate behavior, such as negative vocalizations, throwing, scratching, grabbing, pulling hair, hitting, kicking, flopping, self-injurious behavior, rumination, and drooling (Argott, Townsend, & Poulson, 2017; Barber et al., 2018; Bishop et al., 2020; Bloomfield, Fischer, Clark, & Dove, 2019; Cannon, Easterbrooks, & Fredrick, 2010; Cazzell et al., 2017; Cihon et al., 2017; Courtemanche, Piersma, & Valdovinos, 2019; Curtis et al., 2020; Datchuk, Kubina, & Mason, 2015; Erickson, Derby, McLaughlin, & Fuehrer, 2015; Floress, Zoder-Martell, & Schaub, 2017; García-Zambrano, Rehfeldt, Hertel, & Boehmert, 2019; Glover, McLaughlin, Derby, & Gower, 2010; Holyfield, 2019; Kostewicz, Kubina, & Brennan, 2020; Lancioni et al., 2010, 2011, 2014, 2015; Lopez & Wiskow, 2019; Musti-Rao, Lo, & Plati, 2015; Popovic, Starr, & Koegel, 2020; Schrauben & Dean, 2019; Therrien & Light, 2018; Thiemann-Bourque, Feldmiller, Hoffman, & Johner, 2018; Valentino, LeBlanc, Veazey, Weaver, & Raetz, 2019; Ward & Shukla Mehta, 2019; Wilder & Neve, 2018).

Event recording may also be used when teaching from a task analysis. A task analysis is a list of the individual steps that when chained together form a complex behavior such as solving addition problems or hand washing. During instruction, the teacher records the student's performance of the steps listed in the task analysis. Use of event recording is appropriate as the steps are a series of discrete behaviors each with a clear, or clearly definable, beginning and ending. Using and collecting data from task analyses is discussed at length in Chapter 10.

Some labels for behavior may be used to describe what are actually a number of different responses, each of which may or may not occur each time the so-called behavior occurs. Examples that many teachers try to target for change are on-task or off-task behavior, appropriate or inappropriate verbalizations, in-seat or out-of-seat behavior, or disturbing one's neighbor. For accurate event recording, a standard definition, with an agreed-upon beginning and end, is necessary. In other words, such behaviors can be made discrete by defining them operationally (see Chapter 3).

> Event recording can be used only for discrete behaviors.

Not all behaviors, however, can be measured adequately using event recording. This data collection procedure is *not* appropriate in the following instances:

1. Behavior occurring at such a high **frequency** that the number recorded may not reflect an accurate count. Certain behaviors, such as the number of steps taken while running, some stereotypic behaviors (such as hand flapping or rocking by students with severe disabilities), and eye blinking may occur at such high frequencies that it is impossible to count them accurately.
2. Cases in which one behavior or response can occur for extended time periods. Examples of such behaviors might be thumb sucking or attention to task. If out-of-seat behavior were being recorded, for instance, a record showing that the student was out of her seat only one time during a morning would give an inaccurate indication of what the student was actually doing if this one instance of the behavior lasted from roll call to lunchtime.

An advantage of event recording, in addition to accuracy, is the relative ease of the data collection itself. The teacher does not need to interrupt the lesson to take data. The teacher may simply make a notation on an index card or paper on a clipboard, make slash marks on a piece of tape around his or her wrist, or transfer paper clips from one pocket to another. This information may be tallied and transferred to a data sheet similar to the one presented in Figure 4.4.

Event recording is also easily used for many academic behaviors. Figure 4.5 is a data sheet used for recording the errors made during an oral reading exercise. The teacher simply places a mark in the appropriate row as a particular error is made. The column heads may record the day of week, the child who is reading, dates, page number from the text where the mistake was made, and so on.

Using the data sheet in Figure 4.6, a teacher can record the correct verbal reading of sight words. The sight words chosen for the student are listed in the left column. The succeeding columns provide space to indicate whether the student's reading of the word was correct or incorrect. The total number (or percent) correct is recorded at the bottom of the column (on April 12, for example, Deepa read 5 words correctly—though not the same 5 as on April 10). Data on the number of words identified correctly may be taken during instruction as the teacher records Deepa's response as correct or incorrect each time she is asked to read a word. This is referred to as trial-by-trial data collection. Data may be taken instead at the conclusion of the instructional session by giving Deepa the opportunity to read each word one more time and recording

---

Figure 4.4 Basic data sheet for event recording

Event Recording Data Sheet

Student: PATRICIA
Observer: MRS. COHEN

Behavior: INAPPROPRIATE TALK-OUTS (NO HAND RAISED)

	Time Start Stop	Notations of occurrences	Total occurrences
5/1/14	10:00 10:20	⊬⊬⊬ ⊬⊬⊬ //	12
5/2/14	10:00 10:20	⊬⊬⊬ ////	9

Figure 4.5 Data sheet for event recording

Student: __JEREMY__
Observer: __MS. GARWOOD__

Behavior: __Errors in oral reading__

	CAROL	5/1/14	EXERC. #2	READER P.G. 7
SUBSTITUTIONS				
MISPRONOUNCIATIONS				
INSERTIONS				
REPETITIONS				

Figure 4.6 Data sheet for event recording

Student: **Inclusive Dates:**

OBJECTIVE: Given the following list of 12 sight words found in general merchandise stores (e.g., Walmart), Deepa will verbally state each.

Criterion: with 100% accuracy for 4 consecutive sessions.

Dates/Trials

Items	4/10	4/12									Comments
restrooms	+	+									
exit	+	−									
girls	−	+									
housewares	−	−									
pet	+	−									
supplies	−	+									
checkout	−	−									
express	−	+									
shoes	+	−									
linens	−	+									
videos	+	−									
electronics	−	−									
Total Correct	5/12	5/12									

only those responses. This is one form of probe data collection. A simple method for recording correct and incorrect answers when using flash cards is to mark directly on the back of the card on which the word (or other cue) is printed. These marks can be transferred later to a summary data sheet.

For the more mechanically inclined, counting devices are commercially available. Although these make data collection easier and more accurate, they entail some expense and may break. An inexpensive counter sold for tallying purchases in a grocery store or golf strokes may be useful. Stitch counters designed to fit on the end of a knitting needle come in sizes large enough to fit on a pen.

Nowadays, there are numerous electronic applications used for data collection, such as personal data assistants (PDAs; Tarbox, Wilke, Findel-Pyles, Bergstrom, & Grandpeesheh, 2010) and tablet technology (Lavay, Sakai, Ortiz, & Roth, 2015). Tarbox et al. provided four benefits of electronic data collection: automatic electronic storage of data, electronic analysis of the data, real-time data collection, and greater ease in recording a large number of behaviors (e.g., using a computer keyboard where each key is pressed for a different behavior).

Providing instructions for teaching and collecting data can increase the accuracy of the teaching procedures (LeBlanc, Sump, Leaf, & Cihon, 2020). See the example of the data sheet from this study in Figure 4.7.

TRIAL-BY-TRIAL RECORDING One variation of the event-recording technique is the use of **trial-by-trial recording within discrete trial teaching** (Ferguson et al., 2020). In this method, the teacher structures or controls the number of opportunities the student will have to perform the behavior. Most often this method consists of presenting a predetermined number of opportunities, or trials, in each instructional session. A **trial** may be viewed as a discrete occurrence because it has an identifiable beginning and ending.

Figure 4.7 Enhanced Data Sheet

Participant ID: _____ Session date: _____

Instructions:

1. Arrange the stimuli as indicated per trial
2. Present the sample (bolded one is the target for each trial).
3. Circle the stimulus that the learner FIRST points to – even if it is wrong.
4. Circle the prompt level required to get the correct response.
5. The first 3 trials (highlighted in gray) are LEAST TO MOST PROBES.
6. The rest are MOST TO LEAST TEACHING TRIALS.

Prompt Scoring Key:
  I = Independent Correct Response   G = Gestural Prompt
  PP = Partial Physical Prompt   FP = Full Physical Prompt

		Left	Center	Right	Prompt Req.			
Probes	1	Triangle	Circle	Square	I	G	PP	FP
	2	Circle	Square	Triangle	I	G	PP	FP
	3	Square	Triangle	Circle	I	G	PP	FP
Teaching Trials	4	Circle	Square	Triangle	FP	PP	G	I
	5	Square	Triangle	Circle	FP	PP	G	I
	6	Triangle	Circle	Square	FP	PP	G	I
	7	Circle	Square	Triangle	FP	PP	G	I
	8	Square	Triangle	Circle	FP	PP	G	I
	9	Triangle	Circle	Square	FP	PP	G	I
	10	Circle	Square	Triangle	FP	PP	G	I
	11	Square	Triangle	Circle	FP	PP	G	I
	12	Triangle	Circle	Square	FP	PP	G	I

Figure 4.8 Data collection sheet for use with trial-by-trial recording

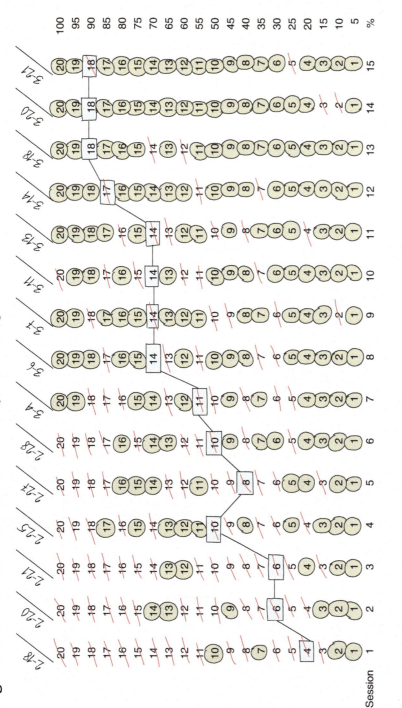

Figure 4.9 Data collection sheet for use with trial-by-trial recording

Name: _Peter_
Task: _Functional Counting to 10_
Date:

10	10	10	10	10
9	9	9	9	9
8	8	8	8	8
7	7	7	7	7
6	6	6	6	6
5	5	5	5	5
4	4	4	4	4
3	3	3	3	3
2	2	2	2	2
1	1	1	1	1

Comments:

Name: _Calvin_
Task: _Functional Counting to 10_

10	10	10	10	10
9	9	9	9	9
8	8	8	8	8
7	7	7	7	7
6	6	6	6	6
5	5	5	5	5
4	4	4	4	4
3	3	3	3	3
2	2	2	2	2
1	1	1	1	1

Comments:

Name: _Tanya_
Task: _Functional Counting to 10_

10	10	10	10	10
9	9	9	9	9
8	8	8	8	8
7	7	7	7	7
6	6	6	6	6
5	5	5	5	5
4	4	4	4	4
3	3	3	3	3
2	2	2	2	2
1	1	1	1	1

Comments:

Name: _Rita_
Task: _Functional Counting to 10_
Date:

10	10	10	10	10
9	9	9	9	9
8	8	8	8	8
7	7	7	7	7
6	6	6	6	6
5	5	5	5	5
4	4	4	4	4
3	3	3	3	3
2	2	2	2	2
1	1	1	1	1

Comments:

Name: _Dylana_
Task: _Functional Counting to 10_

10	10	10	10	10
9	9	9	9	9
8	8	8	8	8
7	7	7	7	7
6	6	6	6	6
5	5	5	5	5
4	4	4	4	4
3	3	3	3	3
2	2	2	2	2
1	1	1	1	1

Comments:

Name: _Roy_
Task: _Functional Counting to 10_

10	10	10	10	10
9	9	9	9	9
8	8	8	8	8
7	7	7	7	7
6	6	6	6	6
5	5	5	5	5
4	4	4	4	4
3	3	3	3	3
2	2	2	2	2
1	1	1	1	1

Comments:

A trial is defined by its three behavioral components: an antecedent stimulus, a response, and a consequent stimulus (S-R-S). The delivery of the antecedent stimulus (usually a verbal cue with pictures, objects, or words) marks the beginning of the trial, and the delivery of the consequent stimulus (reinforcement, error correction) signifies the termination of the trial. For example, in a given session the teacher may decide that a student will be given 10 opportunities, or trials, to respond by pointing to specified objects upon request. Each trial is then recorded as correct or incorrect. Trial-by-trial recording allows the teacher to monitor progress simply by looking at the number of correct responses for each session. This number is often converted to a percentage of a certain number of correct responses out of the total number of trials.

Figures 4.8 and 4.9 present variations of data sheets used for the collection of discrete trial or trial-by-trial recording data. The data sheet in Figure 4.8 (variation of Saunders & Koplik, 1975) is arranged from left to right for 15 sessions. Within each session, or column, there are numbers representing up to 20 trials. The teacher records dichotomous data (whether the response was correct or incorrect) using the following simple procedure:

After each trial:

1. Circle the trial number that corresponds to a correct response.
2. Slash (/) through the trial number that corresponds to an incorrect response.

After each session:

1. Total the number of correct trials (those circled).
2. Place a square around the corresponding number in the session column that corresponds to the number of correct trials.
3. To graph directly on the data sheet, connect the squared numbers across the sessions to yield a learning curve.
4. The column on the far right allows the number of correct trials per session (the number with the square around it) to be converted to the percentage of trials correct. If the number of correct trials in a 20-trial session was 8, looking at the last column, we see that the percentage correct is 40.

Figure 4.9 is a modification of the previous data sheet that allows the observer to use it for up to six students working on the same task or for up to six tasks for the same student.

Classroom teachers can improve instruction by using trial-by-trial recording. For example, a teacher might want to be sure to ask each member of a seminar group five questions during a discussion on early Cold War events and the Berlin Wall. A very simple data sheet with the names of the students and a space to mark whether answers were correct or incorrect would provide valuable information for analysis and evaluation.

Event recording (including trial-by-trial recording) lends itself to the observation of the rate of frequency of behavior, for example:

- number of times Mel talks out in an hour
- number of times Charlie hits another student in a 20-minute recess
- number of questions Melissa answers correctly during a 15-minute world geography review
- number of times Sam answers questions in a whisper
- number of times Mary throws trash on the floor
- number of stairs Eliot climbs by putting only one foot on each step

Behavioral dimensions appropriate to event recording.

Using Event Recording
Pearson eText
Video Example 4.3
In this video, the educator is working with Trae on his reading and collecting data using event recording. How does she connect event recording with a goal for fluency?

Interval Recording and Time Sampling

Interval recording and time sampling data collection systems are ways of recording an approximation of the actual number of times a behavior occurs (Fiske & Delmolino, 2012). Instead of counting each occurrence of the behavior, the teacher counts the number of intervals of time within observation periods during which the behavior occurs. With these methods it is possible to record continuous behaviors (behaviors of longer duration) and high-frequency behaviors that may be incompatible with event recording.

Interval recording and time sampling have been used with behaviors such as off-task and on-task behaviors, engagement with instruction and leisure activities, interactive play, social interactions, out-of-seat behavior, calling out, thumb sucking, tantrums and aggressive behaviors such as hair pulling, negative vocalizations, stereotypic behavior, and self-injurious behaviors (Anderson, Trinh, Caldarella, Hansen, & Richardson, 2018; Aspiranti, Bebech, Ruffo, & Skinner, 2019; Beaver, Reeve, Reeve, & DeBar, 2017; Boden, Jolivette, & Alberto, 2018; Gibbs, Tullis, Thomas, & Elkins, 2018; Hundert, Rowe, & Harrison, 2014; Ivy, Payne, & Neef, 2019; Kranak, Alber-Morgan, & Sawyer, 2017; Prykanowski, Martinez, Reichow, Conroy, & Huang, 2018; Shieltz et al., 2020; Vorndran, Pace, Luiselli, Flaherty, & Kleinman, 2008).

> The observer counts intervals, not discrete behaviors.

In terms of making the closest representation of the actual occurrence of the behavior, event recording is the most accurate, time sampling is next, and interval recording is the least exact (Ledford, Ayres, Lane, & Lam, 2015; Rapp, Colby-Dirksen, Michalski, Carroll, & Lindenberg, 2008). Each system, however, has its advantages and disadvantages.

INTERVAL RECORDING When using interval recording, the teacher defines a specific time period (usually between 10 minutes and an hour) during which the target behavior will be observed. This observation period is then divided into equal intervals. These intervals may be very short, such as 5 or 10 seconds, or longer, such as 1 minute or 5 minutes. The shorter the interval is, the more accurate the data. The teacher draws a series of boxes representing the time intervals. In each box, or interval, the teacher simply notes whether the behavior occurred (+) or did not occur (−) *at any time during the interval*. Therefore, each interval has only one notation. The data sheet for a 5-minute observation period shown in Figure 4.10 has been divided into

> Interval recording does not provide an exact count of behaviors but is especially appropriate for continuous behaviors.

Figure 4.10 Interval recording data sheet

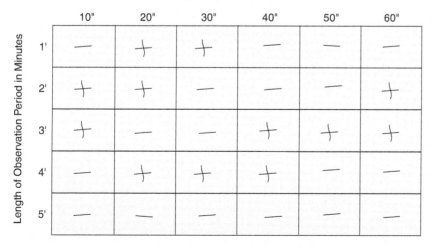

Student: Darius
Date: 8-29
Time Start: 9:10
Observer: Mrs. Heflin
Behavior: On-task (eyes on paper or writing on paper)
Setting: 4th period math
Time End: 9:15

Number (Percent) of Intervals of Occurrence: 12 intervals, 40% of intervals
Number (Percent) of Intervals of Nonoccurrence: 18 intervals, 60% of intervals

> ## Ms. Stallings Counts Tattling
>
> Four of the students in Ms. Stallings's third-grade class seemed to spend most of their time telling her what other students were doing wrong. Ms. Stallings was worried about this for two reasons: the students were not working efficiently, and they were driving her up the wall. When she asked her colleague, Ms. Barbe, for advice, Ms. Barbe suggested that the first thing to do was to find out how often each of the students was tattling.
>
> "Otherwise," she said, "you won't know for sure whether whatever you do to stop them is working."
>
> Ms. Stallings decided to count an instance of tattling each time a student mentioned another student's name to her and described any number of inappropriate behaviors. Thus, "Johnny's not doing his work and he's bothering me" was counted as one instance, but "Harold and Manolo are talking" was counted as two instances. She then went back to Ms. Barbe.
>
> "How can I write it down every time they do it?" she asked. "I move around my room all the time, and I don't want to carry paper and pencil."
>
> Ms. Barbe laughed. "No problem," she answered. "I'm sure that's why dry beans come in so many sizes and shapes. I just pick a different bean for each student, put a handful of each in my right pocket, and transfer by feel to my left pocket when I observe the behavior. Just be sure you get them out before your clothes go into the washer."

10-second intervals. During the first minute of the observation period, the target behavior occurred during two of the intervals, the second and third. Over the total 5-minute period, the target behavior occurred during 12, or 40%, of the intervals.

Because of the way these interval data are recorded, only limited conclusions can be drawn from the record of the behavior's occurrence. Regardless of whether the behavior occurred once or five times during the interval, a single notation is made. Therefore, the actual number of occurrences is not included in the record. If, in the preceding example, cursing was being recorded, all the teacher could say was that, during two of the intervals, the student cursed. There were at least two instances of this behavior, but there may have been more. Even if the student cursed 11 times during the second interval, only one notation would have been made. Recording occurrences of discrete behaviors, such as cursing or hitting, is known as *partial-interval recording* (the behavior does not consume the entire interval).

Behaviors such as walking around the room or being off task may begin in one interval and continue into the next interval. Such timing would appear as two instances, because it would be recorded in two intervals in this instance, but the same duration of behavior would appear as only one instance if it fell within a single interval. Recording ongoing behaviors that may continue for several intervals is known as *whole-interval recording* (the behavior consumes the entire interval).

An additional problem encountered with interval data collection is created by the shortness of each interval in which the notation is to take place. It is very difficult to teach and collect interval data simultaneously. The teacher must keep an eye on a student or students, observe a stopwatch or second hand on a watch, and note the occurrence or nonoccurrence of the target behavior all within a matter of seconds; a third-party observer is often required.

The necessity of looking down at the data sheet to make a recording might even cause an observer to miss an occurrence of the behavior, resulting in inaccurate data. The need to look at one's watch to check the passage of the interval is eliminated by videotaping the observation period and using the time on the DVD player to note intervals (Miltenberger, Rapp, & Long, 1999; MacDonald, Parry-Cruwys, Dupere, & Ahearn, 2014). Observers can also time intervals using an app that indicates the passage of time at the end of each interval, such as the MotivAider, or set a timer with a seconds indicator and an audible signal, or use commercial products such as the WatchMinder or Invisible Clock that will chime or vibrate at selected intervals. Another way of simplifying the task is to build in opportunities for recording as part of the schedule. For example, the observer might alternate 10-second intervals for observing with 5-second intervals for scoring.

Figure 4.11 is an example of an interval recording sheet for a 15-minute period divided into 10-second intervals. Looking at the notations of occurrence and nonoccurrence, the data collector can infer certain information:

1. approximate number of occurrences of the behavior
2. approximate duration of the behavior within the observation period
3. distribution of the behavior across the observation period

Assuming that off-task behavior during a written arithmetic assignment is recorded in the example, the behavior appears to have occurred in 38 of the 90 intervals. The successive intervals in which the behavior occurred indicate that the off-task behavior occurred over long durations (3 minutes each), but it appears to have been confined primarily to two periods. When reviewing such data, teachers should analyze the situation for some indication of what seem to be the immediate precipitating factors. In this example, off-task behavior may have been due to the two sets of written instructions on the worksheet, which prompted the student to ask a neighbor what to do. Alternatively, if occurrence of the behavior is distributed throughout the time period, apparently lacking in some pattern(s), the teacher may consider whether the off-task behavior is a result of a more generalized reason, such as distractibility due to movement and conversation in the room, boredom with the task, or a lack of prior instruction resulting in a lack of the skills necessary for the task.

Figure 4.11 Interval recording of off-task behavior

10-second intervals

Minutes	1	2	3	4	5	6
1	O	O	O	X	X	X
2	X	X	X	X	X	X
3	X	X	X	X	X	X
4	X	X	O	O	O	O
5	O	O	O	O	X	O
6	O	O	X	O	O	O
7	O	O	O	O	X	O
8	X	X	X	X	X	X
9	X	X	X	O	X	X
10	X	X	X	X	X	O
11	O	O	O	O	O	O
12	O	O	O	O	O	O
13	O	O	O	X	O	O
14	O	O	O	O	O	X
15	O	O	O	O	O	O

Student __MALCOLM__
Date __2/24__
Observer __MR. RILEY__
Time Start __9:15__
Time End __9:30__
Behavior __OFF-TASK__

Note occurrence within the 10-second interval.

X = occurrence
O = nonoccurrence

Data summary

Number of intervals of occurrence: 38
Percent of intervals of occurrence: 42%
Number of intervals of nonoccurrence: 52
Percent of intervals of nonoccurrence: 58%

84   Chapter 4

> Time sampling allows for only one observation per interval.

TIME SAMPLING In order to use time sampling, the data collector selects a time period in which to observe the behavior and divides this period into equal intervals. This process is similar to that employed with interval recording. To record these data, the observer draws a series of boxes representing the intervals. The observer simply notes in each box (interval) whether the behavior was occurring (X) or not (O) when the student was observed at the moment the interval ended. Each interval therefore has only one notation. Note that the time sampling procedure differs from interval recording in that the student is observed only *at the end of the interval* rather than throughout it.

Figure 4.12 shows a data sheet for a 1-hour observation period occurring between 9:05 a.m. and 10:05 a.m. 3 days a week. The hour is divided into six 10-minute intervals. On Monday the target behavior (walking around the room without permission) was occurring at the end of four of the intervals: the first, second, fourth, and fifth. On Wednesday it was occurring at the end of three intervals: the first, fifth, and sixth. On Friday it was occurring at the end of four intervals: the first, fourth, fifth, and sixth. The teacher may summarize the number of intervals at the end of which the behavior was occurring for each day or each week or record the daily average for the week. As time sampling allows for longer periods of observation, the teacher could take data on the student's target behavior for the entire morning. The data sheet in Figure 4.13 allows for a morning's observation period of 3 hours, with each hour divided into four 15-minute intervals.

Figure 4.12 Time sampling data sheet for a 1-hour observation period, with 10-minute intervals, 3 days during a week

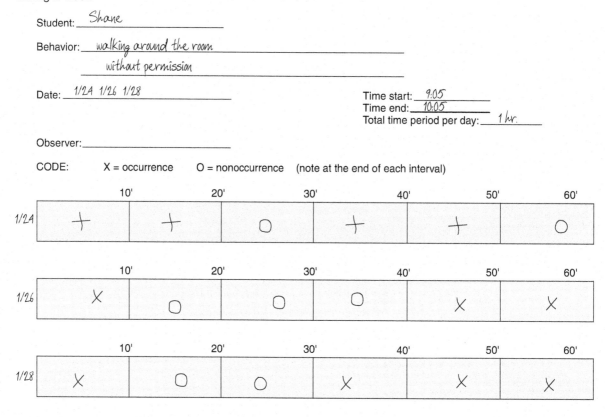

Data Summary
Daily: Mon. number of intervals of occurrence:
              percent of intervals of occurrence:
              number of intervals of nonoccurrence:
              percent of intervals of nonoccurrence:

Weekly: number of intervals of occurrence:
        percent of intervals of occurrence:
        number of intervals of nonoccurrence:
        percent of intervals of nonoccurrence:

Average daily: number of intervals of occurrence:
               percent of intervals of occurrence:
               number of intervals of nonoccurrence:
               percent of intervals of nonoccurrence:

Figure 4.13 Time sampling data sheet for a 3-hour observation period, with 15-minute intervals

Student:_____

Behavior:_____
_____

Date:_____ Time start:_____
Time end:_____
Total time period:_____

Observer:_____

CODE: X = occurrence   O = nonoccurrence   (note at the end of each interval)

15	30	45	00
15	30	45	00
15	30	45	00

Data Summary

Number of intervals of occurrence:
Percent of intervals of occurrence:
Number of intervals of nonoccurrence:
Percent of intervals of nonoccurrence:

Two fairly simple ways of recording time sampling data are to set a timer to ring at the end of the interval and to observe the behavior when the timer rings or to use an app that rings or vibrates at the end of each interval (e.g., MotivAider). To prevent students from figuring out the schedule and performing (or not performing) some behavior only at the end of the interval, the intervals may be of varying lengths. For example, a 10-minute time sampling recording system might have intervals of 8, 12, 6, 14, 9, and 11 minutes. The average interval duration would be 10 minutes, but the students would not know when they were about to be observed. Common sense indicates the need to hide the face of the timer.

Because of the method of recording time sampling data, only limited conclusions can be drawn about the behavior recorded. As with interval recording, the behavior may have occurred more than once within the 10-minute observation interval. A particularly serious drawback with time sampling occurs when a single instance of a behavior occurs just before or just after the observer looks up to record the occurrence, resulting in a record of nonoccurrence.

When time sampling intervals are divided into segments by minutes as opposed to seconds, the procedure allows for longer periods between observations. It is therefore more practical for simultaneous teaching and data collection. Indeed, the interval may be set at 15, 30, 45 minutes, or more, allowing for observation throughout an entire day or class period. As the interval gets longer, however, the similarity between the data recorded and the actual occurrence of the behavior probably decreases (LeBlanc, Lund, Kooken, Lund, & Fisher, 2019). Time sampling is suitable primarily for recording behaviors that are frequent or of long duration, such as attention to task, out-of-seat behavior, or thumb sucking.

| An observer may miss a lot of behavior when using time sampling.

| The longer the time sampling interval, the less accurate the data will be.

Although time sampling is practical for classroom use, its usefulness may diminish as a behavior-change program progresses successfully. For example, if Barry's teacher decides to use time sampling to record his out-of-seat behavior, she may observe that during baseline almost all of her observations indicate that Barry is out of his seat when she records at 15-minute intervals during the first 90 minutes of school. However, when a contingency is applied—"Barry, you will receive one token for each 15 minutes that you stay in your seat"—the procedure will become less useful—for example, if the teacher holds to her recording procedure, records out-of-seat behavior only at the end of the interval, and provides the reinforcer if Barry beats the clock to his seat. If the procedure is successful in spite of this assumption, the data may reflect a complete absence of the behavior long before it has really been eliminated. Barry may be out of his seat for a short while a number of times that do not happen to coincide with the end of intervals. At this point, because the behavior is occurring less frequently and for shorter durations, event or duration recording may be as practical and much more accurate. However, it is important to use the same data collection procedure throughout baseline and intervention periods. Figure 4.13 illustrates a format for collecting data using time sampling.

Data collected using interval recording or time sampling can be used to measure behavior along the frequency dimension by reporting the number of intervals during which the behavior occurred. These data, however, cannot be converted to rate. One cannot say that a certain behavior occurred at the rate of two per minute when what was recorded was the behavior occurring during two 10-second intervals in a 60-second period. Interval and time sampling data are most often expressed in terms of the percentage of intervals during which the behavior occurred. The procedure for converting raw data into percentages will be discussed in the next chapter. Measurement of duration can be approximated using interval recording, but this procedure does not lend itself to measures of latency. Force, locus, and topography may be measured, as with event recording, if they are included in the operational definition.

Behavioral dimensions appropriate to interval and time sampling recording.

To recapitulate some of the important points and differences concerning interval recording and time sampling:

1. Both interval recording and time sampling provide an approximation of how often a behavior occurred. Neither is as accurate as event recording, which provides an exact count of occurrences.
2. The occurrence of a behavior is noted and recorded at any time during an interval when using interval recording. The occurrence of a behavior is noted and recorded only at the end of an interval when using time sampling.
3. Because time sampling requires observing a student only at the moment the interval ends, it is easier to manage while teaching.
4. For both interval recording and time sampling, the observer reports the number or percentage of intervals in which a behavior occurred (or did not occur), not the number of times it occurred. That information is not recoverable from data collected using these methods.

VARIATIONS ON THE DATA COLLECTION SHEET On the interval recording and time sampling data collection sheets presented so far, the teacher records the occurrence or nonoccurrence of a behavior for a single student. These basic data collection formats are, however, flexible tools that can be adapted easily to meet a variety of instructional situations. The most common adaptations are for: (1) a data sheet that is more descriptive of a target behavior whose operational definition may include several topographies (for example, stereotypic behavior defined as hand flapping, body rocking, and finger flicking); (2) a data sheet to accommodate taking data on more than one behavior at a time (for example, out of seat and talking); and (3) a data sheet to accommodate data for more than one student at a time.

Ms. Simmons Observes Pencil Tapping

Ms. Simmons is an elementary school consultant teacher for students with learning disabilities. One of her students, Arnold, tapped his pencil on the desk as he worked. He completed a surprising number of academic tasks but tapped whenever he was not actually writing. This behavior was very annoying to his general education teacher. Ms. Simmons had tried counting pencil taps but found that Arnold tapped so rapidly that the pencil was a blur.

Shane was a teaching assistant in the classroom, and Ms. Simmons requested that Shane collect data on Arnold's tapping. She carefully defined the behavior, provided Shane with a recording sheet on a clipboard, gave him a stopwatch, and told him to mark a "+" in the box if Arnold tapped during a 10-second interval and a – if he didn't. She left Shane to observe and went to teach a small group. Very soon, she heard the sound of the clipboard hitting the floor and an expression of annoyance totally unacceptable in the classroom.

"I'm sorry, Ms. Simmons," said Shane, "but how am I supposed to watch Arnold, the watch, and the sheet at the same time?"

Realizing that this task was overwhelming, Ms. Simmons decided to throw Shane a bone. She had him download the MotivAider app on his phone and set it to vibrate every 10 seconds. Now, he was able to watch Arnold, and when the MotivAider vibrated he looked at the data sheet and recorded a plus or minus.

The next day, Shane said to Ms. Simmons, "This data collection stuff is not too bad when you have the right gadgets!"

Each of these data collection needs may be met by using coded data. Data collected simply to record the occurrence or nonoccurrence of a single behavior are called dichotomous data. The teacher is recording that the behavior either occurred or did not occur. For a fuller description of a behavior's various topographies or to record multiple behaviors, each behavior or variation is assigned a letter code to be used during data collection. If the observer wants to record data for multiple students, each student is assigned a letter code to be used on the data sheet.

There are at least three basic formats for coded data sheets: a legend coded data sheet, a prepared coded data sheet, and a track coded data sheet. Each format can be used with either interval recording or time sampling.

Coded Data Sheet with a Simple Legend A coded data collection sheet may have a legend like the one on a road map listing the behaviors being observed and a code for each. The example at the top of Figure 4.14 shows a few rows of data from an observation period during which interval recording was used to record occurrences of "disturbing one's neighbor." The legend includes codes for hitting (H), talking (T), and pinching (P). In this example, during the first minute of observation, Hector hit his neighbor during the first interval, talked during the third and fourth intervals, and talked and hit his neighbor during the fifth interval.

If the teacher wants to collect data on the same behavior being performed by more than one student, she may use this same format by providing a code for each student. For example, on the bottom of Figure 4.14 the teacher has made an adapted interval recording data sheet on which he will record occurrences of talking during the change of class by Jan (J), Ruth (R), and Veena (V). In this example, during the first minute of observation, Jan and Ruth were talking during the first interval and Ruth was talking during the second and fourth intervals. Veena was not recorded as having talked until the second interval of the second minute.

Coded Data Sheet with a Prepared Format A second type of coding, represented in Figure 4.15, uses letter codes for multiple behaviors or multiple students that are pre-entered in each cell (the space representing an interval) of the data sheet (Alberto, Sharpton, & Goldstein, 1979). With this prepared format the observer simply places a slash through the appropriate letter(s) indicating the behavior(s) that occurred or the student(s) who engaged in the behavior. The example at the top of Figure 4.15 shows rows of data from a 3-hour observation period during which the teacher used time sampling to record Sylvia's social interaction. The operational definition of social

Figure 4.14 Legend coded data sheets for an interval recording observation

Student: Hector Time Start: 9:10
Date: 9-18 Time End: 9:15
Observer: Ms. Hughes

Behavior Codes
H = hitting   T = talking   P = pinching

Minutes	10"	20"	30"	40"	50"	60"
1	H	—	T	T	T / H	—
2	—	P	P	—	—	—
3	—	—	—	T	T	—
4	H	—	—	—	—	—
5	—	H	—	T / H	T / H	—

Student: Jan, Ruth, Veena Behavior: Talking during change of class
Date: 9-14 Time Start: 11:05
Observer: Mr. Nelson Time End: 11:10

Student Codes
J = Jan   R = Ruth   V = Veena

Minutes	10"	20"	30"	40"	50"	60"
1	JR	R	—	R	—	—
2	—	RV	—	RV	—	R
3	JR	—	RV	RV	—	—
4	—	—	—	—	—	—
5	—	—	—	RV	R	—

interaction included six potential elements, each with a code: I—student initiated the interaction, R—student responded to an initiation by someone else, S—the interaction was with another student, A—the interaction was with an adult, V—the interaction was verbal, and P—the interaction was physical. In this example, during the first hour, Sylvia's first recorded social interaction was verbal in response to an adult, occurring at the end of the third interval.

If the observer wants to record the occurrence of a single behavior across several students, each student's code is placed in one cell. At the bottom of Figure 4.15, there is an adapted time sampling data sheet on which "active engagement with their task" was recorded for four students across three morning class periods. In this example, during the first period, Carmen and Kyle were actively engaged at the end of the first

Figure 4.15 Prepared coded data sheets for a time sampling observation

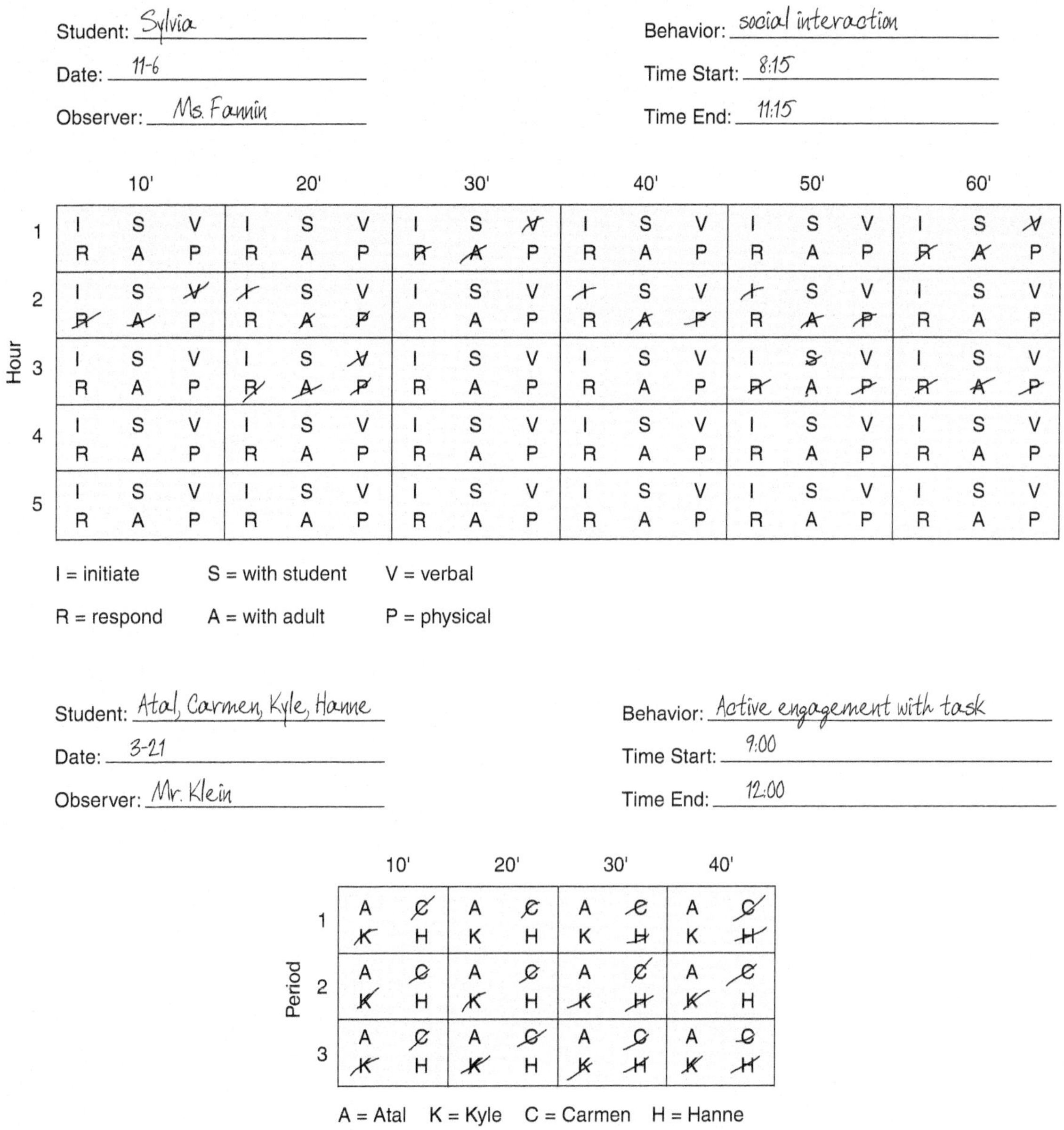

Student: Sylvia
Date: 11-6
Observer: Ms. Fannin

Behavior: social interaction
Time Start: 8:15
Time End: 11:15

	10'			20'			30'			40'			50'			60'		
1	I	S	V	I	S	V	I	S	~~V~~	I	S	V	I	S	V	I	S	~~V~~
	R	A	P	R	A	P	~~R~~	~~A~~	P	R	A	P	R	A	P	~~R~~	~~A~~	P
2	I	S	~~V~~	~~I~~	S	V	I	S	V	~~I~~	S	V	~~I~~	S	V	I	S	V
	~~R~~	~~A~~	P	R	~~A~~	~~P~~	R	A	P	R	~~A~~	~~P~~	R	~~A~~	~~P~~	R	A	P
3	I	S	V	I	S	~~V~~	I	S	V	I	S	V	I	~~S~~	V	I	S	V
	R	A	P	~~R~~	~~A~~	~~P~~	R	A	P	R	A	P	~~R~~	A	~~P~~	~~R~~	~~A~~	~~P~~
4	I	S	V	I	S	V	I	S	V	I	S	V	I	S	V	I	S	V
	R	A	P	R	A	P	R	A	P	R	A	P	R	A	P	R	A	P
5	I	S	V	I	S	V	I	S	V	I	S	V	I	S	V	I	S	V
	R	A	P	R	A	P	R	A	P	R	A	P	R	A	P	R	A	P

(left axis label: Hour)

I = initiate   S = with student   V = verbal
R = respond   A = with adult   P = physical

Student: Atal, Carmen, Kyle, Hanne
Date: 3-21
Observer: Mr. Klein

Behavior: Active engagement with task
Time Start: 9:00
Time End: 12:00

	10'		20'		30'		40'	
1	A	~~C~~	A	~~C~~	A	C	A	~~C~~
	~~K~~	H	K	H	K	~~H~~	K	~~H~~
2	A	~~C~~	A	~~C~~	A	~~C~~	A	C
	~~K~~	H	~~K~~	H	~~K~~	~~H~~	~~K~~	H
3	A	~~C~~	A	~~C~~	A	C	A	C
	~~K~~	H	~~K~~	H	~~K~~	~~H~~	~~K~~	~~H~~

(left axis label: Period)

A = Atal   K = Kyle   C = Carmen   H = Hanne

interval, Carmen at the end of the second, and Carmen and Hanne at the end of the third and fourth.

Coded Data Sheet Using Tracks   A third format for coding more than one behavior or for coding more than one student is the use of a tracking format (Bijou et al., 1968). The top of Figure 4.16 shows on-task behavior being recorded, but the teacher also wanted to know the general nature of any off-task behavior. Therefore, in addition to providing space to note the occurrence or nonoccurrence of on-task behavior, she provided track rows to indicate the general nature of any off-task behavior that occurred. The teacher would simply put a check mark in the appropriate cell(s) to indicate which behavior(s) occurred. This time sampling data sheet indicates that at the end of the first and second 5-minute intervals, Rose was engaged in a motor off-task behavior; at the end of the third, fourth, and fifth intervals, she was on task; she was verbally and motorically off task at the end of the sixth; and she was passively off task at the end of the last two intervals. Alternatively, if the teacher wants to record data on two or three students simultaneously, the data sheet can be adapted by providing a row for each student's data.

> These data collection procedures are very flexible. They can be used to record data on several students simultaneously.

Figure 4.16 Track coded data sheet for time sampling

Student: Rose   Date: 2-6
Observer: Ms. Paster   Time Start: 10:40
Behavior: on task

	5'	10'	15'	20'	25'	30'	35'	40'
on task			X	X	X			
verbal off task						X		
motor	X	X				X		
passive							X	X

Use codes to record data on several behaviors simultaneously.

Collecting Data on Students as a Group One way of adapting interval recording or time sampling for use with a group is the *round-robin* format (Cooper, 1981; Lloyd, Bateman, Landrum, & Hallahan, 1989). With this format the observer obtains an estimate of the group's behavior by observing and recording the behavior of a single group member during each interval. When conducting a language lesson, for example, the teacher might choose to monitor the group's attending behavior. As presented in Figure 4.17, the language period is divided into equal 15-second intervals to accommodate a group of four students, with the name of each group member assigned to each interval.

In this example, Kate is observed for occurrence or nonoccurrence of attending during the first 15-second interval of each minute, Michael's attending is observed and recorded during the second interval of each minute, Harry's during the third, and Jody's during the fourth. Because each student is observed during only one of the intervals per minute, on a round-robin basis, the resulting data provide a representation of the whole group's attending behavior, but not an accurate representation of the attending behavior of any single member of the group. Another data collection method must be used to focus on individual students. The round-robin format may also be used when collecting data on a whole class. In order to measure on-task behavior, Sutherland, Wehby, and Copeland (2000) observed each of four rows of students in rotation. Using time sampling, the teacher noted at the end of each interval whether all the students in the selected row were oriented toward the appropriate task or person and thus, as operationally defined, on task. Using random order, the teacher observed each row of students several times during the observation period.

Figure 4.17 Round-robin format of interval recording

	1st 15-second interval Kate	2nd 15-second interval Michael	3rd 15-second interval Harry	4th 15-second interval Jody
1				
2				
3				
4				

Duration and Latency Recording

Event recording, interval recording, and time sampling collection techniques focus primarily on exact or approximate counts of the occurrence of a behavior. Duration and latency recording differ from these systems in that the focus is on a temporal rather than a numerical dimension of the behavior.

> Duration and latency recording emphasize measures of time rather than instances of behavior.

Duration Recording

Duration recording is used when the primary concern is the length of time a student engages in a particular behavior. For example, if a teacher wants to know about a student's out-of-seat behavior, either event recording or duration recording might be appropriate. Event recording would provide information about the number of times a student left her seat. If, however, the teacher's concern is *how long* she stays out of her seat, the most appropriate data collection method would be duration recording. In this example, event recording would mask the temporal nature of the target behavior. Although event data might indicate that the number of times the student left her seat had decreased substantially, it would not reveal that the length of time spent out of seat might actually have increased.

> You could measure average duration of tantrums, of time spent on task, or of recreational reading.

Duration recording is suitable for behaviors that have an easily identifiable beginning and end. It is important to define clearly the onset of the behavior and its completion. Using clearly stated operational definitions, researchers have measured the duration of on-task behavior and academic engagement, including writing, tracing, and copying; independent seatwork and in-seat behavior; eye gaze toward academic materials; engagement with peers and eye contact; vocational skills such as racking dishes and setting tables; inappropriate behaviors such as fidgeting and prolonged bathroom visits; disruptive behavior such as whining and screaming; and exercise (Athens, Vollmer, & St. Peter Pipkin, 2007; Chung, 2019; Dowdy & Jacobs, 2019; Fonger & Malott, 2019; Gibbs, Tullis, Thomas, & Elkins, 2018; Grossi & Heward, 1998; Guertin, Vause, Jaksic, Frijters, & Feldman, 2019; Keeling, Myles, Gagnon, & Simpson, 2003; Krombach & Miltenberger, 2020; Lai, Chiang, Shih, & Shih, 2018; Luiselli & Sobezenski, 2017; Mitchell, Lewis, & Stormont, 2020; Savage, Taber-Doughty, Brodhead, & Bouck, 2018; Thompson, Plavnick, & Skibbe, 2019).

The observer may time the duration of the behavior using the second hand of a watch or wall clock, but a stopwatch makes the process much simpler. For certain behaviors such as seizures or tantrums, an observer may make an audio or video recording. The duration of the episode may be determined later using the resulting permanent product and a stopwatch or the automatic timer on the video player.

There are two basic ways to record duration data: average duration and total duration. The average duration approach is used when the student performs the target behavior routinely or with some regularity. In a given day, the teacher measures the length of time consumed in each occurrence (its duration) and then finds the *average duration* for that day. If the behavior occurs at regular but widely spaced intervals (for example, only once per day or once per class period), the data may be averaged for the week. One behavior that can be measured by duration data is time spent in the bathroom. Perhaps his teacher feels that each time John goes to the bathroom, he stays for an unreasonable length of time. To gather data on this behavior, she decides to measure the amount of time he takes for each trip. On Monday, John went to the bathroom three times. The first trip took him 7 minutes, the second 11 minutes, and the third 9 minutes. If she continued to collect data in this manner during the rest of the week, the teacher would be able to calculate John's average duration of bathroom use for the week. *Total duration recording* measures how long a student engages in a behavior in a limited time period. This activity may or may not be continuous. As an example, the target behavior "appropriate play" might be observed over a 15-minute period.

> Total duration could be used to record the time spent talking, reading, or playing with toys.

The observer would record the number of minutes the student was engaging in appropriate play during this period. The child might have been playing appropriately from 10:00 to 10:04 a.m. (4 minutes), from 10:07 to 10:08 a.m. (one minute), and from 10:10 to 10:15 a.m. (5 minutes). Although such a behavior record is clearly noncontinuous, these notations would yield a total duration of 10 minutes of appropriate play during the 15-minute observation period.

Latency Recording

Latency recording measures how long a student takes to begin performing a behavior once its performance has been requested. This procedure measures the length of time between the presentation of an antecedent stimulus and the initiation of the behavior. For example, if a teacher says, "Michael, sit down" (antecedent stimulus) and Michael does, but so slowly that 5 minutes elapse before he is seated, the teacher would be concerned with the latency of the student's response. Latency recording has been used to measure the time between an antecedent teacher instruction and students' beginning to engage in on-task behaviors, comply with instructions, answer math problems, complete tangram puzzles, and ask to be "all done." It has also been used to measure the latency to the onset of challenging behaviors, such as tantrums, yelling, crying, throwing, hair pulling, biting, food stealing, self-injurious behavior, public disrobing, elopement, and stereotypic movements (Dowdy & Tincani, 2020; Falligant, Carver, Zarcone, & Schmidt, 2020; Hansen et al., 2019; Hine, Ardoin, & Foster, 2015; Kodak, Bergmann, LeBlanc, Harman, & Ayazi, 2018; Lambert et al., 2019; LeJeune, Lambert, Lemons, Mottern, & Wisniewski, 2019; Porter & Sy, 2020; Tiger, Wierzba, Fisher, & Benitez, 2017; Traub & Vollmer, 2019).

As seen in Figure 4.18, a basic collection sheet for duration or latency data should provide information on the temporal boundaries that define the procedures. A duration recording data collection sheet should note the time the student began the

Figure 4.18 Basic formats for latency and duration recording data sheets

Latency Recording Data Sheet

Student: EDITH   Observer: MR HALL
Behavior: TIME ELAPSED BEFORE TAKING SEAT

Operationalization of behavior initiation: _____

Date	Time		Latency
	Delivery of S^D	Response initiation	

Duration Recording Data Sheet

Student: SAM   Observer: MS. JAMES
Behavior: TIME SPENT IN BATHROOM

Behavior initiation: _____
Behavior termination: _____

Date	Time		Duration
	Response initiation	Response termination	

response and the time the response was completed. A latency recording data collection sheet should note the time the student was given the cue to begin a response (antecedent stimulus) and the time he or she actually began to respond.

Duration and latency recording are closely matched to the behavioral dimensions of duration and latency. Consideration of topography, locus, and force may also apply here. For example, a teacher might want to measure

- how long Calvin can perfectly maintain a position in gymnastics
- how long Rosa talks to each of a number of other students
- how long after being given a nonverbal signal to lower her voice Ellen actually does so
- how long David maintains sufficient pressure to activate a microswitch.

How Can All This Be Done?

Thinking about all that goes on in a classroom can make the tasks in this chapter seem overwhelming. In fact, they may be headed for the pile of advice that is "just not practical" in a class of 34 students in freshman English with 6 "inclusion students" of varying disabilities, or of 14 students with behavioral disorders and hyperactivity, or of 6 students with severe intellectual disability or autism. Before tossing this chapter aside, remember that we acknowledged in the first paragraph that some of this may not be practical on a daily basis. Knowing this content, however, will enable you to design an appropriate data-based accountability system and will enable you to read educational research with more authority and be better prepared to apply it in your classroom. Data collection should be a tool that contributes instructional logic to classroom management. Data collection provides the basis for selecting appropriate objectives, arranging instructional groupings, and meeting the requirements of accountability. Well, then, how *can* all this be done? Here are some suggestions about how much data to collect, who should collect it, and what kind of help technology can provide.

One question to ask about how much data to collect is: How much data should I collect within an instructional session? One can either collect trial-by-trial data (recording *all* occurrences of the behavior) or collect probe data (recording only a *sample* of the occurrences). Trial-by-trial data collection during *instruction* records whether every response during the session is correct or incorrect. Teachers can collect probe data (data on some, but not all, responses) in two ways. It may be collected just before or just after an instructional session. If the teacher is about to conduct a 20-minute lesson on multiplying by 6, she may probe or sample student knowledge before beginning the lesson (measuring what the student has maintained since the last lesson), or she may probe just after the lesson (measuring what the student just learned) by asking the student to multiply a sample of numbers by 6. The term *probe* is also used to mean recording correct or incorrect use of a target behavior in an untrained setting (multiplying by 6 in the grocery store when shopping for a group) or within an untrained variation of the response (in a word problem).

During *behavior-change programs*, trial-by-trial data collection means continuous data recording for the entire period the contingency is in place—for example, recording instances or intervals of verbal aggression during all of PE or recording intervals of attending during the whole general education science class. There are several ways to use probe data with behavior-change programs: (a) a contingency may be in effect all day, but student behavior is sampled by collecting data only during specific time periods—the first 10 minutes of each class period, the first five times the student has the opportunity to greet someone verbally; or (b) students' behavior may be probed or sampled during time periods when the contingency was not initially taught; or (c) students' behavior may be probed or sampled in environments where the contingency was not initially taught.

Another question to ask is: How often should I collect data during a week? Some advice is provided in the professional literature. Farlow and Snell (1994) suggested that when implementing a new behavior program or teaching a new skill, data should be collected every day or every teaching session until the student shows steady progress over six data points or 2 weeks. At that point accurate and reliable judgments of ongoing progress can be made with data collected twice a week. When a learning problem is suspected, data should be recorded daily while programmatic adjustments are made. Once progress is seen over approximately 2 weeks, then data collection twice a week is sufficient. Mellard, McKnight, and Woods (2009) indicated that the most common frequency of curriculum-based measurement was once per week. Filderman, Austin, and Toste (2019) suggested collecting data 1–3 times per week, but less often at the secondary level. When using discrete trial teaching, teachers collect data daily, and even after every trial presented (Giunta-Fede, Reeve, DeBar, Vladescu, & Reeve, 2016).

The teacher is not the only one who can or should collect data. You can get someone to help collect data. Counting by ones is not a higher-order skill. Appropriate training and practice, however, is essential to reliable data collection.

In a cotaught class, the special and general educator can collaborate on data collection to monitor progress of all the students in the class. In classrooms and community settings, the teacher and paraeducators can all collect data. A speech–language pathologist can collect data on communication objectives, and a physical or occupational therapist can collect data on a student's learning to self-catheterize or climb stairs. In special and general education classes, especially classes in which students with disabilities are included, peers can be trained as data collectors in dyads and small groups (Marchand-Martella, Martella, Bettis, & Blakely, 2004; Park, Collins, & Lo, 2020). Students should record data on themselves whenever possible. The ability to self-assess through recording one's own behavior is a component of independence. This is explored in detail in Chapter 12.

Technology for Data Collection

Both low-tech and high-tech assistance is available to facilitate data collection. We have already described a variety of low-tech options that range from paper clips and golf counters for event recording, kitchen timers and stopwatches for duration recording, apps with prerecorded chimes, and watches that chime and vibrate at specific intervals. Whenever possible, we suggest making a permanent product with a video recording device. It is always easier and more accurate to record data on a high-frequency or disruptive behavior later while watching it on a recording rather than while trying to manage the behavior at the same time.

High-tech computerized systems have greatly advanced the ease and accuracy of data collection. Kahng and Iwata (1998) described and reviewed key characteristics of 15 computerized data collection systems that primarily use laptop computers. They suggested these systems can improve reliability and accuracy of behavioral recording compared to paper-and-pencil methods. Most of the systems reviewed use IBM-compatible software; five use Mac OS. The systems have a range of capabilities, from those that can collect frequency, interval, time sampling, duration, and latency data (e.g., Behavioral Evaluation Strategy & Taxonomy, The Behavior Observer System, or The Direct Observation Data System) to those with a limited range, such as the Ecobehavioral Assessment System Software, which can collect interval data, or the Social Interaction Continuous Observation Program for Experimental Studies, which can collect frequency and duration data. Most of the systems include data analysis programs, and about a third include a program to compute interobserver agreement.

In addition, Sleeper et al. (2017) demonstrated that an electronic data collection app increased the number of updated graphs by staff in an agency for individuals with autism.

An option for collecting observational data is use of a smart phone or tablet (Whiting & Dixon, 2012). These provide portability, ease, and versatility of data recording, and data analysis. The data can be exported and converted into a spreadsheet, graphs, or tables. Examples of applications include: *Intervalminder*, which collects fixed or variable interval recording and can also be used for timekeeping; *School Classroom Observation and Analysis (SCOA)* is a program that collects event and duration data; *Catalyst*, which is a broad package that supports collection of dicho, which is tomous and prompt coded data, event data, rate, and duration data (see LeBlanc et al., 2020); and *Central Reach*, which provides data collection, teaching management, and graphing.

An example of a software program available as shareware that can be downloaded easily is *Count It* (Molgaard, 2001). The online manual provides explanations for filing individual behaviors and functions for customized data recording. Figure 4.19 provides instructions for the use of Count It for event recording that were developed for use in general and special education classes in a local school system (Cihak & Alaimo, 2003). *Mooses* (Tapp, Wehby, & Ellis, 1995) is a software system for computers running Microsoft Windows. The option for handheld devices is known as *Minimoose*. While observing students, this system can be used for collection and analysis of event, interval, duration, and latency data. In a current project, educators are using the inexpensive handheld hardware HP iPAQII and Minimoose to collect partial interval data on off-task, disruptive behavior, and inappropriate language of high school students in classrooms. This system also allows for determination of interobserver agreement between data collectors.

For a mobile-based data collection program, *Behavior Tracker Pro* is available in the app store. It is designed for use with the iPhone, iPod Touch, and iPad®. This product can collect trial-by-trial data as well as frequency, duration, and latency data. It allows teachers, parents, paraprofessionals, and behavioral therapists to record and graph behaviors. It can share graphs with others using the iPhone. Its video-capture capability can record behavior as it is occurring or demonstrate the implementation of a procedure. As with all technology, we can expect a continuing stream of products, advancing in ease of use, portability, and capability to collect various forms of data.

Figure 4.19 Using the Behavior Tracker Pro app to collect event data

Summary of Data Collection Systems

Questions for the data collector. How to choose a recording system.

The five observational systems available to the data collector are event recording, interval recording, time sampling, duration recording, and latency recording. Figure 4.20 summarizes the decision making involved in selecting the system appropriate for a particular target behavior. This process is based on a series of questions to be answered by the data collector:

1. Is the target behavior numerical or temporal?
2. If it is numerical:
   a. Is the behavior discrete or continuous?
   b. Is the behavior expected to occur at a high, moderate, or low frequency?
   c. Will I be able to collect data during intervention or instruction, or will I need a third party to collect the data so as not to interrupt instruction?
3. If it is temporal, do I want to measure the time before initiation of the response or time elapsed during performance of the response?

Reliability

Learning Outcome 4.5 **Demonstrate how to calculate reliability for each of the five observational recording systems.**

When data collection depends on human beings, there is always the possibility of error. Even in the case of permanent product data, which are easiest to record, mistakes may happen. Teachers occasionally count math problems as incorrect even when they are correctly done or overlook a misspelled word in a paragraph. Because there is something tangible, however, the teacher can easily recheck the accuracy or **reliability**

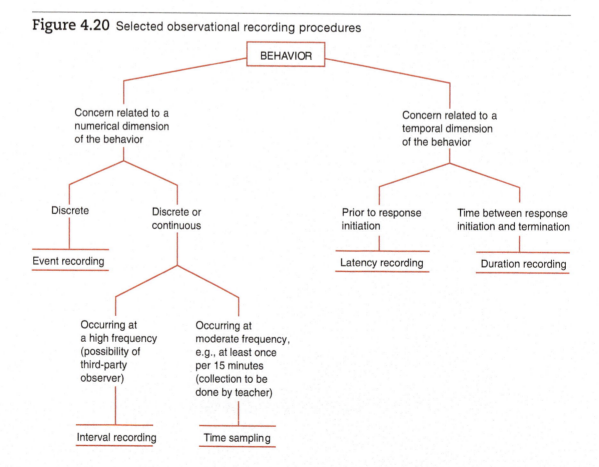

Figure 4.20 Selected observational recording procedures

of any observations of the behavior. In using an observational recording system, however, the teacher does not have this advantage. The behavior occurs and then disappears, so the teacher cannot go back and check his or her accuracy. To be sure the data are correct, or reliable, it is wise to have a second observer simultaneously and independently record the same behavior periodically. When this is done, the two observations can be compared and a percent of *interobserver agreement* may be computed (Johnston & Pennypacker, 2020; Neely, Davis, Davis, & Rispoli, 2015; Vollmer, Sloman, & Pipkin, 2008).

| Computing reliability for permanent product data.

To check event recording, the teacher and a second observer, perhaps a paraprofessional, simultaneously watch the student and record each instance of the target behavior. After the observation period, the teacher calculates the percent of agreement by dividing the smaller number of recorded instances by the larger number of recorded instances. For example, if the teacher observed 20 instances of talking out in a 40-minute session, and the second observer recorded only 19, the calculation would be (19/20) × 100 = 95%. Therefore, the percent of interobserver agreement would be 95%. This method of calculating reliability for research purposes lacks a certain amount of precision and has therefore been referred to as a gross method of calculation. "The problem is that this method does not permit the researcher to state that both observers saw the same thing or that the events they agreed on were all the same events" (Tawney & Gast, 1984, p. 138). In other words, there is no absolute certainty that the 19 occurrences noted by the paraprofessional were the same ones noted by the teacher.

| Computing reliability for event recording.

The reliability of duration and latency data is determined by a procedure similar to that of event recording, except that the longer time is divided into the shorter, as in the following equation:

| Computing reliability for duration and latency recording.

$$\frac{\text{Shorter number of minutes}}{\text{Long number of minutes}} \times 100 = \text{percent of agreement}$$

When using interval recording or time sampling, the basic formula for calculating reliability is:

$$\frac{\text{Agreements}}{\text{Agreements} + \text{Disagreements}} \times 100 = \text{percent of agreements}$$

If the data shown represent 10 intervals during which the teacher and the paraprofessional were recording whether or not Lauren was talking to her neighbor, we see that their data agree in 7 intervals (that is, intervals 1, 2, 3, 4, 6, 7, and 8); their data are not in agreement in 3 intervals (that is 5, 9, and 10). Therefore, using the basic formula, the calculation for reliability would be as follows:

$$\frac{7}{7+3} \times 100 = 70\%$$

	1	2	3	4	5	6	7	8	9	10
Teacher	X	X	-	-	X	X	-	-	X	-
Paraprofessional	X	X	-	-	-	X	-	-	-	X

Under certain research circumstances an additional, more rigorous determination of reliability should be considered. This should be a calculation of *occurrence reliability* or *nonoccurrence reliability*. When the target behavior is recorded to have occurred in less than 75% of the intervals, occurrence reliability should be calculated. When the target behavior is recorded to have occurred in more than 75% of the intervals, nonoccurrence agreement should be computed (Cooper, Heron, & Heward, 2020). These percentages are determined with the same basic formula (agreements/[agreements + disagreements] × 100), except only those intervals in which the behavior occurred (or did not occur) are used in the computation.

Calculating Reliability
Pearson eText
Video Example 4.4
In this video, an educator is describing how to use Google Classroom© to grade assignments submitted through the portal. Consider all the different forms of permanent products that are submitted and how inter-observer agreement could be calculated on each.

https://www.youtube.com/watch?v=7zmI3LdScDM

Factors That May Affect Data Collection and Interobserver Agreement

Learning Outcome 4.6 Identify factors that impact the accuracy and reliability of data collection.

In general, applied behavior analysts aim for interobserver agreement of around 90%. Anything less than 80% is a signal that something is seriously wrong. A low percentage of interobserver agreement can often be explained by examining the operational definition of the behavior; sloppy definitions, those that do not expressly state a behavior's topography or when it begins and ends, result in low interobserver agreement. The observers may not have been told exactly what they are to observe. Insufficient agreement may also be due to a lack of sufficient training in the data collection system. Either the primary or secondary observer may not be employing the mechanics of the data collection system correctly, resulting in differing records of the occurrence of the behavior. The environment in which data are collected may also be a factor. In natural settings such as classrooms, homes, communities, and workplaces, many variables may affect behavior and many behaviors may be occurring simultaneously. Given all that may be going on in natural settings, an observer who is unfamiliar with the setting and collects data only occasionally for reliability purposes will be less at ease and possibly more distracted during data collection, and his or her data may be less accurate than that of an observer who is regularly in that setting (Fradenburg, Harrison, & Baer, 1995; Romani, Alcorn, & Linares, 2018).

Kazdin (1977a) suggested four sources of bias that can also affect interobserver agreement: reactivity, observer drift, complexity, and expectancy.

Reactivity: As teachers are well aware, the presence of an observer can affect the behavior of both the students being observed and of the teacher. This effect is known as *reactivity* (Codding, Livanis, Pace, & Vaca, 2008; King, Gravina, & Sleiman, 2018). A student who knows that he is being observed may react by being very "good" or may put on an unruly show, either of which will give a false view of a target behavior. Some teachers give more prompts to a target student when an observer is present (Hay, Nelson, & Hay, 1977), and some increase their rate of instruction and positive feedback, both of which may affect the typical occurrence of the behavior (Hay, Nelson, & Hay, 1980). Simply knowing another person is present collecting reliability data can influence the accuracy of the primary observer. Such knowledge has influenced reliability data by as much as 20% to 25%. It is suggested that reliability checks should be unobtrusive or covert, if possible, or that the second observer collect data on several students including the target student, or that the second observer be someone familiar to the student, such as a classroom paraprofessional. Some of these suggestions may not be practical in every instance, but just limiting communication between the first and second observers during the observation period can reduce their influence on one another's observations.

Observer Drift: Observer drift is the tendency of observers to change the stringency with which they apply operational definitions (Artman, Wolery, & Yoder, 2012). Over time an observer may reoperationalize the definition as it becomes less fresh in his or her mind. The observer may begin to record as "instances" behaviors that do not exactly conform to the operational definition. If the operational definition appears on every copy of the data sheet, the observer can easily consult it. Observers should periodically review definitions together and conduct practice sessions during the course of the program.

Complexity: A third influence on the reliability of data concerns the complexity of the observational coding system—the more complex the system, the more the reliability is in jeopardy. Complexity refers to the number of different types of a response category being recorded (for example, the number of types of disruptive behavior being observed simultaneously), the number of different students being observed, or the number of different behaviors being scored on a given occasion. In a classroom, the teacher may mitigate the effects of complexity by limiting the number of behaviors or students observed at any given time (Lindstrom, Gesel, & Lemons, 2019).

Expectancy: The fourth bias is that of expectancy. Observers' preconceived notions about students based on their past experiences with them or on information from parents or previous teachers have the potential to bias their interpretation of what they are seeing. In addition, when observers are teachers who expect behavior change (because of the terrific job they did with their intervention), they are likely to find it. The reverse is also true; a teacher who has decided that nothing can be done with a student is not likely to see a change in behavior accurately (Lerman et al., 2010).

Observers may be biased because of the student's sex, race, appearance, or previous history. In addition, a bias may result from the purpose of the observation (Repp et al., 1988). Teachers may be biased data collectors if the failure of a behavior-change strategy will result in a problem student's being moved to a different environment.

The procedures described in this section are adequate to determine reliability for most teachers, especially if efforts are made to control bias. More stringent standards are sometimes applied in research studies. The student who is interested in learning more about interobserver reliability should consult Kostewicz, King, Datchuk, Brennan, and Casey (2016).

Kazdin (1977) provides suggestions for limiting complexity bias in research studies.

Data Collection in the Classroom
Pearson eText
Video Example 4.5
In this video, an educator describes the steps she has taken when creating a data collection system to make it as manageable and accurate as possible. How does her system address sources of bias referenced in the chapter?

https://www.youtube.com/watch?v=n2y6QQX2A0Y

Summary

We described the various dimensions of behavior (i.e., frequency, rate, duration, latency, topography, focus, and locus) and their relationship to data collection. Data collection procedures discussed included anecdotal reports, permanent product recording, and various observational recording systems (event recording, interval recording, time sampling, duration recording, and latency recording). To assist teachers to increase the accuracy of their data, procedures for determining interobserver agreement were outlined. As professionals responsible for student learning, teachers collect data to make determinations about the success of or need for change in their instruction or behavioral intervention.

Discussion Questions

1. Jerry's behavior in his fifth-grade class was reported as "disruptive." The consulting teacher visited his classroom to collect some initial referral data. (a) She went into his class for 30 minutes on 3 days to count instances of "disruptive" behavior. (b) On 3 days she checked every 20 minutes between 9 a.m. and noon to see if he was being disruptive. (c) For 1 hour on Tuesday morning and a Thursday afternoon, she sat in Jerry's class and wrote down everything he did, what his teacher did, and significant actions of other students. What observational recording system did she use in each instance?

2. Susan never gets her math problems done before the end of class. To help determine the nature of her problems, the teacher could (a) give her a set of problems and record how long it was before she began to work, or (b) record how long it took her to complete the set of problems once she had begun. What recording system is being used in each instance?

3. Four student data collectors were observing John, a fourth-grade student. John was doing poorly in spelling. Observer 1 divided his observational time into 15-second intervals and noted whether John was working in his spelling workbook during

each interval. Observer 2 went to John's desk at the end of the spelling period and counted the number of answers John had written in his spelling workbook. Observer 3 counted each time John put his pencil on the workbook and wrote something. Observer 4 divided the period into five-minute intervals and recorded whether John was working in his spelling workbook at the end of each interval. What recording procedure is each observer employing?

4. Mrs. Carrington wanted the students to help her check their knowledge of multiplication facts. The students were divided into pairs in order to ask each other the 7, 8, and 9 multiplication table facts and record their accuracy. Each student was given a packet of flash cards that had the problem statement on one side and the answer on the back of the card. Also, on the back was a place to mark whether the answer given by his or her partner was correct or incorrect. What recording procedure is being used by the students?

5. Why and how may the noticeable and possibly intrusive act of data collection in a classroom affect the behavior of the students being observed? How can potential changes in student behavior be mitigated?

6. How can the video function of a smart phone be used for data collection?

7. Describe the various dimensions of the following behaviors:
   a. mutual toy play
   b. writing in a daily journal
   c. kicking furniture
   d. cleaning the glass doors in the frozen food section of a supermarket
   e. writing the letters of the alphabet
   f. riding a tricycle
   g. using a mouse to select the correct answer on a computer screen
   h. completing a sheet of long-division problems
   i. initiating social greetings
   j. flicking fingers in front of one's eyes

8. The following is an anecdotal report of one session of community-based vocational instruction. Todd, his classmate Lucy, and their teacher were at Pets-Are-Us. The session's task was to move 4-pound bags of birdseed from the storeroom to the shelves at the front of the store. Transpose the information in the anecdotal report into the A-B-C column format.

   May 3, 9:20 a.m.: Teacher, Todd, and Lucy are in the storeroom. Teacher explains the task. She tells both students to pick up a bag and follow her. They do, and each places a bag on the proper shelf. She leads them back to storeroom. Teacher tells Todd to pick up a bag of seed; he walks away. She tells him a second time. Teacher picks up a bag and takes Todd by the hand and walks out to the shelf. She hands him the bag and points to where it belongs; he puts the bag on the shelf. She tells him to go back to storeroom for another. In the storeroom she tells him to pick up a bag from the pile. The third time he is told, he picks one up and goes out front and puts a bag on the shelf. On the way out to the floor with the next bag, Todd stops at a birdcage, drops the bag, and begins to talk to the birds. Several minutes later the teacher comes for him. He ignores her. She puts his hands on the bag then leads him to the shelf. She then takes him to the storeroom. He refuses to lift a bag. She hands him one. He drops it on the floor. This is repeated twice. She takes a bag and leads him back out to the shelf. She tells him to go back to the storeroom. She goes to check on Lucy. Ten minutes later she finds Todd sitting on floor eating candy from his fanny pack. She takes the candy and tells him it is for later. She tells him again to go to the storeroom. When she looks for him again, he is at the rabbit cage. She leads him back to storeroom. She tells him to pick up a bag. After the third delivery of instruction, the teacher holds a bag in front of him; he doesn't move his arms. She places his arms around the bag. He lets it drop through his hands and it splits open. She scolds. She goes to get a broom. She returns, and he is sitting on the floor eating the birdseed. The teacher tells Todd, "Your behavior is not acceptable. Therefore, you will no longer be allowed to work today. Sit over there and time yourself out until we leave. I am very disappointed in your work behavior today."

Chapter 5
Graphing Data

Learning Outcomes

5.1 Identify the basic elements of a line graph.
5.2 Demonstrate how to transfer data to a graph.
5.3 Identify graphing conventions (i.e., conditions, baseline, intervention).
5.4 Identify components and uses of cumulative graphs.
5.5 Identify components and uses of bar graphs.

CHAPTER OUTLINE

The Simple Line Graph
    Basic Elements of the Line Graph
    Transferring Data to a Graph

Additional Graphing Conventions

Cumulative Graphs

Bar Graphs

Summary

Data collection, as you can imagine, results in a pile of data sheets. For data to be useful, the contents of those sheets must be rearranged in a way that allows them to be easily read and interpreted. The most common method of arranging and presenting data is to use a graph. A properly drawn graph provides a picture of progress across the time of instruction or intervention. Graphs should be simple and uncluttered but provide sufficient information to monitor progress. For step-by-step instructions for using the computer to create graphs, see Chapter 6.

Graphs serve at least three purposes. First, they provide a means for organizing data during the data collection process. Tallies on sheets of paper or coded entries on data collection forms are difficult, if not impossible, to interpret. Translating raw data into a graph provides an ongoing picture of progress (or lack thereof) that is easier to understand than thumbing through piles of data sheets. Second, an ongoing picture makes possible formative evaluation, the ongoing analysis of the effectiveness of an intervention. Formative evaluation makes it possible to see how well a procedure is working and to make adjustments if it is not working well. When the intervention is finished, inspecting a graph allows for summative program evaluation, the end result of an intervention or series of interventions. Third, graphs serve as a vehicle for communication among teacher, student, parents, and related service professionals.

| Purposes for graphs.

A properly constructed graph shows all the information about how the target behavior changes during an intervention. One should be able to read and understand the graph without having to read a prose explanation. The information shown on graphs can be used to write and evaluate progress reports, individualized education programs, and behavior management plans.

The Simple Line Graph

Learning Outcome 5.1 Identify the basic elements of a line graph.

Basic Elements of the Line Graph

Line graphs are commonly used to display data in a serial manner across the duration of instruction or intervention. This allows for ongoing monitoring of the behavior and evaluation of the instruction or intervention. Graphs can be constructed using graph paper or a computer program. The grid on the graph paper or the computer software makes it possible to plot data accurately, ensuring proper alignment and equal intervals among data points. When data are presented formally, as in publications, the grid is usually omitted. The following is a description of basic elements and conventions for constructing a simple line graph (*Journal of Applied Behavior Analysis,* 2000, 2006; Gast, 2010; Kazdin, 2011). These are illustrated by the two graphs in Figure 5.1.

> These axes don't chop wood.

AXES A graph is constructed within a set of boundaries. These boundaries are called *axes* (*axis*, singular). A line graph has two axes: the horizontal **x-axis**, or abscissa, and the vertical **y-axis**, or ordinate. When the graph is completed, these axes are drawn in a ratio of 2:3. Thus, if the *y* axis is 2 inches long, the *x* axis should be 3 inches. If the *y*-axis is 4 inches, the *x*-axis should be 6 inches.

1. *x-axis:* The *x*-axis is the horizontal line that serves as the bottom boundary of the graph. It shows how frequently data were collected during the period represented on the graph. It may be labeled as, for example, days, dates, or sessions. If sessions are used, it is helpful to provide some definition of the session, for example, "sessions (9–9:40 a.m.)" or "sessions (math group)." The right boundary of the graph ends at the last session number.
2. *y-axis:* The *y*-axis is the vertical line that serves as the left-hand boundary of the graph. The label on the *y*-axis identifies the target behavior and the kind of data that is being reported. For example, a label might read "number of occurrences of cursing," "rate of cursing," "number of intervals of cursing," or "percent of intervals of cursing." Standard data conversion procedures are presented in Table 5.1.
   a. *y-axis scale:* The scale on the *y*-axis, used to record the performance of the target behavior, always begins at 0. If one is reporting the number of occurrences of the behavior or number of intervals during which the behavior occurred, the scale begins at 0 and goes as high as needed to accommodate the largest number. This number is sometimes difficult to predict, and the researcher may have to redraw the graph if data are being plotted before the intervention is completed. If percent is being reported, the scale always goes from 0 to 100%. The scale may progress by single digits or by 2s, 5s, 10s, or other multiples in order to accommodate the data. It makes the graph easier to read if the beginning point of the scale (the zero value) is raised slightly from the *x*-axis; data points are more easily discerned when they do not rest on the *x*-axis.
   b. *Scale break:* Occasionally, the *y*-axis scale may not be continuous. For example, if all the data points are above 40%, the bottom part of the graph will be empty and the top will be unnecessarily crowded. It is permissible to begin the scale at 0, draw two horizontal parallel lines between the first and second lines on the graph paper, and label the second line 40%.

Figure 5.1 Basic elements and conventions for time graphs

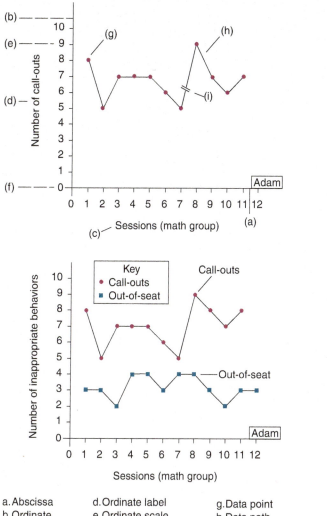

a. Abscissa
b. Ordinate
c. Abscissa label
d. Ordinate label
e. Ordinate scale
f. 0 is raised from *x*-axis
g. Data point
h. Data path
i. Data continuity break

DATA

1. *Data point:* Small geometric forms, such as circles, squares, or triangles, are used to represent the occurrence of the target behavior during a time segment. For example, in the first graph shown in Figure 5.1, the student engaged in cursing eight times during session 1; therefore, a data point is placed at the intersection of 8 on

> An advantage to computing percentage.
> *x*-axis = abscissa,
> *y*-axis = ordinate.

Table 5.1 Summary of data conversion procedures

Type of Recording	Data Conversion	
Permanent product recording	Report number of occurrences ...	if both time and opportunities to respond are constant.
Event recording	Report percentage ...	if time is constant (or not of concern) and opportunities vary.
	Report rate ...	if both time (which is of concern) and opportunities vary, OR if time varies and opportunities are constant.
Interval recording	Report number of intervals ...	if constant.
Time sampling	Report percentage of intervals ...	during or at the end of which behavior occurred.
Duration	Report number of seconds/minutes/hours ...	for which the behavior occurred.
Latency	Report number of seconds/minutes/hours ...	between antecedent stimulus and onset of behavior.

> Graphs with more than three data paths look cluttered.

the y-axis and 1 on the x-axis. Each data point is independently plotted on the graph. The placement or value of one data point does not affect the placement or value of the next data point.

2. *Data path:* When a solid line is drawn connecting the data points, it forms the data path.

   a. A single geometric form is used to represent each point on a single data path.
   b. When more than one set of data appears on a graph, each is represented by a different geometric symbol. Which behavior is represented by each symbol and data path may be shown in one of two ways, both of which can be observed on the second graph of Figure 5.1. Each path may be labeled and an arrow drawn from the label to the path, or a legend (or key) may be provided listing each geometric symbol and the behavior it represents. No more than three different data paths should be plotted on a single graph. Additional graphs should be used when more than three data paths are necessary.
   c. The solid line of a data path implies continuity in the data collection process. If there is a break in the expected sequence of intervention (a student is absent; a special event occurs) and a regularly scheduled session does not occur, there may be simply a break in the data path, or two parallel hash marks are placed on the data path to indicate the continuity break.

3. *Student (participant) identification:* The name of the student(s) is placed in a box in the bottom right corner of the graph.

Creating a Line Graph
Pearson eText
Video Example 5.1
In this video, an educator explains how to create a basic line graph in Microsoft EXCEL©. Notice the conventions of a line graph that she adheres to in the video example.

https://www.youtube.com/watch?v=LGgNxfaXzrY&t=35s

> Graphing permanent product data.

Transferring Data to a Graph

Learning Outcome 5.2 Demonstrate how to transfer data to a graph.

TRANSFERRING PERMANENT PRODUCT DATA TO A GRAPH Permanent product data are reported as a number of items or a percentage of items resulting from behavior. For example, a teacher might record the number of math problems completed, the percent of correctly spelled words, the number of cans placed on a display shelf, or the number of dirty clothes placed in the hamper. If the number of opportunities for responding remains constant—as in spelling tests that always have 20 items or in a series of math worksheets that always have 10 problems—the data may be graphed simply as the number of items. If the number of opportunities varies—different numbers of test items or math problems—the teacher must calculate percentages (see Figure 5.2).

We calculate the percentage of correct responses by dividing the number of correct responses by the total number of responses and multiplying the result by 100, as shown:

$$\frac{\text{Number of correct responses}}{\text{Total number of responses}} \times 100 = \text{percentage of correct responses}$$

Figure 5.2 Choosing measurement conversion for permanent product data

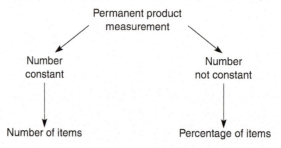

Figure 5.3 Transferring permanent product data to a graph

Student	Catherine		
Behavior	writing paragraphs of 30 words given title and topic sentence		
Date	Number of Words	Date	Number of Words
1 3/16	16	6 3/27	18
2 3/18	24	7 3/30	24
3 3/20	20	8 4/2	20
4 3/23	20	9 4/4	24
5 3/25	22	10 4/7	25

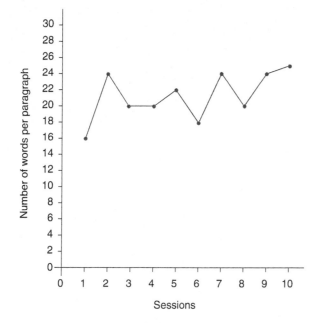

Figure 5.3 is used to record Catherine's performance of paragraph writing. Recorded on the data sheet is the number of words Catherine wrote in each paragraph. Below the data sheet is a simple line graph on which the data have been plotted.

TRANSFERRING EVENT DATA TO A GRAPH Event data may be reported as (a) the number of occurrences of a behavior if the amount of time is consistent across sessions, as in the number of times the student was out of seat during the 40-minute math group; (b) the number correct or a percentage if there is a consistent number of opportunities to respond, as in how many sight words out of 10 the student recognized; (c) a percentage correct if the number of opportunities to respond varies, as in the number of times a student complies with a teacher's instruction when the number of instructions varies from session to session. Figure 5.4 is used to record Michael's talking out during a class activity scheduled from 10:20 a.m. to 11:00 a.m. daily. The teacher tallied the number of times Michael called out without raising his hand. Below the data sheet is a graph representing the data. Figure 5.5 is used to record Tasha's recognition of her list of 10 sight words. Below the data sheet, her performance is transferred onto a graph in two ways—as the number of words read correctly and as the percentage of words read correctly.

| Graphing event data.

TRANSFERRING RATE DATA TO A GRAPH Conversion to rate data is required when the teacher is concerned with both accuracy and speed. Rate data reflect fluency of performance and allow judgments about the development of proficiency. If the time

| Graphing rate data.

Figure 5.4 Transferring event data to a graph

Student	Michael
Behavior	calling out without raising hand
Observation Period	10:20 a.m. –11:00 a.m. (whole-class activity)

Days	Instances	Total
1 Monday	///	3
2 Tuesday	/	1
3 Wednesday	✹//	7
4 Thursday	///	3
5 Friday	//	2
6 Monday	✹	5
7 Tuesday	////	4
8 Wednesday	////	4
9 Thursday	✹//	7

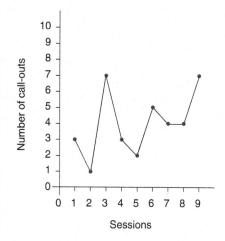

Graphing interval and time sampling data.

allowed for the response(s) is the same across all sessions, simply reporting frequency is all that is necessary. Such is the case when each day the student has 20 minutes to complete a set of 14 math problems. If, however, the time allocated for responding varies from session to session, rate must be calculated so that the data can be compared. Computation of rate is reviewed in Figure 5.6.

Figure 5.7 is used to record Steven's performance during vocational training at the local Red Cross office. Steven was learning to assemble packets of materials used during the blood drive. Because this was vocational training, his teacher was interested

Figure 5.5 Transferring event data to a graph

Student	Tasha				
Behavior	sight word reading				
	Monday	Tuesday	Wednesday	Thursday	Friday
mother	✓	✓	✓	✓	✓
father	✓	✓	✓	✓	
sister					
brother		✓	✓	✓	✓
school	✓	✓	✓	✓	✓
grocery					
hospital			✓	✓	✓
police	✓	✓	✓	✓	✓
church					✓
station					✓
Total Correct	45		66		7

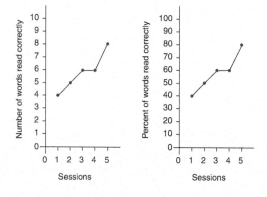

Figure 5.6 Computing rate of correct or error responses

Computing Rate

A rate of correct responding is computed by dividing the number of correct responses by the time taken for responding:

$$\text{Correct rate} = \frac{\text{Number correct}}{\text{Time}}$$

For example, if on Monday Kevin completed 15 problems correctly in 30 minutes, his rate of problems correct would be 0.5 per minute.

$$\frac{15 \text{ problems correct}}{30 \text{ minutes}} = 0.5 \text{ problems correct per minute}$$

If on Tuesday he completed 20 problems correctly in 45 minutes, his rate per minute would be 0.44.

$$\frac{20 \text{ problems correct}}{45 \text{ minutes}} = 0.44 \text{ problems correct per minute}$$

If Kevin's teacher had simply recorded that Kevin completed 15 problems on Monday and 20 problems on Tuesday, the teacher might think that Kevin's math was improving. In reality, though the number of math problems increased, the rate decreased, and Kevin did not do as well on Tuesday as on Monday.

Computing a rate of error may be done by dividing the number of errors by the time. For example:

$$\text{Session 1:} \frac{12 \text{ spelling errors}}{20 \text{ minutes}} = 0.6 \text{ errors per minute}$$

$$\text{Session 2:} \frac{10 \text{ spelling errors}}{30 \text{ minutes}} = 0.33 \text{ errors per minute}$$

These rate computations provide the teacher with the numbers of correct or incorrect responses per minute (or second or hour).

---

in both the number of packets he completed and how long it took him. She was interested in the rate at which Steven assembled packets. Below the data sheet is a graph displaying Steven's rate per minute of assembling packets.

TRANSFERRING INTERVAL AND TIME SAMPLING DATA TO A GRAPH Interval and time sampling data are reported as the number or percent of total observed intervals during which the behavior occurs. They are usually reported as percentages.

Figure 5.8 shows Omar's out-of-seat behavior during the first 6 minutes of center time. The teacher recorded interval data. She constructed the data sheet to show the 6 minutes divided into 20-second intervals and made an X if Omar was out of his seat at any time during the interval. Below the data sheet, the data are transferred onto one graph indicating the number of intervals during which out-of-seat behavior was observed and another graph indicating the percentage of intervals during which Omar was out of his seat at some time.

Figure 5.9 presents the data sheet on which the teacher recorded whether Leann was engaged in self-talk or peer-directed talk during 20-minute play periods. The teacher chose to use time sampling; she recorded the type of talk in which Leann was engaged at the end of each interval. Below the data sheet, the data are transferred onto one graph indicating the number of intervals and another indicating percent of

Transferring Data to a Graph
Pearson eText
Video Example 5.2
In this video, an educator explains how she arranges her system of data collection for her classroom. She demonstrates how to transfer collected data to her graph. Which graph elements do you notice?

https://www.youtube.com/watch?v=iRBLLsqK6WU

Figure 5.7 Transferring rate data to a graph

Student	Steven
Behavior	packet assembly
Observation Period	vocational training at Red Cross

Day	Number Completed	Amount of Time	Rate per Minute
4/16 Monday	45	30′	1.5
4/18 Wednesday	40	25′	1.6
4/20 Friday	45	25′	1.8
4/24 Tuesday	40	20′	2.0
4/26 Thursday	50	25′	2.0
4/30 Monday	48	20′	2.4
5/2 Wednesday	54	20′	2.7

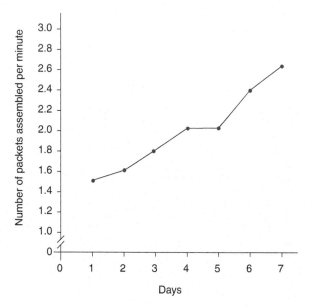

intervals. Note that each graph uses a different identification system to indicate the behavior associated with a data path.

Figure 5.10 presents a differently arranged data sheet for time sampling. On this data sheet the teacher indicated the nature of Kosh's off-task behavior during the time allocated for independent writing. Each of the two types of off-task behavior would have been properly operationalized before data collection. Below the data sheet are two ways of graphing these data and two ways of keying a graph.

| Graphing duration data.

TRANSFERRING DURATION DATA TO A GRAPH Duration data may be collected and reported either as the number of minutes or seconds it takes a student to complete a behavior or as how much of a specified period of time a student spent engaging in a particular behavior. A teacher might record, for example, the total amount of time it took a student to finish an assigned task. Another teacher might record how much of a 20-minute science lab a student spent engaged in the lab project. The second example

Figure 5.8 Transferring interval data to a graph

Student	Omar																	
Behavior	out-of-seat (X = out of seat)																	
Observation Period	6 minutes (first 6 minutes of center time)																	

	20"	40"	60"	20"	40"	60"	20"	40"	60"	20"	40"	60"	20"	40"	60"	20"	40"	60"
Mon	—	X	X	X	—	—	X	—	—	—	—	—	X	X	X	—	X	X
Tues	X	X	X	X	—	X	—	—	—	—	X	—	—	—	—	—	X	—
Wed	—	—	—	—	X	X	—	—	—	—	—	—	X	X	—	—	—	—
Thur	X	—	X	X	—	X	X	—	—	—	X	X	—	X	—	—	—	X
Fri	—	X	—	—	—	X	—	X	—	X	X	—	—	X	X	X	—	X

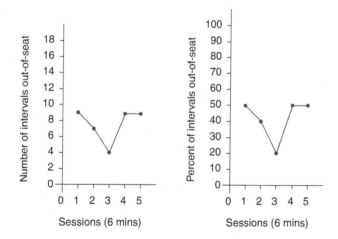

could be reported as the number of minutes of engagement or as the percentage of available time spent engaged in the project.

Figure 5.11 shows how long it takes Casey to complete toileting. The graph below the data sheet is drawn to indicate the number of minutes he spent each time he went to the bathroom.

TRANSFERRING LATENCY DATA TO A GRAPH Latency data are reported as the number of minutes or seconds that elapse before a student initiates a behavior following a request for the behavior to be performed or for a natural occasion for its performance to occur (for example, answering a ringing telephone).

Figure 5.12 shows DuShawn's latency in beginning his daily journal-writing exercise. After giving the class the instruction to begin, the teacher recorded how many minutes elapsed before DuShawn began the task and noted what he was doing before beginning the task. Below the data sheet is a graph that represents these data.

| Graphing latency data.

Figure 5.9 Transferring time sampling data to a graph

Student: Leann
Behavior: self-talk vs. other directed during play (S—self, O—other)
Observation Period: 20-minute play period (varies each day)

	1	2	3	4	5	6	7	8	9	10	11	12	13	14	15	16	17	18	19	20
Mon	—	S	S	S	—	O	O	—	—	S	S	S	S	S	—	O	O	—	S	S
Tues	—	—	—	—	—	S	S	S	S	—	—	—	—	—	—	—	—	—	—	—
Wed	—	—	O	—	—	—	S	S	S	—	—	S	S	S	—	S	S	—	—	O
Thur	O	S	—	—	—	S	S	S	S	—	O	O	O	S	—	—	O	O	S	S
Fri	—	S	S	—	—	S	S	S	O	S	S	S	O	—	—	—	S	S	O	O

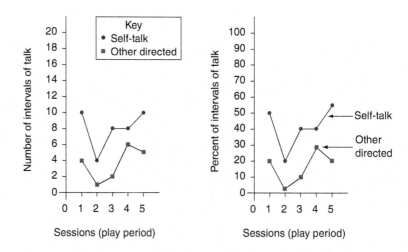

Figure 5.10 Transferring time sampling data to a graph

Student	Kosh							
Behavior	off-task (T—talking, D—daydreaming)							
Observation Period	independent writing (10:15–10:55)							
Monday	T	5'	T	10'	—	15'	—	20'
	—	25'	D	30'	T	35'	T	40'
Tuesday	T	5'	T	10'	D	15'	T	20'
	T	25'	—	30'	T	35'	T	40'
Wednesday	T	5'	T	10'	—	15'	—	20'
	D	25'	D	30'	T	35'	T	40'
Thursday	—	5'	—	10'	T	15'	T	20'
	—	25'	—	30'	—	35'	—	40'
Friday	T	5'	D	10'	T	15'	T	20'
	—	25'	—	30'	—	35'	T	40'

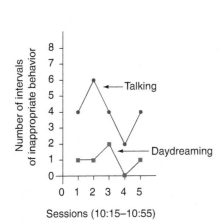
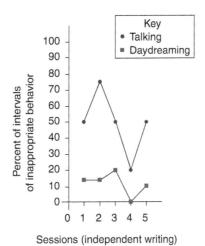

Figure 5.11 Transferring duration data to a graph

Student Behavior	Casey time spent toileting			
Monday	1	12 minutes		
	2	8 minutes		average = 9 minutes
	3	7 minutes		
Tuesday	1	11 minutes		
	2	16 minutes		
	3	9 minutes		average = 12 minutes
Wednesday	1	15 minutes		
	2	10 minutes		average = 11 minutes
	3	8 minutes		
Thursday	1	14 minutes		
	2	10 minutes		
	3	12 minutes		average = 12 minutes
Friday	1	9 minutes		
	2	11 minutes		
	3	10 minutes		average = 10 minutes

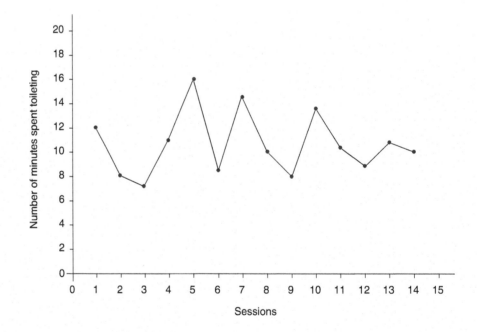

Figure 5.12 Transferring latency data to a graph

Student	DuShawn
Behavior	delay beginning of morning paragraph writing
Observation Period	each morning—8:45 a.m.

Day	Number of Minutes	Comments
Monday	6	pencil sharpening
Tuesday	5	roaming
Wednesday	6	pencil sharp
Thursday	2	chat
Friday	4	chat
Monday	5	pencil sharp
Tuesday	7	pencil sharp
Wednesday	5	coat-pencil
Thursday	4	roaming
Friday	5	pencil sharp

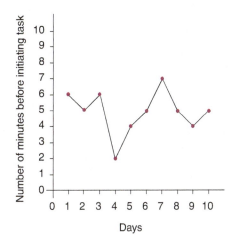

Additional Graphing Conventions

Learning Outcome 5.3 Identify graphing conventions (i.e., conditions, baseline, intervention).

More complex graphs than the ones in this chapter will be illustrated in Chapter 6. Some additional conventions that will help you understand them are described in Figure 5.13.

Conditions are phases of an intervention during which different approaches or techniques are used. A teacher who wanted to reduce the occurrence of an inappropriate behavior might first record the current level of the behavior for several sessions or days—called **baseline data**—and then use some strategy to assist the student to decrease his or her performance of the behavior—called **intervention**. You need a clear indicator on the graph of which condition is in effect during each session. This is provided by drawing a vertical dashed line from the top to the bottom of the graph. This line is drawn between the lines on the graph paper between the last session of one condition and the first session of the next. For example, if

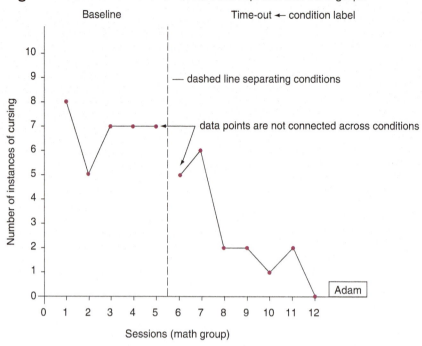

Figure 5.13 Conventions for conditions represented on a graph

baseline occurred for five sessions and intervention began on the sixth session, the condition line would be drawn between sessions 5 and 6 (represented on the *x*-axis). Data points are not connected across conditions. To identify what procedure is represented, a brief, descriptive condition label is placed above the data path for each condition, centered between the vertical dashed lines. For example, if a teacher is using a differential reinforcement procedure to reduce a student's cursing, he would print "differential reinforcement" centered above the part of the graph on which these data are placed.

Using Cumulative Graphs
Pearson eText
Video Example 5.3
In this video, an educator describes how her team has addressed teaching a student, Pablo, his letters. Consider how a cumulative graph could be applied to tracking mastery of letters of the alphabet.

Cumulative Graphs

Learning Outcome 5.4 Identify components and uses of cumulative graphs.

On a simple line graph, data points are plotted at the appropriate intersections without regard to performance during the previous session. On a **cumulative graph**, the number of occurrences observed in a session is graphed after being added to the number of occurrences plotted for the previous session. The occurrences recorded for each session include those of all previous sessions. A cumulative graph presents an additive view of a behavior across sessions, providing a count of the total number of responses. The hypothetical graphs in Figure 5.14 show the same raw data plotted on a line graph and on a cumulative graph. Cumulative graphs always demonstrate an upward curve if any behavior at all is being recorded. This presentation of data provides a continuous line with a slope that indicates the rate of responding. A steep slope indicates rapid responding, a gradual slope indicates slow responding, and a plateau or straight line indicates no responding.

Figure 5.14 Comparison of plotting data points on line and cumulative graphs

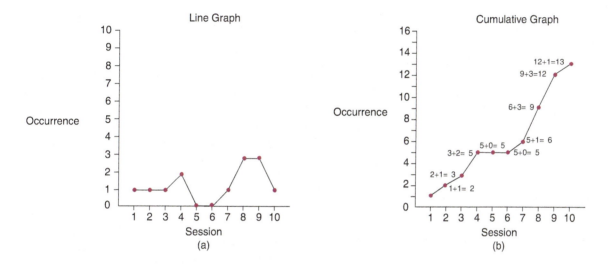

Bar Graphs

Learning Outcome 5.5 Identify components and uses of bar graphs.

A **bar graph**, or histogram, is another means of displaying data. Like a line graph, a bar graph has two axes, the x-axis (sessions) and the y-axis (performance). As its name implies, a bar graph uses vertical bars rather than data points and connecting lines to indicate performance levels. Each vertical bar represents one observation period. The height of the bar corresponds with a performance value on the y-axis. A bar graph may be better for displaying data in situations where clear interpretation of the pattern of behavior plotted on a line graph is difficult. Such confusion may result when several data paths are plotted on a single line graph, as when a teacher chooses to include data from several students or from multiple behaviors. In such cases, plotted lines may overlap or appear extremely close together because data points fall at the same intersections. Figure 5.15 offers an example of the same data plotted on a line graph and on a bar graph. The bar graph is plainly much clearer. A classroom teacher might use a bar graph to display daily the number of correct responses from each member of a small group.

Another use of the bar graph is to summarize student performance data. This may be done for a single task, such as the mean number of science tasks completed across multiple students (Figure 5.16), or to summarize a single student's performance across multiple tasks (Figure 5.17).

Bar graphs are clearer for young students.

Creating a Bar Graph
Pearson eText
Video Example 5.4
In this video, an educator explains how to create a bar graph in Microsoft EXCEL©. Notice the conventions of a bar graph that she adheres to in the video example.

https://www.youtube.com/watch?v=LzSmvZO-q_w

Figure 5.15 Comparing line and bar graphs

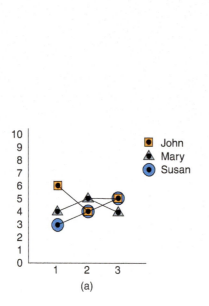
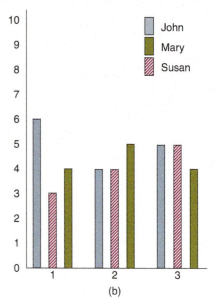

Figure 5.16 Bar graph of summary of task performance of multiple students

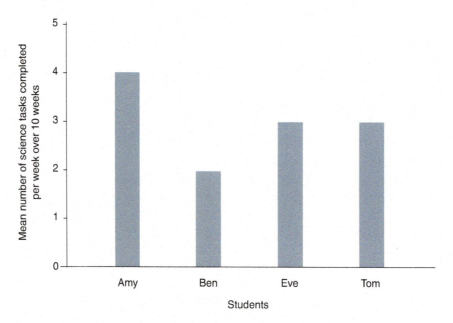

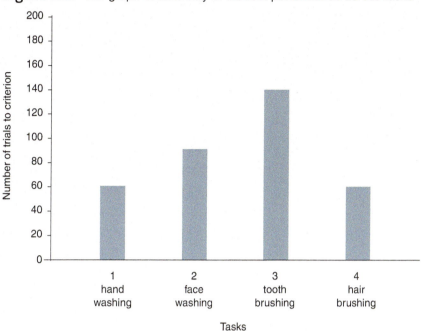

Figure 5.17 Bar graph of summary of student performance across tasks

Summary

We discussed the basic reasons for graphing data, including monitoring of student performance, formative and summative evaluation, and graphs as a tool for communicating among educators, students, and parents. We described three basic methods of graphing data: line graphs, cumulative graphs, and bar graphs. We outlined the basic conventions for drawing line graphs and provided examples of transferring various types of observational data from data sheets to graphs. Instructions for using Microsoft Excel to create graphs are included in Chapter 6.

Discussion Questions

What would be the most appropriate graphing format for each of the following situations? Why?

1. Wendy has been working on sight vocabulary words for several months. Her mother is concerned that she isn't learning them very quickly, but you realize that having started from scratch, Wendy has acquired quite a few words during this time. You want to make it clear to Mom that Wendy has come a long way.
2. You are expected to include data summaries in the folders of each of your students for accuracy of performance in math computation, spelling accuracy, and reading fluency.
3. Your first-grade students love to see their progress in reading accuracy and fluency on the class bulletin board.

Chapter 6
Single-Subject Designs

 Learning Outcomes

6.1 Identify the components of an experiment required to establish a functional relation.

6.2 Identify the components of the different types of single-subject research designs and list the advantages and disadvantages of each.

6.3 Explain how to implement each of the different types of single-subject research design and how to display the design using graphs.

6.4 Evaluate the outcomes of an intervention.

6.5 Identify the components of action research and explain how it parallels single-subject designs.

CHAPTER OUTLINE

Variables and Functional Relations

Basic Categories of Designs

Single-Subject Designs
    Baseline Measures
    Intervention Measures
    Experimental Control

AB Design
    Implementation
    Graphic Display
    Application
    Advantages and Disadvantages

Reversal Design
    Implementation
    Graphic Display
    Design Variations
    Application
    Advantages and a Disadvantage

Changing Criterion Design
    Implementation
    Graphic Display
    Application
    Advantage and Disadvantage

Multiple Baseline Design
    Implementation
    Graphic Display

    Application
    Advantages and Disadvantages

Alternating Treatments Design
    Implementation
    Graphic Display
    Application
    Advantages and Disadvantages

Multiple Treatments Design
    Implementation
    Graphic Display
    Application
    Advantages and Disadvantages

Evaluating Single-Subject Designs
    Analysis of Results
    Visual Analysis of Graphs
    Ethical Considerations with Single-Subject Design

Action Research and Single-Subject Design Tools
    Components of Action Research
    Single-Subject Design Parallels and Contributions
    Example of an Action Research Study

Summary

Data collection allows teachers to make statements about the direction and magnitude of behavioral changes. Data collection alone, however, does not provide sufficient information to indicate a functional relation between an intervention and the behavior in question. To make assumptions about functional relations, data collection must be conducted within certain formats, or designs. A design is a systematic pattern for collecting data that enables the collector to make confident statements about the relation between interventions and behaviors.

In this chapter we will describe a number of experimental designs used in applied behavior analysis that enable teachers and researchers to determine relations between interventions and behavior change. Each design has a particular graphic format. The various formats are what allow visual inspection and analysis of the data. Graphs can be made with paper, a ruler, and a pencil; in most cases, however, the result will look like part of a middle school project. Such graphs do not present the image a teacher wants for a meeting with parents and other professionals gathered to evaluate the progress of student learning. Professional-looking graphs can be made using computer software such as Microsoft Excel. The video tutorials in this text provide step-by-step instructions for creating graphs for several designs useful in the classroom. For more complex graphs, refer to articles by Dixon et al. (2009), Vanselow and Bourret (2012), Deochand, Costello, and Fuqua (2015), Dubuque (2015), Deochand (2017), Chok (2019), and Fuller and Dubuque (2019).

Teachers who can read and understand experimental research reported in professional journals can remain up to date on innovative techniques and procedures. Learning about these designs may also encourage them to become teacher-researchers who can systematically evaluate their own instruction and share their results with others. The ability to conduct classroom-based research will increase teachers' confidence, effectiveness, and credibility.

In this chapter, research applications, taken from professional journals, accompany the description of each design. Each design is also applied to a classroom problem to demonstrate the utility of applied behavior analysis designs in the classroom.

Variables and Functional Relations

Learning Outcome 6.1 Identify the components of an experiment required to establish a functional relation.

We will define some terms basic to experimental investigation before discussing specific designs. The term **variable** is used to refer to any number of factors involved in research. These may include attributes of individuals being studied (age, test scores), conditions associated with the setting in which the study is done (number of students, noise level), or the nature of an intervention, which might be an instructional strategy (direct instruction phonics, cooperative learning), instructional material (counting chips, computer), or behavior management technique (tokens, self-recording). In research, the goal is to control for the presence or absence of variables that may affect outcomes. An unforeseen or uncontrolled variable (illness, for example) is referred to as a *confounding variable*. If a teacher is using a new program to teach a student long division, and the student's father coincidentally begins reviewing long division with the student for an hour every evening, it will be impossible to determine whether the teacher's variable (new math program) or the uncontrolled variable (home instruction) was responsible for the student's learning long division. With experimental designs researchers can control for many confounding variables.

Experimental design differentiates between two types of variables: dependent and independent. The term **dependent variable** refers to the behavior targeted for change. The term **independent variable** refers to the intervention being used to change behavior. In the following sentences, the independent variable is *italicized* and the dependent variable appears in (parentheses).

> Following a student's (oral reading), the teacher provided *corrective feedback*.
> *Picture prompts* are used when the student is engaged in (buying groceries).
> *Coworker modeling* is provided when the student is (shelving books) in the library.
> *Verbal praise* is contingently presented when the student (remains on task for 15 minutes).
> Contingent upon (a temper tantrum), the student is placed in *time-out*.
> For each (math problem completed correctly) the student earned *one token*.

Single-subject experimental designs allow researchers to assess cause and effect between an independent variable and a dependent variable. When changes in a dependent variable are *replicated* each time the same independent variable is implemented, a **functional relation** is said to exist. Single-subject experimental designs provide the framework within which to test for these replications of effect. When interventions and their outcomes are replicated, the teacher and researcher can have confidence that the behavior changed as a function of the intervention because with each replication only the independent variable is changed or manipulated. Repeated manipulation allows the teacher-researcher to rule out confounding variables as agents of the behavior change. Additionally, the demonstration of a functional relation is evidence of experimental control (Kennedy, 2005). This experimental control adds confidence that some extraneous or confounding variable(s) was not the cause of the effect.

Basic Categories of Designs

Group designs versus single-subject designs.

A research design is a format that structures the manner in which questions are asked and data are collected and analyzed. Two categories of research designs are **group designs** and **single-subject designs**. Each provides a plan and a means for demonstrating the effectiveness of an intervention on a behavior. As indicated by their names, group designs focus on questions and data related to groups of individuals, whereas single-subject designs focus on questions and data related to a particular individual.

Group designs are used to evaluate the effects of an intervention on a behavior of a whole population (for example, all the second graders of a school district or of a school building) or of a representative sample of a population. In order to determine the effectiveness of an intervention, the population (or a randomly selected sample) is, also randomly, divided into two groups: an experimental group and a control group. (It is this random selection and division that allows generalization from a sample to an entire population.) Members of the experimental group receive the intervention. This provides multiple replications of the effect of the intervention. Members of the control group do not receive the intervention. Measurements of the behavior (averages in performance) are made before intervention and at the conclusion of intervention for each group. Average changes in behavior of the two populations are compared subsequent to the intervention. This comparison is made through use of statistical procedures, the purpose of which is (a) to verify a difference in the change in average scores between the two groups, (b) to verify that the difference is significant and therefore possibly worthy of being acted upon, and (c) to verify that the differences between groups are more likely the result of the intervention than of chance or some unknown source.

For example, the curriculum committee of Fulton County Public Schools is considering changing their sixth-grade math text. Currently they use the text by Jones and Jones. The committee randomly selects 200 students from among all the sixth graders in the district. These students are then randomly assigned to either the experimental group (100 students) or the control group (100 students). During the first week of the school year all 200 students are tested on sixth-grade math objectives. Then during the school year, the experimental group receives instruction using the Smith and Smith math text, while the control group continues to receive instruction using the Jones and Jones math text. At the end of the school year each group is tested again on sixth-grade math objectives. The average gain in performance (number of objectives met) for the groups is compared. This is done to determine (a) if there is no difference in gain in scores of the two groups; (b) if there is a difference, whether this difference is significant; and (c) whether it is reasonable to assume that a greater or lesser gain in score by the experimental group is due to using the Smith and Smith text.

Applied behavior analysts prefer multiple measurements of behavior in order to provide a detailed picture of the behavior before and during the course of intervention. They also prefer to record information specific to individuals rather than information about average performance of groups. Examining average performance may obscure important information, as illustrated in the following anecdote.

Ms. Witherspoon Orders Reading Books

Ms. Witherspoon, a third-grade teacher, was urged by her principal to order new reading books at the beginning of the school year. Being unfamiliar with her class, Ms. Witherspoon decided to use a reading test to determine which books to order. She administered the test and averaged the scores to determine the most appropriate reader. She came up with an exact average of third grade, first month, and ordered 30 readers on that level.

When the books arrived, she found that the reader was much too hard for some of her students and much too easy for others. Using an average score had concealed the fact that although the class average was third grade, some students were reading at first-grade level and others at sixth-grade level.

Single-Subject Designs

Learning Outcome 6.2 Identify the components of the different types of single-subject research designs and list the advantages and disadvantages of each.

> Single-subject designs often compare the effects of different conditions on the same individual.

Applied behavior analysis researchers prefer to use single-subject designs. Single-subject designs provide structures for evaluating the performance of individuals rather than groups. Whereas group designs identify the effects of variables on the average performance of large numbers of students, single-subject designs identify the effects of variables on a specific behavior of a particular student. These designs monitor the performance of individuals during manipulation of the independent variable(s). Certain techniques, described later in the chapter, are used to verify that changes in the dependent variable result from experimental manipulations and not from chance, coincidence, or confounding variables.

Single-subject designs require **repeated measures** of the dependent variable. The performance of the individual whose behavior is being monitored is recorded weekly, daily, or even more frequently over an extended period of time. The individual's performance can then be compared under different experimental conditions, or manipulations of the independent variable, such as the presence or absence of a teaching procedure. Each individual is compared only to himself or herself, though the intervention may be replicated with several other individuals within the same design. Single-subject research emphasizes clinical significance for an individual rather than statistical significance among groups. If an intervention results in an observable, measurable improvement in functioning, the results of the experiment are considered to have clinical significance.

Certain components are common to all single-subject designs. These include a measure of baseline performance and at least one measure of performance under an intervention condition. Single-subject research designs require at least one replication of the use of the intervention within the design. This replication allows for the assumption of a functional relation. The more replications of the effect, the more convincing the functional relation.

Applied behavior analysts do not assume generality of research results based on a single successful intervention. When a functional relation is established between an independent variable (intervention) and a dependent variable (behavior) for one individual, repeated studies of the same intervention are conducted using different individuals and different dependent variables. The more frequently an intervention proves effective, the more confidence is gained about the generality of the results of the intervention. That systematic teacher praise increases one student's rate of doing math problems may not be a convincing argument for the use of praise. Documentation that such praise increased production of not only math problems but also other academic and social behaviors with numerous students is more convincing. Using systematic replication, applied behavior analysts gradually identify procedures and techniques effective with many students. Others can then adopt these procedures and techniques with considerable confidence that they will work.

Sidman (1960) suggested that it would be an error to view single-subject research as simply a microcosm of group research. Repeated measures of a dependent variable when the independent variable is applied and removed demonstrate a continuity of cause and effect and the relation of one data point to another that would not be seen when comparing the effect of the independent variable across separate groups. He contends that individual and group curves do not provide the same information, "for the two types of data represent, in a very real sense, two different subject matters" (p. 54).

Baseline Measures

The first phase of single-subject design involves the collection and recording of baseline data. **Baseline data** are measures of the level of behavior (the dependent variable) as it occurs naturally, before intervention. Kazdin (2011) stated that baseline data serve two functions. First, baseline data serve a *descriptive function*. These data describe the existing level of student performance. When data points are graphed, they provide a picture of the student's behavior—his or her current ability to solve multiplication problems or his or her current rate of talk-outs. This objective record can assist the teacher in verifying the existence and extent of the behavior deficit (lack of ability to do multiplication) or behavior excess (talking out).

Second, baseline data serve a *predictive function*. "The baseline data serve as the basis for predicting the level of performance for the immediate future if the intervention is not provided" (Kazdin, 2011, p. 105). To evaluate the success of an intervention (the independent variable), the teacher must know what student performance was like before the intervention. Baseline data serve a purpose similar to that of a pretest. "The predication is achieved by projecting or extrapolating into the future a continuation of baseline performance" (p. 123). It is against this projection that the effect of an intervention is judged.

The baseline phase continues for several sessions before the intervention phase begins. In most instances, at least five baseline data points are collected and plotted. The extent of baseline data collection is affected by certain characteristics of these data points.

Because baseline data are to be used to judge the effectiveness of the teacher's intervention, it is important that the baseline be *stable*, providing a representative sample of the natural occurrence of the behavior. The *stability* of a baseline is assessed by two characteristics: variability of the data points and trends in the data points. *Variability of data* refers to fluctuations in the student's performance. "As a general rule, the greater the variability in the data, the more difficult it is to draw conclusions about the effects of the intervention" (Kazdin, 2011, p. 126) and to make projections about future performance. When baselines are unstable, the first thing to examine is the definition of the target behavior. A lack of stability in the baseline may suggest that the operational definition of the target behavior is not sufficiently descriptive to allow for accurate and consistent recording or that the data collector is not being consistent in the procedure used for data collection. In laboratory settings, other sources of variability can often be identified and controlled. In classrooms, attempts to control variability are desirable if the sources of variability can be identified—for example, if fluctuations are caused by inconsistent delivery of medication. In cases of temporary fluctuations caused by such unusual events as a fight or a problem at home, the teacher may just wait for the fluctuation to pass. However, in classrooms, unlike laboratories, "variability is an unavoidable fact of life," and in such settings there are seldom "the facilities or time that would be required to eliminate variability" (Sidman, 1960, p. 193).

Where variables can be rigorously controlled, a research-oriented criterion for the existence of variability would be data points within a 5% range of variability (Sidman, 1960). A therapeutic criterion of 20% has been suggested (Repp, 1983). However, in classrooms where pure research concerns might be less important than rapid modification of the behavior, we suggest a more lenient parameter of 50% variability. If variability exceeds 50%, statistical techniques for performance comparisons must be used (Barlow & Hersen, 1984). A baseline may be considered stable if no data point of the baseline varies more than 50% from the mean, or average, of the baseline. Figure 6.1 illustrates a procedure for computing the stability of a baseline based on this criterion.

> Baselines should be stable. See Chapter 3 for suggestions on writing operational definitions.

Figure 6.1 Computing baseline stability

Session	Data Points
1	14
2	10
3	20
4	16
5	11

Baseline mean (arithmetic average) = 14.2 = 14
50% of mean = 7
Acceptable range of data points = 7 − 21 (14 ± 7)
This baseline is stable because no data point varies more than 50% from the mean.

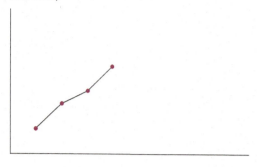

Figure 6.2 Increasing trend (ascending baseline)

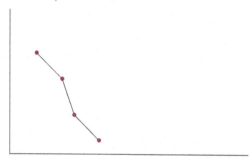

Figure 6.3 Decreasing trend (descending baseline)

> Take baseline trends into account before intervention.

> Professor Grundy encounters a confounding variable when he again visits Miss Harper later in this chapter.

A **trend** in the data refers to an indication of a distinctive direction in the performance of the behavior. A trend is defined as three successive data points in the same direction (Barlow & Hersen, 1984). A baseline may show no trend, an increasing trend, or a decreasing trend. Figures 6.2 and 6.3 illustrate two types of trends—increasing and decreasing.

An *ascending baseline* denotes an increasing trend. Teachers should initiate intervention on an ascending baseline only if the objective is to decrease the behavior. Because the behavior is already increasing, the effects of an intervention designed to increase behavior will be obscured by the baseline trend.

A *descending baseline* includes at least three data points that show a distinctive decreasing direction or trend in the behavior. Teachers should initiate intervention on a descending baseline only if the objective is to increase the behavior.

Intervention Measures

The second component of any single-subject design is a series of repeated measures of the subject's performance under a treatment or intervention condition. The independent variable (treatment or intervention) is introduced, and its effects on the dependent variable (the student's performance) are measured and recorded. Trends in treatment data indicate the effectiveness of the treatment and provide the teacher or researcher with guidance in determining the need for changes in intervention procedures.

Experimental Control

Experimental control refers to the researcher's efforts to ensure that changes in the dependent variable are in fact related to manipulations of the independent variable—that a functional relation exists. The researcher wants to eliminate to the greatest extent possible the chance that other, confounding variables are responsible for changes in the behavior. Confounding variables are those environmental events or conditions that are not controlled by the researcher but may affect behavior. For example, if a teacher institutes a behavioral system for reducing disruptive behavior in a class after the three most disruptive students have moved away, she really cannot be sure that the new system is responsible for the lower levels of disruption. Removal of the three students is a confounding variable.

The designs discussed in this chapter provide varying degrees of experimental control. Some, called *teaching designs*, do not permit confident assumption of a functional relation. They may, however, provide sufficient indication of behavior change for everyday classroom use, particularly if the teacher remains alert to the possibility of confounding variables. Other designs, called *research designs*, provide for much tighter experimental control and allow the teacher or researcher to presume a functional relation. Researchers usually demonstrate experimental control by repeating an intervention several times and observing its effect on the dependent variable each time it is repeated. Research designs may be used in classrooms when a teacher is particularly concerned about possible confounding variables and wants to be sure that intervention has had the desired effect on behavior. The teacher who is interested in publishing or otherwise sharing with other professionals the results of an intervention would also use a research design if at all possible.

> **Using Technology To Graph**
> Pearson eText
> **Video Example 6.1**
> In this video, an educator analyzes student data by creating line graphs. Consider how she interprets results of her graphs and links analysis to future intervention steps
>
> https://www.youtube.com/watch?v=ciS4XV6WZeo

AB Design

Learning Outcome 6.3 Explain how to implement each of the different types of single subject research design and how to display the design using graphs.

The **AB design** is the basic single-subject design. Each of the more complex designs is actually an expansion of this simple one. The designation *AB* refers to the two phases of the design: the A, or baseline, phase and the B, or intervention, phase. During the A phase, baseline data are collected and recorded. Once a stable baseline has been established, the intervention is introduced, and the B phase begins. In this phase, intervention data are collected and recorded. The teacher can evaluate increases or decreases in the amount, rate, percentage, or duration of the target behavior during the intervention phase and compare them with the baseline phase. Using this information to make inferences about the effectiveness of the intervention, the teacher can make decisions about continuing, changing, or discarding the intervention.

> The AB design is a teaching design.

Implementation

Table 6.1 shows data collected using an AB design. The teacher in this instance was concerned about the few correct answers a student gave to questions about a reading assignment. For 5 days, she collected baseline data. She then made 2 minutes of free time contingent on each correct answer and continued to record the number of correct responses. As shown in Table 6.1, the number clearly increased during the intervention phase. The teacher could make a tentative assumption that her intervention was effective.

Table 6.1 Sample data from an AB design

Day	Baseline Data - Number of Correct Responses
Monday	2
Tuesday	1
Wednesday	0
Thursday	2
Friday	1

Day	Intervention Data - Number of Correct Responses
Monday	6
Tuesday	6
Wednesday	4
Thursday	8
Friday	6

Graphic Display

Data collected using an AB design are graphed in two phases: A, or baseline, and B, or intervention. A vertical line (dashed or solid) on the graph separates the two phases, and data points between phases are not connected. The graph in Figure 6.4 shows a clearer picture of the effectiveness of the intervention than do the data in table form.

Application

The basic AB design is not often found in the research literature because it cannot assess for a functional relation. The design does not provide for the replication within an experiment that establishes a functional relation. Schoen and Nolen (2004) used an AB design to illustrate the results of an intervention designed to reduce the off-task behaviors of a sixth-grade boy with learning disabilities. A self-management checklist was employed with which he assessed his behavior. Figure 6.5 illustrates the decline in the total number of minutes he was off task from baseline through the intervention phase. One cannot, however, assume a functional relation between the dependent variable (off-task behaviors) and the independent variable (self-management checklist) because the AB design does not provide for repeated manipulation (use and removal) of the independent variable. This study and the suitability of the use of some single-subject methodologies are discussed in the section on action research at the end of this chapter.

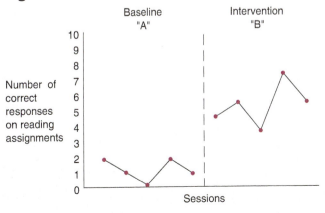

Figure 6.4 Graph of AB design data from Table 6.1

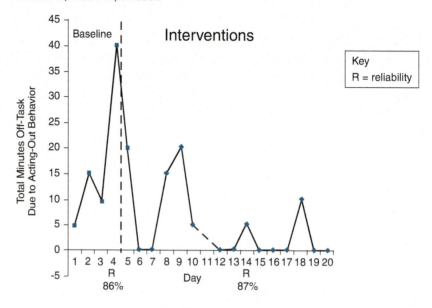

Figure 6.5 Use of an AB design

NOTE: From "Decreasing Acting-Out Behavior and Increasing Learning," by S. Schoen & J. Nolen, 2004. *Teaching Exceptional Children, 37*, 26–29. Copyright 2004, by The Council for Exceptional Children. Reprinted with permission.

Carbone, O'Brien, Sweeney-Kerwin, and Albert (2013) used an AB design to display the results of a procedure to increase the eye contact of a 3-year-old boy with autism. Eye contact was measured when the boy was asking for his reinforcers (i.e., manding). As shown in Figure 6.6, in Baseline (the A phase), the boy made eye contact during an average of 10% of his requests. The intervention (the B phase) was withholding the reinforcer (i.e., extinction) until the boy made eye contact while requesting. In addition, the boy received less of his reinforcer when he required the extinction procedure and more of his reinforcer if eye contact occurred without the extinction period (i.e., differential reinforcement). This procedure resulted in eye contact accompanying an average of 77% of requests. Because this was an AB design, Carbone and colleagues

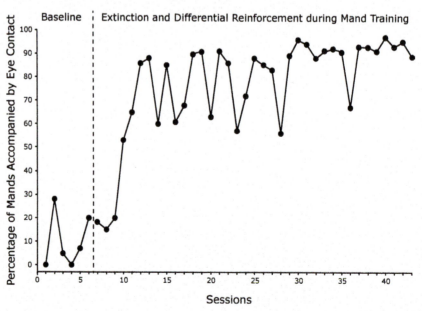

Figure 6.6 Application of the AB design

NOTE: From: Carbone, V. J., O'Brien, L., Sweeney-Kerwin, E. J., & Albert, K. M. (2013). Teaching eye contact to children with autism: A conceptual analysis and single case study. Education & Treatment of Children, 36(2), 139–159. https://doi.org/10.1353/etc.2013.0013

could not conclude a that there was functional relation between the procedure and the increase in eye contact. They complemented this case study with an interpretive analysis of the procedure.

Advantages and Disadvantages

The primary advantage of an AB design is its simplicity. It provides the teacher with a quick, uncomplicated means of comparing students' behavior before and after implementation of some intervention or instructional procedure, making instruction more systematic. As you'll see below, this is how Mr. Vogl assessed the effects of positive reinforcement on Jack's homework completion.

The disadvantage of the AB design is that it cannot be used to make a confident assumption of a functional relation. Although the data may show an increase or decrease in the behavior during the intervention phase, thus indicating effectiveness of the intervention, this design does not provide for a replication of the procedure. Therefore, the AB design is vulnerable to confounding variables or coincidental events. This is illustrated in the example on the next page.

> Many teachers use AB designs to evaluate their students' progress.

Jack Learns to Do His French Homework

Mr. Vogl had difficulty working with Jack, a student in the fourth-period French class. Jack was inattentive when homework from the previous evening was reviewed. Closer investigation revealed that Jack ignored the review sessions because he was not doing the assignments. To increase the amount of homework completed, Mr. Vogl decided to use positive reinforcement. To evaluate the effectiveness of the intervention, he selected the AB design using the number of homework questions completed correctly as the dependent variable.

Over a baseline period of 5 days, Jack completed 0 out of 10 (0/10) homework questions correctly each day. Because Jack frequently asked to listen to music in the French lab, Mr. Vogl decided to allow Jack to listen to music for 2 minutes for each correct homework question. Data collected during the intervention phase indicated an increase in the number of questions Jack answered correctly. Data analysis suggested that the intervention technique was effective.

Reversal Design

The **reversal design** is used to analyze the effectiveness of a single independent variable. Commonly referred to as the **ABAB design**, this design involves the sequential application and withdrawal of an intervention to verify the intervention's effects on a behavior. By repeatedly comparing baseline data to data collected during application of the intervention strategy, the researcher can determine whether a functional relation exists between the dependent and independent variables.

> ABAB is a research design. A functional relationship can be demonstrated.

Implementation

The reversal design has four phases: A, B, A, and B:

- A (baseline 1): the initial baseline during which data are collected on the target behavior under conditions existing before the introduction of the intervention.
- B (intervention 1): the initial introduction of the intervention selected to alter the target behavior. Intervention continues until the criterion for the target behavior is reached or a trend in the desired direction of behavior change is noted.
- A (baseline 2): a return to original baseline conditions, accomplished by withdrawing or terminating the intervention.
- B (intervention 2): the reintroduction of the intervention procedure.

Miss Harper Conducts Research

As part of her initial student teaching assignment, Miss Harper was required to carry out a simple research project using an AB design. She decided to use Ralph's staying in his seat as her dependent variable. (Remember Ralph from Chapter 1.) Miss Harper collected baseline data for several days and determined that Ralph stayed in his seat for periods varying from 20 to 25 minutes during the 1-hour reading class. She prepared to intervene, choosing as her independent variable points exchangeable for various activities that Ralph enjoyed. When Professor Grundy made a visit soon after intervention began, Miss Harper met him at the door in a state of high excitement.

"It's working, Professor!" gloated Miss Harper. "Look at my graph! Ralph was absent the first 2 days of this week, but since he's been back and I've been giving him points, he's been in his seat 100% every day. Do you think I'll get an A on my project?"

Professor Grundy inspected Miss Harper's graph and agreed that her procedure appeared to be effective. He then sat down in the rear of the classroom to observe. After a few minutes, during which Ralph indeed stayed in his seat, Professor Grundy attracted Miss Harper's attention and called her to the back of the room.

"Miss Harper," he asked gently, "did it not occur to you that the heavy cast on Ralph's leg might have some effect on the amount of time he spends in his seat?"

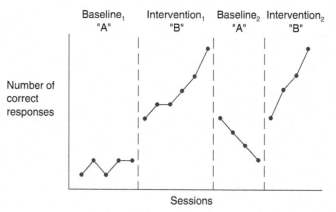

Figure 6.7 Reversal design graph that demonstrates a functional relationship between variables

Data collected using a reversal design can be examined for a functional relation between the dependent and independent variables. Figure 6.7 demonstrates a functional relation between the dependent and independent variables, said to exist if the second set of baseline data returns to a level close to the mean in the original A phase or if a trend is evident in the second A phase in the opposite direction of the first B phase. Figure 6.8 does not demonstrate the existence of a functional relation.

Cooper (1981, p. 117) stated that researchers need three pieces of evidence before they can say that a functional relation is demonstrated: (1) *prediction:* the instructional statement that a particular independent variable will alter the dependent variable—for example, the contingent use of tokens to increase the number of math problems Michael completes; (2) *verification of prediction:* the increase (or decrease) in the dependent variable during the first intervention phase, and the approximate return to baseline levels of performance in the second A phase; and (3) *replication of effect:* the reintroduction of the independent variable during a second B phase resulting again in the same desired change in behavior.

The reversal design is a research design that allows the teacher to assume a functional relation between independent and dependent variables. The second baseline and intervention phases, with conditions identical to those of the first, provide an

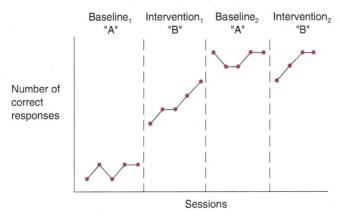

Figure 6.8 Reversal design graph that does not demonstrate a functional relationship between variables

opportunity for replication of the effect of the intervention on the target behavior. It is unlikely that confounding variables would exist simultaneously with repeated application and withdrawal of the independent variable. The reversal design, however, is not always the most appropriate choice. The reversal design should not be used in the following cases:

1. When the target behavior is dangerous, such as aggressive behavior directed toward other students or self-injurious behavior. Because the reversal design calls for a second baseline condition to be implemented after a change in the target behavior rate, ethical considerations would prohibit withdrawing a successful intervention technique.
2. When the target behavior is not reversible. Many academic behaviors, for example, are not reversible, because the behavior change is associated with a learning process. Under such conditions, a return to baseline performance is not feasible. Knowledge that 4 × 3 = 12, for example, is not likely to be "unlearned." At least, we would like to think not.

> It would be unethical to withdraw, for purposes of research, an intervention that stopped a student with severe disabilities from banging her head on the floor.

Graphic Display

The reversal design calls for four distinct phases of data collection. Figure 6.9 illustrates the basic reversal design. (Note that ABAB is derived from the labeling of each baseline period as an A phase and each intervention period as a B phase.)

Design Variations

Variations of the reversal design can be found in the literature. The first variation does not involve a change in the structure of the design, but simply shortens the length of the initial baseline (A) period. This format of the design is appropriate when a lengthy baseline period is unethical, as when the behavior is dangerous, or not called for, as in the case of a student who is not capable of performing the target behavior to any degree.

A second variation of the reversal design omits the initial baseline entirely. This BAB variation is considered if the target behavior is obviously not in the student's repertoire or when a teacher or researcher wants to show a functional relation of an intervention that is already in place. When

Figure 6.9 Basic reversal design format

"A" Baseline₁	"B" Intervention₁	"A" Baseline₂	"B" Intervention₂

Figure 6.10 Research application of the reversal design

NOTE: From "Self-Monitoring for Elementary School Children with Serious Emotional Disturbances: Classroom Applications for Increased Academic Responding," by L. Levendoski & G. Cartledge, 2000, *Behavioral Disorders*. Copyright 2000 by Council for Children with Behavioral Disorders. Reprinted by permission.

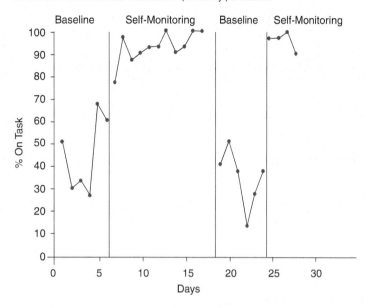

this design is used, a functional relation between the dependent and independent variables can be demonstrated only in the second intervention (B) phase.

Application

Researchers often use the ABAB design. Levendoski and Cartledge (2000) employed it to determine the effectiveness of a self-monitoring procedure for time on task and academic productivity with elementary-age students with emotional disturbance. The four boys were given self-monitoring cards at the beginning of each math period. They were told that each time they heard the bell (every 10 minutes), they should "Ask yourself ... am I doing my work?" They were then to mark yes or no on their cards.

Figure 6.10 shows the results of this intervention for time on task for one of the boys. During the baseline condition when the self-monitoring card was not being used, he was on task an average of 45% of the time. Once the intervention was in place, his time-on-task average increased to 93%. During the return to baseline phase, his on-task average returned to 34%, and then increased again to an average of 96% during reintroduction of the self-monitoring card. Examination of the graph clearly shows that when the student was using the self-monitoring card; his time on task increased. Note that phases 1 and 2 are replicated by phases 3 and 4, allowing a determination of a functional relation.

Goodnight, Whitley, and Brophy-Dick (2019) used an ABAB design to assess the role of response cards on the participation and disruptive behavior of five typically developing fourth graders during language arts lessons in an inclusive classroom in an urban school. The response card in this study was an 8.5" x 11" piece of cardstock paper with the letters A–D and a clothespin so that all students could show answers to multiple-choice questions. Participation was defined as answering a question from the teacher, either by raising a hand or using a response card. Disruptive behavior was either talking with a neighbor, walking around, tapping objects, or calling out during instruction. In the Hand Raising condition (the A condition), the teacher asked questions, projected them on a screen, asked the students to raise a hand, called on a student who raised a hand, and provided feedback

Amos Works Independently on the Computer

Ms. Fredrick is a second-grade teacher with 27 students. While she conducts reading instruction with individuals and small groups, other class members work independently on vocabulary-building exercises using computers. She has become concerned that Amos appears to be doing very little work. During 5 days of baseline data collection, Amos completed an average of 11 examples during a 30-minute session compared to the class average of 24. With her concern confirmed by these data, Ms. Fredrick developed the following intervention plan. She shared with Amos the data about the amount of work he has done and asked him to keep a bar graph for a week showing how many examples he completed each session and how that compared to the class average.

Ms. Fredrick and Amos agreed that he would get one token each day that his completion rate was within 3 examples of the class average and one additional token for each additional example. During 5 days of this intervention, Amos completed within 2 examples of the class average each session. To determine if a functional relation existed between the intervention and the change in Amos's performance, Ms. Fredrick returned to baseline conditions. Amos's target behavior immediately returned to its previous level. The next week, reinitiating the intervention immediately brought Amos's performance behavior back to the target level. Ms. Fredrick felt confident the intervention had changed Amos's behavior.

to that student. In the Response Cards (B) condition, the teacher handed out response cards, asked similar questions, projected the questions, asked students to mark an answer, said, "Cards up," and provided feedback to the class. One student emitted an average of 1 instance of participation in the A condition (both phases) and an approximate average of 15 instances of participation in the B condition (both phases). The other four students responded similarly (see Figure 6.11). There was not a meaningful difference in disruptive behavior between the two conditions. The consistency of the data and clear functional relations for the five students give teachers confidence that response cards will increase participation for similar students in similar classrooms.

The vignette on the previous page illustrates the use of an ABAB design in the classroom.

Advantages and a Disadvantage

As the preceding applications show, the reversal design offers the advantages of simplicity and experimental control. It provides for precise analysis of the effects of a single independent variable on a single dependent variable.

The primary disadvantage of this design is the necessity for withdrawing an effective intervention in order to determine whether a functional relation exists. Even if the target behavior is neither dangerous nor irreversible, it often seems foolish to teachers to stop doing something that is apparently working.

Changing Criterion Design

The **changing criterion design** evaluates the effectiveness of an independent variable by demonstrating that a behavior can be incrementally increased or decreased toward a terminal performance goal. This design includes two major phases. The first phase (as in all single-subject research designs) is baseline. The second phase is intervention. The intervention phase is composed of subphases. Each subphase has an interim criterion toward the terminal goal. Each subphase requires a closer approximation of the terminal behavior or level of performance than the previous one. The student's performance thus moves incrementally from the baseline level to the terminal objective.

The changing criterion design is particularly appropriate when the terminal goal of behavior change is considerably distant from the student's baseline level. For example, if the goal is for the student to read 60 sight words, and her baseline level of performance is 5 words, it is probably unreasonable for the teacher to instruct and for her to learn all 55 words at once. It is better instructional and reinforcement practice for her to acquire a smaller number of words at a time. Similarly, if the goal is for the student to remain in his seat for 40 continuous minutes so he can be successful in an inclusive class, and his baseline level of performance is 5 continuous minutes, it is probably unreasonable to expect him to be able to master the entire 40 minutes at one time. It is more within his reach, and will provide

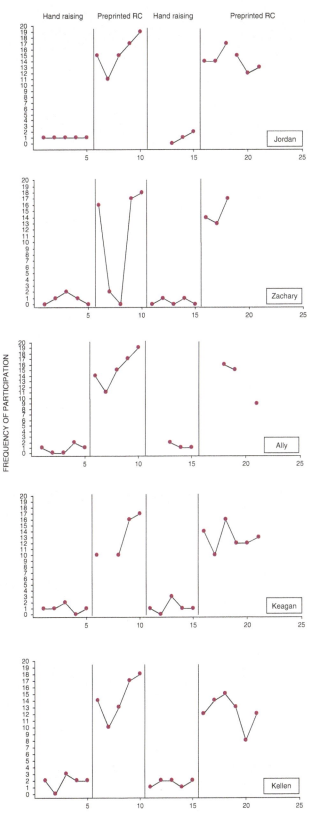

Figure 6.11 Research example of the reversal design
NOTE: From: Goodnight, C. I., Whitley, K. G., & Brophy-Dick, A. A. (2019). Effects of response cards on fourth-grade students' participation and disruptive behavior during language arts lessons in an inclusive elementary classroom. Journal of Behavioral Education.

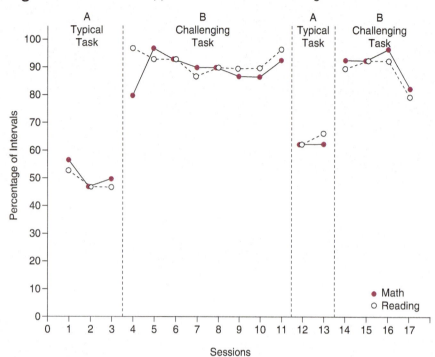

Figure 6.12 Research application of the reversal design

many more opportunities for reinforcement, if he is brought gradually to the terminal goal of 40 continuous minutes in his seat.

The changing criterion design is well suited for measuring the effectiveness of a shaping procedure (see Chapter 10). This design is also useful when the teacher wants to accelerate or decelerate behaviors measured in terms of frequency, duration, latency, or force.

Implementation

The first step in implementing the changing criterion design is to gather baseline data in the same manner used in other single-subject designs. After a stable baseline has been established, the teacher must determine the level of performance change that will be required for each subphase during intervention. The choice of the first interim level of performance may be determined using one of several techniques:

1. The interim criterion for performance can be set at, and then increased by, an amount equal to the mean of the stable portion of the baseline data. This technique is appropriate when the goal of the behavior-change program is to increase a level of performance and when the student's present level is quite low. For example, if a teacher wants to increase the number of questions a student answers and the student's mean baseline level of correct responses was two, that teacher might set two correct answers as a first interim criterion. Each subsequent subphase would then require two additional correct answers.
2. Interim criteria for performance can be set at half the mean of the baseline. If during the first intervention subphase raising the criterion by the mean of the baseline would make the task too difficult for the student, then raising it half that much may be appropriate. If the student's performance during the first intervention subphase is higher than a criterion equal to the mean of the baseline, the interim criterion may be raised by a level twice that of the mean of the baseline.
3. Interim criteria can be based on selecting the highest (or lowest, depending on the terminal objective) level of baseline performance. This is probably most appropriate for use with social behavior, such as out-of-seat occurrences or positive peer interactions, rather than for an academic behavior. The assumption is that if the student were able to perform at that high (or low) level once, the behavior can be strengthened (or weakened) and maintained at the new level.
4. Interim criteria can be based on a professional estimate of the student's ability. This procedure is particularly appropriate when the student's present level of performance is zero.

Regardless of the technique a teacher uses to establish the initial criterion, the data collected should be used to evaluate whether the amount of criterion change for each subphase is appropriate for a particular student.

The next step in implementing the changing criterion design is to begin the intervention phases. In each phase, if the student performs at least at the level of the interim criterion, the teacher provides reinforcement. It is important for the teacher to analyze the appropriateness of the selected interim level of performance during the initial intervention phase. If the student does not meet the criterion after a reasonable number of trials, the teacher should consider decreasing the interim level of performance required for reinforcement. Conversely, the teacher should consider adjusting the interim level of performance required for reinforcement if the student attains the goal too easily.

After the student has reached the established level of performance in a predetermined number of consecutive sessions (usually two, or in two out of three consecutive sessions of a subphase), the level of performance required for reinforcement should be adjusted in the direction of the desired level of performance for the overall behavior-change program. Each successive interim level of performance should be determined using the same mathematical difference established at the first interim level of performance. That is, the behavior-change program should reflect a uniform, step-by-step increase or decrease in criterion level. This process is continued until:

1. The behavior is increased to a 100% level or decreased to a 0% level of performance, or
2. The final goal established by the teacher in the behavioral objective is attained.

A functional relation between the dependent and the independent variable is demonstrated if the student's performance level matches the continually changing criterion for performance and reinforcement specified by the teacher (Kazdin, 2011; Richards, Taylor, Ramasamy, & Richards, 1999). This method of assessing a functional relation is based on the view that repeated matching to a changing criterion represents instances of replication. Each subphase with its interim criterion serves as the baseline for the increased (or decreased) criterion of the next subphase (Cooper, Heron, & Heward, 2020; Hartmann & Hall, 1976). Generally, a student must meet the established criteria in at least three consecutive phases before the assumption of a functional relation is valid.

> Changing criterion designs enable teachers and researchers to establish functional relations.

Graphic Display

The basic changing criterion design format is similar to the one used for the AB design. A baseline phase is followed by the intervention phase, with a vertical line separating the two conditions and each subphase. Figure 6.13 shows that the data for the intervention phase are identified according to the level of performance selected for reinforcement. The procedure for graphing the data calls for connecting data points within each subphase. Data points collected in different interim phases or subphases are never connected. The magnitude of student behavior necessary for consequation (delivery of reinforcement) should be clearly identified at each level of the intervention phase (see Figure 6.13).

Application

Hall and Fox (1977) used the changing criterion design to increase the number of math problems correctly solved by a child with a behavior disorder. Under baseline conditions, the student demonstrated a mean level of performance of one math problem.

The first interim level of performance was established at the next whole number greater than the mean baseline performance (2). If the student met this level of performance, he was allowed to play basketball. If the student failed to reach the criterion, he had to stay in the math session until the problems were solved correctly. Figure 6.14 shows that this process was continued until 10 math problems were solved correctly.

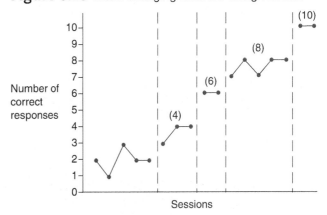

Figure 6.13 Basic changing criterion design format

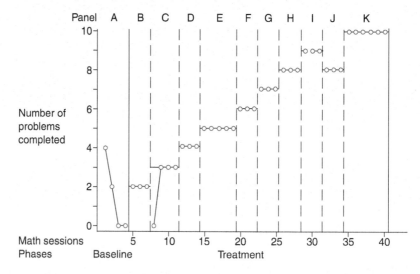

Figure 6.14 Research application of the changing criterion design

NOTE: From "Changing Criterion Designs an Applied Behavior Analysis Procedure," by R. V. Hall & R. G. Fox, in B. C. Etzel, J. M. LeBlanc, & D. M. Baer (Eds.), *New Developments in Behavioral Research: Theory Method and Application.* Copyright 1977 by Lawrence Erlbaum Associates, Inc., Publishers. Reprinted with permission of the authors and the publishers.

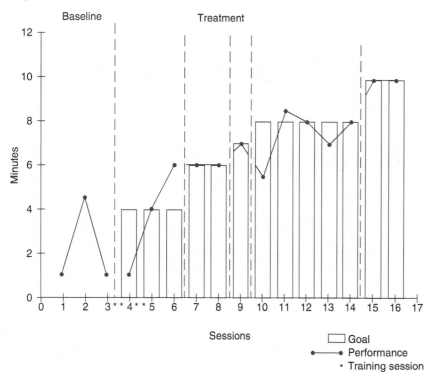

Figure 6.15 Application of the changing criterion design

McDaniel and Bruhn (2016) used a changing criterion design to demonstrate the effects of a Check In/Check Out (CICO) system on appropriate classroom behaviors with two middle school students with histories of conduct problems and disruptive behavior. The CICO card contained scores (0–2) for five expectations: punctual, respectful, organized, winning attitude, and learning. Five teachers provided scores five times each day, resulting in the opportunity to earn 50 points each day. See Figure 6.16 for one students results. In baseline, the teachers completed the cards without conferring with the students, and the students both earned an average of 40% of possible points. In the first intervention phase, the CICO coordinator (a teacher or school psychologist) met with each student and set a goal of earning 40% of possible points for the day. The CICO coordinator provided behavior-specific praise for meeting the goal and corrective feedback for not meeting the goal. The students increased to averages of 62% and 69%. Then the coordinator set the goal at 75% resulting in the students earning averages of 78% and 79%. The highest goal was 85%, and the students scored averages of 83% and 86%. At this point, experimental control was demonstrated because the data matched the different criteria. To gain additional experimental control, the researchers reversed to the Baseline condition (no goal set), and this resulted in decreases to averages of 64% and 72%. When reinstating the 85% goal, the students scored averages of 97% and 100%. In addition to showing improvements on meeting classroom expectations, the students' problem behaviors decreased.

Figure 6.16 Research example of the changing criterion design

NOTE: From: McDaniel, S. C., & Bruhn, A. L. (2016). Using a changing-criterion design to evaluate the effects of check-in/check-out with goal modification. Journal of Positive Behavior Interventions, 18(4), 197–208.

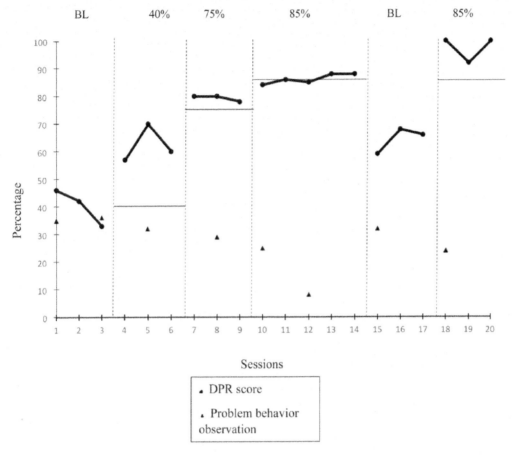

Certain procedural elements may increase the research credibility of the changing criterion design by enhancing experimental control:

1. Continuing with a subphase until a stable rate has been established

    For classroom use, maintaining a behavior at the interim criterion for two sessions (or two out of three sessions) before moving to the next subphase demonstrates sufficient control. Because, for research purposes, each subphase is seen as the baseline for the following subphase, the subphase may be continued until a stable rate has been established before starting the next subphase (Richards et al., 1999).

2. Altering the number of sessions in some subphases

    In Figure 6.14, three sessions at each interim criterion were generally maintained; however, this number of sessions was changed in some subphases. The lengths of subphases may vary with the behavior's remaining at criterion level as long as the criterion is in effect (Cooper et al., 2020). "It is stability after change has been achieved, and before introduction of the next change in criterion, that is crucial to producing a convincing demonstration of control" (Hartmann & Hall, 1976, p. 531).

3. Varying the increase (or decrease) in performance required in subphases

    In Figure 6.16, the subphase criteria when from 40% to 75% to 85%. Varying the size of criterion changes provides a more convincing demonstration of experimental control (Cooper et al., 2020).

4. Requiring a change in a direction opposite to the terminal goal in one or more phases

    In Figure 6.14, in subphase J, a change in the criterion for reinforcement was made in the direction opposite the terminal objective. Returning the student's performance level to a previously mastered criterion demonstrates a reversal effect similar to that of a return to baseline condition in an ABAB design.

> ## Claudia Learns to Sort by Color
>
> Claudia was a student in Mr. Carroll's intermediate class for students with moderate intellectual disability. Mr. Carroll was trying to teach Claudia to sort objects rapidly by color. Claudia could perform the task, but she did it too slowly. Mr. Carroll decided to use a changing criterion design to evaluate the effectiveness of a positive reinforcement procedure. He established that Claudia's average baseline rate of sorting was 4 objects per minute. He set 6 per minute as the first interim criterion and 30 per minute as the terminal goal. Claudia earned a poker chip exchangeable for a minute's free time when she met the criterion. When Claudia met the criterion on two consecutive trials or opportunities, Mr. Carroll raised the criterion required for reinforcement by two. He continued to do this until Claudia sorted 30 objects per minute in order to earn her poker chip. Mr. Carroll concluded that there was a functional relation between the dependent and independent variables, because Claudia's behavior changed quickly each time the criterion was changed but did not change until then.

The following anecdote illustrates the use of a changing criterion design in the classroom.

Advantage and Disadvantage

The advantage of the changing criterion design is that it can establish a functional relation while continually changing the behavior in a positive direction. There is no need to withdraw a successful intervention. Using the changing criterion design, however, necessitates very gradual behavior change. It may therefore be inappropriate for behaviors that require or lend themselves to rapid modification.

Multiple Baseline Design

When to use a multiple baseline design.

As indicated by its name, the **multiple baseline design** permits simultaneous analysis of more than one dependent variable. A teacher may experimentally test the effects of an intervention (the independent variable) on:

1. two or more behaviors associated with one student in a single setting, such as John's out-of-seat and talking-out behaviors in social studies class (*multiple baseline across behaviors*).
2. two or more students exhibiting the same behavior in a single setting, as in the spelling accuracy of Sara and Janet in English class (*multiple baseline across individuals*).
3. two or more settings in which one student is exhibiting the same behavior, such as Kurt's cursing during recess and in the school cafeteria (*multiple baseline across settings*).

The multiple baseline design is the design of choice when the teacher is interested in applying an intervention procedure to more than one individual, setting, or behavior. The multiple baseline design does not include a reversal phase; therefore, it may be used when the reversal design is not appropriate: when the target behavior includes aggressive actions or when academic learning is involved.

Implementation

A teacher using the multiple baseline design collects data on each dependent variable simultaneously. The teacher collects data under baseline conditions for each student, on each behavior, or in each setting. In establishing the data collection system, the teacher should select a y-axis scale that is appropriate for each of the variables involved in the program. To make data analysis possible, the same scale of measurement (for example, number of math problems completed correctly or percent of on-task behavior) should be used for each dependent variable.

After a stable baseline has been achieved on the first variable, intervention with that variable can be started. During the intervention period, baseline data collection continues for the remaining variables. Intervention on the second variable should begin when the first variable has reached the criterion established in the behavioral objective or when the data for the first variable show a trend in the desired direction as indicated by three consecutive data points. The intervention condition should be continued for the first variable, and baseline data should still be collected for any additional variables. This sequence is continued until the intervention has been applied to all the variables identified for the behavior-change program.

The data collected in a multiple baseline design can be examined for a functional relation between the independent variable and each of the dependent variables. The introduction of the intervention with the second and subsequent dependent variables constitutes a replication of effect. For example, after taking baseline data on Matt's on-task behavior in the special education resource class and in environmental science class, the teacher begins intervention in the resource class. Matt is presented with the contingency that if he is on task 85% of the times the teacher looks over at him, he will be able to reduce his homework assignment by 20%. The contingency goes into effect on Tuesday and continues for 4 days until his behavior meets this criterion. During these same 4 days the teacher has continued to take baseline data in the science class. Once Matt has reached the criterion in the resource class, the contingency is put into effect in the science class and continues to be in effect in the resource class. If Matt's on-task behavior is increased in the resource room and then increased in the science class, the teacher can say there is a functional relation between Matt's on-task behavior and earning a reduction in homework. There is a functional relation because the effect was first seen in the resource class and then replicated across settings in the environmental science class. A functional relation is assumed if each dependent variable in succession shows a change when, and only when, the independent variable is introduced.

Adjacent graphs should be examined to be sure that each successive intervention has an independent treatment effect on the appropriate dependent variable. Only the first independent variable should be affected by the first intervention. A change in the second and succeeding dependent variables should be seen only when the intervention is applied to them as well. Figure 6.17 shows an example of a functional relation, whereas Figure 6.18 does not. In Figure 6.18, the second dependent variable begins an upward trend when the intervention is introduced for the first variable, showing that the relations between variables are not discrete, or independent.

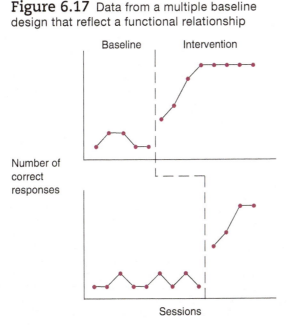

Figure 6.17 Data from a multiple baseline design that reflect a functional relationship

Figure 6.18 Data from a multiple baseline design that do not reflect a functional relationship

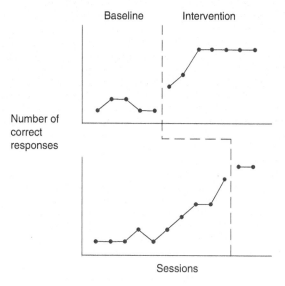

Figure 6.19 Basic multiple baseline design format

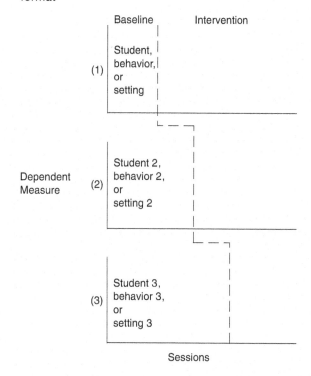

Graphic Display

When using the multiple baseline design, the teacher should plot the data collected using a separate axis for each of the dependent variables to which intervention was applied (individuals, behaviors, or situations). Figure 6.19 shows a composite graph of a multiple baseline design.

Application

ACROSS BEHAVIORS Leaf et al. (2016) used a multiple baseline design across behaviors to evaluate the effects of an intervention package on social game play with eight children with autism spectrum disorder (ages 3–5). The three games—sleeping game, fruit salad, and mousetrap—were similar to hide-and-seek and parachute games. The intervention was modeling, role play, positive reinforcement, and a "cool versus not cool" procedure in which the teachers modeled correct and incorrect ways to play the games. As shown in Figure 6.20, the participants did not play the games correctly in baseline, with the exception of 10%–25% correct in mousetrap. Upon implementation of the intervention at different points in time for each game, correct responding increased for the participants, reaching 100% correct in most cases. The skills also maintained. When the students showed an increase in correct playing of sleeping game, they remained at baseline (near zero) levels in fruit salad and mousetrap; when the students showed an increase in correct playing of fruit salad, they remained at baseline levels in mousetrap until intervention began with mousetrap. This pattern of data illustrates a functional relation between the intervention and the percentage of participants playing the game correctly.

ACROSS INDIVIDUALS Bouck, Park, Levy, Cwiakala, and Whorley (2020) used a multiple baseline design across individuals to evaluate the effects of app-based manipulatives on division skills with three middle school students with various disabilities (learning disability, autism spectrum disorder, and intellectual disability). The app was presented on an iPad and contained movable rods of different lengths that could be used as manipulatives to solve different types of math problems. The intervention also included explicit instruction, defined as modeling, prompting, and providing opportunities for independence. The target skill was solving division problems. As shown in Figure 6.21, all three students solved zero division problems correctly (except for Jesse solving 20% correct in Session 4). When the app and explicit instruction intervention were in place, all three students scored 100% correct in most of the sessions. The Generalization condition was identical to Baseline – just the math worksheet with no app or explicit instruction. Only Rori answered division problems correctly in that phase (80%–100%); Jesse and Dean scored 0% correct in that phase. Because Rori's data remained at baseline levels when Jesse showed an improvement, and Dean's data remained at baseline levels when Rori's responding increased, there was a functional relation between the intervention and the percentage of correctly solved division problems.

Figure 6.20 Research application of the multiple baseline design across behaviors

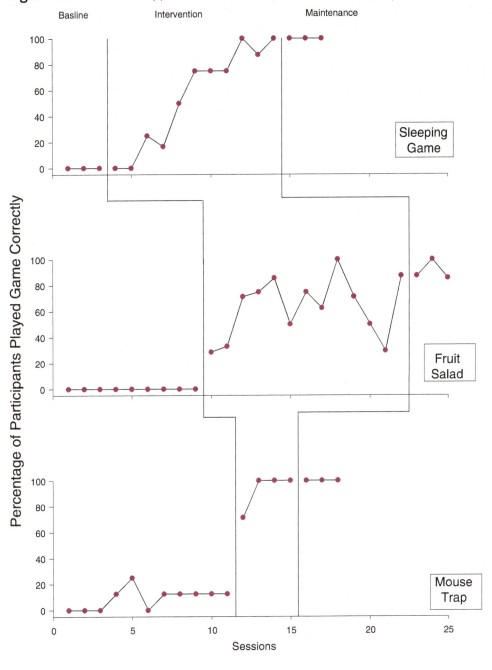

Researchers have used the multiple baseline design to look at the behavior of more than one student at once. They identify pairs of students, small groups of students, or even entire classes as a single unit, as was the case in Leaf et al. (2016). Performance in such cases may be reported either as an average of the target behavior as performed by the group or as the performance of individual members within the group (Aspiranti, Skinner, McCleary, & Cihak, 2011; Beaulieu & Hanley, 2014; Lane, Gast, Ledford, & Shepley, 2017; Leaf et al., 2017; Pinkelman & Horner, 2017; Therrien & Light, 2018).

ACROSS SETTINGS Dalton, Martella, and Marchand-Martella (1999) used a multiple baseline design across settings to evaluate the effects of a self-management program on the off-task behavior of two eighth-grade boys with learning disabilities. Off-task behavior was operationally defined as (a) not in seat (buttocks were not on the seat of chair, feet did not have to be on the floor), (b) talking with others

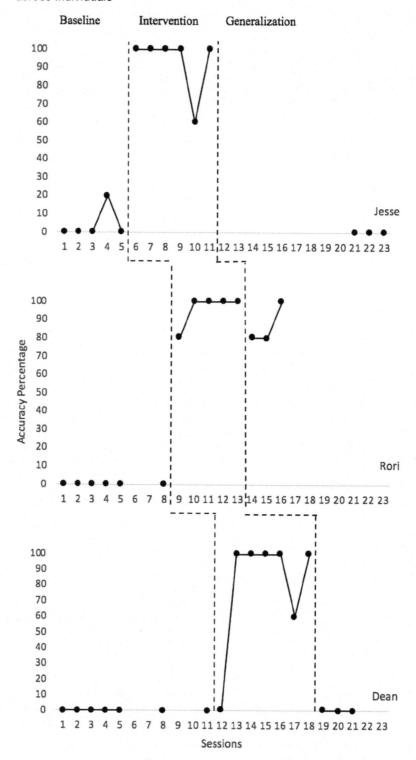

Figure 6.21 Research application of the multiple baseline design across individuals

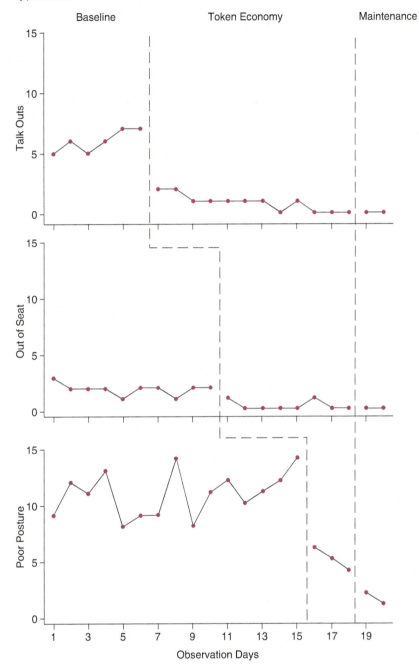

Figure 6.22 Graph of multiple baseline design across behaviors

NOTE: From "The Effects of a Token Economy Employing Instructional Consequences for a Third-Grade Student with Learning Disabilities," by J. Higgins, R. Williams, & T. McLaughlin, 2001. *Education and Treatment of Children*. Copyright 2001, by Family Services of Western PA. Reprinted by permission.

(student talking, whispering, or mouthing to others without permission), (c) interrupting others (passing a note, touching another student's body or possessions), (d) not working on assigned task (scribbling or doodling instead of writing, reading a magazine instead of the text), and (e) engaging in bodily movements unrelated to or interfering with assigned task (playing with pencil or ripping paper). Figure 6.24 presents Peter's graphed data. During baseline, "normal classroom procedures" were in place. These consisted of redirection, reprimand, removal from class, or detention. Peter's off-task behavior averaged 79% in science class, 87% in language arts, and 97% in learning opportunity center (study hall). The self-management program was

Figure 6.23 Graph of a multiple baseline design across individuals

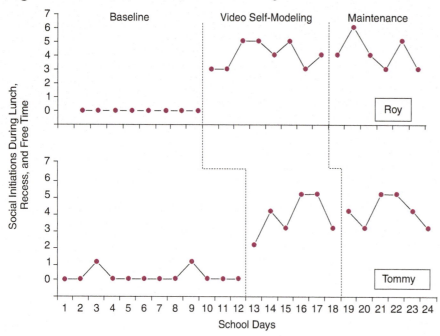

first introduced in science class, where time off task was reduced to an average of 17%; then in language arts, where it was reduced to an average of 21%; and finally in study hall, where his off-task behavior decreased to an average of 16%. Notice that the self-management program was initially used in science class, then replicated in language arts, and replicated a second time in the learning opportunity center. These successful replications allow for a conclusion that there was a functional relation between the dependent variable and the independent variable.

The vignette at the bottom of the page illustrates the use of a multiple baseline design in the classroom.

Advantages and Disadvantages

> A problem with the multiple baseline design—and a suggested solution.

The multiple baseline design can establish a functional relation without withdrawing the intervention, as is necessary in a reversal design, and without gradual alteration, as is required in a changing criterion design. These advantages make it a particularly useful design for classroom use. The multiple baseline design does, however, have some limitations. This design requires that the researcher apply the intervention to several students, behaviors, or settings, which may not always be practical. The multiple baseline design also requires collecting baseline data over extended periods, particularly baseline data for the second and subsequent dependent variables. When the student cannot perform the behavior at all or access to additional settings is not available or practical, collecting daily baseline data may take more time than is actually warranted or may not be possible. The **multiple probe technique** has been suggested as a reasonable solution to this situation (Horner & Baer, 1978). In this variation of the multiple baseline design, data are not continuously collected on the behaviors (or students or settings) on which intervention is not being conducted. Rather, probe trials (single trials under baseline conditions) or a probe session (more than one trial under baseline conditions) are

Students Learn to Come to Class on Time

Ms. Raphael was a middle school English teacher. The students in all three of her morning classes consistently came late. She began to record baseline data on the three classes. She recorded the number of students in their seats when the bell rang. She found that an average of five students in the first class, four in the second, and seven in the third class were in their seats. Ms. Raphael then began recording an extra-credit point in her grade book for each student in the first class who was in his or her seat when the bell rang. Within a week, 25 students were on time and in their seats.

The baseline data for the other classes showed no change during this first intervention. When she began giving extra-credit points in the second class, the number of students on time increased immediately and dramatically. After a week, she applied the intervention in the third class with similar results. Ms. Raphael had accomplished two things: she had succeeded in getting her classes to arrive on time and she had established a functional relation between her intervention (the independent variable) and her students' behavior (the dependent variable).

conducted intermittently on these subsequent behaviors to verify that the student still cannot perform the behavior or to record any changes in his or her ability before intervention. While using the intervention with behavior 1 (or with student 1 or in setting 1), the teacher intermittently probes behaviors 2 and 3. When behavior 1 reaches the criterion, one or more probe sessions are conducted on all three behaviors. Then intervention is begun on behavior 2. Postcheck probes are conducted on behavior 1 to establish that the change in behavior is being maintained, and baseline probes continue on behavior 3. When behavior 2 reaches the criterion, one or more probe sessions are conducted on all three behaviors. Then intervention is begun on behavior 3, while postcheck probes are conducted on behaviors 1 and 2.

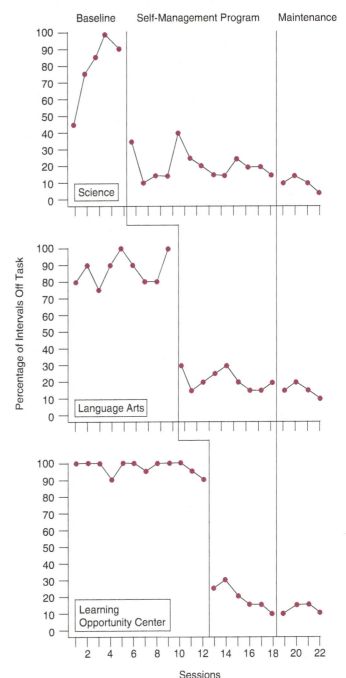

Figure 6.24 Research application of a multiple baseline design across settings

Alternating Treatments Design

In contrast to the multiple baseline design, which uses a single independent variable and multiple dependent variables, the **alternating treatments design** (Kazdin, 2011; Ledford & Gast, 2018) allows comparison of the effectiveness of more than one treatment or intervention strategy on a single dependent variable. For example, using this design, the teacher can compare the effects of two reading programs on a student's reading comprehension ability or the effects of two behavior-reduction procedures on a student's talking out. The teacher can also examine the efficiency of three different types of symbols on a student's communication board. The alternating treatments design is also known as the multi-element design (Cooper, Heron, & Heward, 2020).

Implementation

The first step in setting up an alternating treatments design is to select the target behavior and two or more potential treatments. If the target behavior is social (for example, asking appropriate questions or remaining on task), it should be operationally defined. If the target behavior is academic, two or more representative samples of the behavior (for example, two or more equally difficult sets of division problems) should be selected, each designated for one of the intervention or treatment strategies.

As the name of this design implies, the treatments are implemented alternately or in rotation. The presentation of the treatments may be in random order, such as ABBABAAB (Barlow & Hersen, 1984). When two treatments are used, the student should be exposed to each treatment an equal number of times. If there are three treatments, a block rotation may be used. Each block consists of one presentation of each treatment, for example, ABC, BCA, CAB, ACB, BAC, CBA. If data are collected long enough, each possible order of presentation should be used at least once.

The alternating treatments can be used sequentially within a single session (A followed by B), or from one session to the next (A in the morning, B in the afternoon of the same day), or on successive days (A on Monday, B on Tuesday). The scheduling should be counterbalanced; that is, the treatment that was employed first in one session should be used second in the next session; the treatment employed in the morning on the first day should be used in the afternoon on the second day; and the treatment that was used on Monday the first week should be used on Tuesday of the second week. (In research situations, similar counterbalancing is used to minimize the effects of other potential confounding variables such as the person administering the treatment and the location of the treatment.) This counterbalancing should control for the possibility of carryover and sequencing effects (Barlow & Hayes, 1979). In other words, by presenting the treatments in random order, the possible effects each treatment may have on the others will be minimized.

A distinctive discriminative stimulus, signal, or cue immediately preceding each treatment will make it clear to the student which condition is in effect. For example, the teacher might say, "This is treatment A" and "This is treatment B," or "Now we are going to use a number line" and "Now we are going to use counting chips." The teacher might also color code worksheets to indicate that a particular condition is in effect.

Graphic Display

The basic form of graphing the alternating treatments design is shown in Figure 6.25. As in all designs, baseline data are plotted first and separated from intervention data by a vertical line. The graph for the alternating treatments design differs from others in that several curves may be shown on each graph. The points for each treatment are connected only to other points for that treatment so that the data for each are displayed as separate lines, or curves.

If the data curve of one treatment is vertically separated from the other curves, it is said to be *fractionated*. This fractionation indicates that the treatments are differentially effective.

The top graph in Figure 6.25 shows data that demonstrate an effective treatment. Treatment A is the more effective of the two treatments. The data curves are separated; they do not cross at any point other than at the very beginning of the intervention phase. The two curves are fractionated. Figure 6.25 also shows data that are not substantially different from one another. The middle graph shows two treatments, neither of which demonstrates a meaningful change from baseline levels or a meaningful distance between each other. The bottom graph shows two treatments that show a change from baseline levels but not a substantial change between each other; thus, the conclusion is there is no difference between the treatments.

By visual inspection of the graphs, we may infer experimental control between one or more of the independent variables and the dependent variable.

> Because confounding factors such as time of administration have been neutralized (presumably) by counterbalancing, and because the two treatments are readily discriminable by subjects through instructions or other discriminative stimuli, differences in the individual plots of behavior change corresponding with each treatment should be attributable to the treatment itself, allowing a direct comparison between two (or more) treatments. (Barlow & Hayes, 1979, p. 200)

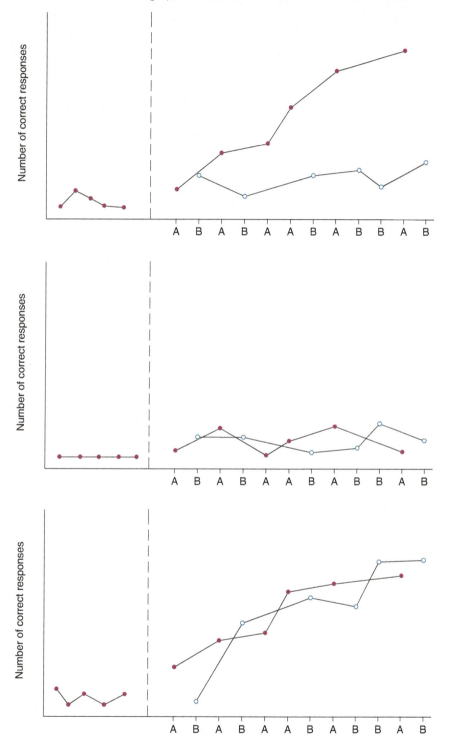

Figure 6.25 Graphs of data collected using an alternating treatments design. The top graph indicates treatment A is the more effective treatment. The middle and bottom graphs indicate no difference between treatments

A substantial distance between the data paths in an alternating treatments design allows a conclusion of a functional relation. As described thus far, the alternating treatments design does not include a replication phase. To strengthen conclusions of a functional relation, a third phase can be instituted. In this phase the more effective of the treatments is applied to the behavior that was exposed to the ineffective treatment during the intervention phase. If the second behavior then improves, a replication of

Figure 6.26 Three-phase alternating treatments design demonstrating functional relationship

the treatment has been accomplished and a stronger functional relation demonstrated. Figure 6.26 shows such a three-phase variation of the design.

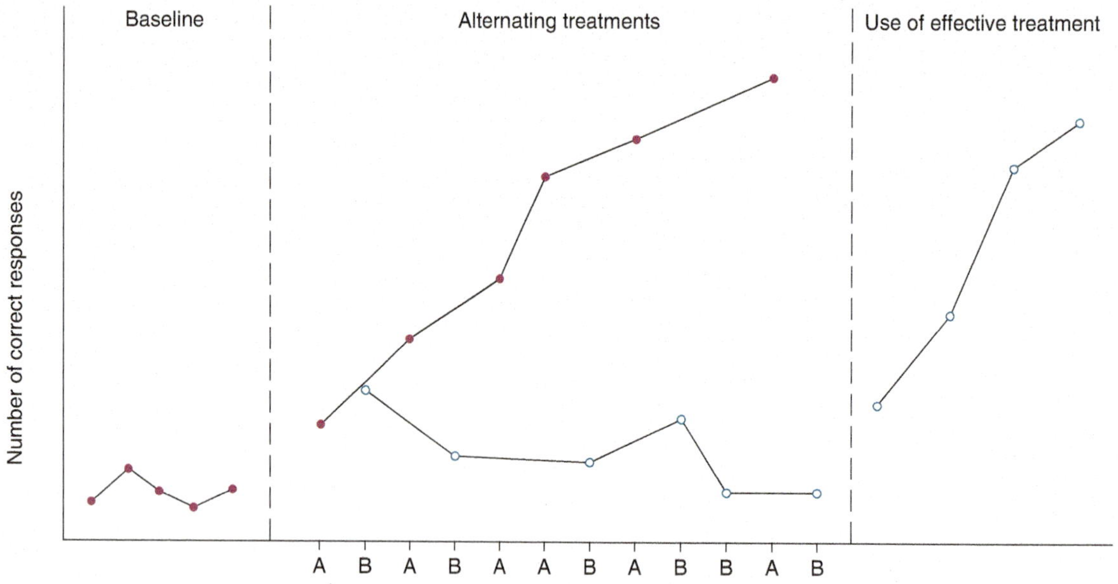

Application

Powell and Gadke (2018) used an alternating treatments design to compare two procedures for improving oral reading fluency with three middle-school students with a history of failure in English classes. Oral reading fluency was measured by giving a student a passage to read at their instructional level and recording the correct words read per minute. One procedure was repeated readings, in which each student read a passage two times with feedback on errors from the researcher. The other procedure was listening passage preview in which each student listened to the researcher read a passage one time while following along with their finger, and then the student read the passage one time. In the control condition, the student read a passage once with no feedback. Results as depicted in Figure 6.27 show that for Grant, the correct words per minute was highest

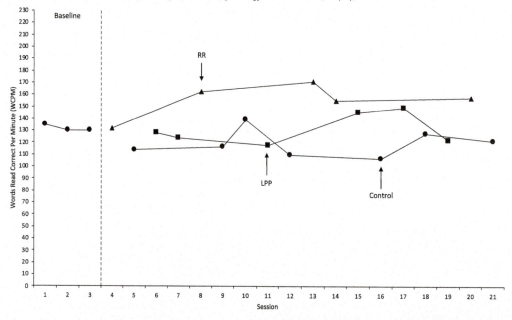

Figure 6.27 Research application of the alternating treatments design

NOTE: From: Powell, M. B., & Gadke, D. L. (2018). Improving oral reading fluency in middle-school students: A comparison of repeated reading and listening passage preview. *Psychology in the Schools, 55*(10), 1274–1286.

in the repeated readings condition compared to the listening passage preview and control conditions. These results, showing a functional relation, were similar for the other two students.

Davis, Dacus, Strickland, Machalicek, and Coviello (2013) used an alternating treatments design to evaluate a treatment for the self-injurious behavior of a nonverbal, 8-year-old boy with autism. The form of self-injurious behavior was placing objects or fingers into his ear to the point of items getting stuck or his ear getting enflamed or bleeding. One condition was providing noncontingent access to items that matched the stimulation to the boy's ears; these were acrylic balls (similar to cotton balls) that were safe and placed in his ears at the start of the sessions by the researcher. The other condition was noncontingent unmatched sensory stimulation in which the boy had continual access to his highest preferred item – a portable DVD player – as well as praise and physical contact every 10 seconds. As shown in Figure 6.28, the percentage of intervals with the self-injurious behavior was consistently and substantially lower in the matched stimuli condition compared to the unmatched stimuli condition. There is a clear functional relation due to the distance between the two data paths.

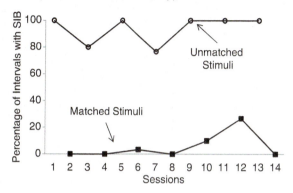

Figure 6.28 Research application of the alternating treatments design

NOTE: From: Davis, T. N., Dacus, S., Strickland, E., Machalicek, W., & Coviello, L. (2013). Reduction of automatically maintained self-injurious behavior utilizing noncontingent matched stimuli. *Developmental Neurorehabilitation, 16*(3), 166–171.

> Using an alternating treatments design can help teachers individualize instruction.

For teachers, the alternating treatments design can provide rapid and accurate feedback about the comparative effectiveness of various teaching techniques, as the following example shows.

Marcia Learns Sight Vocabulary

Mr. Hagan was a resource teacher for elementary students. He wanted one of his students, Marcia, to learn basic sight vocabulary on a first-grade level. He chose 15 words and established that Marcia's baseline rate for reading them was zero. Mr. Hagan then divided the words into three sets of five. One set he printed on cards accompanied by an audio recording tape that Marcia could use to hear the words pronounced. He assigned a peer tutor to work with Marcia on the second set, and the teacher worked with Marcia on the third set. Mr. Hagan recorded and graphed the number of words Marcia pronounced correctly each day for each set. Within a week, Marcia was pronouncing correctly the group of words learned with the peer tutor at a higher rate than that of either of the other sets. Mr. Hagan concluded that, for Marcia, peer tutoring was the most efficient way to learn sight vocabulary.

Advantages and Disadvantages

The alternating treatments design is an efficient way for teachers to answer one of the most important instructional questions: Which method is most likely to be successful with this student? Once clear fractionation appears, the teacher can select the most successful method using as few as three to five data points. One disadvantage is the necessity to institute a replication phase in order to establish a strong functional relation. However, this is likely to be of little practical importance to teachers.

Multiple Treatments Design

A **multiple treatments design** is used to investigate the effects of two or more treatments (independent variables) on the behavior of a student (dependent variable). Unlike in the alternating treatments design, the treatments in this design are introduced sequentially (Cooper, 1981; Kazdin, 2011; Ledford & Gast, 2018).

> The multiple treatments design reflects reality—teachers keep trying different techniques until they find one that works.

The design is useful for the teacher who finds it necessary to try a number of interventions before finding one that is successful with a particular student. The teacher is changing the conditions (for example, environmental conditions, instructional conditions, reinforcement conditions) under which the student is expected to perform the behavior.

Figure 6.29 Use of an alternating treatments design

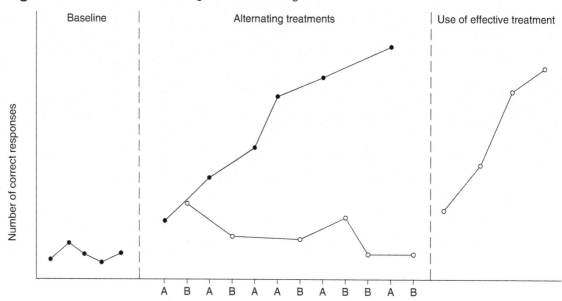

Implementation

The first step in implementing a multiple treatments design is to collect baseline data to assess the student's present level of performance. Once a stable baseline is established, the teacher can introduce the selected intervention and measure its effectiveness through data collection. If the data for the first intervention do not demonstrate a change in the student's performance or if the change is not of a sufficient magnitude or in the desired direction, the teacher may design a second intervention. This second intervention can be either a complete change in strategy or a modification of the earlier intervention. This process of redesigning intervention conditions is repeated until the desired effect on the student's behavior is achieved.

The multiple treatments design has three basic variations: (1) ABC, (2) ABAC, and (3) ABACAB (see Figure 6.30).

1. *ABC design:* The ABC design is used when the teacher is trying to judge the effectiveness between treatments, trying to put together an instructional package that will facilitate a student's performance, or trying to systematically remove forms of assistance to bring a student to a more independent performance.
    a. *Building an instructional package:* Starting from a student's current performance, the teacher implements an intervention. If the student's performance does not respond or does not respond sufficiently, new strategies are successively or cumulatively added until the student's performance meets criterion. This format is compatible with current models of Response to Intervention (RTI; Riley-Tillman, Burns, & Kilgus, 2020). As each piece is added to the instructional package, a new phase is identified. This design is simply an extended AB design. As in an AB design, there is no replication of the effect of interventions and there can be no assumption of a functional relation. Smith (1979) was trying to improve the oral reading of a student with learning disabilities. Following baseline, three cumulative phases were employed. First the teacher used teacher modeling. When the change in the student's performance was not sufficient, a correction procedure was added to the modeling. When this combined strategy still did not produce sufficient change, previewing was added. This package of three strategies was successful.
    b. *Fading assistance:* The teacher systematically reduces the amount of assistance being provided to a student in order to identify the least amount needed for

Figure 6.30 Variations of the multiple treatments design

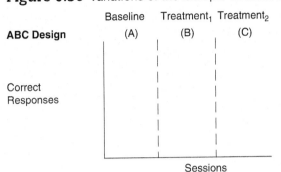

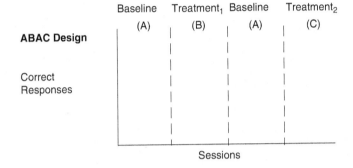

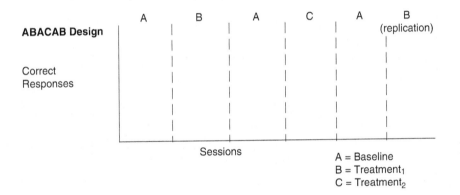

ongoing successful performance. Each reductive change is considered a new phase. Reductive changes might include reducing the intensity of antecedents, such as providing a student who is learning to print letters to trace in the first phase, densely spaced dots to connect in the second phase, more sparsely spaced dots in subsequent phases, and eventually to writing in the presence of just a line on the paper. Other changes might include reducing the amount of reinforcement or the frequency (schedule) of the delivery of reinforcement. Reducing the number of components of an instructional package is also an example of fading assistance. If, in order to be successful in writing a paragraph, a student initially needs to be given the topic, a picture depicting the topic, guidance through a verbal description of the picture, and a topic sentence, the teacher systematically removes each until the student is able to write a paragraph given just a topic.

2. *ABAC design*: In this design the teacher's implementation of two or more interventions is separated by additional baseline conditions: baseline, treatment 1, baseline, treatment 2, and so forth. The treatments may be completely different or variations of one treatment. Separating the treatments by intervening baseline conditions prevents one treatment's continuing to affect the student's behavior while another

treatment is being used, thus providing a clear picture of the effect of each of the treatments. It is not, however, considered definitive in establishing a functional relation as it lacks a replication phase. In a study by Coleman-Martin, Heller, Cihak, and Irvine (2005), three different interventions were compared to increase vocabulary: teacher-only instruction, teacher and computer-assisted instruction, and computer-assisted instruction only. The sequence of phases was: baseline, teacher only, baseline, teacher plus computer assisted, baseline and computer-assisted only.

3. *ABACAB design:* The data resulting from an ABC or ABAC design do not allow for a determination of a functional relation between the dependent variable and any of the independent variables. As is the case with an AB design, the data can give only an indication of the effectiveness of a particular intervention. The design can, however, be refined in order to demonstrate a functional relation. To assess the presence of a functional relation, there should be a replication of the effect of the intervention; therefore, following phases for each of the potential treatments, the one whose data indicate it is most successful is reimplemented after another baseline condition. If the treatment is successful again, this is a replication of its effect, and therefore a functional relation is demonstrated. This design may also be seen as a variation of an ABAB design.

Graphic Display

The format for the multiple treatments design is similar to that of the previous designs. A baseline phase is followed by the intervention phases, with a vertical line separating the sessions and data associated with each specific intervention. Figure 6.30 illustrates the three basic formats: ABC, ABAC, and ABACAB.

Application

O'Handley, Radley, and Cavell (2016) used an ABC design to evaluate the effects of a social skills curriculum on the disruptive behavior of six elementary-aged students with high incidence disabilities, such as ADHD and mild intellectual disability. The disruptive behavior was measured during 10-minute periods of free play and consisted of inappropriate vocalizations, inappropriate toy play, and aggression. After baseline, the researchers taught the social skills using video modeling, role play, and positive reinforcement. The first lessons were "Get Ready" and "Following Directions" from the "Instructional Control Skills" section of the curriculum. These skills included orienting to the speaker, making eye contact, and following instructions. As Figure 6.31 shows, the teaching of these skills did not reduce disruptive behavior substantially from baseline. The next strategy taught was "Turn Taking," defined as deciding who goes first, waiting for your turn, and ensuring all students have a turn. This lesson resulted in a dramatic decrease in disruptive behavior. A final follow-up condition showed that disruptive behavior remained low one and two weeks after the instruction ended. O'Handley et al. referred to this study as a "pilot study" as the ABC design does not allow a demonstration of experimental control.

Crozier and Tincani (2005) used a multiple treatments design with repeated baseline (ABAC) to compare two interventions to reduce the talking-out behavior of an 8-year-old boy with autism. The interventions were implemented during a 30-minute structured independent activity session in his classroom. Figure 6.32 presents the data recorded for Alex's talk-outs during each phase.

   a. During the first baseline, Alex averaged 11.2 talk-outs per session.
   b. During the first intervention, a social story strategy was implemented before the beginning of the activity session. The teacher and Alex sat side by side; the teacher handed Alex a book and said, "this is a story about talking at school." Alex read the story aloud and then answered questions to be sure he understood what he

Single-Subject Designs   151

Figure 6.31 Research application of the multiple treatments design (AEB = appropriately engaged behavior; DB = disruptive behavior)

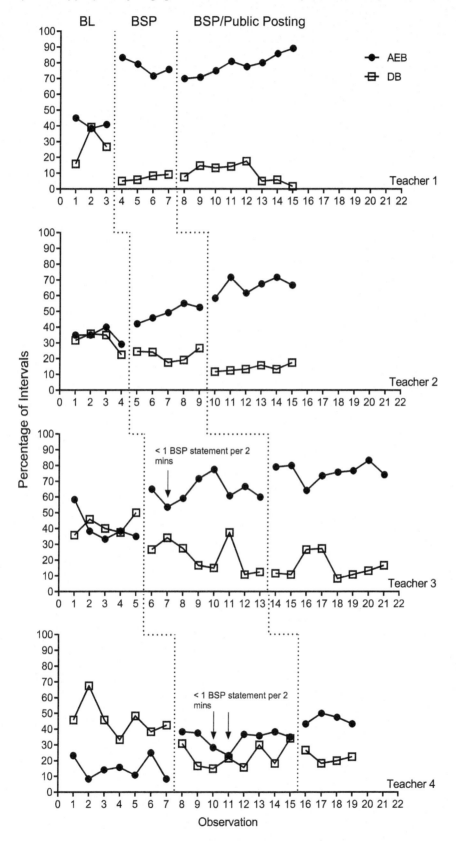

NOTE: From "Utilization of Superheroes Social Skills to Reduce Disruptive and Aggressive Behavior," by R. D. O'Handley, K. C. Radley, and H. J. Cavell, 2016, *Preventing School Failure*, *60*(2), 124–132. Reprinted with permission.

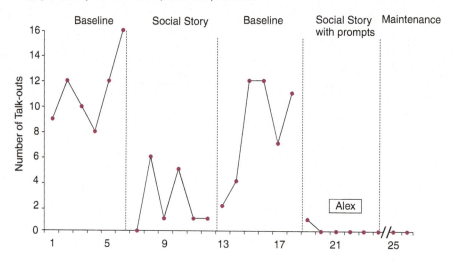

Figure 6.32 Use of a multiple treatments design

NOTE: From "Using a Modified Social Story to Decrease Disruptive Behavior of a Child with Autism," by S. Crozier & M. Tincani, 2005, *Focus on Autism and Other Developmental Disabilities, 20,* 150–157. Copyright 2005, by PRO-ED, Inc. Reprinted with permission.

read. During this intervention phase, talk-outs dropped to an average of 2.3 per session.

c. During the second baseline phase, when the intervention was suspended, Alex's talk-outs increased to an average of 8 per session.

d. In the second intervention phase, the teacher implemented the social story reading as before but added a verbal prompt from the teacher: "Remember to raise your hand when you want to talk to a teacher." This verbal prompt was delivered every 6 minutes during each session. Alex's talk-outs dropped to an average of 0.2 per session.

Roberta Learns to Shoot Baskets

Mr. Woods was recently hired to teach physical education at an elementary school. When he arrived at work, Mr. Woods was approached by the special education teacher, Ms. Jones. She was concerned about Roberta, a student with physical disabilities who would be in Mr. Woods's gym class. Roberta, who used a wheelchair, had difficulty with eye–hand coordination. Ms. Jones hoped the student could learn to throw a basketball. Learning to play basketball would provide coordination training and a valuable leisure skill for Roberta. Mr. Woods agreed that the basketball skill seemed appropriate.

Mr. Woods decided to use a systematic approach to instruction. He asked Roberta to throw the basketball 20 times to see how often she could place the ball through a lowered hoop. This procedure was followed for five gym periods with no additional instruction until a baseline performance rate was determined. Mr. Woods then decided to use a modeling technique. He showed Roberta how to throw the ball and asked her to imitate him. Very little improvement was noted in five class periods. Mr. Woods met with the special education teacher to determine what could be done.

Ms. Jones carefully reviewed all the data and suggested changing the intervention. She explained that a change in intervention seemed necessary and that a modeling procedure could be used in combination with keeping score on a chart.

Mr. Woods agreed to try this. In 2 weeks, Roberta showed improvement but still missed more baskets than she hit. A final condition was implemented using modeling, scorekeeping, and a correction procedure. Mr. Woods now showed Roberta how to throw, recorded her score, and showed her exactly what she did wrong when she missed. This combination of procedures resulted in Roberta's being able to throw a basketball through a hoop 15 out of 20 times. A suggestion was made to Roberta's parents that a hoop be constructed at her home so that she could enjoy her new skill after school.

Two probes 2 weeks after the final intervention session indicated that the change in Alex's behavior was maintained.

The vignette on the previous page shows how a multiple treatments design can be used in teaching.

Advantages and Disadvantages

The multiple treatments design with a single baseline allows the teacher to compare the effects of a number of interventions on student behavior. Although no functional relation can be established, recording data in this format allows the teacher to monitor the effects of various procedures on student behavior. The teacher should be aware, however, that what he or she may be seeing is the cumulative effects of the interventions rather than the effects of any one intervention in isolation. Individual analysis of the effects of the interventions can be made using the repeated baselines format of the multiple treatments design. The teacher who records data systematically in a multiple treatments design will have a record of the student's progress and a good indication of what procedures are effective with that student.

The six single-subject designs we described were the AB, ABAB (reversal), changing criterion, multiple baseline, alternating treatments, and multiple treatments. A summary of the uses, formats, and types of questions answered by each of these designs is presented in Table 6.2.

Comparing Single-Subject Designs
Pearson eText
Video Example 6.2
In this video, an educator presents several single-subject design graphs. She highlights the role of visual analysis for the various graph types. Notice how she relates her analysis back to the efficacy of the intervention and a functional relation.

https://www.youtube.com/watch?v=RhNY5Nur0SU

| Multiple treatments is a teaching design.

Table 6.2 Summary of single-subject research designs

Design	Use	Format	Example Questions
AB	To document changes in behavior during baseline and intervention. Does not allow for determination of a functional relation—lacks a replication of the effect of the independent variable (intervention) on the dependent variable (behavior).	*Two Phases* 1. Baseline 2. Intervention	1. Will Sam's mastery of sight words increase when I use a time delay procedure for instruction? 2. Will Sam's call-out behavior decrease when I reinforce hand raising with tokens?
ABAB Reversal	To determine if a functional relation exists between an independent variable and a dependent variable by replicating the baseline and intervention phases.	*Four Phases* 1. Baseline 2. Intervention 3. Return to baseline 4. Return to intervention	1. Could the number of words Sam writes in a paragraph increase due to use of a point system? 2. Could Sam's off-task behaviors decrease due to use of a self-recording procedure?
Changing Criterion	To increase or decrease a behavior in systematic increments toward a terminal criterion. Allows for determination of a functional relation if performance level matches the continually changing interim criteria.	Baseline plus an intervention phase for each interim criterion toward the objective; e.g., 10 phases of interim criteria raising 5 words per phase until criterion of 50 words.	1. Can I use a time delay procedure to systematically increase the pool of Sam's sight words to a criterion of 100 words? 2. Can I use token reinforcers to systematically decrease the number of times Sam runs in the hall during change of class to a criterion of no occurrences?
Multiple Baseline	To determine if a functional relation exists between an independent variable and a dependent variable by assessing replication across behaviors, individuals, or settings.	Baseline and staggered intervention phase for each replication, e.g., across behaviors: baseline and intervention for Sara's call-outs and then out-of-seat behaviors; across students: baseline and intervention for cursing by Bob and then Ted; across settings: baseline and intervention in the resource class and then consumer math class.	1. a. Will the use of reinforcement of Linda's hand raising result in a decrease in the number of occurrences of both call-outs and out-of-seat without permission? b. Will the use of a learning strategy such as content mastery increase Linda's completion of American history assignments and biology assignments? 2. a. Will the use of points to earn the opportunity to be a team captain result in decrease in cursing by Bob, Ted, and Linda? b. Will the use of a calculator increase the accuracy of grocery purchasing by both Bob and Ted? 3. a. Will the use of self-recording result in a decrease in the occurrences of out-of-seat behavior by Linda in the resource room, consumer math class, and music class? b. Will the use of tokens increase the number of math problems completed by Linda in both the resource class and consumer math class?

(Continued)

Table 6.2 Summary of single-subject research designs (Continued)

Design	Use	Format	Example Questions
Alternating Treatments	To determine which of two or more independent variables is more effective for increasing or decreasing occurrences of a dependent variable. Has the ability to determine the existence of a functional relation by observing a distance between the data paths in the intervention phase; a functional relation is strengthened by replicating use of the more effective independent variable in an additional phase.	*Two or Three Phases* 1. Baseline 2. Intervention phase in which each independent variable is applied on alternating days, or alternating sessions during the same day. 3. Replicating the more effective intervention with the content taught by the less effective; or at the time period in which the less effective intervention was used.	1. Will the use of a number line or counting chips increase Jane's accuracy in addition? 2. Will the use of earning points or losing points prove more effective in decreasing Jane's off-task behavior?
Multiple Treatments	To determine which of two or more independent variables is more effective for increasing or decreasing occurrences of a dependent variable. A functional relation may be determined by replication of more effective independent variable following an additional baseline phase.	Multiple phases: e.g., Baseline, Intervention 1, Intervention 2; Baseline, Intervention 1, Baseline, Intervention 2; Baseline, Intervention 1, Baseline, Intervention 2, Baseline, Intervention 1	1. Will oral and written practice increase Jane's spelling accuracy on a test, or will oral practice alone be just as effective, or will written practice alone be just as effective? 2. Will point loss or point loss plus verbal reprimands be more effective in decreasing Jane's tardiness to classes?

Evaluating Single-Subject Designs

Learning Outcome 6.4 **Evaluate the outcomes of an intervention.**

Analysis of Results

> Social validity was discussed at length in Chapter 2.

The purpose of using applied behavior analysis procedures in the classroom is to achieve, and verify, meaningful changes in a student's behavior. The effectiveness of an intervention can be judged against both an experimental criterion and a clinical criterion. The experimental criterion verifies that an independent variable (an intervention) was responsible for the change in the dependent variable (a behavior). Single-subject designs demonstrating within-subject replications of effects satisfy this criterion (Baer, Wolf, & Risley, 1968; Cooper, Heron, & Heward, 2020; Kazdin, 2011; Kennedy, 2005; Ledford & Gast, 2018).

The *clinical criterion* is a judgment as to whether the results of the teacher's intervention are "large enough to be of practical value or have impact on the everyday lives of those who receive the intervention, as well as those in contact with them" (Kazdin, 2001, p. 153). For example, the teacher should ask herself whether it is truly meaningful to increase a student's grade from a D– to a D (Baer et al., 1968), or to decrease a student's self-injurious behavior from 100 to 50 instances per hour (Kazdin, 2001), or to reduce a student's off-task behavior in the special education class while it remains high in a general educational class. The teacher should ask if the student's behavior has decreased sufficiently so as to no longer interfere with other students' learning, or with the ability of his or her family to carry out its activities at home and in the community.

A third criterion for evaluating the outcome of an intervention is its *social validity*. Those involved with the student's educational program should be concerned about and evaluate the social acceptability of an intervention program and its outcome (Kazdin, 1977b; Snodgrass, Chung, Meadan, & Halle, 2018; Wolf, 1978). Social validity data can be gathered by asking people in a student's environment, such as parents and teachers, how much they agree with the procedures and results. Another method of collecting social validity data is allowing students to choose from an array of interventions (Hanley, 2010).

Using Graphs To Make Decisions
Pearson eText
Video Example 6.3
In this video, an educator describes how analysis of graphs is the foundation of decision-making in her classroom. Consider what types of designs may be most useful for evaluating student performance in her classroom.

Visual Analysis of Graphs

Intervention effects in applied behavior analysis are usually evaluated through *visual analysis* of the graph displaying the plotted data points of the various phases (conditions). Certain characteristics of the data paths within and across phases are examined in order to judge the effectiveness of the intervention. These characteristics include the *mean* of the data points in the phase, the *levels* of performance from one phase to the next, the *trend* in performance across phases, the *percentage* of data that overlap in adjacent phases, and the *rapidity* of behavior change within phases (Cooper et al., 2020; Kazdin, 2011; Kennedy, 2005; Kratochwill et al., 2013; Ledford & Gast, 2018).

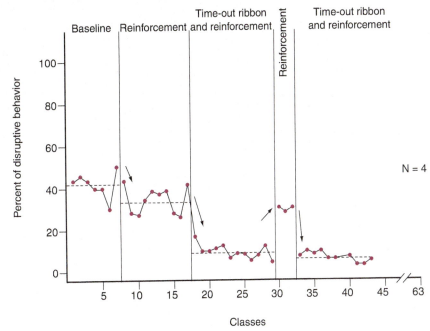

Figure 6.33 Graph for visual inspection of data

NOTE: From "The Timeout Ribbon: A Nonexclusional Timeout Procedure," by R. Foxx & S. Shapiro, 1978, *Journal of Applied Behavior Analysis*. Copyright 1978 by The Society for the Experimental Analysis of Behavior. Reprinted by permission.

1. Evaluation of changes in means focuses on the change in the average level of student performance across the phases of a design. Within each phase, the mean (average) of the data points is determined and may be indicated on the graph by drawing a horizontal line corresponding to the value on the *y*-axis scale. Visual inspection of the relation of these means will help determine if the intervention resulted in consistent and meaningful changes in the behavior in the desired direction of change. In Figure 6.33, Foxx and Shapiro (1978) supplied such indicators of means. The viewer can easily see the relative position of the students' disruptive behavior across the various design phases.

2. Evaluation of the level of performance refers to the magnitude and direction of the change in student performance from the end of one phase to the beginning of the next phase. "When a large change in level occurs immediately after the introduction of a new condition, the level change is considered abrupt, which is indicative of a powerful or effective intervention" (Tawney & Gast, 1984, p. 162). Tawney and Gast suggested the following steps to determine and evaluate a level change between two adjacent conditions: (1) identify the *y*-axis value of the last data point of the first condition and the first data point value of the second condition, (2) subtract the smallest value from the largest, and (3) note whether the change in level is in an improving or decaying direction (p. 162). In Figure 6.33, the arrows have been added to indicate level changes.

3. Evaluation of a trend in performance focuses on systematic and consistent increases or decreases in performance. Data trends may be evaluated using a procedure known as the *quarter-intersect method* (White & Liberty, 1976). Evaluation of trends is based on lines of progress developed from the median value of the data points in each phase. The use of a trend line increases the reliability of visual analysis among people looking at a graph (Manolov, 2018; Ottenbacher, 2016). This is of particular importance as teams of teachers, students, parents, and other concerned individuals review student data to assess progress and make decisions about future instruction or intervention. Steps for computing lines of progress are

Figure 6.34 Steps for computing lines of progress

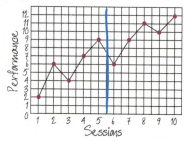

1. Divide the number of data points in half by drawing a vertical line down the graph.

In this example, there are 10 data points; therefore, the line is drawn between sessions 5 and 6. If there had been an odd number of data points, this would have been drawn through a session point.

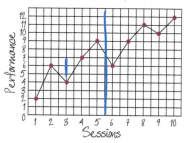

2. On the left half of the graph, find the midsession and draw a vertical line.

In this example, there are five data points; therefore, the line is drawn at session 3. If there had been an even number of sessions, this line would have been drawn between two session points.

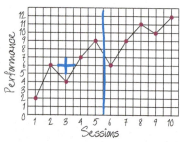

3. On the left half of the graph, find the mid-performance point and draw a horizontal line.

In this example, the data point at performance value 6 is the midperformance point because there are two data points below it and two data points above it. If there had been an even number of data points, this line would have been drawn between the two media points.

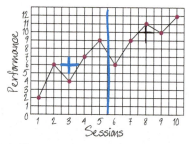

4. Repeat steps 2 and 3 on the right half of the graph.

In this example, session 8 is the midsession, and the data point at performance value 10 is the midperformance point.

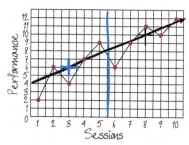

5. Draw a line connecting the intersections of both halves of the graph. This is the trend line for the data.

illustrated in Figure 6.34. Trend lines can provide (1) an indication of the direction of behavior change in the past, and (2) a prediction of the direction of behavior change in the future. This information can help the teacher determine whether to change the intervention.

Taking this process one step further will yield a split-middle line of progress (White & Haring, 1980). This line of progress is drawn so that an equal number of data points fall on and above the line as fall on and below the line. As illustrated in Figure 6.35, if the data points do not naturally fall in such a pattern, the line is redrawn higher or lower, parallel to the original line, until the balance of data points is equal.

4. Evaluation of the percentage of overlap of data plotted for performance (*y*-axis values) across contiguous conditions provides an indication of the impact of an intervention on behavior (Heyvaert, Saenen, Maes, & Onghena, 2015). This is referred to as *effect size* and is used as a measure of effectiveness of the intervention (Ferron, Goldstein, Olszewski, & Rohrer, 2020; Hedges, Pustejovsky, & Shadish, 2012). Percent of overlap is calculated by "(1) determining the range of data point values of the first condition, (2) counting the number of data points plotted in the second condition, (3) counting the number of data points of the second condition that fall within the range of values of the first condition, and (4) dividing the number of data points that fall within the range of the first condition by the total number of data points of the second condition and multiplying this number by 100. In general, the lower the percentage of overlap, the greater the impact the intervention has on the target behavior" (Tawney & Gast, 1984, p. 164).

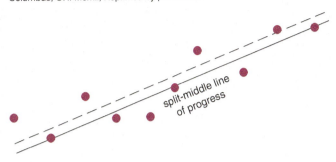

Figure 6.35 Split-middle line of progress

NOTE: From *Exceptional Teaching* (p. 118), by O. White & N. Haring, 1980, Columbus, OH: Merrill, Reprinted by permission.

For example, in Figure 6.33, the range of data values during baseline (phase 1) is 32 to 50. In the reinforcement-only condition (phase 2), 6 of 10 data points fall within the same data value range as the baseline, yielding a 60% overlap. However, the percentage of overlap between phase 2 and phase 3 is 0%. These percentages of change indicate that the use of a time-out ribbon and reinforcement had a much greater impact on the disruptive behavior than did reinforcement alone.

5. Evaluation of the rapidity of the behavior change (sometimes called the latency of behavior change) refers to the length of time between the onset or termination of one phase and changes in performance. The sooner the change occurs after the experimental conditions have been altered (that is, after implementation or withdrawal of the intervention), the clearer the intervention effect (Lieberman, Yoder, Reichow, & Wolery, 2010). Note that "rapidity of change is a difficult notation to specify because it is a joint function of changes in level and slope (trend). A marked change in level and in slope usually reflects a rapid change" (Kazdin, 2011, p. 316).

Visual analysis is often quick, effective, and relatively easy to learn (Poling, Methot, & LeSage, 1994). This makes it useful to the teacher trying to make instructional and behavior management decisions in the classroom. The use of visual analysis encourages ongoing evaluation as data are collected and phases change, rather than reliance on pre- and postintervention data. This facilitates data-based decision making for educational programming (Bruhn, Wehby, & Hasselbring, 2020; Buzhardt, Greenwood, & Walker, 2018; Espin, Wayman, & Deno, 2017; Filderman, Austin, & Toste, 2019; Hammerschmidt-Snidarich, McComas, & Simonson, 2019; Kressler, Chapman, & Kunkel, 2020).

Problematic in the use of visual analysis is a lack of concrete decision rules for determining whether a particular demonstration shows or fails to show a reliable effect (Ledford & Gast, 2018). The components of visual analysis do not have agreed-upon operationalized criteria based in the research literature. Each teacher or researcher sets the standard for a component as he or she uses it. Therefore, visual analysis may be seen as subjective and open to inconsistent application by an individual across sets of student data, or across different individuals reviewing student data (Wolfe, Barton, & Meadan, 2019). Confidence in conclusions based on visual inspection may be increased by increasing reliable use of the various components. The reliability may be increased by (1) teacher training and repeated opportunities for use, (2) interpreting student performance data with a consistently applied standard, and (3) two or more trained individuals independently reviewing the data and drawing conclusions that can be compared (Richards et al., 1999). In special education, there is at least annual interpretation and review of student data by the teacher and the IEP team. This presents an opportunity for reviewing data interpretation and collaborating on setting standards for data-based decision making.

It is noted that evaluation resulting from visual analysis reveals only intervention results that have a strong and reliable effect on behavior—it may miss consistent but subtle or weak behavior change caused by some interventions. However, it may be considered a benefit for classroom use that visual analysis is more likely to identify independent variables that produce strong or socially significant results. The usual purpose of intervention is to obtain immediate and strong treatment effects. If obtained, such effects are "quite evident from visual inspection" (Kazdin, 2001, p. 150). When single-subject designs are used in classroom decision making, clinical and social validity are important criteria. The clinical criterion is a judgment as to whether the results of the teacher's intervention are large enough to be of practical value and impact on the learning or behavior of the student. They are likely to be socially valid based on the functional change in the student's performance and the social acceptance of the student.

Although visual inspection is useful, convenient, and basically reliable for identifying or verifying strong intervention effects for decision making in the classroom, educational and behavioral researchers may choose to explore statistical evaluation of single-subject data as a companion to, or comparison with, the results of visual analysis (Young, 2018). This may be the case when there is concern for generalization across populations, or when seeking intervention effects so subtle as not to be clinically significant but that further research might be able to make more significant or more consistent. Kazdin (1976) offered three reasons to use statistical techniques: (1) distinguishing subtle effects from chance occurrence, (2) analyzing the effect of a treatment procedure when a stable baseline cannot be established, and (3) assessing treatment effects in environments that lack control. Information about advanced uses of visual inspection and statistical evaluation with single-subject designs can be found in Cooper et al. (2020), Kazdin (2011), Kennedy (2005), and Ledford and Gast (2018).

Ethical Considerations with Single-Subject Design

We have indicated that an AB design is sufficient for documenting a behavior change across a baseline condition and an intervention condition, but a more robust design is needed to conclude a functional relation, such as a reversal, alternating treatments, or multiple baseline design. However, in schools, professionals should be cautious with implementing these experimental designs due to ethical considerations (Lanovaz et al., 2019). One consideration is that it can be dangerous to return to baseline (reversal and alternating treatments designs) or keep students in baseline for extended periods (multiple baseline across participants design) because of increased aggression, self-injury, or other dangerous behaviors during these sessions. If a teacher finds an intervention that works, most people in the student's environment would not want the teacher then to take away that effective intervention, as dangerous problem behavior may return. One way to address this while retaining a functional relation is to use the logic of a brief design in which the return to baseline is for only one or two sessions. For example, Borrero et al. (2013) returned to baseline for only two sessions when evaluating treatments for inappropriate mealtime behaviors.

Another ethical concern with single subject designs that require a return to baseline relates to cost. That is, taxpayers fund public schooling for students with and without disabilities. The cost of several sessions of returning to baseline per student adds up to countless hours across the system that cost taxpayers more money. Lanovaz et al. (2019) found that when an AB comparison is replicated, as in an ABAB design, the change between the second AB comparison is comparable to the change between the first AB comparison in the vast majority of cases. This suggests that in many cases, teachers can document behavior changes using AB designs, and more robust designs are not needed.

Action Research and Single-Subject Design Tools

Learning Outcome 6.5 Identify the components of action research and explain how it parallels single-subject designs.

Action research is any systematic inquiry conducted by teachers and other educational professionals in teaching/learning environments to gather information and reflect upon how their school operates, how they teach, or how well their students learn. Information is gathered with goals including effecting positive changes in the classroom and school environments, and improving student outcomes (Mills, 2018). Action research encourages teachers to be participant researchers to gather information to share with the educational team. This information allows immediate analysis of instructional and behavior management issues and is used to develop the next step(s) in programming. Teachers draw from research design tools that will describe what they are seeing in order to analyze and develop solutions and thereby improve their practice.

Action research is considered a naturalistic approach to research. Methods are considered naturalistic when they occur in natural settings (e.g., classrooms) with relatively little interruption of the normal flow of events. For the most part they are nonexperimental. Naturalistic researchers are not interested in manipulating or controlling the situation, and they are not interested in studying interventions to discover functional relations. When the purpose of research is to understand what is occurring rather than to study that which has been manipulated and controlled, naturalistic research methods are appropriate (Arhar, Holly, & Kasten, 2001, p. 36). Fundamentally, action research is nonexperimental and descriptive, whereas single-subject research is experimental and seeks to identify functional relations resulting from the manipulation of variables.

Components of Action Research

There is general agreement on the basic steps of an action research study: (1) identify an area of focus or concern, (2) collect data for documentation, (3) analyze and interpret data, and (4) share the information with others and develop an action plan (Arhar et al., 2001; Mills, 2018; Schoen & Nolen, 2004; Stringer, 2014).

There is an eclectic array of data collection procedures available. As noted by Mills (2018), action research uses elements of quantitative (e.g., comparison of standard scores) and qualitative research methods. However, the literature emphasizes the data collection tools of qualitative research. These include use of observation, interviews, questionnaires, checklists, rating scales, focus groups, records, physical products, scatter plots, field notes, anecdotal records, videotapes, audiotapes, and photographs (Arhar et al., 2001; Mills, 2018; Stringer, 2014). Action researchers often use frequency counts or percentages to describe the extent of behaviors. Arhar et al. suggest the importance of frequencies in capturing the scope of a behavior as reflected in questions such as "How often does 'this' occur? How often does 'this' occur in comparison to 'that'? Does it occur constantly and evenly? Does it occur periodically or in waves?" (p. 201). In order to assess consistency and patterns of behavior, line graphs and bar graphs are used for organization and visual display of these data.

Single-Subject Design Parallels and Contributions

In order to broaden the number and range of tools available to teachers when planning action research, contributions from single-subject research should be considered. They can provide data collection techniques and descriptive graphing tools for quick and easy implementation in the classroom. These can be used by the teacher as a participant and can provide objective data. Some tools of single-subject research parallel existing recommended procedures, and some must be added.

a. *Parallel procedures:* Three areas of single-subject data collection make use of the methodologies similar to those in the action research literature. First, permanent product recording makes use of written records, videotapes, audiotapes, photographs, and physical results of behavior. These data are transformed into frequency or percentage data. Second, we make use of anecdotal recording in order to describe and analyze chains of behavior. As presented in Figure 5.2, we make use of a strategy for structuring these observations to assist in analysis. Third, the methods and data sheets for collecting event data discussed in Chapter 5 will help a teacher structure the collection of frequency and percentage data. Additionally, Chapter 7 includes a discussion of questionnaires, scales, and an alternative scatter plot procedure ABA practitioners use in association with functional assessment.

b. *Procedures to add:* Several single-subject designs are appropriate for the descriptive purposes of action research. The AB design displays and monitors behavior once a plan of action is implemented. The ABC design monitors the effects on behavior of adding components to an instructional package. The alternating treatments design, using only the first two phases, allows display and monitoring of the effects of two interventions. Each of these designs allows one to see if the behavior being examined changed with the implementation of an intervention. However, with these designs there is no manipulation of an intervention and therefore no assessment of a functional relation.

Example of an Action Research Study

The study conducted by Schoen and Nolen (2004) is an example of the use of some single-subject research tools as part of action research. The teacher and the team addressed the behavior of a sixth grader with learning disabilities. He participated in general education and special education classes. His acting-out behaviors were causing him to be off task and resulting in poor academic engagement and lack of academic success. Therefore, this was the identified focus of concern. Several kinds of data were collected to inform decision making and action planning. First, focused observation in the form of antecedent, behavior, consequence analysis (ABC analysis) was conducted over a 5-day period. This analysis identified specific behavior patterns that included slamming materials, yelling at teacher/peers, muttering under his breath, storming out of the room, destroying his work, and tuning out (head down on the desk). Second, interviews were conducted with the student, the special education teacher, and the social worker. Third, a literature review of various theories and strategies was conducted. These data were shared with the educational team and an action plan was developed. A package of peer modeling, a self-management checklist, and positive reinforcement was put in place during reading, math, and transitions. The self-management checklist had the student assess his behavior with the following questions: Did I yell out? Did I stay on task? Did I act respectfully to other students and teachers? Did I use proper outlets to calm down? For analyzing the data, the team chose the total minutes off task displayed on a graph showing baseline data and data during use of the action plan—thus the AB design, as shown in Figure 6.5. This type of graph allowed the team members and the student to monitor the decrease in the number of minutes off task due to his acting-out behavior.

Components of Action Research
Pearson eText
Video Example 6.4
In this video, a group of educators are discussing their practices in the classroom and sharing strategies. Consider the similarities of this form of professional development and the components of action research described in the chapter.

Summary

This summary serves as a rationale and an answer to the question: "Of what use is this to me?"

By best practice and legal mandate, data-based demonstrations of learning are required as evidence of effective instruction and of a quality education. Applied behavior analysis provides tools to meet these accountability requirements. Chapter 4 introduced methods of collecting data that provide the raw material for discussions of effectiveness. This chapter introduced single-subject designs as ways to organize the gathering and display of data. The design routinely used in the classroom is the AB design because it is a direct reflection of common classroom practice. It does not require restructuring teaching sessions. The graph of the AB design provides an uncomplicated visual format that can be used by teacher, student, parent, and supervisor to monitor, interpret, and assess learning. The other single-subject designs have specific capabilities and therefore may be used less frequently. In various ways, each design provides a database for quick, student-specific decision making. Table 6.2 summarizes the use of each and the questions they attempt to answer.

After the AB design, the changing criterion design is the most direct reflection of how a teacher manages instruction. Teachers regularly break down a goal that requires a large amount of learning into manageable units. Teaching manageable units of content, one at a time, in sequence, is the graphic picture resulting from organizing instruction and data collection within a changing criterion design. Another decision often required is which of two or more strategies will result in the most effective and efficient learning. The alternating use of strategies within the format of the alternating treatments design provides a data-based answer, usually by the end of 1 week. Given a little more time, an answer to the question can also be provided by using the ABC design. Variations of this design are used more commonly to evaluate the combination of several strategies in an instructional package. The multiple baseline design has gained popularity as inclusive policies are put in place in schools. Of particular interest is the multiple baseline across settings that allows tracking the effectiveness of an intervention across general education, special education, community, and home settings. The reversal design allows quick and unobtrusive evaluation of an intervention on a classroom problem that you do not want to allow to progress from being a nuisance to a spreading classroom management problem. The reversal design is appropriate for issues such as out of seat, off task, and not doing homework. Later in this text, this design is used when developing a behavior management plan resulting from a functional behavior assessment.

Single-subject research designs employ repeated measurement of student performance during multiple sessions of implementation. Each design requires and displays changes (or lack thereof) in the dependent variable due to implementation of the independent variable. Based on accumulating incremental changes in student performance, there is data-based immediacy to decision making about changes to interventions or instruction. Using repeated measures for ongoing decision making makes single-subject methodology and designs an **iterative** or repetitious process. This iterative capability allows ongoing analysis of learning and necessary modifications, providing the flexibility that individualizes and adapts intervention or instruction to individual students. Single-subject methodology and designs are thus effective developmental tools. Additionally, as noted by Kratochwill et al. (2010), single-subject designs can provide a strong basis for establishing causal inference and are widely used in applied disciplines such as education and psychology.

Aspects of instruction and behavior management are being continually researched and evaluated. This is especially true in ABA, which has a culture of data-based decision making. Research brings to the classroom extensions of current strategies and evaluation of proposed strategies. Teachers must be able to answer questions such as: Is what I am doing still the best practice? Do the suggestions being made by colleagues, supervisors, and parents have a basis in data-based research? If educators are to be lifelong learners, they must be able to access the information provided in professional research journals. In order to read these journals, one must be literate in the types of research being published. From an ABA perspective, one must be able to read research conducted with single-subject designs. Most often found in the research journals are reversal and multiple baseline designs. The reversal design (ABAB) is frequently used because it is most powerfully able to demonstrate a functional relation between a behavior and an intervention due to the controlled application and removal of a strategy (Kazdin, 1982). Multiple baseline designs are found frequently because they build immediate replication and therefore depth of experience with the intervention that allows broader and more confident statements of applicability to other students, behaviors, or settings.

Discussion Questions

1. Baseline data for Craig's self-injurious behavior indicate a mean occurrence of 17 instances per 40-minute observation period. What change in his behavior would be clinically significant (as demonstrated by enhanced functioning)?
2. Which single-subject design might a teacher use to systematically introduce and teach 30 community sight words?
3. During 3 weeks of multiplication instruction, probes of Alison's performance indicated that she still could not multiply. Her teacher wants to determine which of two alternative approaches to teaching multiplication would be most effective for Alison. Select two instructional methods. Select an appropriate single-subject design and outline the steps the teacher should follow to make this determination.
4. Outline a procedure associated with a single-subject design that would demonstrate the generalization of an intervention across settings in a high school.
5. Draw lines of progress on the two sets of data graphed below.
6. Many of the studies that appear in professional journals use "embedded" designs. That is, one single-subject design is embedded within another. This is illustrated in the graph on the next page. (a) Identify the components of the multiple baseline design within the graph; (b) identify the components of the reversal design within the graph; and (c) identify the elements demonstrating a functional relation.

Graphs for Discussion Question 5

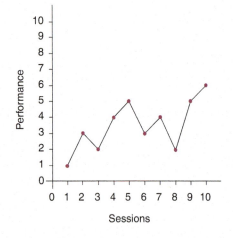
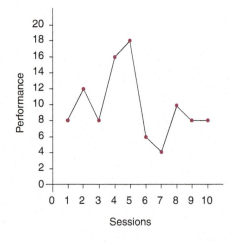

Graphs for Discussion Question 6

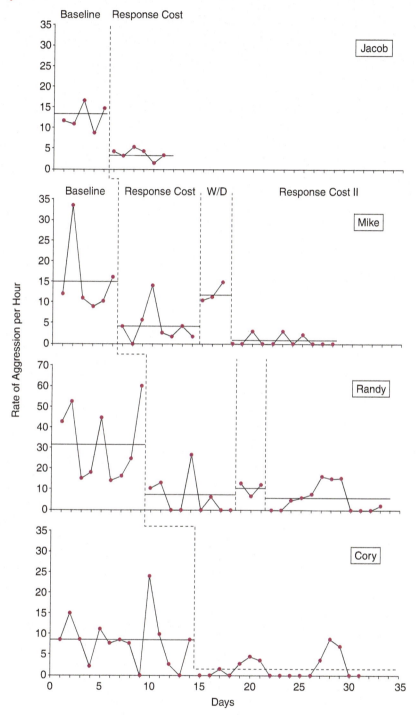

Chapter 7
Determining the Function of Behavior

 Learning Outcomes

7.1 Identify the six functions of behavior.

7.2 Identify the components of a Behavior Support Plan.

7.3 Identify the process for developing a Functional Behavior Assessment and Behavior Support Plan.

CHAPTER OUTLINE

Behavior and Its Function

The Behavior Support Plan

Functional Behavior Assessment and Behavior Support Plan
    Settings for Conducting Functional Analysis
    Brief Functional Analysis
    Positive Behavior Support

Summary

At Whittier Middle School, the consequence for fighting is 2 days of in-school suspension. During such suspension, students must labor all day at written work in individual study carrels adjacent to the principal's office, where they are not allowed to talk or socialize. Fighting has been an infrequent behavior. In these first few weeks of the school year, however, Dr. Toarmina, the principal, is dealing with several fights a day. Repeated interviews with the participants have provided little information: "He just came up and hit me—I hardly know the dude." "The fool knocked my books out of my hand. I smacked him good." Many sixth graders have participated in the fights, but Dr. Toarmina has observed that Maurice is the only student who has participated in all of them and the only student who has endured in-school suspension more than once. Maurice is new to the school and the neighborhood. He is considered an "at-risk" student and has limited English. Even to a translator, however, Maurice refuses to communicate any reason for his aggression. He just shrugs and looks away. In desperation, Dr. Toarmina increases the duration of the suspension to 3 days. The fights continue. In-school suspension, an intervention that has been effective for most students in the past, is not effective for Maurice.

    Angela is a new student in Mr. Gray's class for young children with developmental delays. Angela screams. Indeed, to Mr. Gray it seems that Angela screams all day. He repeatedly goes to Angela, trying to find something to pacify her. "Angela," he asks, "Do you need potty? Do you want juice? Do you want to play with Elmo? Do you hurt? Here? Here? Shall we go outside?" When he finds himself asking

"Is it bigger than a breadbox?" he decides that he cannot spend so much time playing Twenty Questions with Angela and that he will use time-out to decrease her screaming. Every time Angela screams, Mr. Gray or his assistant picks her up, gently deposits her on a mat behind a screen in the classroom, and leaves her there until 1 minute after she stops screaming. Sure enough, Angela stops screaming. Suddenly, however, she starts hitting adults and other children, apparently at random, something she has never done before. Mr. Gray, not easily discouraged, begins to put Angela in time-out for hitting. Soon he observes that Angela has begun banging her head with her fists while she is in time-out. Because he obviously cannot allow her to injure herself, he does become discouraged. He abandons time-out, Angela returns to screaming, and Mr. Gray continues to play Twenty Questions.

In both of these anecdotes, educators are dealing with recurring and apparently random inappropriate behavior with students who cannot or will not provide information about the reasons for their inappropriate behaviors. Attempts are made to reduce the occurrence of the behaviors with techniques that have been effective in the past, but these attempts are unsuccessful. The behavior has a familiar form or topography—it looks like behavior that has been seen before. Why, then, is the intervention strategy not working? The problem may be that in our preoccupation with the behavior's form, we have failed to determine its function (Skinner, 1953). In other words, informal analysis has failed to provide an accurate determination of why the student is engaging in the behavior. In such cases, we may need more in-depth sets of procedures known as functional behavior assessment (FBA; also known as a functional assessment) and functional analysis.

Behavior and Its Function

Learning Outcome 7.1 Identify the six functions of behavior.

When teachers ask, "Why does she do that?" they are really wondering what function the behavior serves for the student—what her purpose is for doing what she is doing. The function of a behavior is to make a desired change in the environment. If engaging in the behavior results in the change the student wants, there is an increased probability that she will engage in the behavior again. The desired change may be getting something she wants or escaping from something she does not want. This relationship between the purpose of behavior—desirable outcomes or consequences—and the maintenance of behavior is the nature of reinforcement.

Things that inappropriate behaviors might serve to communicate.

Educators often focus on the physical characteristics of behavior (form or topography) because those are what we see. We develop an operational definition of the behavior that describes what we see. A quantitative measure of topography (frequency, duration, or percent of intervals during which the behavior occurs) is what we seek to change about the behavior. We select an intervention to reduce the number of times Brett gets out of his seat during reading class, or to reduce the length of time that he remains out of his seat when he gets up, or to reduce the percentage of intervals that he is out of his seat. Focusing on a behavior's topography, however, may provide little information about factors controlling the behavior. The same behavior exhibited by two different students may be maintained for different reasons. One student's aggressive behavior may function to gain a teacher's or peer's attention. Another student may want to escape the teacher's attention because she did not do her homework or escape bullying from a peer. It is unlikely that any single intervention will have the same effect on behaviors performed for such different reasons. By neglecting to attend to a behavior's function, we may fail to see that topographically unrelated behaviors such as signing "juice," pointing to a cup of juice, or banging one's empty cup on the table may serve the same function by resulting in the same outcome—getting some juice to drink.

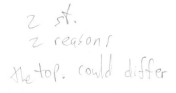

Teachers often find that an intervention eliminates an inappropriate behavior for a short time but that the behavior soon reappears. Sometimes a new, equally or even more inappropriate behavior replaces it. If her teacher takes Sita's cup away from her every time she bangs it on the table but does not teach her to sign "juice" or to point to the juice, Sita may very well stop banging the cup for a while but start banging it again in a few days or, even worse, start screaming and banging her head as soon as she is seated at the snack table. This happens when an intervention is used simply to suppress a behavior. Unless a student has a new, more appropriate way to bring about a desired environmental change, she will continue to bring it about in ways that have been successful in the past. We often call these behaviors "challenging" both because they present major challenges to maintaining a productive learning environment and because they offer challenges to professionals trying to change them. If, by chance, the intervention selected to reduce form results in a new behavior that happens to match function, behavior management is successful. If not, we may dismiss the experience as another puzzling example of the failure of applied behavior analysis methods to produce lasting change. If, for example, after her teacher took Sita's cup away, Sita happened to point to the juice pitcher and get juice, Sita would probably not bang her cup anymore. She could eventually be taught to point even when holding the cup. If, on the other hand, Sita just sat and did not get juice, she would probably go back to banging the cup as soon as it was given back to her or start screaming if she did not have it. This "hit-or-miss" success rate characterized behavior management before we understood the need to attend to both the form and the function of behavior (Anderson, Rodriguez, & Campbell, 2015; Iwata, Dorsey, Slifer, Bauman, & Richman, 1994; Jeong & Copeland, 2020). It may well be that failure to consider a behavior's function is the basis for the assumption that suppression of inappropriate behavior inevitably results in "symptom substitution," or the appearance of new inappropriate behavior based on some underlying disturbance. A need for function-based intervention does not assume some internal motive for a student's behavior but focuses on the purpose of that behavior as defined by environmental events that occasion and maintain it.

Inappropriate behaviors often serve the function of achieving a desired change in the student's environment. Table 7.1 lists six functions of behavior that appear frequently in the research literature and their relationships to reinforcing consequences that maintain the behavior. These include engaging in behavior to gain attention, to gain a tangible item, to gain sensory stimulation, to escape from tasks and interactions, and to escape from internal pain or discomfort.

1. *Challenging behavior to gain attention.* Getting the attention of an adult or peer in order to engage in social interaction is a function of behavior. The most common way to gain someone's attention is using verbal language or some nonverbal communicative behavior. A student may raise his hand or walk up to the teacher and engage her in conversation. When students lack the communication or social skills to gain attention, they may use behaviors considered inappropriate. The student may call out, throw items on the floor, or curse to get the teacher's attention. If these challenging behaviors succeed in getting the adult's attention (pleasant or unpleasant), the student learns that engaging in these behaviors achieves the desired result. If a student is successful in getting the teacher's attention only by raising his hand, he learns a socially appropriate behavior. Achieving the desired result increases the future rate or probability of the student's engaging in the behavior again. This is an example of positive reinforcement.

The social attention students desire may be from peers rather than adults. Dr. Toarmina, the principal of the middle school described at the beginning of this chapter,

Table 7.1 Behavior: Its functions and maintaining consequences

Functions of Behavior		Behavioral Principle
To gain attention: Social from adult (teacher, parent, paraeducator, customer, etc.) Social from peer	–	*Positive Reinforcement* Receiving attention increases the future rate or probability of the student engaging in the challenging behavior again.

To gain a tangible:
Assistance in getting:
    Object
    Activity
    Event
	–	*Positive Reinforcement*
		Receiving the tangible increases the future rate or probability of the student engaging in the challenging behavior again.

To gain sensory stimulations: Visual Gustatory Auditory Kinesthetic Olfactory Proprioceptive	–	*Positive Automatic Reinforcement* Provision of the sensory input by engaging in the challenging behavior itself increases the future rate or probability of the student engaging in the behavior again.
To escape from attention: Attention from peer or adult Social interaction with peer	–	*Negative Reinforcement* Removing the student from the interaction that is aversive increases the future rate or probability of the challenging behavior.
To escape from: Demanding or boring task Setting, activity, event	–	*Negative Reinforcement* Removing the stimulus the student finds aversive increases the future rate or probability of the challenging behavior.
To escape from sensory stimulation: Internal stimulation that is painful or discomforting	–	*Negative Automatic Reinforcement* Attenuation of painful or discomforting internal stimulation by engaging in the challenging behavior itself increases the future rate and/or probability of the student engaging in the behavior again.

initially theorized that Maurice was initiating fights because he lacked the language and social skills to interact appropriately with his peers. She learned from the school social worker, who made a home visit, that Maurice lived with his parents in a neighborhood of older homes primarily occupied by elderly people and a few young couples. Both parents worked two jobs to save money to bring Maurice's younger brother and sister to this country. Their rental house did not allow children, so Maurice was required to stay inside at all times. He was alone much of the time and did not have an opportunity to make friends in the neighborhood. Dr. Toarmina arranged for Maurice to join an after-school recreational program with a diverse population and a focus on appropriate social interaction. Unfortunately, although Maurice did appear to have more positive interactions with peers after a few weeks, he still started fights almost daily. Dr. Toarmina was puzzled but continued her efforts to get to the bottom of the problem.

2. *Challenging behavior to gain a tangible.* Getting the attention of an adult or peer in order to get assistance in obtaining some tangible object, activity, or event is a function of behavior. During morning snack, a student may point to or ask for some of the juice (object), or he may bang his cup on the table or throw it to the floor. A student may use a modified form of sign language to ask to jump on the trampoline, or he may have a tantrum next to the trampoline (activity). A student may use an augmentative communication device to request assistance with changing his position in a wheelchair or to get permission to go to the restroom (event), or he may cry, scream, or wiggle in his chair.

If a student repeatedly gets the tangible object, activity, or event by engaging in inappropriate behavior, she learns to use that behavior to achieve her desired outcome. This increases the future rate or probability that she will perform the challenging behavior again. This, too, is an example of positive reinforcement. What

> It's neither fair nor ethical to punish functional behavior.

teachers or parents describe as <u>inappropriate or challenging behaviors are usually attempts at communication</u>. A student without a standard form of communication might scream and hit herself because she is <u>not able to ask, "Please change my position in my wheelchair; I'm very uncomfortable."</u> A student may <u>bang her cup on the table to communicate,</u> "Please pass the juice," because she lacks the ability to sign "juice" or has not learned that she may obtain it by pointing. A student who has not been taught an acceptable way to indicate that he needs to use the bathroom may display what appears to be simply inappropriate restlessness and agitation. The assessment procedures described in this chapter enabled Angela's teacher (in the anecdote at the beginning of the chapter) to determine that she used screaming to communicate a variety of needs. <u>When screaming became ineffective, she turned to hitting. Once the communicative content of a behavior is identified, the student should be taught a more appropriate form of behavior that serves the same communication purpose</u> (Carr & Durand, 1985; Chezan, Wolfe, & Drasgow, 2018; Gerow, Davis, & Radhakrishnan, 2018; Jeong & Copeland, 2020; Meuthing et al., 2018; Tsami & Lerman, 2020; Walker, Lyon, Loman, & Sennott, 2018). Providing Angela with an augmentative communication device and the training to use it gradually reduced her screaming.

Inappropriate communicative behavior is often maintained by positive reinforcement (either consistently or inconsistently administered) resulting from the teacher's engaging in Twenty Questions when she does not know what the student is trying to tell her. Sometimes the teacher guesses correctly, and the student gets what she wants. The student does not need to be successful every time to keep a behavior in her repertoire (see Chapter 8).

Even adults sometimes lash out when they are frustrated.

3. *Challenging behavior to gain sensory stimulation.* Getting sensory stimulation is a function of behavior. Most of us have a set of motor or communication skills that allow us to provide ourselves with sensory stimulation. We can turn on a voice-activated music device, play a video game, or take a piece of chocolate ourselves or, if need be, we can ask for assistance. If students are not able to provide themselves with appropriate sensory experiences or to ask others to provide them, they may engage in self-injurious or stereotypic behaviors. Behaviors such as humming, blowing saliva bubbles, slapping their ears, pinching themselves, flicking their fingers, mouthing objects, or rocking their bodies may provide students with the only sensory stimulation available to them. The sensory input received by engaging in the behavior increases the future rate or probability of the students' engaging in the behavior again. This is automatic positive reinforcement—the act of engaging in the behavior itself provides the desired environmental change. Please note that repetitive behaviors used to access sensory reinforcement are not always considered challenging behaviors.

4. *Challenging behavior to escape from attention or interactions.* A behavior can serve the function of getting away from a situation one finds unpleasant or aversive. Escaping the teacher's attention when one does not have one's homework may be accomplished by using rather sophisticated social skills such as asking a question on a topic known to get the teacher distracted or by running out of the room. Overly effusive praise from a teacher may cause a middle schooler to leave the classroom to avoid his peers' ridicule. Escaping from an undesired social interaction with a playground bully can be achieved by communicating a need for assistance from friends or by truancy. Escaping from the repetitive activity of shelving bottles of salad dressing on a job-training site may be achieved by asking for a break or by breaking something.

5. *Challenging behavior to escape from tasks.* Getting out of doing a task is a function of behavior. The task can be too hard and therefore aversive, or too easy and

> Dr. Toarmina, the middle school principal, was still puzzled by Maurice's fighting. He seemed to choose his victims randomly; no pattern of events seemed to regularly occasion fighting. The only consistency was the consequence—in-school suspension. Maurice was spending most of his time at school in that environment; when released, he started another fight. She interviewed his teachers. Most of the teachers reported that Maurice was quiet and well behaved (except when he was fighting). They indicated his English was improving rapidly and he had interesting contributions to make. Only Mr. Harris, the social studies teacher, believed that Maurice was not a good student.
>
> Finally, while interviewing one of Maurice's victims, Dr. Toarmina asked the right question. She asked if Maurice was having trouble in any of his classes. The student hesitated but finally stated that Mr. Harris did not seem to know that Maurice spoke very little English and kept calling on him, correcting him, and then yelling at him to pay attention and try to make sense when he talked or to shut up if he could not do any better than he was doing now. The student reported that Maurice was often close to tears. "Maybe," the student suggested, "he just gets so upset he has to take it out on somebody. He never really hurts anyone; we just fight back because that's the way it's done." Dr. Toarmina thanked the student, dismissed him, and shut her office door. No, she thought, he's not so upset he's taking it out on other students; he's so upset that he's figured out a way to avoid being harassed and humiliated. At least nobody embarrasses him or yells at him while he's in in-school suspension. She made a note to have Maurice transferred to another section of social studies and left a note in Mr. Harris's box to see her immediately after school.

therefore boring. Escape from a demanding task such as long division, tooth brushing, or dodge ball can be achieved by communicating the need for help, a break, or dislike for the task. If one does not have the communication or social skills to ask for a break, throwing a temper tantrum may work just as well. When the student has a tantrum and the frustrated teacher or parent just stops the task and walks away, the student learns that having a tantrum is an effective way to escape aversive tasks. In some cases, the context of the task may be aversive. In school, the social embarrassment of an age-inappropriate, gender-inappropriate, or culturally inappropriate task, set of materials, or setting may result in escape behaviors.

If a student does not have the communication skills to request escape or the social skills to remove herself from an unpleasant interaction, she may engage in an inappropriate behavior. If the behavior results in escape, the environment has been changed in a way she desired. Achieving this result increases the future rate or probability of the student's using that form of escape again. This is an example of negative reinforcement. The teacher who removes the difficult task when the student throws it on the floor is teaching the student that this is what to do when you want to escape from a difficult task.

6. *Challenging behavior to escape from internal stimulation that is painful or uncomfortable.* Escape from internal pain or discomfort is a function of behavior. Most of us can move to a more comfortable seat, get a heating pad, take an aspirin or a laxative, or tell our symptoms to a doctor. People who do not have the communication skills or cognitive ability to relate that they are uncomfortable or in pain may engage in what others view as inappropriate behavior in an attempt to reduce (attenuate) discomfort or pain. If engaging in the behavior results in the removal of, or distraction from, pain or discomfort, that increases the future rate or probability that the person will engage in the behavior again. This is automatic negative reinforcement; the act of engaging in the behavior itself provides the desired environmental change—escape from discomfort.

The anecdote on the next page describes attempts to suppress behaviors considering only their form rather than attending to their function.

By attending to the functions of behaviors as well as to their form, we can design interventions to enable students to meet their needs in appropriate ways. A formal document created to achieve this end is the behavior support plan.

Asking Questions To Clarify Function
Pearson eText
Video Example 7.1
In this video, an educator addresses inappropriate classroom behavior with his adolescent student. The educator uses thoughtful questions to help the student communicate the function of her behavior. How does their discussion lead to a function-based intervention?

The Professor Gets a Lecture

Professor Grundy had just returned home from several days out of town at a professional conference. As he pulled his car into the driveway, he heard a muffled squealing sound coming from inside the house. As he opened the back door, he located the sound as coming from the laundry room.

"Minerva," he called to Mrs. Grundy, "I'm home! Is there something wrong with the washing machine? Something's making a fearful noise." Mrs. Grundy did not answer. He finally found her working at her computer in the bedroom but had to touch her on the shoulder to get her attention. She jumped and pulled something out of her ears.

"Minerva," he asked again, "is there something wrong with the washing machine? There is a horrible noise coming from the laundry room."

"That horrible noise," she retorted, "is coming from your horrible dog. He started barking and howling the day after you left. I looked in all your dog-training books and tried everything they suggested. I took him on extra long walks; I gave him extra food; and when I really couldn't stand it, I sprayed him in the face with water."

"Perhaps," suggested Grundy, "he missed me."

"Oh, nonsense, Oliver, you've been gone for several days before since we got him and there's never been a problem," replied Mrs. Grundy. "I finally went to the pet supply store and they sold me a collar..."

"Aargh," roared Grundy, "what kind of collar was this?!?"

"It squirts a blast of citronella when he barks. He stopped barking, but now whenever I let him outside, he digs up my garden. He's also apparently learned that he can make that awful squealing sound without setting the collar off. I'm trying to work (Mrs. Grundy wrote very popular mystery novels) and I've had to put his crate in the laundry room, put him in his crate, shut the door, and wear ear plugs so I can concentrate."

Grundy left her to her work and went downstairs to see about Burrhus. The dog squealed happily to see the professor, who, desirous of directly observing the behavior, took off the collar and took him into the yard. Burrhus barked, howled, and started digging in the dirt in Mrs. Grundy's garden. The garden butted up against the fence between the Grundy's yard and that of their next-door neighbor, Miss Oattis.

"That's it!" Grundy exclaimed aloud, dragging Burrhus back into the house. He had remembered that Miss Oattis was a "dog person." She had three small white dogs, two of which looked pretty normal and one of which had a very peculiar hairstyle. He understood from Mrs. Grundy that Miss Oattis took her dogs, toy poodles, to dog shows and taught dog obedience classes. She would be the person to ask about Burrhus's behavior.

Miss Oattis promptly answered his knock on the front door. She was holding the dog with the peculiar hairstyle. Grundy winced and explained his problem.

"Hmm," replied Miss Oattis, "the only thing that's been different here is that my girls have been playing with a ball in the backyard, and I don't know where that ball came from. Might it be your dog's?"

"Aha!" cried Grundy. He thanked Miss Oattis, took the ball, and ran back to Mrs. Grundy. "Minerva, Burrhus's favorite ball was in Miss Oattis's yard. That's why he was barking, howling, and digging in the garden – he loves that ball! How did it get in Miss Oattis's yard?"

Mrs. Grundy shamefully said, "Oh. Jasper from down the street came by the day you left and asked to play with Burrhus in the yard. He must have thrown the ball over the fence by mistake and not gotten it. I'll be having a word with that boy."

The Behavior Support Plan

Learning Outcome 7.2 Identify the components of a Behavior Support Plan.

 A plan that details an agreed-upon set of procedures for changing inappropriate behavior is the behavior support plan (BSP). <u>Federal special education law, the Individuals with Disabilities Education Improvement Act (IDEIA, 2004), uses the term *behavior intervention plan (BIP)*.</u> The underlying logic guiding the design of a BSP is that of replacing an inappropriate behavior with an appropriate behavior that serves the same function. The first step in designing a BSP is to form a hypothesis as to what function the behavior serves. To form the hypothesis, we try to identify relationships among the behavior, its antecedents, the change resulting in the environment, and the reinforcement that the environmental change provides. We hypothesize that this reinforcement has maintained the inappropriate behavior and predict that the same reinforcement will maintain the more appropriate replacement behavior.

Behavior management based on applied behavior analysis seeks to understand how behavior serves a function for a student by understanding the components and relationships of the three-term expression used to denote the basic reinforcement contingency: S-R-S (top of Figure 7.1), the relationships between behavior and the environmental events that influence it. We seek to understand the pattern of variables that precedes the behavior's occurrence (the stimuli that occasion or signal the opportunity to perform the behavior—antecedents) and the pattern of variables that follow the behavior (those that fulfill the purpose of the behavior and therefore maintain the behavior—reinforcing consequences). An analysis of a problem behavior's function in terms of its antecedents and consequences is necessary for the selection of the most effective treatment (Camp et al., 2009; Castillo et al., 2020; Martens et al., 2010). With this analysis and an understanding of function we can select and teach an appropriate behavior to replace the inappropriate behavior. The new behavior must serve the same function as the original one and thus continue to provide reinforcement to the student. From an educational perspective the replacement behavior must also be appropriate to the student's age and contextually appropriate in the environment in which the student will use the behavior.

Figure 7.1 The three-term expression used to denote the reinforcement contingency

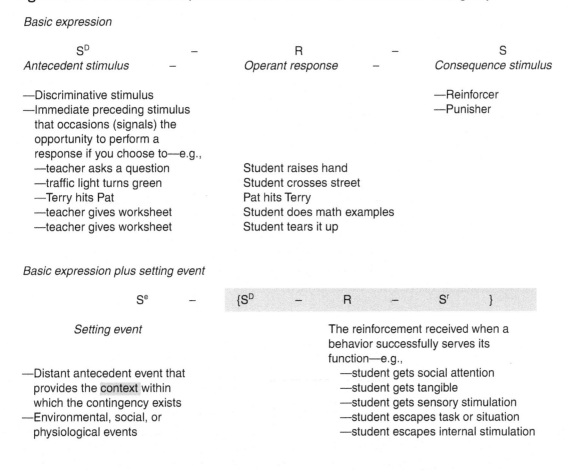

Basic expression

S^D — R — S
Antecedent stimulus — *Operant response* — *Consequence stimulus*

—Discriminative stimulus
—Immediate preceding stimulus that occasions (signals) the opportunity to perform a response if you choose to—e.g.,
　—teacher asks a question
　—traffic light turns green
　—Terry hits Pat
　—teacher gives worksheet
　—teacher gives worksheet

　　　　　　　　　　Student raises hand
　　　　　　　　　　Student crosses street
　　　　　　　　　　Pat hits Terry
　　　　　　　　　　Student does math examples
　　　　　　　　　　Student tears it up

—Reinforcer
—Punisher

Basic expression plus setting event

S^e — { S^D — R — S^r }

Setting event

—Distant antecedent event that provides the context within which the contingency exists
—Environmental, social, or physiological events

The reinforcement received when a behavior successfully serves its function—e.g.,
　—student gets social attention
　—student gets tangible
　—student gets sensory stimulation
　—student escapes task or situation
　—student escapes internal stimulation

hypothesis

The data upon which to base a hypothesis come from conducting a **functional behavior assessment** (FBA), potentially accompanied by a **functional analysis**. Functional behavior assessment is a set of information-gathering strategies and instruments. Based on what precedes the behavior and what follows it, patterns are identified that lead to the hypothesis. Functional analysis, on the other hand, is a strategy of manipulating the student's environment and observing the effect on the student's behavior. Changes in the student's behavior lead to a hypothesis. Each of these procedures attempts to answer the following questions:

1. Is there a pattern of events that consistently precedes the occurrence of the behavior?
2. Is there a pattern of events that consistently follows the occurrence of the behavior?
3. Can the student be taught an alternative, appropriate behavior to accomplish the same function as the inappropriate behavior?

Questions that can be answered using functional behavior assessment/analysis.

In addition to these questions a fourth question should be asked: What is the context within which the behavior, the antecedents, and the consequences take place? This question is asking: What are the **setting events**? Setting events refer to the setting, climate, or context within which the behavior and the contingency occur (see bottom of Figure 7.1 and Chapter 10). Setting events may occur immediately before a problem behavior (proximal antecedents) or hours or days in advance (distal antecedents) and may include ongoing factors such as a student's culture, family circumstances, or medical condition. Setting events can include environmental factors (noise or temperature level, unplanned schedule changes, missing the school bus), social factors (a death or illness in the family, an encounter with a bully, receiving a bad grade in a previous class), or physiological factors (side effects of medication, illness, pain) (Kazdin, 2001). Ongoing classroom characteristics can also set a context or climate that affects the value of reinforcers and punishers. Such setting events include a classroom characterized by understimulation and student boredom (meaningless repetition of tasks, pacing instruction too slowly, lack of systematic instruction), overstimulation (large number of students, too rapid a pace of activities, inappropriate grouping of students), frustration (lack of a communication system or functional vocabulary, constant interruption of performance and goal attainment, lack of demonstrated progress), or anxiety (inconsistent management techniques, fear of failure, undiagnosed learning problems).

By creating the context in which behaviors and contingencies occur, setting events influence the occurrence of the behavior and the value of the contingencies (Kazdin, 2001). They can momentarily change the value of reinforcers and punishers in an environment and therefore change the way a student responds to events and situations in the environment. If, for example, a student comes to your class after receiving yet another D on an essay in her previous class, her ability to concentrate and her motivation to complete your assignment and earn the praise you provide as a reinforcer may be considerably lessened. A student who comes to school extremely overactive because her schedule of medications has been changed may be unable to control her behavior well enough to interact appropriately with her peers. If a student is repeatedly given a task she mastered weeks ago, completion of the task may not be as reinforcing as it once was.

Another antecedent concept that is similar to setting events, as well as the concept of deprivation, is **motivating operations** (MO; Carbone et al., 2010; Laraway et al. 2014; Miguel & Michael, 2020; Nosik & Carr, 2015). In everyday terms, an MO is what someone wants at a certain time. More technically, an MO (or more specifically, an establishing operation; EO) is an antecedent situation that increases the value of an item or event as a reinforcer and evokes a behavior that has produced that item or event in the past. For example, when Taliana has not eaten for five hours, this deprivation is an MO that increases the value of food and makes her drive immediately to her favorite Mexican restaurant to order a burrito. Maurice, mentioned above, had to stay inside his apartment and could not interact with other children. This social deprivation likely served as an MO increasing the value of social interaction and resulting in Maurice fighting with others, which resulted in attention from adults. When a student is continually given difficult schoolwork, this may be an MO that increases the value of escaping the work and results in the student yelling out because this has landed him in the hallway in the past (that is, away from work). A major purpose of conducting a functional behavior assessment is to identify the reinforcers maintaining challenging behaviors, as well as the MOs that are antecedents to the challenging behaviors. In other words, we want to answer: "What does the student want?"

Motivation
Pearson eText
Video Example 7.2
In this video, an educator is responding to undesirable behavior exhibited by both of her students. The educator diagnoses the function of the behavior of both students and prompts alternative responses. What appears to be her hypothesis as to the functions of the observed behaviors?

Functional Behavior Assessment and Behavior Support Plan

Learning Outcome 7.3 Identify the process for developing a Functional Behavior Assessment and Behavior Support Plan.

A sequence of steps for developing a functional behavior assessment (FBA) and BSP is presented in Figure 7.2. The sequence begins with the teacher's recognizing and documenting an ongoing challenging behavior, progresses through the use of FBA or functional analysis procedures, and results in the implementation and monitoring of a set of intervention procedures.

Step 1. Teacher Identifies Problem Behavior
   a. Develop operational definition.
   b. Collect initial confirming data.
   c. Notify IEP committee members.

IDEIA requires development of a BSP on two occasions: (1) when a student's behavior is such that it may result in a suspension of up to 10 days or a change of educational placement; and (2) when a pattern of behavior impedes the learning of the student or of another student (Turnbull, Wilcox, Stowe, & Turnbull, 2001). As educators and parents become more familiar with the procedures, collaboration, and benefits involved with the development of BSPs and their use becomes more routine in schools, BSPs are being developed for additional behaviors. These may include behaviors that (1) are of potential harm to oneself; (2) are of potential harm to others; (3) interfere with the performance of others in school, in the community, or on the job site; (4) may result in damage to property; (5) regularly require third-party intervention; (6) draw ridicule or undue negative attention to the student; (7) restrict or deny entry into current or new educational, community, or job settings; or (8) cause disruption within the family and may result in isolation within the family.

The teacher prepares an operational definition of the inappropriate behavior targeted for reduction. The operational definition clearly states the form of the behavior. The specificity of an operational definition allows for the design of a data collection system. The teacher collects initial data with one of the data collection systems and then graphs the data. These data are used during initial discussions of the scope and severity of the behavior in order to substantiate the existence of a challenging behavior requiring further management. The teacher

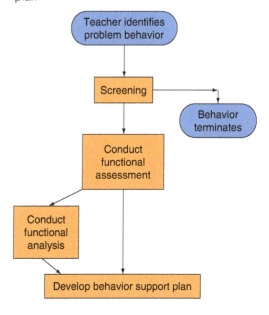

Figure 7.2 Development of a functional behavior assessment and behavior support plan

notifies the members of the IEP committee of her concern and initial actions. The IEP committee (or a designated subgroup that will act as the behavior-management team) convenes to review the data collected by the teacher and to confirm that the behavior is of a nature and frequency that will require the preparation of a BSP. It may be that discussing the behavior and its occurrence with team members will provide the teacher with ideas she has overlooked and enable her to manage the behavior quickly and simply. The team will also review information from the student's records to ensure that all appropriate screening measures have been conducted and that the results are up to date.

Step 2. Screening
    a. Request as needed: health, medications, physical, sensory, and learning disability screenings.
    b. Implement changes based on screening.

The teacher and the IEP committee may request that screening tests be conducted that might provide insight into the cause of the behavior problem and a direct solution. Toward this end the committee may request a new or updated (1) physical health screening, (2) review of medications being taken and their interactions and side effects, (3) screening for a physical impairment or review of its current management by school personnel and family members, (4) screening for a sensory impairment or review of its current management, and (5) administration of screening instruments to assess for the presence of a learning disability, whose currently unknown presence could result in inappropriate compensating behaviors by the student. Based on information from the screenings, the members can make recommendations that may terminate the behavior. A vision screening, for example, may result in a prescription for new glasses. Testing for a learning disability may result in 4 hours a week with the resource teacher. Waiting for the results of screenings need not delay the next step in the sequence, which is information gathering.

Step 3. Conduct a Functional Behavior Assessment
    a. Employ indirect information-gathering strategies.
    b. Employ direct information-gathering strategies.

Functional behavior assessment is a set of information-gathering strategies used to formulate a hypothesis about the function of an inappropriate behavior. There are two categories of these strategies (see Table 7.2). Indirect strategies gather information from people who regularly interact with the student. This is informant assessment. Various interview forms, scales, and questionnaires are available. Direct observation strategies gather information by taking data on the behavior while the student is engaged in it. This is descriptive assessment. These strategies include anecdotal reports, scatter plot analysis, and A-B-C descriptive analysis.

INDIRECT STRATEGIES: INFORMANT ASSESSMENT Indirect (or informant) assessment procedures involve questioning a person familiar with the student (e.g., teacher, parent, paraprofessional, or related service professional) about

Table 7.2 Functional behavior assessment strategies

Functional Behavior Assessment Strategies: Information Gathering

A. Indirect strategies of information gathering (informant assessment)
    1. Behavioral interview
    2. Behavioral scales and questionnaires
B. Direct observation strategies of information gathering (descriptive assessment)
    1. Anecdotal reports
    2. Scatter plot analysis
    3. A-B-C descriptive analysis

the behavior and the circumstances surrounding its occurrence. Because this questioning necessarily takes place after the behavior has occurred, it is limited by the informant's memory, presence during the behavior, distraction by other events, potential bias, and ability to verbalize what was seen (Dracobly et al., 2018; Kazdin, 2001).

BEHAVIORAL INTERVIEW The purpose of a behavioral or functional interview is to get as complete a picture as possible of the problem behavior and the environmental conditions and events surrounding it. A teacher may interview a parent about a behavior occurring at home; a special education teacher may interview a general education teacher about a behavior occurring in math class. A baffled teacher may ask a colleague or supervisor to interview him. The interview provides preliminary information to help form a hypothesis about what may be occasioning or maintaining the behavior and may be used to structure direct observation and data collection for further analysis. The interviewer wants to know, for example:

- the topography, frequency, and duration of the behavior
- at what times of day the behavior occurs
- during what activities the behavior often or always occurs
- in what settings the behavior often or always occurs
- with what materials the student is engaged when the behavior occurs
- what people are present
- what often or always happens right before the behavior occurs (antecedents)
- what the student does right after the behavior occurs
- what other people do right after the behavior occurs (consequences)
- what are the primary ways the student communicates
- what efforts have already been made to reduce the behavior

Things that can be learned by interviewing.

Four examples of structured behavioral interviews are the Functional Assessment Interview (FAI; O'Neill et al., 1997), the Student Guided Functional Assessment Interview (O'Neill et al., 1997; Reed, Thomas, Sprague, & Horner, 1997), the Student-Assisted Functional Assessment Interview (Kern, Dunlap, Clarke, & Childs, 1994), and the Functional Assessment Checklist: Teachers and Staff (FACTS; March et al., 2000; McIntosh et al., 2008). The student-involved interviews were found to agree closely with the results of teacher interviews; however, some responses were inconsistent or vague.

Open-ended interviews involve asking questions like those bulleted above and may be especially useful in identifying the specific, nuanced, and sometimes multiple antecedents and consequences controlling challenging behaviors (Coffey et al., 2020; Hanley et al., 2014; Jessel et al., 2018). For example, by asking a parent what the child gets when he engages in screaming, the parent might report that when he screams, he leaves the dinner table and goes to the living room to watch TV. This would indicate that the teaching team needs to teach appropriate ways of asking for a break from dinner and access to TV.

BEHAVIOR RATING SCALES Behavior rating scales are instruments designed to obtain more quantitative information from informants. Informants are asked to respond to items describing behavior with a rating (for example, never, seldom, usually, always). The items are related to several possible functions that behavior might serve. Several individual items may elicit information about the same function. The function whose items receive the highest cumulative rating is hypothesized to be the variable maintaining the student's inappropriate behavior. Following are descriptions of four such scales.

The Problem Behavior Questionnaire (PBQ) (Lewis, Scott, & Sugai, 1994) is comprised of 15 items correlated to five functions. Informants are asked to indicate the frequency with which an event is likely to be observed. The range of the item rating scale is: never, 10% of the time, 25%, 50%, 75%, 90% of the time, and always. Examples of functions and correlated items are:

1. *Access to peer attention.* "When the problem behavior occurs, do peers verbally respond to or laugh at the student?"
2. *Access to teacher attention.* "Does the problem behavior occur to get your attention when you are working with other students?"
3. *Escape/avoid peer attention.* "If the student engages in the problem behavior, do peers stop interacting with the student?"
4. *Escape/avoid teacher attention.* "Will the student stop doing the problem behavior if you stop making requests or end an academic activity?"
5. *Setting events.* "Is the problem behavior more likely to occur following unscheduled events or disruptions in classroom routines?"

The Motivation Assessment Scale (MAS; Durand & Crimmins, 1988, 1992) is comprised of 16 items correlated to four functions. Informants are asked to indicate the frequency with which an individual is likely to exhibit an operationalized target behavior. Examples of functions and correlated items are:

1. *Sensory reinforcement.* "Would the behavior occur continuously, over and over, if this person were left alone for long periods of time?"
2. *Escape.* "Does the behavior stop occurring shortly after (1 to 5 minutes) you stop working with or making demands on this person?"
3. *Attention.* "Does the behavior seem to occur in response to your talking to other persons in the room?"
4. *Tangible.* "Does the behavior stop occurring shortly after you give this person the toy, food, or activity he or she has requested?"

The Functional Analysis Screening Tool (FAST; Iwata & DeLeon, 1996) is comprised of 18 items. These items are correlated to four likely maintaining functions (five items per function; two items overlap). It is recommended that the FAST be administered to several individuals who interact frequently with the target individual. The informant is asked to indicate "yes" or "no" as to whether an item statement accurately describes the person's target behavior problem. Examples of the maintaining functions and correlated items are:

1. *Social reinforcement (attention/preferred items).* "When the behavior occurs, do you usually try to calm the person down or distract the person with preferred activities (leisure items, snacks, etc.)?"
2. *Social reinforcement (escape).* "When the behavior occurs, do you usually give the person a 'break' from ongoing tasks?"
3. *Automatic reinforcement (sensory stimulation).* "Does the behavior occur at high rates regardless of what is going on around the person?"
4. *Automatic reinforcement (pain attenuation).* "Does the behavior occur more often when the person is sick?"

The Questions About Behavioral Function (QABF; Matson & Vollmer, 1995; Paclawskyj, Matson, Rush, Smalls, & Vollmer, 2000) is comprised of 25 items correlated to five functions. The informant is asked to rate how often each specifically targeted behavior occurs. Examples of functions and correlated items are:

1. *Attention.* "Engages in the behavior to try to get a reaction from you."
2. *Escape.* "Engages in the behavior when asked to do something" (get dressed, brush teeth, work, etc.).

3. *Nonsocial.* "Engages in the behavior even if he/she thinks no one is in the room."
4. *Physical.* "Engages in the behavior more frequently when he/she is ill."
5. *Tangible.* "Engages in the behavior when you have something he/she wants."

Special education and general education students can contribute valuable information to the development of hypotheses of behavior function. This includes information about preferences, academic difficulties, setting distractions, and conflicts with peers and adults. Information gathered through interviews should be used with caution. Some responses can be inconsistent, vague, or impracticable. Type and severity of disability, and age, may affect the quality and reliability of a student's contribution. For both student and adult informants, there appears to be greater accuracy and consistency when the information concerns situations and classrooms that are highly likely to evoke problem behavior (Dufrene et al., 2017; Flanagan & DeBar, 2018; Kern et al., 1994; Trussell et al., 2018). Similar cautions are expressed about using behavior rating scales. Item ratings by teachers and parents have resulted in low percentages of reliability across items, across administrations of a scale, across rating scales, and across raters (Dracobly et al., 2018; Fee et al., 2016; Herscovitch et al., 2009; May et al., 2014; Wasano et al., 2009; Zarcone, Rodgers, Iwata, Rourke, & Dorsey, 1991).

DIRECT OBSERVATION STRATEGIES: DESCRIPTIVE ASSESSMENT   Direct observation strategies are ways of describing behavior that is directly observed. They are more reliable than informant assessment. Someone who takes notes as he observes the problem behavior directly will provide a more accurate description of the context, antecedents, and consequences than someone who is working from memory. Three methods of direct observation include the use of anecdotal reports, scatter plot analysis, and A-B-C descriptive analysis (see Table 7.2). (A-B-C is an alternative way of expressing S-R-S: Antecedent stimulus—Behavior/response—Consequence stimulus.)

ANECDOTAL REPORTS   Anecdotal reports are written to provide as complete a description as possible of a student's behavior and the events surrounding it. An observer preparing an anecdotal report attempts to record in regular prose each occurrence of a target behavior and the context, activities, and interactions within which it occurs. This is done within defined observation periods, preferably over several days. (Preparation of anecdotal reports is described in detail in Chapter 4.) What makes these reports a tool of analysis is transferring the prose into a structured format that clearly identifies and labels instances of the target behavior, the immediate antecedent, and the consequence. The A-B-C formatting of this information is illustrated in Figure 4.2. This formatting facilitates identifying temporal relationship patterns among the three elements. It is the identification of patterns of particular antecedents and consequences associated with a target behavior that yields a hypothesis of function.

SCATTER PLOT ANALYSIS   The scatter plot procedure is an assessment tool found to be easy and useful by classroom teachers (Maas et al., 2009; Symons, McDonald, & Wehby, 1998; Touchette, MacDonald, & Langer, 1985). It is used primarily to identify the common locations and times of day challenging behaviors do and do not occur. Once identified, more intensive assessment methods, such as A-B-C descriptive analysis, can be implemented during those times and in those locations. The scatter plot procedure can be helpful in identifying a relationship between an environmental condition and behavior that is frequent, seemingly random, but steady over long periods of time. For such behaviors, informal observations often do not suggest correspondence with particular stimuli.

Things that inappropriate behaviors might serve to communicate.

For scatter plot assessment, the teacher prepares a grid. Figure 7.3 shows four sample grids (A, B, C, D). On grid A, successive days or observation periods are plotted along the horizontal. Time is plotted along the vertical. Time may be divided into hours, half hours, quarter hours, and so forth, depending on the time available for observation and observation frequency. As an alternative, shown on grids C and D, time may be denoted as class periods or instructional formats.

Figure 7.3 Sample scatter plot grids

SCATTER PLOT

Student: _____ Behavior: _____

SCORING: Blank = 0 occurrences Slash = < 4 Solid = 4/ > 4

Time	Day/Date					Activity/Location	Comments
8:00–8:20							
8:20–8:40							
8:40–9:00							
9:00–9:20							
9:20–9:40							
9:40–10:00							
10:00–10:20							
10:20–10:40							
10:40–11:00							
11:00–11:20							
11:20–11:40							
11:40–12:00							

SCATTER PLOT

Student: _____ Behavior: _____

SCORING: Blank = 0 occurrences Slash = < 3 Solid = 3/ > 3

Time	Day/Date					Activity/Location	Comments
1-Reading: special instruction							
2-Computer							
3-Earth science							
4-Lunch							
5-Language arts: special instruction							
6-Consumer math							

SCATTER PLOT

Student: Nancy Behavior: Loud vocalizations

SCORING: Blank = 0 occurrences Slash = < 4 Solid = 4/ > 4

Time	Mon 3-16	Tue 3-17	Wed 3-18	Thur 3-19	Fri 3-20	Activity/Location	Comments
8:00–8:20	■	■	■	/	■	Hygiene	Hand over hand
8:20–8:40						Snack	Hand over hand, spoon feed
8:40–9:00							
9:00–9:20							
9:20–9:40							
9:40–10:00			/	/	■	Toy skills	
10:00–10:20							
10:20–10:40							
10:40–11:00							
11:00–11:20							
11:20–11:40	■	■	■	/	■	Hygiene	Physical resistance
11:40–12:00	■	■	■	/	■	Lunch	Hand over hand

SCATTER PLOT

Student: _____ Behavior: _____

SCORING: Blank = 0 occurrences Slash = < 3 Solid = 3/ > 3

Format/Content Area						Activity/Location	Comments
Large group instruction							
Small group instruction							
One:one instruction							
Independent activity							
Activity transition							
Setting transition							
Hygiene							
Toileting							
Eating: lunch/snack							

As the scatter grid is filled in, each cell contains a designation indicating whether the behavior occurred at a high, low, or zero rate (see grid B). A cell is left blank if the behavior did not occur during the interval; a cell has a slash through it to indicate a low rate of occurrence during the interval (for example, < 4); or a cell is filled in completely to indicate a high rate of occurrence (for example, = or > 4). Inserting numbers to represent the exact number of occurrences in the cell will provide a more precise representation (Axelrod, 1987). Once the grids are completed, they can be analyzed for the presence of correlational patterns. "A pattern, should one exist, can emerge as soon as several days are plotted" (Touchette et al., 1985, p. 345). Kahng et al. (1998) cautioned that patterns may not be evident without statistical analysis, even with as much as a month's data. Touchette et al. (1985) suggested that problem behavior may be found to correlate to a time of day, the presence or absence of certain people, a social setting, certain types of activities, a reinforcement contingency, a physical environment, or combinations of variables. They suggested a scatter plot offers "insights into patterns of responding not readily available from graphs of daily or weekly frequency" (p. 351). Patterns may be considered to occur when three or more adjacent intervals across days contained either a low- or high-frequency occurrence of the behavior (Symons et al., 1998). Such patterns can be seen in grid B during the 8:00–8:20 interval across 5 days, the 8:40–9:00 interval across 4 days, and the 11:20–11:40 and 11:40–12:00 intervals all week. Assistance in interpreting these patterns can be derived from notations of activity and location and the accompanying comments. In the example in grid B, one can begin to see correlations between the targeted behavior and, in this case, hand-over-hand techniques during hygiene and eating instruction.

There are currently no empirical data that suggest how to set a value for low or high rates of occurrence, especially across different populations of students. The value chosen will affect the cells identified as part of a pattern, and therefore any resulting hypothesis. A different picture will emerge depending on the value chosen. One suggestion is that values may be chosen by identifying rates of behavior considered disruptive by the teacher in particular settings (Symons et al., 1998). The teacher would decide how much behavior could be tolerated for a student included in a general education class, which may be less than the amount of disruption tolerated in a special education class or more than that which would be acceptable in a community setting.

Axelrod (1987) noted that a scatter plot will detect only environmental conditions that are related to behavior on a time-cyclical basis. Some events affect behavior in a noncyclical manner. For example, a student may become disruptive whenever a classmate is given a special privilege or when the student feels she was treated unfairly or "cheated." Axelrod suggests that it might be helpful to write comments on the data sheet to document such events. Although a scatter plot may not be as precise or efficient as other descriptive analyses for revealing cause-effect or correlational relationships between behavior and specific environmental events (Kahng et al., 1998), it can narrow the field of analysis so closer assessment can be conducted more efficiently (Lennox & Miltenberger, 1989). It is a procedure a classroom teacher can carry out with little or no help to gather initial descriptive data of the behavior. These data can then be augmented with more precise data collection as the team decides how to proceed.

A-B-C DESCRIPTIVE ANALYSIS A-B-C descriptive analysis provides a structure for noting behavior and the environmental events that surround it, as it is being observed, or later while viewing a videotape. Instead of the two-step anecdotal report process of writing in prose what is observed and then restructuring the notes, this procedure uses coded notations made on a prepared data sheet. The format of the data sheet imposes the A-B-C (S-R-S) structure on observations as the data are collected. Various procedures for data collection and accompanying data sheets are available. Figure 7.4 presents an adaptation of the data collection sheet by Smith and Heflin, 2001. (Alternative formats are available from O'Neill et al., 1997 and Umbreit, Ferro, Liaupson, & Lane, 2007.)

Figure 7.4 Data sheet for collection of A-B-C descriptive data

STUDENT: _Mona_ DAY/DATE: _Mon 9/16_ LOCATION: _Classroom_ OBSERVATION PERIOD: _8 a.m. – 10 a.m._ OBSERVER: _MC_ PAGE: _1_

Time/Duration	Context/Activity	Antecedent	Target Behavior	Consequence	Student Reaction	Perceived Function	Comments
8:20	1, 5	B, D	1, 4	E, A	2, 3		Hand and face washing
↓	1, 5	A, D	1, 2, 4	E, A, B	2, 1, 3		
8:26	1, 5	A, D	1, 2, 3	E, C	2		Face slapping
	1, 5	A, D	1, 3	B, C, F	1		

Recording Codes:

Context/Activity	Antecedent	Target Behavior	Consequence	Student Reaction	Perceived Function
1. Sink hygiene	A. Hand/hand	1. Scream	A. Redirect/guide	1. Stop	A. ATT
2. Toilet	B. Hand/arm	2. Stamp	B. "No"	2. Continue	B. ESC
3. Group table	C. Material	3. Slap	C. Restrain	3. Escalate	C. Stim
4. Snack table	D. Verbal cue	4. Resist	D. Ignore	4. New behav.	D. Tang
5. Teacher	E. "No"	5.	E. Calm talk	5. Move-run	E. UNK
6. Parapro	F.	6.	F. End activity	6.	F.
7.	G.	7.	G.	7.	G.
8.	H.	8.	H.	8.	H.
9.	I.	9.	I.	9.	I.
10.	J.	10.	J.	10.	J.

Operational Definitions

Behavior 1: _scream—high pitch vocalization above conversation level_

Behavior 2: _stamp—feet strike floor with force beyond used for walking_

Behavior 3: _slap—hand or fist strikes face or head_

Behavior 4: _resist—body pulling in opposition to physical prompt_

(Adaptation of Smith & Heflin, 2001)

NOTE: From "Supporting Positive Behavior in Public Schools: An Intervention Program in Georgia," by M. Smith & L. J. Heflin, 2001, *Journal of Positive Behavior Interventions*, 3, pp. 39–47. Copyright (2001) by PRO-ED, Inc. Reprinted with permission.

The A-B-C Descriptive Data Sheet and Procedure As seen in Figure 7.4, the form has four sections. From top to bottom, they are (1) identification information, (2) columns and rows for data collection, (3) lists of recording codes, and (4) operational definitions of target behaviors.

Identification information. The top of the sheet provides basic identification information: (a) The name of the student. (b) The day of the observation. (c) The location of the observation. (d) The beginning and ending time of the observation period. (e) The name of the person making the observations. (f) The page number.

In Figure 7.4, the data sheet is prepared for observations of Mona's behavior on Monday, September 16, from 8:00 a.m. to 10:00 a.m., in her classroom. This is page 1 of data collected by MC.

Columns and rows for data collection. Columns are provided for the following information about each instance of behavior as it occurs:

1. *Time/duration:* The beginning and ending time, and the duration of each occurrence of behavior.
2. *Context/activity:* The setting events—activity, persons, materials.
3. *Antecedent:* The stimulus event immediately preceding the occurrence of the target behavior. Don't confuse this with precursor behaviors. Behaviors do not go in this column; only stimuli in the student's environment go in this column. In schools, antecedents are often what other people say and do.
4. *Target behavior:* The behavior for which the observation is designed to describe. Working operational definitions appear at the bottom of the page.
5. *Consequences:* The occurrences that immediately follow the student's engagement in the target behavior. These may include environmental events or reactions by the teacher, peers, or others in the setting. (Note: Avoid writing the target student's behaviors in this column.)
6. *Student reaction:* What does the student do immediately following the target behavior and its consequences?
7. *Perceived function:* At the time of data collection, the observer may make note of an initial judgment of the function served by the behavior.
8. *Comments:* Notes of novel or unexpected aspects of the interaction, details for which codes are not provided, a specific material used, or some unexpected occurrence (for example, the student has a seizure, an unexpected person enters the setting).

Lists of recording codes. To assist the observer's fluency in data collection, this space allows for listing various "common" codes needed for this particular student. The lists of codes are derived from information gathered earlier and from at least one opportunity for informal observation during which the observer practices with the data sheet.

In Figure 7.4, the codes for context/activity are those that are scheduled during the observation time period: morning hygiene and toileting, group instruction of various content, and snack. Codes are also included for members of the staff who usually interact with the student. Noted under antecedents are codes for physical assistance, materials, and verbal cues. The column for target behaviors lists those previously agreed upon. This list may be expanded if additional behaviors are repeatedly observed. In this case, screaming, stomping, slapping, and resisting are Mona's target behaviors. Consequences listed are those noted during observation that the teacher uses regularly with this student. Mona's teacher regularly uses redirection, verbal "No," restraint, ignoring, and calm talk. There is also a code to note when the teacher ends a task or activity. The next column lists codes for student reactions to the interactions occurring and the consequences. A basic list like the one on this form will be common across observations: the behavior stops, continues, or escalates; a new behavior occurs; or the student moves or runs from the interaction. The next column lists four possible functions of behavior: attention, escape, stimulation, and tangible; and a code for unknown at this time. As data collection continues, the observer may add subcategories of functions such as attention from adult or peer, or escape from social interaction or academic task.

Operational definitions. For easy and repeated access for the data collector, the operational definition of each target behavior is provided at the bottom of the data sheet.

DATA COLLECTING With the prepared data collection sheet in hand, the data collector makes note of each occurrence of the behavior in the column labeled "Target Behavior." Having noted the behavior, the observer then moves his pen horizontally across the page, noting the consequence provided and the student's reaction. He then notes the antecedent, the time of occurrence, and the context. If the function of the behavior for that occurrence is immediately evident, the perceived function is filled in. If not, "unknown" is written in the cell.

DATA ANALYSIS Data analysis occurs daily and weekly. At the end of each day or observation period, the data collector (and others, if possible) reviews that day's data for (a) confirmation of the occurrence of the target behavior; (b) validity of the operational definitions; (c) occurrences of new inappropriate behaviors, antecedents, or consequences; (d) consistent relationships emerging between particular behaviors and consequences or between particular behaviors and antecedents; (e) when the student terminates the behavior; and (f) emerging functions. In addition, ongoing tallies are kept of the percent of various antecedents and consequences.

In-depth analysis of the data occurs following at least 5 days of data collection. The same questions asked of informants during interviews are now asked of these data. The purpose is to illuminate any patterns among antecedents, behavior, and consequences. These patterns are identified in part by looking horizontally across rows for consistent A-B-C relationships. It is then noted if these relationships and elements are repeated over occurrences of behavior: for example, are the same antecedents occasioning the same behaviors, resulting in the same consequences, resulting in the same student reactions? Analysis questions may include:

- Is the behavior occurring within the context of the same activity, materials, instructor, or group of peers? Does this behavior occur with both Ms. Brown and Mr. Green?
- Does the behavior consistently occur following particular antecedents? What percent of each antecedent appears in the data?
- Following instances of the behavior, is there a consistent consequence used by the teacher, peers, or other adults? What percent of each consequence appears in the data?
- Does the student terminate the behavior following a particular consequence? In what percent of occurrence does the consequence result in the student's terminating the behavior?
- Does the same S-R-S occur repeatedly, leading to a consistent hypothesis of function across all, or almost all, occurrences of the behavior? (What can you say about the occurrences that do not fit the pattern?) What percent of this pattern appears within the data?

Figure 7.4 presents an example of data recorded about the behavior of Mona, a student with autism. It reflects a cluster of behaviors that occurred from 8:20 to 8:26 a.m. The notations were taken during morning hygiene when Mona was being instructed on hand and face washing. The following statements can be made based on these data:

- There is confirmation of occurrence of the target behaviors during morning instruction of hygiene skills and tasks.
- This interaction occurs entirely at the sink during instruction of hand and face washing.
- For each occurrence of the behavior, the antecedent is delivery of a verbal cue and the use of hand-over-hand prompting (with one occasion of hand-at-arm).
- The consequences used by the teacher were talking calmly to the student and redirecting to the task. As the behavior escalated, the teacher used a verbal reprimand and then restraint. There is an A-B-C pattern of hand-over-hand—target behavior—calm talk and redirection. Each occurrence of a target behavior occurs at the sink, is immediately preceded by a verbal cue and physical prompt (hand-over-hand), and is followed by calm talk and redirection. At the third occurrence of the behavior, restraint was added.
- Despite these consequences, the behavior continues and eventually escalates.
- The student reaction is continuation and escalation by adding face slapping.
- The behavior is not ended until after the fourth occurrence of the behavior, at which point the teacher stops the activity.
- This implies an escape function. The behavior is terminated once it serves its purpose. If this is escape-motivated behavior, does Mona use it with other activities she does not like in order to terminate them?

Repp, Nieminen, Olinger, and Brusca (1988) demonstrated that interventions based on hypotheses derived from an A-B-C descriptive analysis were more effective than those that were not. Oftentimes in classrooms, teachers can identify the function of challenging behavior and design an effective intervention based on conducting an A-B-C descriptive analysis. Other times, however, it is more difficult to identify the function using a descriptive analysis, and a functional analysis is required (see below). It is important to remember that a relationship established as a result of A-B-C descriptive analysis is correlational, not causal. Because descriptive analyses identify functions based on variables occurring in a classroom, descriptive analyses may produce more effective interventions (English & Anderson, 2006). On the other hand, several researchers have found that functional analyses are stronger determinants of function than descriptive analyses (Martens et al., 2019; Thompson & Iwata, 2007). Additionally, researchers have found that incorporating the results of a descriptive analysis into a functional analysis is important (Galiatsatos & Graff, 2003; Tiger, Hanley, & Bessette, 2006). Nevertheless, once a relationship found in an A-B-C descriptive analysis leads to a hypothesis concerning what is occasioning or maintaining the behavior, structured data collection and manipulation of the variables in a functional analysis are possible.

ABC Data
Pearson eText
Video Example 7.3
In this video, an educator describes how to collect and analyze ABC data utilizing a high-tech platform. What are some advantages of using a high-tech data collection system that you notice?
https://www.youtube.com/watch?v=xThcmhwFlKw

Step 4. Conduct a Functional Analysis of Behavior

An FBA may result in a clear indication of the function of an inappropriate behavior. If, however, the function remains unclear following an FBA, the teacher and IEP committee may request a functional analysis. Functional analysis comprises a set of procedures for determining the function of a behavior by systematic manipulation of environmental variables, both antecedents and consequences, and documentation of their effect on the occurrence of the target behavior. The goal is to examine the effect of each variable's presence, absence, heightening, or lessening. Although there is research that indicates a teacher may conduct a functional analysis, given the complexity of the procedure it is most common that the teacher and at least a behavior specialist are involved due to the potential for injury to the student or others in the environment. A functional analysis is conducted for one of the following reasons:

1. to verify a hypothesis resulting from an FBA. If, for example, an FBA results in a hypothesis that the inappropriate behavior is maintained by positive reinforcement

from teacher attention, the student is placed in a condition where brief teacher attention is provided when the behavior occurs and in a condition where teacher attention is withheld.
2. to refine the hypothesis resulting from an FBA. If, for example, the hypothesis is that the behavior is maintained by positive reinforcement resulting from attention, additional analysis seeks to identify the source of the attention.
3. to clarify uncertain results of an FBA. The data resulting from indirect and direct strategies are unclear; they do not suggest a particular function.
4. to serve as the initial step in the development of a hypothesis of function.

The basic model for arranging the manipulation of environmental variables is to place the student in two or more conditions in which the settings and interactions are purposefully structured. Two conditions may be used if one variable is being assessed, or two are being compared (Hanley et al., 2014; Strohmeier, Pace, & Luiselli, 2014; Tiger et al., 2009; Ward & Higbee, 2008). If, for example, the purpose of the functional analysis is to refine an understanding of the source of attention, the student is placed in a condition in which attention is provided by an adult and one in which a peer provides attention. Two conditions may also be used if the purpose is to clarify whether the correct hypothesis of function is attention or self-stimulation. The student may be placed in a situation where attention is provided when he performs the target behavior and one where no attention is available. Four conditions are used when the function of a behavior is initially to be identified through functional analysis. The conditions arranged represent the basic functions of behavior (or some variation) as initially discussed by Iwata, Dorsey, Slifer, Bauman, and Richman (1982). These conditions and functions are:

1. *Attention condition.* This condition is used to test if a student is engaging in inappropriate behavior to gain positive reinforcement in the form of social attention from an adult or peer. During this condition, the student has access to moderately preferred activities, and the evaluator is engaged in reading or some other activity unrelated to the student. When (and only when) there is an instance of the target behavior, the evaluator provides brief attention, such as a statement of concern or a reprimand. Increased levels of the behavior in this condition suggest it has the function of gaining access to positive reinforcement in the form of social attention.
2. *Tangible condition.* This condition is used to test if a student is engaging in inappropriate behavior to gain positive reinforcement in the form of a preferred object, activity, or event. During this condition, the student interacts with the adult and is denied access to the preferred object, activity, or event. When the student engages in the inappropriate behavior, the adult provides access to the object, activity, or event for a limited time, such as 15 seconds. Increased levels of the behavior in this condition suggest the function is to gain access to positive reinforcement in the form of a preferred object, activity, or event.
3. *Demand condition.* This condition is used to test if a student is engaging in inappropriate behavior to escape from demands. This represents negative reinforcement. The adult presents and prompts the student through demands in the form of undesirable tasks, difficult tasks, tasks the student cannot do, or social demands. Each time the student engages in the inappropriate behavior, the demand is briefly removed, for 15 seconds or so, and the student is given a break from the task. Increased levels of the inappropriate behavior in this condition suggest the function is to escape a demand, and it is thus being maintained by negative reinforcement.
4. *Alone condition.* This condition is used to test if a student is engaging in inappropriate behavior to provide self-stimulation, also referred to as automatic reinforcement. The setting contains no activities, materials, reinforcers, or other sources of stimulation. There are no externally supplied consequences for the behavior. If it is safe, no other people are in the room; sometimes an adult is in the room to ensure safety but generally ignores the student. Increased levels of the behavior

in this condition suggest the function is to provide self-stimulation and it is thus being maintained by automatic reinforcement.
5. *Play condition.* This condition represents a control condition. The student is placed in an environment rich with materials and social attention from the evaluator, as well as the absence of demands. If the behavior does occur, there should be no explicit consequences. Under this condition the instances of inappropriate behavior should be minimal or nonexistent.

Manipulation of Variables One framework for the manipulation of variables during functional analysis is the multi-element design (a variation of the alternating treatments design). Van Camp, Lerman, Kelley, Contrucci, and Vorndran (2000) conducted a functional analysis with Rachel, a 21-year-old public school student with moderate to severe intellectual disability. She was referred for aggression, defined as hitting, pinching, kicking, or pushing; and for self-injury, defined as forceful contact between one or both hands and her head. The functional analysis was conducted in an unused room at the school. Three to five 10-minute sessions were conducted 2 to 5 days per week. Data were collected using frequency recording, and the data were reported as number of responses per minute. Rachel experienced the following five conditions:

1. *Alone.* Self-injury was ignored, and there were no attention, leisure materials, or demands. The purpose of this condition was to evaluate whether self-injury would persist in the absence of social consequences.
2. *Attention.* Twenty seconds of attention was delivered on each occurrence of aggression or self-injury, and Rachel had continuous access to leisure materials. This condition was designed to determine if Rachel's challenging behavior was maintained by positive reinforcement in the form of attention.
3. *Tangible.* Twenty seconds of access to leisure materials was delivered upon each occurrence of aggression or self-injury, and Rachel had continuous access to attention. This condition was designed to identify behavior maintained by positive reinforcement in the form of access to tangible leisure materials.
4. *Demand.* Twenty seconds of escape from continuous tasks was delivered upon each occurrence of aggression or self-injury. This condition was designed to identify if the challenging behaviors were maintained by negative reinforcement in the form of escape from tasks.
5. *Play.* Rachel had continuous access to attention and preferred items, no demands were delivered, and all problem behavior was ignored. This condition served as the control for comparison with the other conditions.

Figure 7.5 displays the occurrence of Rachel's aggression and self-injury under each condition. The occurrence of the behavior is consistently highest only during the tangible condition, therefore suggesting that the problem behavior was maintained by access to tangible reinforcement in the form of leisure materials.

Settings for Conducting Functional Analysis

Functional analysis can be conducted in special education and general education classrooms, community settings, and community-vocational settings. In these natural settings, the behavior and the natural surrounding events, people, and contingencies are in effect (Austin, Groves, Reynish, & Francis, 2015; Flanagan et al., 2020; Greer et al., 2013; Hansen et al., 2019; Hughes, Alberto, & Fredrick, 2006; Kodak et al., 2013; Lampert, Lopano, Noel, & Richie, 2017; Ledford et al., 2019; Lloyd, Weaver, & Staubitz, 2016; Reid, Parsons, & Lattimore, 2010; Rispoli et al., 2013). Some studies, however, have been conducted in an analog setting. An analog setting is an environment outside the classroom where very controlled presentation of the conditions can be managed.

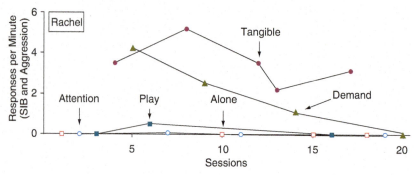

Figure 7.5 Use of a multi-element design for functional analysis

NOTE: From "Variable-Time Reinforcement Schedules in the Treatment of Socially Maintained Problem Behavior," by C. Van Camp, D. Lerman, M. Kelley, S. Contrucci, & C. Vorndran, 2000, *Journal of Applied Behavior Analysis, 33*(4), pp. 545–557. Copyright 2000 by The Society for the Experimental Analysis of Behavior. Reprinted by permission.

It is this precision that makes it an option sometimes selected. In the controlled analog setting it is possible that the behavior will not be exposed to the same variables found in the natural environment; thus different functions may be identified in the analog and in the natural setting (Hansen et al., 2019; Jessel et al., 2014; Petrongolo et al., 2015; Rooker et al., 2011). In schools, a teacher and behavior specialist often use an unoccupied classroom as an analog setting. Thomason-Sassi, Iwata, and Fritz (2013) compared the results of functional analyses conducted by behavior specialists in a clinic and functional analyses completed by trained parents in their homes. These across-setting analyses were conducted on the self-injurious behavior, aggression, and property destruction of three elementary school-aged children with developmental disabilities. The results were the same in the controlled environment of the clinic and the less-controlled home environment. These comparisons suggest that functional analysis does not have to be conducted in analog settings by behavior specialists. Teachers can be trained to conduct valid analyses in their classrooms (Alnemary et al., 2017; Chok et al., 2012; Griffith et al., 2020; Lambert et al., 2014; Pence et al., 2014; Rios et al., 2020; Rispoli et al., 2016).

Brief Functional Analysis

Adaptations to the functional analysis process have been investigated to make it more practical and efficient for use in schools with students with special needs, at-risk students, and general education students. Initially, functional analysis procedures involved as many as 50 to 60 sessions of up to 30 minutes each to identify and verify the function of behavior. This *extended* functional analysis format could take many days. The development of a *brief* functional analysis (BFA) format reduced the individual sessions in which the various conditions are in place from 5 to 10 minutes, allowing completion in 90 minutes or less. These shorter sessions have been found to yield the same interpretations, leading to the same identification of functions. The total number of sessions conducted is also reduced by not including all four conditions. The information gathered from methods of functional assessment is used to narrow the possible controlling variables. It should be noted that the behavior must occur at a high frequency if sufficient information is to be captured in shorter and fewer sessions (Badgett & Falcomata, 2015; Call et al., 2013; Falcomata et al., 2016; Meuthing et al., 2017; Perrin et al., 2008).

Additional formats for BFA have been used successfully. In a grocery store site used for community-based vocational training, Cihak, Alberto, and Fredrick (2007) used a BFA to experimentally confirm the results of teacher interviews. The BFA included conditions for escape-from-task demands, attention, and control. Students participated in one 10-minute session for each condition, with a 10-minute break between conditions. As seen in Figure 7.6, data were plotted cumulatively by 1-minute intervals (Vollmer, Iwata,

Figure 7.6 A form of brief functional analysis

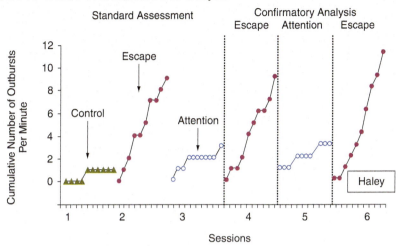

NOTE: From "Use of Brief Functional Analysis and Intervention Evaluation in Public Settings," by D. Cihak, P. Alberto, & L. Fredrick, 2007, *Journal of Positive Behavior Interventions, 9*(2), 80–93. Copyright (2007) by the Hammill Institute on Disability. Reprinted with permission.

Zarcone, Smith, & Mazaleski, 1993), and indicated that escape was the function of the behavior. This was then confirmed as the students participated in three additional sessions immediately following completion of the functional analysis. The condition with the highest level of target behaviors during the BFA (i.e., escape) was repeated twice, alternated with the condition that produced the second highest occurrences of the target behavior (e.g., attention). In general education classrooms, Casey and Merical (2006) conducted BFA of a series of 5-minute conditions, for example, for attention, escape, and control. The condition associated with the highest percentage of the target behavior (self-injury) was repeated. As shown in Figure 7.7, the percentage of 10-second intervals with self-injury for each 5-minute session was graphed. The results of the BFA indicated the highest percentages of intervals of self-injury occurred during escape conditions, providing evidence that Karl used self-injury to escape or avoid demands.

Step 5. Develop Behavior Support Plan
    a. Review hypothesis and select components of a behavior support plan.
    b. Collect and use data to evaluate and revise plan as necessary.
    c. Maintain and generalize successful results and fade intervention as appropriate.

Figure 7.7 A form of brief functional analysis

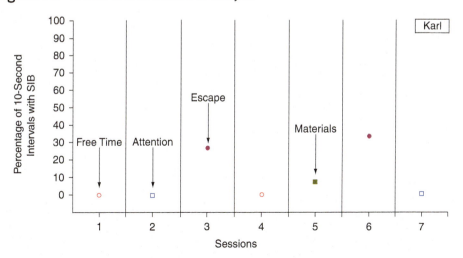

NOTE: From "The Use of Functional Communication Training without Additional Treatment Procedures in an Inclusive School Setting," by S. Casey & C. Merical, 2006, *Behavioral Disorders, 32*, 46–54. Copyright 2006, by Council for Children with Behavioral Disorders. Reprinted with permission.

A behavior support plan (BSP) summarizes the information generated, presents the hypothesis of function, and details agreed-upon procedures for behavior change and support. Most state education agencies and school districts have a specific form for writing BSPs; some incorporate it as part of the IEP document. These and other published forms have various components. Figure 7.8 is a sample BSP with many components common to such forms.

Figure 7.8 Sample behavior support plan

BEHAVIOR SUPPORT PLAN

STUDENT _____ DOB _____ CLASS _____

Date of Meeting:

(1) **Team Members:**

Name	Title/Role Assigned

(2) **Operational Definition** of Target Behavior: _____

Figure 7.8 (Continued)

(3) Summary of **Strategies Previously Used:**

Inclusive dates of implementation:
Person(s) implementing intervention strategy:
Components of intervention strategy:

Effectiveness data (attach documentation as appropriate):

Inclusive dates of implementation:
Person(s) implementing intervention strategy:
Components of intervention strategy:

Effectiveness data (attach documentation as appropriate):

Figure 7.8 (Continued)

(4) Results of **Screening:**

Health:

Medications:

Physical Disability:

Sensory Disability:

Learning Disability:

Other:

Have the results of the screening indicated some action, and has it been implemented?

Figure 7.8 (Continued)

(5) Complete this page if a **Functional Assessment** was conducted.

A. Was an indirect method used? YES _____ NO _____

    If yes, which instrument was used? _____
    (attach the completed instrument)
    e.g., Functional Assessment Interview
           Student Guided Functional Assessment Interview
           Motivation Assessment Scale
           Problem Behavior Questionnaire
           FAST
           QABF

B. Was a direct method used? YES _____ NO _____

    If yes, which procedure was used? _____
    (attach the analysis data sheets)
    e.g., Analysis of Anecdotal Report
           Scatter Plot Analysis
           A-B-C Descriptive Analysis

C. Resulting Hypothesis.

    1. Social attention seeking: adult   _____
                                              peer   _____
    2. Tangible seeking: item/object   _____
                                              activity/event   _____
    3. Self-stimulation   which sense   _____
    4. Escape/avoid: adult   _____
                                              peer   _____
                                              item/object   _____
                                              task/activity   _____
    5. Escape/attenuate: internal pain   _____

D. **SUMMARY STATEMENT OF HYPOTHESIS:**

Figure 7.8 (Continued)

(6) Complete this page if a **Functional Analysis** was conducted.

A. Was the purpose to: verify a hypothesis resulting from a Functional Assessment?
refine a hypothesis resulting from a Functional Assessment?
clarify an uncertain result from a Functional Assessment?
initial development of a hypothesis?

    Purpose: _____
_____

B. Was it conducted in an analog or natural setting? _____
_____
_____

C. What were the conditions used in the analysis? **(attach graph)** _____
_____
_____

D. Resulting Hypothesis.

    1. Social attention seeking: adult   _____
                                               peer   _____
    2. Tangible seeking: item/object   _____
                                               activity/event _____
    3. Self-stimulation: which sense _____
    4. Escape/avoid: adult   _____
                                               peer   _____
                                               item/object _____
                                               task/activity _____
    5. Escape/attenuate: internal pain _____

E. **SUMMARY STATEMENT OF HYPOTHESIS:**

Figure 7.8 (Continued)

(7) **INTERVENTION**

(7a) Current Target Behavior(s):

(7b) Alternative/Replacement Behavior(s) to be taught: (e.g., social skills instruction, self-management training):

Figure 7.8 (Continued)

(7c) Antecedent/setting event strategies (e.g., environment, routines, tasks, personnel, instructional strategy, grouping, timing, etc.):

(7d) Consequence strategies (e.g., DRA, DRO, NCR, redirection, extinction, timeout); functional equivalency training, functional communication training:

Figure 7.8 (Continued)

(7e) Plan for monitoring implementation:

(7f) Maintenance and generalization:

(7g) Crisis intervention: (1) What will constitute a behavioral crisis for which some intervention other than that described in this plan will be necessary? (2) What will be the crisis intervention?

(7h) Staff training, support, and resources needed:

Component 1 lists the behavior-management team, those primarily responsible for the BSP. These members may be the entire IEP team or a subcommittee. In addition to their names and professional roles (for example, teacher, speech–language pathologist), the document also describes their specific role in this plan. The plan will identify the primary and secondary implementers of the strategies and name the person who will monitor the correct implementation of the strategies. Data collectors, members of the crisis team, and teachers in settings to which the behavior change will be generalized may also be named.

Component 2 lists the operational definitions of the target behaviors. These were previously defined by the IEP team and were used during the FBA or functional analysis. Component 3 includes documentation of unsuccessful strategies previously used in an attempt to alter the student's behavior. This may provide some insight to the team as it designs a new course.

Components 4, 5, and 6 represent the activities for developing a hypothesis of function. Component 4 lists the types of screening examinations that were conducted, their results, and any resulting intervention. Component 5 provides information about the FBA. It records the indirect and direct methods of information gathering that were used and the resulting hypothesis. Component 6 provides information about the functional analysis. It provides information about the purpose, setting, conditions of the analysis, and the resulting hypothesis. Appropriate documentation is attached to the BSP document for both FBA and functional analysis.

Component 7 details the elements of the resulting intervention. There are two sets of elements. One set delineates the strategies for teaching and supporting more appropriate behaviors to replace the target behavior (elements 7b, 7c, and 7d), and one set to support that implementation (elements 7e–7h).

Component 7 lists an operational definition of the alternative behavior selected to replace the inappropriate behavior. It also describes the paradigm for teaching the new behavior (for example, social skills training, self-management). Also included are changes to the contextual setting events of those settings in which the behavior occurs and alternatives to the antecedent stimuli that occasion the inappropriate behavior. Delineated are strategies for arranging consequences that will reinforce the alternative behavior and the paradigms within which they will be used (for example, functional communication training). No single intervention approach is always appropriate for a particular function across all students and circumstances. Table 7.3 provides examples of some of the successful strategies that appear in the research literature. Note that these strategies are predominantly positive, reinforcement-based approaches. As noted by Pelios et al. (1999), it appears that the use of functional analysis increases the likelihood of choosing reinforcement-based treatments for self-injurious behavior and aggression, as opposed to punishment-based treatments. Explanations of these strategies appear in the following chapters on procedures to increase behavior and procedures to decrease behavior.

The second set of elements provides for the development of further plans to support implementation. A concern of the team should be that the strategy selected is implemented correctly and consistently. A plan should be developed for periodic observation of, and assistance with, implementation. Once the intervention has been successful, you need a plan for maintenance and ongoing support for the new behavior and for its generalization into other settings at school, in the home, and in the community. The BSP acknowledges the difference between behavior management and crisis management. Behavior management, the overall purpose of the BSP, is a plan for long-lasting behavior change that systematically provides the student alternative behaviors with which to interact with those in the environment. Crisis management requires immediate stopping of inappropriate behavior when the student is out of control. This is an issue of safety rather than long-term learning. Finally, consideration

Developing a Behavior Support Plan
Pearson eText
Video Example 7.4
In this video, two educators discuss the process of developing a behavior support plan. Which steps in the functional behavioral assessment process did they utilize?

Table 7.3 Examples of interventions based on function

Function: ATTENTION

DRA: Athens & Vollmer, 2010; Flynn & Lo, 2016; Wright-Gallo et al., 2006

DRO: Rosa et al., 2015

NCR: Banda & Sokolsky, 2012; Noel & Rubow, 2018; Rubow et al., 2019

FCT: Balka et al., 2016

Extinction: Hanley, Piazza, Fisher, & Eidolons, 1997

Time-out: Coppage & Meindl, 2017; Slocum et al., 2019

Self-management: Wadsworth et al., 2015

Function: TANGIBLE/ACTIVITY

DRA: LeGray et al., 2013; Romani et al., 2019; Schlichenmeyer et al., 2015

DRO: Iannaccone et al., 2020; Sullivan & Roane, 2018

NCR: Clay et al., 2018; Falligant et al., 2020; Kettering et al., 2018

FCT: Betz et al., 2013; Fragale et al., 2016

Function: ESCAPE

DRA: Briggs et al., 2019; Flynn & Lo, 2016; Wright-Gallo et al., 2006

DRO: Call, Wacker, Ringdahl, & Boelter, 2005; Coleman & Holmes, 1998

NCR: (noncontingent escape): Moore et al., 2016

FCT: Davis et al., 2018; Fisher et al., 2014; Gerow et al., 2020; Zangrillo et al., 2016

Extinction: Bloom et al., 2018; Rubio et al., 2020; Tereshko & Sottolano, 2017

Function: SENSORY STIMULATION

DRA: Hedquist & Roscoe, 2020; Roscoe et al., 2013

DRO: Hirst et al., 2019; Gehrman et al., 2017; Nuernberger et al., 2013

NCR: Rosales et al., 2010; Newcomb et al., 2019; Ahearn, Clark, DeBar, & Florentino, 2005 (matched stimuli)

Extinction: Scheithauer et al., 2017

Medication: Carter & Wheeler, 2007

Function: MULTIPLE FUNCTIONS

DRA: Herman et al., 2018

NCR: Falcomata & Gainey, 2014; Phillips et al., 2017; Slocum et al., 2018

FCT: Falcomata et al., 2013; Fewell et al., 2016; Miteer et al., 2019; Scalzo et al., 2015; Tsami & Lerman, 2020

Extinction: Bachmeyer et al., 2019

DRA—Differential Reinforcement of Alternative Behavior
FCT—Functional Communication Training
DRO—Differential Reinforcement of Other Behavior
NCR—Noncontingent Reinforcement

---

must be given to staff training, new personnel, and other support in order for the plan to be successful (for example, a temporary paraprofessional, protective equipment, alternative instructional materials).

Positive Behavior Support

Positive behavior support (PBS) is an application and extension of basic elements of applied behavior analysis. PBS uses these elements to increase appropriate behaviors in a student's repertoire and applies systems-change methods to redesign environments in which the student functions in order to assure generalization and maintenance, and enhance the student's quality of life (Carr et al., 1999; Dunlap et al., 2010,

2012, 2017; Lewis et al., 2010). PBS began with a focus on the individual student level, employing applied behavior analysis (ABA) strategies such as FBA and antecedent manipulation. The goal of PBS, also referred to as Positive Behavior Interventions and Supports (PBIS), is to apply applied behavior analysis at scales of social significance in contexts of classrooms, schools, family, and worksites, thereby impacting a student's lifestyle (Freeman et al., 2016; Lo et al., 2010; McIntosh et al., 2013; Mitchell et al., 2018; Sugai & Horner, 2020).

E. G. Carr et al. (2002) noted that "were it not for the past 35 years of research in applied behavior analysis, PBS could not have come into existence" (p. 5). ABA provides the conceptual framework of the three-term contingency (S-R-S) and the concepts of setting events, stimulus control, generalization, and maintenance. PBS has incorporated assessment and intervention strategies such as shaping, fading, chaining, and prompting, as well as an array of procedures for reducing problem behavior, including differential reinforcement contingencies. In addition, PBS has adopted the methods of direct observation and time series designs developed by ABA researchers (E. G. Carr et al., 2002; Dunlap, 2006; Horner & Sugai, 2015). The core values of PBS are derived from those expressed within the ABA community: prevention of inappropriate and nonfunctional behaviors, application of research-/evidence-based practice to build behavior repertoires, and creating contexts and processes that are person centered and supportive.

PBS employs a three-tiered prevention model (McIntosh et al., 2017; Sugai & Horner, 2020). The primary tier (universal) focuses on all students within the environment (e.g., entire school). Three to five positively stated rules are applied to all students in nonclassroom areas (e.g., hallway, cafeteria, bathrooms). The purpose is to provide a foundation of behavioral support for all students by teaching and reinforcing appropriate behaviors (Farkas et al., 2012). The second tier (targeted) focuses on students for whom the procedures of the first tier were not adequate to address their behavior needs. These students are identified as requiring additional behavioral supports based on data such as number of office discipline referrals and in-school suspensions. These students may receive social skills instruction and participate in peer mentoring programs with other students based on shared behavioral problems (e.g., same type of problem behavior, same location, same time of day). The purpose of this tier is to prevent the student's behaviors from becoming disruptive to the learning environment (Fallon & Feinberg, 2017; Stormont & Reinke, 2013). The third tier (intensive) focuses on students for whom both the universal and targeted tiers were not successful, and for students whose data reflect chronic behavioral problems. In this tier, functional behavioral assessments may be conducted to determine the function of the student's problem behavior as well as to implement a function-based behavioral intervention plan, and may provide wrap-around services. The purpose of this tier is to reduce the intensity and chronicity of the student's problem behavior (Cumming & O'Neill, 2019; Scott & Cooper, 2013).

PBS WITH INDIVIDUAL STUDENTS The foundation of PBS lies in the ABA emphasis to apply principles of behavior to improve the lives of individual students with severe behaviors (Carr et al., 1999; Russa et al., 2015). One of the ABA strategies of individual analysis employed by PBS is the use of functional behavior assessment for determining the purpose of socially significant behaviors, thereby facilitating intervention planning (Crone et al., 2015; Oakes et al., 2018; Stoiber & Gettinger, 2011). For example, Bunch-Crump and Lo (2017) employed positive behavior support to reduce the disruptive behavior and increase the academic engagement of four African American elementary-aged students in an urban school. The children had been participating in Tier 1 of a schoolwide positive behavior support model. Because of ongoing disruptive behaviors, such as talking out, noncompliance, and negative interactions, the four students participated in a Tier 2 intervention, Check

In/Check Out. This consisted of the assistant principal working with the students to set behavioral goals related to the schoolwide expectations and issuing a Daily Report Card indicating whether or not the goals were met. If they were, the student received a reward, such as a sticker, a victory dance, or candy. This intervention resulted in decreases in disruptive behavior for three of the students and some gains in academic engagement. For the student who did not have sustained reductions in disruptive behavior, an FBA was completed that indicated his disruptive behavior served a function of receiving teacher attention. One intervention component was teaching and differentially reinforcing a replacement behavior—a hand raise—to recruit teacher attention. Another intervention component was using a device with an app to self-monitor compliance with classroom rules, such as being respectful. This Tier 3 intervention was successful in decreasing disruptive behavior and increasing academic engagement with this student.

PBS IN LARGER CONTEXTS At the inception of the field of applied behavior analysis, Baer, Wolf, and Risley challenged researchers and educators that "If the application of behavioral techniques does not produce large enough effects for practical value, then application has failed" (Baer, Wolf, and Risley, 1968, p. 96). PBS takes this to what may be seen as the next level by broadening the perspective and application of behavioral principles to social change. PBS strives to impact larger contexts in which the student must function once provided with appropriate behavior in order to assure practical and lasting value to the student and those around him or her who share the setting.

As PBS adds focus to the contexts or environments in which students must function, it brings with it the need for tools of systems change and restructuring for prevention of occurrence and reoccurrence of inappropriate behavior on the part of individual students or groups of students. PBS acknowledges that providing the student with more appropriate or functional behavior, but returning him or her to a dysfunctional context, has no long-term value. The best technology will fail if it is applied in an uncooperative or disorganized context. This principle has made efforts at systems change one of the defining features of PBS. Meaningful change is possible only if systems are restructured in a manner that enables change to occur and be sustained (Andreou et al., 2015; Feuerborn et al., 2015; Freeman et al., 2009). Designing and structuring supports resulting from an FBA for the maintenance of new behavior in the context into which the student must return is required. In order to design these supports, PBS applies principles of ABA and systems analysis. A primary emphasis of the system change as applied in PBS is prevention (the proactive, skill-building aspect of PBS seeks to prevent the recurrence of problem behavior by strengthening communicative competence, self-management skill; the proactive environmental design aspect of PBS is seen in strategies that enhance opportunities for choice making, modifying the setting events that alter the valence of reinforcers, and restructuring curricula; Harn et al., 2015; Sprague et al., 2020).

Classroom Arranging a supportive classroom context within which the intervention resulting from an FBA will operate is a use of preventive strategies. Ongoing classroom systems analyzed for restructuring include reinforcer selection and delivery, transitions between tasks and between locations, seating arrangements, task schedules, instructional groupings, curriculum choices, and class rules of behavior. Hunter and colleagues (2017) suggested four research-based, Tier 1, preventive strategies for classrooms using the abbreviation, PPET: (1) physical classroom, (2) procedures and rules, (3) explicit timing, and (4) transition. Focusing on the physical classroom means arranging furniture that allows smooth flows of traffic and limited distractibility; having students face the teacher; and ensuring the teacher circulates among, and actively supervises, the students. Procedures and rules must be "identified, posted, taught, reviewed, monitored, and reinforced" (p. 83). Rules are usually 3–5 positive statements of expectations, such as "Be respectful," and procedures are expectations for processes such as entering the classroom, turning in homework, and walking in the hallway. Explicit timing is using a daily schedule to indicate the timelines for academic and non-academic activities. For example, 8:00–8:15 am is allotted for a "do now," 8:15–8:45 am is the time for guided reading practice, and 8:45–9:00 am is time for a bathroom break. Finally, because a considerable amount of time is lost during transitions between activities, the last step is planning for transitions and using group contingencies (see Chapter 8) to decrease transition time. Researchers and educators agree that systems of positive behavior support should not be static; they should be subject to ongoing evaluation.

Schoolwide Use of schoolwide PBS is one example of large-scale implementation and expanding the unit of analysis from the individual student to the school (Freeman et al., 2016; Gage et al., 2015; Horner, Sugai, & Anderson, 2010; Lewis et al., 2016). Schoolwide PBS is a systems approach of using evidence-based practices for establishing the social culture and individualized behavior supports needed for schools to achieve both social and academic success while preventing problem behavior. This approach has been implemented in both elementary and secondary schools (Freeman et al., 2016, 2019; Lane et al., 2013; McDaniel et al., 2017; Nese et al., 2014; Swain-Bradway et al., 2015). Schoolwide positive behavior support (SW-PBS) is an approach that begins with a schoolwide prevention effort and then adds individualized support for those students with more significant needs. Researchers in schoolwide PBS agree upon a set of core strategies (Algozzine et al., 2017; McIntosh et al., 2013):

1. Focus on preventing the development and occurrence of problem behaviors.
2. Teach appropriate social behavior and skills.
3. Acknowledge appropriate behavior. (Students should receive regular recognition for appropriate behavior at rates that exceed rates of recognition for rule violations and problem behaviors. Staff should arrange consistent consequences-based interventions for problem behavior.)
4. Collect ongoing data about student behavior and use it to guide behavior support decisions.
5. Follow a continuum of intensive, individual interventions.
6. Invest in the systems (e.g., teams, policies, funding, administrative support, data structures) that support adults in their implementation of effective practices.

Bohanon et al. (2012) presented a case study on the implementation of schoolwide PBS in a large, urban high school. There were three phases of the intervention. Phase 1 occurred over two years and consisted of meeting and learning how to implement the three tiers of schoolwide PBS, determining a data collection strategy, and training all school staff on the system. In Phase 2, the school established a leadership team comprised of special education teachers, general education teachers, students, school administrators, and the university research team. The team met in the summer to plan several steps for the school year, including defining schoolwide expectations, setting goals for problem behavior reductions, establishing coaches to guide staff in implementation, and planning celebrations for meeting goals. Phase 3 was implementation with explaining and modeling behavioral expectations in school assemblies, posting schoolwide expectations, establishing acknowledgment tickets teachers gave to students for demonstrating expected behavior, and data-based retraining of staff. Phase 3 lasted three years. The intervention was implemented by all school staff and resulted in a decrease in the key measure used in schoolwide PBS, office discipline referrals.

"Hawk Wings"
Pearson eText
Video Example 7.5
In this video, two educators discuss how the "Hawk Wings" wrist bands are used to encourage positive behaviors for students within their school. What elements of schoolwide positive behavior support do you notice?

Summary

When students present challenging behavior that interferes with their learning and that of others and presents the possibility of a change in their educational placement, IDEA requires educators to engage in functional behavior assessment procedures. These procedures provide a systematic means of determining the function that the behavior serves for the student. The functional behavior assessment procedures provide direct and indirect means of information gathering that leads to a hypothesis of function. The functional analysis procedures provide for the manipulation of environmental variables that leads to a hypothesis of function. Based on the function of the behavior, it is possible to design an intervention and support plan. The BSP details changes in the environment, an alternative behavior to replace the inappropriate behavior, and strategies for teaching the alternative behavior. It has been suggested that functional behavioral assessment is not intended solely as a reaction to behavior problems that have reached a crisis point. Functional behavior assessment is most effective when problem behaviors are first exhibited (Ala'i-Rosales et al., 2019).

A great deal of research and application substantiates the validity, reliability, and positive effects of these procedures, but there is still the need for further investigation to expand our knowledge of valid and effective methods that are practical in school settings (Freeman et al., 2019; Horner & Yell, 2017; Steege et al., 2019; Strickland-Cohen et al., 2016; Zirkel, 2017). The need for further knowledge is especially true for populations of typical students and those with mild disabilities. For populations of students with moderate and severe disabilities, there is evidence of agreement across indirect and direct methods of functional assessment and functional analysis, and that the identification of function leads to successful intervention and support plans (Bruni et al., 2017; Jeong & Copeland, 2020; Scott & Cooper, 2017; Walker et al., 2018). A great deal is known about the process of functional assessment for individuals with severe disabilities, and although there is a research base for functional assessments with students with emotional and behavioral disorders (Kamps et al., 2006), the knowledge is less developed in that area (Scott & Alter, 2017).

Discussion Questions

1. Jenna's teacher, Ms. Alvaraz, and a behavior specialist have been asked to develop a hypothesis as to why Jenna, who eats lunch independently in school with no problem, becomes completely unmanageable during mealtimes at home. Introducing many variables such as noise, movement, and different foods to Jenna in the empty cafeteria has produced no challenging behavior. Before even going to Jenna's home, Ms. Alvaraz and the behavior specialist brainstorm to predict differences they might find. List as quickly as possible as many such possible differences as you and your colleagues can identify.

2. Many teachers of typical students and those with mild disabilities attempt to determine the function of their students' behaviors by interviewing the students. They repeatedly ask students "why" they perform certain behaviors. Why is this unlikely to be effective?

3. A functional analysis has confirmed a hypothesis that DeMarcus is engaging in yelling and hitting adults in order to get out of doing undesired tasks (escape from demand). What components might his teacher include in a treatment plan for him? What if he is doing it to gain social attention from peers or adults? How would the plans be similar or different?

4. Anecdotal reports are one means of direct information gathering for functional behavior assessments. The following is an anecdotal report of one session of community-based vocational instruction. Todd, his classmate Lucy, and their teacher were at Pets-Are-Us. The session's task was to move 4-pound bags of birdseed from the storeroom to the shelves at the front of the store. Convert this report into the structure for analyzing anecdotal reports as shown in Chapter 4.

   > May 3, 9:20 a.m. Teacher, Todd, and Lucy are in the storeroom. Teacher explains the task. She tells both students to pick up a bag and follow her. They do, and each places a bag on the proper shelf. She leads them back to the storeroom. Teacher tells Todd to pick up a bag of seed; he walks away. She tells him a second time. Teacher picks up a bag and takes Todd by the hand and walks out to the shelf. She hands him the bag and points to where it belongs; he puts the bag on the shelf. She tells him to go back to the storeroom for another. In the storeroom she tells him to pick up a bag from the pile. The third time he is told, he picks one up and goes out front and puts the bag on the shelf. On the way out to the floor with the next bag, Todd

stops at a birdcage, drops the bag, and begins to talk to the birds. Several minutes later the teacher comes for him. He ignores her. She puts his hands on the bag then leads him to the shelf. She then takes him to the storeroom. He refuses to lift a bag. She hands him one. He drops it on the floor. This is repeated twice. She takes a bag and leads him back out to the shelf. Together they put the bag on the shelf. She tells him to go back to the storeroom. She goes to check on Lucy. Eight minutes later she finds Todd sitting on the floor eating candy from his fanny pack. She takes the candy and tells him it is for later. She tells him again to go to the storeroom. When she looks for him again, he is at the rabbit cage. She leads him back to the storeroom. She tells him to pick up a bag. After the third delivery of instruction, the teacher holds a bag in front of him; he doesn't move his arms. She places his arms around the bag. He lets it drop through his hands, and it splits open. She scolds. She goes to get a broom. She returns and he is sitting down eating the birdseed. The teacher tells Todd, "Your behavior is not acceptable. Therefore, you will no longer be allowed to work today. Sit over there and time yourself out until we leave. I am very disappointed in your work behavior today."

Chapter 8
Arranging Consequences That Increase Behavior

 Learning Outcomes

8.1 Identify the types of reinforcers and ways to effectively choose reinforcers.

8.2 Identify components of a behavioral contract and ways to use behavior contracts.

8.3 Identify variations in the delivery of reinforcement.

8.4 Differentiate between positive and negative reinforcement.

8.5 Identify the correct and incorrect use of negative reinforcement and demonstrate how to use negative reinforcement during instruction.

8.6 Identify natural reinforcers.

CHAPTER OUTLINE

Positive Reinforcement
    Choosing Effective Reinforcers
    Making Reinforcers Contingent
    Making Reinforcement Immediate
    Types of Reinforcers

Contracting

Variations in Administration of Reinforcers
    Group Contingencies and Peer Mediation
    Schedules of Reinforcement

Negative Reinforcement
    Inadvertent Use
    Appropriate Means of Escape
    Using Negative Reinforcement for Instruction

Natural Reinforcement

Summary

The term *reinforcement*, used to describe pleasant events or rewards given to a person who complies with the demands of some behavior-change agent, has become part of the vocabulary of the general public. It has thus become associated with a stereotypic, manipulative view of behavior modification, conceptualized as an artificial tool created to make people engage in behaviors chosen by others. Although applied behavior analysts use the principles of reinforcement to change behavior, it is not true that they invented them. Reinforcement is a naturally occurring phenomenon. Applied behavior analysts have simply applied the effects of reinforcement in a thoughtful and systematic manner.

Reinforcement describes a relationship between two environmental events, a behavior (response) and an event or consequence that follows the response. The relationship is termed reinforcement only if the response increases or maintains its rate as a result of the consequence. In Chapter 1, we described two types of reinforcement: positive reinforcement, the *contingent presentation* of a consequence that increases behavior, and negative reinforcement, the *contingent removal* of some unpleasant stimulus that increases behavior. Both positive and negative reinforcement increase the future probability of the event they follow.

Everyone does things because of the consequences of doing them. Every action we engage in results in some consequence. When our behavior results in a naturally occurring, desirable consequence, this experience motivates us to continue behaving that way. Consider these examples:

- An office worker goes to work each day expecting to receive a check at the end of the week. If the check is delivered on Friday in an amount the individual finds satisfying, it increases the probability that the person will return to work on Monday.
- A little leaguer hits a double and is applauded by fans and teammates. This motivates her to play again next Saturday.

- A baby coos at his mother's approach, so she cuddles him and spends more time playing with him. The mother's response increases the frequency of the baby's cooing, which increases the time spent playing, and so on.
- A student spends 45 minutes each night for a week studying for a history exam. If the student earns an A on the exam, this consequence will motivate her to study just as hard for her next exam.

Although many appropriate behaviors are maintained by naturally occurring reinforcers, this natural process may be insufficient to maintain all desirable behaviors. Teachers often find students for whom naturally occurring reinforcers currently fail to maintain appropriate behavior. Some students may see little immediate benefit from learning plane geometry or applied behavior analysis. Competing reinforcers stronger than those being offered by the teacher may motivate some students. These students may find the laughter of other students more reinforcing than the teacher's approval. Some students may not value the reinforcers the teacher offers. Grades, for example, may have little meaning to them. In such instances, the teacher must develop a systematic, interim program to arrange opportunities for students to earn reinforcers they value. When naturally occurring reinforcers are not sufficiently powerful, the wise teacher looks for more powerful ones.

We shall describe procedures for the effective use of reinforcement in changing classroom behavior. The majority of the chapter examines the use of positive reinforcement, whereas the final section describes classroom applications of negative reinforcement. Suggested categories and examples of potential reinforcers are summarized in Table 8.1. This table is not designed as a scheme for ordinal selection of reinforcement categories on a contrived-to-natural continuum. One might be tempted to identify, for example, the use of edible reinforcers in the classroom as contrived or artificial. Such a designation, however, depends on the target behavior, the setting, and the age of the student.

Any category or specific stimulus could be described as a contrived or natural reinforcer. Food as a reinforcer while teaching a student to feed himself or access to the water fountain as a reinforcer for properly lining up after a PE period may be considered natural consequences of the target behaviors. It may be helpful to distinguish among items or events ordinarily available in a given environment (that is, natural) and those temporarily added to the environment for increased consequence intensity (that is, contrived).

Table 8.1 Categories and examples of reinforcers for classroom use

Class	Category	Examples
Primary reinforcers	1. Edible reinforcers	Foods and liquids, such as pieces of cracker, sips of juice, pudding
	2. Sensory reinforcers	Exposure to controlled visual, auditory, tactile, olfactory, or kinesthetic experience: face stroked with furry puppet, music through earbuds
Secondary reinforcers	3. Tangible (material) reinforcers	Certificates, badges, stickers, music star posters, balloons
	4. a. Privilege reinforcers b. Activity reinforcers	Monitorships, team captain, excused from homework, self-directed class time, play activities, special projects, access to media or computer
	5. Generalized reinforcers	Tokens, points, credits
	6. Social reinforcers	Expressions, proximity, contact, words and phrases, feedback, seating arrangements

Positive Reinforcement

Learning Outcome 8.1 Identify the types of reinforcers and ways to effectively choose reinforcers.

Positive reinforcement (S^{R+}) is the contingent presentation of a stimulus, immediately following a response, that increases the future rate or probability of the response. There are three operative words in this definition. The word *increases* makes it clear we are dealing with some form of reinforcement, because the stimulus will have the effect of increasing the probability that the response will reoccur. The second operative word is *presentation.* When we use positive reinforcement, we intentionally present the student with a stimulus following the production of a response. The third operative word is *contingent.* The teacher will not present the consequence to the student unless and until the desired response is produced. If a teacher states, "Marcus, you finished all your math problems—you may now play with the airplane models," the teacher is using positive reinforcement if airplane models are reinforcing to Marcus. The reinforcing stimulus (playing with airplane models) was presented to the student contingent on production of the desired behavior (completion of math problems). The examples in Table 8.2 illustrate the principles of positive reinforcement.

Whereas *positive reinforcement* refers to the relationship between a behavior and a consequence, the term **positive reinforcer** describes the consequent event itself. A positive reinforcer is a consequential stimulus (S^R) that

1. increases or maintains the future rate or probability of occurrence of a behavior;
2. is administered contingent upon the production of a desired or requested behavior; and
3. is administered immediately following the production of the desired or requested behavior.

Table 8.2 Examples of positive reinforcers

	Stimulus	Response	S^{R+}	Effect
Example 1	Math problems and instructions.	Marcus completes math problems.	Teacher states he is allowed to play with model planes.	Increased probability that Marcus will complete next set of problems on time.
Example 2	—	John sits upright in his seat.	Teacher presents him with a smile and words of praise.	Increased likelihood that John will continue to sit appropriately.
Example 3	—	Sara brings in her homework each day this week.	Teacher appoints her board monitor for next week.	Increased probability that Sara will continue to bring her homework every day.

Choosing Effective Reinforcers

The reinforcing potential of an item or event depends on reinforcement history and deprivation.

Because a stimulus is defined as a positive reinforcer only as a result of its effect on behavior, no item or event can be termed a positive reinforcer until this relationship has been established. It follows, therefore, that a teacher cannot state with any real degree of certainty—in advance of evidence of such a relationship—what will or will not be a reinforcing consequence for any given student. What serves as a reinforcer for a particular student depends on several factors, including the student's reinforcement history (what has motivated her in the past), the student's deprivation state (what she wants but does not get easily or frequently), the perceived value of the reinforcer (whether it is worth performing the behavior to get it), consistency (whether reinforcers have been reliably delivered in the past), and age appropriateness (whether the reinforcer, even if the student might enjoy it, is more suitable for a younger child and thus embarrassing to her).

What will serve as a reinforcer may be different for each student. Preconceived notions of what should be reinforcing are frequent reasons for the failure of intervention programs. When the desired behavior change does not occur, the teacher's first reaction is often to assume the reinforcement procedures have not worked, when in fact one of the fundamental notions of reinforcement has been violated: the *individualization of reinforcers.* One way to individualize reinforcers is by using **preference assessments**.

The method of conducting preference assessments will vary depending on a student's level of functioning. Systematic preference assessments have been found to be more reliable than teachers' or caregivers' predictions or guesses for identifying items that will function as reinforcers when applied contingently (Cote, Thompson, Hanley, & McKerchar, 2007; Daly, Jacob, King, & Cheramie, 1984; Reid, White, Halford, Brittain, & Gardner, 1988). However, in some cases, teacher or caregiver reports may predict items that will function as reinforcers (Russo, Tincani, & Axelrod, 2014; Verschuur et al., 2011). Further, students with verbal skills can often be asked what they would like as a result of their effort or achievement. This can also be done using a prepared survey such as the School Reinforcement Survey Schedule (Holmes, Cautela, Simpson, Motes, & Gold, 1998) that was developed for use with students in the fourth through twelfth grades. The results of asking the student, like any source of information concerning a potential reinforcer, must be taken with a grain of salt until the effect on behavior is seen (Cohen-Almeida, Graff, & Ahearn, 2000; Northup, 2000).

Preference assessments for students with severe disabilities must be concrete.

Another strategy for conducting a preference assessment is using a prepared reinforcer menu like the one shown in Figure 8.1 in which items are named or pictured. Students are asked to rank-order the potential reinforcers in order of preference. A reinforcer menu should include a variety of items the teacher can reasonably make available. A variety of choices is necessary because what is reinforcing to some students may not be reinforcing to others. The presentation of limited choices will prevent unrealistic selections (such as iPods, video-game devices, and trips to Cancun) that students might suggest. Teachers, however, may still wish to offer the opportunity for an open-ended response following some forced choices. An alternative suggestion is to offer, rather than a long list of items to be rank-ordered, a choice between two items or two categories of items (either verbally or with pictures). For example, the teacher might ask, "Which would you do a lot of hard work to get, things to eat, like chips, cookies, or popcorn, or things to do, like art projects, play computer games, or go to the library?" (Northup, George, Jones, Broussard, & Vollmer, 1996, p. 207).

To determine reinforcer preferences of students whose abilities to respond are more limited, it may be necessary to present an array of potential reinforcers and allow the student to select items. It is most common to present actual objects or events, and this may be necessary for students with more severe disabilities (Higbee, Carr, & Harrison, 1999). For some students, presenting pictures of items—either physical pictures or pictures presented on a laptop or tablet—is just as effective as showing objects when assessing preference (Brodhead et al., 2016). Potential reinforcers may even be presented as

Figure 8.1 Reinforcer menu

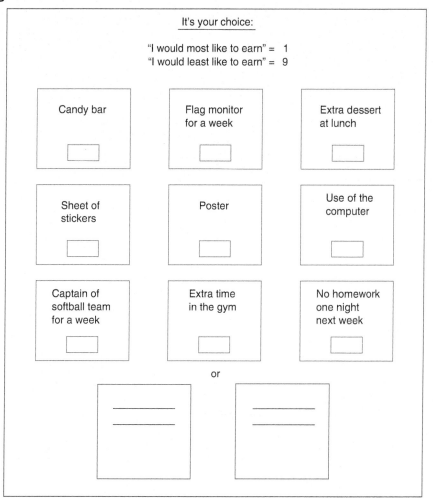

videos that students select, particularly when assessing social interactions, vocational activities, or videos themselves (Curiel, Curiel, Li, Deochand, & Poling, 2018; Morgan & Horrocks, 2011; Wolfe, Kunnavatana, & Shoemaker, 2018). It is usually best to bring to a preference assessment session up to six items the teacher thinks are potential reinforcers based on past history of reinforcer effectiveness and interviews with parents and past teachers. The items should include reinforcers from a variety of categories, such as edible items, sensory items, toys, or items that affect the environment (a fan, for example).

Four preference assessment procedures have been suggested:

1. <u>Free Operant Preference Assessment</u>, in which items are available for a student to engage with, and the duration of engagement with each item is recorded (Roane, Vollmer, Ringdahl, & Marcus, 1998; Sautter, LeBlanc, & Gillett, 2008). Compared to the other preference assessment methods, the free-operant method resulted in less challenging behavior (Verriden & Roscoe, 2016). A limitation of this method is it does not result in a hierarchy of preferences.
2. <u>Single-item presentation</u>, in which one item at a time is presented to the student either prior to or embedded within instruction or activities (Green, Middleton, & Reid, 2000; Pace, Ivancic, Edwards, Iwata, & Page, 1985; Thomson, Czarnecki, Martin, & Yu, 2007). Items are presented until they are chosen a predetermined number of times to indicate preference. This procedure provides an indication of whether an item is preferred or not preferred but lacks the ability to rank-order preferences.
3. <u>Paired Stimulus Preference Assessment</u>, in which items are presented in pairs from which the student is to select the preferred item (Fisher et al., 1992). The selection response may be pointing, picking up, or looking at the item (Cannella-Malone,

Paired Stimulus Preference Assessment
Pearson eText
Video Example 8.1
In this video, an educator is conducting a paired stimulus preference assessment. How does her example align with the description from the chapter?

https://www.youtube.com/watch?v=CnBraS9rmz4

Multiple Stimulus without Replacement Preference Assessment
Pearson eText
Video Example 8.2
In this video, an educator is conducting a multiple stimulus without replacement preference assessment. How does her example align with the description from the chapter?

https://www.youtube.com/watch?v=fEEelCgBkWA&t=113s

Sabielny, & Tullis, 2015). Items may include tangibles, pictures, or videos depicting social interactions. Each item is presented at least once with every other item so that preference for each relative to the others can be determined. The left or right position of the items in an array should be randomly positioned for each opportunity. When determining the potential comparative reinforcing effects among items selected, a common standard is that high-preference items are those selected on 75% or more of trials, and low-preference items are those selected on 25% or fewer trials. Low-preference items are usually associated with weak reinforcement effects, and high response rates are associated with high-preference items (Ciccone, Graff, & Ahearn, 2015; Horrocks & Higbee, 2008; Lang et al., 2014). This procedure better predicts subsequent reinforcement effects than does the single-item presentation method.

4. <u>Multiple Stimulus Without Replacement Preference Assessment</u>, in which three or more items (tangible, picture, activity options) are presented simultaneously. (Note: The Multiple Stimulus *With* Replacement Preference Assessment was evaluated in the 1990s, but is rarely used in practice or current research.) Once an item is selected and experienced, it is removed. This continues until all items are selected or a period of no responding passes. This process is usually repeated several times to confirm a student's preferences (Brodhead, Abston, Mates, & Abel, 2017; Carr, Nicolson, & Higbee, 2000; DeLeon & Iwata, 1996; Daly et al., 2009); Radley, Hart, Battaglia, and Ford (2019) conducted this type of preference assessment in a classroom of 19 students using a smartphone app-based response system.

With any of these methods there may be practical limits on the teacher's ability to provide an opportunity for an activity to be one of the options. Also, with these populations of students it may be difficult to determine whether the selection of a ball is due to its tactile character, its color, or the activity associated with it.

The teacher must decide which student response she will record as an item selection. Depending on the students' functioning level, they may pick up an item, point to or gaze at it, indicate the item using a less articulated approach (Pace et al., 1985), or access and select it using microswitches (Dutt et al., 2014; Leatherby, Gast, Wolery, & Collins, 1992; Wacker, Berg, Wiggins, Muldoon, & Cavanaugh, 1985). See Karsten, Carr, and Lepper (2011) for a discussion of pros and cons of the different preference assessment methods, as well as a model for conducting preference assessments.

Hall and Hall (1980, pp. 15–17) suggested the following nine-step sequence for selecting potential reinforcers:

Step 1. "Consider the age, interests, and appetites of the person whose behaviors you wish to strengthen." The teacher should select potential consequences that attempt to correspond to the student's chronological age and social background. Fruit Loops or an opportunity to work puzzles will probably have little motivational value for an adolescent.

Step 2. "Consider the behavior you wish to strengthen through reinforcement." The teacher should select potential consequences that attempt to correspond to the value, or effort required to produce the response. "If an employer offered to buy an employee a cup of coffee for working all weekend on a special job, it would be unlikely that any worker would accept the offer." Similarly, offering a student 5 additional minutes of free time for completion of an entire day's written assignment is an opportunity the student will probably pass up.

Step 3. "List potential reinforcers considering what you know of the person, his or her age, interests, likes and dislikes, and the specific behavior you have defined." This step allows the teacher to organize the potential reinforcers she is considering in an orderly and objective manner. See Figure 8.2 for the Preference Inventory Checklist organized by activity, edible, sensory, social and tangible items (Da Fonte et al., 2016).

Name: _____ Completed by: _____ Date: _____

Instructions: Complete the *Preference Inventory Checklist* by selecting and rating items in which the student demonstrates interest. Items should be rated as follows: 1=*Does not demonstrate interest*; 2=*Slightly motivated/interested*; and 3=*Highly motivated/interested*. It is highly suggested that at least three items from each category be identified for further evaluation. The notes section should be used to provide specific information on the item/activity being selected (e.g., brand, type, name). Additionally, when possible it is highly recommended that multiple people complete the *Preference Inventory Checklist* in order to gather information on preferences across setting and individuals.

Preference Inventory Checklist-Elementary

Activity	1	2	3	Edibles	1	2	3	Sensory	1	2	3	Social	1	2	3	Tangible	1	2	3
Books	☐	☐	☐	Chocolate	☐	☐	☐	Jumping	☐	☐	☐	Adult attention	☐	☐	☐	Blanket	☐	☐	☐
Computer	☐	☐	☐	Cookies	☐	☐	☐	Music	☐	☐	☐	Alone time	☐	☐	☐	Coins/token	☐	☐	☐
Dance	☐	☐	☐	Crackers	☐	☐	☐	Shaving cream	☐	☐	☐	High 5s	☐	☐	☐	Fidget	☐	☐	☐
Movie	☐	☐	☐	Drink	☐	☐	☐	Swing	☐	☐	☐	Peer attention	☐	☐	☐	Stamps	☐	☐	☐
Play game	☐	☐	☐	Gummies	☐	☐	☐	Therapeutic toy	☐	☐	☐	Praise	☐	☐	☐	Stickers	☐	☐	☐
Walk	☐	☐	☐	Pretzels	☐	☐	☐	Water play	☐	☐	☐	Smile	☐	☐	☐	Stuffed animal	☐	☐	☐
Other: ___	☐	☐	☐	Other: ___	☐	☐	☐	Other: ___	☐	☐	☐	Other: ___	☐	☐	☐	Other: ___	☐	☐	☐
Other: ___	☐	☐	☐	Other: ___	☐	☐	☐	Other: ___	☐	☐	☐	Other: ___	☐	☐	☐	Other: ___	☐	☐	☐
Other: ___	☐	☐	☐	Other: ___	☐	☐	☐	Other: ___	☐	☐	☐	Other: ___	☐	☐	☐	Other: ___	☐	☐	☐
Other: ___	☐	☐	☐	Other: ___	☐	☐	☐	Other: ___	☐	☐	☐	Other: ___	☐	☐	☐	Other: ___	☐	☐	☐

Notes:

Figure 8.2 Preference Inventory Checklist.

Step 4. "The Premack principle." When selecting potential reinforcers, the teacher should consider watching the student and noting activities in which he likes to engage. David Premack (1959) systematized the use of preferred activities as reinforcers. A discussion of the Premack principle follows later in this chapter.

Step 5. "Consider asking the person." The teacher should remember that the best authority on the likes and dislikes of a student is that student. The mechanism most often used to determine a student's potential reinforcers is the previously mentioned reinforcer menu. For alternative forms of reinforcer menus, see Raschke (1981).

Step 6. "Consider novel reinforcers." With this step, Hall and Hall (1980) reminded teachers that "varying the reinforcers is more effective than using the same reinforcers over and over." Repeated use of the same reinforcer can lead to boredom and satiation, lessening the motivating effectiveness of a consequence. See Livingston and Graff (2018) for a method of identifying novel reinforcers.

Step 7. "Consider reinforcers that are natural." Hall and Hall (1980) suggested three advantages to the use of natural reinforcers. First, natural reinforcers such as recognition and privileges can be provided more easily and at lower cost than most edible and material consequences. Second, natural reinforcers are more likely to be available to the student after the behavior has been established. "In a natural situation, even though you discontinue to systematically reinforce the behavior you wanted to strengthen, the natural positive consequence you provided is more likely to be available on at least some occasion in the future." Third, natural reinforcers automatically occur on a contingent basis. Praise for a homework assignment well done will not naturally occur unless the behavior was performed.

Step 8. "Select the reinforcer or reinforcers you will use." Once the teacher has considered steps 1 through 7, Hall and Hall (1980) suggest selecting the reinforcers that will most likely have the desired effect on the target behavior.

Step 9. "Make a record of the behavior." The teacher is reminded that the only way to confirm a consequence as a reinforcer is to observe its effect on the behavior. To verify this effect, the teacher should systematically document the change, if any, in the production of the behavior. Various methods for providing such documentation are presented in Chapter 4 of this text.

Periodic reassessment of any reinforcer is often necessary (Mason, McGee, Farmer-Dougan, & Risley, 1989; Schanding, Tingstrom, & Sterling-Turner, 2009; Stafford, Alberto, Fredrick, Heflin, & Heller, 2002). This is especially true when a single item or small set of items is used in the assessment. Reinforcers identified by a paired-item method of assessment appear to be more stable than those identified by the single-item preference method (Call, Trosclair-Lasserre, Findley, Reavis, & Shillingsburg, 2012; Kelley, Shillingsburg, & Bowen, 2016). When shifts in item preference appear, indicated by the slowing of desired changes in a behavior or an increase in incorrect responding, it may be due to changing preferences as the student gets older and his experiences broaden. In the short term, it may be simply because a student is tired of the reinforcer or has recently consumed a large amount of that reinforcer (satiation, abolishing operation; Chappell, Graff, Libby, & Ahearn, 2009; Hanley, Iwata, & Roscoe, 2006; McAdam et al., 2005). In the latter case, a known high-preference item may be returned to use after a period of time.

Developing Reinforcement Systems
Pearson eText
Video Example 8.3
In this video, an educator is consulting with a parent about the reinforcement system used in the classroom. Different options for activities, privileges, and tangible items are discussed. Compare this discussion to the recommendations provided by Hall and Hall (1980).

Making Reinforcers Contingent

If reinforcement is to be effective, the student must receive the reinforcer only after performing the target behavior. An "if . . . , then . . ." statement is in place. Such a statement establishes a clear and explicit relationship between performing the behavior and receiving the reinforcer. If Clara finds, regardless of whether she has performed the target behavior, she can watch a preferred video at the end of the day when the teacher is tired, Clara may decide the teacher does not mean business: No contingency is actually in force. Implied in such a contingency and explicit in reinforcer delivery is that the teacher or some other specifically designated person is the source of the reinforcer. If the student can go to the classroom assistant or some other adult during the day and get the same promised reinforcer without having performed the desired behavior, that student will quickly determine there is no need to comply with the contingency. Note that a teacher need not always state an "if . . . , then . . ." contingency statement—she may simply deliver a reinforcer when she sees a desired behavior. The principle of contingency still applies: deliver reinforcers when and only when the student engages in the desired behavior.

> It may also be necessary to be sure parents or other caregivers don't make potential reinforcers available noncontingently.

Making Reinforcement Immediate

To be effective, a reinforcer should initially be delivered immediately after the target behavior is performed. This timing convinces the student of the veracity of the contingency and underlines the connection between a particular behavior and its consequence. Immediacy of delivery is also necessary to avoid the hazard of inadvertently reinforcing an intervening behavior. The longer the delay between the desired behavior and receipt of the reinforcer, the greater the possibility the student may engage in a behavior not under the contingency or not desired. Eventually the teacher will want to introduce a delay between the behavior and the reinforcer. This systematically arranged delay is known as a schedule of reinforcement and is discussed later in this chapter.

Types of Reinforcers

Two major varieties of reinforcers are available to teachers: *primary reinforcers* and *secondary reinforcers*.

PRIMARY REINFORCERS Primary reinforcers are stimuli that have biological importance to an individual. We can assume that they are innately motivating because they are necessary to the perpetuation of life. Therefore, primary reinforcers are

> Primary reinforcers can be powerful tools for changing behavior.

Ms. Troutman Reinforces Chaos

Ms. Troutman was a teacher of students with severe social maladjustments. She taught in a self-contained special class. It was the first week of her first year in this setting, and she was determined to make it a success. She had taken a course in applied behavior analysis and decided to set the following contingency for her students:

> *If you complete at least 20 assignments during the week, then you may participate in a class party at 2:15 on Friday.*

The students worked busily, and Ms. Troutman glowed with satisfaction as she wondered why people thought these students were difficult to teach. At 11:00 on Friday morning, the first student completed his twentieth assignment. By noon, all seven students had fulfilled the contingency. The remaining hours before 2:15 were among the longest Ms. Troutman had ever spent. Even though the students yelled, fought, cursed, ran around, and generally created havoc, the party was held as scheduled. (Ms. Troutman at least had sense enough to know that if she failed to live up to her end of the contingency, the students would never believe her again.) Monday morning the class came in yelling, fighting, cursing, and running around. Ms. Troutman had reinforced chaos, and that's what she got.

described as natural, unlearned, or unconditioned reinforcers. Given their biological importance, we may expect that they will be highly motivating to individual students. The major types of primary reinforcers include foods, liquids, sleep, shelter, and sex (the last reinforcer is most commonly used in the form of entry to social activities). Obviously, the two most common and appropriate primary reinforcers for the classroom are food and liquids. Edible reinforcers are used mainly when teaching new behaviors to younger students and students with severe disabilities. Because of their high motivational value, they quickly affect behavior.

Teachers should strive for the most naturally occurring reinforcers, and teachers rarely find it necessary to use edible reinforcers with older students and students with mild disabilities. In many settings, edible reinforcers may not be used because of concerns about infection, pests, or allergies. An imaginative teacher can choose from a great many other potential reinforcers. Reinforcing some students' behavior with candy or other treats is an example of behavioral overkill. Besides being unnecessary, primary reinforcers may be perceived by students as insulting. A ninth grader could hardly take seriously a teacher who said, "Great job on that algebra assignment, Casey. Here's your cookie." This is not to imply that teachers of older students should never use food as a reinforcer. An occasional treat may be very effective, when appropriately presented. For example, a popcorn party for students who have met some contingency may be perfectly appropriate. It is amazing to observe how rapidly second or third graders complete assignments once the smell of the popping corn begins wafting about the room.

Primary reinforcers are often needed to change the behavior of students with autism and related disabilities as praise and other forms of social attention may not function as a reinforcer (Axe & Laprime, 2017). For primary reinforcers to be effective, the student whose behavior is to be reinforced must be in a state of deprivation in relation to that reinforcer. Using an edible reinforcer with a student who has just returned from lunch is less likely to be effective because the student is not hungry. This by no means suggests that students should be starved so that food will be an effective reinforcer, but the necessity for a state of deprivation is a drawback to the use of primary reinforcers. A student need not be hungry, however, for limited amounts of special foods such as potato chips, raisins, ice cream, or candy to be effective reinforcers. The opposite of deprivation is **satiation**. Satiation occurs when the **deprivation state** that existed at the beginning of an instructional session no longer exists, and the student's cooperation and attention have worn thin. A teacher of students with severe disabilities who conducts a training session lasting perhaps 30 minutes may come to a point in the session when the primary reinforcer loses its effectiveness. The teacher will know this when the student's rate of correct responding slows down or—in the case of more assertive students—when the student spits the no-longer-reinforcer at the teacher.

There are at least seven ways a teacher may plan to prevent or delay satiation:

1. There is evidence to suggest that reinforcers selected by a student are more motivating than those chosen by the teacher (Thompson, Fisher, & Contrucci, 1998). Data also indicate substantially more responding when choices among items occur during instructional sessions rather than before instruction (Toussaint, Kodak, & Vladescu, 2016). The teacher should have available an array of three or four edible reinforcers for the student to select from following correct responses.
2. Assign a particular reinforcer to each task or behavior. There is no need to use a single reinforcer all day, in all content areas, or across all behaviors. To do so is to build in the potential of satiation.
3. At the onset of satiation, when the student becomes less cooperative or errors increase, try switching to an alternative reinforcer. As a result of the preference assessment that was conducted, an ordered list of several potential reinforcers is available so that more than one can be used during the day.

> Deprivation is a condition that must be met if primary reinforcers are to be effective.

4. Shorten the instructional session in which the edible reinforcer is being used. Shorter sessions with fewer trials (controlled presentations) decrease the chance of satiation. Several short sessions may be held during the day.
5. Decrease the size of the pieces of the edible reinforcer given for correct responses. Smaller portions also disappear more quickly, thus not creating artificially long periods between trials as the student continues to savor the reinforcer.
6. Do not provide a reinforcer for every correct response. Require more performance from the student for a reinforcer. This changes the schedule on which reinforcers are delivered (schedules of reinforcement are discussed later in this chapter). Combining this strategy with the availability of more than one reinforcer produces more stable responding than constant use of the same reinforcer.
7. Use multiple reinforcers, preferably those that occur naturally. For example, Carbone, Sweeney-Kerwin, Attanasio, and Kasper (2010) delayed the onset of satiation and tied their use of reinforcers directly to the behaviors they were teaching students with developmental disabilities. Based on preference assessments, they presented six items—edible items, toys, and movies—to each student one at a time. If the student reached for the item, the teacher taught the student to request the item using sign language. If the student did not reach for the item, the teacher presented the next item in the rotation. When the student requested an item using sign language, the teacher delivered the requested item. A problem with satiation is illustrated by the following story.

Mr. Alberto Eats Ice Cream

Jeff was a student with severe intellectual disability whose behavioral repertoire seemed to consist mainly of throwing materials and chairs. He sometimes varied this by hitting teachers and other students. In an effort to control this behavior, Mr. Alberto had tried more than a dozen potential primary reinforcers—from potato chips to candy—with no success whatsoever. Appropriate behavior stayed at a low rate and inappropriate behavior at a high rate.

In desperation, Mr. Alberto asked Jeff's mother if there was anything Jeff liked. "Of course," she said. "Jeff loves butter pecan ice cream."

One quick trip to the grocery store later, Mr. Alberto began to make progress. By the end of a week, Jeff's behavior was under reasonable control, and Mr. Alberto thought his troubles were over. Before long, however, the inappropriate behavior was back in full force. Once again, Mr. Alberto questioned Jeff's mother. Could she explain why butter pecan ice cream wasn't working anymore?

"Well, maybe," she said, "it's because he gets so much at home. I learned long ago that it was the only way to make him behave. I give him a whole carton some days."

Mr. Alberto solaced himself with the remaining pint of butter pecan; he prepared once again to go in search of the elusive reinforcer that would work with Jeff.

Edibles provide the teacher a wide range of potential reinforcers, for example, items that have been used include pieces of cookie, banana, apple, and pear; pudding, yogurt, pretzels, chips, popcorn, cereal, cheese doodles, chex mix, goldfish crackers, cheese or peanut butter crackers, gummi bears, gummi worms, gumballs, tiny candies, and crispy rice treats; and various liquids, such as various fruit juices, flavored water, and chocolate milk.

Common sense also suggests some precautions in selecting edible reinforcers. First and most important, no edible reinforcer should be given to a student until the teacher has checked the student's medical record and spoken with the parent concerning allergies and other food intolerances. In some programs, parents are asked to send a supply of appropriate foods from home. On a more mundane note, a teacher conducting language training would not use peanut butter as a reinforcer, because it is difficult to imitate sounds with your tongue stuck to the roof of your mouth. Liquid reinforcers may increase the number of toileting breaks necessary, unduly delaying the session.

Teachers should also note that the strong motivational property of certain reinforcers, especially edible reinforcers, has the potential to encourage responses that are incompatible with the target response. Balsam and Bondy (1983) illustrated this point with the example of using ice cream as a reinforcer for a young child. They suggested that the ice cream itself might stimulate so much approach behavior (that is, staring, reaching) that it interferes with the child's attending to the relevant antecedent and response requirement of the contingency. Similarly, if a teacher tells the students that if they are good, they will be allowed a special treat at lunchtime, they may become increasingly fidgety and inattentive in anticipation of the reinforcement. (For a full discussion of the theoretical and operant negative side effects of reinforcement, see Balsam & Bondy, 1983).

Sensory reinforcers, often categorized as primary reinforcers, include:

Auditory: tones, voices, music, environmental (music through headphones)

Visual: black/white or colored lights (with or without blinking); pictures, books, magazines, slides, videos; movement (battery-operated toys, soap bubbles, slinky); mirror, kaleidoscope

Olfactory: sweet, pungent scents (cinnamon, clove, orange, inexpensive perfume)

Taste: solids or liquids (sweet, sour, salty, sharp, bitter)

Tactile: smooth/rough, soft/hard, warm/cold, wet/dry, movement (vibrators, fans, various textures such as fur)

Proprioceptive: bounce, swing, rock (trampolines, swings, rocking chairs, rocking horses)

Sensory events can be used individually or in combination. It is important to select events that are age appropriate in the manner in which they are delivered. Sensory reinforcers have been used successfully with young children with developmental disabilities (Cicero & Pfadt, 2002; Summers, Rincover, & Feldman, 1993). They have been used frequently with students with severe and profound disabilities, including autism (Lancioni, O'Reilly, & Emerson, 1996; Mechling, Gast, & Cronin, 2006; Preis, 2006; Smith, Iwata, & Shore, 1995; Wilder et al., 2008). There are indications that naturally occurring sensations are reinforcing for stereotypic or self-injurious behavior (Durand, 1990; Iwata et al., 1994; Sprague, Holland, & Thomas, 1997).

SECONDARY REINFORCERS No teacher wants to make students dependent on primary reinforcers for working or behaving appropriately. Primary reinforcers, even for very young students or students with severe disabilities, are temporary measures to enable rapid acquisition of appropriate behavior. The teacher cannot send a student into a general education classroom expecting a Tootsie Roll each time he can identify the word "dog" or to a job site expecting a chocolate cake or side of beef at the end of the work week. **Secondary reinforcers** should eventually replace primary reinforcers. Secondary reinforcers include social stimuli, such as words of praise or the opportunity to engage in preferred activities, and symbolic representations, such as a token exchangeable for another reinforcer. Unlike primary reinforcers, secondary reinforcers do not have biological importance to individuals. Rather, their value has been learned or conditioned. Thus, secondary reinforcers are often called **conditioned reinforcers**. Some students have not learned to value secondary reinforcers and must be taught to do so before secondary reinforcers will be effective.

| Pairing teaches students to value secondary reinforcers.

Pairing Students for whom secondary reinforcers have no value often need primary reinforcement to acquire appropriate behavior. To avoid dependence upon primary reinforcers, however, their use should always be in conjunction with some secondary reinforcer. The combined use of primary and secondary reinforcers is known as **pairing**. For example, when Jake behaves appropriately, his teacher may give him a bite of food and simultaneously tell him what a good job he has done.

Through pairing, we condition or teach the student to be motivated by the secondary reinforcer alone. Once this association has been established, the secondary reinforcer may be as effective as the primary reinforcer (Axe & Laprime, 2017; Dozier, Iwata, Thomason-Sassi, Worsdell, & Wilson, 2012; Lugo, Mathews, King, Lamphere, & Damme, 2017; Moher, Gould, Hegg, & Mahoney, 2008). The teacher may then gradually withdraw the primary reinforcer. Some students, of course, have a reinforcement history including paired association, allowing for the use of secondary reinforcers without the need for primary reinforcers.

TANGIBLE REINFORCERS Tangible reinforcers are items that are concrete and can sometimes be delivered immediately. Depending on a student's history with items—especially in play or leisure—or through planned pairing by the teacher, just about any item can serve as a reinforcer. Age-appropriate potential tangible reinforcers may include small toys, coloring books, stickers, stars, plastic jewelry, Play Doh, and cars and trucks for young children, or baseball cards, handheld games, posters of rock stars, books, magazines, comics, YouTube videos, and video games for adolescents and young adults. There is some indication that tangible items may be subject to satiation effects similar to those of edible items (Ivy, Neef, Meindl, & Miller, 2016). Teachers may want to consider rotating available items or providing choices from an array of items (Peterson, Lerman, & Nissen, 2016). Sometimes not knowing exactly what the reinforcer is can be enticing (Kowalewicz & Coffee, 2014; Kruger et al., 2016). Tangible reinforcers can also include awards such as certificates, badges, and trophies or one's own copy of the driver's education manual.

ACTIVITY REINFORCERS An activity is the secondary reinforcement perhaps most often used by teachers. The systematic use of such activity reinforcers was described by Premack (1959) and is referred to as the **Premack principle**. The Premack principle states that individuals engage in certain behaviors at low frequencies, so these behaviors have a low probability of occurrence. Other behaviors are engaged in at high frequencies and therefore have a high probability of occurrence. When low-frequency behaviors are followed by high-frequency behaviors, the effect is to increase the probability of the low-frequency behavior. In other words, any activity a student voluntarily performs frequently may be used as a reinforcer for any activity he seldom performs voluntarily (Azrin, Vinas, & Ehle, 2007). When a teacher tells a student she may work on her airplane model in the back of the room when she has finished the math assignment, or when a mother tells her child he may play outside when he has finished eating his Brussels sprouts, they are using the Premack principle. The student can himself set the sequence of preferred and less preferred activities, thus choosing the sequence in which he or the class will engage in specified tasks (Ramsey, Jolivette, Kennedy, Fredrick, & Williams, 2017). The student may schedule two or three tasks or the tasks and activities for the entire day. What might be considered a variation of the Premack principle involves making the appropriate behavior itself a preferred activity by increasing its desirability or making it "fun." An automobile company recently sponsored an event during which people increased rates of recycling by using containers functioning as electronic games and of using stairs instead of escalators when the stairs functioned as a piano. Almeida, Allen, Maguire, and Maguire (2018) identified going to certain restaurants and stores as activity reinforcers for adolescents with autism and intellectual disability. Additional suggestions for secondary reinforcers are shown in Table 8.3.

Another source of ideas for secondary activity reinforcers is illustrated in the anecdote on the next page.

Kazdin (2001) suggested some limitations to the use of activity reinforcers. First, access to some high-preference activities cannot always immediately follow the low-preference behavior, thereby reducing the effectiveness of the high-preference behavior as a reinforcer. For example, scheduling problems might prevent students' using the gym right after doing their math. Second, an activity may often be an all-or-nothing enterprise. It is either earned or not earned. This may limit flexibility in administration

Watch 'Em Like A . . .

Mr. Hawk was a teacher in a short-term rehabilitation class for 10- to 13-year-old students with serious behavior problems. His job was to get his students' academic skills as well as their behavior up to snuff and very quickly reintegrate them into general education classrooms. He provided behavioral consultation to the classroom teachers and continued help with academics as necessary. Some of his students remained with him full time for several months; others began attending some general education classes within a week. Mr. Hawk used a token reinforcement system (see the discussion beginning on page 219 about token reinforcers) and prided himself on finding unusual, but effective, activity reinforcers simply by listening to students, asking what they wanted to do, or watching what they chose to do when they had free time.

Some of his students, for example, used their points to spend 10 minutes sitting on Mr. Hawk's motorcycle, safely parked in the faculty parking lot with the ignition key in Mr. Hawk's pocket. Some students helped the building engineer empty trash; others played with games or toys in the classroom. One boy, who showed some characteristics of autism, preferred to straighten and reorganize various manipulatives and teaching materials; Mr. Hawk was going to be sorry to lose Richard.

One day Mr. Hawk got a new student. In an effort to give him some immediate academic success and to provide an opportunity for reinforcement, Mr. Hawk gave Aidan a math assignment on the computer. The format was colorful, highly interactive, and entertaining. Mr. Hawk chose a level that he knew would be fairly easy for the boy. After a few minutes, Aidan blurted out, "Wow, this is baaad!" whereupon the young man at the next computer leaned over toward him and said softly, "Careful, man, you let him find out you like something, next thing you know, you'll be earnin' it doin' something you don't like."

Table 8.3 Examples of privileges and activities available in a classroom that may be used as secondary reinforcers

- Select and plan next field trip or class party.
- Lead a class activity (unit activity, Fun Friday, morning circle time, making popcorn).
- Choose a partner for a task.
- Put on a skit or direct the next class play.
- Decorate a bulletin board.
- Create a learning center.
- Edit class webpage.
- Set schedule of day's lessons and activities.
- Participate in a peer tutoring program.
- Conduct a class lesson on a topic of your choice.
- Study driver's education manual.
- Be excused from a night's homework.
- Be excused from a test.
- Be excused from an activity of choice.
- Write essay question for next class exam.
- Have points added to grade.
- Drop lowest quiz grade.
- Spend time on the computer.
- Make a video.
- Lead problem-solving team.
- Have access to gym or library.
- Watch a music video.
- Be first in lunch line.
- Get tickets to high school football game.
- Be classroom librarian or game manager.
- Become a member of the safety patrol.
- Be a monitor (of chalkboard, messages, pets, plants, playground equipment).
- Be a class officer.
- Have "student of the week" privileges.
- Be captain of sport team or reading group.
- Use media equipment.
- Play with games or toys.
- Use arts and crafts materials.

of the reinforcer. For example, a student either earns the right to go on a field trip or he does not earn it. Such activities cannot be proportionally awarded depending on the degree of acceptable performance. This limitation, however, is not invariably true with activity reinforcers. Some activities may be earned in increments of time. For example, the consequence of 1 minute of shooting baskets in the gym for each correctly spelled word is easily administered if the minutes earned are banked until a designated time.

A third limitation of activities as reinforcers is that many activities must be freely available to students without reference to their performance. Examples include lunch periods, physical education, and art and music classes. Finally, the use of an activity reinforcer may cause an interruption in the continuous performance of the target behavior. For example, a teacher would not want to allow a student to go to the gym and shoot a basket after each correctly spelled word. Some students, however, may not continue to perform the target behavior unless some reinforcement is available after each response. In cases where the effectiveness of activity reinforcers seems lessened by such factors, the use of generalized conditioned reinforcers may be considered.

GENERALIZED CONDITIONED REINFORCERS When a reinforcer has been associated with a variety of other primary or secondary reinforcers, it may be termed a **generalized conditioned reinforcer**, or simply a *generalized reinforcer*. Social reinforcers such as attention or praise are one kind of generalized reinforcer. These generalized reinforcers get their value by association with other reinforcers. Praise from the teacher after a difficult work assignment, for example, has been paired with an opportunity to use the computer; praise from a spouse for a delicious dinner has been paired with affection and physical contact; and praise from a parent for picking up dirty clothes has been paired with milk and cookies.

A second type of generalized reinforcer includes those that are exchangeable for something of value. Money is the most obvious example. Money, which has little or no intrinsic value, can be earned in a variety of ways and is associated with access to many types of reinforcers: food, shelter, a ticket to the Super Bowl, or a Mercedes. The effectiveness of generalized conditioned reinforcers is not dependent on a single type of deprivation, and they are less susceptible to satiation than other types of reinforcers (Russell, Ingvarsson, Haggar, & Jessel, 2018).

The use of generalized reinforcers has a number of advantages. Kazdin and Bootzin (1972) suggested the following advantages:

1. As opposed to certain edible or activity reinforcers, generalized reinforcers permit the reinforcement of a response at any time and allow sequences of responses to be reinforced without interruption.
2. Generalized reinforcers may be used to maintain performance over extended periods of time and are less subject to satiation effects due to their reinforcing properties and their relative independence of deprivation states.
3. Generalized reinforcers provide the same reinforcement for individuals who have different preferences.

TOKEN REINFORCERS Because the use of money is unrealistic in most school settings, a generalized reinforcer known as a token reinforcer is widely used. Token reinforcers are symbolic representations exchangeable for some item or activity of value to students. The use of tokens is analogous to the use of money in general society (Figure 8.3). Token reinforcers can be exchangeable for a wide variety of primary and secondary reinforcers, just as money is. They are used as a transition between primary reinforcers and the natural community of secondary reinforcers. A token system may be adapted for use with a single student and a single behavior, one student and several behaviors, groups of students and a single behavior, and groups of students and several of the same or different behaviors.

Token systems are used in most special education self-contained and resource classes and many general educational classes. Tokens are used by teachers and paraprofessionals when teaching academic and social skills, when teaching students to manage their own behavior, for general classroom management, and in facilitating the inclusion of students with disabilities into general education classes. Peers have even been taught to evaluate behavior and distribute tokens. If you are earning points for exams, papers, and projects that you will trade in for a final grade in your behavior-management course, you, too, are participating in a token reinforcement system (Fiske et al., 2015; Gilley & Ringdahl, 2014; Jowett, Dozier, & Payne, 2016; Mason, Davis, & Andrews, 2015; Romani, Alcorn, Miller, & Clark, 2017; Russell, Ingvarsson, Haggar, & Jessel, 2018).

> Tokens won't work unless they can be exchanged for something.

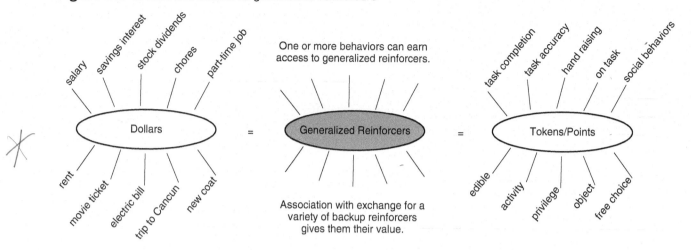

Figure 8.3 Tokens and dollars as generalized reinforcers

A token reinforcement system requires two components: the tokens themselves and **backup reinforcers** (Ivy, Meindl, Overley, & Robson, 2017). The tokens themselves should have no innate value; the backup items should have the value to the students. The teacher explains or demonstrates that tokens are needed to acquire the backup reinforcers. The goal is to earn enough tokens to access the backup reinforcers. The tokens are a means to an end. Tokens are delivered following the students' responses. Access to the backup reinforcers is allowed at a later time. The token can be an object, such as a poker chip, sticker, or coupon (Becraft & Rolider, 2015). It can also be a symbol, such as a check mark, a hole punched in a card, or the ubiquitous happy face. In general, tokens should be portable, durable, and easy to handle.

The teacher and the students should keep accurate records of the number of tokens earned. When the token is an object, such as a poker chip, a token box or some other receptacle can be designated for storing the tokens in an assigned location or at each student's desk. With younger students, chaining necklaces with tokens or building towers will help to control token loss. A dot-to-dot representation of the backup reinforcer may be drawn. In this system, as each response occurs, two dots are connected. When all dots are connected, the picture is complete and the student has earned the backup reinforcer (Trant, 1977). Students may accumulate puzzle pieces that depict the backup reinforcer when all have been earned or simply form into a preferred puzzle (Carnett et al., 2014). Token cards with blank circles to be filled in with a smiley face for each point earned (Odom & Strain, 1986) may be used, holes may be punched in a card (Maher, 1989), or tally marks may be drawn on a dry-erase board (Cihon et al., 2019). When the tokens are points earned, stamps, or check marks, a chart in the front of the classroom or some recording card similar to those displayed in Figures 8.3 and 8.4 may be used. The collaborative use of point cards among general education and special education teachers as students attend various classes has been successful in maintaining appropriate student behavior. The student manages the process by asking the teacher to record a symbol at the end of each class to indicate performance on each target behavior listed on the card (Carpenter, 2001).

A more recent development in improving classroom behavior and accountability is the Check-In, Check-Out (CICO) system (Boden, Jolivette, & Alberto, 2017; Campbell & Anderson, 2011; Drevon, Hixson, & Wyse, 2018). According to Boden et al., there are five steps of CICO:

1. Check-in: At the beginning of the day, the student meets with an adult facilitator to discuss goals for the day and receive a daily progress report card (DPR) to complete in each class.

Figure 8.4 Traditional check-in/check-out daily progress report

Student: _____ **Check-in/Out** with: _____
Student: My GOAL is to earn _____ points today.
Teacher: Please indicate the student's progress today by circling a score using the following criteria.
2 Points = Excellent   **1 Point** = Needs improvement   **0 Points** = Poor

	Be respectful	Be responsible	Be prepared	Period total	Initials
1st Period	0 1 2	0 1 2	0 1 2		
2nd Period	0 1 2	0 1 2	0 1 2		
3rd Period	0 1 2	0 1 2	0 1 2		
4th Period	0 1 2	0 1 2	0 1 2		
5th Period	0 1 2	0 1 2	0 1 2		
6th Period	0 1 2	0 1 2	0 1 2		
7th Period	0 1 2	0 1 2	0 1 2		
	Total daily points =				

Residential mentor: _____   **Date:** _____

2. Feedback: The student takes his DPR to each class and receives feedback and points from each teacher based on how well goals were achieved.
3. Check-out: At the end of the day, the student meets with the adult facilitator to discuss successes, address challenges, and earn a reinforcer if a certain amount of points were accrued.
4. Home component: The student shares the DPR with a parent or guardian at home for a discussion and to sign the DPR.
5. Return to school: The student brings the signed DPR to the adult facilitator and restarts the cycle.

See Figure 8.4 for a sample CICO DPR (Andrews, Houchin, & Varjas, 2017).

Figure 8.5 Point cards for token reinforcement systems with elementary students

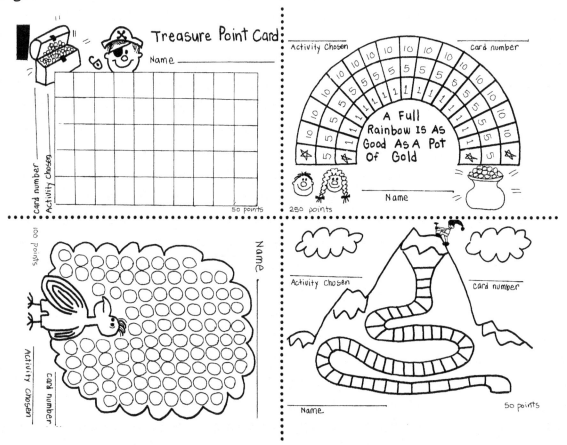

Figure 8.6 Point cards for token reinforcement systems with secondary students

```
                              POINT CARD
Student:                                              Date:
Points earned for:

    1    2    3    4    5    6    7    8    9   10
   11   12   13   14   15   16   17   18   19   20
   21   22   23   24   25   26   27   28   29   30
   31   32   33   34   35   36   37   38   39   40
   41   42   43   44   45   46   47   48   49   50

Total number of points earned:
```

Total daily points _____   Name _____
                                      Date _____
                        Lunch

	Period 1	Period 2	Period 3	Period 4	Period 5	Period 6	Period 7
on task most of the time							
attitude							
completes work							
good relations w/ staff/peers							
keeping to yourself							

Homework: Comments:

Period 1 _____
Period 2 _____
Period 3 _____
Period 4 ___ LUNCH _____
Period 5 _____
Period 6 _____
Period 7 _____

Parent Signature _____

Note: From "Tokens for Success: Using the Graduated Reinforcement System," by C. Lyon & R. Lagarde, 1997, TEACHING EXCEPTIONAL CHILDREN 29(6). Copyright 1997 by The Council for Exceptional Children. Reprinted by permission.

The use of token systems requires precautions against counterfeiting or theft. Any student with $1.99 can buy 100 paper clips, thus debasing the value of paper clip tokens and thereby the effectiveness of the system. One of us once consulted with a residential treatment center that used holes punched on cards as tokens. When the residents went home on weekend passes, many of them informed their parents that their teacher wanted them to bring a hole punch back to the center. A simple preventive measure is to mark tokens, objects, or symbols with a code that allows validation of their source or confirmation of their ownership by a particular student. If check marks on a card are used, the teacher can randomly use different-colored markers on different days. The chances of a student's having a puce-colored marker at school on the day the teacher chooses that color are minimal. (The teachers at the residential center found hole punches with different shapes.)

Tokens in and of themselves are unlikely to have reinforcing power. They attain their reinforcing value by being exchangeable for items that are reinforcing. Therefore, the students must clearly understand they are working for these tokens to exchange them, at some point, for the second component of the token system, the backup reinforcer.

The selection of the backup reinforcer is probably the most difficult aspect of the token system, especially if the system is being used with a group of students or an entire class. The teacher must select a wide enough variety of backup reinforcers to provide a motivating item for each member of the class. Therefore, teachers should try to include an assortment, such as edibles (cereals, crackers, juice), activities (going to the library, listening to music), objects (game, notebook, or crayons), and privileges (being first in line, being collector of lunch money).

When a teacher announces the initiation of a token system to a class or to an individual, students will want to know at least four things immediately. First, they will want to know what behaviors are required. As always, the contingency (if . . . , then . . .) should be clearly stated by the teacher and understood by the students. The description of each behavior to be performed and the parameters of acceptability should be clearly stated or posted. Second, the students will want to know what backup reinforcers their tokens will buy. It is a good idea to keep representations of the backup reinforcers, if not the items themselves, in full view in the classroom.

What students need to know about a token system.

The third question might involve the cost of each backup reinforcer in tokens. Based on their evaluation of the expense and desirability of the backups, the students will decide whether the reinforcer is worth the required behavior change. To get the process working initially, the teacher may price reinforcers to allow everyone to quickly acquire some. Students should learn at this very first exchange that if they earn a certain number of tokens, they may trade them for a certain backup reinforcer. Stainback, Payne, Stainback, and Payne (1973) suggested that prices of items, such as edibles, posters, and toy soldiers, should be in proportion to their actual monetary value. The pricing of activities and privileges is difficult to judge. Students should neither earn backups too quickly nor should they be required to work inordinately hard.

Finally, the students will want to know when they can exchange the tokens for the backup reinforcers. Two ways to answer this question are based on behavior or based on time (Ivy et al., 2017). It is most common for an exchange period to be based on time, such as taking place at the end of each day or week. In the early stages of a token system, especially with young students or those with disabilities, the period before the first exchange should be very short. It would be unwise to start a token system on Monday and schedule the first exchange period on Friday. Students need to see quickly how the exchange process works and that the teacher is indeed telling the truth. Therefore, we suggest that the first exchange period be either at lunch, at the end of the school day, or even at the morning break (using a cookie exchange, for example). Stainback et al. (1973) suggested that tokens be paid frequently in the early stages and that exchange times be held once or twice a day for the first three to four days and then gradually decreased in frequency until they are held only once a week by the third week. The other option is to base the exchange on behaviors, such as earning 10 or 50 tokens and then exchanging for backup reinforcers. This means new tokens can start to be earned on Monday and exchanged for a backup reinforcer on Wednesday. It may be beneficial to base exchanges on behavior rather than time so that students are not waiting until the time period, such as Friday, to start engaging in desired behaviors.

Exchanging tokens for backup reinforcers may take place in a variety of formats. Four ways to arrange the exchange of backup reinforcers are: (1) select reinforcers from a menu of options, (2) be given a "mystery reinforcer," (3) use the same reinforcer for every exchange, and (4) select the reinforcer prior to the teaching session (Ivy et al., 2017). One application of #1 is using a classroom store. In this format, the price-labeled backup reinforcers are located on shelves in a corner of the classroom. During the designated exchange period, students may enter the store and purchase

The Case of Charlie the Miser

Charlie was a student in Mr. Thomas's class for children with learning disabilities. He was a very intelligent boy with severe reading problems and many inappropriate behaviors. Like Mr. Thomas's other students, he responded well to a token reinforcement system. The students earned check marks on a card exchangeable for a variety of backup reinforcers, including toys and privileges. The most expensive item cost three cards, and many were available for one or two cards.

After several months, Mr. Thomas noticed that both Charlie's behavior and his academic work had deteriorated drastically. This deterioration seemed to have happened overnight. Mr. Thomas could see no reason for it, so he decided to do a very sensible thing. He asked Charlie what had happened. Charlie grinned and opened his work folder. "Look here," he chortled. "I got 11 cards saved up. I don't have to do anything for weeks, and I can still get anything I want from the store."

any item they can afford. An interesting variation on the exchange is the class auction (Polloway & Polloway, 1979). In this format, the students are allowed to bid for each of the backup reinforcers. Students may bid as high as they choose, up to the number of tokens they have earned. An auction format allows students to trade in their tokens or points for lottery tickets, for example, five tokens per lottery ticket (Schilling & Cuvo, 1983). The teacher can run a single drawing with all the tickets in a bag, or three drawings, one for each of three ranges of point values, and therefore dollar value, of prizes. The teacher can make a prize wheel that, when spun, randomizes the backup reinforcers. Lien-Thorne and Kamps (2005) used a wheel with extra recess time, five minutes of free time in the classroom, candy, time to play a board game, and computer time.

One potential impediment to an effective token system occasionally arises as a result of exchange procedures. It is illustrated by the following case.

It is wise, as Mr. Thomas learned, to think through your token system to prevent the accumulation of tokens that Charlie demonstrated. There are various strategies for avoiding this problem. For example:

1. Instead of having a designated day for exchanging tokens, an exchange may be allowed as soon as the student has earned enough tokens for a particular item. This ongoing exchange will encourage students to plan for specific items and exchange their tokens rather than save them.
2. Immediate and delayed exchange may be combined. Students are allowed immediate exchange when they have earned sufficient tokens for a particular reinforcer. They may bank all tokens earned or tokens left over after an exchange for major items or events in the future. There should be a substantial penalty for early withdrawal of banked tokens.
3. The color or some other characteristic of tokens can be changed monthly or quarterly. All students understand that when the tokens change, old tokens become worthless.
4. Extremely well-organized managers can limit the number of tokens a student can accumulate and enforce this limit. This requires careful and accurate record keeping. Any token system that takes too much of a teacher's time and energy to implement and maintain is doomed to be abandoned.

See page 36 for Professor Grundy's advice

It is feasible to use token systems with an entire class or only with selected students. If only some children earn tokens, others may question why. Professor Grundy's advice in Chapter 2 should help the teacher deal with this problem.

A backup reinforcer that may encourage spending tokens is "time." Students may use their accumulated tokens to earn additional minutes to engage in preferred activities. A student may exchange the required number of tokens for the opportunity to work at the computer for 10 minutes. The student is allowed to spend an additional 5 tokens for an additional 5 minutes or 10 tokens for 10 minutes. Within such an exchange there can be a direct, easy-to-understand proportional relationship established between a number of tokens or points and the amount of time that can be bought to engage in an activity. This also allows the students to decide on the value or extra value they associate with a particular reinforcing activity.

When using a system with an entire class, it is easiest to begin with some behavior that is a target for change for the entire class. For example, the teacher might initially give points for academic assignments finished or hands raised during class discussions. Once students have become familiar with the exchange system, the program can be individualized. While still distributing tokens for the initially targeted behavior, the teacher can integrate many academic tasks and social behaviors into the system. For example, Marty might earn tokens for neatness, Debbie for increased speed, and Sara for speaking loudly enough to be heard. Or, instead of this individual focus, the teacher might expand the initial system for classroom behavior management to include additional behaviors that are appropriate for all class members. The following is an example of a teacher's criteria for classroom points (Schumaker, Hovell, & Sherman, 1977, p. 453).
When a discussion is held:

4 pts: Student listens and contributes three times to discussion.
3 pts: Student listens and contributes twice to discussion.
2 pts: Student listens and contributes once to discussion.
1 pt: Student pays attention and listens to discussion.
0 pts: Student does not listen to discussion.

When in-class assignment is given:

4 pts: Student works all of class time on assignment.
3 pts: Student works 3/4 of class time on assignment.
2 pts: Student works 1/2 of class time on assignment.
1 pt: Student starts work on assignment.
0 pts: Student does no work on assignment.

In classes where there is no opportunity for participation (reading on own, movie, lecture):

4 pts: Student is extremely attentive to subject throughout class.
2 pts: Student is generally attentive to subject.
0 pts: Student does not attend to subject.

A token system can also be used for teaching complex academic tasks. For instance, if a teacher is trying to teach a class of students to write appropriate paragraphs, instead of awarding 20 points for writing a paper on "How I Spent My Summer Vacation," the teacher might use the token system by awarding points for the following behaviors:

1 point for bringing pen and paper to class
1 point for beginning the writing assignment on time
1 point for completing the writing assignment on time
1 point for each sentence that begins with a capital letter
1 point for each sentence that ends with a period

Once the students have begun to master these items, the teacher can replace them with a point system for a more complex writing task. For example, <u>by the fourth or fifth writing lesson, instead of awarding points for bringing paper and pen, the teacher might begin to award points for sentences using the appropriate plural suffix.</u> Providing many alternative ways to earn a few points can be important in a token system. Some students find working toward several relatively simple objectives less frustrating and easier to undertake than attempting to earn many points for a long assignment that they may feel inadequate to complete. This approach also builds some measure of assured success into the assignment. Token exchange time can be used for direct or incidental teaching or for review and practice (Fabry, Mayhew, & Hanson, 1984; Kincaid & Weisberg, 1978). The teacher may place words, math problems, or science questions on each backup reinforcer. Students would respond to a stimulus or solve

Position example:
Sports

a problem before receiving the reinforcer. Be sure that students understand this contingency and perhaps even know what the question will be before the exchange takes place. Imagine your reaction if your employer suddenly refused to deposit your salary until you named the Supreme Court justices in order of appointment.

Token reinforcers can be very useful in managing a classroom. Ayllon and Azrin (1968, p. 77) suggested there are advantages to using tangible reinforcers (tokens) that may make them more effective than generalized **social reinforcers** (smiles and praise):

1. The number of tokens can bear a simple quantitative relation to the amount of reinforcement.
2. The tokens are portable and can be in the student's possession even when in a situation far removed from the classroom.
3. No maximum exists on the number of tokens a subject may possess. Their value does not fluctuate with deprivation or satiation.
4. Tokens can be continuously present during the period between earning them and exchanging them.
5. The physical characteristics of the tokens can be easily standardized.
6. The tokens can be made durable so they will not deteriorate before being exchanged.
7. The tokens can be made unique and nonduplicable so that the experimenter can be assured that they are received only in the authorized manner.
8. The use of tokens provides the student with a tangible means of continuous feedback. By having custody of the token objects or point card, the student can follow personal progress toward the criterion set in the contingency—whether it is for a behavior to be brought under control or for the acquisition of an academic objective.
9. The use of tokens enables more precise control by the teacher over administration of reinforcers. As noted by Kazdin (1977a), a teacher's vocal tone will differ each time she or he says "Good work," as will the exact phrasing of "good," "pretty good," or "very good," although in each instance the teacher means to convey an equal praise statement. Token reinforcement does not suffer from this subjective influence.
10. Tokens can be carried by the teacher and delivered unobtrusively. Thus, the administration of a token can be immediate without interfering with the student's performance of the target response or with other students' work.
11. A system of token reinforcement allows for differential valuing of performance. It does not require an all-or-nothing delivery of reinforcement. The student may initially be given a token for each correctly spelled word and later earn reinforcement for a 20-out-of-20 performance. The criterion for performance can be changed as performance improves.
12. A system of token reinforcement allows the student to become accustomed to delayed gratification of wants.
13. The use of a token system allows for greater versatility than is possible with other reinforcement systems. This versatility is related to the wide variety of backup reinforcers that may be selected and to the variety of behaviors that may be placed under a contingency for earning tokens.
14. The most important advantage a token system provides is its ease of generalizability. Unlike primary reinforcers or certain activity reinforcers, tokens can easily be used across settings (in other classrooms, in the cafeteria, on field trips) and with different behaviors simultaneously (in-seat behavior and correct spelling). They can also easily be administered by more than one teacher and by parents.
15. Tokens can often maintain behavior at a higher level than other secondary reinforcers such as praise, approval, and feedback (Kazdin & Polster, 1973; O'Leary, Becker, Evans, & Saudargas, 1969).

Many public school and residential programs for students with behavior disorders and learning disabilities use an adaptation of a token economy usually referred to as a levels system (Randall, Lambert, Matthews, & Houchins-Juarez, 2018; Smith & Farrell, 1993). A levels system is a rigorous framework for shaping appropriate student behavior. Students are divided into groups according to their behavior and can move to higher levels as their behavior improves. Each level requires progressively more appropriate behavior and progressively more student self-management (self-recording, evaluation, and reinforcer selection). As students progress through levels, they have more rigorous standards to meet, gain access to a wider variety of backup reinforcers, and must display increased responsibility for their own behavior. Although there are various ways to set the expectations for behavior within each level and to determine progress from one level to another, at each level teachers set general behavior expectations (for example, use of appropriate language, keeping one's hands to oneself, not leaving the room without permission), and each student has a set of individual behavior requirements based on an individual assessment of academic, social, or behavior deficits. Students on the lowest level have very basic privileges and little freedom of choice or activity, and they earn from a limited range of reinforcers. After a period of behavior that meets various criteria, students move to higher levels, where they must meet increasing expectations and can earn more varied and valuable reinforcers. It is often the case that the last level is a transition stage into a more inclusive educational placement for the student. On the first level, reinforcers in the form of praise, feedback, and points are delivered frequently. As a student progresses through the levels, reinforcers are delivered less often, requiring more appropriate behavior for a reinforcer. At each level, certain behaviors, such as hitting another student or a staff member, will automatically drop a student a level. Some programs include aspects of a psychoeducational model such as log or journal keeping and personal goal setting as requirements for reinforcement (Barbetta, 1990; Gonzalez, Taylor, Borrero, & Sangkavasi, 2013; Hagopian et al., 2002; Lambert, Lopano, Noel, & Ritchie, 2017; Mastropieri, Jenne, & Scruggs, 1988).

SOCIAL REINFORCERS A category of secondary reinforcers that teachers and others often use almost unconsciously (and usually unsystematically) includes demonstrations of approval or attention. The teacher's attention is usually the most readily available and potent reinforcer in a classroom. If teachers are not careful about distributing their attention, they may find that they have reinforced inappropriate behavior by paying attention to it. An example of reinforcing inappropriate behavior in another environment is provided in the following episode.

Burrhus Teaches the Professor

Professor Grundy was sitting on the sofa reading the newspaper. Burrhus padded into the room, lumbered over to Grundy, and stuck his huge head under the professor's arm between the professor and the paper. "Look, Minerva," said the professor, scratching Burrhus on the head, "he likes me. Good boy. Good boy. Aren't you a good boy?" He continued to scratch; Burrhus remained close to the professor, occasionally inserting his head and being petted and praised. Later that day the professor returned from the grocery store. Burrhus lumbered over, stuck his head between the professor and the grocery bag and precipitated the bag to the floor. "He didn't mean to," stated the professor. "He was just glad to see me. Weren't you boy?" he crooned, stepping over the broken eggs that Mrs. Grundy was cleaning up. "Want to go chase your ball?" After dinner Grundy retired to his study to complete work on an important manuscript. Burrhus accompanied him and settled in a place close to the professor's feet. All went well until Burrhus got up, inserted his head between the professor and the computer screen, drooled into the keyboard, and smeared the screen. Grundy leaped up and shouted, "Minerva, call this dog! He's driving me crazy! He's going to have to learn to leave me alone when I'm working."

"Oliver," said Mrs. Grundy tartly, "you have been reinforcing him with your attention for nudging you all day. Now you're complaining. Do you expect him to know you're working? I talked to Miss Oattis this morning. She's teaching a dog obedience class starting next week. I think the two of you need to go."

A wide variety of interactions is associated with a job well done. As shown in the following list, the range of potential social reinforcers includes various nonverbal expressions, teacher proximity to the student, physical contact between teacher and student, student privileges, and words and phrases that convey pleasure and approval of the student's performance (Kranak, Alber-Morgan, & Sawyer, 2017; Nelson et al., 2018; Rubow, Vollmer, & Joslyn, 2018; Tsiouri & Greer, 2007; Weeden, Wills, Kottwitz, & Kamps, 2016). Social reinforcers have proven effective not only for teachers in changing and maintaining student behavior but also for students in changing and maintaining teacher behavior (Gilberts, Agran, Hughes, & Wehmeyer, 2001; Lastrapes, Fritz, & Casper-Teague, 2018).

Expressions
smiling, winking, laughing, nodding, clapping, looking interested

Proximity
sitting next to the student at lunch, sitting next to the student on bus trips, placing the student's desk next to the teacher's, sitting next to the teacher during storytime, being the teacher's partner in a game

Contact
shaking hands, holding hands, pat on the back

Privileges
having good work displayed, being leader of an activity, being classroom monitor, being team captain

Words and Phrases
"I like the way you are sitting." "That is excellent work." "You should be proud of what you have done." "That is just what I wanted you to do." "You should show this to your parents."

Of these social reinforcers, words and phrases are the most often deliberately used by teachers. Affirmative words and phrases are described as forms of teacher praise. See Table 8.4 for additional, effective praise statements (Perle, 2016). Teacher

Table 8.4 Examples of Effective Positive Attending

Ways to begin the praise	Targets of the praise
I love that you are . . .	Following directions
I like that you are . . .	Staying calm after getting upset
You're doing an awesome job . . .	Keeping your hands to yourself
You're doing a great job . . .	Staying in your seat
Fantastic job . . .	Doing your work
I really appreciate that you are . . .	Helping [me], helping a peer
I'm really impressed that you are . . .	Turning in your work
It makes me very happy that you are . . .	Using nice words, language
I'm so proud of you for . . .	Using an inside voice
Awesome job . . .	Holding the door
You did fantastic . . .	Standing nicely in line
You did amazing . . .	Acknowledging you heard the instructions
Look at how great you are . . .	Listening
Nice work . . .	Saying "please," "thank you" Making eye contact Sharing Cleaning up after yourself Playing nicely with a peer Accepting "no"

Table 8.5 Components of positive attending

Component	Description
Be specific	A teacher should tell the student *exactly* which behaviors he or she is happy to see in order to encourage the student (e.g., "Great job raising your hand" instead of "Great job").
Be immediate	A teacher should positively attend as soon as a desired behavior occurs so the student can associate the teacher's praise with the positive behavior.
Be consistent and frequent	A teacher can demonstrate the importance of the students' positive behaviors by attending to them consistently and frequently. Praising a behavior once every few hours may not be enough, especially for students with emotional and behavioral disorders.
Be preventative	A teacher can "catch a student being good" instead of waiting for problems to occur in order to prevent difficulties.
Praise the opposite	A teacher should consider the opposite of the student's disruptive behavior as a basis for positive attending (e.g., praise students for raising their hands if they frequently call out).
Avoid criticism and derogatory feedback	Derogatory teacher-provided statements may exacerbate a student's problematic behavior, whereas positive language may facilitate improved student behavior.
Focus on the student's performance	A teacher should focus positive attending on the student's performance instead of ability (i.e., attend to doing well on an assignment rather than intelligence).
Actively ignore disruptive behavior	If feasible, a teacher should immediately and consistently ignore disruptive attention-seeking behaviors. Ignoring should be brief (e.g., a few seconds), with the teacher looking for opportunities to positively attend to appropriate behavior.

praise as a consequence of appropriate student behaviors is a classroom and behavior-management strategy with a long and thorough history of research-based support. Across chronological ages in both general and special education, teachers' use of contingent praise effectively increased a wide variety of student behaviors and academic skills (Markelz & Taylor, 2016). See Table 8.5 for essential components of delivering praise (Perle, 2016).

Praise for student performance can be non-behavior-specific praise or behavior-specific praise. Non-behavior-specific praise does not specify the desired behavior for which the student was being praised, for example, "Nice work" or "You are doing a good job" (Polick, Carr, & Hanney, 2012). Behavior-specific praise is when the teacher identifies the behavior for which the student is being reinforced. Behavior-specific praise can be delivered for academic or social behavior, as in "You're right! It is 1:15 because the little hand is on the 1 and the big hand is on the 3," or "All of you did a great job of sitting quietly while Ron read to us today" (Adamo et al., 2015). Verbal praise/feedback is also used to reinforce an attempt or approximation, for example, "Good try, you got two out of three right. Now do this one the same way." Behavior-specific praise was seen to have a direct effect on student on-task and study behavior in general education and special education settings (Rathel, Drasgow, Brown, & Marshall, 2014; Sutherland, Wehby, & Copeland, 2000). For example, Sutherland et al. (2000) demonstrated that with fifth-grade students with emotional behavioral disability (EBD), as the rate of behavior-specific teacher praise increased, student behavior increased; as the rate of behavior-specific teacher praise decreased, student behavior decreased.

Some forms of feedback provide students with a measure of accuracy, as in Cronin and Cuvo's (1979) use of various-colored stars (red stars equal a performance better than last time, gold stars equal 100% accuracy). Graphs and charts have been used as a means of immediate feedback and reinforcement. Seeing their individual bar graphs grow or the increasing trend of their line graphs has been found to be reinforcing for a range of students and for many academic and social behaviors, including increasing performance in reading, writing, and mathematics by elementary and secondary students (see Figure 8.7 from Wells, Sheehey, & Sheehey (2017); Albers & Hoffman, 2012; Finn, Ramasamy, Dukes, & Scott, 2015; Pennington & Koehler, 2017; Sheehey, Wells, & Rowe, 2017).

Token Systems
Pearson eText
Video Example 8.4
In this video, an educator and her student review the classroom's reinforcement system with various colored clips. Consider what gives each of the clips value in this system and how that could be customized for each student.

Figure 8.7 James' bar graph of math problems completed accurately.

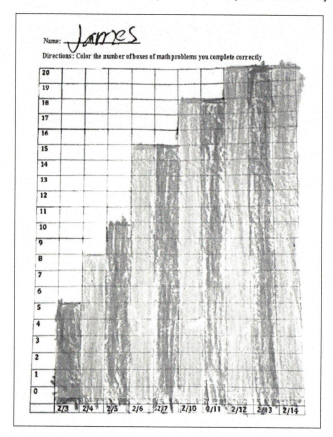

Contracting

Learning Outcome 8.2 Identify components of a behavioral contract and ways to use behavior contracts.

It can be difficult for a teacher to use a reinforcement system serving a number of students and having a variety of objectives for managing behavior and instruction. On a hectic day, a teacher might offhandedly state a contingency for a student without thinking it through. Later the teacher may not remember the details of what was said and thus will not be in a position to enforce the contingency. To complicate this uncertainty, students tend to rewrite reality to suit themselves: "You said I could go outside if I finished my math. You didn't say I had to get them right." A simple way to systematize the use of reinforcement is contracting. **Contracting** is placing the contingency for reinforcement into a written document. In the contract itself, the teacher creates a permanent product that can be referred to if questions arise (Bowman-Perrott, Burke, de Marin, Zhang, & Davis, 2015).

As with any contract, the classroom contract should be the product of reasonable negotiations between the parties involved—namely, the teacher and the student. In many cases these negotiations involve the collaboration of the student and all of the teachers whose classes he attends (Lassman, Jolivette, & Wehby, 1999). Though the exact wording of a written contract will depend on the sophistication of the student for whom it is designed, each will contain some form of the basic "if . . . , then . . ." statement, as shown in Figure 8.8. A written contract should always contain those elements minimally necessary for any reinforcement contingency: the behavior, the conditions, the criterion, and the reinforcer.

To avoid later disagreement about what was really meant, the contract should contain precisely written statements describing the behavior required. This description

Figure 8.8 Formats used in contracting

Note: From *It's Positively Fun: Techniques for Managing Learning Environments*, by P. Kaplan, J. Kohfeldt, & K. Sturla, 1974, Denver: Love Publishing. Copyright 1974 by Love Publishing. Reprinted by permission.

should include the parameters within which the behavior is to be performed and the criterion level for meeting the contract terms. After discussion of the criterion, the student should understand the method or instruments that will be used to evaluate performance. The contract should also include the type, amount, and method of delivery of the reinforcement.

In addition to these basic items, dates for an interim and final review should appear in the contract. The interim date reminds the teacher of the need to monitor progress and allows renegotiation if the behavior required is unrealistic or if there is an instructional component to be added. Listing the final review date sets the student's time limit for fulfilling the terms of the contract. Once the terms of the contract have been discussed and written down, the teacher should answer all questions the student may have. To ensure that the student understands the terms of the contract, he or she

See Chapter 10 for more about reinforcement of small approximations.

should read it back to the teacher and then restate the terms in different words. If this process results in a very different statement, the contract should be rewritten in easier language. Once a contract is finalized, the teacher and the student should both sign it, and each should have a copy.

Homme, Csanyi, Gonzales, and Rechs (1970, pp. 18–20) suggested basic rules for the use of reinforcers in contracting (numbers 1–5) and characteristics of proper contracting (6–10):

1. "The contract payoff (reward) should be immediate." This rule follows what has been stated as one of the essential elements of an effective reinforcer: It must be administered immediately upon performance of the target behavior.
2. "Initial contracts should call for and reward small approximations." This form of successive approximations—that is, progressive steps toward the target behavior—is particularly useful for behaviors the student has never performed before, a criterion level set too high, or a behavior category that is too broad (such as "clean your room").
3. "Reward frequently with small amounts." Homme et al. stated that experience has shown that "it is far more effective to give frequent, small reinforcements than a few large ones." Frequent delivery of reinforcement allows for closer monitoring of the progress of the behavior change by both the teacher and the student.
4. "The contract should call for and reward accomplishment rather than obedience." Homme et al. suggested that contracts focusing on accomplishments lead to independence. Therefore, appropriate wording should be, "If you accomplish such and such, you will be rewarded with such and such," as opposed to "If you do what I tell you to do, I will reward you with such and such."
5. "Reward the performance after it occurs." This rule restates an essential element of a reinforcer: It must be administered contingently. Inexperienced teachers sometimes state contingencies as, "If you get to go on the field trip today, you must do all your work next week." They are usually disappointed with the effects of such statements.
6. "The contract must be fair." The "weight" of the reinforcement should be in proportion to the amount of behavior required. The ratio set up in the contract should be fair to both the teacher and the student. Asking the student to finish 2 out of 20 problems correctly for 30 minutes of free time is just as unfair as requiring 20 out of 20 problems correct for 2 minutes of free time.
7. "The terms of the contract must be clear." Ambiguity causes disagreement. If the teacher and student do not agree on the meaning of the contract, the teacher may decide contracting is more trouble than it is worth. The student may decide neither the teacher nor the system can be trusted.
8. "The contract must be honest." According to Homme et al., an honest contract is one that is (a) "carried out immediately" and (b) "carried out according to the terms specified in the contract." This can be assured if the teacher and the student have freely engaged in the contract negotiation. Teachers should avoid imposing a contract on the student.
9. "The contract must be positive." Appropriate: "I will do . . . , if you do. . . ." Inappropriate: "I will not do . . . , if you do. . . ." "If you do not . . . , then I will. . . ." "If you do not, then I will not. . . ."
10. "Contracting as a method must be used systematically." As with any form of reinforcement strategy, if contracting is not done systematically and consistently, it becomes a guessing game: "Does she really mean it this time?"

Writing contracts brings added advantages to a reinforcement system:

1. A written contract is a permanent document that records the variables of the original contingency for consultation by the teacher and the student.
2. The process of negotiation that leads to the contract enables students to see themselves as active participants in their learning as they each take part in setting their own expectations or limitations.

3. The writing of a contract emphasizes the individualization of instruction.
4. Contracting provides interim documents that state current objectives between IEP meetings. Such information may be shared with parents.

Variations in Administration of Reinforcers

Learning Outcome 8.3 Identify variations in the delivery of reinforcement.

A basic reinforcement system has the following design:

- The teacher presents the antecedent discriminative stimulus.
- The student performs the requested response.
- The teacher presents the student with an appropriate reinforcer.

This basic scheme focuses on the administration of an individually selected reinforcer designed for the particular student. Reinforcement is, however, a flexible strategy that can be adapted to a number of situations that arise in the management of a classroom. Based on the type of contingency and manner of administering consequences, Kazdin (2001) devised a matrix to represent these variations (see Figure 8.9). Although the matrix was originally proposed for variation in use of token systems, it is equally appropriate with any reinforcement system.

As Figure 8.9 shows, there are two options for administering consequences. First, reinforcement can be administered individually: The particular student who has performed the requested response is given the cereal, free time, or appropriate number of tokens. Second, reinforcement can be administered to students as a group: Given an acceptable performance by the whole class, for example, all 30 students earn extra time for crafts on Wednesday afternoon.

There are three options for the type of contingency a teacher may establish for receipt of reinforcement. These are represented at the top of the matrix in Figure 8.9. For the first one, *individualized contingencies*, the behavior requested and the criterion of performance required are specific to the behavior or instructional needs of a particular student. Under the second option, *standardized contingencies*, the teacher sets a requirement that is applied equally to all members of a class or to several class members. Using the third alternative, *group contingencies*, some behavior is required of a group of students and reinforcement is based on performance of the group as a whole (Little, Akin-Little, & O'Neill, 2015).

Interaction among the two manners of administration and the three types of contingencies yields the six-celled matrix in Figure 8.9.

Figure 8.9 Variations in administration of consequences

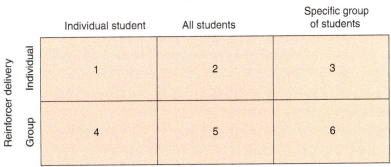

Note: Adapted from *The Token Economy: A Review and Evaluation*, by A. E. Kazdin, 1977, New York: Plenum Press.

Cell 1 shows a system in which both the contingency for reinforcement and the manner of its delivery are individualized. The behavior and criterion are specific to a particular student, and the reinforcement is delivered only to that student.

1. Randy, if you complete 17 of your 20 arithmetic problems correctly, then you may use the computer terminal for 10 extra minutes.
2. Randy, for each arithmetic problem you solve correctly, you will receive one token.

Cell 2 shows a system that provides the same contingency for reinforcement for all class members (standard) but individualizes the manner of delivery to each student.

1. Class, each of you who completes 17 of your 20 math problems correctly may have an extra 10 minutes at the computer terminal.
2. Class, each of you may earn one token each time you raise your hand before asking a question.

Cell 3 shows a system that sets the same contingency for reinforcement for a particular group of students, but individualizes the manner of reinforcer delivery to each group member.

1. Math Group B, if you can develop 10 original problems that require multiplication for their solution, you may all have 10 extra minutes at the computer terminal whenever you choose and with whichever program you wish.
2. Each boy in the class may earn a token for placing his tray on the cart when he has finished eating his lunch.

Cell 4 shows a system that requires each member of a group to perform a specific behavior in order for the group as a unit to be reinforced.

1. Math Group B, you are to present a 15-minute program to the class concerning the use of multiplication. Randy, you are responsible for an explanation of the basic computation procedure. Carol, you are to explain the relationship between multiplication and addition. Nicholas, you are to demonstrate how to work problems from our math workbooks. Sandy, you are to pose three original problems for the class to solve. At the end of the presentation, the four of you may use the computer terminal together for one of the game programs.
2. The following students may go to the gym to play basketball if they write an essay on basketball: Gary, your essay must have at least four sentences. Jamie, your essay must have at least six sentences. And Cory, your essay must have at least 10 sentences.

Cell 5 shows a system that sets the same contingency for reinforcement for all class members and allows each individual who has met this standard criterion to become a member of a group to be jointly reinforced.

1. Class, for homework you are to develop a problem that requires multiplication for its solution. All students who bring an appropriate problem will be allowed to go to the math lab tomorrow morning from 10:00 to 10:30.
2. All students who receive a grade of 100 on the geography test today will be exempt from geography homework tonight.

Cell 6 shows a system that sets the same contingency for reinforcement and same manner of reinforcer delivery for a group of class members.

1. Math Group B, here are 20 problems. If you get the correct answers for all 20, you may go to the math lab for 30 minutes.
2. Redbirds, if you all remember to raise your hand before speaking during our reading lesson, you may select your own books to take home this weekend.

Following a review of studies in which contingencies were applied to more than one individual at a time, Litow and Pumroy (1975) delineated three administrative

Table 8.6 Group contingency types and examples

Type	Definition	Examples	Research-based examples
Dependent	Reinforcement provided to an entire group contingent on the behavior of one or more individuals	If the mystery hero completes his or her seat work, we can all leave for recess 2 min early. If everyone at Table 2 leaves their lunch table neat, we will continue reading our novel after lunch.	Red card/green card game of the FIRST STEP Next intervention (Walker et al., 2015)
Independent	Reinforcement provided to an individual contingent on the behavior of that individual	Anyone who increases their reading fluency rate by 10 correct words per minute this semester can earn 5 bonus points on the unit test. Anyone who earns three behavior bucks this week can earn entry into an extra recess.	Contingency Contracting (e.g., Bowman-Perrot, Burke, de Marin, Zhang, & Davis, 2015)
Interdependent	Reinforcement provided to an entire group contingent on the behavior of the entire group	If everyone is working when the timer goes off, we can earn appoint toward Friday free time. If everyone in your row completes their warm up, your row will earn a point toward a spin on the wheel of reinforcement.	Good Behavior Game (Barrish, Saunders, & Wolf, 1969) Classwide Function-Based Intervention Teams (CW-FIT; Kamps et al., 2015)

systems. They categorized these as dependent, independent, and interdependent group-oriented contingency systems. See Table 8.6 (from Ennis, 2018) for descriptions and examples of the three types of group contingencies.

In *dependent group-oriented contingency systems*, "the same response contingencies are simultaneously in effect for all group members but are applied only to the performances of one or more selected group members. It is the performance of the selected group members that results in consequences for the whole group" (Litow & Pumroy, 1975, p. 342). The teacher makes reinforcement for the entire class contingent on the performance of one or more particular students. The remaining class members are dependent on the targeted student's performance for the reinforcement. The targeted student and reinforcer may be randomized and not revealed to the students until the end of each class session (Cariveau & Kodak, 2017).

1. The opportunity for the class to have an extra session of physical education depends on Robert's and Caroline's passing Friday's spelling test.
2. The opportunity for the class to have an extra session of physical education depends on William's and Bernice's having talked out without raising their hands no more than seven times during math class.

In *independent group-oriented contingency systems*, "the same response contingencies are simultaneously in effect for all group members but are applied to performances on an individual basis. In this type of contingency system, each member's outcomes are not affected by (are independent of) the performances of the other group members" (Litow & Pumroy, 1975, p. 342). The teacher makes reinforcement for each class member contingent on that class member's being able to meet the contingency criterion level of performance. Those who fail to achieve the performance criterion will not receive the reinforcer.

1. The opportunity for an extra session of physical education is available to each student who passes Friday's spelling test.
2. The opportunity for an extra session of physical education is available to each student who talks out no more than three times.

In *interdependent group-oriented contingency systems*, "the same response contingencies are simultaneously in effect for all group members but are applied to a level of group performance. Consequently, in this type of contingency system, each member's outcome depends ([is] interdependent) upon a level of group performance" (Litow & Pumroy, 1975, p. 343). The *Good Behavior Game* is the most common application of interdependent group contingencies (Barrish, Saunders, & Wolf, 1969; Nolan, Houlihan, Wanzek, & Jensen, 2014). In the Good Behavior Game, the teacher assigns students to groups, gives points for inappropriate behaviors, and rewards the team with the fewest points. This has been shown to reduce disruptive behavior, increase academic behaviors, and increase positive peer interactions (Donaldson, Matter, & Wiskow, 2018; Groves & Austin, 2017; Rubow, Vollmer, & Joslyn, 2018). Students with emotional and behavioral disorders may benefit the most from the Good Behavior Game (Bowman-Perrott, Burke, Zaini, Zhang, & Vannest, 2016).

There are effective variations of the Good Behavior Game. One variation is the Caught Being Good Game in which the teacher sets a timer to sound or vibrate every 5 minutes, assigns points to each team with all members on task, and delivers rewards contingent on a certain number of points (Wahl, Hawkins, Haydon, Marsicano, & Morrison, 2016). Another variation of the Good Behavior Game is the Teacher versus Students Game in which the students earn points for following rules, and the teacher earns points when the students do not follow the rules (Lastrapes, Fritz, & Casper-Teague, 2018). See Figure 8.10 for examples of teacher displays of point systems in group contingencies (Ennis, 2018).

Litow and Pumroy (1975) listed three types of group performance levels:

1. The contingency is stated so that each group member must achieve a set criterion level. Failure to achieve this criterion level by the class results in no class member receiving the reinforcer. For example, the opportunity for an extra session of physical education is contingent on each member of the class earning at least 90% on Friday's spelling test.
2. The contingency is stated such that each group member's performance meets a criterion average for the entire group. For example, the opportunity for an extra session of physical education is contingent on a class average of 90% of written work completed.
3. The contingency is stated so that the class, as a group, must reach a single highest or lowest level of performance. For example, the opportunity for an extra session of physical education is contingent on the class as a whole having engaged in no more than 12 talk-outs.

> Always use the simplest effective system.

Figure 8.10 Group contingency visual displays.

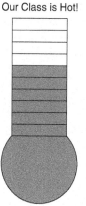

Our Class is Hot!

We're working for an afternoon in the sun!

When our class spells history, we earn a free homework pass:

H I S T O

Our behavior is LINKED! When our chain reaches the floor, we'll earn the mystery suprise!

The first groups to 10 get a reward from the bin!

Group 1	Group 2
││││	𝍷𝍷𝍷𝍷𝍷
Group 3	Group 4
𝍷𝍷𝍷𝍷𝍷 │	𝍷𝍷𝍷𝍷𝍷 │

By using these variations of the reinforcer delivery system, the teacher can tailor a reinforcement system to a particular classroom. In considering which system to use, Deshais, Fisher, and Kahng (2018) found that an independent group contingency was superior to a dependent group in terms of increasing answers completed on literacy worksheets with first grade general education students; however, interestingly, the students preferred the dependent group contingency. Despite these findings, every classroom is different: Some groups, even in general education classrooms, need a formal token system; other groups may have members who need contracting or individual systems; many general education classrooms can be managed using relatively informal arrangements of social and activity reinforcers. Teachers should use the simplest, most natural system that will be effective.

Group Contingencies and Peer Mediation

Good Behavior Game
Pearson eText
Video Example 8.5
In this video, the educator is implementing a variation of the Good Behavior Game. Notice how she incorporates technology effectively to manage the system.

Group contingencies can be an extremely effective means of managing some students' behavior. Adolescents, particularly, may find working as a group more reinforcing. There is some evidence that students with and without disabilities rank academic work with peers very highly (Lloyd, Eberhardt, & Drake, 1996; Martens, Muir, & Meller, 1988). Lloyd et al. (1996) also found that when compared with individual study and group study with individual reinforcement, group study with group reinforcement raised mean quiz scores, decreased the range of scores, and had substantial positive effects on the scores at the low end of the distribution. Group contingencies can foster interdependence and may result in increasing cooperative behavior among students (Groves & Austin, 2019). Kohler et al. (1995) found that group contingencies could increase supportive prompts, such as sharing and assistance, among disabled and nondisabled peers.

Group contingencies can be accomplished through peer mediation as well as teacher-managed intervention. Pigott, Fantuzzo, and Clement (1986) successfully arranged peer tutoring and group contingencies for the academic performance of underachieving fifth-grade students. The students were divided into arithmetic drill teams. Each member of the team was assigned a role. The coach reminded the team of their group goal for the number of correct answers, the strategy they had selected (for example, "work fast," "work carefully," "don't talk"), and selected backup reinforcers from a reinforcer menu. The scorekeeper counted the number of correct answers on individual team members' papers. The referee served as the reliability checker, and the team manager compared the total team score with the goal and decided if the goal was met. In all three classes the students' math performance improved and was maintained during the 12-week follow-up when students were allowed to use teams if they wished, but no reinforcement contingency was in place. Cashwell, Skinner, and Smith (2001) taught second-grade students to record and report the prosocial behaviors of their peers that occurred during the day. Following sessions in which prosocial behavior was defined and examples generated, the students recorded on an index card all incidents of peers helping them or other classmates. A group contingency of a cumulative goal of 100 reports was set for the class in order for them to participate in an agreed-upon activity reinforcer (e.g., extra play time). Each morning the students were told of the tally from the day before and it was entered on a ladder-like bar graph. When the class met their cumulative goal, the entire class received access to the predetermined group reinforcer. This interdependent group reinforcement procedure and publicly posted progress-feedback procedure resulted in increases in the students' prosocial behaviors.

In a third example, Carpenter and McKee-Higgins (1996) combined a group contingency and individual contingencies in a first-grade classroom. Over a period of months, off-task behaviors had spread from one disruptive student to most of the class members. A plan was implemented combining teacher statements acknowledging appropriate behavior and redirecting inappropriate behavior with reinforcement contingencies. The students chose an activity reinforcer in the form of chalkboard class games played by the whole class for the group contingency. They chose pieces of candy for the individual contingencies. The teacher paired the edible reinforcer with positive verbal statements to shape and maintain desired student behavior and gradually eliminated its use once student behaviors began to improve. Before each activity time, students were asked to determine an acceptable level of off-task behaviors for the group. If the students reached their goal for two of three activities, they were reinforced with a chalkboard game. At the end of each activity students placed a card in a pocket on the bulletin board if they thought they personally had used on-task behaviors during the activity. The teacher and students briefly discussed the on-task behaviors and reached consensus about each student's performance. When individual students earned 10 cards, they got a piece of candy. Peer pressure is a powerful tool in group contingencies. Indeed, it is so powerful that group contingencies should be used with caution to avoid the negative side effect of undue pressure on some members of a group (Balsam & Bondy, 1983). In an interdependent group contingency, such as the Good Behavior Game, there may be negative peer pressure such as, "Come on, Shawn—if you goof off again we may earn less points than the other team—get it together!" In addition, consider the following example.

Ms. Montgomery Teaches Spelling

Ms. Montgomery, a fifth-grade teacher, was concerned about her students' grades on their weekly spelling test. Some students did very well, but others spelled only a few words correctly. Ms. Montgomery came up with what she felt was a brilliant plan. She divided the students into pairs—one good speller and one poor. She then announced, "The grade that I enter in my grade book on Friday will be an average of what you and your partner earn on the test." She sat back and watched the students busily drilling one another and assumed that her troubles were over.

She first began to see a flaw in her plan when she observed LeeAnn chasing Barney around the playground during recess, slapping him with her speller and yelling, "Sit down, dummy, you've got to learn these words." She knew she had blown it when she got a phone call at home that night from LeeAnn's mother protesting that LeeAnn was going to fail spelling because that dumb Barney couldn't learn the words, and one from Barney's mother asking if Ms. Montgomery had any idea what might have caused Barney to spend the entire afternoon crying in his room.

Ms. Montgomery violated one of the most important rules about setting group contingencies: *Be absolutely sure each member of the group is capable of performing the target behavior.* If this rule is violated, the teacher risks subjecting students to verbal and physical abuse by their peers. It is especially important not to put students with disabilities and English language learners in such a position, particularly when they are included in general education classes. When implemented correctly, the Good Behavior Game may result in more positive interactions and fewer negative interactions amongst students, as Groves and Austin (2019) found with two classrooms of adolescents and younger students with and without mild/moderate disabilities. Ms. Montgomery may have had more success by using the Good Behavior Game and splitting the class into larger-member teams in which students could encourage each other to do well.

Another important caution is being sure some member does not find it reinforcing to sabotage the group's efforts. In the original Good Behavior Game study, Barrish, Saunders, and Wolf (1969) arranged a group contingency to modify disruptive out-of-seat and talking-out behavior in a class of 24 fourth-grade students. The class was divided into two teams during reading and math periods. Each instance of out-of-seat behavior or talking out by an individual team member resulted in a mark against the entire team. The team with the greatest number of marks would lose certain privileges. Although this procedure was successful, an important modification was implemented. Two members of one team consistently gained marks for their team. During one session, one of the members "emphatically announced" that he was no longer going to play the game. The teacher and the children felt the behavior of one student should not further penalize the entire team. The saboteur was removed from the team (and the group contingency) and made into a one-person team, thus applying an individual-consequences procedure until his behavior was brought under control and he could then be returned to one of the class teams. The authors stated that it appeared the expected effects of peer pressure, instead of bringing individual behavior under group control, may have served as a social reinforcer for the student's disruptive behavior.

Finally, the system must minimize the possibility of some members' performing the target behavior for others. If these factors are taken into account, group contingencies can be a very useful management device.

Schedules of Reinforcement

Schedules of reinforcement are patterns of timing for delivery of reinforcers. Until now, we have described the delivery of reinforcers for each occurrence of the target behavior. Delivery of reinforcement on a continuous basis is referred to as a continuous schedule of reinforcement (CRF). That is, each time the student produces the target response, she or he immediately receives a reinforcer. This schedule has a one-to-one ratio, or response: reinforcement ($R:S^R$).

We call a one-to-one CRF schedule one that has a *dense* ratio of reinforcement to response; there is a lot of reinforcement relative to performance, and this leads to a high rate of responding. This high rate of responding results in an increase in the number of trials or opportunities for the student to perform the response (increased practice) and to receive feedback and reinforcement from the teacher. Therefore, CRF schedules are most useful when students are learning new behaviors (acquisition). A student who is learning a new behavior should receive a reinforcer for each correct response or any response that is closer to a correct response than previous ones. The process of reinforcing closer (successive) approximations to the target behavior is called shaping and is discussed in Chapter 9. A CRF schedule may also be useful when the target behavior initially has a very low frequency. It is most effective during the early stages of any reinforcement system. There are, however, certain potential problems when using a CRF schedule:

1. A student whose behavior is on a CRF schedule may become satiated on the reinforcer, especially if a primary reinforcer is being used. Once correct responding is frequent, the continuous receipt of an edible will reduce the deprivation state and thereby reduce motivation for correct responding.
2. Continuous delivery of reinforcers may lead to accusations that teachers are leading students to expect some type of reinforcement every time they do as they are told.
3. CRF schedules are not the most efficient way to maintain a behavior following its initial acquisition or control. First, once a behavior has been acquired, or its frequency increased, by reinforcement on a CRF schedule, teachers may terminate the intervention program. The transfer from continuous reinforcement to no reinforcement results in a rapid loss of the behavior. This rapid loss of behavior when reinforcement is withheld is called **extinction** and is discussed in Chapter 9. Second, CRF schedules may interfere with classroom routine. How long could (or would) a teacher continuously reinforce 4, 6, 8, or 30 students for raising their hands before speaking or for making the letter "a" correctly?

Using a variety of less-than-continuous schedules may solve the problems caused by using CRF schedules beyond the point of effectiveness.

INTERMITTENT SCHEDULES In **intermittent schedules** reinforcement follows some, but not all, correct or appropriate responses (Skinner, 1953). Because each occurrence of the behavior is no longer reinforced, intermittent schedules put off satiation effects. Behaviors maintained on intermittent schedules are also more resistant to extinction. Intermittent schedules require greater numbers of correct responses for reinforcement. The student learns to delay gratification and to maintain appropriate behavior for longer periods of time.

The two categories of intermittent schedules most often used to increase the frequency of behaviors are **ratio schedules** and **interval schedules** (Ferster & Skinner, 1957; Skinner, 1953). To increase the duration of a behavior, the teacher may use **response-duration schedules** (Dixon et al., 1998; Gresham, Van, & Cook, 2006; Stevenson & Clayton, 1970).

Ratio Schedules Under ratio schedules, the number of times a target behavior occurs determines the timing of reinforcer delivery. Under a **fixed-ratio schedule (FR)**, the student is reinforced on completion of a specified number of correct responses. A behavior on an FR3 schedule would be reinforced immediately following the occurrence of every third correct response, a contingent ratio of three correct responses to each reinforcer (R, R, R:S^R). A student who must complete eight math problems correctly to earn the right to work on puzzles or who must correctly point to the blue object on eight trials before getting a bite of pretzel would be on an FR8 schedule of reinforcement.

Behaviors placed on FR schedules have particular characteristics. The student generally has a higher rate of responding than on CRF schedules because increases in rate result in increases in the frequency of reinforcement. Because the time it takes the student to perform the specified number of correct responses is not considered when delivering reinforcers, FR schedules may result in inappropriate fluencies for a given behavior. For example, to earn a reinforcer, a student may work math problems so rapidly that he makes more mistakes and his handwriting deteriorates. In addition to inappropriate fluency, FR schedules may cause another type of problem. As the schedule ratio increases (from FR2 to FR10, for example), the student will often stop responding for a period of time following delivery of the reinforcer, taking what is termed a postreinforcement pause.

The problems of fluency and postreinforcement pause are eliminated by transition to a variable-ratio schedule (VR). Under a VR schedule, the target response is reinforced on the average of a specified number of correct responses. A behavior on a VR5 schedule would be reinforced on the average of every fifth correct response. Therefore, in a teaching or observation session, the student may be reinforced following the third, eighth, fifth, and fourth correct responses.

"No, Mrs. Cole, a VR10 schedule does not mean 10 cookies every time Ralph gets it right."

After the occurrence of a behavior on the FR schedule has been established at the criterion level (as stated in the behavioral objective), the VR schedule will maintain a moderate and consistent rate of correct responding. The unpredictability of reinforcer delivery on a VR schedule causes the student's rate of responding to even out, with little or no postreinforcement pausing. "The probability of reinforcement at any moment remains essentially constant, and the 'student' adjusts by holding to a constant rate" (Skinner, 1953, p. 104).

Interval Schedules   Under interval schedules, the occurrence of at least one correct or appropriate response plus the passage of a specific amount of time are the determinants for delivery of the reinforcer. Under a **fixed-interval schedule (FI)**, the student is reinforced the first time he or she performs the target response following the elapse of a specified number of minutes or seconds. On an FI5-minute schedule, the first correct response that occurs after 5 minutes has passed is reinforced. Following the delivery of that reinforcer, the next 5-minute cycle begins. Because a single instance of the behavior after the end of the interval is reinforced, instances that may occur before the interval ends are not reinforced. It is this phenomenon that defines a fixed-interval schedule as intermittent reinforcement.

Behaviors placed on FI schedules also have particular characteristics. Because the only requirement for reinforcement on an FI schedule is that the response occur at least once following each specified interval, behaviors occur at a relatively low rate as compared with behaviors on ratio schedules. This is especially true if and when the student becomes aware of the length of the interval and therefore aware of when reinforcement is possible. The length of the interval will affect the rate of responding (Skinner, 1953). If reinforcement is available every minute, responding will be more rapid than if it is available every 10 minutes. Behaviors on FI schedules also have a characteristic that parallels the postreinforcement pause of FR schedules. A student eventually realizes that additional correct responses before the interval ends do not result in reinforcement. It also becomes apparent that responses immediately after reinforcement are never reinforced. The rate of responding eventually is noticeably lower (or ceases) for a short time after each reinforcement (the initial portion of the next interval). This decrease in correct responding is termed a *fixed-interval scallop*, because of the appearance of the data when plotted on a cumulative graph.

Lee and Belfiore (1997, p. 213) cautioned teachers that FI schedules may not be the best choice if the goal is to increase student time on task. If secondary English students, for example, are assigned to work on writing a paper and the teacher habitually reinforces those who are writing when the end-of-period bell rings by excusing them from homework, the teacher should expect a typical FI pattern of responding: that is, a long period of inactivity followed by a slight increase in writing rate just before the bell rings—the end of the interval. If the teacher's goal was to increase the amount of time students were engaged in writing, her goal was not met. Her program increased time on task only shortly before the bell. A similar pattern would emerge if a teacher placed students on an FI5-minute schedule when they were assigned the vocational task of assembling packets for distribution by the Red Cross. The work would proceed at low rates with only a slight increase toward the end of each interval, resulting in low productivity.

The effects on rate of responding resulting from FI schedules are eliminated by transition to a **variable-interval schedule (VI)**. Under a VI schedule, the intervals are of different lengths, but their average length is consistent. A behavior on a VI5-minute schedule would have a reinforcer available for the target response on the average of every 5 minutes. As in use of VR schedules, the unpredictability levels out student performance. Behaviors under a VI schedule are performed at moderate, steadier rates across intervals without the appearance of fixed-interval scallops, because the student can no longer predict the length of the interval following delivery of a reinforcer and therefore cannot predict which response will be reinforced.

A technique for increasing the rate of responding under an interval schedule is use of a **limited hold (LH)** contingency. A limited hold restricts the time the reinforcer is available following the interval. That is, when the interval has elapsed and the next correct response will be reinforced, the reinforcer will remain available for only a limited time. In this case, students must respond quickly to earn reinforcers, whereas under a simple interval schedule, they may delay responding and still be reinforced. An F15-min/LH5-sec schedule would make a reinforcer available for 5 seconds following each 5-minute interval. For example, when a student is being taught to ride a bus, he learns that the bus comes every 15 minutes and that he must step in quickly when the doors open (naturally occurring reinforcement) for only 30 seconds (FI15 min/LH30 sec).

Response-Duration Schedules Under response-duration schedules, the continuous amount of time of a target behavior is the determinant for delivery of the reinforcer. Under a fixed-response-duration schedule (FRD), the student is reinforced following completion of a specified number of minutes (or seconds) of appropriate behavior. A behavior on an FRD 10-minute schedule would be reinforced immediately at the end of each 10 minutes of continuous appropriate behavior. A student whom the teacher wants to remain seated during reading period and whom the teacher verbally praises for in-seat behavior every 10 minutes is under an FRD 10-minute schedule. Timing is restarted if the behavior stops occurring at any point during the time period.

As in FR and FI schedules, a pause following reinforcement may be seen under FRD schedules. In this case, the pause appears to be related to the length of the required time period for appropriate behavior. The longer the time period, the longer the pause. It may be expected that if the time period is too long or is increased too rapidly, the behavior will either decrease or stop occurring altogether. Varying the length of the time periods required for reinforcement, using a **variable-response-duration schedule (VRD)**, minimizes these problems. Under a VRD schedule, continuous appropriate behavior is reinforced on the average of a specified time period. A behavior on a VRD 10-minute schedule would be reinforced on the average of every 10 minutes.

In the real world, it is often necessary to delay gratification.

Lag Schedules of Reinforcement One other type of schedule of reinforcement, called a lag schedule of reinforcement, is used to increase the variety of behaviors students learn (Neuringer, 2004). Contreras and Betz (2016) wanted to vary students' responses when asked to name some items, such as, "Tell me something you find in a kitchen" (p. 6). If a student said "fridge" every time, this is a more limited repertoire than if the student varied her response each time she was asked. In a lag schedule of reinforcement, reinforcement is contingent on saying a response that is different from a certain number of previous responses. For example, using a Lag 1 schedule, if a student answered the question with "sink," a reinforcer was delivered if the student said something other than "sink" the previous time she was asked. On a Lag 3 schedule, a response has to be different than the last three responses. Susa and Schlinger (2012) used lag schedules to vary the responses to "How are you?" of a student diagnosed with autism.

THINNING SCHEDULES OF REINFORCEMENT A formal classroom reinforcement system should be viewed as a temporary structure used to produce rapid behavior change. Most teachers eventually plan to bring students' behavior under the control of more natural reinforcers. Schedule thinning helps decrease dependence on artificial reinforcers and helps students learn to delay gratification. In **thinning**, reinforcement gradually becomes available less often or, in other words, becomes contingent on greater amounts of appropriate behavior.

In thinning reinforcement schedules, the teacher moves from a dense schedule (continuous) to a sparse schedule (variable). The ratio between correct responding and reinforcement is systematically increased. The following examples illustrate this concept:

1. A student may be on a CRF schedule (1:1) for correctly defining vocabulary words on flash cards. As the student approaches the criterion of 90% accuracy, the teacher may move the student to an FR3 schedule (R, R, R:S^R) and then to an FR6, to a VR8, and to a VR10. With each schedule shift, the teacher requires the student to perform more correct responses to receive a reinforcer.
2. A student may be on an FRD5 for sitting in her seat during the time she is to work in a workbook. Once the student has been able to meet this criterion, the teacher may move her to an FRD10, FRD20, and FRD30 schedule. With each schedule shift, the teacher is requiring the student to maintain longer periods of appropriate behavior to earn reinforcement.
3. When teaching a student to ask for preferred items rather than engage in challenging behavior to receive preferred items, it is important to use a CRF schedule at first. One way to thin the schedule of reinforcement for these requests is to first arrange a "multiple schedule." An example of using this is when the teacher wears a green wristband indicating that she will reinforce requests and a red wristband indicating she will not reinforce requests. Then, the teacher gradually increases the amount of time she wears the red wristband (Fuhrman, Greer, Zangrillo, & Fisher, 2018). It can be helpful to provide attention or other reinforcers when the teacher wears the red wristband.

Figure 8.11 presents a model of a schedule thinning. As schedule shifts are made from a continuous schedule to a fixed schedule to a variable schedule, a point is finally reached where predetermined timing of reinforcer delivery is no longer required. At this point the behavior is under the control of naturally occurring reinforcers.

Thinning schedules of reinforcement should result in

1. higher, steadier levels of responding as a result of moving to variable schedules
2. decreasing expectation of reinforcement
3. maintenance of the behavior over longer periods of time as the student becomes accustomed to delayed gratification
4. removal of the teacher as a necessary behavior monitor

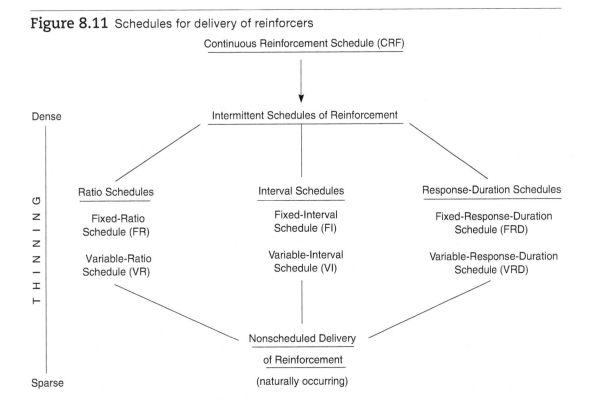

Figure 8.11 Schedules for delivery of reinforcers

5. transfer of control from the reinforcer to more traditional methods, such as teacher praise and attention, especially if schedule thinning is done in conjunction with pairing social reinforcers with tokens or primary reinforcers (Axe & Laprime, 2017; Dozier, Iwata, Thomason-Sassi, Worsdell, & Wilson, 2012; Rodriguez & Gutierrez, 2017)
6. an increase in persistence in responding toward working for goals (reinforcers) that require greater amounts of correct responding (work)
7. the ability in educational settings to deliver reinforcers on a relatively lean schedule so that appropriate levels of student performance can be maintained in a practical way (Freeland & Noell, 2002)

One caution should be considered when thinning schedules. Behaviors are subject to an effect known as **ratio strain**. Ratio strain occurs when the schedule has been thinned so quickly that the ratio for correct responding and reinforcement is too large. In such instances, the student does not earn a reinforcer often enough to maintain responding, and the rate decreases significantly. The student may stop responding altogether. If teachers see this effect occurring, they should return to the last schedule that resulted in an acceptable rate of responding and then thin again, but in smaller schedule shifts.

It is usually best to tell the student the schedule of reinforcement delivery that is in effect. If students do not know what the rule is, they will probably make up one of their own. They will theorize and verbalize to themselves: "I must read three words correctly in order to get another token," or "I must work for 15 minutes to get another token." If this is a self-generated rule rather than one stated or confirmed by the teacher, it may not be correct (Bradshaw & Reed, 2012; Lattal & Neef, 1996). If students work under an incorrect formulation of the rule, their unmet expectations may interfere with their learning and their trust in the teacher's contingencies.

Professor Grundy Goes to Las Vegas

As Professor Grundy prepared to leave the house one morning, Mrs. Grundy handed him a stack of envelopes.

"Oliver, dear," she asked, "would you mind putting these in the mail for me?"

"More contests?" sneered Professor Grundy. "You've entered every contest and sweepstakes and bought every lottery and raffle ticket ever offered. And how often have you won?"

"Well," answered Mrs. Grundy, "there was the pickle dish six years ago, the steak knives the year after that, and last year. . . ."

"Minerva," scolded the professor, "I've heard of resistance to extinction, but your behavior is being maintained on a VI3-year schedule. I'd think that was a little lean, even for you."

Imagine the professor's surprise when he received a phone call later that morning. "Oliver," bubbled Mrs. Grundy, "I've won a trip for two to Las Vegas! How's that for a reinforcer?" The very next weekend, the Grundys flew off to claim their prize. As they walked into the lobby of their hotel, they passed a bank of slot machines.

"Just one moment, my dear," said Professor Grundy. "Let me try a couple of quarters in one of these. After all, when in Las Vegas. . . ."

An hour later, Mrs. Grundy checked into their room. Three hours later, she ate a solitary dinner. At midnight, she returned to the lobby, where the professor was still pulling the handle on the slot machine.

"Oliver," she insisted, "you must stop this."

"Just a few more minutes, Minerva," pleaded the professor. "I know a few more quarters will do it."

Mrs. Grundy watched for a few minutes as Professor Grundy pulled the handle. Occasionally, the machine paid off with a few quarters.

"Oliver," snorted Mrs. Grundy, as she turned on her heel and stalked off, "I've heard of resistance to extinction, but your behavior is being maintained on a VR27 schedule of reinforcement. How utterly ridiculous!"

Negative Reinforcement

Learning Outcome 8.4 Differentiate between positive and negative reinforcement.

Learning Outcome 8.5 Identify the correct and incorrect use of negative reinforcement and demonstrate how to use negative reinforcement during instruction.

Although positive reinforcement is usually used when the teacher's goal is to increase the rate or frequency of a target behavior, another procedure is available. *Negative reinforcement* (S^{R-}) is the contingent removal of an aversive stimulus immediately following a response that increases the future rate or probability of the response.

The first operative word in this definition is, once again, *increases*, which implies that a form of reinforcement is taking place. The second operative word is *removal*. Whereas in positive reinforcement a stimulus is presented to the student, in negative reinforcement something is removed from the student's environment. The third operative word is *contingent*. The teacher will not remove the aversive condition (negative reinforcer) unless and until the requested response is performed. Consider Marcus who has not finished his math problems. If his teacher states the contingency, "Marcus, you must stay in the room and finish all your math problems before you may join the rest of the class in the gym," that teacher is using negative reinforcement. The aversive condition of the empty classroom will be removed contingent on completion of the math assignment that Marcus should have completed earlier. His rate of completing math problems will probably increase today so he can get to the gym and may well increase tomorrow so he can avoid having to stay in the room at all.

Negative reinforcement works because the student performs the behavior to escape and thereby terminate an aversive stimulus. It is not necessary, however, for an aversive stimulus to be present for negative reinforcement to work. Negative reinforcement also works when a signal is presented, such as a disapproving look from a teacher, and a student performs some behavior to avoid an aversive stimulus, such as time in the classroom during gym. If Marcus indeed finishes his math quickly the day after he has to stay in the room while the other students go to the gym, he avoids that negative reinforcer. In addition to negative reinforcement affecting positive behaviors, negative reinforcement often serves to establish and maintain behaviors teachers would rather their students not demonstrate. For example, many students who engage in inappropriate behaviors during lessons do so because in the past, those behaviors have led to slowing down demands; in other words, they are hoping to escape from what to them is an existing aversive event.

Inadvertent Use

Teachers often use negative reinforcement inadvertently. When a student engages in disruptive behavior, is off task, or whines about an assignment and her teacher removes the assignment (in hopes of stopping the behavior), the student learns that the disruptive behavior will result in the termination of the assignment (aversive stimulus). The student then whines the next time an assignment is presented in order to escape again. This repeated demonstration of the disruptive behavior indicates that the inappropriate behavior has been negatively reinforced. This is a negative reinforcement cycle:

1. student is confronted with an aversive stimulus;
2. student engages in inappropriate behavior;
3. teacher removes aversive stimulus;
4. student is negatively reinforced for the inappropriate behavior;
5. the next time the student is confronted by the aversive stimulus, the cycle is repeated.

In such situations, negative reinforcement may be at work for both teacher and student. Taking the task away from the student may be negatively reinforcing for the teacher because the behavior disrupting the classroom has ceased. The degree to which this cycle can contribute to the development of spectacularly inappropriate behavior is illustrated in the true anecdote (only the names have been changed) at the bottom of the page.

Students may view various tasks as aversive; Sarah obviously held this view about math. As with reinforcers, what is aversive is individual to a student. In general, tasks or activities may be seen as aversive if they are too difficult, too boring and repetitive, or too

The Howler

Dr. Carp was an assistant professor of special education at a large university. To supplement her income and "to keep her hand in," she tutored children who were having problems in school. Many of her clients were the children of fellow faculty members who attended an elementary school where there was virtually no direct instruction and where students were expected to learn from texts and other materials and to progress through the curriculum on their own. These children usually had only minor problems and made a lot of progress in a short time with a little direct remediation and some instruction about using study skills. The tutoring was thus positively reinforcing for the children, who experienced success; for the parents, who saw a lot of improvement; and for Dr. Carp, who received many compliments and more referrals. Therefore she eagerly accepted the request from a colleague to work with his third-grade daughter, who was, in his words, "having a little trouble with math."

Sarah was duly delivered by her mother to Dr. Carp's home one afternoon the next week. Dr. Carp greeted mother and daughter at the door and suggested that Mom return in an hour. She sat Sarah at the student desk in the den and explained brightly that she and Sarah would be doing some easy problems together to let Dr. Carp get an idea about what might be causing math to be giving her "a little trouble." As the worksheet reached the surface of the desk, Sarah suddenly erupted with a howl that would have done a coyote justice. Simultaneously, tears, nasal mucus, and saliva began to flow at an incredible rate, covering Sarah, the worksheet, and the desk, but not Dr. Carp, whose rapid movement in the face of erupting children had often been negatively reinforced in the past. The dog, banished to the kitchen for the duration of tutoring, matched the howl, ululation for ululation, and Dr. Carp's own children, banished upstairs, appeared in the doorway to check on her welfare. Muttering the words "a little trouble with math, my eye," Dr. Carp hushed the dog, rebanished the children, fetched a wastebasket, paper towels, and disinfectant spray from the kitchen, and waited for Sarah to stop howling. She then politely explained that she could not evaluate damp worksheets and that Sarah could start with a fresh one as soon as she had disposed of the wet one and cleaned herself and the desk up with the disinfectant. Sarah, a little startled, complied, but when the fresh worksheet reached the surface of the desk, she repeated her earlier performance. The cycle was repeated seven times.

By then the hour was almost over, and Mom's car appeared through the window. Sarah jumped up and announced she was leaving. Dr. Carp replied, "No, you'll need to work these first three problems before you go; I'll go ask your mom to wait."

"She won't make me," shrieked Sarah, throwing herself on the floor and resuming the howl. "You're so mean, she won't make me stay. She loves me."

Dr. Carp walked to the car and explained, over the audible howls from inside, that Sarah was not quite finished and that if Mom could not wait, Dr. Carp would be happy to bring Sarah home when she was done. Mom burst into tears, her loud wails immediately echoed by the infant in the car seat behind her.

"She hates math so," Mom howled. "Her teachers just let her do puzzles instead. Listen to her"—as if Dr. Carp had a choice—"I don't want her to be upset. I'll just take her home and calm her down, and we'll try again next week."

"Mrs. Howler," said Dr. Carp gently, "she's your daughter and it's your choice, but if you take her home now, I'll have to ask you not to bring her back."

Leaving Mom and the baby howling in the car, Dr. Carp returned to the desk and said cheerfully, "Mom's going to wait. Let's look at this first one—you tell me what you would do first."

One huge hiccup later, Sarah completed the first three problems and joined her mother and sibling in the car. Over the next few months there were increasingly infrequent bouts of howling as demands were increased, and Sarah reached grade level in math and performed adequately at school. Dr. Carp did not hear from Sarah's dad (she's always wondered if he ever knew what the "little trouble with math" really was) until years later when he stopped her in the parking lot and said that the family was taking a weekend trip to Sarah's very selective college, where she was about to be inducted into an academic honor society and was to receive a degree cum laude in a few weeks. In engineering. Honest. That's the kind of positive reinforcement that keeps teachers teaching.

embarrassing. A student given a math worksheet with problems above her current ability level, or one who did not do the homework, or one who has not benefited from effective instruction will find the task too difficult and engage in inappropriate off-task behaviors to escape the assignment. A student given yet another age-inappropriate pegboard to fill time may find the task too boring and find something much more entertaining to do with the board. Asking a poor reader to read aloud in front of the class, or a poor math student to do a problem on the board, or a student with poor coordination to climb the rope in physical education class may result in that student's trying to escape the task to avoid the ensuing embarrassment. A variety of other events may be aversive to students, such as a reading task for a student with a reading disability, being touched for a child with autism, an incorrect wheelchair position for a child with a physical disability, failure to introduce the items in her immediate environment to a student with a visual impairment, receiving excessive praise from the teacher in front of his classmates for a middle school student, or dissecting a frog for a squeamish biology student. Factors like these have been observed in special education and general education settings (Carbone, Morgenstern, Zecchin-Tirri, & Kolberg, 2010; Kettering, Neef, Kelley, & Heward, 2018; Langthorne, McGill, & Oliver, 2014; Smith, Iwata, Goh, & Shore, 1995). An additional factor influencing behavior maintained by negative reinforcement is teacher attention resulting from attempts to escape (Gardner, Wacker, & Boelter, 2009; Moore & Edwards, 2003). This is both negative reinforcement, because the student has been allowed to stop doing the aversive task, and positive reinforcement, because the teacher's behavior is often quite entertaining.

Appropriate Means of Escape

Instead of engaging in inappropriate behavior, students can be taught appropriate means of accessing the negative reinforcement resulting from escaping a task. In place of an inappropriate behavior that results in escape, students can be taught a more standard and appropriate means of communicating the need for assistance or for a break. This is known as functional communication training (Carr & Durand, 1985; O'Connor & Daly, 2018; Radstaake et al., 2013; Zangrillo, Fisher, Greer, Owen, & DeSouza, 2016). For example, Zangrillo and colleagues worked with students whose challenging behaviors (e.g., hitting, kicking, pushing, throwing objects, spitting) were resulting in escape from academic demands. These students were being negatively reinforced, and therefore their inappropriate behaviors were being strengthened. In place of the inappropriate behaviors, the students were taught to say, "break please," to provide escape and therefore negative reinforcement. As the new behavior was used and resulted in reinforcement, the students no longer needed to use the inappropriate behaviors to achieve escape and negative reinforcement.

Students can also perceive teachers' behavior as aversive. Teacher behaviors such as nagging, unpleasant vocal tones, threatening facial expressions, sarcasm, or outright hostility may occasion student escape and avoidance. For example, had Dr. Carp responded to Sarah's howls with a sustained whine of her own, begging her to do her work, Sarah wouldn't have been any more likely to finish her math problems. Despite this, some teachers use these behaviors to set the general tone of classroom management. Every teacher makes a decision to run a classroom in such a way that students behave appropriately to avoid unpleasantness from the teacher or in such a way that they behave appropriately because the teacher provides many opportunities for positive reinforcement. Harrison, Gunter, Reed, and Lee (1996) suggested that the way in which teachers provide instructions to students may also be aversive. They suggested that asking a student with behavior disorders to perform tasks without sufficient information is associated with higher rates of disruptive behavior. If the student does not understand the instruction, he may choose to be disruptive and thereby escape further instruction rather than risk embarrassment due to responding incorrectly. Sanford and Horner (2013) found that when reading instruction for students with learning disabilities was at a frustration level (<90% accuracy or fluency), there were high levels of problem behavior and low levels of academic engagement. However, when instruction was at "instruction-level" (>90% accuracy or fluency), this was less aversive, challenging behavior was reduced, and academic engagement was improved. In terms of intensive instruction for students with autism, certain instructional procedures are often aversive and result in problem behavior: beginning sessions by removing reinforcers, requiring high degrees of effort, presenting a high rate of demands, and delivering low-quality reinforcers contingent on correct responses (Carbone, Morgenstern, Zecchin-Tirri, & Kolberg, 2010). On the other hand, there are many ways to alter instruction to make it less aversive and result in less problem behavior and more academic engagement, such as delivering reinforcers prior to demands, offering choices, interspersing easy and difficult demands, and using a fast pace of instruction.

A functional behavior assessment, and perhaps a functional analysis, can be used to determine if problem behavior is reinforced by escape from demands. Additionally, Cipani (1995, p. 37) suggested that a teacher may be able to determine whether disruptive behavior is being negatively reinforced by answering the following questions:

1. Does the behavior result in the termination or postponement of specific teacher requests, instructional demands, or instructional tasks, activities, or materials (even temporarily)?
2. Is the student not competent with regard to the specific instructions, tasks, teacher requests, or materials identified in question 1?
3. Does the problem behavior occur more frequently under those specific content areas, tasks, materials, or teacher requests identified in questions 1 and 2 (in contrast to other content areas or tasks where the student is more capable academically)?

These situations, like satiation and deprivation described earlier, may serve as motivating operations that increase the value of escape and interfere with the effects of planned reinforcement strategies.

Using negative reinforcement has some disadvantages. Tantrums, attempts to flee, and destruction of materials are examples of escape and avoidance behaviors. They may occur particularly if the individual is unskilled at subtler or socially acceptable forms of escape. Apparently, these behaviors are especially likely to happen when difficult demands or tasks are placed on students with limited behavioral repertoires. Aggressive or self-injurious behaviors may be an avenue of escape from the demands because their intensity or topography can be alarming to a teacher (Davis et al., 2018; Tereshko & Sottolano, 2017).

Using Negative Reinforcement for Instruction

Negative reinforcement can be used as a teaching strategy. For example, Alberto, Troutman, and Briggs (1983) employed negative reinforcement for initial response conditioning of a student with profound disabilities. Following an exhaustive preference assessment, the only response made by the student was to pull his hand away from an ice cube. During instruction he was taught to turn toward a source of blowing air (a fan) by simultaneously guiding his head and removing ice from the palm of his hand. He was negatively reinforced by the removal of the ice for performing the desired behavior.

Negative reinforcement is often used in conjunction with behavior programs based on the results of a functional assessment. As discussed in Chapter 7, students may engage in attempts to escape and avoid demanding tasks, social interactions with adults or peers, unwanted attention, or a variety of classroom activities and events. The controlled and contingent use of opportunities to escape from, or terminate, an event may be managed by the teacher to decrease interruptive escape attempts. Escape is allowed based on a contingency set by the teacher rather than as a reaction to the student's inappropriate behavior. In this way negative reinforcement is used to establish a new, more appropriate behavior. Another component of such an intervention is simultaneous positive reinforcement of an alternative means of achieving escape. The teacher may provide the student with an opportunity to escape following an appropriate, more typical request for a break (e.g., use of functional communication training). Chezan, Drasgow, Martin, and Halle (2016) observed that when two young children were offered non-preferred foods, the children pushed them away. Because pushing away resulted in the food being removed, this was a negative reinforcement contingency. The intervention involved substituting a more appropriate means of requesting the removal of the non-preferred foods. Specifically, when the therapist presented non-preferred foods, she prompted the children to hand over a card, which resulted in removing the food. Another type of intervention is gradually increasing the amount of work required before a break is allowed, and eventually allowing breaks only after tasks have been completed (Davis et al., 2018).

> Aversive stimuli may lead to aggressive reactions.

Positive and Negative Reinforcement
Pearson eText
Video Example 8.6
In this video, students are participating in morning meeting and earning tokens for target behaviors. One student (Dylan) is interested in taking a break from morning meeting and earning tablet. Consider how both negative and positive reinforcement may be interacting in this scenario.

The use of aversive stimuli in the classroom should be minimized. As we will discuss in greater detail in Chapter 9, such stimuli may lead to aggressive reactions. The child who is confined to his room until he gets "every last doll and dinosaur off the floor" is likely to kick the unfortunate cat that comes to investigate the clattering and banging. Escape and avoidance behavior may not be limited to the aversive stimulus but may result in a student's escaping (running out of the room) or avoiding the entire school setting (playing truant). For a discussion of the theoretical and applied concerns relating to negative reinforcement, see Iwata (1987) and Carbone et al. (2010).

Natural Reinforcement

Learning Outcome 8.6 Identify natural reinforcers.

Reinforcement is a naturally occurring process. A structured reinforcement system in the classroom has at least four purposes. The first is simply to manage behavior. Second, for some students, the imposition of "artificial" high-intensity reinforcing stimuli provides highly visible connections between their behavior and its consequences. This allows them to learn a cause-and-effect relationship. Third, a classroom reinforcement system provides in microcosm a learning laboratory for how reinforcement works in the everyday world. The fourth purpose is to teach students to value a more general and natural pool of reinforcers. Students should be taught to be motivated by reinforcers that naturally occur in a situation—that is, those that will ordinarily result from their behavior in their school, home, and community settings.

Whether a reinforcer is natural depends on the situation, the setting, and the ages of the individuals. Almost any reinforcer can be natural. Most students in general education classes earn privileges for appropriate academic and social behavior—from being a lunch monitor in kindergarten to being excused from final exams in high school. Adults earn privileges as well—from a special parking place for the custodial employee of the month to access to the executive washroom. Activities are also often earned naturally, from an extra 5 minutes of recess for a hard-working kindergarten class to a trip to Bermuda for the salesperson of the year. Everyone works for tokens—gold stars for kindergartners and big bucks for some successful professionals

Natural Reinforcement
Pearson eText
Video Example 8.7
In this video, the student is working on an "About Me" project. She has to type multiple sentences on a tablet to complete the project. At the end, notice how excited she is to see her own work product. Students enjoying the products of their own efforts is an ideal form of natural reinforcement.

(fortunately most teachers like gold stars). Finally, when everyone remembers his or her manners, social reinforcers abound in the natural environment. Reinforcers that are natural outcomes for a specific behavior are more effective than unrelated reinforcers (Mohammadzaheri, Koegel, Rezaei, & Bakhshi, 2015). In addition, behavior reinforced naturally has an increased probability of being maintained and generalized (Durand, 1999; Stokes & Baer, 1977). As students learn to anticipate and accept natural reinforcers, they are exposed to naturally occurring schedules of reinforcement. They learn that behavior in some situations results in immediate and frequent reinforcement, whereas in others it results in delayed and infrequent reinforcement.

> **Professor Grundy Teaches About Reinforcement**
>
> Professor Grundy's graduate class had turned in their observation assignments, muttering and grumbling all the while. After collecting the papers, Professor Grundy launched into his lecture on reinforcement. One of the students came up to the podium at the end of the lecture. Beaming, she said, "It's about time, Professor. I took this course to learn how to manage a classroom. For weeks, all we've talked about is history, theory, and all that technical junk. It was worth living through that just to hear tonight's lecture. I was going to drop the course, but now I won't miss a week."
>
> "Why," asked Professor Grundy, lighting his pipe to hide the grin on his face, "do you think I wait to talk about reinforcement until after we're done with all that technical junk?"

Summary

This chapter described procedures to increase or maintain appropriate academic or social behaviors. Positive reinforcement, the preferred approach, is the presentation of a stimulus contingent on appropriate behavior. Positive reinforcers may be either primary or secondary, and the best reinforcers are natural. Negative reinforcement is the removal of an aversive stimulus contingent on the performance of the target behavior. We suggested specific ways in which students' behavior can be changed using these procedures. We hope we have also positively reinforced your reading behavior and you are now prepared to continue.

Discussion Questions

The following scenarios depict implementations of reinforcement strategy gone wrong. Discuss why you believe the teacher's plan is not working and what you might do to fix the situation.

1. Questions, questions, questions, etc.

    Jack and Ryan call out "all the time"—when they have answers to questions, when they have questions, when they have information they want to share with Ms. Andrews or their classmates. Ms. Andrews has been told they have "poor impulse control." She decides to reinforce them for raising their hands. Each time either of them raises his hand, she immediately calls on him and provides verbal praise. Within 2 days both boys have reduced their callouts to less than one a day. Two days later Ms. Andrews is satisfied that the boys have learned to raise their hands, so she goes back to her usual procedure of randomly calling on students who have their hands up. Two days after that, the two boys' calling out is back to its original rate.

2. From minor annoyances large disturbances can grow.

    Ms. Arnold is becoming concerned with Todd's behavior. Though a minor annoyance, it is disturbing and appears to be happening more frequently. Not wanting to make a big production, she decides to place the behavior on extinction—planned ignoring. She knows she must not make a show of ignoring the behavior, so she merely makes a notation on the blackboard and shakes her head each time the student does it. To her further annoyance, the behavior continues to escalate.

3. **Help from the principal.**

   Ms. Taber is at her wits' end with Tracy and his aggressive verbal behavior. She has tried scolding, moving his seat, and giving him extra assignments. There has been no decrease in the frequency of his behavior. She decides she needs help. Each time the student engages in the behavior, she sends him to the principal's office to discuss his behavior. If the principal has someone with her, Tracy sits outside the office, where everyone who passes talks to Tracy about his inappropriate behavior. Tracy continues his verbal aggression in the classroom.

4. **Endless laughs.**

   Ms. Hughes is at her wits' end with Oran and his clowning around. She has tried scolding, moving his seat, subtracting points, and giving him extra assignments. There has been no decrease in the frequency of his behavior. She decides to ignore the behavior and put it on extinction, understanding and expecting that the behavior will increase before it decreases. Oran continues the behavior; it continues to be disruptive and makes the other students laugh and talk back to him. She studiously ignores each occurrence and continues lessons and group work through the behavior. But after 2 weeks without any decrease in the behavior, she is giving up again.

5. **Boy, he is a hard worker.**

   Troy is a hard worker and took to the point system from day 1. He looked over the available backup reinforcers and immediately identified two he wanted. He needed 115 points for the two items; he earned 145. On Friday he cashed in for item one and "banked" his tokens for item two for the next Friday. During the second week Troy seemed to be in a world of his own rather than attending to math and science.

6. **This is how it's going to work.**

   Mr. Kana wants to start a token economy. He provides the basic information to his class: "We are going to start our economy by earning points for two general behaviors expected of all of you, and one behavior personal to each of you. On day 1 you can earn 2 points each time you raise your hand, and you will lose 1 point every time you call out. The second behavior is work completion. You can earn 5 points per completed assignment. You will lose 1 point per assignment component not completed within time limits. Points lost will increase by one each day through Friday. Each personal behavior will be developed through a contract between you and me." The students were each given a written copy of the rules. Hand raising and task completion increased the first day, then showed a decreasing trend for the remainder of the week.

7. **Good citizenship.**

   Ms. Stafford has confirmed that her students Ali, Ben, Manny, and LaToya think cheesy fish crackers are great. She decides to use them to reinforce the eight basic "good citizen" behaviors posted in her classroom on a CRF schedule. From when she starts on Wednesday through the following Monday, the students are perfect good citizens. By Thursday, however, the chaos rate is on the rise.

8. **Fishing for reinforcers.**

   Ms. Gonzales talked to Ms. Stafford during the early days of her cheesy fish program. By show of hands she confirms that her students think the crackers are great too. She decides to use them to reinforce hand-raising behavior during their whole-class lesson each day and during small-group reading. Her data indicate that she is having overall success with her management plan; however, Kyle and Rudy's data indicated they continued calling out as much as ever.

9. **Sharing best practice.**

   At a staff development workshop a teacher shared the idea of using stickers as tokens. Ms. Briggs decided to use seasonal sticker tokens with her third-grade class. She began using stickers for in-seat behavior during group instruction sessions and center times. The students were enthusiastic, and the roaming around the room so prevalent in her class was greatly reduced. After the weekend, however, the students were still trading in stickers but the roaming behavior was back.

10. **A fraction of the skill.**

    Ms. Heller introduced multiplying fractions to Eric and Anu. She understood that when teaching a new behavior, she needed to provide a reinforcer every time the behavior was performed correctly. Within nine sessions the students were accurately adding fractions with like denominators. Ms. Heller then stopped the continuous reinforcement in order to allow internal reinforcers and self-esteem to take the place of the external reinforcer. When she did the next weekly maintenance check, the students were no longer adding accurately.

11. **No thank you.**

    Ivan is reviewing the catalogue of backup reinforcers that are available within the token economy at Pioneer High School. After reviewing pages containing pictures of boy-band posters, various monitorships, fast-food restaurant coupons, art materials, and so on, he put his Game Boy back in his pocket and went to sleep on his desk.

Chapter 9
Arranging Consequences That Decrease Behavior

Learning Outcomes

9.1 Identify and differentiate between the five reinforcement-based strategies for behavior reduction.

9.2 Explain the problems associated with extinction.

9.3 Identify types of behavior reduction strategies associated with the removal of desired stimuli.

9.4 Identify types of behavior reduction strategies associated with the presentation of aversive stimuli.

CHAPTER OUTLINE

Procedural Alternatives for Behavior Reduction
Level I: Reinforcement-Based Strategies
    Differential Reinforcement of Lower Rates of Behavior
    Differential Reinforcement of Other Behaviors
    Differential Reinforcement of Alternative Behavior and Incompatible Behavior
    Noncontingent Reinforcement

Level II: Extinction
    Delayed Reaction
    Increased Rate
    Controlling Attention
    Extinction-Induced Aggression
    Spontaneous Recovery
    Imitation or Reinforcement by Others
    Limited Generalizability
    Sensory Extinction

Punishment
Level III: Removal of Desirable Stimuli
    Response-Cost Procedures
    Time-Out Procedures

Level IV: Presentation of Aversive Stimuli
    Types of Aversive Stimuli
    Disadvantages of Aversive Stimuli

Overcorrection
    Restitutional Overcorrection
    Positive-Practice Overcorrection

Summary

When teachers complain about a student's misbehavior, other teachers usually offer sympathy and advice. Too often their suggestions emphasize punishment—by which they mean applying an aversive stimulus or taking away privileges following the inappropriate behavior, for example, telling a student firmly that you "mean business," taking away recess, or sending the student to the principal's office. Using punishment can become a reflex, because it often simply and immediately stops the behavior—it works! Using punishment negatively reinforces teachers' behaviors; that is, removing a disruptive student from the classroom is a pleasant consequence for the teacher telling the student to "go to the office," and therefore the teacher will repeat that behavior in the future. Unfortunately, that reinforcement may make teachers lose sight of the side effects or reactions that may accompany the use of punishment. This chapter describes a broad range of behaviorally based alternatives to punishment that will have the same effect of reducing the occurrence of inappropriate and challenging behavior. These alternatives are presented as a sequenced hierarchy. The sequence moves from the most positive approaches for behavior reduction (those that use reinforcement strategies) to the most aversive approaches. Although the use of aversive consequences has a conceptual place in such a hierarchy, due to ethical and professional considerations and awareness of the undesirable effects that aversive stimuli produce, these approaches are rarely, if ever, appropriate in the school setting. Indeed, in our hierarchy, three levels of options are presented before aversive consequences are even mentioned. These alternatives, with their individual constraints, are presented as viable alternatives to aversive procedures, because they too have the desired effect of reducing the occurrence of inappropriate and challenging behavior.

Certain principles should guide the selection of a procedure for behavior reduction. The first is the principle of the least intrusive alternative. This principle suggests that when determining which intervention to choose, an important consideration is the intervention's level of intrusiveness. When one is considering behavior reduction, the least intrusive intervention is the least aversive or the lowest on the hierarchy. The teacher should determine, based on a hierarchy of procedures from the least intrusive to the most intrusive (most positive to most aversive), an effective procedure that is in the positive range of available choices. For example, if a Level I procedure as shown in Figure 9.1 will accomplish the behavior change, it is neither necessary nor ethical to use a Level IV procedure. In addition, Gast and Wolery (1987) suggested that "if the choice of treatments is between procedures that are equally effective, then the least aversive (intrusive) should be selected. If the choice is between a less intrusive but ineffective procedure and more aversive but effective procedure, then the effective

Figure 9.1 Procedural alternatives for behavior reduction

Procedure of choice	**Level I**	**Reinforcement-based strategies**
		a. Differential reinforcement of lower rates of behavior (DRL)
		b. Differential reinforcement of other behavior (DRO)
		c. Differential reinforcement of incompatible behavior (DRI)
		d. Differential reinforcement of alternative behavior (DRA)
		e. Noncontingent reinforcement
	Level II	**Extinction (terminating reinforcement)**
	Level III	**Removal of desirable stimuli**
		a. Response-cost procedures
		b. Time-out procedures
	Level IV	**Presentation of aversive stimuli**
		a. Unconditioned aversive stimuli
		b. Conditioned aversive stimuli
		c. Overcorrection procedures

procedure should be selected" (p. 194). Given the extensive published research and reported success with Level I reinforcement-based procedures in recent years, the use of aversive procedures in schools has little support. The second principle is that, when possible, selection of an intervention should be based on the identified function of the challenging behavior. Before the development of the procedures described in Chapter 7 that allow the identification of function, the selection of interventions was often "hit or miss." An intervention would work for many but not all students or would reduce some but not all behaviors. The behavior would eventually return or be replaced by one equally bad or even worse. This erratic success occurred because sometimes interventions were selected without considering the function of the behavior, but only its form and topography, that would accidentally match the function of the behavior (Iwata, Dorsey, Slifer, Bauman, & Richman, 1994). In addition, a significant component of this principle is that concurrent instruction of a functionally equivalent alternative behavior must occur. The student must learn an appropriate replacement behavior that will result in the same reinforcement as that resulting from the inappropriate behavior to be eliminated. Because a pretreatment functional assessment/analysis is now commonplace in behavioral interventions, it is more likely that educators and researchers will use reinforcement-based treatments for serious behavior problems rather than punishment-based treatments (Ala'i-Rosales et al., 2019; Scott & Cooper, 2017).

Several requirements must be met in implementing procedures for behavior reduction. The first requirement is that movement along the hierarchy must be data-based. That is, before deciding that a currently employed procedure is not effective and that an alternative, possibly more intrusive, procedure should be used, the data collected during the intervention must substantiate the ineffectiveness of the procedure. The second requirement is that a point of consultation and permission must be established. At some point, the teacher must consult with the student's parents and IEP team to review the progress of the current intervention and agree on a further plan of action. Such a plan may include conducting a functional assessment or functional analysis and developing a behavior support plan as described in Chapter 7.

Procedural Alternatives for Behavior Reduction

The hierarchy outlined in Figure 9.1 has four levels of options for reducing inappropriate behaviors. Level I is the first choice to consider, whereas Level IV is, in most instances, the choice of last resort.

Level I offers five strategies using differential reinforcement: differential reinforcement of low rates of behavior, differential reinforcement of other behaviors, differential reinforcement of incompatible behaviors, differential reinforcement of alternative behaviors, and noncontingent reinforcement. These are options of first choice because, by selecting them, the teacher is employing a positive (reinforcement) approach to behavior reduction.

Level II refers to extinction procedures. Using extinction means withholding or no longer delivering the reinforcers that maintain a behavior.

Level III contains the first set of options using what will be defined as a punishing consequence. However, these options—such as response-cost and time-out procedures—still do not require the application of an aversive stimulus. The administration of these options may be seen as a mirror image of negative reinforcement. In the use of negative reinforcement, an aversive stimulus is contingently removed in order to increase a behavior. Level III options require removal or denial of a desirable stimulus in order to decrease a behavior.

The options in Level IV of the hierarchy are to be selected after unsuccessful attempts at the first three levels have been documented or when the continuation of some behavior presents an imminent danger to the student or to others. The options at this level include the application of unconditioned or conditioned aversive stimuli or the use of an overcorrection procedure. Selecting one of these options is not the prerogative of a single individual. Administration of these options may be seen as the mirror image of a reinforcement procedure.

Positive reinforcement: Stimulus is contingently *presented* to *increase* a behavior.
Presentation of aversive stimuli: *Aversive* stimulus is *presented* to *decrease* a behavior.

Level I: Reinforcement-Based Strategies

Learning Outcome 9.1 Identify and differentiate between the five reinforcement-based strategies for behavior reduction.

In Chapter 8, reinforcement was defined as the presentation or removal of a stimulus contingent upon performance of behavior (response) that increases or maintains the future rate or probability of that behavior. A reinforcing stimulus can also be used to decrease behavior. With reinforcement-based procedures to decrease behavior, the teacher either contingently reinforces behavior on a differential basis or uses reinforcement in a noncontingent manner. Five such reinforcement-based procedures are included in Level 1.

In all differential reinforcement procedures, one behavior or set of behaviors is reinforced, and one behavior or set of behaviors is not reinforced.

Differential Reinforcement of Lower Rates of Behavior

Differential reinforcement of lower rates of behavior (DRL) is the application of a specific schedule of reinforcement, used to decrease the rate of behaviors that, although tolerable or even desirable in low rates, are inappropriate when they occur too often or too rapidly. For example, contributing to a class discussion is a desirable behavior; dominating a class discussion is not. Doing math problems is appropriate; doing them so rapidly that careless errors occur is not. Burping occasionally, while hardly elegant, is tolerable; burping 25 times an hour is neither.

In the initial laboratory version of DRL, a reinforcer was delivered contingent on a response, provided that a minimum period of time had elapsed since the previous reinforced response. To decrease the total number of occurrences within a total time period, it is necessary only to increase the minimum period of time that must pass before another response will be reinforced. This format is referred to as *interresponse-time DRL* or *spaced-responding DRL.* This procedure was used by Singh, Dawson, and Manning (1981) to reduce stereotypic behaviors (rocking, mouthing, complex movements) of three adolescent girls who were profoundly intellectually disabled. The time required between occurrences was increased from 12 seconds to 180 seconds. The average percent of intervals of occurrence for the three girls went from 92.5% to 13%.

The DRL format more commonly used in the classroom provides for reinforcement delivery "when the number of responses in a specified period of time is less than, or equal to, a prescribed limit" (Deitz & Repp, 1973, p. 457). This DRL has two variations: full-session DRL and interval DRL.

> Differential Reinforcement for DRL:
> Student emits more than X behaviors → no reinforcement
> Student emits X or fewer behaviors → reinforcement

Full-session DRL compares the total number of responses in an entire session with a preset criterion. A reinforcer is delivered if occurrences are at or below that

DRL schedules may be used when shaping behavior (see Chapter 10).

Recall the changing criterion design from Chapter 6.

criterion. For example, baseline data indicate that Jenny interrupts an average of nine times per 30-minute lesson. Although not wanting to extinguish this behavior completely, the teacher wants it reduced to no more than two such interruptions per lesson. Jenny is told that she is allowed two interruptions, and if she keeps her interruptions to that level, she will be awarded an extra token for good behavior that day. If she keeps interruptions at or below two occurrences, the reinforcer is delivered. Interval DRL involves dividing a session into smaller intervals (for example, dividing the 30-minute session into six 5-minute intervals) and delivering reinforcement at the end of each interval in which responding is below or equal to a specified limit. This format may be used if the teacher believes that a more gradual approach will be more successful. If the maximum number of interruptions that can be tolerated is two per session, that number is initially allowed during each 5-minute interval. Once the behavior has stabilized, the length of the interval is increased, so that the student may interrupt, for example, only twice per 10-minute interval if she is to earn a reinforcer. The contingency might then be that to earn a reinforcer the student may interrupt twice in each of two 15-minute intervals. Finally, the student would be allowed only two interruptions during the full 30-minute session. These forms of the DRL procedure have been used to reduce a variety of behaviors, including requests for attention (Austin & Bevan, 2011; Becraft, Borrero, Mendres-Smith, & Castillo, 2017), repetitive behaviors (e.g., jumping, flapping; Looney, DeQuinzio, & Taylor, 2018), severe problem behavior (e.g., self-injurious behavior, aggression; Bonner & Borrero, 2018), and eating rate (Lennox, Miltenberger, & Donnelly, 1987; Wright & Vollmer, 2002).

Finally, DRL may be arranged in a manner analogous to using a changing criterion design. If baseline levels of the target behavior are high, the teacher may successively lower DRL limits to bring the rate into an acceptable range. For example, if a student's baseline rate of out-of-seat behavior averaged 12 occurrences, he would be told that if during a lesson he got out of his seat no more than nine times, he would be allowed to select the day's free-time activity. Once he had stabilized at nine occurrences, the contingency would be changed to no more than six times, then no more than three times. When using this approach, the teacher must bear in mind that when she tells a student he can do something nine times, he will (and she must congratulate him!). In their initial experiments in the use of DRL, Deitz and Repp (1973) employed both criterion-setting strategies. In the first, an 11-year-old boy with moderate intellectual disabilities had a baseline of talk-outs within a 50-minute session that averaged 5.7, with a range of 4 to 10 talk-outs per session. He was told that if he talked out three or fewer times in a 50-minute session, he would be allowed 5 minutes of free playtime at the end of the day. During this intervention, he averaged 0.93 talk-outs per session with a range of 0 to 2.

In the second experiment, 10 students with moderate intellectual disabilities had an average of 32.7 talk-outs with a range of 10 to 45. The students were told that if the group talked out five or fewer times in a session, each person would get two pieces of candy. This intervention yielded an average of 3.13 talk-outs per session with a range of 1 to 6. In the third experiment, 15 high school girls in a regular class demonstrated a baseline level of 6.6 instances of inappropriate social discussion during a 50-minute class period. The intervention was planned in four phases: six or fewer inappropriate discussions, three or fewer, two or fewer, and then a zero rate in order to earn a free period Friday.

As a guide in the use of DRL scheduling, Repp and Deitz (1979, pp. 223–224) suggested the following:

1. Baseline must be recorded to determine the average number of responses per full session or session intervals. This average occurrence may then serve as the initial DRL limit.

Ms. Keel Teaches Stacy to Be Self-Confident

Stacy was a student in Ms. Keel's second-grade class. Stacy had excellent academic skills but raised her hand constantly to ask, "Is this right?" or to say, "I can't do this." If Ms. Keel had not been a behaviorist, she would have said that Stacy lacked self-confidence.

One morning, Ms. Keel called Stacy to her desk. She remembered that Stacy always volunteered to clean the blackboards after lunch. She told Stacy that she wanted her to learn to do her work herself.

"If you really need help," she assured Stacy, "I'll help you. But I think three times in one morning is enough. If you raise your hand for help three times or fewer this morning, you may clean the blackboards when we get back from lunch."

Stacy agreed to try. Within a few days, she was raising her hand only once or twice during the morning. Ms. Keel praised her enthusiastically for being so independent. The teacher noticed that Stacy often made comments like "I did this all by myself, Ms. Keel. I didn't need help once." If Ms. Keel had not been a behaviorist, she would have said that Stacy was developing self-confidence.

---

2. Reasonably spaced criteria should be established when using successively decreasing DRL limits to avoid too frequent reinforcement and ratio strain, and so that the program can be faded out.
3. A decision must be made as to whether or not to provide feedback to the student concerning the cumulative number of responses during the session.

The primary advantage of DRL scheduling is its peculiar ability to reduce the occurrence of the behavior through delivery of reinforcement. It therefore offers the same advantages of reinforcement in general. In addition, the approach is progressive, because it allows the student to adjust, in reasonable increments, to successively lower rates rather than making a drastic behavioral change. The limits chosen should be within the student's abilities and acceptable to the teacher. DRL is not a rapid means of changing behavior and therefore is inappropriate for use with violent or dangerous behavior.

> See Chapter 8 for a discussion of the merits of reinforcement strategies.

Differential Reinforcement of Other Behaviors

While Ms. Keel found that Stacy's raising her hand three times each morning was acceptable, there are other behaviors that are unacceptable at any level. When using the procedure called **differential reinforcement of other behaviors (DRO)**, a reinforcing stimulus is delivered contingent on the absence of a target behavior for a specified period of time (Reynolds, 1961; Weston, Hodges, & Davis, 2018). Whereas DRL reinforces gradual behavior reduction, DRO reinforces only zero occurrences. In fact, DRO is sometimes referred to as *differential reinforcement of zero rates of behavior* or *differential reinforcement of the omission of behavior*. In Chapter 8, reinforcement was defined as the delivery of a reinforcing stimulus contingent on the occurrence of a desired behavior. DRO involves the presentation of a reinforcing stimulus contingent on the nonoccurrence of a behavior. Another way to define DRO is the presentation of a reinforcing stimulus contingent on any behaviors *other* than the target behavior at the end of a certain period of time.

Differential Reinforcement for DRO:

Student emits target behavior during the interval → no reinforcement
Student does not emit target behavior during the interval → reinforcement

---

DRO may have at least three administrative variations, similar to those used with DRL procedures:

1. Reinforcement contingent on the nonoccurrence of a behavior throughout a specified time period. For example, reinforcement is delivered only if talking out

Clarence Learns Not to Hit People

Clarence was a student in Mr. Byrd's resource class. He often hit other students in the class, usually because someone had touched some possession of his. Having observed that Clarence hit someone an average of 12 times during the 90-minute resource period, for an average interresponse time of 7.5 minutes, Mr. Byrd chose an interval of 7 minutes. He told Clarence that he could earn a card worth 5 minutes to work on an art project for each 7 minutes that elapsed without hitting. When Clarence hit someone, Mr. Byrd reset the timer. He did this rather than simply not delivering the reinforcer at the end of the interval, because he was afraid that once Clarence had "blown it," he would engage in a veritable orgy of hitting until the end of the interval.

Within a few days, Clarence's hitting rate was much lower, so Mr. Byrd lengthened the intervals to 8 minutes, then 10, then 15. Soon he was able to reinforce the absence of hitting at the end of the period and still maintain a zero rate.

---

does not occur for an entire 40-minute period (DRO 40 minutes). The student is told, "If you do not talk out during this reading period (40 minutes long), then you may be one of the captains in the gym this afternoon." If the student meets this contingency, she receives the reinforcer. Scheduling reinforcement delivery only after no instances of the behavior occur during an entire session is called full-session DRO.

2. Reinforcement contingent on the nonoccurrence of a behavior within a time period that has been divided into smaller intervals. This procedure is used when a more gradual reduction of inappropriate behavior is more practical or realistic. In some cases of very high rates of inappropriate behavior, implementation of a full-session DRO would mean that the student would never earn a reinforcer. A 40-minute session may be divided into 5-minute intervals and reinforcement delivered at the end of each 5-minute interval in which the student has not talked out. This breaking down of the time period provides the student an increased number of opportunities for reinforcement, an increased amount of feedback, and an increased number of opportunities for success. The intervals may be of equal or different lengths (that is, on the average of every 5 minutes, as is done in variable-interval scheduling). Once the student can control his behavior for these smaller intervals, the teacher increases the length of the intervals. For example, the schedule of eight 5-minute intervals is changed to four 10-minute intervals. This process continues to the point that the contingency can be met for the entire 40 minutes, the equivalent of a full-session DRO. A method for selecting interval length is basing it on the average time between instances of the behavior (interresponse interval). For example, in an effort to reduce the self-hair pulling of a 19-year-old woman with autism and mild intellectual disabilities, Nuernberger, Vargo, and Ringdahl (2013) set the initial DRO interval length at 6 seconds "based on the mean interresponse time observed during baseline sessions" (pp. 109–110). The intervals were then increased to 12, 24, 48, 96, 192, 384, and 768 seconds.

3. DRO may be used with permanent-product data. For example, the teacher may draw a happy face on every paper that does not contain doodles.

Two additional types of DRO are whole-interval DRO and momentary DRO (Gongola & Daddario, 2010). Whole-interval DRO is as described above: a reinforcer is delivered if there is no occurrence of the target behavior during the specified interval. Momentary DRO is when a reinforcer is delivered when a target behavior does not occur at the moment an interval ends (Toussaint & Tiger, 2012). For example, Mr. Byrd could have set an interval of 3 minutes and looked at Clarence at the moment each 3-minute interval ended. If he was not hitting, he would earn a point toward time on an art project. Although this might be effective, momentary DRO is probably more effective with behaviors that have a longer duration than hitting, such as off-task behavior. An advantage of momentary DRO is the teacher does not need to observe the student during the entire interval. To reduce the likelihood the student will respond to the interval – that is, engage in disruptive behavior up until the end of the interval – the teacher can use a variable momentary DRO in which the length of the interval changes each time. A MotivAider™ can be used to signal the teacher to these variable intervals.

A question may arise when implementing DRO: When the student engages in the challenging behavior during the interval, does the teacher start the interval over or not? Mr. Byrd did this with Clarence to avoid excessive hitting. With a 6-year-old boy with ASD who engaged in stereotypical hand flapping, Gehrman, Wilder, Forton, and Albert (2017) found that whether or not the teacher reset the interval did not make a difference in reducing the challenging behavior. Given the concerns raised by Mr. Byrd, that decision may be made on a case-by-case basis.

Three important factors should be considered before a teacher implements a DRO procedure. First, a "pure" DRO requires that reinforcement be delivered if the student does not perform the target behavior, no matter what else he does. In effect, the student may be positively reinforced for performing a wide range of inappropriate behaviors, as long as he does not perform the target behavior. Some students will take advantage of this loophole. They may not walk around the room but may instead throw spitballs, something they have never done before. Technically, they would still be entitled to reinforcers. For practical classroom management, this cannot be allowed to happen. For this reason, DRO procedures are sometimes used in conjunction with other reduction procedures for such interfering behaviors, such as response cost (Roane & DeRosa, 2014).

Second, DRO reinforces the absence of a behavior. The student earns the reinforcer if the target behavior does not occur during the specified time period. For students who do not have a large repertoire of appropriate behaviors, the teacher may be creating a behavior vacuum. If a behavior is not identified to replace the targeted one, the student may soon fill that vacuum with the only behavior he knows—the one the teacher tried to reduce. It is practical and ethical to identify an appropriate behavior to replace the inappropriate one and to positively reinforce its occurrence.

Third, the effectiveness of a DRO procedure may depend on the reinforcer selected (Jessel & Ingvarsson, 2016; Repp et al., 1991). The stimulus used to reinforce the student for not engaging in the inappropriate behavior must be of at least equal strength or motivating value as that which is currently maintaining the behavior (Cowdery, Iwata, & Pace, 1990). A student who is entertaining his peers with hilarious comments during math class is being reinforced by their appreciative laughter. Offering him 5 minutes to play computer games if he refrains from wisecracking for 50 minutes may not be a sufficiently powerful competing reinforcer.

DRO has been used with a variety of behaviors, such as social skills, off-task behaviors, out-of-seat behavior, various types of repetitive behaviors (Healy et al., 2019; Nuernberger, Vargo, & Ringdahl, 2013), severe problem behavior (e.g., aggression, self-injury; Sullivan & Roane, 2018), fingernail biting (Heffernan & Lyons, 2016), and tics (Capriotti, Brandt, Ricketts, Espil, & Woods, 2012).

Sullivan and Roane (2018) used DRO procedures with two adolescents with developmental disabilities and severe challenging behavior. Lou was 15 years old and exhibited aggression, self-injury, and property destruction. Joan was 12 years old and engaged in aggression, self-injury, disruption, and negative vocalizations. After conducting preference assessments and functional analyses of the challenging behaviors, the researchers implemented DRO in which they started each session by delivering a low-preferred activity. If the student did not exhibit challenging behavior for the 10-minute session, he or she got to choose the activity for the next session. The choice-making was demonstrated to function as a reinforcer because when the researcher (not the student) chose the activity, the challenging behavior was at a lower level. The DRO intervention worked for Lou, but not for Joan. For Joan, the interval length was reduced to 20 seconds. Once this intervention resulted in a decrease in Joan's challenging behavior, the duration was increased to 40, 80, 160, 320, and 600 seconds.

Higgins, Williams, and McLaughlin (2001) used DRO to reduce the disruptive classroom behaviors of a 10-year-old third grader with learning disabilities. The student's targeted behaviors included high rates of out of seat, talking out without permission, and poor seat posture (e.g., legs splayed out, tucked underneath body, lying on the desk). During the 20-minute sessions the student earned a check mark if, at the end of each minute, appropriate behavior occurred instead of the specific targeted behaviors. By the end of the case study, three check marks could be earned per period for the absence of all three target behaviors. A piece of paper was taped to the corner of the student's desk to record check marks, enabling him to receive feedback on his behavior. At the end of the session, the check marks were counted and divided by two to determine the number of minutes available to use backup reinforcers such as math worksheets, computer time, leisure reading, and playing academic games (p. 102).

As a guide to the use of DRO scheduling, Repp and Deitz (1979, pp. 222–223) and Deitz and Repp (1983) suggested:

1. Baseline must be recorded not only to measure the inappropriate behavior, but also to schedule the DRO procedure properly. Because the size of the initial DRO interval can be crucial, it should be based on data rather than set arbitrarily. From the baseline, an average interresponse time (time between responses) should be determined, and a slightly smaller interval should be designated as the initial DRO interval.
2. Criteria must be established for increasing the length of the DRO interval. The basic idea is
   a. to start at a small enough interval that the student can earn more reinforcers for not responding than he could earn for responding, and
   b. to lengthen that interval over time. The decision to lengthen should be based on the success of the student at each interval length.
3. Possible occurrence of the undesirable behavior necessitates two additional decisions:
   a. whether to reset the DRO interval following a response occurrence or merely to wait for the next scheduled interval, and
   b. whether to deliver a consequence for a response occurrence in any other way or just to ignore it.
4. Reinforcement should not be delivered immediately following a grossly inappropriate behavior even if the DRO interval has expired without the target response having occurred.

Using a DRO
Pearson eText
Video Example 9.1
In this video, a student, Kayvon, and his teacher discuss his DRO system. The teacher provides rationale for why the system was developed and how she hopes the system evolves over time.

Differential Reinforcement of Alternative Behavior and Incompatible Behavior

An excellent way to prevent creating a behavior vacuum is the use of **differential reinforcement of alternative behavior (DRA)**. DRA is one of the most frequently used and successful behavior analytic procedures to decrease inappropriate behaviors (MacNaul & Neely, 2018).

With this procedure, an inappropriate or challenging behavior is replaced by a behavior considered (by student, parent, teacher) as more appropriate, positive, or standard. DRA refers to reinforcing an alternative behavior, the performance of which decreases the likelihood that the inappropriate behavior will be performed. Selection of an alternative behavior is usually based on physical incompatibility or functional equivalence.

> Differential Reinforcement for DRA:
>
> Student emits a challenging behavior → no reinforcement
> Student emits an appropriate, alternative behavior → reinforcement

Differential reinforcement of incompatible behavior (DRI) is a DRA procedure in which the teacher reinforces a behavior that is topographically incompatible with the behavior targeted for reduction. For example, if out-of-seat behavior is targeted for reduction, in-seat behavior is reinforced because these two behaviors cannot occur simultaneously (similarly, running and walking, normal voice and screaming, on task and off task). Such mutually exclusive behaviors are chosen so that an appropriate response makes it physically impossible for the student to engage in the inappropriate behavior. This allows for increasing the strength or rate of the appropriate behavior and decreasing the probability of the inappropriate behavior. Reinforcing a child's play with a particular toy, and her play skills in general, decreases the opportunity and probability of her engaging in stereotypic hand movements (Favell, 1973). When her hands are appropriately occupied, she cannot engage in the inappropriate behavior.

Differential reinforcement of incompatible behavior has been used to modify behaviors including skin picking (Radstaake et al., 2011); littering, inappropriate sitting, and running in a lunch room (Wheatley et al., 2009); pica (Donnelly & Olczak, 1990); and aggression (de Zubicaray & Clair, 1998).

Wheatley et al. (2009) used DRI to reduce the inappropriate behaviors of elementary students in the lunchroom. They targeted littering, inappropriate sitting, and running. All adults in the building were instructed to give students a "Praise Note" and specific praise when they were engaged in appropriate behaviors. The Praise Note contained the school mascot, the school motto, and lines to write the student's and adult's name. When a student received a Praise Note, she took it to the office and put it in a large jar. The principal drew five praise notes at the end of each day, and the students whose notes were drawn received a small prize. Teachers whose names were on the notes were rewarded by entering a weekly drawing for a gift certificate or other prize. As a result of the intervention, littering decreased from an average of 34.3 pieces to an average of 1.3 pieces; inappropriate sitting decreased from an average of 65.6 to an average of 23.3; and running decreased from an average of 34 instances to an average of 8.5 instances. This was a DRI intervention because students could not litter and not litter at the same time, sit appropriately and inappropriately at the same time, or run and walk at the same time.

As a guide to the use of DRI scheduling, Repp and Deitz (1979, p. 224) suggested:

1. A behavior that is incompatible with the undesirable behavior must be chosen. If there is no appropriate behavior that is opposite to the inappropriate behavior, then a behavior that is beneficial to the student should be selected and should be reinforced.
2. Baseline should be recorded to determine (a) how often the inappropriate behavior occurs and (b) how often the chosen incompatible behavior occurs.
3. The schedule of reinforcement must be determined. In addition, a program for carefully thinning the schedule should be written so that the program can be phased out and the student's behaviors can come under control of natural contingencies in the environment.

Often a mutually exclusive behavior is not readily identifiable. This fact, plus the research on interventions based on functional assessment and functional analysis, has resulted in greater emphasis on and use of DRA in which selection of the replacement behavior is based on the functional equivalence of the behavior rather than physical incompatibility of the form of the behavior, as is the case with DRI. In this broader approach to DRA, the alternative behavior and the inappropriate behavior are topographically dissimilar, but not necessarily physically incompatible.

In the general definition of DRA and DRI, the appropriate or incompatible behavior is reinforced, and the challenging behavior is not reinforced; that is, the challenging behavior is placed on extinction. This is an effective procedure because the student eventually learns that the challenging behavior "does not work," and the alternative behavior "does work" in terms of gaining reinforcers. However, extinction has many side effects, such as an initial extinction burst (see below for additional side effects). In fact, when hitting peers is reinforced by attention, it is likely impossible to implement extinction – that is, withhold attention – because doing so is unsafe and unethical; a teacher must provide some attention to separate the two students and ensure safety. (Had Mr. Byrd ignored Clarence's hitting his classmates, he would have been derelict in his duties.) Therefore, teachers may use DRA without extinction while ensuring the appropriate behavior accesses more reinforcement than the inappropriate behavior.

For example, Kunnavatana, Bloom, Samaha, Slocum, and Clay (2018) evaluated DRA without extinction with three individuals with ASD and other developmental disabilities. In baseline, both problem behavior and the alterative behavior (e.g., "Can I have a turn, please?") resulted in 90 seconds of access to high-quality reinforcers (e.g., iPad); rates of problem behavior were higher than alterative behaviors. Next, the researchers manipulated the magnitude of reinforcement in which problem behavior resulted in 15 seconds of access to low-quality reinforcers, and the alternative behavior resulted in 90 seconds to low-quality reinforcers. This resulted in a decrease in problem behavior, but only a modest increase in the alternative behavior. Finally, the researchers manipulated the quality of reinforcement in which problem behavior resulted in 30 seconds access to low-quality reinforcers, and the alternative behavior resulted in 30 seconds access to high-quality reinforcers. Under these conditions, the participants "chose" the high-quality reinforcers much more often as demonstrated through an increase in the alternative behavior and zero rates of problem behavior. This study demonstrated that teachers can implement DRA without extinction by providing high-quality reinforcers for the alternative behavior and low-quality reinforcers for the problem behavior, which will result in more appropriate and less inappropriate behaviors. Translating this to attention as a reinforcer, a teacher might provide just enough attention to ensure safety when a challenging behavior occurs, but an abundant amount of attention when an appropriate behavior occurs.

With older, high-functioning, or nondisabled students, DRA often involves instruction and reinforcement of more appropriate social skills, compliance with work or school routines, direction following, and task engagement or self-management skills (e.g., Greer et al., 2013; Luczynski & Hanley, 2009; Shumate & Wills, 2010; Wiskow, Donaldson, & Matter, 2017).

Frequently, for young students with significant communication disorders or severe disabilities, challenging behaviors have proven to be an effective, but inappropriate, means of communication. Therefore, the use of DRA involves instruction and reinforcement of a more standard means of communication. This is known as functional communication training (FCT; Carr & Durand, 1985; Gerow, Davis, Radhakrishnan, Gregori, & Rivera, 2018). For example, Matter and Zarcone (2017) taught two boys with autism and intellectual disabilities (ages 9 and 12) a variety of ways to request preferred items, such as Goldfish™ and an iPod™. The boys had previously engaged in aggression, disruptive behavior, and self-injurious behavior to access these items. Examples of types of requests were vocal ("I want the iPod please"), signing ("fish"), and touching icons on a voice output communication device that outputted the sentence, "I want the iPod please." The teaching procedure involved presenting the Goldfish or iPod in view but out of reach, providing the preferred items contingent on requests, reminding the students to use their communication systems, and ignoring instances of problem behavior. FCT resulted in decreases in problem behavior and increases in both existing and new forms of communication. In addition to using FCT to teach requesting tangible items, teachers may use FCT to teach students to request attention (Lambert, Bloom, & Irvin, 2012) and escape from instruction (i.e., asking for "Break please"; Zangrillo, Fisher, Greer, Owen, & DeSouza, 2016).

An important consideration when conducting DRA, DRI, and FCT is that the alternative behavior should be more efficient than the problem behavior in terms of the effort required to emit the behavior, the immediacy of reinforcement, and the rate and quality of reinforcement (Horner & Day, 1991). Certain criteria should be considered when selecting an alternative behavior (Brown et al., 2000; Carr et al., 1990; DeLeon, Fisher, Herman, & Crosland, 2000; Durand, Berotti, & Weiner, 1993; Friman & Poling, 1995; Horner & Day, 1991; Horner, Sprague, O'Brien, & Heathfield, 1990; Lim, Browder, & Sigafoos, 1998; O'Neill et al., 1997; Richman, Wacker, & Winborn, 2000; Shore, Iwata, DeLeon, Kahng, & Smith, 1997). These criteria include:

1. The alternative behavior serves the same function as the behavior being replaced.
2. The student, parent, and general public view the alternative behavior as more appropriate, often partly because the new behavior is viewed as a more standard behavior that achieves the same function as the behavior it replaces.
3. The alternative behavior requires equal or less physical effort and complexity.
4. The alternative behavior results in the same type, quantity, and intensity of reinforcer. If the student learns that the new behavior does not result in equivalent reinforcement, he will revert to the inappropriate behavior that has resulted in reinforcement in the past.
5. The alternative behavior is reinforced on the same schedule (frequency and consistency). If the alternative behavior of raising a hand does not result in gaining teacher attention with the same consistency as the old behavior, the student will revert to screaming in order to gain attention.
6. There is no greater delay between performance of the alternative behavior and its reinforcement than there was with the original behavior. The efficiency of replacement is enhanced if a behavior already in the student's repertoire is selected. If the student can already perform the behavior, learning a new behavior is not required at the same time as learning to replace an old behavior. Finding a behavior already in the student's repertoire is difficult with a student whose existing repertoire of appropriate behaviors is limited. Shaping an existing basic motor or social behavior into a more complex behavior may be necessary.
7. The alternative behavior is eventually maintained by natural reinforcers.

Figure 9.2 summarizes and compares various options for differential reinforcement.

Using a DRA
Pearson eText
Video Example 9.2
In this video, the educator is prompting her young students to communicate with one another as an alternative to whining and rough play. Notice that with her help, they are able to work through the situation and meet their needs through appropriate behavior.

Noncontingent Reinforcement

Another procedure that uses reinforcers to decrease behavior is **noncontingent reinforcement (NCR)**. NCR provides the student the reinforcer that is maintaining an inappropriate behavior independently of his performance of the behavior

Figure 9.2 Summary of differential reinforcement procedures

	Purpose	Formats	Management	Provides for reinforcement of alternative behavior	Objective
DRL[1]	Reduce behavior to acceptable level	Full session Interval Changing criterion Spaced responding	Focus on reducing number of occurrences	No	Tom will talk out no more than 3 times in 40 minutes.
DRO[2]	Reduce behavior to zero occurrences	Full session Interval Permanent product Whole-interval DRO Momentary DRO	Focus on increasing time of nonoccurrence	No	Tom will have no occurrence of talking out in a 40-minute period.
DRI[3] DRA[4]	Reinforce a functional alternative behavior	Concurrent reduction and strengthening programming	Focus on developing functional alternative behavior	Yes	Tom will press a buzzer to indicate he wants the attention of an adult instead of engaging in yelling and face slapping.

[1]Differential reinforcement of lower rates of behavior
[2]Differential reinforcement of other behaviors (or of zero rates of behavior, or of omission of behavior)
[3]Differential reinforcement of incompatible behavior
[4]Differential reinforcement of alternative behavior

(Coy & Kostewicz, 2018; Moore, Robinson, Coleman, Cihak, & Park, 2016; Phillips, Iannaccone, Rooker, & Hagopian, 2017; Noel & Rubow, 2018; Slocum, Grauerholz-Fisher, Peters, & Vollmer, 2018). The student receives the reinforcer not when she performs the inappropriate behavior but at preselected intervals of time. This serves to disassociate the reinforcer from the behavior and results in the behavior's decrease. While NCR is in place, the inappropriate behavior is essentially on extinction. The inappropriate behavior is ignored (not reinforced), and there is systematic delivery of reinforcers independent of performance of the inappropriate behavior. For example, if calling out is being maintained by attention from the teacher, the teacher provides lots of attention throughout the class session at preselected time intervals, whatever the student is doing. If throwing tantrums is being maintained by escape from a task, the teacher allows the student to escape the task (take a break) at intervals throughout the class.

No behavior is systematically strengthened as a result of NCR because the reinforcers are delivered at intervals regardless of what the student is doing. It is for this reason that some argue that the term NCR is not appropriate because, technically, reinforcement must result in the strengthening of a behavior (Poling & Normand, 1999; Vollmer, 1999). The procedure, however, is effective, and the term communicates its implementation. Because an alternative behavior is not developed using NCR, NCR may be combined with DRA (Fritz, Jackson, Stiefler, Wimberley, & Richardson, 2017).

During NCR, delivery is time scheduled. Access to positive reinforcement (teacher attention, for example) or negative reinforcement (a break from a task, for example) may be delivered on a fixed time schedule (FT of every 5 minutes, for example), or a variable time schedule (VT of on the average of every 5 minutes). NCR is typically administered initially on a dense, often continuous, schedule. Once the inappropriate behavior is reduced to acceptable levels, the schedule is thinned. This parallels schedule thinning as described in Chapter 8.

A potential unintended effect of NCR is adventitious, or accidental, reinforcement of the inappropriate behavior that it is the goal of the intervention to decrease (Ecott & Critchfield, 2004; Vollmer, Ringdahl, Roane, & Marcus, 1997). It is possible for a reinforcer to be delivered right after the inappropriate behavior occurs, just as it has in the past. "One would surmise that aberrant behavior that occurs at a high frequency would be more susceptible to adventitious reinforcement than a lower frequency behavior. Using the same logic, a denser NCR schedule would be more likely to produce adventitious reinforcement than a leaner schedule" (Carr, Coriaty, et al., 2000, p. 386).

NCR has become one of the most reported function-based interventions for challenging behavior (Ritter, Barnard-Brak, Richman, & Grubb, 2018). NCR has been used successfully to reduce levels of inappropriate speech and vocalizations, noncompliance, rumination, pica, object mouthing, aggression and disruption, property destruction, stereotypy, and self-injurious behaviors (e.g., Fritz et al., 2017; Phillips et al., 2017; Noel & Rubow, 2018; Slocum et al., 2018).

Noel and Rubow (2018) used NCR to reduce the perseverative speech of a 7-year-old boy with ASD who attended a social skills program with four other children. An FBA and FA demonstrated that the student's perseverative speech about cartoon characters was reinforced by attention from others. Baseline data showed that the average interresponse time of perseverative speech was 78 seconds; therefore, the NCR schedule was set at a schedule of fixed time 60 seconds. For the NCR procedure, the teacher wore a MotivAider™ that was set to vibrate every 60 seconds. When it did, the teacher delivered a neutral statement to the student, such as, "Today is Friday." Rates of perseverative speech were averages of 10.5 and 8.25 during the 10-minute baseline sessions and reduced to averages of 3.75 and 1.5 during the NCR sessions. In addition, the percentage of time the student was engaged in the curriculum increased during the NCR sessions.

Moore, Robinson, Coleman, Cihak, and Park (2016) used NCR to reduce disruptive behavior and increase task engagement with an 8-year-old boy with a developmental disability. The hypothesized function of the student's disruptive behavior was escape from demands, and he exhibited 80%–90% of intervals of disruptive

Ms. Elliott in the Community

Toni and Jake's mothers asked that trips to stores be included in their community-based instruction. When they took their children to stores, the children would take items from shelves and throw them on the floor or themselves drop to the floor and scream. During her first trip with the two students, Ms. Elliott found that this indeed occurred. She understood the parents' frustration and embarrassment. As alternative behaviors, Ms. Elliott decided to reinforce Toni for holding onto the shopping cart while pushing it down the aisles and to reinforce Jake for holding a basket on his lap as he sat in his wheelchair. As she came to various items, she would give the students opportunities to identify the correct item from two she held up, asking them to choose the "red" box or the "bottle" or the "little one" and then guiding them into placing the items in either the cart or the basket. Once the students' behavior was consistently appropriate, Toni's mother was invited to come on a shopping trip to see how the procedure was done. Ms. Elliot emailed Jake's mother, who was unavailable during school hours, a video shot during one of the shopping trips.

behavior when presented with fine motor tasks in the classroom. In the NCR intervention, the student first chose a preferred activity, such as swinging, riding a scooter, or taking a walk. Then, at the end of each 2-minute interval during the 6-minute sessions, the teacher pointed to the picture of the chosen activity, said, "I earned X activity," and directed the student to the next room to engage in the activity for 3 minutes. The authors wrote, "The escape breaks were not contingent on Max's behavior during work time (i.e., the escape breaks were noncontingent reinforcement)" (Moore et al., 2016, p. 649). Disruptive behavior was reduced from 85.5% and 82.5% in the baseline phases to 55.5% and 61.5% in the NCR phases. Task engagement increased from 31% and 28% in the baseline phases to 73% and 74% in the NCR phases.

Level II: Extinction

Learning Outcome 9.2 **Explain the problems associated with extinction.**

In contrast to Level I, which focuses on providing reinforcement, Level II, **extinction**, reduces behavior by withholding or terminating the positive reinforcer that maintains an inappropriate target behavior. This withholding results in the cessation of behavior. When the behavior being maintained is an appropriate one, preventing extinction is the goal. Many inappropriate behaviors, however, are also maintained by positive reinforcement. A parent who gives children cookies or candy when they cry may be positively reinforcing crying. If the cookies are withheld, crying should diminish.

Extinction is most often used in the classroom to decrease behaviors that are maintained by teacher attention. Teachers often pay attention to students who are behaving inappropriately, and many students find such attention positively reinforcing. This may be true even if the attention takes the form of criticism, correction, or threats. Some students' behavior may be positively reinforced by even such extreme measures as yelling.

It is often difficult for teachers to determine when their attention is positively reinforcing inappropriate behavior. Thus, a teacher may find it helpful to have someone else observe the teacher–student interaction. Once the relationship between the teacher's attention and the student's behavior is verified by this method, extinction in the classroom most often takes the form of ignoring inappropriate behavior. The teacher withholds the previously given positive reinforcer (attention), and the inappropriate behavior extinguishes or dies out (Burt & Pennington, 2017).

Ignoring is withholding attention, which will reduce behavior that is maintained by attention. But what about behavior with other functions? Consider these ways to implement extinction based on the function:

Table 9.1 Implementing extinction across functions

Challenging Behavior and Function	Extinction Procedure
Aggression maintained by attention	Withhold attention (ignore): when aggression occurs, do not provide attention
Pinching maintained by tangible items	Withhold tangible items: when pinching occurs, do not provide tangible items
Screaming maintained by escape	Withhold escape: when screaming occurs, do not provide escape. In other words, keep presenting tasks
Hand mouthing maintained by sensory reinforcement	Withhold sensation: have student wear a glove so that when he hand mouths, the sensation he previously felt is not felt

Extinction procedures have been used to decrease the occurrence of a variety of problem behaviors, including disruptive behavior (Arndorfer, Miltenberger, Woster, Rortvedt, & Gaffaney, 1994; Richman, Wacker, Asmus, Casey, & Andelman, 1999), obscene language (Salend & Meddaugh, 1985), tantrums (Carr & Newsom, 1985), food refusal (LaRue et al., 2011; Voulgarakis & Forte, 2015), inappropriate mealtime behavior (Bachmeyer et al., 2009), sleep disturbance (France & Hudson, 1990), nonstudy behavior (Hall, Lund, & Jackson, 1968), self-injurious behavior (Tereshko & Sottolano, 2017), and noncompliance (Cote, Thompson, & McKerchar, 2005; Iwata, Pace, Kalsher, Cowdery, & Cataldo, 1990; O'Reilly, Lancioni, & Taylor, 1999; Zarcone, Iwata, Mazaleski, & Smith, 1994). Extinction has also been used to increase the variety of types of responses within a class of behaviors, such as increasing the variability of communicative gestures (Duker & van Lent, 1991), toy play (Lalli, Zanolli, & Wohn, 1994), types of requests (Grow, Kelley, Roane, & Shillingsburg, 2008), and social responses (Lee & Sturmey, 2014). Extinction may be used to reduce two behaviors that occur in a chain. For example, "If a child engaged in a chain of aggressive behavior consisting of arm grabbing and hair pulling, grabbing likely would decrease if hair-pulling was treated with extinction" (Kuhn, Lerman, Vorndran, & Addison, 2006, p. 276).

Extinction is most often used in conjunction with reinforcing other, more appropriate behaviors. Combining procedures this way appears to speed extinction. When extinction is used independently, "there is little or no evidence of constructive learning. What is learned is that a certain behavior no longer provides an expected reward; the net effect is a reduction in the repertoire of behavior" (Gilbert, 1975, p. 28). If attention is given to appropriate behavior, this indicates to the student that the teacher's attention (SR^1) is still available, but that it is selectively available. It is not the student who is being ignored, just the inappropriate behavior. Because of the side effects of extinction outlined below, it is best practice to combine extinction with a positive reinforcement procedure in the form of a differential reinforcement procedure (see above).

"Just ignore it and it will go away. He's only doing it for attention." This statement is one of the most common suggestions given to teachers. In truth, extinction is much easier to discuss than to implement. It will go away, all right, but not necessarily rapidly or smoothly. Whatever "it" is, the teacher who decides to implement an extinction procedure should give careful consideration to the following points.

Delayed Reaction

The effects of extinction are not usually immediate. The extinction procedure may take considerable time to produce reduction in behavior. Once reinforcement is withheld, behavior continues for an indeterminate amount of time (Craig & Shahan, 2018; Skinner, 1953). This characteristic, known as *resistance to extinction*, is particularly marked when behaviors have been maintained on intermittent reinforcement schedules. The student continues to seek the reinforcer that has eventually resulted in the past. In an initial extinction phase to reduce aggressive behavior toward peers in a preschooler, Pinkston, Reese, LeBlanc, and Baer (1973) found it took 8 days to reduce the rate of behavior from 28% of total peer interactions to 6% of interactions. In a study of the effects of self-injurious behavior, Lovaas and Simmons (1969) reported that "John hit himself almost 9,000 times before he quit" (p. 146). Not all self-injurious behavior, however, is resistant to extinction (Lerman & Iwata, 1996). Iwata et al. (1990) found, after performing a functional analysis, that extinction reduced self-injurious escape behavior by the fifth 15-minute session.

Increased Rate

The teacher should expect an increase in the rate, duration, or intensity of the behavior before significant reduction occurs (Watson, 1967). It is going to get worse, in other words, before it gets better. This is often referred to as a burst of the behavior (Briggs, Fisher, Greer, & Kimball, 2018; Lerman, Iwata, & Wallace, 1999). In comments on one subject, Lovaas and Simmons (1969) stated, "Rick eventually did stop hitting himself under this arrangement (i.e., extinction) but the reduction in self-destruction was not immediate, and even took a turn for the worse when the extinction was first initiated" (p. 146). About John and Gregg, two other subjects, they acknowledged "the self-destructive behavior showed a very gradual drop over time, being particularly vicious in the early stages of extinction" (p. 147). Figure 9.3 displays this phenomenon in graphic data from Lovaas and Simmons (1969) and Pinkston et al. (1973).

A common pattern is that of the teacher who decides to ignore some inappropriate behavior such as calling out. When a student finds a previously reinforced response is no longer effective, the student then begins to call out louder and faster. If, after a period of time, the teacher says, "Oh, all right, Ward, what do you want?," the teacher has reinforced the behavior at its new level of intensity and may find that it remains at this level. Once an extinction procedure has been implemented, the teacher absolutely must continue ignoring whatever escalation of the behavior occurs.

Timeout From Attention
Pearson eText
Video Example 9.3
In this video, a student, Tyra, is sitting away from the other students following difficulty following instructions. The educator explains what he believed to be the function of her behavior (attention) and how Tyra taking a break from the other students, with minimal attention, allowed her to regain calm.

Controlling Attention

It is ridiculous to say to a student, "Can't you see I'm ignoring you?" Of course, what the student can see is that the teacher is not ignoring her. Even nonverbal indications that the teacher is aware of the misbehavior may be sufficient to prevent extinction. The teacher who stands rigidly with teeth and fists clenched is communicating continued attention to the student's behavior. It takes a great deal of practice to hit just the right note. We have found that it helps to have something else to do.

1. Become *very* involved with another student—perhaps praising the absence of the target behavior in her—"I like the way you raised your hand, Lou. That's the *right* way to get my attention."
2. Read something or write busily.
3. Recite epic poetry subvocally.
4. Carry a worry rock or beads.
5. Stand outside the classroom door and kick the wall for a minute.

An additional guideline we use when implementing extinction is: "Your behavior doesn't change my behavior." That is, if I'm walking to the door and you exhibit a problem behavior, I continue walking to the door—your behavior doesn't change my behavior.

Extinction-Induced Aggression

The last suggestion in the preceding section is related to another phenomenon that may occur: extinction-induced aggression by the student in the early stages of extinction procedures (Azrin, Hutchinson, & Hake, 1966; Lerman & Iwata, 1996; Lerman, Iwata et al., 1999). In search of the previously available reinforcer, the student says, in effect, "You only think you can ignore me. Watch this trick." The pattern of escalation and aggression that occurs in the early stages of extinction is illustrated by

Figure 9.3 Data from studies using extinction procedures for behavior reduction

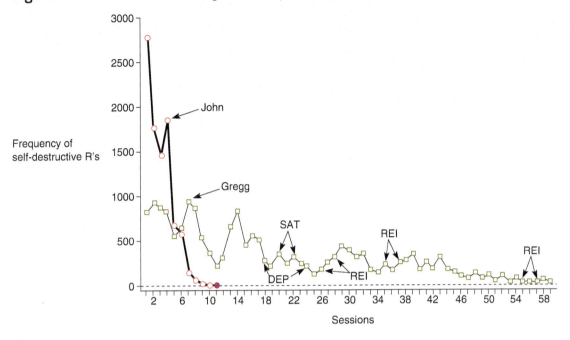

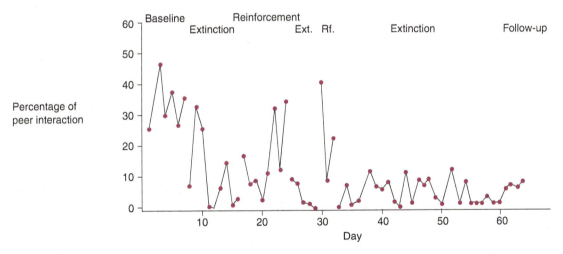

Note (top): From "Manipulation of Self-Destruction in Three Retarded Children," by O. I. Lovaas & J. Q. Simmons, 1969, *Journal of Applied Behavior Analysis*. Copyright 1969 by the Society for the Experimental Analysis of Behavior, Inc. Reprinted by permission. *Note (bottom):* From "Independent Control of a Preschool Child's Aggression and Peer Interaction by Contingent Teacher Attention," by E. M. Pinkston, N. M. Reese, J. M. LeBlanc, & D. M. Baer, 1973, *Journal of Applied Behavior Analysis*. Copyright 1973 by the Society for the Experimental Analysis of Behavior, Inc. Reprinted by permission.

a typical interaction between a thirsty customer and a defective vending machine. The customer puts four quarters in the machine (a previously reinforced response) and pushes the appropriate button. When no reinforcer is forthcoming, the customer pushes the button again ... and again ... and faster ... and harder. Before her response is extinguished, she is likely to deliver a sharp rap or swift kick to the unreinforcing machine or even to try to shake the soda out of it. Indeed, it has been reported that the abuse of soda vending machines has resulted in a considerable number of injuries. The machines fall forward onto the thirsty aggressor when rocked or tilted (Byrne, 1989; Spitz & Spitz, 1990).

Mr. Medlock Extinguishes Arguing

Judy was a student in Mr. Medlock's fourth-grade class. Whenever Mr. Medlock told Judy to do something, she argued with him. Mr. Medlock had found himself having conversations like this:

"Judy, get to work."
"I am working, Mr. Medlock."
"No you're not, Judy. You're wasting time."
"I'm getting ready to work."
"I don't want you to get ready. I want you to do it."
"How do you expect me to work if I don't get ready?"

He realized one day that he was having childish arguments with a 9-year-old and that his behavior was reinforcing Judy's arguing. He decided to put this behavior on extinction. The next day he said, "Judy, get to work." When Judy began to argue that she was working, he walked away.

Judy muttered to herself for a while and then said loudly, "I ain't gonna do this dumb work, and you can't make me." Mr. Medlock held on and continued to ignore her comments.

Emily raised her hand. "Mr. Medlock," she simpered, "Judy says she's not going to do her work."

"Emily," said Mr. Medlock quietly, "take care of yourself."

"But, Mr. Medlock, she said you can't make her," countered Emily.

Mr. Medlock realized that his only hope was to ignore Emily's behavior too. He got up and began to walk around the room, praising students who were working and reminding them of the math game they were going to play when the work was finished. Soon Emily went back to her work. Judy, however, began to tap her pencil ostentatiously on her desk. Mr. Medlock continued to interact with other students. Judy finally shrugged and began to do her assignment. When she had been working for several minutes, Mr. Medlock walked casually over to her and said, "Good job, Judy. You've already got the first two right. Keep it up."

It occurred to Mr. Medlock that Judy's delay in starting to do her work was probably reinforced by his nagging and that if he ignored her procrastination as well, Judy would probably begin to work more quickly.

Spontaneous Recovery

Teachers may also expect the possible, temporary reappearance of an extinguished behavior. This phenomenon, known as spontaneous recovery (Lerman & Iwata, 1996; Lerman, Kelley, Van Camp, & Roane, 1999; Skinner, 1953; Wathen & Podlesnik, 2018), may occur after the behavior has been extinguished for some time. The student tries once again to see if the extinction rule is still in effect or if it is in effect with all the teachers with whom she comes in contact. Ignoring this reemergence of the behavior can quickly terminate it. Failure to ignore it, however, may result in rapid relearning on the part of the student. When using functional communication training to reduce problem behavior, thinning to an intermittent schedule of reinforcement for the problem behavior reduces the likelihood of spontaneous recovery, or "resurgence" of the problem behavior (Fisher, Greer, Fuhrman, Saini, & Simmons, 2018).

Imitation or Reinforcement by Others

The behavior the teacher is ignoring may spread to other class members. If other students see a particular student getting away with misbehavior and not being punished for it, they may imitate the behavior (Bandura, 1965). This may serve to reinforce the behavior. As a result, a number of students may perform the misbehavior, instead of just one, making the behavior that much harder to ignore. The use of an extinction procedure relies on the teacher's ability to terminate the reinforcing stimulus for the inappropriate behavior. This is one of the hardest aspects of conducting an extinction procedure. In a classroom setting, the best bet is that the behavior is being reinforced by attention from the teacher (yelling) or from the classmates (laughing). To determine the reinforcing stimulus, the teacher may have to use a functional analysis to test several suspicions systematically, attempting to eliminate one potential reinforcer at a time (Hanley, Jin, Vanselow, & Hanratty, 2014; Iwata, Dorsey, Slifer, Bauman, and Richman, 1994).

It is frequently difficult to control the reinforcing consequences delivered by peers. Successful approaches to this problem have been used by Patterson (1965), who reinforced peers for withholding attention when the target student was out of seat, talking, or hitting others; by Solomon and Wahler (1973), who selected five high-status peers and trained them in the use of extinction and reinforcement of appropriate behavior; and by Pinkston et al. (1973), who attended to the peer being aggressed against while the aggressor was ignored.

Limited Generalizability

Although extinction is effective, it appears to have limited generalizability. That is, the behavior may occur just as frequently in settings where extinction is not in effect. Liberman, Teigen, Patterson, and Baker (1973) reported no generalization of treatment to routine interchanges with staff on the ward. Lovaas and Simmons (1969) reported that behavior in other settings is unaffected when extinction is used only in one setting. Programming extinction may be required in all necessary environmental settings (Ducharme & Van Houten, 1994).

Benoit and Mayer (1974) suggested six considerations before making a decision to use extinction, stated here as questions to guide teachers' decision making:

1. Can the behavior be tolerated temporarily based on its topography (for example, is it aggressive?) and on its current rate of occurrence?
2. Can an increase in the behavior be tolerated?
3. Is the behavior likely to be imitated?
4. Are the reinforcers known?
5. Can reinforcement be withheld?
6. Have alternative behaviors been identified for reinforcement?

Questions to ask yourself before implementing an extinction procedure.

Sensory Extinction

A social consequence, such as teacher attention, is not always the maintaining consequence of a behavior. "Some persons do things not for attention or praise, but simply because it feels good or is fun to do" (Rincover, 1981, p. 1). In such instances, sensory consequences rather than teacher consequences may be maintaining the behavior. This seems to be particularly true of certain stereotypic or self-injurious behaviors. A student's stereotypic hand flapping may be maintained by the visual input resulting from the behavior. A student's self-injurious self-scratching may be maintained by the tactile input resulting from the behavior. When sensory consequences can be identified as the reinforcer of a behavior, the form of extinction known as *sensory extinction* may be employed (Rincover, 1981).

Sensory extinction attempts to remove the naturally occurring sensory consequence of the behavior. Hand flapping and head hitting have been reduced by placing weights on the student's arm, thereby making the behavior more work, reducing its frequency, and fading the reinforcer (Hanley, Piazza, Keeney, Blakeley-Smith, & Worsdell, 1998; Rincover, 1981; Van Houten, 1993). Self-scratching has been reduced by covering the area being scratched with heavy petroleum jelly, thereby eliminating the tactile consequence of the behavior. Pinching has been reduced by covering others' skin with a thick fabric (Saini, Greer, & Fisher, 2015). Face scratching has been reduced by placing thin rubber gloves on the individual's hands (Rincover & Devany, 1982). Hand-mouthing and self-injurious behavior have been reduced by requiring students to wear mitts or soft arm restraints (Irvin, Thompson, Turner, & Williams, 1998; Mazaleski, Iwata, Rodgers, Vollmer, & Zarcone, 1994; Scheithauer, Mevers, Call, & Shrewsbury, 2017; Zhou, Goff, & Iwata, 2000). Two children's finger sucking was reduced by placing adhesive bandages on their fingers (Ellingson,

Ms. Troutman's Moment of Weakness

Ms. Troutman, a teacher and parent, picked her children up at day care after her work at school was done. Her 2-year-old son always asked for a p-bo-jelly as soon as they got home. She always explained that it was too close to dinnertime for peanut butter and jelly sandwiches. He always fell to the floor and screamed. She ignored him. This pattern was repeated daily, often several times. One afternoon her 7-year-old daughter, over the sound of screaming, explained that when Ms. Troutman had an especially hard day at school, she occasionally went ahead and fixed the boy a sandwich in order to avoid the tantrums, and that's why he kept asking and screaming. Ms. Troutman, albeit not graciously, was forced to acknowledge the correctness of the fledgling behaviorist's analysis.

Sensory Extinction
Pearson eText
Video Example 9.4
In this video, a student is engaging in stereotypic vocalizations. The vocalizations appear to interfere with his work and learning. Consider what might be serving as the reinforcement for the vocalizations and how sensory extinction would be applied.

Miltenberger, Stricker, Garlinghouse, et al., 2000). A padded helmet and other protective equipment have been used to reduce self-injurious behavior (e.g., face slapping, head banging; Kuhn, DeLeon, Fisher, & Wilke, 1999; Moore, Fisher, & Pennington, 2004; Rincover & Devany, 1982). Goggles have been used to block the sensory reinforcement of eye poking (Lalli, Livezey, & Kates, 1996), as has using one's hand to block an individual's hand as it approached the eyes (Smith, Russo, & Le, 1999). Difficulties may arise using sensory extinction with precision if identification of the reinforcing sensory consequence is unclear, and if there is difficulty eliminating "all the sensory consequences inherent in many commonly occurring stereotypic responses, such as rocking or clapping" (Aiken & Salzberg, 1984, p. 298).

A group of investigators has examined the use of extinction through manipulation of what is known about reinforcement schedules. In Chapter 8, we noted that once new behaviors are well established, we move from continuous to intermittent schedules of reinforcement so that behaviors become more resistant to extinction (Ferster & Skinner, 1957). The investigators wondered if inappropriate behaviors being maintained by occasional (intermittent) reinforcement would become easier to extinguish if reinforcement was temporarily delivered continuously and then withdrawn.

Neisworth, Hunt, Gallop, and Nadle (1985) investigated the efficacy of this procedure with two 19-year-old students with severe intellectual disabilities. One student engaged in stereotypic hand flapping and one in finger flicking. "During the CRF phase of treatment, the trainer delivered a reinforcer each time the participant emitted the target behavior. During the EXT phase of treatment, the reinforcer was, of course, no longer available to the participant" (p. 105). For both students, the stereotypic behaviors were reduced to near-zero levels. This remained so for one of the students at a 2-week follow-up, whereas the other student's behavior returned to baseline levels. As noted by the authors, though the effects on behaviors "run close to textbook illustrations and laboratory demonstrations" (p. 111), this is a preliminary study. In addition, the necessity to increase a behavior's rate makes the selection of an appropriate target behavior an ethical question. However, with four children with ASD, MacDonald, Ahearn, Parry-Cruwys, Bancroft, and Dube (2013) found that when EXT was preceded by CRF, responding was higher than when EXT was preceded by intermittent reinforcement (INT). This supports behavioral momentum theory, which states that the higher the rate of reinforcement (CRF), the longer the behavior will persist (Nevin & Grace, 2000). Nevertheless, it is difficult to ascertain whether CRF or INT leads to more persistence of behavior and more resistance to extinction.

Sometimes intermittent reinforcement works to maintain inappropriate behavior. Teachers or parents who reinforce a behavior during occasional moments of weakness may maintain it forever.

Punishment

The two remaining levels of the hierarchy, Levels III and IV, contain options for behavior reduction that may be termed *punishment*. As is the case with the term *reinforcer*, we use a functional definition of the term. A **punisher** is a consequent stimulus (S^P) that

1. decreases the future rate or probability of occurrence of behavior;
2. is administered contingently on the production of the undesired or inappropriate behavior;
3. is administered immediately following the production of the undesired or inappropriate behavior.

It must be clearly understood that the terms *punishment* and *punisher* as used in this context are defined functionally. Any stimulus can be labeled a punisher if its contingent application results in a reduction of the target behavior. *A punisher, like a reinforcer, can be identified only by its effect on behavior—not on the nature of the consequent stimulus.* For example, if a father spanks his son for throwing toys, and the son stops throwing toys, then the spanking was a punisher. If the son continues to throw toys, then the spanking was not a punisher. If each time a student talks out, her teacher reduces her playtime by 1 minute or takes tokens away, and this results in the reduction or cessation of the talking out, then the consequence was a punisher. If the behavior continues, the consequence was not a punisher. Again, this is a definition of the term *punisher* from a functional perspective.

Punishers, like reinforcers, may also be naturally occurring phenomena. Punishers are not simply techniques devised by malevolent behaviorists to work their will on students. Consider the following examples and label the punishers:

> Jeannie toddles into the kitchen while her father is cooking dinner. As her father's back is turned, Jeannie reaches up and touches the saucepan on the front burner. She jerks her hand away crying and thereafter avoids touching the stove.
>
> Theresa has finished her math assignment quickly. Proudly, she raises her hand and announces this fact to her teacher. The teacher assigns her 10 additional problems to work. The next day Theresa works more slowly and fails to finish her assignment before the end of math class.
>
> Gary, a student with special needs, is to attend a general education class for reading. On the first day that he attends Mr. Johnston's fourth-grade reading class, he stumbles through the oral reading passage. The other students ridicule him, and he subsequently refuses to leave the special class to attend the fourth grade.
>
> Mrs. Brice, a first-year teacher, decides to use praise with her junior high social studies class. She greets each student who arrives on time with effusive compliments and a happy-face sticker. The next day no students arrive on time.

Level III: Removal of Desirable Stimuli

Learning Outcome 9.3 Identify types of behavior reduction strategies associated with the removal of desired stimuli.

Response-Cost Procedures

Response-cost occurs when reinforcers are removed in an attempt to reduce behavior. The procedure itself may be defined as the withdrawal of specific amounts of reinforcement contingent on inappropriate behavior. As implied by this definition, "some level of positive reinforcement must be made available in order to provide the opportunity for ... withdrawing that reinforcement" (Azrin & Holz, 1966, p. 392). If the use of a response-cost procedure empirically results in the desired behavior reduction, withdrawal of the reinforcement functions as a punisher.

Response-cost may be seen as a system of leveling fines, a familiar event. A city government has, as a means of behavior control and fund raising, a whole system of fines for predefined, inappropriate behavior. We, the citizens, have possession of the pool of reinforcers—the dollar bills we have earned. The city administration withdraws specific amounts of these reinforcing stimuli contingent on such inappropriate behaviors as littering, staying too long at a parking meter, and speeding. Similarly, McSweeny (1978) reported that the number of directory assistance phone calls made in Cincinnati decreased significantly when a charge for these calls was instituted. Marholin and Gray (1976) found that when cash shortages were subtracted from employees' salaries, the size of shortages was sharply reduced.

A token system can incorporate response-cost procedures. If a teacher informs students they will earn one token for each of 10 math problems they solve correctly, that teacher is employing a token reinforcement system. If, on the other hand, the teacher hands out 10 tokens to each student and informs them that, for each problem they solve incorrectly, one token will be "repossessed," that teacher is employing a response-cost procedure. In practice, a response-cost procedure is most often and effectively used in combination with a token reinforcement system (Jowett Hirst, Dozier, & Payne, 2016; Laprime & Dittrich, 2014). In such a combined format, the students concurrently earn the pool of reinforcers and lose the reinforcers as fines for misbehavior. The students have ongoing access to future reinforcers.

In classrooms, response-cost procedures have shown to be effective in reducing a variety of behaviors, without the undesirable side effects usually associated with punishment. They have been used to modify behaviors such as screaming, vocal stereotypy (i.e., scripting) and other inappropriate vocalizations, motor stereotypy (e.g., finger twisting, object manipulation, ear play), throwing objects, and disruptive behaviors (e.g., Conyers et al., 2004; Falcomata, Roane, Hovanetz, Kettering, & Keeney, 2004; McNamara & Cividini-Motta, 2019; Nolan & Filter, 2012; Watkins & Rapp, 2014).

They have also been used to improve academic performance such as completion of math problems (Iwata & Bailey, 1974), vocational training activities in community settings (Rusch, Connis, & Sowers, 1978), and on-task behavior (Jowett Hirst et al., 2016). The response-cost contingency has been enforced by both adults and peers (Dougherty et al., 1985) and used to coordinate between school and home (Kelley & McCain, 1995). This procedure has been used to manage groups of students as well as individuals (Mowrer & Conley, 1987; Salend & Kovalich, 1981). For reducing vocal and motor stereotypy, response cost has been combined with other interventions, such as response interruption and redirection (McNamara & Cividini-Motta, 2019), differential reinforcement and a social story (Laprime & Dittrich, 2014), and environmental enrichment (Watkins & Rapp, 2014).

Jowett Hirst et al. (2016) evaluated response cost with typically developing preschoolers in both group and individual formats. When sitting down for instruction, the researcher showed the children a token board with 10 tokens on it and explained that if they moved out of their seat or were not completing their work, they would lose a token. They also explained that tokens were exchangeable for prizes and that no prizes were available if all tokens were lost. This intervention increased on-task behavior compared to a baseline condition and was nearly equally as effective as differential reinforcement of on-task behavior with tokens. Interestingly, when the researchers let the children choose between response cost and differential reinforcement, more of them chose response cost.

There are a number of practical cautions in the use of a response-cost procedure. First, the teacher must have the ability to withdraw the reinforcer once given. It is probably unwise to attempt to use response-cost procedures with edible primary reinforcers. The student who has at his desk a cup of candies that are to be contingently withdrawn is apt to immediately eat all the candy as his first inappropriate behavior. The slight young teacher in the secondary classroom who walks over to the football tackle and announces that he is to return five tokens may find that the student answers, "When pigs fly" (or something to that effect). It is best in such an instance to use points, which can be withdrawn without being physically repossessed. Careful consideration must also be given to the magnitude of the penalties— the number of tokens or points being withdrawn. Research has produced mixed recommendations. For example, Burchard and Barrera (1972) used severe fines, whereas Siegel, Lenske, and Broen (1969) used mild fines; both got good results. An important point to remember is that exacting large fines may make tokens worthless. If students learn that an entire day's work can be wiped out by a fine, they are unlikely to work very hard.

Problems with response-cost.

Another problem may occur when all the reinforcers have been withdrawn. Consider, for example, the substitute teacher who is assigned to a ninth-grade remedial class for the day. One of the thoughts uppermost in her mind, in addition to the educational welfare of her temporary charges, is making it in one piece to lunchtime. When the students enter the room, she announces that, if they cooperate and work hard during the morning hours, she will permit them 30 minutes of free time. If she fines them 5 minutes whenever anyone misbehaves, by 10 a.m. the students may have very little free time left. Once the reinforcement system has become debased to this extent, the student energy involved in being good far outweighs the remaining amount of the reinforcer.

When using response-cost, as with all management systems, students must clearly understand the rules of behavior and the penalties for infractions. Clear understanding will avoid lengthy conversations at the time of misbehavior, when the teacher should just describe the infraction and exact the fine.

Before selecting a response-cost procedure, the teacher should answer the following questions:

1. Have more positive procedures, such as differential reinforcement strategies, been considered?
2. Does the student currently have, or have access to, a pool of reinforcers?
3. Have the rules of appropriate behavior and the results (fines) for infractions been clearly explained and understood?
4. Has the ratio of the size of the fine to each instance of misbehavior been thought out?
5. Can the reinforcers be retrieved?
6. Will appropriate behavior be reinforced in conjunction with the use of response-cost?

Guide to setting up a response-cost procedure.

Response-Cost Coupons

In order to make a response-cost system more concrete for her class of 6- and 7-year-olds, Ms. Calabash decided to use pictorial coupons as tokens. Before leaving the classroom and entering the community, the four children were given five coupons each to keep in their waist packs. Four of the coupons had a picture of an item they could acquire while on their trip (a soft drink; a yogurt cone; a picture of a bus seat, meaning they could choose where to sit; and a picture of the store where they could buy something). The fifth coupon had a picture of an activity they could choose when they got back to class (puzzle, iPod). If they misbehaved while on the trip, the teacher removed one of the coupons.

Figure 9.4 Categories of time-out procedures

TIME-OUT PROCEDURES	
Nonexclusion Time-Out Procedures	**Exclusion Time-Out Procedures**
The student **remains** in the instructional/activity area.	The student is **removed** from the instructional/activity area.
• environmental manipulation • time-out ribbon • contingent observation • visual screening	• exclusion from immediate activity to another location in the room • separate time-out room

Time-Out Procedures

Time-out procedures decrease behavior by denying a student, for a fixed period of time, the opportunity to receive reinforcement. **Time-out** is a shortened form of the term *time-out from positive reinforcement*. Before using time-out procedures, the teacher must be sure that reinforcing consequences for appropriate behavior are available in the classroom. This is a critical and often overlooked aspect of time-out; if there are no positive reinforcers available in the classroom, time-out will not work. Time-out procedures may be categorized according to the method of denying access to reinforcers (Figure 9.4). When using nonexclusion time-out procedures, the student remains in the instructional area. When using exclusion time-out procedures, the student is removed from the instructional area.

NONEXCLUSION TIME-OUT PROCEDURES In **nonexclusion time-out** procedures, the student is not removed from the instructional setting; instead, the teacher denies the student access to reinforcers through a temporary manipulation of the environment. Teachers use this procedure in its most common form when faced with a generalized, minor disturbance. Contingent on a challenging behavior, they may tell the students to put their heads on their desks, sit on a carpeted corner of the classroom, or sit in a chair on the perimeter of the playground (Donaldson & Vollmer, 2012; Donaldson, Vollmer, Yakich, & Van Camp, 2013; Higgins et al., 2001). If during instruction students begin to act inappropriately, the teacher may remove the materials (for example, eating utensils, counting chips, frog and dissection kit), herself, her attention for a brief period contingent on the inappropriate behavior. Similarly, time-out may be accomplished by turning off music during free time when jocularity gets out of hand or turning off the radio on the school bus when students are out of their seats (Ritschl, Mongrella, & Presbie, 1972). If the problem occurs while the student is getting to the bus, the teacher can place the student in nonseclusionary time-out by stopping all verbal prompting and social attention and removing from sight any reinforcers that are being delivered for appropriate walking to the bus (Huguenin, 1993). Dupuis, Lerman, Tsami, and Shireman (2015) worked with a 6-year-old boy with autism and Fragile X syndrome who engaged in aggression to escape certain noises and songs. They reduced aggression by playing sounds while delivering preferred edibles; if aggression occurred, the song and edibles ceased for 30 seconds. This resulted in a decrease in aggression.

A frequently reported form of nonexclusion time-out is use of the **time-out ribbon** model (Kostewicz, 2010). This procedure has been used with individual students (Alberto, Heflin, & Andrews, 2002; Fee, Matson, & Manikam, 1990; Huguenin & Mulick, 1981; McKeegan, Estill, & Campbell, 1984; Salend & Maragulia, 1983) and with groups of students (Foxx & Shapiro, 1978; Salend & Gordon, 1987).

During a group lesson, Foxx and Shapiro had students wear a ribbon tie while behaving in a socially appropriate manner. A student's ribbon was removed for any instance of misbehavior. This removal signaled an end to teacher attention and an end to the student's participation in activities and access to reinforcers for 3 minutes. During community-based instruction, Alberto et al. had students wear an athletic wristband. The wristband was removed for instances of inappropriate behavior. When not wearing the wristband, the student was required to stay next to the teacher and was not given a task to perform. He was neither spoken to nor given social attention, and if regularly scheduled tokens were distributed, the student did not get one.

Various time-out "ribbons" have been used, including actual ribbons, badges, leather shoelaces in belt loops, and wristbands with smiling-face stickers. In a study by Adams, Martin, and Popelka (1971), a misbehavior prompted the teacher to turn on a recorded tone. While the tone was audible, access to reinforcers was denied to the student. In classrooms where token systems are in effect, taking a student's point card for a specified number of minutes provides a period of time-out from reinforcement.

Another form of nonexclusion time-out is **contingent observation**, which involves moving students to the edge of an activity so that they can still observe other students' appropriate behavior and its reinforcement. Barton, Brulle, and Repp (1987) used contingent observation with two elementary students with severe disabilities. When the students misbehaved, they were moved slightly away from the group but were allowed to observe the classroom activities. Not every instance of the behavior resulted in contingent observation. A prespecified number of occurrences was permitted within given time intervals. Time-out was used only when instances of misbehavior exceeded the maximum. Such scheduling is similar to that used for DRL procedures. White and Bailey (1990) used what they referred to as a "sit and watch" procedure during physical education classes comprised of typical fourth graders and students with severe behavior problems. During "sit and watch," the teacher removed the student from the activity and explained the reason for his removal. The student picked up an egg timer, walked to an area away from the other students, sat down on the ground, and turned the timer over. He remained in "sit and watch" for approximately 3 minutes, until all of the sand had flowed to the other end of the timer. The student was then allowed to rejoin the class. At the teacher's request, backup procedures were available in the form of lost privileges for some students. Twyman, Johnson, Buie, and Nelson (1994) described a range of more restrictive contingent observation alternatives that were used for vocal or physical disrespect to staff or peers, noncompliance, off task, out of area, or talk-outs with elementary students with emotional or behavior disorders. Students remained in the setting at a desk, in a chair, on the floor, against the wall, or just standing. In each case, students were required to maintain "appropriate hands and feet" and to keep their heads tucked between their arms. "Although the required posture reduced the possibility of visual observation, the student was able to hear the activities of the group and reinforcement being delivered to others" (p. 247). (Note: The study in which this procedure was used found that warning students of potential point loss for inappropriate behavior during contingent observation resulted in increased negative interaction between staff and students.)

EXCLUSION TIME-OUT PROCEDURES **Exclusion time-out** involves removing the student from an activity as a means of denying access to reinforcement. The student may be taken to another room, but it is not necessary to remove the student from the classroom completely. Exclusion may be accomplished by removing the student from the immediate activity area to another part of the room. Observation and subsequent modeling of reinforced behavior (as with contingent observation) are not components of this procedure. The student is removed to a chair facing away from the group, facing a corner, or in a screened-off area of the room. This procedure has been used with students who displayed aggressive and disruptive behaviors, tantrums, and noncompliance (LeBlanc & Matson, 1995; Luiselli, 1996; Reitman & Drabman, 1999; Roberts, 1988). Baer, Rowbury, and Baer (1973) used a variation of such exclusion. When a student misbehaved during an activity for which she was earning tokens, she was placed in the middle of the room out of reach of the work activity and thereby denied access to earning tokens. In another variation, a student was moved to a chair outside the play area when he displayed aggressive behavior. The teacher stood next to him until he sat quietly for 5 seconds. While in the time-out area, the student was required to perform a nonpreferred task before being allowed to return to the play area. The addition of this task was intended to decrease the potential reinforcing value of teacher attention during the time-out (Richman et al., 1997).

Coppage and Meindl (2017) implemented an additional variation of time-out with two girls with autism spectrum disorder (ages 7 and 10) who engaged in tantrums. Previous reinforcement-based interventions were unsuccessful. When the students were engaging in homework or coloring, the researchers video-recorded their tantrums and did not issue any consequences following tantrums. Fifteen minutes after this activity, the student was brought into the session room and asked to watch a 1-minute video of her tantrum. After watching the video, the researcher said, "Now time-out," and brought the student to a chair to face the wall for 3 or 5 minutes. This "delayed time-out" reduced tantrums from 40%–80% of intervals in baseline to 0–20% of intervals. Delayed time-out may be useful when a teacher cannot bring a student to a time-out area because she or he is engaging in disruptive or aggressive behavior.

An exclusion procedure used less often in today's public schools is time-out associated with the use of a time-out room. This procedure involves removing the student from the classroom to a room identified for total social isolation, contingent on misbehavior. In such a room, access is denied to all potential reinforcers from the teacher, classmates, or the classroom environment and materials. Such a procedure is sometimes termed *seclusionary time-out*. This procedure has been reserved for behaviors such as physical aggression and destruction of property (Costenbader & Reading-Brown, 1995, Vegas, Jenson, & Kircher, 2007).

Unfortunately, time-out rooms have often been seriously misused or mismanaged. Their use, therefore, has been the subject of negative publicity and litigation (Cole v. Greenfield-Central Community Schools, *1986*; Dickens v. Johnson County Board of Education, *1987*; Hayes v. Unified School District No. 377, *1989*; Honig v. Doe, *1988*). A decision to use a time-out room strategy is not a decision a teacher can make alone. The IEP or behavior-management committee would discuss prior attempts at behavior management and the details of use of the time-out room procedure, and informed permission from the appropriate people, including the parent, would need to be obtained. When discussing the possible use of a time-out room strategy, individuals should consult the school district's policies and procedures and available professional literature, such as the position statement on restraint and seclusion from the Association for Behavior Analysis International (Vollmer et al., 2011). Three guiding principles of this statement are: "the welfare of the individuals served is the highest priority," "individuals (and parents or guardians) have a right to choose," and "the principle of least restrictiveness" (p. 104). In other words, schools must ensure students are safe, parents/guardians should have input into restrictive interventions (including providing informed consent), and professionals should use restrictive measures only when less restrictive methods have been ruled out.

Many of us remember the days when teachers routinely put students out in the hall in an attempt to change their behavior. Ms. Sutton tries this in the following vignette.

Removing Desired Items
Pearson eText
Video Example 9.5
In this video, a student, Daniel C, has his head down on the table and is not participating. The educators remind him that if he is not participating he may not earn free time (a desired activity). The educators use a time out from instruction and then Daniel C returns to the group.

Ms. Sutton Tries Time-Out

The next time Aaron hit someone, Ms. Sutton told him, "Aaron, you hit somebody. You have to go to time-out." She sat him in a chair in the hall and went back to teaching reading. At the end of the period, about an hour later, she went to get him. He came back into the room and hit Elaine before he even got to his seat. Once again, he went to the hall. This pattern was repeated throughout the morning.

Aaron spent most of the time in the hall and the rest of the time hitting people. Ms. Sutton concluded that time-out was an ineffective procedure. Later that day, she heard Aaron say to Elaine, "Hey, I got this all figured out. If I hit you, I get to go sit in the hall. I don't have to do my work, and I get to talk to all the people in the hall. The principal even came by and asked me what I did. Boy, did I tell him!"

Ms. Sutton, a second-grade teacher, read about time-out. She decided that she would use it to teach Aaron not to hit other students and concluded that the hall outside her classroom would be a good area for time-out.

"I don't understand it, Professor. Time-out just isn't working anymore."

Time-out will not be effective if positive reinforcement is not available in the classroom, if students escape tasks while in time-out, or if reinforcing consequences are available during time-out.

> Factors that may make time-out ineffective.

Level IV: Presentation of Aversive Stimuli

Learning Outcome 9.4 Identify types of behavior reduction strategies associated with the presentation of aversive stimuli.

The presentation of an aversive stimulus as a consequence of an inappropriate behavior is, in popular usage, identified with the term *punishment*. Teachers turn to this form of punishment almost by reflex. Perhaps because many people have been disciplined at home and at school by being yelled at or hit, they learn to handle other people's inappropriate behavior by yelling and hitting, especially when their opponent is physically smaller. From a more functional perspective, this form of punishment is often used because it has three powerful advantages. First and foremost, the use of an aversive stimulus rapidly stops the occurrence of a behavior and has some long-term effects (Azrin, 1960). A child throwing a tantrum who is suddenly hit across the backside will probably

> What makes the presentation of aversive consequences so appealing to parents and teachers?

stop immediately; a pair of students gossiping in the back of the room will stop when the teacher screams at them. Second, the use of aversive stimuli facilitates learning by providing a clear discrimination between acceptable and unacceptable behavior or between safe and dangerous behavior (Marshall, 1965). The student who is slapped for spitting, subjected to mild shocks on the arm for self-injurious behavior, or hit by a car while dashing across the street clearly and immediately sees the inappropriateness of the behavior. Third, the aversive consequence following a student's inappropriate behavior vividly illustrates to other students the results of engaging in that behavior, and therefore tends to lessen the probability that others will engage in the behavior (Bandura, 1965).

In listing these advantages, *we are not recommending the use of aversive consequences* (especially involving physical contact) as a routine management procedure in the classroom, in homes, or in agencies for students with disabilities. We merely acknowledge the behavioral effects resulting from their use. Physical or other strong aversive consequences are justified only under the most extreme instances of inappropriate behavior. They are appropriate only when safety is jeopardized or in instances of long-standing serious behavior problems. Aversive consequences should be used only after considering appropriate safety and procedural guidelines. Guidelines should minimally include

1. *demonstrated* and *documented* failure of alternative nonaversive procedures to modify the target behavior (Verriden & Roscoe, 2019);
2. informed written consent of the student's parents or legal guardians through due process procedures and assurance of their right to withdraw such consent at any time (Vollmer et al., 2011);
3. the decision to implement an aversive procedure made by a designated body of qualified professionals;
4. a prearranged timetable for review of the effectiveness of the procedure and discontinuance of the procedure as soon as possible;
5. periodic observation to ensure staff members' consistent and reliable administration of the procedure;
6. documentation of the effectiveness of the procedure as well as evidence of increased accessibility to instruction;
7. administration of the procedure by only designated staff members (the staff members should have had instruction in the procedure, have reviewed published studies in the use of the procedure, and be familiar with procedure-specific guidelines and possible negative effects); and
8. positive reinforcement of incompatible behavior, whenever possible, as a part of any program using aversive stimuli.

Krasner (1976) pointed out an important distinction between effectiveness and acceptability. It is not the effectiveness of aversive procedures that is in question, but their acceptability to parents, the public, and many professionals. Techniques involving aversive consequences understandably cause concern to many people. Some professionals believe that aversive techniques are always inappropriate. Others believe their use may be acceptable in cases of self-injurious behavior, for example, if proper safeguards are implemented. It is doubtful, however, that such drastic measures could or even should become accepted as routine classroom management procedures.

The Professor Experiences Déjà Vu

Mrs. Grundy had made numerous inquiries about obedience training for the professor's dog. She found that Miss Oattis taught for a licensed dog club and signed Burrhus and the professor up for an 8-week series of classes. One Monday evening, therefore, the professor and the dog stood in what appeared to be a former convenience store whose fixtures had been replaced with green rubber mats. There were decrepit lawn chairs along one wall, separated from the training floor by what appeared to be baby gates.

Miss Oattis introduced herself and began by telling the group some basic school rules—where the dogs were to be taken to relieve themselves and procedures for making up missed classes. She stressed the need for each owner to maintain control of his or her dog and keep it at least 6 feet from the other dogs. The large, active brown dog next to the professor continued to investigate Burrhus and to pull on his owner. The instructor asked the owner to control her dog and continued with the introduction.

"We will be using lots of praise and treats to help our dogs learn. In operant conditioning (the professor began to pay very close attention), we call that positive reinforcement. Operant conditioning is the latest, most modern kind of dog training. It's not hard to learn and I'm here to help you. We will also be using corrections when the dogs behave inappropriately. You will learn why both are necessary and how to use them effectively. We will also use cues, signals, and prompts as well as shaping. Don't worry about all this new terminology; you'll catch on." (The professor was all ears.) The large brown dog finished its investigation of Burrhus and jumped on the professor. Miss Oattis said calmly, "This is the perfect opportunity to demonstrate a correction." She walked briskly over to the woman with the large brown dog and took the leash from her. As the dog began to jump on the professor again, she snapped the leash as she said, "Off!" in a ringing tone. The dog put all four feet on the floor and regarded the instructor quizzically. "Good dog," she said, sweetly.

"You see," Miss Oattis stated, "the dog was behaving inappropriately. I snapped the leash so that his collar put pressure on his neck, and he stopped jumping. Soon we'll teach him to sit so he will know what to do instead of sniffing and jumping around people and other dogs."

The dog's owner drew herself up to her full height.

"I am appalled," she hissed, "I have been watching tapes of some of the most famous dog trainers and they say you should never, ever, correct a dog. It is inhumane and will destroy your relationship with him. You can do all the training you need with only praise and treats. You have abused my dog. I'm leaving right now and I want my money back."

The professor's mind flashed back to a confrontation he had recently witnessed at a professional conference. "Amazing," he said to himself. "The same issue and the same anger."

Types of Aversive Stimuli

Aversive stimuli may be categorized into two groups: unconditioned aversive stimuli and conditioned aversive stimuli. **Unconditioned aversive stimuli** result in physical pain or discomfort. This class of stimuli includes anything that causes pain—naturally occurring consequences, such as contact with a hot stove, or contrived consequences, such as paddling. Miss Oattis used the unconditioned aversive stimulus of snapping the dog's leash. Because these stimuli immediately produce a behavior change without the need for any previous experience, they may also be termed universal, natural, or unlearned punishers. Unconditioned aversive stimuli also include consequences that result in annoyance, discomfort, or irritation. These aversive consequences include loud or harsh verbal corrections, administration of substances, and the use of physical control. These consequences are not appropriate for classroom use. Before we understood the effectiveness of interventions based on the function of behaviors rather than simply their topography, these interventions were sometimes thought necessary to deal with very challenging behaviors. Use of substances sometimes included directing a fine mist of water toward an individual engaging in various severe forms of self-injury, and placing lemon juice on the tongue of an individual engaged in rumination-regurgitation or pica (e.g., Apolito & Sulzer-Azaroff, 1981; Bailey, Pokrzywinski, & Bryant, 1983; Becker, Turner, & Sajwaj, 1978; Dorsey, Iwata, Ong, & McSween, 1980; Mayhew & Harris, 1979). Physical control included procedures requiring direct physical intervention to suppress a targeted behavior. Two such procedures were contingent exercise and immobilization or physical restraint. Contingent exercise required the student to engage in unrelated physical activity such as push-ups, deep knee bends, or running laps as a consequence for a targeted behavior. This procedure was used with self-injurious and aggressive behaviors (e.g., DeCatanzaro & Baldwin, 1978; Luce, Delquadri, & Hall, 1980; Kern, Koegel, & Dunlap, 1984).

Severe challenging behaviors that often serve a sensory function, such as rumination and pica, are so difficult to reduce that researchers have resorted to punishment procedures. When treating the rumination of an 18-year-old man with autism and other medical diagnoses, DeRosa, Roane, Bishop, and Silkowski (2016) found that freely delivering food (noncontingent reinforcement) decreased rumination from baseline levels, but not to zero levels. The researchers met with the student's mother and asked which punishment procedures she would be comfortable with, such as a baskethold, time-out, contingent exercise, and hands down. The procedure they chose was a facial screen (FS), which "included the therapist standing behind Darnell and lightly placing one hand over his eyes, while the therapist used her other arm to block attempts to remove the FS" (p. 682). This lasted 30 seconds, was then reduced to 10 seconds, and resulted in zero and near-zero levels of rumination. Mitteer, Romani, Greer, and Fisher (2015) also used a facial screen combined with DRA to reduce the pica and property destruction of a 6-year-old girl with autism spectrum disorder.

Physical restraint has a history of use primarily with self-injurious behaviors (e.g., Matson & Keyes, 1988; Pace, Iwata, Edwards, & McCosh, 1986). Harris (1996) discussed three categories of restraint: personal restraint, mechanical restraint, and self-restraint. Personal restraint is movement suppression by the application of force or pressure by one person upon another. This may involve holding a student's hands to his side, placing pressure on the student's shoulders, or using an embrace or "baskethold" for immobilization. If physical restraint is necessary, most educators agree that personal restraint in a chair is more acceptable than methods involving personal restraint on the floor (McDonnell & Sturmey, 2000). Mechanical restraint involves use of a device such as arm splints or adapted clothing (DeRosa, Roane, Wilson, Novak, & Silkowski, 2015; Morgan, Wilder, Podlesnik, & Kelley, 2017). Self-restraint involves actions an individual uses to restrict his or her own movements, such as placing hands in pockets or the waistband of pants, wrapping arms in clothing, and self-use of mechanical restraints (e.g., Banda, McAfee, & Hart, 2012; Kerth, Progar, & Morales, 2009; Powers, Roane, & Kelley, 2007; Richards, Davies, & Oliver, 2017; Rooker & Roscoe, 2005; Scheithauer, O'Connor, & Toby, 2015).

Schloss and Smith (1987) and Luiselli, Sperry, and Draper (2015) suggested limitations to the use of physical restraint:

1. Physical restraint is "often strenuous, emotionally arousing, and difficult to maintain" (Luiselli et al., p. 170).
2. Restraint does not involve the reinforcement of an alternative behavior.
3. The inappropriate behavior may be reinforced by manual restraint, thereby increasing the probability of future occurrences.
4. Once the student learns that he will be physically blocked from performing the response, he is likely to increase his efforts to perform it.
5. Implementation may result in harm to the student or the teacher.
6. Ongoing training is required to implement restraint properly.

The use of physical restraint in general, but especially in schools, is very controversial because it can cause harm to the student and compromise the student's dignity and right to effective treatment (Cooper, Heron, & Heward, 2020; Graber & Graber, 2018; Vollmer et al., 2011). Indeed, federal legislation on reducing restraint and seclusion has been introduced into the U.S. Congress, such as a House bill in 2009 entitled the Preventing Harmful Restraint and Seclusion in Schools Act (H.R. 4247) and a Senate bill in 2011 entitled the Achievement Through Prevention Act (S.3373; Gagnon, Mattingly, & Connelly, 2017). These bills were not voted into law, yet 27 states and the District of Columbia have laws or policies regulating the use of seclusion and restraint in schools, and other states have policies at the local level. Although society has a goal of reducing seclusion and restraints in schools, these procedures are necessary and appropriate in the most severe cases when they can increase safety and reduce the future likelihood of the behaviors (Vollmer et al., 2011). A multidisciplinary team, with input and consent from parents/guardians, may develop a behavior intervention that includes restraint and "must (a) incorporate reinforcement-based procedures, (b) be based on a functional behavior assessment, (c) be evaluated by objective outcome data, and (d) be consistent with the scientific literature and current best practices" (Vollmer et al., 2011, p. 105). Using exclusion time-out has the same guidelines, in addition to being brief.

Conditioned aversive stimuli are stimuli a person learns to experience as aversive as a result of pairing with an unconditioned aversive stimulus. This class includes consequences such as words and warnings, vocal tones, or gestures. For example, a child may have experienced being yelled at paired with being spanked. Yelling may thus have become a conditioned aversive stimulus, because experience has proven to the student that yelling is associated with pain. The pain associated with a conditioned aversive stimulus may also be psychological or social pain or discomfort, usually in the form of embarrassment or ridicule from peers.

Verbal reprimands (shouting or scolding) are the most common form of conditioned aversive stimuli used in the classroom (Hodges, Wilder, & Ertel, 2018; Thomas, Presland, Grant, & Glynn, 1978; White, 1975; Wilder & Neve, 2018). This may be true due to two immediate results. First, shouting or scolding will often put an immediate, if temporary, end to the disruptive behavior in which the student is engaging; and second, it provides negative reinforcement to the teacher who has put an end to a disruptive incident and thinks about what a good behavior manager he is (Alber & Heward, 2000; Miller, Lerman, & Fritz, 2010). Research on verbal reprimands identified factors that influence the effectiveness of reprimands, such as delivery with direct eye contact and "a firm grasp," delivery once rather than repeatedly, and delivery near the student rather than from across the room. Indeed, a quiet reprimand audible only to the student being reprimanded may be as effective as a loud "no" heard by everyone in the class (O'Leary, Kaufman, Kass, & Drabman, 1970; Van Houten, Nau, Mackenzie-Keating, Sameoto, & Colavecchia, 1982). Verbally reprimanding a student may put an immediate stop to the behavior, but it may result in escalating behavior. Looking into this possibility, Mace, Pratt, Prager, and Pritchard (2011) describe three ways of saying "no" to a student, in this case to a student wanting access to the computer to play a game. They provide three examples: (1) denying access to a requested activity by saying "no" and then offering an explanation for the refusal, for example, "You cannot use the computer now; someone else is using it at the moment"; (b) denying access to the requested activity but offering an opportunity to engage in a preferred alternative activity, for example, "You cannot use the computer now; someone else is using it at the moment, but you may choose a game from the closet"; or (c) denying immediate access to the requested activity but permitting delayed access contingent on the completion of a low-preference demand, for example, "You cannot use the computer now; someone else is using it at the moment, but you may use it when you have completed your math assignment." Saying "no" with an alternative provided as in option b or c tends to limit the potential escalation of inappropriate behavior by the student resulting from being told "no."

If unconditioned or conditioned aversive stimuli are to be used as consequences in a behavior-reduction program, they should be used as effectively as possible. As indicated in the functional definition, the teacher must be consistent and immediate in applying the consequences (Azrin, Holz, & Hake, 1963). The rules of behavior must be clearly associated with a contingency that has been previously stated: the "if, then" statement of cause and effect. The student must understand that the aversive consequence is not being arbitrarily applied. The immediacy of application convinces the student of the veracity of the contingency and underlines the connection between a particular behavior and its consequence.

In addition to ensuring consistency and immediacy, the teacher should avoid extended episodes of punishment. Consequences should be quick and directly to the point. Sometimes teachers become so involved in analyzing behavior and arranging consequences, they forget that for some children, a polite request to "Please stop doing that" is all that's required. If words are a punisher for a student, a few words—such as, "Don't run in the hall"—may be far more effective than a 15-minute lecture, most of which the student tunes out. When targeting the toe walking of a 5-year-old boy with autism, Hodges, Wilder, and Ertel (2018) delivered praise for appropriate walking and the reprimand, "No toe walking," contingent on toe walking. This procedure reduced toe walking. Wilder and Neve (2018) also used a brief reprimand—"No rumination"—paired with access to a lollipop to decrease the rumination of a 19-year-old man with autism.

Punishment is far less effective when the intensity of the aversive stimulus is increased gradually instead of being initially introduced at its full intensity (Azrin & Holz, 1966). With a gradual increase in intensity, the student has the opportunity to become habituated or desensitized to the intensity of the previous application. Such gradual habituation may eventually lead the teacher to administer an intensity level far above what was originally considered necessary to terminate the student's misbehavior. On the other hand, once punishment is implemented and reduces challenging behavior, the punishment may be put on an intermittent schedule of reinforcement and have sustained effects (Lerman, Iwata, Shore, & DeLeon, 1997).

A desire or actual attempt to escape from an aversive condition is a natural response. If punishment is to be effective in changing undesirable student behavior, the teacher will have to arrange the environment to prevent students' escaping punishment (Azrin, Hake, Holz, & Hutchinson, 1965; Bandura, 1969; Delprato, 2002).

The most important element of any program that includes punishment of inappropriate behavior is to be sure that any punishment is always used in association with reinforcement for appropriate behavior. Punishment involves very little learning. In effect, all the student learns is what behavior should not be engaged in. Reinforcing appropriate behavior instructs the student on appropriate or expected behaviors and provides an opportunity for successful or reinforced experiences.

Disadvantages of Aversive Stimuli

The disadvantages of aversive consequences far outweigh the advantages of their immediate effect. The following limitations of such procedures should make teachers stop and consider very carefully before choosing to use aversives:

1. In the face of aggressive punishers, the student has three behavior options:
    a. The student may strike back (for example, yell at the teacher or even become physically aggressive). A reaction may be triggered that will result in escalation of the situation.

b. The student may become withdrawn, tune out the punisher, and remain tuned out for the rest of the day, thus learning nothing.
   c. The student may engage in an escape and avoidance behavior. Once a student has run out of the room, a punisher in the classroom can have no immediate effect.
2. We know that a most basic and powerful form of instruction and learning takes place through modeling or imitation. Because a teacher is a figure of respect and authority, students closely observe his or her behavior. A teacher's reactions become a model of adult behavior for various situations. The teacher who yells or hits is, in effect, saying to the students this is how an adult reacts and copes with undesirable behaviors in the environment. Students may, through such a model, learn an inappropriate, aggressive form of behavior. As noted by Sobsey (1990), this punishment-induced aggression results in more inappropriate behavior and can result in harm to both the individual and to any targets of aggression.
3. Unless students are taught to understand what behavior is being punished, they may come to fear and avoid the teacher or the entire setting in which the punishment occurred.
4. Many interactions that teachers consider punishers function as positive reinforcers instead. A child may find making an adult lose control and look ridiculous very reinforcing.

A disadvantage of punishment is illustrated by the following vignette.

Like Dennis, what students learn most often from punishment using aversive stimuli is not to perform the behavior when the person who applied the punishment is present. They learn not to get caught! They don't learn to behave appropriately.

Concern about inappropriate and excessive use of aversive interventions has resulted in position statements about their use from various advocacy and professional organizations (e.g., Vollmer et al., 2011).

Professor Grundy Teaches Dennis a Thing or Two

Professor Grundy's 5-year-old nephew, Dennis, was spending the week at the professor's house. One of Dennis's more unpleasant habits was jumping on the bed. Mrs. Grundy had asked Dennis not to do it, but this had been completely ineffective.

Professor Grundy was sitting in his easy chair, smoking his pipe, and reading a professional journal. He heard the unmistakable "crunch, crunch, crunch" of the bedsprings directly overhead in the guest bedroom. "Minerva," he said, "the time has come for drastic action. Where is the fly swatter?"

"Oliver, you're not going to beat the child, are you?" asked Minerva.

"Certainly not, dear," replied the professor. "I shall merely apply an unconditioned aversive stimulus, contingently, at a maximum intensity."

The professor took the fly swatter in hand and tiptoed up the carpeted steps in his stockinged feet. He continued to tiptoe into the bedroom, where he observed Dennis happily jumping on the bed. Dennis did not observe the professor; his back was to the door. Grundy applied the immediate, contingent, and intense aversive stimulus saying, firmly, "Do not jump on the bed." Dennis howled.

"That, I think," said the professor to Mrs. Grundy, "will teach Dennis a thing or two." In fact, Dennis did not jump on the bed all weekend. Professor Grundy was at home all the time and knew he would have heard the springs.

On Monday, when the professor arrived home from the university, Minerva met him at the door. "Oliver," she said, "I don't know which thing or two you planned to teach Dennis, but the one he learned was not to jump on the bed when you were home. He's been at it all day."

Overcorrection

Overcorrection was developed as a behavior-reduction procedure that includes training in appropriate behaviors. Appropriate or correct behavior is taught through an exaggeration of experience. The exaggeration of experience characteristic of overcorrection contrasts with a simple correction procedure in which a student rectifies an error of behavior but is not necessarily required to follow that with exaggerated or extended practice of the appropriate behavior.

There are two basic types of overcorrection procedures. *Restitutional overcorrection* is used when a setting has been disturbed by a student's misbehavior. The student must overcorrect the setting she or he has disturbed. *Positive-practice overcorrection* is used when the form of a behavior is inappropriate. In this procedure, the student practices an exaggerated correct form of an appropriate behavior (Foxx & Azrin, 1973a).

Restitutional Overcorrection

A restitutional overcorrection procedure requires that the student restore or correct an environment that he or she has disturbed not only to its original condition, but beyond that. For example, when the teacher catches a student throwing a spitball, she is employing simple correction when she says, "Michael, pick that up and throw it in the trash." She is employing restitutional overcorrection when she says, "Michael, pick that up and throw it in the trash, and now pick up all the other papers on the floor."

This form of environmental restoration was used by Azrin and Foxx (1971) as part of their toilet-training program. When a child had an accident, she or he had to undress, wash the clothes, hang them to dry, shower, obtain clean clothing, dress, and then clean the soiled area of the lavatory. A variation was employed by Azrin and Wesolowski (1974) when, in order to eliminate stealing, they required the thief to return not only a stolen item but also an additional identical item to the person who had been robbed.

A review of studies by Rusch and Close (1976) shows restitutional overcorrection techniques used to reduce various classes of disruptive behavior:

1. In cases where objects were disturbed or rearranged, all objects (such as furniture) within the immediate area where a disruption occurred were straightened, not merely the originally disturbed objects.
2. In cases where someone annoyed or frightened others, all persons present were to be apologized to, not just those annoyed or frightened.
3. In cases of self-inflicted oral infection, a thorough cleansing of the mouth with an oral antiseptic followed unhygienic oral contacts such as biting people or chewing inedible objects.
4. In cases of agitation, a period of absolute quiet was imposed following commotions such as shrieking and screaming.

Positive-Practice Overcorrection

With positive-practice overcorrection, the student who has engaged in an inappropriate behavior is required to engage in exaggerated or overly correct practice of the appropriate behavior. For example, if a class runs to line up for recess, the teacher who makes everyone sit back down and line up again is using simple correction. The teacher who makes everyone sit back down and then practice getting in line several times while reciting the rules for doing it the right way is using positive-practice overcorrection.

> Positive-practice overcorrection of behavior that is autistic-like is sometimes called autism reversal.

To ensure the educative nature intended by this procedure, the practice should be of an alternative appropriate behavior topographically similar to the inappropriate behavior. Azrin and Foxx (1971) used positive-practice procedures in their toilet-training program by artificially increasing the frequency of urinations through offering students large quantities of appealing liquids. This technique increased the opportunity for practice and reinforcement. Azrin and Wesolowski (1975) eliminated floor sprawling by requiring the student to practice sitting on several chairs (one at a time, of course) for an extended time.

Positive-practice overcorrection has been used for these and other inappropriate behaviors such as bruxism (Steuart, 1993), stereotypic behavior (Anderson & Le, 2011; Denny, 1980; Doke & Epstein, 1975; Peters & Thompson, 2013), and aggression (Adams & Kelley, 1992; Luiselli & Rice, 1983). Because stereotypic behavior often serves a sensory function, it is among the most challenging behaviors to reduce. Peters and Thompson (2013) worked with three men, ages 9, 17, and 24, who were diagnosed with autism or other developmental disabilities and engaged in motor stereotypy (e.g., rocking, flapping arms). While playing with toys, if a student exhibited stereotypy, the researcher used physical prompting for the student to appropriately play with the toy. This resulted in reduced stereotypy and increased engagement with the toys.

In addition to reducing challenging behaviors, positive-practice overcorrection has been successful with various academic behaviors (Lenz, Singh, & Hewett, 1991), including oral reading (Singh, 1987), spelling (Stewart & Singh, 1986), and cursive writing (Mabee, 1988). For an example with oral reading, students who made an error were instructed to listen to the teacher read the word correctly while the student pointed to the word in the book. The student then said the word correctly five times and reread the sentence (Singh, 1987). Lenz et al. (1991) suggested that overcorrection procedures used for academic remediation be called "directed rehearsal" because their major components were rehearsal and attention directed to the learning task.

Guidelines for using overcorrection.

Overcorrection procedures should not themselves be allowed to become positively reinforcing. Indeed, a quality of aversiveness is involved in their use. Restitutional or positive-practice overcorrection procedures usually include the following components (Epstein, Doke, Sajwaj, Sorrell, & Rimmer 1974; Rusch & Close, 1976):

1. telling the student she or he behaved inappropriately;
2. stopping the student's ongoing activity;
3. providing systematic verbal instructions for the overcorrection activity in which the student is to engage;
4. forcing the practice of correctional behavior (manually guiding the desired movements, using as much bodily pressure as necessary, but reducing such pressure immediately as the person begins to perform the movement with verbal instruction alone); and
5. returning the student to the ongoing activity.

Before using an overcorrection procedure, teachers should consider the following management concerns:

1. Implementation of overcorrection requires the full attention of the teacher. She must be physically close to the student to ensure that he complies with the overcorrection instruction and be ready to intervene with physical guidance, if necessary.
2. Overcorrection procedures tend to be time consuming, sometimes lasting 5 to 15 minutes and possibly longer (Foxx & Azrin, 1973a; Ollendick & Matson, 1976; Sumner, Meuser, Hsu, & Morales, 1974), though sometimes lasting 30

seconds (Anderson & Le, 2011; Peters & Thompson, 2013). Short-duration implementation may be at least as effective as longer durations in facilitating behavior changes, especially when appropriate alternative behavior is being taught emphasizing the educative rather than punishment potential of the procedure (Carey & Bucher, 1983; Cole, Montgomery, Wilson, & Milan, 2000; Conley & Wolery, 1980).

3. Because physical contact with the student is involved in the use of overcorrection, the teacher should be aware of the possibility of aggression by the student (Carey & Bucher, 1983; Rollings, Baumeister, & Baumeister, 1977) or attempts to escape and avoid the aversive situation.
4. During long periods of overcorrection, the student may become so disruptive that the teacher cannot guide him through the overcorrection procedure (Matson & Stephens, 1977).
5. Because overcorrection often involves physical guidance for extended periods, it may be a very aversive procedure to the adults implementing it (Repp, 1983).
6. In comparing positive practice with and without reinforcing correct responses, Carey and Bucher (1986) found that use without reinforcement "showed no advantages over the reinforced variation, and resulted in a greater incidence of undesirable side effects such as aggression and emotionality" (p. 85).
7. Overcorrection may provide an alternative to aversive consequences in the classroom. It is important to remember that overcorrection procedures, although they have some aversive features, are to be used not as retaliative but as educative tools. The teacher's tone and manner make a difference in the way the procedures will be received by students. A teacher who uses an angry or haranguing tone of voice or unnecessary force when guiding students through overcorrection procedures may increase the probability of resistance. Firmness without aggression is the aim here.

Summary

This chapter reviewed a number of procedures to decrease or eliminate inappropriate or challenging behaviors: differential reinforcement, reinforcement of incompatible behaviors, extinction, punishment, and overcorrection. These procedures are most usefully and constructively viewed as a hierarchy of approaches, from those emphasizing reinforcement to those having aversive features.

We stressed throughout the chapter that procedures to decrease behaviors should be chosen only when the behaviors in question are clearly interfering with a student's ability to learn or are presenting a danger to the student or to other people. Positive reinforcement of appropriate behavior should always be combined with any procedure to decrease or eliminate behavior.

Discussion Questions

For each of the following scenarios, decide what has gone wrong and suggest ways to improve the intervention.

1. Can he sit and work?

    Morse, a student in Mr. Sharpton's special education class, has the opportunity to attend a seventh-grade computer class during the second period each day. The teacher who has agreed to this said that before he can come to her class, Morse, who can barely sit still for 15 minutes, must be able to stay in his seat for 40 consecutive minutes. Mr. Sharpton spoke to Morse about this opportunity and Morse indicated he wanted to be in the class. So Mr. Sharpton told him if he would sit and work for 40 minutes for a whole week in Mr. Sharpton's class, the following week he could be a member of the computer class. Alas, Morse never became a member of the computer class.

2. What, what, what!

    Jade is a question asker. She asks questions all the time. She raises her hand and asks questions, she calls out questions, and she asks her neighbors questions. While question asking is important, and her teacher, Mr. Cihak, does not want to punish it or get rid of it totally, he does want to reduce its occurrence from the current 23 questions per class period. Mr. Cihak decides to reinforce a gradual reduction in Jade's question asking, beginning during his Environmental Science class each day. His plan is to reinforce Jade's asking 20 or fewer questions, then 17 or fewer questions, then 14 or fewer, and so on. He reduces the allowed number of questions by 3 after the third day at each interim criterion. Mr. Cihak and Jade reviewed the first criterion and the contingency attached. The science class progresses and Jade does fine. She does fine the next day, too. The fourth day she asks nine questions in a row at the very end of class. Mr. Cihak, exasperated, scolds her for this. On day 5 he begins to scowl each time Jade asks a question but he answers them. As the days progress, he allows her to ask her questions, he continues to scowl, and the frequency of question asking is unchanged.

3. Six of one, half a dozen of the other.

   Deon is a 7-year-old student with severe intellectual disabilities and autism. He has no standard form of communication. It is believed that his self-injurious behavior, such as face slapping, is a form of communication used to gain adult attention. Each time he slaps his face, his teacher holds his hand and tells him to stop. His teacher and the behavior-management team selected a replacement behavior for gaining teacher attention: grasp a large red chip and raise it in the air. For days the behavior specialist or paraprofessional was at Deon's side to block attempts at face slapping and to redirect his hand to the chips. They used hand-over-hand prompting to help him raise a chip. When he did so, if the teacher noticed the chip, she came over to him and put some of his favorite "slime" in his hands. The team felt good that the teacher was catching him more than 75% of the time, but the data on his face slapping seemed to have plateaued.

4. Around and around ... faster and faster.

   Dave runs around the room often, and he runs with such force that sometimes he runs into the walls and into chairs. Ms. Wyatt's immediate concern is the potential for Dave to run into one of the three students using wheelchairs. She provides Dave with numerous models of appropriate walking behavior. She reinforces walking behavior of other students and ignores Dave's running. His behavior continues and escalates. Later in the morning, Dave finally does knock over an empty wheelchair. Ms. Wyatt yells: "See what you did! What if Joan was in her chair, she would be on the floor and hurt." Dave is startled, but soon resumes his running at an even more frantic pace.

5. Clowning around.

   Bart, the self-proclaimed class clown, makes ongoing comments about each student's reading as they take turns reading orally. It becomes more and more disruptive as students giggle, hiss, and talk back. The teacher sees that scolding Bart is not producing noticeable results. She decides to put the behavior on extinction. But the behavior does not decrease with this strategy, either.

6. I don't want to do that anymore, anymore.

   The hypothesis evolving from a functional assessment is that Calvic engages in self-injurious behaviors to escape tasks with significant motor demands. Ms. Parker decides to redirect Calvic's hand to task materials each time his hand rises above his shoulder. He is reinforced each time he touches the material. After 6 days of this intervention, Calvic's SIB was not decreasing.

7. There are limits.

   Mrs. Clinton has a token economy in her fourth-grade class. Students can both earn points and lose them (response-cost). After 2 weeks, she needs to adjust for the amount of carryover points the students can keep and use. She sets a ceiling on the number of points an individual student can earn in any given week not to exceed 5% in excess of the most "expensive" item on the reinforcer menu. For the next week, students earn points within this new limited number of points available while continuing to lose the usual number of points for misbehavior. By Thursday lunchtime, the students no longer seem to be engaged in their work.

8. Continued, and continued, and continued.

   Ms. Cohen says the following two behaviors will result in a fine: getting out of your seat without permission and calling people names. That afternoon Steve gets out of his seat without permission. Ms. Cohen goes over and asks for three tokens. Ms. Cohen says, "Steve, your being out of your seat will cost you three tokens." Steve says, "I wasn't really out of my seat because it was for a good reason—Ron's money fell and I had to give it to him." "Steve, we did not say there were good and bad reasons for being out of your seat." Steve adds, "Besides, that is too many tokens because I was out of my seat for a good reason and only for just a second." "Steve, I am sure I said that will cost you three tokens. Three tokens now." "I understand you said that. But you need to understand that I really wasn't out of my seat except for a very good reason." This exchange continued, and continued, and continued.

9. Amphibian competition.

   Mr. Morris set up a math competition between the Frogs and the Toads. The two groups earn points for the number of math problems solved correctly. They lose points for grabbing papers and for yelling. Mr. Morris fined the Frogs a point the first time they yelled. He fined them a point again the next time. When the Toads yelled, he fined them 2 points more than the Frogs because they yelled louder. When it occurred again, the Toads lost 3 points and the Frogs lost 1 point. Then the Toads lost an additional point for "grousing" about the point loss. The Toads eventually lost the competition by a considerable margin, mainly because of the very few points earned for completion and accuracy.

10. In the community.

    Mrs. O'Hara has designed a time-out ribbon procedure to use during community-based instruction. Before each session in the community, she and three students review what qualifies as good and bad behaviors and what happens when you engage in a bad behavior: "I will take your sweatband off your wrist, and for the next 5 minutes you cannot earn tokens for dessert." While out in the community, each time someone commits an infraction, she takes the three students' wristbands and does not return them for 5 minutes.

11. The scales of justice.

    At the lunch table, the students in Mr. Brown's class are talking about the token economy in their class. The first Monday morning of each month, Mr. Brown announces the items that will earn or lose points for the month. Then in the afternoon the class discusses and finalizes the rules for the month. During the month of October, they will be getting 1 point for bringing in their homework, 1 point for subject–verb agreements in their paragraph writing each morning, and 1 point for each library book they read. They will lose 2 points for each pencil they sharpen over two a day, 2 points for a dropped piece of paper, and 3 points for whispering to a neighbor. The students say that it seems unfair, but they cannot put their fingers on exactly why.

12. A walk together.

    John is a 6-year-old with autism. He always seems to be in such distress, whining and thrashing his arms around. So when the teacher asks the paraeducator to walk him to the time-out room, she walks with him, talking to him in a soothing manner, and hands him his favorite keys. Three weeks of data indicate no decrease in John's inappropriate behavior.

Chapter 10
Differential Reinforcement: Antecedent Control and Shaping

Learning Outcomes

10.1 Describe two types of antecedent events that may influence behavior.

10.2 Briefly describe the process by which discriminations are formed.

10.3 Define verbal, visual, and physical prompts.

10.4 Define methods of fading prompts.

10.5 Describe the roles of task analysis and chaining in teaching complex behaviors.

10.6 Describe the use of differential reinforcement in shaping.

CHAPTER OUTLINE

Antecedent Influences on Behavior

Differential Reinforcement for Stimulus Control

Principles of Discrimination
   Discrimination Training

Prompts
   Rules as Verbal Prompts
   Instructions as Verbal Prompts
   Hints as Verbal Prompts
   Self-Operated Verbal Prompts
   Visual Prompts

Modeling

Physical Guidance
   Other Tactile Prompts

Fading
   Most-to-Least Prompting
   Graduated Guidance
   Time Delay
   Least-to-Most Prompting

Effectiveness of Methods for Fading Prompts
Effective Prompting

Teaching Complex Behaviors
Task Analysis
Chaining
How to Manage Teaching Chains

Differential Reinforcement for Shaping

Summary

In Chapters 8 and 9 we described some ways to increase appropriate behavior and decrease inappropriate behavior. That solved a number of problems having to do with behavioral deficits and excesses. Not all problems, however, can be solved simply by increasing or decreasing the frequency of behaviors. Many behaviors are defined as appropriate or inappropriate based not on their frequency but on the circumstances under which they occur. Running, for example, may be viewed very differently by the track coach and the teacher with hall duty. What makes running appropriate or not depends not on how often or how fast someone runs but on the circumstances under which someone runs. It is very appropriate to run on the track during practice but very inappropriate to run in the halls of the school. Yelling is perfectly acceptable, even admirable, when the team scores a touchdown but is considered a problem behavior when it occurs in the cafeteria. Many academic skills are acquired when a student learns, for example, to say a word he knows in response to printed letters (we call that reading) or to write a numeral he knows how to write on a worksheet with examples like "2 + 1 =" (we call that math). Bringing responses the learner already knows under the control of the appropriate cue or signal is called *stimulus control.* Many other antecedent influences on behavior must also be considered when implementing behavior-change procedures.

When people learn about reinforcement procedures, they often protest that the behavior they are looking for cannot be reinforced because it never occurs. How can one increase something that does not exist? How does a teacher reinforce talking when a student never talks? sitting when a student never sits? or anything at all when a student appears to do absolutely nothing? One way of teaching students to do new things is by **shaping**. The teacher literally molds or shapes an existing response, however minimal, into the desired behavior.

Stimulus control and shaping are often used together to teach students academic and social behaviors. For that reason, and because both make use of differential reinforcement procedures, they are both described in this chapter. The first part of the chapter describes in detail the phenomenon of stimulus control and stimulus control procedures for use in the classroom.

Antecedent Influences on Behavior

Learning Outcome 10.1 Describe two types of antecedent events that may influence behavior.

In Chapters 8 and 9, when we talked about arranging consequences to increase or decrease behavior, we were concerned with what happens after a behavior is performed—with the effects of behavior on the environment. In this chapter, our concern will be with what happens before the behavior is performed—with the effects of the environment on behavior. We will describe some influences that may be distant in time and space from the behavior we observe as well as those closely associated.

The increasing emphasis on functional assessment and functional analysis and the requirements for positive behavior support (see Chapter 7) have made attention to antecedent conditions of greater interest to teachers and administrators. It is incumbent upon all school personnel to arrange school environments to provide safe, supportive conditions for all students, not merely those whose behavior is considered challenging. It is equally important to identify antecedents that may trigger challenging behavior in any student, but particularly in students with disabilities who are included in general education programs. This can be done in large part by managing antecedent conditions. Schoolwide structure, as well as conditions within individual classrooms, is critical. Many of the procedures described in this chapter can be used to provide that structure.

Applied behavior analysts have traditionally focused on antecedent conditions and events that occur and can be observed immediately before a given behavior. In recent years, there has been an increasing emphasis on examining the influence of conditions and events that exist or occur at times or settings outside the environment being observed (Luiselli & Cameron, 1998). As we discussed in Chapter 7, functional analysis to assess the influences on challenging behaviors must consider such setting events in addition to immediately observable factors. **Setting events** may be environmental (including instructional and physical aspects of the environment and environmental changes), physiological, or social (Bailey, Wolery, & Sugai, 1988; Kazdin, 2000). Setting events may also be manipulated to bring about desired changes in behavior. This may be accomplished by removing or preventing the occurrence of a setting event, reducing the effects of the setting event if it cannot be eliminated entirely, or satiating the student with a reinforcer when she is in a state of deprivation in regard to it (Kennedy & Meyer, 1998). If, for example, a student frequently comes to school cranky from sleep deprivation (physiological setting event) and refuses to work and has tantrums on those days, a conference with parents or other caregivers about an earlier or more consistent bedtime might have excellent results. The reinforcers available for appropriate behavior will be more powerful when the student is not sleep deprived and cranky. Carr, Smith, Giacin, Whelen, and Pancari (2003) provided pain-relieving medication and other palliatives to three women with intellectual disabilities whose challenging behaviors were related to menstrual discomfort. It was impossible to prevent or remove the discomfort entirely, but reducing it resulted in positive changes in behavior. There are numerous examples in Chapter 8 of the use of noncontingent reinforcement. In these interventions, students are provided, at no charge as it were, with large amounts of the reinforcer maintaining a challenging behavior. A student, for example, who avoids tasks and wants only to play games on the computer may be allowed to play on the computer for an extended time before being asked to perform tasks.

Other antecedent manipulations may involve changes to the environment when setting events are known to be in effect. Dadson and Horner (1993), for example, changed classroom expectations for a young woman with severe disabilities who displayed challenging behaviors when she had less than 8 hours of sleep or when her bus was late. They provided extra attention from teachers and paraprofessionals on those days, allowed the student to substitute a preferred activity for one she disliked, and allowed her more opportunities to make choices about the order in which she would do tasks. Her behavior improved significantly. It seems self-evident that teachers who are aware of setting events beyond their control should manipulate those that are within their control. If a teacher is aware that a student is undergoing a family trauma, he can take care to decrease demands and increase the availability of powerful reinforcers. The same kinds of modifications might be made for a student whose medication is being adjusted, whose household size has been significantly increased by the arrival of immigrating relatives, whose placement has or is about to be changed, or who is simply unnerved by the presence of a young lady upon whom he has a crush.

Differential Reinforcement for Stimulus Control

Operant and respondent conditioning are contrasted on pages 17–19.

When describing events that affect operant behavior, it is important to remember the distinction between operant and respondent behavior described in Chapter 1. Respondent conditioning involves stimuli that elicit reflexive behavior—for example, the puff of air (unconditioned stimulus) that results automatically in an eye blink (response). This automaticity is absent in operant behavior; the relationship between antecedent events and behavior is learned rather than reflexive, and we say that antecedent events occasion behavior rather than cause it. Although antecedent events do not elicit operant behavior, they do exert considerable influence over such behavior.

Principles of Discrimination

Learning Outcome 10.2 Briefly describe the process by which discriminations are formed.

Students learn to discriminate as a result of differential reinforcement.

Discrimination is the ability to tell the difference between environmental stimuli and develops as a result of differential reinforcement. Consider a response that results in positive reinforcement (S^{R+}) in the presence of Stimulus X but not in the presence of Stimulus Y. After many experiences with those stimuli and differential reinforcement, the response will occur reliably in the presence of Stimulus X, referred to as the **discriminative stimulus**, or S^D, because in the past, the response has resulted in reinforcement. The response will occur infrequently, if at all, in the presence of Stimulus Y, referred to as the **S-delta**, or S^Δ, because it has not led to reinforcement in the past. The S^D is then said to occasion the response (Holland & Skinner, 1961). This relationship between the S^D and the response is different from that between the unconditioned stimulus and response in respondent conditioning. The S^D does not elicit the response; it just sets the occasion for it, or to use the technical terminology, it **occasions** it or **evokes** it. The response that occurs in the presence of an S^D, but not in its absence, is said to be under stimulus control. A behavior under stimulus control will continue to occur in the presence of the S^D even when reinforcement is infrequent.

The development of discrimination is an important factor in much human learning. A baby learns that saying "mama" is reinforced in the presence of the adult with the glasses and the curly hair, but usually results in the disappearance of the adult with the beard. Glasses and curly hair are an S^D for the response "mama." A beard is an S^Δ for "mama." The first grader learns that saying "went" in the presence of a flash card with the letters *w-e-n-t* (S^D) results in praise, but that the same response to a flash card with the letters *c-a-m-e* (S^Δ) does not. A group of junior high students learns that obscene language and disruptive behavior get their math teacher's (S^D) attention, but that the social studies teacher (S^Δ) attends only to raised hands and completed assignments. "Mama" is the right response to the adult with the curly hair and glasses and the wrong response to the adult with the beard. "Went" is the right response to the flash card with the letters *w-e-n-t* and the wrong response to a flash card with any other set of letters. Obscene language and disruptive behavior are the right way to get the math teacher's attention but not that of the social studies teacher. Many teachers unwittingly make themselves into S^Ds for inappropriate behavior by giving it their attention. O'Donnell (2001) has suggested that a discriminative stimulus for punishment (S^{Dp}) is also a factor in understanding behavior. Anyone who has ever taken a child (or a pet, for that matter) to receive an inoculation can identify a syringe as such a stimulus.

Much of the everyday behavior of adults is a result of discrimination learning. We answer telephones when they ring, not when they are silent. We drive through intersections when lights are green, not when they are red. Discriminations based on relatively informal or imprecise patterns of reinforcement develop slowly and are often imperfect. For example, babies may, for a while, call all men with beards "daddy." First graders may say "went" when they see a flash card with the letters *w-a-n-t* or *w-e-t*. Junior high students may occasionally raise their hands in math class or utter obscenities in social studies class. Adults sometimes pick up the phone when the doorbell rings. The imperfect stimulus control exerted by traffic signals provides employment for numerous police officers, tow-truck drivers, and ambulance attendants but may be made more powerful in several ways, including adding additional information to the basic stimulus. We shall describe such **prompts** later in this chapter.

Discrimination Training

Teaching students to respond appropriately to specific stimuli is the teacher's basic job. As teachers, we want our students to obey rules, follow instructions, and perform specified academic or functional skills at the appropriate time, in the appropriate place, and in response to specified instructions or other cues. A major part of the teaching task is establishing specific times, places, instructions, and other antecedent events as discriminative stimuli for various student behaviors.

SIMPLE DISCRIMINATION When establishing simple discriminations, we want a student to differentiate something—simple instructions, for example. The teacher wants the student to clap when she says, "Clap," and wave when she says, "Wave." If the student claps when the teacher says, "Clap," (S^D for clapping), he receives a reinforcer. If he claps when the teacher says, "Wave," (S^Δ for clapping), no reinforcer is delivered. Reading is the ability to distinguish each combination of letters constituting a word from all other combinations. A student may use the word "went" in conversation but not say "went" when shown a flash card with the letters *w-e-n-t* and asked, "What is this word?" The teacher wants to bring saying "went" under stimulus control of the letters *w-e-n-t*.

> The teacher tells the students what the word is before asking for the discrimination to be made.

In this example, the teacher established the letters *w-e-n-t* as the S^D for the response "went" through the process of differential reinforcement. The response is reinforced in the presence of *w-e-n-t* (S^D) and not in the presence of *g-o* or any other combination of letters (S^Δ). With sufficient repetition, the student should reliably respond correctly and could then be said to have formed a discrimination. Note that *g-o*, which functions as the S^Δ in this example, will be the S^D for responding with "go." The definition, as always, depends on the function. To state with any degree of confidence that the response "went" is under stimulus control, the teacher will have to establish that no other combination of letters occasions the response, including combinations such as *w-a-n-t* and *w-e-t*, whose shape and spelling (topography) closely resemble that of the S^D. The teacher will also want to determine that *w-e-n-t* is a reliable S^D for "went" when it is written in places other than on the original flash card. Students can be taught discriminations using only repeated presentation of S^D and S^Δs with reinforcement for correct responding, but that is a very inefficient teaching method. We will discuss ways to increase teaching efficiency when we describe prompts and errorless learning strategies later in this chapter.

It is important to be sure that students are responding to salient features of the stimulus. One first-grade teacher thought she had finally taught one of her students to read the word "come" only to learn that the real S^D was a smudge on the flash card. Many beginning readers identify words by their first letters alone. This strategy works well as long as "went" is the only word on the word wall that starts with *w*.

When the teacher introduces the word "what," however, the student can no longer discriminate reliably. Students may respond either to some totally irrelevant stimulus, like the smudge on the flash card, or to only one aspect of the stimulus, like the first letter of a word. This tendency toward **stimulus overselectivity** (Dube et al., 2016; Lovaas, Schreibman, Koegel, & Rhen, 1971) is a characteristic of some students with disabilities.

Teachers want students to learn many things that involve multiple simple discriminations. Students must discriminate each letter of the alphabet from all the other letters and from stimuli that do not represent letters of the alphabet. Each numeral must be discriminated from all the others and all other stimuli. Chemistry students must discriminate each element of the periodic table from the others and from stimuli that do not represent elements.

CONCEPT FORMATION   A **concept** is a class of stimuli that have characteristics in common (Becker, Engelmann, & Thomas, 1975a; Layng, 2019). All members of the class should occasion the same response. There are many stimuli properly identified as person, mammal, prime number, honesty, and so forth. Each of these words, and hundreds of thousands of others, represents a class of stimuli having common characteristics, or a concept. In order to learn a concept, a student must discriminate based on specific characteristics common to a large number of stimuli, thus forming an abstraction (Belisle, Stanley, Alholail, Galliford, & Dixon, 2019; Ferster, Culbertson, & Boren, 1975).

Such learning may be accomplished by providing many samples of positive and negative instances of the concept or abstraction and reinforcing correct responses. Using such a procedure, Herrnstein and Loveland (1964) taught pigeons to respond differently to pictures that included people than to pictures that did not. They simply reinforced pecking only on pictures containing people. Basic concepts, those that cannot be fully described with other words (other than synonyms; Engelmann & Carnine, 1982), must be taught in almost the same way to people. Belisle et al. (2019) taught adolescents with developmental disabilities to label the feeling of items as either wet or dry, as well as hard or soft. Because they taught many examples of each, the adolescents applied appropriate labels to untrained items that hadn't been taught yet, demonstrating abstraction.

Try to think of a way to teach a 3-year-old child the concept "red" by describing it. Obviously, it is impossible. What most parents do is provide many examples of red things, label them, and provide strong reinforcement when the child points and says "red" appropriately or when the child responds correctly to the instruction, "Give me the red block." Most children learn thousands of basic concepts in this informal manner before ever entering school. Children who do not must be taught them systematically. For these children, we do not wait for casual opportunities to introduce "red" into conversation. We get some red objects and some not-red objects and proceed to label, instruct, and ask for responses until the student demonstrates mastery of the concept.

Concepts may often be taught more efficiently by using additional antecedent stimuli. If the common elements of a stimulus class can be listed—if the concept can be verbally defined—it may be more efficient to provide a set of rules for identifying instances and then reinforcing correct responses. Concepts that can be verbally defined need not be taught using only differential reinforcement. Most students, unlike pigeons, have some verbal skills that enable a teacher to use sets of rules as shortcuts in teaching them concepts or abstractions.

A related concept that has thus far been primarily investigated in the experimental (using match-to-sample procedures) and theoretical, rather than applied, literature is that of **stimulus equivalence**. Three requirements must be met before equivalence is established. For an example, a person must match a piece of bread to another piece of bread when presented with an array of choices. He must choose the piece of bread when shown the word "bread" and vice versa. If he has been taught to select bread when he hears "bread" and to choose the printed word *bread* when he sees bread, he should choose the printed word *bread* when he hears the word (Devany, Hayes & Nelson, 1986, p. 244). This concept has been used to teach names and identities of historical figures and cartoon characters to children with autism (Tullis, Frampton, Delfs, Greene, & Reed, 2019), religious literacy to middle school children (Ferman, Reeve, Vladescu, Albright, Jennings, & Domaski, 2019), and geography skills with children with autism (Dixon et al., 2017).

Prompts

Learning Outcome 10.3   Define verbal, visual, and physical prompts.

A prompt is an additional stimulus that increases the probability that an S^D will occasion the desired response. Prompts are delivered after the presentation of an S^D that has failed to occasion the response. Most people are familiar with the use of prompts in the theater. An actor who fails to respond to his cues (the preceding lines, for example) is prompted from the wings. The use of the word "prompt" in applied behavior analysis has a similar meaning. Students who fail to respond to S^Ds are prompted. Prompts can be in the form of assistance with a response (response prompts) or by making temporary changes to the stimulus (stimulus prompts). Wolery and Gast (1984) and Cengher, Budd, Farrell, and Fienup (2018) provided thorough reviews of both kinds of prompts as well as suggestions for fading them. Prompts may be presented verbally, visually, or physically. The desired response may also be demonstrated or modeled. The reading teacher who holds up a flash card with the letters *w-e-n-t* and says, "Not came, but …" is providing a verbal prompt. The kindergarten teacher who puts photographs as well as name tags on her students' lockers is providing a visual prompt. The mother who says to her child, "Wave bye-bye to Granny," while vigorously flapping the infant's hand, is furnishing a physical prompt. Each hopes that control will eventually be attached to the S^D "went," the student's name, or "wave bye-bye." The prompt is a crutch to be gradually withdrawn (faded) as soon as the need for it no longer exists. Prompts increase teaching efficiency. Rather than waiting for the student to emit the desired behavior, the teacher uses extra cues to increase the number of correct responses. The more correct responses that occur, the more there are to be reinforced, and the faster the behavior will be learned. When prompting is used, a reinforcer is usually delivered just as if the student had not needed prompting. We shall first describe the use of the various categories of prompts separately and then describe some systems that use several types of prompts at once.

Rules as Verbal Prompts

The English teacher who wants students to identify nouns and verbs correctly will probably not simply give students numerous chances to respond with "noun" or "verb" when they read sentences with the S^D underlined. Because most people have the ability to use verbal rules or definitions to form concepts, the English teacher might define *noun*, then present students with sentences and ask, "Is the underlined word a noun?" (S^D). "Is it the name of a person, place, or thing? Then it's a noun" (prompt). "Right, John, it's a noun" (S^{R+}). Prompting using rules or definitions is not confined to academic tasks. By defining honesty, politeness, kindness, or any other concept related to social behavior, a teacher can prompt students until they can identify instances of each behavior. This, of course, does not ensure that students will engage in the behaviors, merely that they can label them.

It's not easy to give instructions.

Instructions as Verbal Prompts

Instructions are often a means of prompting behavior. If, when the teacher says, "Get ready for reading," the children do not move, the teacher will probably add, "Put your materials away and go to the reading circle." If the S^D does not occasion correct responding, the teacher may provide step-by-step instructions. The teacher who uses instructions as prompts is making two assumptions. The first is that the instructions offered are accurate. It is not easy to give clear verbal instructions for a complex task. If people who ask you for directions to get from one place to another by car usually become hopelessly lost, do not be surprised if students fail to follow your instructions. The second assumption is that the student's behavior is under stimulus control of the general S^D, "Follow instructions." Many students do not follow instructions, as any experienced teacher will attest. Before depending on instructions as prompts, the wise teacher will determine that students do indeed follow them. It may be necessary to bring this response under stimulus control first. Becker et al. (1975a) suggested that teachers reinforce following instructions to the most specific detail. Practice in this skill can be provided by specifying details arbitrarily, such as telling students to line up with their toes on a crack in the floor or to perform activities in a specified order even though no specific order is required. This kind of practice can become a game. The traditional Simon Says game provides practice in following instructions.

Another technique for teaching students to follow instructions more reliably is to issue a series of instructions with which students are likely to comply (high-probability, or high-p, instructions) followed rapidly by an instruction with which they are less likely to comply (low-probability, or low-p, instruction). This has been shown to increase compliance with the low-p instruction. One might say to a group of students, for example, "Touch your head, touch your nose, clap your hands, get out your math books." The behavioral momentum created by compliance to the high-p instructions carries students through the low-p instruction (Bross et al., 2018).

Hints as Verbal Prompts

Many verbal prompts are less elaborate and more informal than rules or instructions. A reading teacher might prompt the correct response to the S^D *dog* by saying, "This is an animal that says 'bow-wow.'" When a teacher tells the class to line up, then adds "Quietly," this too is a prompt. Such reminders or hints increase the probability that the correct response will be emitted, thus supplying an opportunity for reinforcement.

Self-Operated Verbal Prompts

Several studies have demonstrated that recorded verbal prompts can enable students with disabilities to acquire vocational skills (Alberto, Sharpton, Briggs, & Stright, 1986; Briggs et al., 1990; Mitchell, Schuster, Collins, & Gassaway, 2000; Steed & Lutzker, 1997; Taber, Alberto, & Fredrick, 1998). A complex task is broken into its component steps and a teacher records an instruction for each step on audiotape. Students use portable tape players with headphones and are taught to operate the player and to follow instructions. The student is instructed to listen to each step and to turn off the tape to perform it. When the student turns the player back on, the next step is prompted. The student is periodically asked to evaluate her progress and to ask for assistance if necessary. Self-operated recorded prompts have also been used to increase fluency of task performance (Davis, Brady, Williams, & Burta, 1992). Students are allowed to choose music to listen to; the teacher superimposes verbal prompts such as "Keep on working" on the musical selection. A major advantage of this procedure is that it is by no means unusual in many workplaces for employees to wear portable players and earbuds on the job. The apparatus, therefore, does not draw undue attention to workers with disabilities even if the prompts are needed for a long period of time or even permanently (Davis et al., 1992). More recently, audio verbal prompts have been effective with teaching requesting. Szmacinski, DeBar, Sidener, and Sidener (2018) taught students with autism to request items by presenting a broken version of a reinforcer, such as presenting a juice box with a broken straw. When the student encountered a broken straw, the researcher played a pre-recorded verbal prompt of "straw," and then gradually faded the volume of the recording to result in independent requests.

Visual Prompts

Many teaching strategies involve some form of visual prompting. The illustrations in most beginning readers are designed to aid students in identifying the printed word. Teachers may give examples of correctly completed math problems to prompt students. Students may be allowed to use a matrix of multiplication facts when learning complex computational procedures.

A number line may be used when students are learning to add or subtract (Bouck, Satsangi, & Bartlett, 2017). Visual goal markers may be used to improve oral reading fluency (Mason et al., 2016). Richardson et al. (2017) used picture prompts to teach sight words to students with developmental disabilities. In one procedure, they showed a card with the sight word overlaid on the picture and then gradually faded out the picture. In the other procedure, they had the students match pictures to sight words in the context of sight-word instruction. Fienup, Shelvin, and Doepke (2013) first assessed children with autism on recalling their peers' answers to questions, such as "What's your favorite color?" Writing the answers on the board served as visual stimuli that were later faded to increase the children's recall statements.

Picture prompts have been used to help teach a wide variety of behaviors to learners with disabilities, particularly complex daily living and vocational tasks. Kimball, Kinney, Taylor, and Stromer (2003) used Microsoft PowerPoint® to create individual interactive activity schedules for young students with autism. Copeland and Hughes (2000) used picture prompts to teach high school students with severe disabilities to complete vocational tasks. They added a self-monitoring component requiring the students to touch each picture before starting and to turn it over when finished. This increased the students' independent task completion. Spriggs, Gast, and Ayers (2007) taught students with moderate intellectual disabilities to use picture activity schedule books to guide them through multiple activities. Van Laarhoven, Kraus, Karpman, Nizzi, and Valentino (2010) had two adolescents with autism look at a picture book with prompts to engage in the daily living skills of folding clothes and making pasta. The picture prompts were effective, though video prompts were slightly more effective and efficient. Kelley, Test, and Cooke (2013) had young adults with intellectual and developmental disabilities look at pictures on an iPod to guide them in reaching designated locations on a university campus. Many employers use picture prompts to train both disabled and nondisabled workers. Figure 10.1 is a picture prompt like those used to train workers at fast-food restaurants to prepare basic hamburgers and cheeseburgers. Some restaurants now print these prompts directly on the wrappers for the sandwiches. One advantage of picture prompts is that once students have been taught to use them, they can do so independently, just as adults use maps or diagrams to prompt themselves. Many educators, in fact, consider such prompts as examples of self-management of behavior rather than merely as teaching tools (Bulla & Frieder, 2018; Lancioni & O'Reilly, 2001; McDougall et al., 2017).

Picture prompts have been used to teach receptive and expressive language skills to students with autism and other developmental disabilities. When teaching receptive discrimination by displaying an array of pictures and asking to point to one, teachers may prompt by holding up a picture so that the prompted response is essentially matching picture-to-picture (Carp, Peterson, Arkel, Petursdottir, & Ingvarsson, 2012; Vedora & Barry, 2016). When teaching students with disabilities to answer questions,

Verbal Prompts
Pearson eText
Video Example 10.1
In this video, an educator assists students with a math task through verbal prompts. Notice the variety of verbal prompts used—instructions, hints, and direct prompts.

Figure 10.1 Picture prompt for preparing hamburgers

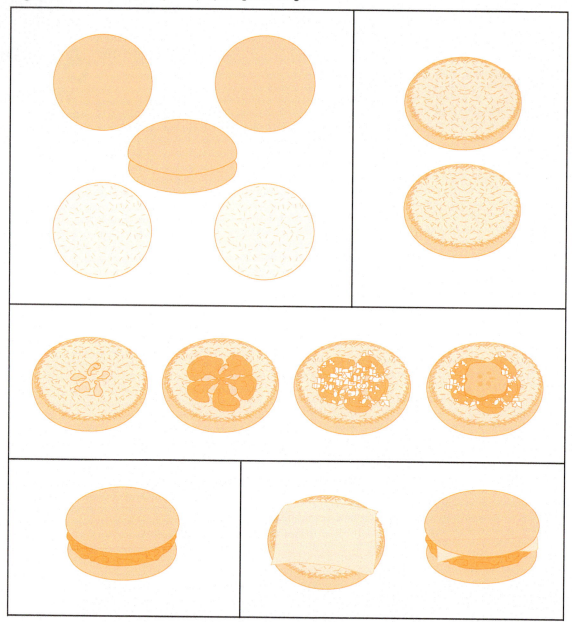

such as "What do you use to call someone?" and "What are some fruits that are green?" the teacher may hold up a picture of a phone or a pear to prompt the answers (Feng, Chou, & Lee, 2017; Wallace, Bechtel, Heatter, & Barry, 2016). Researchers have shown that the type of prompt, such as a picture prompt or a verbal prompt, that will have the most success with teaching question answering is the type with which the student had the most recent experience (Coon & Miguel, 2012; Roncati, Souza, & Miguel, 2019). That is, if a student experiences many sessions of labeling pictures, pictures may be most successful in prompting conversational skills.

Visual prompts can save a lot of teacher time. Bulletin boards in classrooms can easily be used to provide picture prompts. Line drawings or photographs of the correct procedure for accomplishing some task, or a picture of the way desks should look before leaving the room, or a photograph of the class in a nice straight line on the way to the cafeteria posted just inside the doorway could all be used to prompt correct responding.

Other visual prompts are provided in written form. Classroom schedules and rules are often posted to serve as reminders of cues. Many students are easily prompted to do complex new tasks by written instructions. Think of all the tasks you do that depend on written instructions and think of how important it is that the instructions are clear and accurate. Anyone who has tried to assemble children's toys late at night before a holiday can attest to the importance of clarity and accuracy. Of course, written instructions are technically verbal prompts, because the written word is a form of verbal (though not vocal) communication. Because they are processed visually, however, it seems logical to consider them here.

Many children with autism are hyperlexic—an advanced ability to read (Cardoso-Martins, Goncalves, & de Magalhaes, 2013). Recently, researchers have shown that written prompts may be used to teach students with autism to answer questions (Ingvarsson & Le, 2011), ask questions (Shillingsburg, Gayman, & Walton, 2016; Swerdan & Rosales, 2017), and request preferred items using multiple words (Roche et al., 2019). Lopez and Wiskow (2019) presented written prompts on the Apple Watches® of children with autism to prompt social interactions.

Krantz and McClannahan (1993) used a written script to prompt a child with autism to interact with peers. Kate was given a written list of statements and questions relevant to school activities. She was taught (using physical prompts) to pick up a pencil, point to an item, and move the pencil along below the text. She was then physically prompted to face a classmate and instructed to ask the question or issue the statement. The physical guidance was faded first and Kate continued to use the script independently. Even after the script was faded, Kate continued to interact with her peers more frequently. A similar study used a combination of picture prompts and very simple words to increase interaction with adults in young children with autism who had very limited reading skills. The students learned to read "Look" and "Watch me," and cards with these words were interspersed with pictures in their activity schedules. They were prompted to read the words aloud when they appeared, thus asking for adult attention. As any parent knows, that is an extremely typical behavior of young children. The students' verbal interactions with adults increased and spontaneous requests for attention occurred (Krantz & McClannahan, 1998). Davis, Boon, Cihak, and Fore (2010) improved conversational skills of secondary students with Asperger syndrome using "power cards" describing supposed conversational strategies employed by a hero figure chosen by each student. As it is often difficult to transfer skills learned at school to home, Wichnick-Gillis, Vener, and Poulson (2019) used script fading to facilitate this generalization of social initiation skills. Script fading has also been used to teach complex requests (Sellers, Kelley, Higbee, & Wolfe, 2016) and joint attention (Rozenblat, Reeve, Townsend, Reeve, & DeBar, 2019).

Using video clips rather than static pictures has been shown to be effective in teaching functional skills to students with autism spectrum disorders, moderate intellectual disabilities, and persons with severe intellectual disabilities (Bellini & Akullian, 2007; Cihak, Alberto, Taber-Doughty, & Gama, 2006; Cihak, Fahrenkrog, Ayers, & Smith, 2010; Kleeberger & Mirenda, 2010; Van Laarhoven & Van Laarhoven-Myers, 2006; Van Laarhoven, Zurita, Johnson Grider, & Grider, 2009). In addition, scripts may be presented in audio form and then faded to prompt social interactions (Garcia-Albea, Reeve, Brothers, & Reeve, 2014).

Teachers often provide such prompts for themselves as well as for their students. A road map helps the itinerant consulting teacher who is given the S^D "Go to Oakhaven School." Some teachers post reminders to themselves to help them remember to reinforce certain student behaviors. Other adults use prompts as well: handheld computers, calendars, address books, tickler files, and sticky memos often remind us of tasks or information we knew but would not have remembered without a prompt. Teachers may even use a tactile prompt, which is a device similar to a pager worn on the belt that can be set to vibrate after a set amount of time, to increase using praise and token reinforcement in the classroom (McDonald, Reeve, & Sparacio, 2014).

We sometimes forget that procedures like prompting can be of use outside of schools and other traditional teaching environments. Researchers have investigated the use of prompting procedures to increase compliance with S^Ds or instructions in widely varied applications, including adding a light-emitting diode (LED) sign showing eyes looking right and left and a "LOOK BOTH WAYS" legend or other information to traditional stop signs at busy intersections; increased use of seatbelts among senior citizens and college students by adding information to signs; decreasing cell phone use while driving; encouraging saving electricity in a college dorm; and increasing the use of designated drivers by patrons leaving a college bar (Austin, Hackett, Gravina, & Lebbon, 2006; Bekker et al., 2010; Clayton & Helms, 2009; Clayton, Helms, & Simpson, 2006; Cox, Cox, & Cox, 2005; Kazbour & Bailey, 2010; Van Houten & Retting, 2001).

Modeling

"Watch me, I'll show you," says the teacher. This teacher is using yet another kind of prompt. When verbal instructions or visual cues are insufficient, many teachers demonstrate, or model, the desired behavior. In many cases, demonstration may be the procedure of choice from the start. A home economics teacher attempting to tell the class how to thread a sewing machine provides a convincing example of the superiority of demonstration.

Origin of the generalized imitation response.

The majority of students, including those who have mild disabilities, easily imitate the behavior of a model. Many explanations of this phenomenon have been offered (see Bandura, 1969, for a complete discussion), but the simplest is that most students' history of reinforcement includes considerable reinforcement of imitative behavior, resulting in a generalized imitation response. In other words, "Do it like this" has become an S^D for imitation in virtually any setting.

Most individuals reinforced for imitating various responses will eventually also imitate unreinforced responses (Malott, Whaley, & Malott, 1997). Anyone observing a parent interacting with an infant has seen examples of positive reinforcement of imitation. Such reinforcement occurs throughout the preschool years so that most children come to school already accustomed to responding to the S^D "Do it like this" or "Do it like Mary." Of course, children are as likely to imitate inappropriate behavior as appropriate behavior. Many a parent has at some point been startled at how quickly children imitate less admirable parental habits. Students also imitate the behavior of their classmates. Kindergarten students spontaneously play Follow the Leader. Nonacademic behaviors, such as speech patterns, are frequently imitated. It is amazing how quickly a new student with a distinctive regional accent begins to sound exactly like his or her peers. The tendency to imitate peers perhaps reaches its zenith in the secondary school. Adolescents tend to dress alike, talk alike, and engage in the same activities.

Furnishing appropriate models for students with disabilities is one of the primary goals of the current trend toward placement of such students in settings with as many typical students as possible. It is hypothesized that the students with disabilities will imitate and thus learn from their nondisabled peers. This may happen in an informal way but may also be programmed. Brock, Biggs, Carter, Cattey, and Raley (2016) taught paraprofessionals to teach typically developing peers to model, explain, and reinforce the academic and communicative skills of middle school students with severe disabilities. The anecdote on the next page illustrates one example of peer modeling.

In using demonstration techniques to prompt behavior, a teacher may choose to model the behavior personally, to allow another student to be a model, or to bring in someone from outside the group. The choice of a model is important, as certain

> ## Robert Learns to Be a Teenager
>
> Many years ago, before mainstreaming, much less inclusion, was heard of, Robert was a student in Ms. Weinberg's self-contained junior high (it would be middle school today) class for students with severe behavior problems. He was labeled a student with autism and would now be considered "high-functioning." His teachers at the isolated center for students with autism were concerned that Robert had only those students as models and that his behavior was becoming more like theirs every day. It was decided that students with conduct disorders, whose conduct was controlled by a highly structured environment, would be better role models for Robert.
>
> The placement worked out very well and Robert was even able to attend a general education math class almost right away. (Ms. Weinberg didn't know that was inclusion.) One morning Robert walked up to his teacher, extended his middle finger and asked, "Ms. Weinberg, what does this mean?" As Ms. Weinberg was composing herself to answer, two other students hustled Robert away, one of them saying, "You don't ask teachers questions like that!"
>
> Apparently, the other students were appalled by Robert's complete ignorance of all the things typical 13-year-old boys know, and over the course of the next few weeks, they taught him. Ms. Weinberg simply didn't notice.

characteristics increase models' effectiveness. Students are most likely to imitate models who

- are similar to themselves
- are competent
- have prestige (Sulzer-Azaroff & Mayer, 1986)

Video technology has made possible some very promising modeling procedures. With **video modeling**, a teacher shows students a video demonstrating a certain skill, such as play (Ezzeddine, DeBar, Reeve, & Townsend, 2019), social skills (Jones, Lerman, & Lechago, 2014), transitions (McNiff, Maag, & Peterson, 2019), math (Hughes, 2019; Satsangi, Hammer, & Hogan, 2019), toilet training (Lee, Anderson, & Moore, 2014), and vocational skills (Van Laarhoven, Winiarski, Blood, & Chan, 2012). Video self-modeling uses edited video recordings to show students themselves performing skills correctly, such as reading fluency (Edwards & Lambros, 2018), job skills (Goh & Bambara, 2013), writing (Harris, Little, & Akin-Little, 2017), and playing games (Jung & Sainato, 2015). Alternatively, peers may be filmed modeling skills such as pretend play (Sani-Bozkurt & Ozen, 2015) and playing games (Kourassanis, Jones, & Fienup, 2015). It is even possible, through video editing, to show students themselves engaged in behaviors they have never actually performed. Seeing a model that is not just similar to herself, but is herself, who is competent (at least on the video) and who certainly must be prestigious (she's on TV!) has promise for changing a wide variety of social and academic behaviors.

Another variation of video modeling is **video prompting** in which instead of showing a student a whole chain of behaviors and observing if the student demonstrates the chain, the teacher shows a short clip of one step, allows the student to perform that step, then shows a video clip of the next step, and so on. Video prompting has been used to teach daily living skills (e.g., dish washing; Gardner & Wolfe, 2015; Mechling, Ayres, Bryant, & Foster, 2015; Wu, Wheaton, & Cannella-Malone, 2016), vocational skills (e.g., filling an envelope; Cullen, Alber-Morgan, Simmons-Reed, & Izzo, 2017; Seaman-Tullis, Cannella-Malone, & Brock, 2019), and academic skills (Kellem & Edwards, 2016; Knight, Kuntz, & Brown, 2018; Saunders, Spooner, & Ley Davis, 2018).

Modeling may be used to prompt simple or more complex behaviors (Peterson, Rodriguez, & Pawich, 2019). A teacher may use modeling to prompt speech in a student with severe disabilities. A math teacher may ask a competent student to demonstrate a problem on the board before other students are expected to work similar problems

> ### The Students Learn to Polka
>
> Some children with poor gross motor skills were enrolled in an after-school program designed to improve motor coordination. Their teacher decided that because the students had mastered skipping and hopping, they would enjoy learning to polka. "Let's polka!" said the teacher. "Watch what I do. Step-together-step-hop! Now you do it. Step-together-step-hop." Soon, when the teacher said, "Let's polka!" the students produced the desired movement. Many of them, incidentally, continued to whisper "step-together-step-hop" as they danced.
>
> Modeling can be an effective prompting procedure, but it does have limitations. Some behaviors are difficult to imitate. Some students, particularly those who have severe disabilities, have not acquired a generalized imitation response and do not respond to verbal cues. Although it is possible to teach students to respond to modeled prompts by reinforcing imitation, other forms of prompting may be required. Many teaching procedures involve combining various kinds of prompts.

Self-instruction is discussed in Chapter 12.

on their own. A physical education teacher may demonstrate a complex gymnastic performance. Modeling may not be effective alone, but rather when it is combined with rehearsal and/or feedback. For example, Garcia, Dukes, Brady, Scott, and Wilson (2016) combined modeling and rehearsal to teach fire safety to students with autism. Quigley, Griffith, and Kates-McElrath (2018) combined modeling and verbal prompts to increase play skills with students with autism. They also found that when using antecedents, such as models and verbal prompts, the consequences—positive reinforcement—matter. Whereas they started the intervention with independent play responses receiving two edible reinforcers and prompted responses receiving one edible reinforcement, they produced superior results when they provided one edible reinforcer for independent responses and praise for prompted responses. Hunter (1984) described a procedure that combines verbal and physical modeling. She suggested that the teacher first perform the skill while describing the actions involved, then perform the skill while the students provide the verbal prompts, then ask students to perform it while the teacher provides verbal guidance. Students are then asked to perform the skill on their own. There is some evidence that a verbal description of what is being demonstrated makes modeling more effective (Hay, Murray, Cecire, & Nash, 1985; Hunter, 1984). Most of us can intuitively confirm that statement by remembering a high school or college mathematics instructor who demonstrated highly involved proofs or algorithms on the board while saying not a word, then turned to the class and asked, "Everyone got that?" The anecdote at the top of the page illustrates a procedure combining modeling with verbal instructions.

Physical Guidance

The teacher puts her hand on the student's hand and pulls it up.

When students fail to respond to less stringent forms of prompting, they may be physically prompted. Physical prompting may be a first step in the development of a generalized imitation response. Streifel and Wetherby (1973) taught a student with severe intellectual disabilities to follow instructions, such as "Raise your hand," by using a physical guidance procedure. The teacher first gave the verbal instruction, then guided the student so that the instruction was followed. Eventually, the student's behavior was under the control of the instructions. The implications of bringing the behavior of students with severe disabilities under stimulus control of imitation and instructions are enormous. Students who will imitate a model and follow instructions can be taught many things. Researchers have also used physical prompts to teach toy construction (Blair, Weiss, & Ahearn, 2018; McKay, Weiss, Dickson, & Ahearn, 2014; Seaver & Bourret, 2014), answering questions using an iPad as a speech-generating device (Lorah, Karnes, & Speight, 2015), and folding clothes (Sabielny & Cannella-Malone, 2014).

Physical guidance procedures are by no means limited to use with students with disabilities. Most teachers routinely use such procedures when teaching beginning handwriting skills, for example. Music teachers may guide their students' fingering. Many athletic skills are most easily taught using physical guidance. It is difficult to imagine any other way of teaching anyone to change gears in a car with a four-speed manual transmission. When using physical guidance, teachers need to be sure that the student is cooperative. Such a procedure will be unpleasant (possibly to both parties) if it is performed with a resisting student. Even cooperative students may have a tendency to tighten up when physically prompted.

Other Tactile Prompts

Advances in technology have made it possible to prompt students using paging devices more commonly used by very busy and important people who are considerate enough to turn them to "vibrate" when in public. Researchers have used a pager that can be activated by remote control (Shabani et al., 2002) or one that can be preset to activate at specified intervals (Taylor & Levin, 1998) to prompt students with autism to initiate interaction with peers (Tzanakaki et al., 2014). Taylor, Hughes, Richard, Hoch, and Coello (2004) used a pager to prompt a student to seek adult assistance when lost. The teacher and parent went out of sight, waited a short while, and activated the pager. The student was to hand a communication card to a community member. Tactile prompts have also been used to increase the on-task behavior of students in classrooms (Boswell, Knight, & Spriggs, 2013; Moore, Anderson, Glassenbury, Lang, & Didden, 2013; Rafferty, 2012).

Individualizing Prompts
Pearson eText
Video Example 10.2
In this video, notice both the various prompts used by the peer buddy to help Katrina and the types of prompts used by the teacher to help the peer buddy. How are the prompting approaches individualized to the students?

Fading

Learning Outcome 10.4 Define methods of fading prompts.

A prompted response is not under stimulus control. Prompts must be withdrawn, and the response must be occasioned by the S^D alone. Too-abrupt removal of prompts, however, may result in termination of the desired behavior. Gradual removal of prompts is referred to as **fading**. Any prompt may be gradually faded so that the response occurs and is reinforced when the S^D alone is presented. Considerable skill is involved in determining the optimum rate of fading: too fast, and the behavior will not occur frequently enough for reinforcement to be effective; too slow, and students may become permanently dependent on the prompt. Prompts can be faded in a number of different ways, such as using most-to-least prompting, graduated guidance, time delay, and least-to-most prompting (Cengher, Budd, Farrell, & Fienup, 2018).

Most-to-Least Prompting

When using most-to-least prompting for fading prompts, the teacher begins with a level of prompting that virtually assures that the student will produce the appropriate response. The amount of assistance is then systematically reduced as the student becomes more competent. This procedure can be used to fade a wide variety of prompts. The English teacher using rules to help her students identify nouns might start with the S^D "Is this a noun?" and the prompt "If it's the name of a person, place, or thing, it's a noun." When her students respond reliably, she might say:

> Is this a noun? (S^D)
> Is it the name of a person, place, or thing? (prompt)
> then
> Is this a noun? (S^D)
> Remember, person, place, or thing. (prompt)

then
Is this a noun? (S^D)
Remember your rule. (prompt)
and finally
Is this a noun? (S^D, no prompt)

A math teacher may use most-to-least prompting to fade a visual prompt by providing students with a complete multiplication matrix to help them work problems and systematically removing easier combinations as they are mastered. A reading teacher working with students with learning disabilities may embed questions to guide reading comprehension and then systematically remove those questions to generate self-questions (Rouse, Alber-Morgan, Cullen, & Sawyer, 2014). A teacher working on communication skills with students with autism may fade from a full verbal model (e.g., "car") to a verbal choice of answers (e.g., "car, horse, or plane?") to no prompt when teaching picture labeling (Leaf et al., 2016). The "Children Learn to Hula Hoop" anecdote at the bottom of the page illustrates such a fading procedure.

Most-to-least prompting may also be used when combinations of prompts are used. If teachers initially provide students learning a new math skill with a demonstration, a sample problem, and step-by-step instructions, these three different kinds of prompts may be removed one by one until the students are responding simply to the incomplete example.

> Stimulus shaping should not be confused with the shaping procedures described later in this chapter.

The most refined form of most-to-least prompting results in virtually **errorless learning** (Mueller, Palkovic, & Maynard, 2007). Many procedures termed *errorless learning* use alterations within the stimuli (S^Ds or S^Δs) to prompt correct responses. These prompts are often called **stimulus prompts**, and the procedure itself is sometimes called stimulus shaping. To enable students to make a discrimination more easily, some features of the S^D, the S^Δ, or both are changed. Malott et al. (1997) described a procedure by which Jimmy, a student with developmental delay, learned to discriminate his name from another by pasting the name *Susan* in white letters on a black card and the name *Jimmy* in white letters on a white background. Reinforcing the choice of *Jimmy* established the correct card as the S^D. The background color on the *Jimmy* card was gradually darkened until both names were printed in white on black. The student made no incorrect choices and eventually made the discrimination based on the relevant stimulus properties.

Another example was described by Ayllon (1977). A teacher was trying to teach a group of young children to discriminate their right from their left hands. On the first day of training, each child's right hand was labeled with an x made by a felt-tipped marker. This enabled the students to discriminate the S^D (right hand) from the S^Δ (left hand)

The Children Learn to Hula Hoop

Coach Townsend was an elementary school physical education teacher. He decided to teach the first graders to hula hoop so they could perform at open house. He began by demonstrating. "Watch me!" he said, and proceeded to show the students how to do it. When the giggles died down, he handed each first grader a hula hoop. "Ready," he said, "hoop!" Twenty-six hoops hit the floor clattering and banging. The children looked discouraged. The coach took a hoop from one student. "Okay," he said, "start it like this." He pushed his hoop with his hands. "Now do this." He rotated his hips. When the giggles died down, he said, "Again, just like this!" Coach Townsend gave the hoop back to the student and just demonstrated the movements. He eventually faded the hand movement to a flick of the wrist and the hip movements to a mere twitch. Before long, the cry "Ready, hoop!" was enough.

The great day finally arrived. Twenty-six first graders equipped with hula hoops stood in the gym. Their parents sat in the bleachers. Coach Townsend started the music and said, "Ready, hoop!" He stood to one side of the group. The children did him great credit, but he heard suppressed giggling from the audience. The coach finally realized that, in his enthusiasm, he had gone back to modeling the necessary hip movements.

when asked to raise their right hands. On the second day, the plan was again to mark right hands, but because of the permanence of the marker (or the personal hygiene of the children), each child still had a visible mark. As the training proceeded during the week, each child's mark gradually faded, and by week's end, each child consistently raised the right hand when asked. Yorlets, Maguire, King, and Breault (2018) used a similar procedure to teach a child with autism to match pictures and printed words to spoken words and manual signs by first bolding the font of the correct pictures and gradually fading the boldness of the fonts. Touissaint, Scheithauer, Tiger, and Saunders (2017) taught children with visual impairments to discriminate Braille characters by first having very different characters, such as one having five dots and the other having one dot, and then gradually increasing the similarity between the characters to discriminate.

Evidence indicates that errorless learning is most efficient if the features of only the S^D are altered and the S^Δ is held constant (Mueller et al., 2007). Although it is possible to provide for learning without errors with other prompting systems, the technical term *errorless learning* is most often used when systematic alteration of the discriminative stimulus is the primary form of prompting.

Fading for errorless learning provides for development of stimulus control without practicing incorrect responses and without occasioning inappropriate behavior that some students display when they make errors (Dunlap & Kern, 1996; Munk & Repp, 1994). Providing a completely error-free learning environment, however, may not always be desirable. Spooner and Spooner (1984) suggested that optimal learning may occur when initially high error rates decrease quickly and correct responding accelerates rapidly. Terrace (1966) pointed out that a lack of frustration tolerance may result from errorless training. In the real world, some errors are inevitable, and students must learn to handle mistakes. Krumboltz and Krumboltz (1972) suggested gradually programming students to persist after errors. Rodewald (1979) suggested that intermittent reinforcement during training may mitigate the possible negative effects of errorless learning. Such intermittent reinforcement may help develop a tolerance for nonreinforcement of responses.

Graduated Guidance

Graduated guidance is used in fading physical prompts. The teacher begins with as much physical assistance as necessary and gradually reduces pressure. The focus of the guidance may be moved from the part of the body concerned (spatial fading), or a shadowing procedure may be substituted in which the teacher's hand does not touch the student but follows his movement throughout the performance of the behavior (Foxx & Azrin, 1973a). Graduated guidance has been used to teach spoon use to students with severe disabilities and visual impairment (Ivy, Hatton, & Wehby, 2018), matching pictures and words using an iPad with a student with autism spectrum disorder (van der Meer et al., 2015), and play skills with students with autism (Akmanoglu, Yanardag, & Batu, 2014). O'Hara and Hall (2014) used a visual schedule and graduated guidance to teach children with autism to engage with playground equipment during recess by fading prompts from hand-over-hand prompts to wrist prompts, elbow prompts, shoulder prompts, and finally "shadow" prompts (i.e., guiding but not touching the student).

Juan learns by a graduated guidance procedure in the vignette on the next page.

Time Delay

Time delay differs from other fading formats in that the form of the prompt itself is not changed, just its timing. Rather than presenting the prompt immediately, the teacher waits, thus allowing the student to respond before prompting. Delays are usually only a few seconds. Time delays can be constant (the delay remains the same length)

Juan Learns to Eat with a Spoon

Juan was a student with severe intellectual disabilities. His teacher, Ms. Baker, believed that he could eat lunch with his typical peers if he could learn to use a spoon instead of his fingers for eating. She equipped herself with a bowl of vanilla pudding and a spoon, hoping that the pudding, which Juan loved, would be a positive reinforcer for using the spoon and that vanilla would make a less visible mess than chocolate on Juan, herself, the table, and the floor. (Teachers have to think of everything!) Ms. Baker sat next to Juan, put her hand over his right hand, and guided it to the spoon. She helped him scoop up some pudding and guided his hand toward his mouth. When the spoon reached his mouth, he eagerly ate the pudding. Ms. Baker then removed Juan's left hand from the pudding dish and wiped it off with the damp cloth that she had thoughtfully provided. She repeated this procedure a number of times, praising and patting Juan whenever the spoon reached its goal. As she felt Juan making more of the necessary movements on his own, she gradually reduced the pressure of her hand until it was merely resting on Juan's. She then moved her hand away from his—to his wrist, to his elbow, and finally to his shoulder. Eventually, she removed her hand entirely. Juan was using the spoon on his own.

or progressive (the interval before the prompt becomes longer as the student gains competence). Time delay procedures can also be used with a variety of prompting formats. Many teachers use them instinctively. Let's go back to our English teacher. She asks, "Is this a noun?" and waits a few seconds. Finding no response forthcoming, she prompts, "If it's the name of a person, place, or thing, it's a noun." Textbooks and articles about teaching often include a discussion of wait time (Kauchak & Eggen, 1998; Wasik & Hindman, 2018), encouraging teachers to give students up to 3 seconds to answer before providing assistance or calling on another student.

Time delay can also be used to fade visual prompts. A teacher working on sight vocabulary might cover up the picture on the flash card and wait a few seconds to allow students to identify the word without seeing the picture. If they fail to respond within the latency the teacher has established, the picture is uncovered. Stevens and Schuster (1987) used a similar procedure to teach 15 spelling words to a student with learning disabilities.

Coleman, Hurley, and Cihak (2012) taught sight words to students with moderate intellectual disability. The instructor presented a sight word card, asked, "What is it?," immediately modeled the correct response (e.g., "pour"), and asked "What is it?" again. Subsequently, the teacher presented the card, asked "What is it?" and waited 4 seconds, during which the student labeled the picture, or after which the teacher modeled the answer. Coleman et al. also showed this could be implemented using computer-assisted instruction.

Oliveira, Font-Roura, Dalmau, and Giné (2018) taught the initial sounds of words to a student with autism. The goal was to show three printed words and ask the student to point to the word that started with a certain sound (e.g., "Point to the word that starts with ssss"). In the first session, there was a 0-second time delay; that is, the teacher presented three cards, gave the instruction, and immediately pointed to the correct answer. When the student pointed, the teacher provided praise. After that initial session, the teacher waited 5 seconds. If the student responded correctly within the 5 seconds, she was praised; if not, she was prompted.

Ackerlund Brandt, Weinkauf, Zeug, and Klatt (2016) used a similar procedure to teach a variety of academic and language skills (e.g., addition, matching, labeling) to students with autism. In the first teaching session, they used a 0-second time delay by delivering an immediate prompt (e.g., "What is this? Say 'dog;'" p. 60). In subsequent sessions, the instructor waited 4 seconds and delivered praise and an edible reinforcer given a response within 4 seconds and a prompt if an incorrect response or no response after 4 seconds. Starting with a 0-second delay and gradually increasing the delay is a form of errorless teaching. When Morgenstern, Causin, and Weinlein (2019) started with a 0-second time delay to teach pronouns to students with autism, they termed their procedure "errorless teaching."

SIMULTANEOUS PROMPTING PROCEDURES An exception to the statement that prompts are delivered when students do not respond to an S^D occurs when teachers use a **simultaneous prompting**. When using this form of response prompting, the S^D is presented, the teacher immediately provides a controlling prompt (one that ensures the correct response, often the correct response itself), and the students immediately provide the correct response (Morse & Schuster, 2004; Tekin-Iftar, Olcay-Gul, & Collins, 2019; Waugh, Alberto, & Fredrick, 2011). This is as if one is using a time delay prompt with no delay at all. Simultaneous prompting is an errorless teaching procedure because students do not have the opportunity to make errors. An obvious question is "How does the teacher know the students are learning anything?" To answer that question the teacher conducts test trials or **probes** immediately before each instructional session to test students' mastery of targeted skills previously taught.

This procedure has been used successfully with children with autism and those with mild and moderate intellectual disabilities. For example, Ramirez, Cengher, and Fienup (2014) taught three adolescents with autism to calculate elapsed time in the form of math problems (e.g., "4:45 – 3:30 = __") or word problems (e.g., "The movie starts at 2:45 PM. The movie ends at 4:10 PM. How long is the movie?" p. 766). The simultaneous prompting was the instructor modeling a step (e.g., writing the problem as a vertical subtraction problem) and having the student complete that step. This was repeated for all steps of the task analysis.

With fifth-grade students with emotional behavioral disorder or attention deficit hyperactivity disorder, Hudson, Hinkson-Lee, and Collins (2013) probed students on writing a paragraph on a certain topic using verbal prompts (e.g., "Show me the first step in writing the paragraph," "Show me what comes next in writing a paragraph," p. 148). The simultaneous prompting procedure was the same, except the instructor modeled each step before asking the students to complete it. In her modeling, the instructor also embedded writing instructions, such as instructions about capitalization and punctuation.

Collins, Terrell, and Test (2017) taught adolescents with mild intellectual disabilities the employment skill of taking care of plants in a greenhouse. The probe was standing in the greenhouse and asking, "What do you do to take care of the plant?" (p. 40). Simultaneous prompting consisted of the instructor asking, "What's the first thing you do to take care of a plant?" and stating the first step. When the student completed the first step, the instructor provided praise. The instructor taught the subsequent steps in this manner. The students mastered the task analysis of plant care and learned additional science content about photosynthesis.

When simultaneous prompting has been compared to other prompting procedures, the results have not been strikingly different (Brandt et al., 2016; Seward, Schuster, Ault, Collins, & Hall, 2014; Swain, Lane, & Gast, 2015). In extensive reviews of the literature, Morse and Schuster (2004) and Waugh et al. (2010) pointed out that in addition to other benefits, teachers prefer the procedure to other prompting procedures, and it can easily be implemented by peer tutors or paraprofessionals working with individuals with disabilities in inclusive settings.

Least-to-Most Prompting

Least-to-most prompting can be considered the opposite of most-to-least prompting. When using this procedure, the teacher starts with the S^D, moves to the least intrusive prompt in her repertoire, and gives students an opportunity to respond. Many teachers use least-to-most prompting without being aware of the terminology. The English teacher says, "Is it a noun?" and gets no response. She prompts, "Remember your rule," and gets no response. She says, "Remember, person, place, or thing," and gets no response. She prompts "Is it the name of a person, place, or thing?" and gets no response. She whimpers, "If it's the name of a person, place, or thing, then it's a noun." It is sometimes difficult to implement least-to-most prompting without sounding either strident or whiny.

Least-to-most prompting can be used to fade visual prompts. A beginning reading teacher using a set of flash cards might first show a card with just the word *boy* and then a card with a stick figure, finally moving to a card with a representational drawing of a boy. To use the procedure with modeling, one could first provide a gesture and move toward a full demonstration. To use least-to-most prompting with physical guidance, one would also start with a gesture and then move toward a full putting-through procedure.

Researchers have demonstrated the effectiveness of least-to-most prompting for teaching a variety of skills. For example, Davis-Temple, Jung, and Sainato (2014) used least-to-most prompting to teach young children with a variety of special needs to play board games with peers. Here were the steps of the least-to-most prompting:

> These prompts included (a) an indirect verbal prompt (for example, "What are you supposed to do?" or "Where are you supposed to move your piece?"), (b) a direct verbal prompt (for example, "put your piece on the yellow space"), (c) a gestural prompt or model (for example, pointing to the space), and (d) a physical prompt (for example, the experimenter places her hand on the child's and together they select the playing piece and move it to the colored space). For each step, the experimenter presented the material and waited 5 seconds for a response. If no response occurred or an error occurred, the prompts from the least to most intrusive were provided. (p. 25)

Hudson, Browder, and Jimenez (2014) taught reading comprehension of science texts to students with moderate intellectual disabilities. Typical peers delivered the least-to-most prompting hierarchy consisting of: "(a) read the text again; (b) read the sentence that contained correct answer again; (c) said the correct answer; and (d) said and pointed to the correct response option on the response board" (p. 68).

Gil, Bennett, and Barbetta (2019) used least-to-most prompting to teach young adults with moderate intellectual disabilities to shop at a grocery store. They created a task analysis (see below) for the steps of grocery shopping and displayed the grocery list on an iPad on the cart. The prompt hierarchy was verbal, gestural, partial physical, and full physical. The prompt was increased if the students performed a step incorrectly, took more than 10 seconds to start a step, or took more than 3 minutes to find an item.

Least-to-Most Prompts
Pearson eText
Video Example 10.3
In this video, the educator uses least-to-most prompting to assist a student in requesting a desired item. What characteristics of least-to-most prompting do you notice?

Effectiveness of Methods for Fading Prompts

Amongst the different fading methods, no method is superior to the others. Libby, Weiss, Bancroft, and Ahearn (2008) compared most-to-least and least-to-most prompting for teaching five children with autism to build Lego structures. Most-to-least prompting was effective for all the children, whereas least-to-most prompting was effective for only three children. However, for those three children, least-to-most prompting was more efficient than most-to-least prompting. On the other hand, least-to-most prompting resulted in more errors, which are known to slow learning and evoke challenging behavior. A potential guideline that comes out of the research on the different fading methods is that for students with moderate-to-severe disabilities, it is probably best to start teaching a new skill using an errorless procedure, such as most-to-least prompting, simultaneous prompting, or progressive time delay starting with a 0-second delay. Once these students show proficiency with new skills, least-to-most prompting is a good strategy for continually assessing and strengthening the skills. Students with mild disabilities or typically developing students may benefit from least-to-most prompting from the start of teaching.

Summary Chart for Fading Prompts

Least-to-most prompting: Start with the least intrusive prompt, then provide more intrusive prompts if necessary.

Graduated Guidance: Reduce full physical guidance to "shadowing" (following movement but not touching the student), a light touch at a distance from the part of the body performing the behavior.

Time Delay: May be constant or progressive. Wait several seconds before prompting to allow the student to respond.

Most-to-least prompting: Start with the most powerful prompt available. When the target behavior occurs reliably, move to the next less intrusive prompt.

Procedures for establishing and maintaining stimulus control are powerful tools. Once all prompts have been withdrawn and behaviors are under stimulus control, they will continue to occur, sometimes for years, without any reinforcement except that naturally available in the environment, and even when the person knows no reinforcement will be forthcoming. Have you ever sat at a red light at 3 a.m. at a deserted intersection and waited for the light to change? If you have, you have some idea of the power of stimulus control.

It appears that stimulus control procedures have great promise in facilitating not only the acquisition of behaviors but also their generalization and maintenance. Stimulus control has recently emerged as one of the most powerful potential tools for programming for generalization—ensuring that the skills acquired by students are performed in settings other than that in which they were taught and that the skills will continue to be performed long after the original programmer is gone. Generalization and maintenance, and their relationship with stimulus control, are discussed at length in Chapter 11.

Effective Prompting

To make the most effective use of prompts, teachers need to attend to the following guidelines:

> Guidelines for using prompts.

1. Prompts should focus students' attention on the S^D, not distract from it. Prompts that are spatially or otherwise distant from the stimulus may be ineffective (Schreibman, 1975). Cheney and Stein (1974) pointed out that using prompts unrelated to the stimulus may be less effective than using no prompts or trial-and-error learning. The well-meaning teacher who encourages beginning readers to use the illustrations in the preprimer as clues to the words on the page may find that overemphasis on such prompts may result in some children's developing an overdependence on the illustrations at the expense of the written word. For some students, such dependence may be so well developed as to require the use of reading materials without illustrations in order to focus attention on the relevant S^D.

2. Prompts should be as weak as possible. The use of strong prompts when weak ones will do is inefficient and may delay the development of stimulus control. The best prompt is the weakest one that will result in the desired behavior. Strong prompts are often intrusive. They intrude on the environmental antecedent, the S^D, and drastically change the circumstances or conditions under which the response is to be performed. Every effort should be made to use the least intrusive prompt possible. Visual and verbal prompts are, on the whole, less intrusive than modeling, and all are less intrusive than physical guidance. This may not always be the case. A gentle push on the hand to help a young child slide in a recalcitrant puzzle piece is probably less intrusive than yelling "Push it the other way." Inefficiency is not the only undesirable effect of prompts that are stronger than necessary. Many students react negatively to strong or unnecessary prompts (Heal & Hanley, 2011). When students say "Don't give me a hint. I'll figure it out myself!," the wise teacher listens.

3. Prompts should be faded as rapidly as possible. Continuing to prompt longer than necessary may result in failure of the S^D to acquire control. The efficient teacher uses prompts only as long as necessary and fades them quickly, thus avoiding students' becoming dependent on prompts rather than S^Ds. Students who are allowed to use a matrix of multiplication facts for extended periods may never learn their multiplication facts. Perhaps the most rapid way to fade prompts is within a session (Barbera & Kubina, 2005).
4. Unplanned prompts should be avoided. Anyone who has observed a large number of teachers has seen students watch the teacher carefully for clues to the correct answer. A teacher may be completely unaware that students are being prompted by a facial expression or vocal inflection. Neither is an inappropriate prompt when used intentionally. But the teacher who asks, while shaking her head, "Did Johnny really want to go to the park in the story?" in such a tone that all the children answer "no" is fooling herself if she thinks that the students necessarily comprehended what they read.

Teaching Complex Behaviors

Learning Outcome 10.5 Describe the roles of task analysis and chaining in teaching complex behaviors.

So far we have discussed bringing behavior under stimulus control as if all behaviors consisted of simple, discrete actions that may be occasioned by a discriminative stimulus, prompted if necessary, and reinforced. Much of what we want students to learn involves many such discrete behaviors, to be performed in sequence on presentation of the S^D. Most functional, academic, and social skills are of this complex nature. Before even considering teaching such sequences of behaviors, the exact nature of the complex task must be analyzed.

Task Analysis

> To task analyze, pinpoint the terminal behavior and list necessary prerequisite skills and component skills in sequence.

The most exacting task facing the teacher who wants students to acquire complex behavioral chains is determining exactly what steps, links, or components must be included and their sequence. Breaking complex behavior into its component parts is called task analysis. **Task analysis** forms the basis of many of the teaching strategies used to teach individuals with disabilities to perform complex behaviors and sequences of behaviors. Before the teacher can select instructions, cues, prompts, or other teaching tools, he must decide exactly what he is teaching and break the task down into manageable components. Tasks with many steps or components may be divided into phases for teaching purposes. DeQuinzio, Townsend, and Poulson (2008), for example, broke the skill of sharing into three steps: "(a) hold-up a toy and say, 'Look at this,' (b) walk a distance to another person, hand it to him or her and say, 'Here, you try it,' and (c) then say, 'Let's play together.'" (p. 266).

Task analysis requires considerable practice but can be applied to behaviors ranging from eating with a spoon (Rubio, Pichardo, & Borrero, 2018), to shopping for groceries (Morse & Schuster, 2000), to writing your name (Moore et al., 2013). It is perhaps easier, in general, to analyze motor tasks than those related to academic and social behaviors, but the analysis is equally important for teaching all complex behaviors. Many academic skills include steps that are not directly observable. The first step of solving a two-digit into three-digit long division problem might be listed as:

1. Write the number of times the divisor can be subtracted from the first two or all three digits of the dividend.

Clearly, there are some questions the student must answer before she can perform it. Can the divisor be subtracted from the first two digits? If it can, how many times? If it can't, what do I do? How many times can it be subtracted from all three digits? Obviously, the student's performance can be evaluated by looking at the behavior listed in step 1, but consideration must be given to what must happen first. Carter and Kemp (1996) suggest initially using a two-step task analysis for tasks such as this, initially including the nonobservable components, and creating ways to make them observable—for example, asking a student who is doing the long division problem to vocalize the otherwise hidden steps.

Teachers and researchers originally used task analysis to break basic skills into small steps in order to teach them—one step at a time—to learners with severe and profound disabilities. It proved such a valuable tool that it has been used not only for this population but to help teachers of all kinds of students to analyze all kinds of tasks.

To acquire a general idea of what is involved in task analysis, take a simple task, such as putting on a jacket, and list its component parts in the correct sequence. Then read your steps, in order, to a tolerant friend while she or he does exactly what you have written. Don't worry; you'll do better next time. One of the authors assigns this task as part of a midterm exam. Failing grades are given only to task analyses that result in feet being placed through armholes.

Task analysis is the basis for programs teaching complex functional and vocational skills to people who have severe and profound disabilities. It is theoretically possible, by breaking a task into sufficiently small components, to teach anybody anything. Time limitations make it impractical to teach some students some things. Nevertheless, the technology exists. Teachers can even teach students to perform behaviors that those teachers cannot perform, so long as the teachers can recognize and reinforce the terminal behavior and its components. One is reminded of the middle-aged, overweight gymnastics coach cheering on his adolescent charges as they perform incredible feats of agility—feats that he has taught them but that it is laughable to picture him performing.

Moyer and Dardig (1978) provided a basic framework for analyzing tasks. The first step is always to determine what skills or concepts the learner must already have in order to learn the task at hand. These are known as the prerequisites for learning the skill. Anyone who has tried to teach a child who does not know how to hold a pencil to print her letters, or a child who does not know basic multiplication facts to find the least common multiple, is aware of the folly of these endeavors. When analyzing any new task, it is important to ask, "What does the learner already need to know in order to learn this?" If more teachers asked themselves that simple question before beginning a lesson, fewer children would be chronic failures in school. Although it is wise to attempt to list prerequisite skills before beginning a task analysis, many teachers find that one of the most valuable aspects of the analysis itself is that additional prerequisites are identified as they go through the process.

Before analyzing the task, the teacher also lists any materials that will be required to perform it. Again, others may show up as necessary as the analysis progresses. Finally, the analyst must list all the components of the task in the order in which they must be performed. Although it is possible to do this simply from experience, many people find that watching someone competent (a master of the skill) perform the task (Moyer & Dardig, 1978) is helpful. It may be valuable to ask the "master" to list the steps verbally as he performs them.

Shrestha, Anderson, and Moore (2013) wrote a task analysis to teach a 4-year-old child with autism to make a bowl of cereal. Table 10.1 shows the task analysis Shrestha et al. used to teach this skill.

Table 10.1 Example of a task analysis for making and eating a bowl of cereal and cleaning up afterwards

	Steps	Phases
1)	Get a bowl from the drawer	Phase 1
2)	Get a spoon from the drawer	Phase 1
3)	Get Weetbix from the cupboard	Phase 1
4)	Get soy milk from the fridge	Phase 1
5)	Put two Weetbix in the bowl	Phase 2
6)	Open the lid of the milk bottle	Phase 2
7)	Pour some milk in the bowl just enough so the Weetbix can still be seen	Phase 2
8)	Close the lid of the milk bottle	Phase 2
9)	Break the Weetbix up	Phase 2
10)	Eat	Phase 2
11)	Take the bowl over to the sink	Phase 3
12)	Put the Weetbix back in the cupboard	Phase 3
13)	Put the milk back in the fridge	Phase 3

NOTE: From Shrestha, A., Anderson, A., & Moore, D. W. (2013). Using point-of-view video modeling and forward chaining to teach a functional self-help skill to a child with autism. *Journal of Behavioral Education, 22*(2), 157–167. https://doi-org.ezproxy.simmons.edu/10.1007/s10864-012-9165-x

The following anecdote illustrates the derivation of a task analysis by "watching a master perform" and asking him to list the steps.

We suggest that you begin acquiring the skill of task analysis by breaking down simple motor tasks into their prerequisites and components. A number of examples

Ms. Cadwallader Analyzes a Task

The consultant from Computer Services stood in Ms. Cadwallader's office waiting to get her attention. "Excuse, me, er, Ma'am," he said diffidently. "I'm here to install your new computer."

"Yes, indeed," answered Ms. Cadwallader cheerfully. "I can hardly wait." The consultant looked dubious; his experience had been that most clerical workers were attached to their current systems and highly resistant to new technology. He had not met Ms. Cadwallader.

As the young man unplugged and plugged, he muttered continuously about microprocessors, memory, bits, chips, viruses, spreadsheets, interfaces, buffers, and other esoteric lore. Ms. Cadwallader ignored him and continued working. Soon he happily announced that her system was "up" and prepared to leave.

"One moment, young man," said Ms. Cadwallader firmly, removing a pencil from her bun and a notebook from her pocket. "Although you may safely assume that I have the necessary prerequisite skills to operate this system, I will need for you to show me exactly what steps to take in order to activate and operate the word-processing program. Please be good enough to describe exactly what you are doing at each step. You may begin now."

"But, lady," protested the consultant, "this is a state-of-the-art system; you can surf the Net, access the mainframe, download updates, burn CDs, video chat with your friends, watch television, check your Facebook page, follow blogs ..." The expression on Ms. Cadwallader's face silenced the consultant.

"Step one?" She prompted. As the consultant listed and performed the steps in order (Ms. Cadwallader had noticed before that most computer programmers were quite good at this if pressed), Ms. Cadwallader carefully wrote them down. She knew that this task analysis would be useful not only for herself but for teaching the professors in the department how to use their new computers. As she thanked the somewhat chastened young man, she sighed quietly.

"As I expected," she thought, "nothing much to it. Most of my professors will pick it up quickly with a little coaching. After all, most of them have been using less efficient word processors for years. But, oh my, wait until Professor Grundy finds out that there's no more typing from longhand and he really has to learn word processing at last."

are provided in the following section when we discuss teaching behavioral chains. For those who are accomplished cooks, many recipes provide models of task analysis. An understanding of the importance of prerequisite concepts and skills is easily understood by those of us less accomplished. When confronted by a recipe beginning, "First, bone a young hen," we have questions about prerequisite skills and concepts: "Bone? It looks pretty bony already. Young? Its date of birth isn't on the package. Is it young if today is the day before the 'Use or freeze by' date? Hen? How the heck would I know?" When informed that "to bone" to the well-informed means to remove the bones, a serious question about component skills arises. The task of removing the bones from a chicken (of either sex) is one that itself requires analysis. However, the analysis is not enough. Simply reading the steps or even watching the late Julia Child (certainly a master of the skill) perform them is not sufficient. We, at least, will have to be taught. Someone will have to help us learn each component and perform them all in sequence. Only then can we incorporate that task into the even more complex task that will produce the delicious chicken cassoulet. We may send out for pizza instead, a task the components of which we have thoroughly mastered.

Chaining

The components of a task analysis form what applied behavior analysts call a *behavioral chain*. The ideal task analysis would break a task down into components that the learner could already perform with a verbal instruction or a demonstration. When teaching typical students and those with mild disabilities, this is often possible. Even more frequently the chain may consist primarily of behaviors learners can perform with instruction (behaviors under stimulus control) but incorporate one or two behaviors that must be taught. The major focus when teaching chains whose components are already part of student repertoires is their learning to perform the behaviors in sequence with the presentation of only one S^D. Consider, for example, a classroom teacher who gives the instruction, "Get ready for math practice." The result is vague shuffling and furtive looking around among the students. Some students locate their math workbooks; others imitate them. "Come on," prompts the teacher, "hurry up now." One or two students locate pencils; some students still appear completely confused. The process of getting ready for math practice is actually a series of behaviors performed in a sequence:

1. Clear desk of other materials.
2. Locate math workbook.
3. Locate pencil.
4. Wait quietly for instructions.

| A behavior chain.

The students in this class are probably able to perform each of these behaviors, but the behaviors are not under the control of the S^D presented ("Get ready for ..."). The teacher must establish a series or chain of behaviors that will occur when the instruction is given. The teacher might proceed by giving each instruction separately and reinforcing compliance, always starting with "Get ready for math practice." Soon two steps could be combined, and reinforcement would follow only after completion of the two-part chain. Finally, the teacher would need to provide only the S^D. The students would have acquired a behavioral chain.

A behavioral chain is a sequence of behaviors, all of which must be performed to earn a reinforcer. Many complex human behaviors consist of such chains—often with dozens or even hundreds of component steps. Usually, reinforcement occurs only when the final component is performed. The instructional procedure of reinforcing individual responses occurring in sequence to form a complex behavior is called **chaining**.

To understand the process involved in the development of behavioral chains, first recall that any stimulus must be defined in terms of its function and that identical stimuli may have different functions. Similarly, behaviors included in chains may simultaneously serve multiple functions. Consider the behaviors in the get-ready-for-math-practice chain. When the chain is fully established, reinforcement occurs only after the last link. The last link in the chain, however, is paired with the reinforcer and thus becomes a conditioned reinforcer, increasing the probability of occurrence of the preceding link. Each link is subsequently paired with its preceding one: each link serves as a conditioned reinforcer for the link immediately preceding it.

We can also look at the behavior chain from another perspective: each link also serves as an S^D for the link immediately following it. Consider again the getting-ready-for-math-practice chain:

1. Clear desk of other materials (S^D for 2).
2. Locate math workbook (S^{R+} for 1; S^D for 3).
3. Locate pencil (S^{R+} for 2; S^D for 4).
4. Wait quietly for instructions (S^{R+} for 3).

Each link increases the probability of the one it follows and specifies, or cues, the one it precedes (Ferster et al., 1975; Staats & Staats, 1963). Test and Spooner (1996) illustrated this with an everyday example. They described a set of directions for reaching a house to which one has been invited to dinner. The instructions read: "(a) From your house go north to the first stop sign; (b) turn right (immediately after you turn right, you will see a bright yellow house on the left); (c) go two stoplights (not stop signs); (d) turn left at the second light; (e) turn right on Independence Boulevard ..." (p. 12). Figure 10.2 illustrates how a link in the chain serves both as a reinforcer and an S^D (the authors use "cue" as a synonym for S^D).

On another level, each of the component links of a chain, as in our classroom example, can in turn be described as a chain; that is, clearing one's desk includes picking up books and papers, opening the desk, and putting books in the desk. Picking up books is also a chain of behaviors—raising the arm, extending it, opening the hand, grasping the books, and raising the arm. Grasping books, in fact, is still another chain, including placing the thumb ... but wait. We can go on this way in both directions—toward increasing specificity in behaviors and toward increasing complexity. Later in the school year, the teacher in our example may say, "Boys and girls, for math practice I want you to do the first 10 problems on page 142," whereupon the students promptly

1. get ready for math practice,
2. open their books,
3. pick up their pencils, and
4. complete the assignment.

Figure 10.2 A practical example of a diagrammed chain

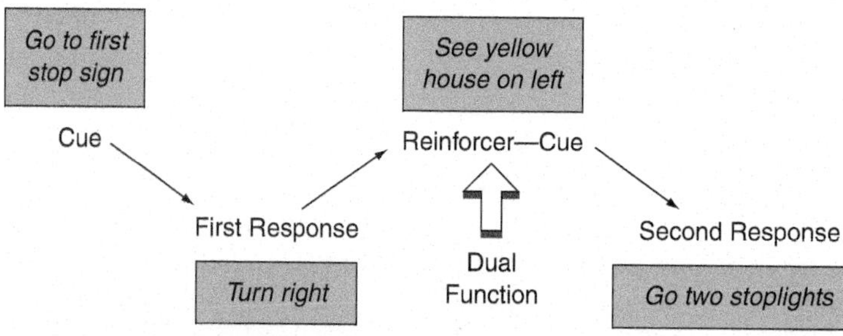

Note: From COMMUNITY-BASED INSTRUCTIONAL SUPPORT by D. W. Test and F. Spooner. Washington: American Association on Mental Retardation. Copyright 1995 by the American Association on Mental Retardation. Reprinted by permission.

The original chain has now become merely a link in a more complex chain. The process of chaining simple behaviors into longer and more complicated sequences results in production of the most elaborate and sophisticated forms of human behavior. For some students, behavioral chains can be acquired by having each step in the chain verbally prompted or demonstrated. The prompts can then be faded and the links combined (Becker, Engelmann, & Thomas, 1975b). For other students, some or all of the separate steps of the chain may have to be taught using more elaborate prompting procedures as the chain is developed. When working with students with severe physical or cognitive disabilities, the teacher may identify links in the chain that must temporarily or permanently be performed by someone else. Such partial participation enables these students to do as much as possible for themselves. The same thing, of course, can be true of anyone. One is reminded of an elderly, but fiercely independent, neighbor who insisted upon mowing her own lawn but accepted assistance starting the mower. Several procedures may be used to teach chains of behavior to students who do not necessarily know how to perform any or more than a few of the links. Those most commonly used are backward chaining, forward chaining, and total task presentation.

BACKWARD CHAINING When backward chaining is used, the components of the chain are acquired in reverse order. The last component is taught first, and other components are added one at a time. Rubio et al. (2018) used backward chaining to teach a 4-year-old boy with a developmental disability to feed himself with a spoon. See Table 10.2 for the steps in backward chaining the researchers used. The steps consisted of picking up a spoon with a bite of food, placing the spoon in his mouth, accepting the bite, and placing the spoon back on the plate. In Step 1, the researcher used hand-over-hand guidance to physically prompt all steps. In Step 3, the researcher physically prompted all steps except for the last one—placing the spoon on the plate. In Step 4, the researcher physically prompted all steps except for the last two—pulling the spoon out of his mouth and putting it on the plate. This backward chaining progressed until the student fed himself independently. Jerome, Frantino, and Sturmey (2007) used backward chaining to teach adults with developmental disabilities to use the Internet.

Table 10.2 Task analysis of backward chaining steps

Step	Procedure
1	Therapist implemented an initial HOH prompt completing the entire chain by guiding Caleb's hand to pick up the prescooped bite, placing the spoon in his mouth, depositing the bite, and then placing the spoon back on the plate.
2	Therapist implemented an initial HOH prompt until the spoon was two in above the plate, and Caleb was required to bring the spoon to his mouth, accept the bite, and then place the spoon back on the plate.
3	Therapist implemented an initial HOH prompt until the bite was directly outside of Caleb's mouth, and he was required to place the spoon on the plate.
4	Therapist implemented an initial HOH prompt until the spoon was in his mouth, and Caleb was required to pull the spoon out of his mouth and place the spoon back on the plate.
5	Therapist implemented an initial HOH prompt until the spoon was directly at his lips, and Caleb was required to place the spoon in his mouth consume the bite, and place the spoon back on the plate.
6	Therapist implemented an initial HOH prompt until the spoon was approximately half the distance to his mouth, and Caleb was required to place the spoon in his mouth, consume the bite, and place the spoon back on the plate.
7	Therapist implemented an initial hand placement (i.e., therapist placed Caleb's hand around the spoon then released her hand), and Caleb was required to lift the spoon from the plate, place the spoon in his mouth, consume the bite, and place the spoon back on the plate.
8	Independent self-feeding (i.e., Caleb picked up the prescooped bite, placed the spoon in his mouth, accepted the bite, and then placed the spoon back on the plate).

Note: HOH = hand-over-hand

Backward chaining is intuitively appealing because the reinforcer is always delivered at the most natural point—when the task is completed. Care must be taken to avoid delivering the reinforcer unless all necessary steps of the task have been completed. If, for example, a secondary caregiver reinforces a preschooler's dressing herself without verifying that she is wearing underwear, the chain will be disrupted or unlinked (Kuhn, Lerman, Vorndran, & Addison, 2006) and the desired behavior will no longer occur.

FORWARD CHAINING When forward chaining is used, the teacher starts with the first link in the chain, teaches it until it is mastered, and then goes on to the next link. The student may be required to perform all the steps previously mastered each time, or each step may be separately taught to the criterion and then the links made (Patterson, Panyan, Wyatt, & Morales, 1974). To use forward chaining to teach undressing skills, the teacher would start with the student fully dressed, deliver the instruction, "Timmy, take your shirt off," and then provide whatever prompting was required to get Timmy to cross his arms and grab the bottom of his T-shirt. When Timmy reliably performed this behavior, she would add the next step until Timmy's shirt was off. Purrazzella and Mechling (2013) used forward chaining to teach spelling of grocery store words to adolescents with moderate intellectual disabilities in a group format. See Figure 10.3 for the forward chaining progression of teaching "milk." The students took turns spelling words on a tablet that was projected on a screen for all to see. Many additional academic applications of forward chaining come to mind. The first-grade teacher who wants students to print the letters of the alphabet in sequence may start with A and

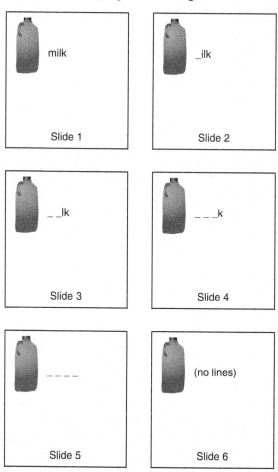

Figure 10.3 Example of slide progression using the forward chaining procedure

add a letter a day until the children can print all 26 capital letters in sequence. The chemistry teacher who wants students to know the elements on the periodic table in order starts with a few at a time and adds a few each day. A teacher who wants students to recite a poem may have them recite the first line until it is mastered and then add a line at a time until they can recite the entire poem. A conscientious teacher who requires students to write a report (an extremely complex chain) teaches them to find references, then take notes, then outline, then prepare a rough draft, and then turn in a final copy.

Consider a forward chaining program in an eight-step task analysis in which a student completes the first three steps and the teacher directly teaches (i.e., prompts and reinforces) the fourth step as the target step. There are a few possibilities of what to do with the rest of the chain. First, the teacher can complete the remaining steps on her own. Second, the teacher can physically prompt the student to complete the steps. Third, the teacher could end the session and not complete the remaining steps. Bancroft, Weiss, Libby, and Ahearn (2011) compared these three procedures with seven students with autism building Lego constructions. All three procedures were effective, and the "student completion" procedure was most efficient for 5 of the 7 students. Bancroft et al. made these recommendations:

1. Use "student completion" if the student tolerates physical prompts
2. Use "teacher completion" if the student engages in problem behavior with physical prompting
3. Use "no completion" if the student has difficulty remaining on task for long periods of time

TOTAL TASK PRESENTATION When using total task presentation, the teacher requires the student to perform all the steps in sequence until the entire chain is mastered. Total task presentation may be particularly appropriate when the student has already mastered some or all the components of a task but has not performed them in sequence. It is also possible, however, to teach completely novel chains in this manner (Spooner, 1981; Spooner & Spooner, 1983; Walls, Zane, & Ellis, 1981). Total task presentation is generally considered the most appropriate and effective method for teaching students with disabilities to perform functional skills (Gaylord-Ross & Holvoet, 1985; Kayser, Billingsley, & Neel, 1986; Spooner & Spooner, 1984). Taber, Alberto, Seltzer, Hughes, and O'Neill (2003) used total task presentation to teach adolescents with moderate intellectual disabilities to follow steps to answer a cell phone and provide information related to being lost.

> Combine verbal instructions, modeling, and chaining.

Many academic chains are forged using a total task presentation. The arithmetic teacher working on long division usually requires her students to solve an entire problem, with whatever coaching is required, until they have mastered the process. Students practice the entire process of finding the longitude and latitude of a given location in geography until it is mastered, as do biology students learning to operate a microscope.

How to Manage Teaching Chains

An important consideration in teaching chains is that no matter which format is used, the teacher must select a teaching procedure to use for teaching each "link in the chain;" that is, each behavior. For example, when Edwards, Landa, Frampton, and Shillingsburg (2018) taught children with autism play skills, such as playing with toy trains, they used most-to-least prompting to teach each behavior in a backward chaining arrangement.

Whatever method a teacher chooses when teaching chained behavior, some organization will be required in order to manage the process efficiently and, of course, to keep accurate and precise data showing progress toward mastery of the chain. The teacher will need a list of the steps to be taught and a way to mark correct or incorrect responses. Most teachers find it more convenient to include the list of steps on the data sheet itself. One can either make and duplicate a sheet for a specific chain or make a generic data sheet on which the steps for any task can be written.

Figure 10.4 is arranged for recording dichotomous data on the instruction of chained tasks. The data sheet is arranged for tasks with up to 25 steps, indicated by the numbers on the far left. The response required for each step is written next to the number. The 20 columns to the right represent 20 trials or opportunities for performance of the task. Each column has 25 numbers representing up to 25 potential steps. Each trial consists of an opportunity for the student to perform all the steps that make up the chained task. For each trial, the teacher records the accuracy of the student's performance of each step, using the simple circle and slash procedure (see Figure 4.7); or, as seen in this figure, by noting an error by putting a slash through the step number and leaving untouched the step number for a correct response. This format allows for graphing directly on the sheet. The number corresponding to the number of correctly performed steps is indicated by placing a filled-in circle in each trial column. Then the circles are connected across trials to create the graph line. Hisa's performance, depicted on the data sheet, indicates she correctly performed 2 of the 13 steps on the first trial of the hand-washing task analysis being used by the teacher. She also correctly performed 7 steps on trial 7, and 11 steps on trial 17.

Figure 10.5 is arranged for recording coded data on the instruction of chained tasks. The data sheet is arranged for tasks with up to 25 steps, indicated by the numbers on the far left. The response required for each step is written next to the number. The columns on the right represent 16 trials or opportunities for performance of the task. For each step the teacher records the type of prompt the student required for performance. On this graph the data for the first trial on September 6th indicate Hisa independently performed steps 5 and 12, required a verbal prompt on step 1, a gesture prompt on steps 4, 6, 7, 9, 10, 11, and 13, and required full physical assistance on steps 2 and 3. A graph can be created directly on this data sheet also. Use the numbers on the left (the step numbers) as the ordinate of the graph. For each trial, count the number of steps the student performed independently and place a data point on the line representing that number. On the graph presented, the data path rises from 2 steps performed independently to 11 steps performed independently. If the objective defines a level of assistance that allows recording a correct response, the graph is created by counting responses with the allowed level of assistance and all lesser levels. If, for example, the objective allows for performance with a verbal prompt, steps performed independently or with a verbal prompt are counted for graphing.

It is helpful to provide spaces on the data sheet to record the level of any prompts. Snell and Loyd (1991) found that teachers were more consistent in assessing students' performance and that teachers made more correct instructional decisions when they had that information.

Using Technology to Teach Chains
Pearson eText
Video Example 10.4
In this video, the educator uses a smartphone with picture and audio prompts to help a student complete a chain of steps to make a latte. How did use of technology increase this student's independence?

Differential Reinforcement for Shaping

Learning Outcome 10.6   Describe the use of differential reinforcement in shaping.

The behavioral procedures described in this chapter assume that students are able to perform with some degree of prompting the components of the target behavior. The emphasis has been on differential reinforcement to bring the desired behavior

Figure 10.4 Data sheet for use with chained tasks

Student: Hisa Task: hand washing Criteria: 100% of steps–1 wk

Step/Response	9-6	9-6	9-8	9-8	9-10	9-10	9-13	9-15	9-17	9-20	9-22	9-24	9-27	9-29	10-1	10-3	10-5	10-8	10-10	10-12
25.	25	25	25	25	25	25	25	25	25	25	25	25	25	25	25	25	25	25	25	25
24.	24	24	24	24	24	24	24	24	24	24	24	24	24	24	24	24	24	24	24	24
23.	23	23	23	23	23	23	23	23	23	23	23	23	23	23	23	23	23	23	23	23
22.	22	22	22	22	22	22	22	22	22	22	22	22	22	22	22	22	22	22	22	22
21.	21	21	21	21	21	21	21	21	21	21	21	21	21	21	21	21	21	21	21	21
20.	20	20	20	20	20	20	20	20	20	20	20	20	20	20	20	20	20	20	20	20
19.	19	19	19	19	19	19	19	19	19	19	19	19	19	19	19	19	19	19	19	19
18.	18	18	18	18	18	18	18	18	18	18	18	18	18	18	18	18	18	18	18	18
17.	17	17	17	17	17	17	17	17	17	17	17	17	17	17	17	17	17	17	17	17
16.	16	16	16	16	16	16	16	16	16	16	16	16	16	16	16	16	16	16	16	16
15.	15	15	15	15	15	15	15	15	15	15	15	15	15	15	15	15	15	15	15	15
14.	14	14	14	14	14	14	14	14	14	14	14	14	14	14	14	14	14	14	14	14
13. Throw towel in trash	13	13	13	13	13	13	13	13	13	13	13	13	13	13	13	13	13	13	13	13
12. Rub hands	12	12	12	12	12	12	12	12	12	12	12	12	12	12	12	12	12	12	12	12
11. Pull one towel	11	11	11	11	11	11	11	11	11	11	11	11	11	11	11	11	11	11	11	11
10. Go to towel dispenser	10	10	10	10	10	10	10	10	10	10	10	10	10	10	10	10	10	10	10	10
9. Turn off cold water	9	9	9	9	9	9	9	9	9	9	9	9	9	9	9	9	9	9	9	9
8. Turn off hot water	8	8	8	8	8	8	8	8	8	8	8	8	8	8	8	8	8	8	8	8
7. Rub hands 3 times	7	7	7	7	7	7	7	7	7	7	7	7	7	7	7	7	7	7	7	7
6. Place hands under water	6	6	6	6	6	6	6	6	6	6	6	6	6	6	6	6	6	6	6	6
5. Press pump	5	5	5	5	5	5	5	5	5	5	5	5	5	5	5	5	5	5	5	5
4. Hand under soap pump	4	4	4	4	4	4	4	4	4	4	4	4	4	4	4	4	4	4	4	4
3. Turn on hot water (red)	3	3	3	3	3	3	3	3	3	3	3	3	3	3	3	3	3	3	3	3
2. Turn on cold water (blue)	2	2	2	2	2	2	2	2	2	2	2	2	2	2	2	2	2	2	2	2
1. Approach sink	1	1	1	1	1	1	1	1	1	1	1	1	1	1	1	1	1	1	1	1
DATE	1	2	3	4	5	6	7	8	9	10	11	12	13	14	15	16	17	18	19	20

Note: Adapted from *Vocational Habilitation of Severely Retarded Adults: A Direct Technology,* by G. T. Bellamy, R. Horner, & D. Inman, 1979, Baltimore: University Park Press. Copyright 1979 by University Park Press, Baltimore. Reprinted with permission.

320 Chapter 10

Figure 10.5 Data sheet (showing prompt levels) for use with chained tasks

Student: _Hisa_   Instructor: _Ms. Ebenezer_   Location: _1st floor bathroom_

Objective: _will independently complete 100% of steps for hand washing for 1 week_

PROMPT CODES: I   V   g   P

(e.g. I=independent, V=verbal cue, G=gesture, P=physical assist)

Steps:

Steps																
25.																
24.																
23.																
22.																
21.																
20.																
19.																
18.																
17.																
16.																
15.																
14.																
13. throw towel in trash	g	g	I	I	I	I	I	I	I	I	I	I	I	I	I	I
12. rub hands	I	I	I	I	I	I	I	I	I	I	I	I	I	I	I	I
11. pull one towel	g	g	V	V	I	I	I	I	I	I	I	I	I	I	I	I
10. go to towel dispenser	g	g	g	g	g	g	V	V	V	g	V	g	V	V	V	I
9. turn off cold water	g	P	P	P	P	P	P	g	P	P	P	P	g	g	g	g
8. turn off hot water	P	P	P	P	P	P	P	P	g	g	g	g	g	g	g	I
7. rub hands 3 times	g	g	V	V	V	I	I	I	I	I	I	I	I	I	I	I
6. place hands under water	g	g	I	I	I	I	I	I	I	I	I	I	I	I	I	I
5. press pump	I	I	I	I	I	I	I	I	I	I	I	I	I	I	I	I
4. hand under soap pump	g	g	g	V	I	I	I	V	V	I	I	I	V	I	I	I
3. turn on hot water (red)	P	P	P	P	P	P	P	P	g	V	V	V	I	g	g	g
2. turn on cold water (blue)	P	P	P	P	V	V	V	V	V	V	V	V	I	I	I	I
1. approach sink	V	V	V	V	V	V	V	V	I	I	I	I	I	I	I	I
Date	9/6	9/6	9/8	9/8	9/10	9/10	9/13	9/15	9/17	9/20	9/22	9/24	9/27	9/29	10/1	10/3

Comments:

under the control of a specified stimulus. Many behaviors that teachers want students to perform are not a part of the students' behavioral repertoire. For such behaviors, a different approach, called shaping, is required. Shaping is defined as differential reinforcement of successive approximations to a specified target behavior. Becker et al. (1975b) listed two essential elements of shaping: differential reinforcement and a shifting criterion for reinforcement. Differential reinforcement, in this case, requires that responses that meet a certain criterion are reinforced, whereas those that do not meet the criterion are not. The criterion for reinforcement shifts ever closer to the target behavior.

Although the term *differential reinforcement* is used in both stimulus control and shaping, the usage is somewhat different. In developing stimulus control, a response in the presence of the S^D is reinforced; the same response in the presence of S^D is not reinforced. The differentiation of reinforcement depends on the antecedent stimulus. In shaping procedures, differential reinforcement is applied to responses that successively approximate (or become increasingly closer to) the target behavior. It is easy to confuse shaping with fading, because both involve differential reinforcement and gradual change. The following guidelines should clarify the differences:

1. Fading is used to bring an already learned behavior under the control of a different stimulus; shaping is used to teach a new behavior.
2. The behavior itself does not change when fading is used; only the antecedent stimulus varies. In shaping, the behavior itself is changed.
3. In fading, the teacher manipulates antecedents; in shaping, consequences are manipulated.

Shaping is not a stimulus control procedure; it is included in this chapter because it is an integral part of many teaching strategies that combine elements of stimulus control, prompting, fading, and chaining.

To design successful shaping programs, the teacher must first clearly specify the **terminal behavior**, the desired goal of the intervention. This will be a behavior that is not currently in the students' repertoire. Then the teacher will identify an **initial behavior**, a behavior that resembles the terminal behavior along some significant dimension and that is in the students' repertoire. The teacher may also identify **intermediate behaviors** that represent successive approximations toward the terminal behavior (Malott et al., 1997). Each intermediate step in the sequence will be reinforced until established; then the criterion for reinforcement will be shifted to the next step. In Chapter 1 we described a procedure whereby students shaped a professor's behavior so that he taught standing in one corner of the classroom. What do you suppose was the initial behavior that led to the result illustrated below?

Panyan (1980) described a number of *dimensions* of behavior along which behavior may be shaped. These dimensions are similar to those we described in Chapter 3. Most basically, the *form* or *topography* of the behavior may be considered. Other dimensions include *duration,* the length of time a student spends responding; *latency,* the length of time between the S^D and the response; *rate,* the speed or fluency of the behavior; and *force,* the intensity of the response.

An example of shaping along the dimension of topography, or form, would be teaching vocal imitation to a child with severe disabilities. The teacher would present the S^D—"ah," for example—and reinforce successive approximations to correct imitation. The teacher might reinforce any vocalization (initial behavior) at first, then only vowel-like sounds (intermediate behaviors), then only close sounds, and finally exact imitations of "ah" (terminal behavior). In the heat of a language-training session with a child with autism, it is frequently difficult to determine whether a given vocal utterance is closer to the target behavior than the preceding one. Only extended practice, supervised by an instructor who shapes the teacher's behavior, will result in the development of such a skill. Coaches who reinforce successive approximations to correct swings in baseball or golf, correct posture in gymnastics or fencing, or correct form in dance or ice skating are equally concerned with the shaping of topography.

In another example, Ghaemmaghami, Hanley, Jessel, and Landa (2018) worked with children with ADHD and related disabilities who engaged in aggression, disruption, and self-injury to access attention, tangible reinforcers, and the removal of demands. They first taught the functional communication response, "My way please," and placed the challenging behaviors on extinction. Then they wanted to increase the complexity of the functional communication response to ultimately result in better generalization and put "My way please" and challenging behavior on extinction while reinforcing, "May I have my way please?" All of those responses were then placed on extinction with the reinforcement of, "Excuse me, may I have my way please?" The final response that was shaped was "'Excuse me?' [pause to receive acknowledgement] 'May I have my way please?'" (p. 505). This shaping process was effective in increasing the topography and complexity of the functional communication response.

Many teachers have concerns about the duration of behaviors. So many students are described as hyperactive or as having deficits in attention that teaching students to stay in place and on task for extended periods of time is a major part of assisting them to be functional students. Suppose his teacher wants Harold to remain in his seat for an entire 20-minute work period. She has observed that Harold has never remained in his seat longer than 5 minutes, with an average of 2 minutes. A program in which Harold earns a reinforcer for remaining in his seat for 20 minutes is doomed—Harold will never come into contact with the reinforcer. Instead, the teacher defines her target behavior as Harold's remaining in his seat for the full 20 minutes but sets up a graduated sequence of criteria:

1. Harold remains in his seat for 3 minutes.
2. Harold remains in his seat for 5 minutes.
3. Harold remains in his seat for 10 minutes.
4. Harold remains in his seat for 15 minutes.
5. Harold remains in his seat for 20 minutes.

This example illustrates another aspect of shaping that requires great skill on the part of the teacher: determining the size of the steps toward the goal. If the steps are too small, the procedure is needlessly time consuming and inefficient. If the steps are too large, the student's responses will not be reinforced and the behavior will be extinguished. Finally, the teacher must consider how long to remain at each plateau—just long enough to establish the behavior solidly, but not so long that the student becomes stuck at that level.

It is not always possible to make all these decisions before beginning a program. For example, Harold's teacher might find that even after Harold has consistently remained in his seat for 5 minutes for a full week, he fails to meet the criterion of sitting for 10 minutes. The teacher would then have to drop back to 5 (or even 4) minutes and gradually work back up to 10, using smaller increments this time. The ability to evaluate and adjust ongoing programs is vital to the success of shaping procedures.

Fonger and Mallot (2019) used shaping to increase the duration of eye contact with young children with autism spectrum disorder. In one phase of their study, they removed a preferred item and gave it back if the child made eye contact for 1 second. With success, the researchers then put 1 second of eye contact on extinction and reinforced 3 seconds of eye contact. Following that, 3 seconds of eye contact was placed on extinction and 5 seconds of eye contact was reinforced. Through this shaping procedure, Fonger and Mallot increased the duration of time the children with autism exhibited eye contact with their teacher.

Most concerns about latency, the period of time between the presentation of an S^D and a student's response, are about decreasing it. For example, when a teacher says, "Get ready for math practice," he usually wants students to do so quickly. Teachers want students to respond to sight words or math facts on flash cards more and more quickly as training proceeds. Sometimes, however, a teacher might want to shape longer latencies for some responses. This would be particularly true in the case of children often called impulsive, who need to stop and think before they respond. In either case, shaping latency proceeds as in shaping any other dimension: Start with a latency the student demonstrates and shorten or lengthen the response time that receives reinforcement until the desired latency is achieved.

Shaping fluency, rate, or speed of responding is often critical. Many children with disabilities fail to perform adequately in general education classrooms not because they cannot perform certain behaviors, but because they cannot perform them fast enough to meet standards set in those classrooms. Fluency is shaped, for example, when students are given timed tests and expected to steadily increase the number of correct responses from test to test. Examples of performances whose fluency has been shaped to astounding rates abound in everyday life. Think of an experienced cashier or bank teller counting money, an expert chef cutting an onion, or any master of a craft at work. One of us recently encountered a gentleman who was a master of the task of filling a soft drink vending machine. Upon noticing open-mouthed admiration, he grinned and stated, "Yup! Three hundred plus cans a minute. They use me to show trainees how it's done." Admiration and respect were clearly continuing to reinforce a high rate of behavior developed by shaping.

Shaping Speech
Pearson eText
Video Example 10.5
In this video, the educator prompts and differentially reinforces vocal speech from a young child. Notice how she provides extra attention and praise to the best vocal approximations of target words.

Ms. Wallace's Class Learns to Print the Letter A

Ms. Wallace was trying to teach her students to print the letter A. At first she just told them, "Make a capital A." They did not respond to this S^D. "Look at the one on the chart," she said.

But, "Does this look like the one on the chart, Harold?" asked Ms. Wallace. She then tried some verbal instructions:

This verbal prompt resulted in success for some students. But, "Ralph, your teepee is a little flat," sighed Ms. Wallace. In desperation, Ms. Wallace walked around the room, guiding her students' hands through the correct movements. Physical

In the teachers' lounge that afternoon, Ms. Wallace sobbed, "I can't go through this 25 more times." An unkind colleague pointed out that she had forgotten the lowercase

"Make it just like this one." Some of the students responded to this visual prompt by producing a creditable A.

"Make two slanted lines that look like a teepee; then make another line across the middle."

prompting resulted in success for many students. But, "Melissa, relax your hand, for heaven's sake. I'm only trying to HELP you," wailed Ms. Wallace.

letters, making 51 more to go. Before Ms. Wallace became completely hysterical, an experienced first-grade teacher showed her a worksheet like this:

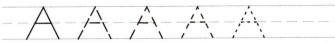

"You see," said Ms. Weatherby, "you just reinforce successive approximations to the terminal behavior of writing an A independently, tracing with fewer and fewer cues until the prompt just fades away."

Force, or intensity, may refer to the volume of a student's voice, to the pressure she exerts when writing on paper, or to the tightness with which a student learning an assembly task holds onto parts. Any of these behaviors, along with countless others, may need shaping in either direction of force.

Shaping is an extremely useful teaching tool. It provides a means of developing new behaviors in students with all levels of ability. Used alone, however, it may be less efficient than procedures using it combined with other tools.

As we stated earlier, shaping and fading are often used in combination. The example on the previous page illustrates a combined procedure.

Summary

You have learned a variety of skills that will help you to teach students to perform behaviors, simple and complex. We have discussed the process of differential reinforcement for bringing students' behavior under stimulus control and the process for bringing simple and complex behaviors under the control of antecedent stimuli. Verbal, visual, modeling, and physical prompts have been discussed, as well as systematic procedures for fading these prompts. Task analysis, backward chaining, forward chaining, and total task presentation have been described. Finally, procedures for shaping behaviors that students cannot initially perform were suggested.

Discussion Questions

1. Miles is a new student in Mr. Grishom's kindergarten class. He has been attending a special private preschool for children with pervasive developmental disorders. Mr. Grishom is overwhelmed by the prospect of teaching Miles even simple routines. As the school's inclusion teacher, you need to help Mr. Grishom task analyze some of the routines. Which do you think would be most important? How would you find out what they are and what components are required? Pick two routines and task analyze them for Miles and Mr. Grishom.

2. As a group, design a task analysis for an everyday task. Give your analysis to another group and see if they can perform it. Determine whether any difficulties they have require improvement to the task analysis or one of the teaching procedures described in this chapter.

Chapter 11
Providing for Generalization of Behavior Change

 Learning Outcomes

11.1 Define and differentiate among stimulus generalization, maintenance, and response generalization.

11.2 Describe seven approaches to programming for generalization.

CHAPTER OUTLINE

Generalization
    Stimulus Generalization
    Maintenance
    Response Generalization

Programming for Generalization
    Train and Hope
    Sequentially Modify
    Introduce to Natural Maintaining Contingencies
    Train Sufficient Exemplars
    Train Loosely
    Use Indiscriminable Contingencies
    Program Common Stimuli
    Mediate Generalization and Train to Generalize

Summary

Preceding chapters described principles and procedures related to strengthening appropriate behaviors, reducing or eliminating maladaptive behaviors, and teaching new behaviors. The technology of behavior change presented in earlier chapters has been thoroughly investigated and its efficacy demonstrated beyond doubt. Applied behavior analysts have not always been as thorough in demonstrating that behaviors changed using their technology are changed permanently or, indeed, that the changed behaviors are displayed in any setting except that in which training programs are executed. That has changed in recent years; virtually every published article reporting behaviors changed using applied behavior analysis procedures includes at least an examination of generalization and often specific efforts made to accomplish it. Researchers have learned that it is meaningless to change behavior unless the change

> Some people believe that changing behavior invariably infringes on personal freedom.

can be made to last and unless behavior will occur in settings other than the original training site and in the absence of the original trainer.

To program meaningful behavior change, teachers must use the behavioral principle of generality. Baer, Wolf, and Risley (1968), in their classic essay defining applied behavior analysis, stated: "A behavioral change may be said to have generality if it proves durable over time, if it appears in a wide variety of possible environments, or if it spreads to a wide variety of related behaviors" (p. 96). Baer and his colleagues describe three ways a behavior may show generality: over time, across settings, and across behaviors. Each of these types of **generalization** will be discussed in more detail later in this chapter. The following examples illustrate behavior changes that do not have generality.

> Ways that behavior change can generalize.

The students at the Foxwood Residential Center for Youth have a very structured program during both the school day and in their dormitories. Most of them have been referred because of substance abuse issues or serious behavioral problems that have brought them in contact with the judicial system. Under the point and level system of the center they display very few problem behaviors, but when discharged many of them go right back to the same behaviors that caused them to be referred. A significant percentage of the discharged students are back at Foxwood or in another residential facility within a few months.

Ms. Kitchens is a consultant teacher for children with learning disabilities. She spends approximately half an hour a day working directly with clusters of her students and their peers in the students' general education classes. Ms. Kitchens has noticed that although her students do very well when she is there, they do not perform academic tasks that she knows they can do when only the general education class teacher is present.

Mr. Fonseca's first graders have learned to recognize a large number of words using flash cards and a sight word approach. When confronted with an unfamiliar word, however, the students just guess. They have not learned to decode new words based on relationships between symbols and sounds.

The preceding examples describe situations in which some academic or social behavior has been successfully changed. The change, however, was accomplished only for as long as the contingencies were in effect, or only in the presence of the initial trainer, or only for very specific behaviors that were trained. There is no question that applied behavior analysis procedures often cause situation-specific behavior changes. Indeed, several of the research designs described in Chapter 6 depend on this phenomenon. The classic ABAB (reversal) design demonstrates functional relationships between behavior and consequences by successfully applying and withdrawing such consequences and demonstrating that the dependent variable (the behavior) changes according to the condition. If the behavior failed to return to its baseline rate under one of these designs, the experimenter would have failed to demonstrate a functional relation.

The multiple baseline design enables an experimenter to demonstrate functional relation by successfully applying contingencies to several different behaviors, to behavior in several different settings, or to the same behavior displayed by different students. A functional relation is shown only when the behaviors are not changed until contingencies are implemented. Baer et al. (1968) stated, "generalization should be programmed rather than expected or lamented" (p. 97). The experimenter attempting to establish functional relations between procedures and behavior may, indeed, lament the occurrence of generalization. The classroom teacher is more likely to expect it and to lament its absence. With few exceptions, it is the professional expecting generalization who will be disappointed. If generalization does not automatically result when behavior is changed, does that mean applied behavior analysis procedures are useless? If you have stuck with us this far, you know that we do not think so. To most behavior analysts, the lack of automatic generalization indicates the need for developing a technology of generalization as efficient as the technology of behavior change. Such a technology need not interfere with the necessity for demonstrating functional relations; it may be applied after these relations have been established.

As Baer et al. (1968) suggested, generalization must be programmed. This chapter describes the principles of generalization that are the foundation of this programming and suggests specific ways that teachers can increase the odds that the behaviors their students learn will be maintained even when all the charts, graphs, and reinforcers have been discarded.

Generalization

Learning outcome 11.1 **Define and differentiate among stimulus generalization, maintenance, and response generalization.**

In Chapter 3 we described a response hierarchy for designing objectives. It included response levels of acquisition, fluency, maintenance, and generalization. It is important that the IEP for each student with a disability includes objectives for the levels of maintenance and generalization (Burt & Whitney, 2018). Haring and Liberty (1990) suggested that maintenance and generalization objectives differ from acquisition objectives in two ways: the conditions under which the behavior is to be performed and the criteria defined for performance. The conditions specified should be those that exist in the setting or settings in which the behavior will ultimately be performed. For example, if our generalization objective for a student is that he or she will order food at a fast-food restaurant, we might begin instruction in the classroom under simulated conditions. Numerous prompts and reinforcers would probably be provided. However, in a real restaurant the student will have to function with only a cue such as "May I help you?" or "Help you?" or "What do you want?" or, conceivably, "Would you like to try our new low-fat turkey chipotle wrap today?" Neither the order taker nor another customer is likely to say "Good ordering," "Nice waiting," or "Good getting your card out" (Cihak, Alberto, Kessler, & Taber, 2004), or to provide hugs, tokens, or points as a consequence. These prompts and reinforcers may be perfectly appropriate during the acquisition phase, but the conditions specified in a generalization objective should reflect conditions in the real-life environment (Barczak, 2019; Burckley et al., 2015).

How to write objectives for generalization and maintenance.

Criteria specified in a generalization objective should reflect performance that is "good enough," a phrase that occurs frequently in popular self-help literature. As we stated in Chapter 3, performance for some behaviors, like looking both ways before crossing the street, is good enough only if it is perfect—one must look both ways every time. For other behaviors we might ask, for example, if the student can wash, dry, and fold towels at the Laundromat well enough that they can be stored in the linen closet at the group home. During the acquisition phase, the instructor might insist that towels be folded with corners exactly square and stacked precisely. If that same instructor, however, were to permit us a peek at his linen closet, we might find that he, too, settles for "good enough" performance in towel folding. Trask-Tyler, Grossi, and Heward (1994) defined cooking as "good enough" if the result could be eaten. As with the towel-folding instructor, we wonder if the cooking instructor plans to eat the good-enough meal himself.

The evaluation of generalization objectives is also critical (Burt & Whitney, 2018). We must consider both where the behavior is to be evaluated and who is to do the evaluation. If we want George to be able to get a soft drink from any machine he encounters, we might begin instruction on the vending machine in the community center where he goes swimming twice a week. It is important to be aware that even though we may pat ourselves on the back because we are conducting instruction in the community, this skill is no more likely to generalize than if we brought a vending machine into the classroom (Cooper et al., 2020). After we have taught George to use various vending machines in various locations, we can assess generalization. It is obviously impossible to take George to every vending machine in his community, so we conduct probes. We select several vending machines in different locations and check to see whether George gets a soft drink—without prompts and with no reinforcer except the soda. If we really want to be certain that George has a generalized skill, it will be important that his teacher or another adult he knows not be standing near him with a clipboard. Generalization probes are best taken by someone unfamiliar to the student or at least someone who would normally be in the environment in which generalization is to be assessed.

> There are several kinds of generalization.

Before suggesting guidelines for facilitating generalization, we need to differentiate several types. The first variety of generalization, *stimulus generalization*, occurs when a response that has been trained in a specific setting with a specific instructor occurs in a different setting or with a different instructor. Second, *maintenance* refers to the tendency of a learned behavior to occur after programmed contingencies have been withdrawn. Finally, the term *response generalization* is used when referring to unprogrammed changes in similar behaviors when a target behavior is modified. In this chapter, the term *generalization* will refer to any of the three types, and the terms *stimulus generalization*, *maintenance*, and *response generalization* will be used when distinctions are made among them.

Stimulus Generalization

> Not all generalization is a good thing.

Stimulus generalization occurs when responses that have been reinforced in the presence of a specific stimulus (S^D) occur in the presence of different but similar stimuli. Sometimes this is a good thing. Parents and teachers, for example, spend a lot of time teaching young children concepts such as colors and shapes. We do not expect to have to teach every example of "red" or "triangle." The children will eventually identify shades of red we have not taught or triangles that look different from those used in teaching. A group of stimuli that occasion the same response are considered members of a **stimulus class**. The more similar the stimuli, the more likely stimulus generalization will occur. The students described at the beginning of this chapter who performed differently in the presence of their consulting teacher have not learned that all teachers should occasion academic performance. The student who stands befuddled when the fast-food worker asks, "What'll it be?" instead of "May I help you?" has not learned that there is a class of questions that should occasion the ordering response. However, the student is not to blame for these problems; rather, the teacher has not effectively programmed for the generalization.

Stimulus generalization can also be a problem. Children who are learning colors often identify objects that are pink or orange as red, or shapes with more than three sides as triangles. Remember the baby who called all bearded adults with glasses "Daddy." Some stimuli are in a class by themselves.

Maintenance

Most behaviors that teachers want students to perform should occur even after systematic applied behavior analysis procedures have been withdrawn. This continued performance over time is **maintenance**. Teachers want their students to read accurately in class and to continue reading accurately after they are no longer in school. Math problems in school are merely a means to an end—we want students eventually to balance checkbooks, fill out income tax forms, or multiply measurements in recipes. Appropriate social behaviors, although adaptive in the classroom, are also necessary when a specific program for their systematic reinforcement no longer exists. Chapter 8 detailed what happens when positive reinforcement is abruptly withdrawn from a behavior that previously has been reinforced on a continuous schedule: The

Goals for Generalization
Pearson eText
Video example 11.1
In this video, an educator is targeting reading and spelling sight words. How is she incorporating both stimulus and response generalization in this teaching session?

behavior decelerates and is eventually extinguished. Extinction may be a very useful phenomenon when a teacher withdraws attention from a maladaptive behavior. On the other hand, it may be frustrating when the teacher has systematically developed some appropriate behavior only to see that it has disappeared when the student is observed a year later.

Ensuring that behavior will be maintained is an important part of teaching. It is impossible for the teacher to follow students around forever, reinforcing them with cereal or a smile and praise. Behaviors that extinguish rapidly when the artificial contingencies used to develop them are withdrawn can hardly be considered learned in any meaningful sense. Early experimental evidence indicated that extinction usually occurs unless specific measures are taken to prevent it (Kazdin, 2001; Rincover & Koegel, 1975; Stokes, Baer, & Jackson, 1974).

Response Generalization

Sometimes changing one behavior will result in changes in other, similar behaviors. Such similar behaviors are often referred to as a *response class*, and changes in untrained members of the response class as **response generalization**. For example, if students receive reinforcers for completing multiplication problems and subsequently increase their rates of completing both multiplication and division problems, response generalization has occurred to untrained members of the response class: completion of arithmetic problems. Unfortunately, this kind of generalization does not happen often. Usually only the specific behavior reinforced will change. "Behavior, unlike the flower, does not naturally bloom" (Baer & Wolf, 1970, p. 320).

Programming for Generalization

Learning outcome 11.2 Describe seven approaches to programming for generalization.

Ensuring the generality of behavior change is particularly important to the teacher of students with disabilities. Because legislation requires that all such students be educated in the least restrictive environment, large numbers of students with disabilities are educated entirely in general education classes or are in special classes only temporarily or for only part of the school day. The special educator cannot count on being able to apply systematic applied behavior analysis procedures for extended periods of time or even for the entire school day. Even the teacher of students with pervasive disabilities must be aware that these students, too, will be living, learning, and working in an environment that is least restrictive—that is, one that as much as possible resembles that of their typical peers. Special educators must prepare their students to perform in situations where systematic contingency management programs may not be available.

General education teachers also must be aware of techniques for promoting generalization. These teachers will serve large numbers of students with disabilities who have been taught appropriate academic and social behaviors using applied behavior analysis procedures. To help these students perform optimally in their classrooms, general education teachers must know not only the techniques used to teach these students but also techniques that will encourage generalization to less-structured settings. The current emphasis on increasing integration of students with disabilities in the regular programs makes awareness of this technology more important for all teachers (Wood et al., 2015).

The procedures for encouraging generalization described in the following sections include some that do not meet more stringent or technical definitions of generalization of behavior change. Traditionally, generalization has been noted only when behavior occurs spontaneously in circumstances where no contingencies are in effect. For practical purposes, we shall also consider behavior changes that can be facilitated by relatively minor changes in the setting in which generalization is desired. If such changes can be made fairly effortlessly and if gains made in the training setting can be maintained, for all practical purposes the behavior has generalized. Haring and Liberty (1990) suggested a number of questions that instructors should ask to help make decisions about programming for generalization. In simplified form, questions that a teacher might ask when assessing and programming for generalization include:

1. Has the skill been acquired? Unless the student can perform the skill fluently, accurately, and reliably in an instructional setting, we should not expect that she will perform it in any other setting.
2. Can the student acquire reinforcers (natural or otherwise) without performing the skill? If, when George stands helplessly in front of a soft drink vending machine at the local miniature golf course, typical peers kindly (or impatiently) take his change and get him a drink, he is unlikely to be motivated to get it for himself.
3. Does the student perform part of the skill? When the student performs part of a skill in a generalization setting, the teacher's job is to go back to his task analysis, assess the antecedent and consequent stimuli for the missing or nonperformed component, provide more effective ones during retraining, and identify potentially effective stimuli in the generalization environment.

Zirpoli and Melloy (1993, p. 192) provided the following general guidelines to facilitate generalization:

- Teach desired behaviors, whether they are social or academic, within the natural setting where they should occur.
- Employ a variety of caregivers for training (for example, several teachers, parents, peers). This decreases the probability that the behavior will become situation specific.
- Train in a variety of settings.
- Shift as quickly as possible from artificial cues and reinforcers to more natural ones.
- Shift from continuous reinforcement to intermittent reinforcement.
- Gradually increase delays in the delivery of reinforcement.
- Reinforce instances of generalization.

Stokes and Baer (1977, p. 350), in a more detailed analysis, reviewed the literature on generalization assessment and training in applied behavior analysis and categorized the techniques for assessing or programming generalization as follows:

Train and hope.
Sequentially modify.
Introduce to natural maintaining contingencies.
Train sufficient exemplars.
Train loosely.
Use indiscriminable contingencies.
Program common stimuli.
Mediate generalization.
Train to generalize.

Although the review by Stokes and Baer (1977) was completed over 40 years ago, the categories they identified are as relevant today as they were then. The following sections review classic and more contemporary research on each of the techniques described by Stokes and Baer and provide examples illustrating possible classroom uses.

Train and Hope

Stokes and Baer (1977) warned against "train and hope." That is, if we teach a new skill and hope it generalizes across people and settings, we will likely not see that generalization. Rather, we must program for that generalization using the procedures described below. In other words, we must change "train and hope" to "train and program for generalization."

On the other hand, unplanned generalization does sometimes happen. It may be likely to happen in cases where the skill trained is particularly useful to the student or where the skill becomes reinforcing in itself. Appropriate behaviors may also last after programs are withdrawn. Many behaviors taught to typical children and those with mild disabilities do generalize. Students who learn to read in school delight their parents (and sometimes drive them to distraction) by reading street signs. This spontaneous generalization, however, is much less likely to occur with students with more severe disabilities (Spooner et al., 2015).

> Remember that changes in students' behavior can change adults' behavior, too.

In spite of reported evidence that some behaviors are automatically generalized, it is important to remember that most are not. When they are, we usually do not know why (Kazdin, 2001). It may be that some aspect of the generalization setting has acquired conditioned reinforcing characteristics or that the behavior of teachers or parents has been permanently altered by the implementation of the applied behavior analysis procedure and that reinforcing consequences, though no longer formally programmed, may still occur more frequently than before intervention (Kazdin, 2001).

Although there is hope that behaviors acquired or strengthened through formal contingency management programs may generalize, there is no certainty. Hoping will not make generalization happen. The teacher who expects it should be prepared to monitor students' behavior closely and to instigate more effective procedures immediately upon learning that early hopes have been dashed. The example at the bottom of the page illustrates a behavior that generalized for no discernible reason.

> Do you think Ms. Andrews should read the section on negative reinforcement in Chapter 9?

Ms. Andrews Works a Miracle

Ms. Andrews, who did private tutoring at home to supplement her income, was asked to work with Brandon, who had completed the first semester of the seventh grade with 2 Cs, 2 Ds, and an F. Because Brandon had previously been an excellent student, his parents were frantic. Ms. Andrews tested Brandon, found no learning problem, and decided that Brandon simply had a particularly bad case of seventh-grade slump. He was not doing homework or classwork, and he didn't study for tests. He seemed to have efficient study skills—he just wasn't using them. Ms. Andrews suggested that once-a-week tutoring was not the answer and urged the parents to implement some contingency management. She explained the low probability that study behavior would generalize beyond her living room. They insisted on tutoring and implemented no program.

For 2 weeks, Ms. Andrews worked with Brandon on grade-level materials—not the books he was using at school because he, naturally, forgot to bring them. She provided very high rates of verbal praise for reading, studying, and completing math problems, as well as access to a vocabulary development game if Brandon completed other tasks.

During the third week, Brandon's mother called. Three of his teachers had written notes indicating that Brandon's work in their classes had improved dramatically. Tests and papers from all classes were As and Bs. Ms. Andrews, said Brandon's mother, had worked a miracle. Agreeing modestly before hanging up, Ms. Andrews spent the next few minutes staring into space and wondering, "Did he just coincidentally decide to kick into gear, or was it really something I did?"

Sequentially Modify

> Review Chapter 6 for an extended discussion of the multiple baseline design.

A procedure that allows stimulus generalization or transfer of training across settings is *sequential modification*. In this procedure, generalization (in the practical sense) is promoted by applying the same techniques that successfully changed behavior in one setting to all settings where the target behavior is desirable. Exactly the same process is undertaken when using a multiple-baseline-across-settings design to demonstrate a functional relationship between independent and dependent variables. For example, for a student who learned to behave appropriately and complete academic tasks in a resource room but did not perform in any general education classrooms, the teachers involved might set up a reinforcement system similar to that used in the resource class in each general education classroom. A similar procedure to promote maintenance would necessitate training those responsible for the student's education and care after the student has been dismissed from a special training program. Teachers, parents, or other caregivers would be trained to carry out the same applied behavior analysis procedures employed in the training situation. In some cases, it may be unrealistic to program exactly the same contingencies in the generalization setting. For example, a general education classroom teacher may not be able to monitor disruptive behavior as closely, or deliver reinforcers as often, as a special education teacher. Similarly, parents may be unable or unwilling to structure programs as closely as may be done in residential settings. In such cases, modified versions of programs may still provide enough environmental control to maintain the target behaviors at rates close to those established during training. Examination of any published study using a multiple-baseline-across-settings experimental design provides an example of sequential modification.

> Homes may be harder to structure than schools or other institutions.

Sequential modification has been used to teach individuals with disabilities to generalize to untrained recipes requiring similar skills to those taught initially (simple generality) and to more difficult untrained recipes requiring a combination of skills learned during instruction (complex generality). It has also been used in language training and modification of inappropriate verbalization (Browning, 1983; Drasgow, Halle, & Ostrosky, 1998; Trask-Tyler et al., 1994).

Anderson-Inman, Walker, and Purcell (1984) used a procedure they call *transenvironmental programming* to increase generalization from resource rooms to general education classrooms. Transenvironmental programming involves assessing the target environment, providing students in the resource room with skills identified as critical in the general education classroom, using techniques to promote transfer of the skills acquired, and evaluating student performance in the general education classroom. Specific techniques for facilitating transfer included reinforcing the newly acquired skills in the general education classroom.

The transfer and maintenance of behaviors by sequential modification may not technically qualify as generalization, as we discussed earlier. The provision of identical or similar applied behavior analysis procedures in alternate settings, however, is practical and frequently successful. Even if the alterations are necessary for extended periods, their effectiveness may make their implementation well worth the trouble. The following vignette illustrates the use of sequential modification.

> Whose behavior has generalized here?

Connie Learns to Do Her Work

Connie was a second-grade student in Ms. Gray's resource room for children with learning disabilities. Connie performed very well in the resource room, where she earned points exchangeable for free time when she completed academic tasks, but did no work in the general education classroom, where she spent most of the school day. Instead, she wandered around the classroom bothering other students. After conferring with the general education classroom teacher, Ms. Gray provided her with slips of paper preprinted with Connie's name, a place for the date, and several options to check regarding Connie's academic work and classroom behavior (see Figure 11.1).

Figure 11.1 Connie's chart

```
Connie                              Date:_____

Assignments complete:               Behavior:
Yes _____                           Good _____
No _____                            Fair _____
Partly _____                        Poor _____
                                         _____Initials
```

Ms. Gray then awarded Connie bonus points for her work in the general education classroom. Although Connie continued to be less productive in the general education classroom than in the resource room, her behavior was acceptable, and the amount of academic work completed was comparable to that of most students in the class. The general education classroom teacher was so impressed with the procedure that she made rating slips for several of her problem students and awarded them special privileges when they completed their work and behaved properly.

Introduce to Natural Maintaining Contingencies

An ideal applied behavior analysis program seeks to change behaviors that receive reinforcement in the student's natural environment. Baer (1999) suggested "A good rule is not to make any deliberate behavior change that will not meet natural communities of reinforcement" (p. 16). He added that this rule should be broken only if there is a commitment to provide follow-up for as long as necessary. Ideally, as a result of the program, the student would behave appropriately for the same reasons that motivate students who were never referred because of inappropriate behavior. The student would work hard at academic tasks to earn good grades, behave well in the classroom to receive the approval of the teacher, or perform a job for money. It may be possible to accelerate the process of making the natural reinforcers more powerful (Horcones, 1992). If a teacher points out how a student's hard work on a math paper resulted in a big red A+, or how proud a resource student's general education teacher has been of his good behavior, or how terrific it is to be able to spend money one earns by working hard, these natural reinforcers become more noticeable. For example, although fairly complicated procedures—including shaping, chaining, and graduated guidance—may be necessary to teach students with severe disabilities to feed themselves, feeding themselves may generalize to other settings and be durable after training is withdrawn because that skill has a built-in positive reinforcer in that children who feed themselves efficiently can control their own intake of food. Toilet training of persons with intellectual disabilities (Azrin, Sneed, & Foxx, 1973), children with autism (Cocchiola et al., 2012), and typically developing young children (Greer et al., 2016) may be maintained after contingencies are withdrawn because discomfort is avoided. Similarly, students who are taught such skills as reading or math may maintain these skills without programmed generalization because the skills are useful. Some social behaviors may also generalize.

> We try to teach functional skills—those that are useful to the student.

An increasing emphasis in the education of persons with severe disabilities has been on training functional skills—that is, skills useful to the individual in his school or workplace and community. Rather than teach these students meaningless school skills such as sorting blocks by color, we teach them skills they need for maximum independence: riding the bus, using the Laundromat, cooking a meal, even using an automated bank teller machine (Shafer, Inge, & Hill, 1986). O'Reilly, Lancioni, and Kierans (2000) taught four adults with intellectual disabilities to order their own drinks in a bar and to interact with other patrons. Brodhead et al. (2019) taught three 7-year-old boys with ASD to engage in social conversations via video chat. These skills, by their nature, are more prone to be maintained by the natural environment. One of the most important reasons for teachers to know about their students' lifestyles, customs, and cultures is so they will know what behaviors those students' environments will maintain. Choosing behaviors to change that will be maintained by the natural environment applies the Relevance of Behavior Rule. Ayllon and Azrin first described this rule in 1968. Baer and Wolf (1970) conceptualized the Relevance of Behavior Rule as a form of *trapping*. They asserted that if applied behavior analysts can generate behaviors that are reinforced by the natural environment, a situation analogous to catching a mouse in a trap will be created. The mechanism of trapping works this way:

> Consider, for example, that very familiar model, the mouse trap. A mouse trap is an environment designed to accomplish massive behavior modification in a mouse. Note that this modification has thorough generality: The change in behavior accomplished by the trap will be uniform across all environments, it will extend to all of the mouse's behaviors, and it will last indefinitely into the future. Furthermore, a mousetrap allows a great amount of behavioral change to be accomplished by a relatively slight amount of behavioral control. A householder without a trap can, of course, still kill a mouse: He can wait patiently outside the mouse's hole, grab the mouse faster than the mouse can avoid him, and then apply various forms of force to the unfortunate animal to accomplish the behavioral change desired. But this performance requires a great deal of competence: vast patience, supercoordination, extreme manual dexterity, and a well-suppressed squeamishness. By contrast, a householder with a trap needs very few accomplishments: If he can merely apply the cheese and then leave the loaded trap where the mouse is likely to smell that cheese, in effect he has guaranteed general change in the mouse's future behavior. The essence of a trap, in behavioral terms, is that only a relatively simple response is necessary to enter the trap, yet once entered, the trap cannot be resisted in creating general behavioral change. For the mouse, the entry response is merely to smell the cheese. Everything proceeds from there almost automatically. The householder need have no more control over the mouse's behavior than to get him to smell the cheese, yet he accomplishes thorough changes in behavior. (Baer & Wolf, 1970, p. 321)

Some behaviors do lend themselves to trapping. Behaviors that result in increased peer reinforcement are particularly likely to be maintained in the natural environment. Social and communication skills, grooming skills, and even assertiveness may only need to be generated to be maintained (Hood et al., 2017). The network of reinforcement available for such behaviors may form an irresistible environmental trap that, like the mouse trap, once entered is inescapable. Unfortunately, it is often difficult to pinpoint behaviors that will be reinforced by the natural environment (Kazdin, 2001). Most natural environments seem to ignore appropriate behavior and concentrate attention on inappropriate behavior. Few drivers are stopped by police officers for compliments; workers are seldom praised for getting to work on time and attending regularly. Even in the classroom, teachers tend to pay little or no attention to students who are doing well but instead correct students whose behavior is disruptive or inattentive. It is unwise for the applied behavior analyst to assume that any behavior will be maintained by the student's natural environment. We can say, however, that the maintenance or transfer of behaviors to reinforcement contingencies in the natural environment may be facilitated by:

| Ways to promote generalization.

1. Observing the student's environment. What parents, teachers, or other adults describe as desirable behavior for the student may or may not be what they reinforce.
2. Choosing behaviors that are subject to trapping as determined by observation. For example, if teachers in a given school heavily reinforce pretty handwriting,

a consulting teacher may teach students pretty handwriting, even if it would not otherwise be a priority.

3. Teaching students to recruit reinforcers from the environment. Students can be taught to call adults' attention to appropriate behavior and thus to receive praise or other reinforcers. Craft, Alber, and Heward (1998) taught fourth graders in a special class to ask, "How am I doing?" or make statements like, "Look, I'm all finished!" an appropriate number of times during a class session. The students were able to perform the skill in their general education class. Praise from their teachers increased, and so did their academic performance.

4. Conditioning praise and other social expressions as reinforcers. For many students with severe disabilities, particularly autism, praise and other forms of attention may not function as reinforcers. Repeatedly delivering praise along with strong reinforcers, such as toys and food, may condition praise to function as a reinforcer (Axe & Laprime, 2017; Dudley et al., 2019). Once praise and other forms of attention function as reinforcers, more skills are likely to be maintained by these natural contingencies.

Natural Contingencies
Pearson eText
Video example 11.2
In this video, children prepare themselves a snack and participate in social conversation in a small group. Consider all the different ways that appropriate behavior is contacting natural contingencies, helping to promote generalization.

The teacher who wants the natural environment to take over reinforcement should be aware that this is by no means an automatic process. Careful monitoring should take place to assess the natural environment and to determine how well the behavior change is being maintained. The first vignette below illustrates a behavior that is maintained because it receives naturally occurring reinforcers. The second anecdote illustrates a failure of the environment to provide sufficient reinforcers.

Alvin Learns to Read

Alvin was an adjudicated juvenile delinquent in Mr. Daniel's class at the detention center. He was a virtual nonreader when he came into the class, but with systematic direct instruction (Adams & Engelmann, 1996) of a reading method using token reinforcement for correct responses, Mr. Daniel taught Alvin to read phonetically regular one- and two-syllable words. Mr. Daniel wondered whether Alvin would ever read after being released from the center, because the boy certainly showed little enthusiasm for any of the high-interest, low-vocabulary books available in the classroom for recreational reading. Alvin appeared to read only when the token condition was in effect. About a year after Alvin's release, however, Mr. Daniel happened to meet him emerging from a bookstore. He had several paperback books under his arm, one open in his hands, and a look of intense concentration on his face.

Marvin Fails the Sixth Grade

Mr. Cohen, a consulting teacher, had worked with Marvin for 2 years while he was attending fourth- and fifth-grade classes. He spent time in Marvin's classroom with small groups of students and sometimes scheduled Marvin and others for more intensive work outside the general education classroom. Marvin had done well in fourth and fifth grades because his teachers had used high rates of verbal praise and free time contingent on completion of work. Marvin was dismissed from special education at the end of fifth grade. Mr. Cohen had not even considered that Marvin might have trouble in sixth grade, but his sixth-grade teacher, Ms. Roach, was, to put it bluntly, a hardnose. She did not believe in praising students for good behavior or in providing any consequence for academic work except grades. As she put it, "That's why they come to school. I don't believe in coddling them." Marvin went back to the behaviors that had resulted in his original referral: He disrupted the classroom, did not complete assignments, and ultimately failed the sixth grade. Mr. Cohen felt he had learned two things at Marvin's expense: Never assume that the same conditions exist in all classrooms, and always follow up on students whose behavior appears to have been permanently changed.

Train Sufficient Exemplars

Most academic and social behaviors that we want to teach our students to perform are members of various response classes. That is, there is seldom a single behavior that is always performed in exactly the same way in exactly the same place. For example, when we teach a student to read, we expect that she will eventually apply her reading skills to decoding and comprehending material she has never read. We would certainly not expect her to do that after learning one or two words with the same beginning sound or after one example of how to use the context to derive the meaning of an unfamiliar word. We would provide lots of examples and lots of lessons; we would provide sufficient exemplars. Similarly, we would not expect a student with severe disabilities to use any vending machine in the city after learning to use only the one in the community center, or a student who had learned to greet his teacher in the morning to greet any adult. Again, we would train sufficient exemplars.

GENERAL CASE PROGRAMMING *General case programming* promotes generalization by training sufficient exemplars. It was developed many years ago to teach language, academic, and social skills to young children at risk (Becker & Engelmann, 1978). General case programming emphasizes using sufficient members of a class of stimuli to ensure that students will be able to perform the task on any member of the class of stimuli. If we want a child to identify red objects, we do not have to expose him to every red object in the world to ensure that he can perform this task. We just have to expose him to enough red objects having enough variety in their redness, and he will reliably identify any red object as red. For many children it is not necessary to be very systematic in picking the red objects—we just label whatever objects come our way. With learners who have disabilities, however, careful attention must be given to selecting objects that will facilitate their acquisition of this skill.

Engelmann and Carnine (1982) stated that examples used to train the general case must teach *sameness*—the characteristics of a stimulus that are the same for all members of a class—and *difference*—the range of variability within the members of a class. In other words, what do all red things have in common and how different can things be and still be red? The selection of the training stimuli is the critical factor in general case programming. If all the stimuli used in training sessions are red plastic objects of the same shade, the student asked to fetch the red book from the teacher's desk (it's her copy of Engelmann and Carnine's *Theory of Instruction*) may very well fail to do so because the book is an orangey red, not the pinkish red of the training stimuli. General case programming has been very successful in teaching academic behaviors to students with and without disabilities. It has also been used to teach appropriate social behaviors (Engelmann & Colvin, 1983). An early application of general case programming was teaching students with disabilities to use different vending machines by noticing all the variations of vending machines (e.g., where to put the money, types of buttons) and teaching those variations (Sprague & Horner, 1984).

Milata, Reeve, Reeve, and Dickson (2020) used a similar procedure to teach three adolescents with ASD, ages 18–25, to use chip-debit cards in multiple automatic payment machines (APM) to make purchases. They described two components of general case procedures (see Figure 11.2). The first is "general case analysis," the planning phase. This consisted of the researchers identifying the "instructional universe" as (1) stores within a 10-mile radius of the participants' school (e.g., CVS, Target), (2) critical stimuli that responses (e.g., "insert" evokes inserting the card), and (3) noncritical stimuli (e.g., font and position of the text). These critical and noncritical stimuli differed across APMs in the four stores, and the researchers identified 17 behaviors requires to use a chip debit card (e.g., inserting the card, pushing different buttons). The second component was "general case programming," the teaching

Figure 11.2

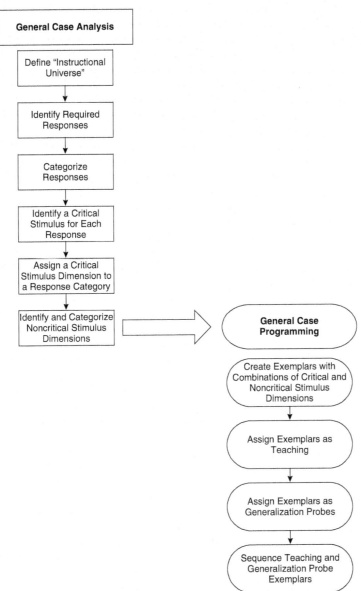

phase. The researchers used a refurbished APM in a classroom that was identical to the APMs in the stores. PowerPoint presentations were created to display the range of critical and noncritical stimulus variations present on the APMs across the four stores. The researchers presented video models of using the APMs at the four stores, as well as positive reinforcement and error correction. This intervention was successful in increasing correct responses in the teaching condition, a generalization condition at the school, and the APMs in the stores.

General case programming has been used to teach other functional skills to learners with severe disabilities, such as telephone skills, taking telephone messages, street crossing, using different soap dispensers for hand washing, sorting mail by zip code, bussing cafeteria tables, personal hygiene, and many other skills (Bicard, Horan, Plank, & Covington, 2009; Chezan et al., 2012; Horner, Eberhard, & Sheehan, 1986; Horner, Jones, & Williams, 1985; Horner, Williams, & Stevely, 1984; Stokes et al., 2004).

USING MULTIPLE SETTINGS, TEACHERS, AND ACTIVITIES Another approach to using sufficient exemplars is to train the behavior in a number of

See Chapter 9 for a discussion of generalization after punishment.

Sufficient Exemplars
Pearson eText
Video example 11.3
In this video, an educator teaches her young students the concepts of empty and full. How might this teaching instance be a component of a generalization plan related to training sufficient exemplars?

settings or with several different trainers. Doing this often results in generalization of the behavior change into settings where no training has taken place (Gomes et al., 2020). Considerable evidence exists to indicate that training novel responses under a wide variety of stimulus conditions increases the probability of generalization under conditions where no previous training has occurred. Such training has been successful with a variety of social behaviors, such as initiating bids for joint attention, social initiations, job-related social skills, and perspective taking (Gomes et al., 2020; Grob et al., 2019; Welsh et al., 2019; Wichnick-Gillis et al., 2019). This procedure differs from sequential modification in that change is targeted and assessed with settings, individuals, or activities in which no intervention has taken place.

Many studies have demonstrated that the effects of suppressing deviant behaviors in individuals with severe disabilities are situation- and experimenter-specific unless trained across several conditions (Falcomata & Wacker, 2013; Podlesnik et al., 2017). The effects of punishment contingencies are apparently less likely to generalize than behavior changes resulting from positive reinforcement (Ackerman, 1972), though some studies have demonstrated the generalization of punishment procedures (McKenzie et al., 2008; Piazza et al., 1996). The limited generalization of punishment procedures has probably contributed to the decrease in recent years of published studies using behavior suppression procedures.

The training of sufficient exemplars is a productive area for teachers concerned with increasing generalization. It is not necessary to teach students to perform appropriate behaviors in every setting or in the presence of every potential teacher or other adult. The teacher need train only enough to ensure that a generalized response has been learned. Neither is it necessary to teach every example of a response class that we want students to perform. Imagine the difficulty of teaching students to read if this were so. We expect students to generalize letter or syllable sounds and thus to decode words they have never read before. Most teaching of academic skills is based on the assumption that students will be able to use these skills to solve novel problems or to perform a variety of tasks. The following examples show how teachers may use training a number of exemplars to program response generalization and generalization across trainers and across settings. In the anecdote on the next page, DeWayne helps out Professor Grundy and illustrates the effectiveness of general case programming.

Carol Learns to Use Plurals

Carol was a 5-year-old student with a language delay in Ms. Sims's integrated preschool class. Carol had learned the names of many common objects but did not differentiate the singular from the plural forms. Ms. Sims made a point of labeling single and multiple examples of objects frequently during the school day: "Look, Carol, coat" (as Carol took hers off); "Carol, coats" (as she ran her hand over all the students' coats in the cloakroom); "Say coat" (as Carol hung up hers); "Say coats" (as she moved Carol's hand along all the coats). Using a discrimination training procedure, she brought Carol's verbal responses under stimulus control of the correct form of a number of singular and plural pairs:

cow	cows
shoe	shoes
dog	dogs
bird	birds
plane	planes

She then tested for generalization. She showed Carol a new set of pictures:

chair	chairs

Carol responded correctly. Her response using singular and plural forms had generalized to an untrained example. Carol used singular and plural forms correctly in a variety of untrained examples. Her response generalization was so broad that when the principal and superintendent visited the class, Ms. Sims heard Carol say to another student, "Mans come." Ms. Sims sighed, then remembered that such overgeneralization is not uncommon among young children and that she would just have to teach irregular plurals as a separate response class.

The Professor Goes High-Tech

After ignoring numerous memos and announcements regarding the importance of integrating technology into his classes, Professor Grundy reluctantly agreed to video-record some student presentations. The students were to include copies of the video files in e-portfolios they were required to compile before student teaching. He attended a seminar during which he received instruction on how to take videos on a tablet. He checked out a tablet and tripod from the technology office (Grundy was old-fashioned and still didn't have his own tablet), which looked very much unlike the ones on which he had received training. He picked up the tablet and looked for the home button – he looked on each side of the front and each side of the back and scratched his head vigorously. Just as the professor was about to announce that the presentations would not be recorded after all, DeWayne jumped out of his seat and approached the tablet.

"Whoa! This is the 12.0 version! Don't worry, Professor," he announced. "I've never worked with this one either, but I worked in the computer lab and I've used all sorts of smart devices so I'll figure it out. The university gets bids on each piece of equipment and buys it from the lowest bidder. It seems like that's never the same vendor so there's no two pieces of equipment of the same make or model."

"Let's see," he mumbled, "I'm thinking you swipe up from the bottom to get to the home screen. Yep, there we go." DeWayne handed it back to Grundy who now searched the icons for the camera app. To no avail, he handed it back to DeWayne who found the camera app nested in an app folder. Now the professor successfully flipped to the "video" screen in the camera app and attempted to put the device on the tripod. He tried to pull the four clips to snap onto the corners of the tablet, followed by the display of a very frustrated face. DeWayne took a look and popped the device into the four holders that sprung apart. Grundy profusely thanked his fine student, called up the first presenter, and pushed "record." DeWayne, peering over, said, "Professor, you might want to push the "flip" button so you don't record yourself watching the presentation!"

Train Loosely

Teaching techniques based on principles of behavior have historically emphasized tight control of many teaching factors (Becker, Engelmann, & Thomas, 1975a; Lovaas, 1987, 2003; Stephens, 1976). Teaching procedures for students with disabilities are often rigidly standardized: adhering to the same format, presenting items in a predetermined sequence, and requiring mastery of one skill before training on another has begun. Although this may be an efficient means of instruction, and although it is the way that most special educators were taught to teach, especially those training to work with populations having more severe disabilities, there is increasing evidence that it may not always be the best way to ensure that skills will be generalized. For example, in traditional descriptions of discrete trial teaching, pictures in matching and receptive discrimination tasks were equal sizes, arranged in a straight line in front of the student, and equidistant from each other (Lovaas, 1987, 2003). More recently, teachers implementing intensive teaching with students with autism and related disabilities are encouraged to arrange pictures in a "messy array"; that is, not in a straight line and not all the same size (Sundberg, 2008). The array is "messy" because the world, and therefore the generalization setting, is messy. Relatedly, when working with students with autism, teachers were traditionally taught to give instructions in a clear, consistent manner with concise language, such as saying, "Touch cat," in a monotone voice. Nowadays, some teachers vary their intonation each trial because general education teachers vary their intonation across instructions. Structure, rigidity, and consistency in early phases of teaching can help with stimulus control and correct responding. But, teaching in a structured and rigid manner is a poor way to program for generalization into less structured and consistent environments. Using "messy arrays" and varied intonation with instructions are ways to train loosely.

> This is the same phenomenon that causes a typical city 2-year-old to call the first cow she sees "doggie."

> Sometimes too much structure interferes with generalization.

Training loosely may have started in the early 1970s with investigations of alternating or rotating various stimuli or responses in highly structured training sessions, which resulted in a major change in the instruction of individuals with disabilities in the 1990s and beyond. Schroeder and Baer (1972) found that vocal imitation skills were better generalized to untaught members of the response class when the training stimuli were varied within sessions rather than when each skill was taught to mastery before instruction on another was begun. Rather than tightly restricting the vocal skills being taught (serial training), the researchers allowed a number of different imitations to be taught within a single session (concurrent training).

In an example of response alternation, Panyan and Hall (1978) investigated the effects of concurrent as opposed to serial training in the acquisition, maintenance, and generalization of two different response classes: tracing and vocal imitation. The serial training procedure required mastery of one response class (tracing) before instruction began on a second response class (vocal imitation). In the concurrent training procedure, training on the two different response classes was alternated in a single training session before either task was mastered. The procedure used did not affect the time required for acquisition or maintenance of the response trained, but generalization to untrained responses was greater under the concurrent training condition. These results have been replicated (Dufour & Lanovaz, 2017; Wunderlich et al., 2014, 2017) and have definite implications for the teacher. Apparently, it adds no efficiency to train students to master one skill before beginning instruction on another, unless of course the first skill is prerequisite to the second. Alternating teaching within sessions not only does not interfere with learning but, on the contrary, leads to greater generalization. Thus, statements like "I can't worry about Harold's math until I get him reading on grade level" may not be justified. Investigations of "loose training" have showed great promise in a wide variety of settings and for many behaviors. Variously termed *incidental teaching, naturalistic teaching, nonintensive teaching*, or *minimal intervention*, strategies that incorporate instruction for individuals with disabilities into less structured activities have been successful in promoting acquisition of behaviors and even more successful in promoting generalization (Bruinsma et al., 2020; Dufek & Schreibman, 2014; Haq & Aranki, 2019; Lane et al., 2016). Naturalistic interventions are most common in early childhood special education (Harjusola-Webb et al., 2012; Rahn et al., 2019). It is generally agreed that direct instruction and naturalistic teaching used together facilitate the generalization of language skills in children with autism.

Campbell and Stremel-Campbell (1982) taught two boys with moderate to severe disabilities to use various statements and questions while they were being taught academic and self-help skills. The target verbal skills were reinforced when they were emitted spontaneously or when their use was prompted. Both boys acquired the verbal skills along with the academic and self-help skills, and generalization also occurred. Using a procedure they called *nonintensive*, Inglesfield and Crisp (1985) compared the effects of teaching dressing skills 10 times a day for 3 days (an approach many special educators might choose for initial skill acquisition) to the effects of teaching the same skills twice a day for 15 days (an approach that would occur in the natural environment). They found the twice-daily procedure more effective for both initial learning and generalization. Milata et al. (2020; described above) considered teaching across the multiple critical and noncritical features of the APMs based on the general case analysis to be an example of training loosely.

The use of naturalistic or loose training represents a departure from tradition in special education teaching. Its success suggests again the importance of teachers' maintaining their skills and keeping up with current research. Although most special educators continue to use structured teaching during the acquisition of new skills, they rapidly begin to incorporate teaching and assessing these skills more informally.

Train Loosely
Pearson eText
Video Example 11. 4
In this video, two educators lead their class through a segment on shapes. Which strategies for promoting generalization are evident in their lesson?

Use Indiscriminable Contingencies

As we described in Chapter 8, resistance to extinction or maintenance of behavior is greatly prolonged by intermittent reinforcement schedules. Intermittent reinforcement may be used to maintain behaviors at a high rate, or it may be a step toward eliminating reinforcement entirely. It is possible to thin a reinforcement schedule to such a degree that few reinforcers are used. If reinforcement is then withdrawn altogether, the behavior will continue. This resistance to extinction is not permanent, because behavior, if unreinforced, will eventually be extinguished. It may be possible, however, that "eventually" will be so far in the future as to make no practical difference. The behavior will be maintained as long as necessary.

Long-standing evidence indicates that intermittent reinforcement schedules lead to increased maintenance of behavior change (Kazdin & Polster, 1973; Phillips, Phillips, Fixsen, & Wolf, 1971). Teachers should consider this evidence when planning and implementing behavior-change strategies. Even if intermittent reinforcement must be continued indefinitely, if schedules are very lean this may be a fairly efficient and economical means of providing for maintenance.

Other procedures besides intermittent reinforcement make it difficult for students to discriminate which responses will be reinforced. One strategy that may lead to generalization across settings is delaying the delivery of reinforcers. Long ago, Schwarz and Hawkins (1970) videotaped the behavior of a student during math and spelling classes. After the end of the school day, the student was shown the videotape, and appropriate behaviors in math class were reinforced. In the next days, a behavior change was evident in spelling class as well as math class. The authors hypothesized that the generalization across settings was due to the delayed reinforcement, which made it more difficult for the student to determine when contingencies were in effect. The availability and sophistication of video recording today enables wider and more creative uses of this technology, many of which will be discussed in Chapter 12.

Fowler and Baer (1981) used a delayed reinforcement procedure to modify various behaviors of preschool children. The children received tokens exchangeable for toys either immediately after the period during which they earned them or at the end of the day, after other periods during which no tokens were available. The children generalized the appropriate behavior; that is, they behaved better all day when the reinforcer was not given until the end of the day. Similarly, Dunlap, Koegel, Johnson, and O'Neill (1987) used delayed reinforcement to maintain the work performance of students with autism in community settings.

Another way of delivering reinforcers that resulted in decreased discriminability of contingencies was demonstrated by Koegel and Rincover (1977). The authors taught children with autism to perform simple nonverbal imitations or to follow simple instructions. After the behavior was learned (using continuous reinforcement), schedules were thinned. Once training was concluded, the children were observed to allow researchers to assess maintenance of behavior change. The behaviors were ultimately extinguished. (The thinner the schedule during training, the more responses occurred before extinction.) The use of noncontingent reinforcers after extinction, however, resulted in recovery of the behavior. At random intervals, the children were given candy identical to that earned in the original training setting—whether their responses were correct or not. The noncontingent reinforcers delayed extinction considerably. Apparently, the reinforcer had acquired the properties of a discriminative stimulus. It served as a cue to the students that, in this setting, reinforcement was available. The students were unable to discriminate which responses would be reinforced, so they produced larger numbers of the correct (previously reinforced) responses before extinction. This procedure also illustrates aspects of providing common stimuli discussed later in this chapter.

Thin intermittent reinforcement schedules are the most frequently used means of making reinforcement contingencies indiscriminable. Evidence indicates, however, that any procedure that makes it difficult for students to determine when contingencies

> ## Ms. Bell's Class Learns to Complete Assignments
>
> In the morning group in her intermediate-level resource room, Ms. Bell's students with intellectual disabilities consistently failed to complete their assignments. Each student was expected to independently complete a reading comprehension, a math, and a spelling activity, while Ms. Bell worked with small groups on other academic skills. Ms. Bell began giving her students tokens worth 5 minutes of free time to be exchanged at the end of the morning for each assignment completed. This resulted in almost 100% completion of assignments. Ms. Bell then announced that tokens would not be given until the end of the period and that only two assignments could earn tokens. She put the words *reading*, *spelling*, and *math* on slips of paper and allowed a student to draw two slips. The students did not know until the end of the hour which two assignments would earn free time but continued to complete their assignments. Ms. Bell, who wanted to move to a lean reinforcement schedule, then announced that there would be the possibility of two drawings daily: one for a "yes/no" card, which would determine whether reinforcement would be available, and a second if the "yes" card was drawn. The second drawing would determine which assignment would earn free time. At first, one "yes" and one "no" card were available. She then gradually added "no" cards to the pool until there was only a 20% probability that free time would be available. The students continued to complete their assignments in all three subject areas and seemed to enjoy the suspense of never knowing when free time would be available or for which specific behavior.

are in effect is likely to result in greater durability of behavior change, either in the original training setting or in other settings. The example above illustrates a procedure that makes it difficult for students to make such determinations.

Indiscriminable contingencies have been applied as a component of group contingencies (see Chapter 8). For example, Beeks and Graves (2016) described the Mystery Motivator intervention as part of an interdependent group contingency. The teacher creates a calendar of the school days and randomly writes an M on some of the days using an invisible ink marker. When the class meets a behavioral expectation, such as refraining from off-task talking, the teacher asks a student to color in the day on the calendar and reveal if there is an M, resulting in a classwide reward, or not, resulting in praise. In the context of a dependent group contingency with at-risk second graders in small groups, Cariveau and Kodak (2017) randomly and secretly selected a student whose behavior—meeting or not meeting a percentage of intervals on task—determined if the whole group earned a randomly selected, preferred activity during a break. Not knowing if today is a reward day or if I am the one being observed keeps everyone on their toes—a hallmark of indiscriminable contingencies.

Program Common Stimuli

Walker and Buckley (1972) asserted "intra-subject behavioral similarity across different settings is probably a function, in part, of the amount of stimulus similarity which exists between such settings" (p. 209). Kirby and Bickel (1988) suggested that stimulus similarity, and thus stimulus control, is the major factor in any generalization. A possible method of achieving either maintenance or stimulus generalization is deliberate programming of similar stimuli in the training setting and in the setting in which generalization is desired. That is, generalization can be achieved by making the training setting as much like the generalization setting as possible. This may be accomplished by either increasing the similarity of the training situation to the natural environment or by introducing elements of the training situation into the natural environment.

Several studies have investigated the effects of introducing elements of the natural environment into the training situation to increase the probability of generalization. For example, Ayllon and Kelly (1974) restored speech in a girl who was electively mute. After speech occurred frequently in the training situation (a counselor's office), elements similar to those present in the classroom were introduced. Other children, a blackboard, and desks were installed in the room; and the trainer began to function more as a traditional teacher by standing in the front of the room, lecturing, and asking questions. Training was also continued in the classroom. Increases in speech occurred in the classroom, and a follow-up a year later indicated that speech was maintained in several novel settings. Although the specific effects of the increase in similarity between training and natural settings are difficult to assess because of the package of treatments employed, generalization to the classroom did occur and was maintained.

Koegel and Rincover (1974) trained children with autism to respond to instructions in a one-to-one situation. Generalization to a classroom setting was programmed by gradually introducing more children into the training situation, so that it resembled the classroom. Stokes and Baer (1976) taught word recognition to students with learning disabilities through a peer-tutoring procedure. The students did not display the skills in other settings until the peer tutor and pupil were brought together. Then both students showed increased generalization.

Livi and Ford (1985) found that domestic skills generalized from a training site to each student's home much more efficiently when stimuli similar to those in each home were used. (Every effort should be made to teach those skills in the students' homes.) In general, using discriminative stimuli during training that are similar to those in the setting where generalization is desired has proven to be a very effective technique (Stainback, Stainback, & Strathe, 1983). Woods (1987) suggested that such a procedure is an adaptation of the naturalistic procedures discussed previously, in that the stimuli in the generalization setting are natural ones.

One way of attempting to introduce natural stimuli into training settings is through the use of simulations. For example, van den Pol et al. (1981) successfully used pictures of fast-food items to teach students with moderate intellectual disabilities to use community fast-food establishments. Simulated instruction for students with more severe disabilities is generally less successful (Foxx, McMorrow, & Mennemeier, 1984; Marchetti, McCartney, Drain, Hooper, & Dix, 1983). Horner et al. (1987) suggested that simulations employing real, rather than representational, items from the environment may be more successful. Simulations using real stimuli have been used to teach numerous generalized skills, including comprehension of category labels, using the telephone, playing video games, interviewing, firearm safety, dental care, bathroom hygiene, and menstrual care (Byra et al., 2018; Horner et al., 1987; Hupp, 1986; Maxfield et al., 2019; Richman, Reiss, Bauman, & Bailey, 1984; Sedlack, Doyle, & Schloss, 1982; Stocco et al., 2017; Szalwinski et al., 2019). Some studies have attempted to increase generalization by introducing elements of the training situation into the setting where generalization was desired. Rincover and Koegel (1975) taught children with autism to imitate nonverbal behaviors modeled by a therapist. When the children responded correctly on 20 consecutive trials without a prompt, a transfer test was made. For children who emitted no correct responses on the transfer test, an assessment of stimulus control was made. Stimuli from the training environment were introduced into the regular setting, one at a time. If the child did not respond correctly in the presence of the first stimulus, that stimulus was removed and another one introduced. This process was continued until the stimulus controlling the behavior was identified and the responses occurred in the regular setting. It was found that each of the children was responding selectively to some incidental stimulus in the treatment room. When this stimulus was provided in the regular setting, each child responded correctly. The amount of responding in the regular situation was, however, consistently less than in the training situation.

> Simulations may be more practical than always teaching every skill in the natural environment.

Baer (1999) and Ayllon, Kuhlman, and Warzak (1983) suggested the use of a contrived common stimulus. A portable object was introduced from the training setting into the setting in which generalization was desired. Ayllon et al. (1983) called the object a "lucky charm." Taking an object that had been associated with reinforcement from the training setting to the general education setting resulted in better academic and behavioral performance. Trask-Tyler et al. (1994) suggested that a portable tape player with audio instructions for task completion is such a contrived common stimulus that may have great promise for improving generalization for students with severe disabilities. Many of the procedures described in Chapter 10 using schedules, picture cues, pagers, handheld computers, and other relatively unobtrusive items have shown excellent generalization results—to new settings and to novel tasks.

In another example of demonstrating generalization from a special education classroom to a general education classroom, Mesmer et al. (2007) targeted this type of generalization of completing academic work with three elementary-aged students with emotional and developmental disabilities. They were first given two items in the special education classroom: a goal statement indicating how much work needed to be completed to earn a reward, and a thumbs up icon on a worksheet or a digital timer. Correct responses increased in the special education classroom, but only in the general education classroom when the goal statement and the thumbs up or timer were also present in the classroom.

A logical extension of programming common stimuli may change completely the approach to providing services for persons with severe and profound disabilities. The setting with the most stimuli common to the setting where generalization is desired is that setting itself. If we want behavior to occur in the classroom, why not teach it in the classroom rather than an isolated treatment room or corner (Horner & Budd, 1985)? If the behavior should occur in the community (Bourbeau et al., 1986) or in an employment site (Dehaven, Corley, Hofeling, & Garcia, 1982), why not teach it there? Miltenberger et al. (1999) taught sexual abuse prevention skills to women with intellectual disabilities. The skills did not generalize until they were taught in the community. Community-based programming for persons with disabilities is now accepted practice. On the other hand, it can be more efficient to teach safety skills in a classroom and test for generalization in the community. It is critical to program for generalization effectively with this goal. Carlile et al. (2018) taught students with autism what to do when lost in a store, such as notifying an employee and calling a caregiver. They taught the skills in a classroom in the students' school and programmed common stimuli by creating a "mock store" in the classroom with the uniforms, banners, signs, sale items, shopping bags, and shopping baskets from each store. This, along with video modeling and error correction, resulted in the acquisition and generalization of the safety skills.

The potential effectiveness of stimulus control for stimulus generalization and maintenance is a factor that should be considered by all teachers. Relatively simple and economical measures can help ensure reliable generalization in many settings and help maintain gains long after training has been terminated. The following vignettes illustrate generalization achieved by increasing stimulus similarity.

Program Common Stimuli

Pearson eText

Video example 11.5

In this video, an educator helps Vince complete a pre-vocational filing task using a card box and index cards. Use of the stimuli that may be found in a vocational setting will promote generalization. What other strategies to promote generalization to a workplace could be applied?

Ms. Statler's Students Get Ready for Supported Employment

Ms. Statler was a teacher of secondary students with moderate to severe disabilities. Some of her students were receiving instruction that would enable them to gain independent employment, and others were preparing for employment in a more supportive environment. For these students, supported employment in a local nursery greenhouse with a full-time job coach on site was the goal. Because of transportation and other logistical problems, it was possible to take the students to the nursery for instruction only once a week.

Although Ms. Statler could teach relevant skills in the classroom, she was concerned that the environment was not very similar to that of the nursery and was much less visually and aurally distracting. To solve these problems, she borrowed a number of props from the nursery, including a bench like the one at which the students would eventually work, and created a mini environment in one corner of her classroom. She also made an audio recording of the nursery environment. While she played this recording, she arranged for as many people as possible to visit her classroom for a minute or two and to walk through the mini environment, examining plants and communicating with the students.

Sammy Learns to Behave in the Second Grade

Sammy was a student in Mr. Reddy's class for students who were developmentally delayed. His academic work was superior, but he displayed disruptive behavior, such as shouting gibberish and making strange movements with his hands and arms. This behavior was controlled in the special class by positive reinforcement on a DRO schedule, but Mr. Reddy had noticed that outside the special class Sammy continued to shout and gesture. Because the goal of the special program was to return students to the general education classroom as quickly as possible, Mr. Reddy was concerned about Sammy's behavior outside the special class.

Mr. Reddy decided to borrow a second grader from Sammy's class. After getting parental permission, he invited Brad, a gifted student, to visit his class for half an hour three times a week. He taught Brad basic learning principles to help with a project Brad was doing for his enrichment class. He also allowed Brad to give reinforcers to Sammy during his observation periods. When Sammy began spending short periods of time in the general education class, Brad came to get him and brought him back. Sammy consistently behaved appropriately in the second-grade class, even though no reinforcers were ever given there. Brad's presence had become an S^D for appropriate behavior for Sammy.

Mediate Generalization and Train to Generalize

We shall consider together these last two procedures for facilitating generalization: *mediating generalization* and *training to generalize*. It is possible to increase the probability of generalization by reinforcing generalization as a response class (Stokes & Baer, 1977). In other words, if students receive reinforcers specifically for displaying behavior in settings other than the training setting, performing learned behaviors in a novel setting may become a generalized response class. The students have thus been taught to generalize. If the student has sufficient receptive verbal ability, it is appropriate to explain the contingency to the student; that is, students may be told that if they perform a particular behavior in a new setting, reinforcement will be available (Mastropieri & Scruggs, 1984). It is also possible to teach students to offer varied behaviors by reinforcing variation. One way to do this is to use a **lag schedule of reinforcement**. When using a lag schedule, the teacher provides reinforcement only for responses that are different from the previous response to that cue (Lag 1), or the previous two responses (Lag 2), and so on.

Ivy et al. (2019) used a lag schedule to increase the variety of leisure items with which three students with autism (ages 11–12) engaged. In general, students with autism exhibit repetitive behavior or restricted interests which precludes them from participating in and learning from more varied activities. Before the lag schedule, when the students were told it was leisure time and offered four leisure items, such as magazines, a bracelet kit, a puzzle, and drawing, they engaged nearly exclusively with one item or rapidly switched between items (not allowing time to engage with each). During the lag schedule, the researcher delivered an edible reinforcer or high five when the student chose a leisure item "that was different from the activity selected during a majority of the intervals for the previous two sessions" (p. 266). This intervention increased the variety of leisure items the two students with rigid patterns engaged in and decreased the rapid switching of the other student.

Radley et al. (2019) used a Lag 2 and a Lag 4 schedule to increase the variability of social responses with five students with ASD, ages 10–14. The target skills, which were from a social skills curriculum, were maintaining a conversation, initiating participation, expressing wants and needs, and responding to questions. An example of a skill was answering "Tell me about your day" with multiple responses. At first, the researchers used behavior skills training, which consisted of providing instructions, modeling correct responses, having the students role-play, and providing feedback. They evaluated a condition where they modeled one response and a condition where they modeled three responses. The next condition was modeling three responses and reinforcing on a Lag 2 schedule; that is, each response had to be different from the previous two responses. The final condition was modeling three responses and reinforcing on a Lag 4 schedule. In the lag schedule conditions, if a student repeated a response, the researcher prompted a different response. All four conditions increased correct responses, and the Lag 4 condition produced the most variable responses.

Wiskow et al. (2018) evaluated lag schedules with two 6-year-old students with autism. They targeted variability when responding to verbal category tasks, such as, "Tell me some vehicles," and "Tell me some fruits." Students with autism may provide the same response each time, and it is important to teach students to respond with many varied answers. With one student, the researchers compared starting with a Lag 9 schedule to progressively increasing the lag schedule from Lag 1 to 2 to 4 to 8 to 9. The student varied more quickly with the Lag 9 schedule, but this appeared to evoke negative statements indicating the student found it very difficult. With the other student, neither of these procedures (Lag 9 or progressive lag schedules) increased varied responses. Therefore, the researchers implemented a priming strategy by having the student label nine pictures of items in the category before the session. This was effective in generating varied responding, even when the Lag 9 schedule was later implemented without the priming procedure.

> We can teach students to generalize some skills.

Lag schedules have also been used to increase the variability of requests (Silbaugh & Falcomata, 2019), play skills (Lang et al., 2014), speech sounds (Koehler-Platten et al., 2013), foods consumed (Silbaugh & Falcomata, 2017), labeling pictures (Heldt & Schlinger, 2012), and answers to "How are you?" (Susa & Schlinger, 2012).

In mediating generalization, students are taught to monitor and report on their own generalization of appropriate behavior. Such a program involves self-control or self-management, possibly the most promising of all techniques for ensuring the generalization and maintenance of behavior change. If you check the dates on many of the studies discussed in this chapter, you will find that many date from the 1970s and 1980s. Although those procedures are still valuable, most researchers are currently focusing on self-management training to facilitate generalization. Ways of teaching these skills will be described in Chapter 12. For many students, the ultimate objective of the applied behavior analyst is to bring behavior under the control of self-monitoring, self-administered contingencies, and even self-selected goals and procedures.

Summary

We have investigated many techniques for promoting stimulus generalization, response generalization, and maintenance of behavior. In the first edition of this text, we stated that the technology of generalization was in its infancy. In the second edition, we suggested that it had reached the toddler stage. With increased emphasis on theoretical and practical analysis of generalization, there is reason to hope that the technology will continue to mature. Every year there is more emphasis on generalization in the literature. Its status, however, was well described by Buchard and Harig (1976):

> Formulating questions about generalization is somewhat like a game that might go something like this: At the start, there are two things to worry about. Will the behavioral change be maintained in the natural environment or won't it? If it won't, then there are two more things to worry about. Does the lack of generalization reflect the type or level of the reinforcement schedule that produced the behavioral change in the first place, or did the behavior fail to generalize because of a lack of supporting contingencies in the community? If the problem pertains to the schedule, you have little to worry about. You go back to the treatment setting and strengthen the desirable behavior, preferably through a positive reinforcement schedule. However, if the problem is with the supporting contingencies in the natural environment, then you have more things to worry about. Should you reprogram the natural environment to provide supporting contingencies through intermittent reinforcement, fading, or overlearning? And so on ... (pp. 428–429)

Obviously the game is one in which these questions can be formulated ad infinitum. With generalization, the unfortunate part is that there will probably always be something to worry about; this is the nature of the beast! It is hard enough to try to determine whether or not behavior has changed, and if so why, let alone trying to determine whether or not the change also occurred in a completely different setting. Applied behavior analysts who are also teachers may never stop worrying about generalization. Given the techniques described in this chapter and the next, however, there appears to be less and less excuse for mere worrying. If applied behavior analysis procedures are to become an accepted part of the repertoire of every teacher, it is time, as Baer et al. (1968) suggested, "to stop lamenting and start programming."

Discussion Questions

1. Ms. Ashcroft is a teacher of students with mild cognitive disabilities. All of her students are placed full-time in general education classes, and Ms. Ashcroft co-teaches for 2 hours each day with three general education teachers. She is frustrated because her students do not do as well academically or socially when she is not in their classroom. What might Ms. Ashcroft and her co-teachers do to help these students?

2. Mr. Jenkins is well aware that his adolescent students with severe disabilities will do better with job skills if they can be trained at job sites. Budgetary and logistical issues, however, prevent his being able to take the students to job sites as frequently as he would like. Think of five specific things Mr. Jenkins might do without leaving the high school campus to help his students get ready for employment in the community.

Chapter 12
Teaching Students to Manage Their Own Behavior

Learning Outcomes

12.1 Characterize instances of informal or systematic self-management in one's own behavior.

12.2 Explain the roles of goal-setting, self-monitoring, self-evaluation, self-reinforcement, self-punishment, and self-instruction.

12.3 Describe the use of self-management techniques specific to individuals with severe disabilities, mild disabilities, and at-risk for disabilities.

CHAPTER OUTLINE

A Common Experience

Preparing Students to Manage Their Own Behavior
- Goal Setting
- Self-Monitoring
- Self-Evaluation
- Self-Reinforcement
- Self-Punishment
- Self-Instruction

Self-Management for Special Populations
- Self-Management for Learners with Severe Disabilities
- Self-Management for Learners with Mild Disabilities
- Self-Management for Students at Risk

Summary

The best person to manage each student's behavior is the student herself. We call this kind of behavioral intervention *self-management*. Your grandmother called it self-control or self-discipline. Anyone who is to function independently to any extent must learn to manage his own behavior. There is considerable interest among theorists about the development of self-control or self-discipline among people in general (Baumeister, Vohs, & Tice, 2007) and in the processes and mechanisms that enable some people to be more responsible and productive than others. Such theoretical concerns are beyond the scope of this text; we will confine our discussion to relatively simple procedures that teachers can use to help students progress toward independence. There is also considerable speculation as to why some of the procedures, singly or in combination, are effective. Although many researchers offer theories, at this point we really do not know why they work (Briesch, Daniels, & Beneville, 2019), just that they often do. As teachers, we will do what we always do—try something, make data-based decisions as to its effectiveness, and either continue to do it if it works or discard it and try something else if it does not.

Throughout this book, we have described procedures for teachers to use to change their students' behavior. In Chapter 11, we discussed many ways to increase the generalizability of behavior change and thus minimize the necessity for continued teacher support. This chapter further examines techniques that enable teachers to make students less dependent on teachers' environmental manipulation. The procedures discussed place the responsibility for change on the student. The focus in all the approaches is on teaching students to become effective modifiers of their own behavior. John Dewey (1939) suggested many years ago that "the ideal aim of education is the creation of self-control" (p. 75). Students who have self-control can learn and behave appropriately even when adult supervision is not available.

Lovitt (1973) noted that "self-management behaviors are not systematically programmed [in the schools], which appears to be an educational paradox, for one of the expressed objectives of the educational system is to create individuals who are self-reliant and independent" (p. 139). If we, as teachers, agree that our goals include independence for our students, then we must teach students to be independent. Although total independence is not possible for all students, most can be taught to be more self-reliant. Kazdin (2001, pp. 302–303) offered several additional reasons for preferring self-management to that controlled by external change agents:

- The use of external change agents sacrifices consistency, because teachers or others may "miss" certain instances of behavior.
- Problems associated with communication between agents in different settings (such as teachers and parents) can also undermine the success of a program.
- The change agents themselves can become an environmental cue for the performance or lack of performance of a behavior.
- An individual's contribution to the development of a personal behavior-change program may increase performance.
- External agents are not always available in the environment where the target behavior is occurring or should occur.

Both typical learners and those with disabilities can be taught to monitor and change their own behavior. This is becoming increasingly critical as more and more students with disabilities spend time in general education and community settings. We will describe several aspects of self-management, including goal setting, self-monitoring, self-evaluation, self-reinforcement, and self-instruction. Students can use any technique to change their own behavior that a teacher can use to change it for them. Students can be taught to set their own goals and objectives, to record data about their behavior, to evaluate their behavior, and to provide their own consequences through self-reinforcement and even self-punishment. Students can also learn to manipulate behavioral antecedents by using self-instruction. Although each of these self-management techniques is described separately, in practice they have most often been employed in packages. In other words, combinations of the procedures were used—for example, self-monitoring with self-reinforcement or self-instruction with self-reinforcement. Although we will discuss goal setting, self-monitoring or evaluation, self-monitoring, and self-instruction separately, these procedures have been used almost universally in combination with one another and with other procedures such as direct instruction and modeling. It is often impossible to identify which components of such packages are actually influencing behavior. Some efforts have

Self-management usually comes in packages.

been made to examine the differential effects of the various procedures (Fritz et al., 2012), but for now most teachers will settle for knowing that many of the procedures work in combination. We will describe the use of several self-management packages in some detail.

A Common Experience

Learning Outcome 12.1 Characterize instances of informal or systematic self-management in one's own behavior.

Self-management procedures are as much a part of the natural environment as are all the behavioral procedures described in this book. Many people use goal setting, self-monitoring, self-reinforcement, self-punishment, and self-instruction in managing their everyday behavior.

Many popular self-help and self-improvement programs are commercially available to adults who wish to change their lives for the better financially, emotionally, romantically, or in the area of productivity. Virtually all of these programs begin by encouraging their users to set goals, to put them in writing, and to use them to change behavior. As we originally wrote this section, a new year was approaching and millions of people were engaged in **goal setting** in the form of making New Year's resolutions. Some of the strategies we suggest might help them to stick to these resolutions more successfully.

Many self-employed or freelance workers use **self-monitoring** as a means of maintaining productivity. Author Irving Wallace (1977) described how he and other authors, including Anthony Trollope and Ernest Hemingway, have practiced self-monitoring techniques. Trollope, a Victorian novelist, described the reactivity of such self-monitoring rather graphically: "There has ever been the record before me, and a week passed with an insufficient number of pages has been a blister to my eye and a month so disgraced would have been a sorrow to my heart" (p. 518).

The use of **self-reinforcement** is also familiar to most people. Consider the following teacher's internal monologue as she heads home from a day at school:

> What a day! Bus duty at 7:00 a.m...
> Jenny Lind fell, sprained her ankle, screamed like a banshee, and her mother says she's going to sue...
> Clifford refused to believe that 6 times 4 was 24 today just because it was yesterday...
> Two fights over whose turn it was to use the blue paint in art class. Tran ended up with the blue paint; Mark ended up blue...
> The picture money didn't balance...
> Why does that Velma Johnson always sit next to me at lunch and talk my ear off?
> I kept my temper all day though—I deserve a stop at Baskin-Robbins!

If the same teacher also practices **self-punishment**, she may remember the three scoops of rocky road at lunchtime tomorrow and restrict herself to two pieces of lettuce and a diet drink.

Many of us also practice **self-instruction**, providing ourselves with verbal prompts. We talk to ourselves, sometimes aloud, as we do complex or unfamiliar tasks. Many children also use such self-instruction naturally (Winsler, 2009). For example, Kohlberg, Yaeger, and Hjertholm (1968) recorded the self-instruction processing of a 2-year-old child during solitary play with a set of Tinker Toys.

> The wheels go here, the wheels go here. Oh, we need to start it all over again. We have to close it up. See, it closes up. We're starting it all over again. Do you know why we wanted to do that? Because I needed it to go a different way. Isn't it pretty clever, don't you think? But we have to cover up the motor just like a real car. (p. 695)

Briesch et al. (2019) offered a comprehensive definition of self-management: "self-management will only be effective in promoting sustained behavior change if three components are present. That is, after observing one's own behavior (i.e., self-monitoring), one must then compare the observed behavior to a goal or standard (i.e., self-evaluation) and reward one's self (i.e., self-reinforcement) if the criterion is met" (p. 71). We suggest the following flow chart of 5 components of a self-management system:

Each of these steps will be described.

B. F. Skinner, the founder of behaviorism, was a master of self-management techniques (Epstein, 1997). Using goal setting, environmental management, self-monitoring, self-assessment, and reinforcement, he was able to be incredibly productive and to maintain this productivity until the day before his death at 84. He even produced a book about using self-management techniques to overcome the difficulties presented by old age (Skinner & Vaughan, 1983). Two of us read about it as an amusing curiosity when this text was initially published; we each now own a copy, and thanks to Dr. Skinner, know exactly where those copies are.

Teaching students to manage their behavior is a mechanism for systematizing and making more powerful these naturally occurring phenomena. Some students may be effective self-managers without training; others may be unready to manage their own behavior to even a small extent. Diminished ability for self-regulation has been found in students with intellectual disabilities (Vieillevoye & Nader-Grosbois, 2008), learning disabilities (Berkeley & Larsen, 2018), emotional disturbance (Popham, Counts, Ryan, & Katsiyannis, 2018), and physical disabilities (Varsamis & Agaliotis, 2011). The wise teacher will remain alert for signs that students are ready to begin managing their own behaviors and will take advantage of this readiness. The strategies discussed in this chapter are sometimes called *cognitive training strategies* or *metacognitive strategies* (Chevalier et al., 2017; Schiff, Nuri Ben-Shushan, & Ben-Artzi, 2017). Along with other strategies less closely related to applied behavior analysis, they are ways to help students solve problems more productively.

Preparing Students to Manage Their Own Behavior

Learning Outcome 12.2 Explain the roles of goal-setting, self-monitoring, self-evaluation, self-reinforcement, self-punishment, and self-instruction.

The teacher who uses some systematic behavior-management program can try a number of techniques to increase students' potential for taking the responsibility for managing their own behavior.

- Teachers may ask students to set goals. "Sammy, you did 7 problems correctly in 10 minutes yesterday; how many do you think you can do today?"
- Teachers may ask students to evaluate their performance. "Sammy, check your problems with the answer sheet. How many did you do correctly?"
- When delivering reinforcers, the teacher may explain to the student what behavior resulted in reinforcement. "Sammy, you did 10 math problems correctly. You get 10 points—1 for each problem."

Preparing for Self-Monitoring
Pearson eText
Video Example 12.1
In this video, an educator sets expectations and prepares students to transition to their next room. Which strategies related to preparing students for self-monitoring do you notice?

- The teacher may ask the student to relate part of the contingency. "Sammy, you get 10 points. Why do you get 10 points?" or "Sammy, you did 10 problems right. How many points have you earned?"
- The teacher may ask the student to state the entire contingency. "Sammy, how many points? Why?"
- The teacher may involve students in choosing reinforcers and in determining their cost in terms of behavior.

Students who have been exposed to such techniques will frequently volunteer statements about their behavior and its consequences. It is a small step from asking a student how many points he has earned and why to allowing him to record the points himself with teacher supervision. Ultimately, Sammy may be allowed to check his own answers, count the number of problems he has done correctly, and record his points on his card.

Goal Setting

We addressed the issue of teachers' and students' negotiating goals and contingencies when we described the use of contracts in Chapter 9. People usually believe that teachers set goals for students as part of the educational process. This is certainly true in some cases, but students can be taught to set their own goals. There is clear evidence that students who set their own goals perform better than those whose goals are simply assigned by others (Mazzotti et al., 2013; Reed & Lynn, 2016; Shogren & Wehmeyer, 2017). This is consistent with evidence that providing choices to students improves academic performance (Ennis et al., 2020; Lane et al., 2015; Wehmeyer & Abery, 2013). Xu et al. (2017) used a combination of goal setting and self-monitoring to improve the academic engagement of a 9-year-old student with ASD in China. Weeden et al. (2016) used goal setting in a classroom management intervention to increase the on-task behavior of six elementary students with emotional and behavioral disorders in a self-contained, urban classroom. Grossi and Heward (1998) taught adults with developmental disabilities enrolled in a community-based restaurant training program to set goals as part of a self-management package. Each trainee was encouraged to set goals regarding speed and duration for tasks such as pot scrubbing, dish racking, sweeping and mopping floors, and bussing and setting tables. Trainees were encouraged to set goals that were higher than their baseline means but not higher than the highest performance during baseline. As goals were met, trainees were encouraged to increase their goals to approximate a competitive standard established by observing the performance of nondisabled employees. Along with self-evaluation, this procedure enabled the trainees to improve performance significantly.

Gureasko-Moore, DuPaul, and White (2006) used goal setting as part of a package that also used self-monitoring and self-evaluation. The students were 12-year-old boys diagnosed with ADHD and, like many such students, their academic problems stemmed mainly from their failure to perform what the authors call "classroom preparation behaviors." They didn't come to class on time, they didn't have materials, and they didn't do homework. The four students met as a group and were asked to record their problems with class preparation and to record these in a log. They were given a checklist with six items and asked how many they agreed to complete during the first week. They completed the checklists independently and discussed them with the experimenter daily. They were asked to evaluate their performance and to write the evaluation in their logs. The procedure was successful for all the students. Meetings were faded to every other day and eventually occurred only weekly. Improvements were maintained through a 4-week period of weekly meetings.

Reed and Lynn (2016) used goal setting to increase the number of inferences middle school students with disabilities made when reading text. The teacher first explained and modeled how to make inferences from text and provided the students with a graphic organizer in which to write inferences. Then students used a goal setting form (Figure 12.1, top) either individually or as a group to write down how many inferences they thought they could make with a given passage. When the students received the graded graphic organizers from the teachers, they recorded how many correct inferences they made on the graph (Figure 12.1, bottom). When students met their goal for two consecutive sessions, they increased the goal; if they did not meet their goal for two consecutive sessions, they met with a teacher to practice the skill or reset their goal. Goal setting as a whole class was most effective in increasing the number of correct inferences the students made.

When teaching students to set goals, it is important to help them set goals that are specific, challenging, but achievable, and whose attainment, in the early stages, is immediate rather than distant. It is also helpful to provide feedback about the success or failure of achieving goals.

Figure 12.1 Examples of goal setting form (top) and self-graphing form (bottom)

STUDENT CONFERENCE: DATE_____ TIME_____

Goal #1:

Steps I will take to reach this goal:

1.
2.
3.

Date I accomplished the goal:

1 Point = Needs improvement

Goal Chart

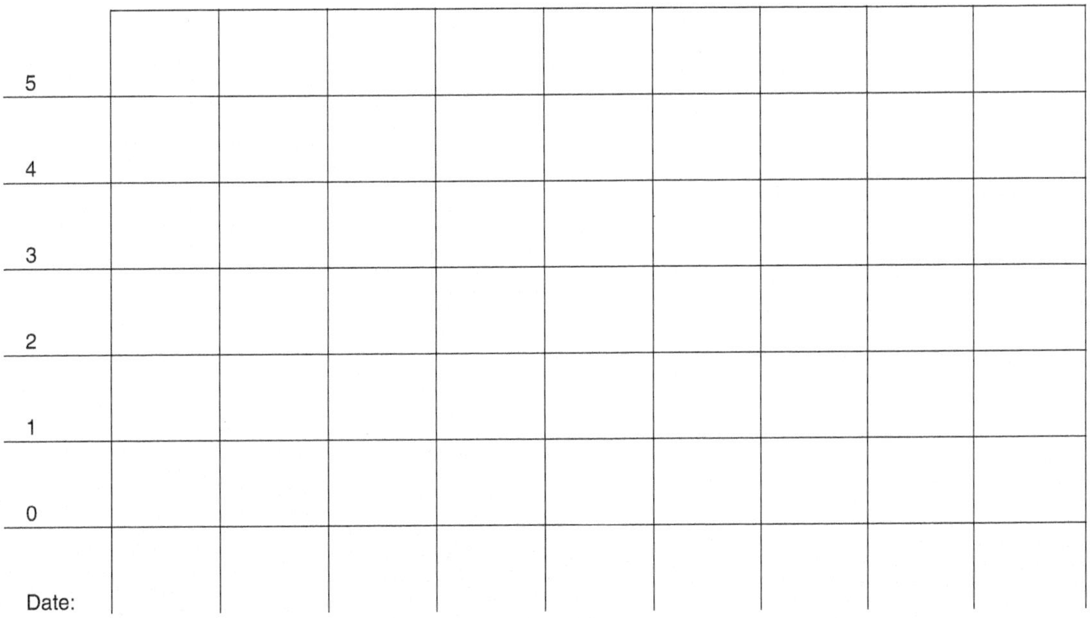

Self-Monitoring

| Chapter 4 describes techniques for data collection. | Students may be asked to keep a record of their behavior rather than having it recorded by an observer as described in Chapter 4. Having students record data is called *self-monitoring* and often includes asking students to also evaluate their performance, known as self-evaluation. This sometimes takes the form of *cued self-monitoring*, when students are given a signal, such as a recorded tone or tactile cue, and asked to indicate whether they were performing the behavior when they heard the tone or felt the cue; and it sometimes takes the form of *non-cued self-monitoring*, when students are asked to make a notation each time they perform the target behavior. Figure 12.2 provides an example of a data collection sheet that students might use. |

| The reactive effect of self-monitoring may only be temporary. | Self-monitoring provides the student and teacher with concrete feedback regarding behavior. This information may be used to determine what reinforcers are available. In some cases, collecting data on a behavior may have a *reactive effect* on |

Figure 12.2 Student self-monitoring form

Name: _____

Date: _____

	Yes ☺		No ☹	
Day	1st Bell	2nd Bell	1st Bell	2nd Bell

* At this exact second am I doing my work?

Note: From Levendoski, L. S., & Cartledge, G. (2000). Self-monitoring for elementary school children with serious emotional disturbances: Classroom applications for increased academic responding. *Behavioral Disorders, 25,* 211–224.

the behavior. The behavior may change in the desired direction as a function of the self-monitoring process alone. In this capacity, self-monitoring, in and of itself, functions as a behavior-change technique (McDougall et al., 2012). In some cases, it is as effective as an external cue or reminder. If you have ever tried to budget money by writing down every penny you spend in a little notebook, you have probably experienced this reactivity. If, while reading a chapter on self-management, you start recording every instance of daydreaming with a tally mark on a 3 × 5 card, you will probably daydream less. (If 3 × 5 cards are unavailable, just make a pencil mark in the margin or a tally mark on a notes app on your computer or tablet.)

As a self-management and behavior-change technique, self-monitoring has been successfully used in a variety of settings, with a wide variety of behaviors, and with learners with and without disabilities, both decades ago (Coleman & Blampied, 1977; Koegel & Koegel, 1984; Swanson, 1981) and more recently (Beckman et al., 2019; Boswell et al., 2013; Bouck et al., 2014; Bruhn et al., 2016, 2017; Clemons et al., 2016; Cook et al., 2017; Falkenberg & Barbetta, 2013; Guzman et al., 2018; Holifield et al., 2010; Hudson, 2019; Joseph & Eveleigh, 2011; King et al., 2014; Kolbenschlag & Wunderlich, 2020; Li et al., 2019; McDougall et al., 2012; Miller & Taber-Doughty, 2014; Rosenbloom et al., 2019; Rouse et al., 2014; Schardt et al., 2019; Wadsworth et al., 2015; Wells et al., 2017; Xu et al., 2017). Although self-monitoring may change behavior when first used, changes may dissipate over time unless supported with additional self-management procedures, such as self-reinforcement. Although self-monitoring has been used for initial behavior-change programs, it appears to be most effective in maintaining behavior changes resulting from traditional, teacher-managed strategies.

Two general ways to self-monitor is to record instances of (1) being on task and (2) completing a piece of academic work, such as recording each time five math problems are completed or each component of locating information in a passage to answer reading comprehension questions (Joseph & Eveleigh, 2011; Kolbenschlag & Wunderlich, 2020). The question posed is whether it is more effective for students to record that they are "paying attention" or "working hard" or to keep track of how much academic work they have completed or done correctly. It appears that both procedures are effective but that many students prefer to record tasks accomplished. Many teachers may also prefer this approach; we are sometimes reluctant to encourage students to give themselves credit for merely looking busy.

The following vignette shows how one teacher used cued self-monitoring to help her students learn self-management.

Ms. Dietrich's Students Learn to Work Independently

Ms. Dietrich was a resource teacher for elementary students with learning challenges. She arranged her schedule so that each group of students received direct instruction for the first 20 minutes of each scheduled resource hour. That group then worked independently while Ms. Dietrich taught another group. She was concerned that she could not give tokens to the groups working independently without disrupting the lesson she was teaching. She decided to teach the students self-monitoring. She borrowed a "clicker" from a friend who used it to mark correct behavior in children with autism. At first, she observed the students working independently and clicked the clicker only if all of them appeared on task. They awarded themselves a point when they heard the click. After a while, she just clicked randomly during her direct teaching and told the independently working students to give themselves a point if they were working hard when they heard the sound. She found her procedure very effective. It was almost as good as being in two places at once.

Considerable amounts of research have shown the power of self-monitoring. In most studies, the teacher first directly taught the students to use the self-monitoring system and then evaluated its use in the classroom. The format of self-monitoring has varied over the years from paper and pencil to apps on iPads and smartphones (Bouck et al., 2014). Rosenbloom et al. (2020) used a technology-based self-monitoring intervention to increase the percentage of time on task of four adolescents with ASD during classroom instruction. The students implemented self-monitoring in an app on a smartphone that was set to ask, "Are you on task?" every 30 seconds with the opportunity to respond with "yes" or "no." The researchers first taught the students to use the app using behavioral skills training, which included instructions, modeling, role play, and feedback. Then the researcher placed the smartphone on each student's desk and provided minimal prompts or feedback. In addition to improving time on task, the self-monitoring improved task completion, as well as reduced disruptive behavior for one of the students.

Perhaps not surprisingly, researchers have found that when students with disabilities use a self-monitoring system in a classroom through the use of an audible prompt, headphones, or a data sheet or smartphone on their desk, the students often find these materials embarrassing. One inconspicuous self-monitoring device is a tactile cue that vibrates on a certain schedule upon which a student can self-record on- or off-task behavior. McDougall et al. (2012) used this type of self-monitoring with 15-year-old Gabriel who had ADHD and 12-year-old Kawika who had emotional disturbance. Each student put a MotivAider in his pocket that was set to vibrate every 90 seconds for Gabriel and every 3 minutes for Kawika. When the students felt the vibration, they asked, "Am I working?" and marked the data sheet (Figure 12.3) accordingly. This resulted in a substantial increase in the percentage of algebra work Gabriel completed in a 10-minute independent work period (a mean of 21%–66%) and a substantial decrease in the time required for Kawika to complete a vocabulary task (from a mean of 30 minutes to a mean of 11 minutes).

Kolbenschlag and Wunderlich (2020) used another less-conspicuous self-monitoring system: a Bluetooth-enabled in-ear headphone connected to an iPod that was held by a teacher. The teacher set the device to emit a tone in the student's ear every 2 minutes during a 20-minute session. Using a data sheet, the students were taught: "When you hear the timer, draw a smile if you were on task and a frown if you were off task" (p.85). With self-monitoring and earning a reward for accuracy (matching the teacher's recording) but not for being on-task, all the students' on-task behavior improved. One student improved further with self-monitoring and earning a reward for being on-task, as well as intermittent rewards for accuracy. On-task behavior maintained but did not generalize to a general education classroom. Perhaps using the self-monitoring system in the general education classroom would have facilitated this generalization.

Figure 12.3 Self-monitoring form

Am I completing my bellwork?

1	2	3	4	5	6	7

√ = Yes   0 = No

Am I working?

1	2	3	4	5	6	7	8	9	10

Yes: +   No: −

Teaching students to use self-monitoring should include the following components:

- selecting a target behavior
- operationally defining the behavior
- selecting an appropriate system of data collection (Successful data collection systems include adaptations of event recording, time sampling, and permanent-product recording; notation methods include tally sheets, wrist counters, graphs, charts, and handheld devices. Figures 12.4 and 12.5 provide examples of charts that may be used.)
- instructing the student in the use of the selected self-monitoring system
- monitoring at least one practice data-recording session
- allowing students to use self-monitoring independently and monitoring the results

Several suggestions have been made as to why self-monitoring changes behavior. It appears that self-monitoring forces students to record their behavior and may lead to students' covertly rewarding or punishing themselves. Self-monitoring provides environmental cues that increase the students' awareness of potential consequences (Fritz et al., 2012; Kirby, Fowler, & Baer, 1991). This is why so many weight-loss and smoking-cessation programs require that adults write down every morsel they eat and every cigarette they smoke. As the preceding examples show, self-monitoring alone has some reinforcing qualities if there is a behavior change in the desired direction. However, we should always ensure positive reinforcement for engaging in the self-monitoring behavior, as well as making improvements in the target behavior (Briesch et al., 2019).

> Two reasons for the success of self-monitoring procedures.

An issue often raised when considering a self-monitoring procedure is the accuracy of students' records. In past decades, researchers concluded that the accuracy of students' records has little effect on behavioral changes; even inaccurate record keeping may result in positive behavior change (Marshall et al., 1993; Reinecke et al., 1999). This may still be true in some cases. More recently, researchers have found that when teachers reinforce the accuracy of self-monitoring, the target behaviors improve (Briesch et al., 2019; Kolbenschlag & Wunderlich, 2020).

> But won't they cheat?

Self-Evaluation

Asking students to evaluate their performance may take many forms. Students may be asked to compare their responses on a worksheet to an answer key prepared by the teacher or provided in a teacher's edition of a textbook (most students find it reinforcing merely to have access to the teacher's edition). Occasional spot checking and, of course, eternal vigilance will reduce students' temptation to record their answers *after* referring to the answer key rather than before. Shimabukuro et al. (1999) taught students with ADD/ADHD to self-correct their work in reading comprehension, mathematics, and written expression. The students recorded

Overview of Self-Monitoring
Pearson eText
Video Example 12.2
In this video, an educator discusses the expectations for work and the self-monitoring system for the classroom. Which components of self-monitoring are described here?

Figure 12.4 Self-monitoring checklist for home use

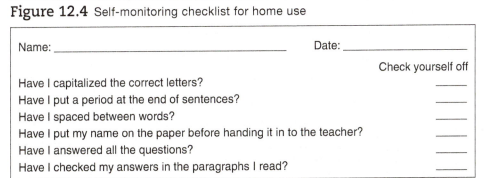

Figure 12.5 Self-monitoring checklist for a language arts activity

Have I?	Terry	Todd
1. Washed my face and hands?	_____	_____
2. Brushed my teeth?	_____	_____
3. Brushed my hair?	_____	_____
4. Picked up my dirty clothes?	_____	_____
5. Made my bed?	_____	_____
6. Put my lunch money in my pocket?	_____	_____
7. Gotten my homework and my books?	_____	_____

accuracy and productivity (comparing the number of items completed to the number assigned). They recorded their scores and plotted them on graphs. Self-correction of spelling (Morton, Heward, & Alber, 1998; Turner et al., 2017) and multiplication facts (Bennett & Cavanaugh, 1998) enabled students to receive immediate feedback (after each word or math problem) rather than waiting for feedback from a teacher. Immediate feedback resulted in improved performance. More complex procedures may require students to rate less easily evaluated products against standards. Sweeney, Salva, Cooper, and Talbert-Johnson (1993), for example, taught secondary students to evaluate the legibility of their handwriting on the basis of shape, spacing, slant, size, and general appearance. The legibility of the students' handwriting improved significantly as a result of this self-evaluation and other elements of a treatment package.

> Start with teacher-controlled contingencies.

Teaching students to evaluate their own behavior requires teaching them to discriminate between acceptable and inappropriate behavior. Dalton et al. (1999) used direct instruction to teach two adolescents with learning disabilities to identify on-task and off-task behaviors. The teacher randomly provided examples of each and asked the students to label them as on or off task. Training may also include a teacher or peer modeling examples of either appropriate behaviors or, in some cases, inappropriate behaviors and teaching students to discriminate between them. Videotapes of students modeling appropriate or inappropriate behavior may be useful in helping students form these discriminations. Embregts (2000) used videotaping to improve social behavior in students with mild intellectual disabilities. Tapes were made during lunch, dinner, and group meetings. The students watched the tapes (as much as a week later) with an instructor. The tape was stopped every 30 seconds and the students were asked to record whether their behavior was appropriate or inappropriate. When their evaluation matched that of the instructor 80% of the time, a comparison was made only at the end of the session. The students earned tokens for accurate identification.

Another method of self-evaluation is self-graphing in which students create graphs of their self-monitored data. Stotz et al. (2008) evaluated self-graphing with three 10-year-old students with emotional disturbance or specific learning disability. The students were given 3 minutes to write a story from a story starter, such as "I was shipwrecked on a deserted island" (p. 176). At the end of each 3-minute period, the student counted the number of words he wrote and drew a corresponding bar graph-type data point on a handwritten graph. This increased the number of words written as well as the quality of the written work. Pennington and Koehler (2017) implemented a similar strategy with three middle school students with moderate intellectual disability. These students self-graphed story elements, such as characters, setting, and events, from stories they read; the researchers also used explicit modeling and feedback.

Graphing Results
Pearson eText
Video Example 12.3
In this video, a student describes how he graphs results of his work. What is the evaluation method he uses to determine if he is on track to meet his goals?

Self-Reinforcement

In most classrooms, teachers arrange contingencies. They may simply apply contingencies without talking about them, or they may specify what behaviors are expected and the consequences for performing those behaviors. Contingencies are stated in the form of "if ..., then ..." statements: "If you complete your composition, then you may have 5 minutes of extra free time." "For each correct answer to the reading comprehension questions, you will earn one token." Students may be involved in contingency management in a number of ways. They may be allowed to choose reinforcers, to assist in determining the cost of the reinforcers in relation to behavior, or even to choose behaviors to be modified. The ultimate goal in allowing students to participate in contingency management is to encourage their use of the procedures they have been taught to manage their own behavior. As with self-monitoring, the transition from teacher-managed to student-managed programs must be gradual, and students must be explicitly taught to use self-reinforcement or self-punishment.

> Contingencies students set themselves may be more effective than those set by teachers.

It has been repeatedly demonstrated that self-determined contingencies and teacher-determined contingencies can be equally effective in producing behavior change. In fact, self-determined standards and reinforcers may sometimes be more effective than those externally determined (Hayes et al., 1985).

When allowing students to select their own contingency for tasks to be completed, specific instructions should be given as to the procedure to be followed. The following set of instructions (Felixbrod & O'Leary, 1974, p. 846) has served as a model for many investigations of self-reinforcement:

1. When people work on a job, they get paid for what they do. I am going to pay you points that you can use to buy these prizes (pointing to prizes and point-exchange values). YOUR job is to answer these arithmetic questions. Answer the questions in order. In order to earn the points, only correct answers will count (repeated). You will have 20 minutes to do these. But you can stop before 20 minutes are up if you want to.
2. I am going to let YOU decide how many points you want to get paid for each right answer. Take a look at the numbers on the next page (pointing to a separate page on which the subject is to choose a performance standard). I want YOU to decide how many points you want to get paid for each right answer. (Experimenter points to each possible choice in a list of 10 possible performance standards: "I want to get paid 1 point; 2 points ... 10 points for each right answer.") After I leave the room, draw a circle around the number of points you want to get paid for each right answer.

Contingency-management systems are most often implemented with the teacher controlling the selection and administration of reinforcers. A period of teacher-controlled contingency management should precede any effort to teach students self-reinforcement (King-Sears, 1999). After the students become accustomed to the mechanics of the system, the students themselves can manage contingencies effectively. Explanations to students like the one above about setting contingencies may be used to encourage students to set more stringent contingencies and to transition gradually to self-management of reinforcers.

Beaver et al. (2017) used self-monitoring to teach vocational, leisure, and functional living skills, such as preparing a meal and making soap, to three adolescents with ASD. Each student followed a list of steps for completing the skills that was presented on an application within an iPod Touch. Within the application, there was a golf counter icon that, when clicked, increased the number showing. The teacher or student clicked the golf counter for correct implementation of the steps of the

Dewayne Passes Intro to ABA

DeWayne was panic stricken. At midterm, his average in his behavior mod course was 67. If he failed, his grade point average would drop below the point where he would be retained in college. After listening to a lecture on self-reinforcement, he decided to try it on himself.

DeWayne downloaded a self-monitoring app on his phone and acquired a supply of 3 × 5 cards. He decided that he needed short-term and long-term reinforcers. He began setting the timer on the app for an hour and making a check on a 3 × 5 card whenever he sat at his desk or in the library without getting up or talking to anyone for the entire hour. He then allowed himself a 10-minute break for scrolling his social media, making a cup of coffee, or taking care of bodily necessities. When he had four checks, he decided to allow himself to go out with his friends for pizza. He saved the cards, and when he had accumulated five cards with at least four checks, he texted his girlfriend and asked her to go to a movie. Although he was somewhat skeptical about the effectiveness of his plan, he found that it worked. When he studied for an average of 4 hours a day, his grades began to improve. He finished the semester with a 3.0 grade point average and a conviction that applied behavior analysis was more than a gimmick for getting students to stay in their seats.

Using Technology for Self-Management
Pearson eText
Video Example 12.4
In this video, an educator describes an application that can be used in a classroom to help students manage their behavior. What elements of self-management do you notice in the description?

https://www.youtube.com/watch?v=nFgFySAX4mc

skills. Both the teacher-delivered reinforcement and self-reinforcement were effective in increasing task completion, and for two of the students, the self-reinforcement allowed the proximity of the teacher to be faded more quickly than the teacher-delivered reinforcement.

The above vignette illustrates a combined self-monitoring and self-reinforcing procedure.

Self-Punishment

Most self-management procedures have emphasized self-reinforcement. Some investigations, however, have analyzed the effectiveness of teaching students to punish rather than reinforce behaviors. Fans of Harry Potter (Rowling, 1998) may remember Dobby, the house elf, who regularly punished himself by banging his head on the wall, beating himself with a desk lamp, twisting his ears, and even slamming his ears in the oven door. In classrooms, not surprisingly, self-punishment is rather different. The form of self-punishment most often investigated has been the use of response cost in conjunction with token reinforcement systems where students must decide when to subtract or return tokens as well as when to award them. It is consistent with the continuing emphasis on positive behavior interventions that very few recent investigations have addressed using self-punishment procedures with students. Many adults, as illustrated in the example on the next page, use some sort of response cost procedure in combination with other self-management techniques to manage their own behavior.

Self-Instruction

Self-instruction is a process of providing one's own verbal prompts. Prompting, as we discussed in Chapter 10, is necessary when discriminative stimuli are insufficient to set the occasion for the required response. Prompts are often supplied by others; self-instruction involves providing prompts for oneself. Many adults give themselves prompts when they engage in difficult or unfamiliar tasks. We talk ourselves through such activities as starting a new car or performing a complicated dance step. We use prompts such as "i before e except after c" when we encounter a hurdle in letter writing. Some of us still sing the "ABC" jingle when searching for words listed in alphabetical order. Teaching students to use self-instruction tactics enables them also to provide verbal prompts for themselves, rather than to remain dependent on others.

> ### Professor Grundy Completes A Book
>
> Professor Grundy was panic stricken. He had just received an email from the editor in charge of production on his textbook manuscript (which, as you may remember, was considerably overdue). Because he had seen the words "breach of contract" and "by the end of the month" used in the same sentence, he concluded he had best accelerate his writing rate. He decided that he needed to write at least 10 pages every day and that he would need some motivation for doing so. He had bought a laptop computer for word processing but had spent hours surfing the net and communicating with others on social media and very little time processing words. He therefore provided himself with a nutrition bar cut neatly into 10 pieces, two Styrofoam cups, and a number of marbles borrowed from his nephew Dennis. Before he sat down to work, he filled one Styrofoam cup with marbles and put the other next to it. He placed the pieces of the bar on a saucer. Mrs. Grundy agreed to cooperate by keeping his coffee cup constantly full. (She was motivated by the hope that her living room decor might eventually consist of something besides stacks of books and downloaded articles, note cards, and crumpled multicolor sticky notes.)
>
> Professor Grundy's preparations for writing had consumed almost an hour. He was tempted to take a break before beginning but restrained himself. He began putting words on the screen and at the end of each page ate 1 of the 10 pieces of his bar. Whenever he found his mind wandering, he transferred a marble from the full to the empty cup. He had decided he would have to write an extra page for each marble over 10 that accumulated in the previously empty cup.
>
> Professor Grundy was very pleased with the effectiveness of his self-management system. "It's amazing," he thought to himself. "I've been using applied behavior analysis procedures on other people for years and even teaching students to do it. Why didn't I ever think to try it on myself?" He spent considerable time in self-congratulation and then, with a guilty start, transferred a marble and got back to work.

Self-instruction enables students to identify and guide themselves through the process necessary to solve problems. Training in self-instruction occurs before students are given problems to solve, questions to answer, or tasks to perform. Students who are taught self-instruction procedures may be able to generalize these strategies to other settings—for example, from one-to-one tutoring to the classroom (Bornstein & Quevillon, 1976). They may also be able to generalize across tasks—for example, from arithmetic or printing tasks to a phonics task not specifically trained but requiring similar process management for completion (Burgio, Whitman, & Johnson, 1980; Smith et al., 2015).

Teaching students self-instruction tactics has been effective in teaching children who are hyperactive and impulsive to increase their attending and on-task behaviors, increasing students' ability to demonstrate academic skills, increasing appropriate social behaviors, and teaching a wide variety of skills to persons with moderate, severe, and profound disabilities (Barkley, Copeland, & Sivage, 1980; Borkowski, 1992; Browder & Shapiro, 1985; Bryant & Budd, 1982; Burgio et al., 1980; Callicott & Park, 2003; Case, Harris, & Graham, 1992; Faloon & Rehfeldt, 2008; Lagomarcino, Hughes, & Rusch, 1989; Peters & Davies, 1981; Shepley et al., 2019; Smith et al., 2016).

Most studies investigating self-instruction have used adaptations of a training sequence developed by Meichenbaum and Goodman (1971). A five-step training program for self-instruction successfully increased the self-control of second graders who had been labeled hyperactive, and thus increased their ability to attend to a task and to decrease errors. Students were taught individually using the following sequence (Meichenbaum & Goodman, p. 117):

1. An adult model performed a task while talking to himself aloud (cognitive modeling).
2. The student performed the same task under the direction of the model's instructions (overt, external guidance).
3. The student performed the task while instructing himself aloud (overt self-guidance).
4. The student whispered the instructions to himself as he went through the task (faded, overt self-guidance).
5. The student performed the task while guiding his performance via private speech (covert self-instruction).

The following example shows the cognitive model provided by the teacher and then rehearsed, overtly and covertly, by the student. The task requires copying line patterns:

> Okay, what is it I have to do? You want me to copy the picture with the different lines. I have to go slowly and carefully. Okay, draw the line down, down, good; then to the right, that's it; now down some more and to the left. Good. I'm doing fine so far. Remember, go slowly. Now back up again. No, I was supposed to go down. That's okay. Just erase the line carefully. Good.... Even if I make an error, I can go on slowly and carefully. I have to go down now. Finished. I did it! (Meichenbaum & Goodman, 1971, p. 117)

For students to learn to imitate an effective and complete strategy, the teacher must include in the initial modeling several performance-relevant skills that guide the task process. These skills (Meichenbaum, 1977, p. 123) include:

1. problem definition ("What is it I have to do?")
2. focusing attention and response guidance ("Carefully ... draw the line down.")
3. self-reinforcement ("Good, I'm doing fine.")
4. self-evaluative coping skills and error-correction options ("That's okay.... Even if I make an error, I can go on slowly.")

To help impulsive students to be more reflective and thus better able to finish a matching task, a teacher modeled the following strategy:

> Now let's see, what am I supposed to do? I have to find which of these (pointing to the six alternatives) goes into this space (pointing to the blank space in the rectangular figure). Good. Now I have to remember to go slowly and be sure to check each one of these carefully before I answer. Is this the one (pointing to the first alternative)? It's the same color but it looks different because the lines are thicker. Good, now I know it isn't this one. Now I have to check this next one (pointing to the second alternative). It looks different because there aren't any lines on it and this one (pointing to the standard) has lines on it. Good, now I know it isn't this one. Next I have to check this one (pointing to alternative three). It looks the same to me. The colors are the same and the lines are the same too. I think it might be this one but I have to check the other ones slowly and carefully before I choose ... (continues to check remaining three alternatives one at a time). Good, I have checked them all and I have gone slowly and carefully. I think it is this one (points to the correct variant). (Peters & Davies, 1981, p. 379)

Reid and Lienemann (2006) taught a group of students with ADHD to improve their written composition skills using Self-Regulated Strategy Development (Graham & Harris, 2005). The strategy uses mnemonics to teach students to plan, organize, and write stories and to include all necessary parts of a story. Direct instruction and modeling were used to teach students the strategy and they were then able to use it independently. The students evaluated their own stories. All the students increased the number of words in their stories, the number of story parts included, and the quality of their writing. They also kept graphs to show their progress.

Self-instruction can be a useful procedure for helping students become more independent and for maintaining and generalizing behavior change. Several factors appear to influence the effectiveness of self-instruction:

1. Actual implementation of the procedure during task performance. Roberts, Nelson, and Olson (1987), however, found no difference in performance between students who used self-instruction and those who had merely been taught a self-instructional strategy. They suggest that, at least in some cases, training in self-instruction to solve specific kinds of problems may be good academic instruction rather than a modification of cognitive processing.
2. The ability of the students to perform the response in question. Higa, Tharpe, and Calkins (1978) found that unless kindergartners and first graders had practiced making a motor response, self-instructions actually interfered with performance. No amount of self-instruction will enable students to perform tasks not in their repertoire.
3. Reinforcement for adhering to self-instructions.
4. Making the focus of instructions specific. For example, Mishel and Patterson (1976) found that nursery school children were better able to resist talking to a puppet if they specifically instructed themselves not to talk to the puppet than if they reminded themselves with general instructions to work on their assigned tasks.

Factors influencing the effectiveness of self-instruction.

Results of self-instruction training have been somewhat inconsistent. Bornstein (1985) suggested that differential effects of the procedure may result from age, gender, intelligence, race, history, or attributional or cognitive style and pointed out, "Quite simply, it appears that self-instructional programs can be effective, although obviously they are not always effective" (p. 70). As we have said before, "Nothing always works."

Efforts to teach persons with moderate and severe disabilities to use self-instruction have included the use of picture prompts, as described in Chapter 10 (Pierce & Schreibman, 1994; Steed & Lutzker, 1997). Students are provided with books of pictures portraying various tasks performed in sequential order. Students refer to the books, after being taught to use them, without needing a teacher, job coach, or employer to provide constant supervision, just as teachers refer to lesson plans, lecturers to lecture notes, and physicians to the *Physician's Desk Reference.*

Using a more high-tech system, Smith et al. (2016) taught four adolescents with ASD to use self-instruction to increase daily living and vocational skills, such as making lemonade and sorting office supplies. They first taught the students to hold a smartphone, navigate to an icon, and watch a video demonstration, such as after being asked, "Watch a video about making coffee" (p. 1202). Then they gave an instruction the student could not complete, such as "Make lemonade," and used progressive time delay with verbal prompts to teach him to get the smartphone from his pocket, find the "make lemonade" video, watch the video, and then perform the steps. In addition to the students acquiring new skills using this self-instruction, the students demonstrated generalization of the self-instruction skill across people and settings, though some students needed progressive time delay in two settings before generalization occurred. Shepley et al. (2019) replicated this study with elementary students with intellectual disability.

Most self-instructional procedures are taught in combination with self-monitoring and self-reinforcement. Thus, students provide for themselves both antecedents to behavior and consequences for correct performance. The following sections describe several studies that examined the effects of implementing intervention packages, including several types of self-management.

Self-Management for Special Populations

Self-Management for Learners with Severe Disabilities

Learning Outcome 12.3 Describe the use of self-management techniques specific to individuals with severe disabilities, mild disabilities, and at-risk for disabilities.

Descriptions of self-management procedures might lead one to believe that only high-functioning individuals could use such techniques. On the contrary, many students with relatively severe disabilities, including intellectual disabilities and autism, have been taught to use self-management procedures (Aljadeff-Abergel et al., 2015; Beckman et al., 2019; Boswell et al., 2013; Carr, 2016; Douglas et al., 2015; Fritz et al., 2012; Griffin & Copeland, 2018; Gushanas & Thompson, 2019; Kartal & Ozkan, 2015; Koegel et al., 2014; Lee et al., 2018; Legge et al., 2010; Li et al., 2019; Liu et al., 2015; Looney et al., 2018; Miller & Taber-Doughty, 2014; Newman, Buffington, & Hemmes, 1996; Roberts et al., 2019; Rouse et al., 2014; Sheehey et al., 2017; Singh et al., 2017; van der Burg et al., 2018; Wadsworth et al., 2015).

Koegel et al. (2014) taught three students with autism to self-manage their conversation skills. They presented them with the self-monitoring recording sheet shown in Figure 12.6. This form prompted the students with the conversation skills of answering a question, making a comment, elaborating on a response, and asking a question. The students were taught to put a checkmark in a box when they emitted one of those conversational skills and they then earned a preferred activity, such as a game. The therapist prompted the students to engage in the conversational skills and self-record, and then faded those prompts. Koegel et al. suggested that the self-management helped with the *performance,* also considered the maintenance, of conversational acts as opposed to the *acquisition* of the conversational skills.

In addition to addressing skills in self-contained environments, self-management procedures show great promise in providing skills to students with significant disabilities to participate fully in inclusive settings (King-Sears, 2008; Koegel et al., 1999). Xu et al. (2017) used self-management and goal setting to increase the academic engagement of a 9-year-old boy with autism included in a general education language arts classroom in China. The researcher first taught the student to use the self-management system in a one-on-one, private setting. This was comprised of having the student select a preferred activity to earn, role-playing the use of the self-management form (Table 12.1) to self-record engaged and disruptive behavior in 1-minute intervals, and teaching the student to check the reliability of his scores with the teachers' scores. The researcher taught and established goal setting by first showing the student his baseline data and telling him to set his first goal at the highest point of his baseline data, which was engagement in 20% of intervals. This continued for each phase

Figure 12.6 Self-monitoring form used with students with autism

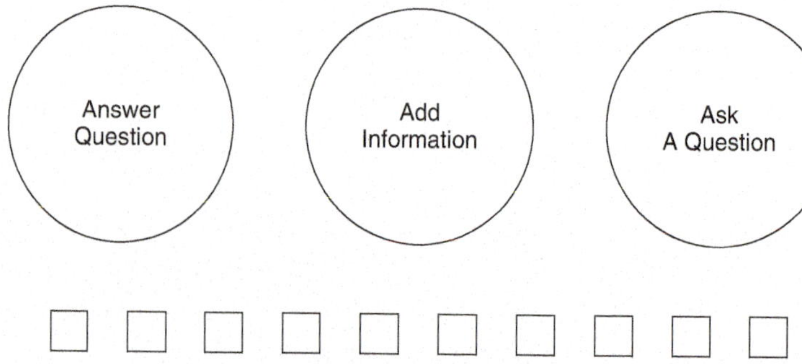

Table 12.1 Self-monitoring data recording form

Name: Date: Language Art Class
I put a "+" if I did everything on the target list;
I put a "−" if I did not do everything on the target list.
Today's goal: (e.g., 15 "+" or 50%)

Target behaviors	1. I did not play with things.
	2. I sat on the chair nicely.
	3. I looked at the teacher, blackboard, or PPT.
	4. I did what the teacher said.

1-min intervals	1	2	3	4	5	6	7	8	9	10
	11	12	13	14	15	16	17	18	19	20
	21	22	23	24	25	26	27	28	29	30

Total "+"	Goal: Yes, No (Circle one)

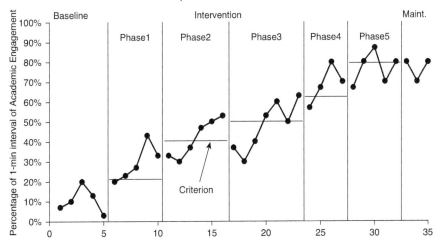

Figure 12.7 Percentage of one-min whole interval of academic engagement across conditions and intervention phases

(see Figure 12.7). In the inclusive classroom, the student set a goal, chose a reinforcer to earn, self-recorded his engagement, decided if he met his goal, and, if so, accessed his reinforcer. The student went from 10% engagement in baseline to 80% engagement in the final phase; he also maintained this engagement.

A meta-analysis of 29 studies using self-management for students with disabilities in inclusive settings indicated that most of the participants were students with severe disabilities, and in most cases, self-management was an effective treatment (McDougall et al., 2017).

Self-Management for Learners with Mild Disabilities

Coughlin et al. (2012) taught three 7-year-old students with mild intellectual disability to self-monitor their on-task behavior in a self-contained classroom. The students were given worksheets with tasks such as counting items and circling letters. At first, after each of the five tasks on the worksheet, there were pictures of their favorite cartoon character with a box in which to put a sticker when the work was completed (Figure 12.8). The number of times this occurred on the worksheet was faded to 3, then 2, and then 1 at the end of the worksheet. The researcher used a script to teach the self-management system to the students (Table 12.2). This intervention was successful in decreasing off-task behaviors and the time required to complete the worksheets.

Figure 12.8 Self-monitoring charts

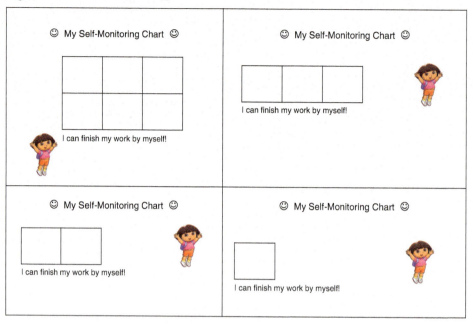

Table 12.2 Instruction Script

1.	Tell: you are going to learn how to self-monitor while you work.
2.	Show: self-monitor visual cue.
3.	Tell: this picture (of Dora the Explorer/SpongeBob SquarePants) shows me that it is time to stop working and self-monitor.
4.	Show: self-monitoring chart.
5.	Tell: when I self-monitor, I put a sticker on this chart.
6.	Tell: when you see Dora the Explorer/SpongeBob SquarePants, I stop working and put a sticker on my chart.
7.	Tell: after I put a sticker on my chart, I go back to my work.
8.	Tell: watch me.
9.	Show: work on a problem.
10.	Tell: I am doing my work.
11.	Show: see the self-monitor cue.
12.	Tell: I see Dora the Explorer/SpongeBob SquarePants. It is time to give myself a sticker.
13.	Show: stop work; take a sticker and place it on the self-monitoring chart.
14.	Tell: I am putting a sticker here because I have finished some work.
15.	Show: go back to the worksheet and start next problem.
16.	Tell: after I put a sticker on my chart, it is time to work.
17.	Tell: now let practice together.
18.	*Walk through steps 10–17 with the student self-monituring.*
19.	Tell: now show me how you self-monitor.
20.	*Watch student walk through steps 10–17 independently; prompt when necessary.*

Self-management strategies can also improve the performance of students with mild disabilities in general education settings (Bedesem, 2012; Wills & Mason, 2014). Wills and Mason taught two high school students with a specific learning disability and ADHD to self-manage their on-task behavior in a general education science class. The researcher taught the students to use an app on a smartphone to first discriminate on- and off-task behavior. Then, in class, the students placed the smartphone with the app opened on the top corner of their desks and recorded a "yes" or "no" based on whether they were on- or off-task during each 5-minute interval. To reduce distractions, the intervals were marked with a flashing screen, not a tone or vibration.

Self-Management for Students at Risk

Some studies have described the use of self-management strategies with students who are not identified as disabled, but who are at risk of school failure because of poor academic work and disruptive behavior (Bunch-Crump & Lo, 2017; Trevino-Maack et al., 2015; Wills et al., 2016). Researchers have shown that self-management is effective for general education students in specific content areas, such as reading (Guzman et al., 2018), writing (Ennis & Jolivette, 2014), and math (Stocker & Kubina, 2017).

Classwide Self-Monitoring
Pearson eText
Video Example 12.5
In this video, an educator describes a self-monitoring system employed in a class-wide manner using auditory cues. Consider how the description of the procedure may fit with students at risk or with mild disabilities.

Summary

This chapter has described a number of techniques for transferring behavior management from teachers to students. Several advantages come with such transfer. Students become more independent. Their behavior may be maintained and generalized in settings where no intervention is in effect. The emphasis is changed from short-term intervention designed to change a single target behavior to the acquisition of strategies that may be used to change many behaviors over the long term. Discussion of self-management procedures may seem contradictory to the emphasis on overt, observable behavior throughout this book. Some of the processes described in this chapter, such as covert self-instruction, are not directly observable. However, the emphasis, as always, is on changes in behaviors that are observable. For example, although we cannot observe students' covert self-instruction, we can observe that they perform academic tasks more rapidly and more accurately than before they were taught to use the procedure.

Discussion Questions

1. Design a self-management program for yourself. Include self-monitoring and self-reinforcement.

2. Implement the program and see if you can change your own behavior. Describe the change process.

Chapter 13
Putting It All Together

Learning Outcomes

13.1 Describe four kinds of structure and their relationship to stimulus control.

13.2 Explain three factors that increase the effectiveness of classroom rules.

13.3 Describe several characteristics of effective teachers.

13.4 Label principles of applied behavior analysis operating in hypothetical classroom environments.

In previous chapters we have discussed a great many principles, cited numerous research studies, and provided dozens of examples of how procedures can be implemented in classrooms. In this chapter we will try to show how teachers put all the principles, research studies, and procedures together to provide classrooms and other environments where students learn efficiently and effectively. We also want to stress ways that school and learning can provide enjoyment for both teachers and students. If it is not, for the most part, fun, no one will want to keep doing it. Surely no one goes into teaching for the money. First we will describe practical implementation of various principles; then we will describe several environments in some detail. Throughout the chapter, we will point out with marginal notes which behavioral principles are being used.

    The most important part of running an effective and efficient classroom takes place before the students arrive. Careful planning can ensure that all students successfully acquire knowledge and learn skills and that few disruptive or inappropriate behaviors occur. Being prepared for students who have trouble mastering knowledge and skills or who behave inappropriately despite preventative planning enables the teacher to react quickly and solve problems as soon as possible. It is, however, impossible to anticipate every potential problem. One thing that makes teaching so challenging and so much fun is that students are not completely predictable. At this very moment, somewhere in the world, a teacher is asking an assistant, "Have you ever seen one do *that* before?"

Stimulus Control

Learning Outcome 13.1 Describe four kinds of structure and their relationship to stimulus control.

Learning Outcome 13.2 Explain three factors that increase the effectiveness of classroom rules.

Students whose academic or social behavior is inappropriate or maladaptive present a special challenge. These students may or may not be classified as disabled or at risk. Many such students respond to the entire school environment as an S^D for either acting-out behavior or complete withdrawal. To design a classroom environment to alter such behaviors, teachers must simultaneously avoid presenting old S^Ds and concentrate on establishing certain elements of the classroom as discriminative stimuli for appropriate behavior. This process may be thought of as providing appropriate classroom structure. We will describe several kinds of structure, including the physical arrangement of the room; time, instructional, and verbal structure; and teacher characteristics.

Physical Arrangement

The physical arrangement of the classroom provides discriminative stimuli for students. Some of the behaviors occasioned by these stimuli may be undesirable. For some students, proximity to other students (or a particular classmate) may be an S^D for off-task talking or physical abuse. Sitting in a chair may be an S^D for tilting it. The teacher may need to arrange the classroom in a way that interferes with such behaviors before more appropriate behavior can be taught. Bettenhausen (1998), Blume et al. (2019), Cummings (2000), MacAulay (1990), Sainato et al. (2008), Soukup et al. (2007), Stewart and Evans (1997), and van den Berg and Stoltz (2018) have all described the relationship between classroom arrangement and student behavior. Specific suggestions from these sources include:

1. provision for easy teacher observation of all students
2. sufficient physical separation of students to minimize inappropriate behaviors
3. careful delineation of areas in which only work behaviors are reinforced from those in which more informal behavior is permitted
4. avoidance of clutter and distracting classroom accessories and availability of study carrels for students so distractible that virtually any stimulus is an S^D for off-task behavior
5. students seated closer to the teacher perform better
6. for early childhood, smaller spaces result in more social interactions

> It's not interior decoration, it's stimulus control.

The specific arrangement of the classroom will depend on what instruction is being delivered, the students in the class, and, of course, the constraints of the space itself. (If you're in the boiler room, you'll have to work around the furnace.) If most instruction is to be one-on-one, then either there must be several work areas where the teacher and a student can sit comfortably and see necessary materials or, better yet, each student must have a workstation large enough to accommodate another chair and an adult. We do not recommend leaning over or squatting when moving from station to station to provide instruction—in very few years either the back gives way or the knees do. In addition, many students react badly to an adult's looming over or crowding them. One creative teacher we know uses a chair on wheels and wheels herself from desk to desk in her classroom. If there is to be a great deal of group instruction, there must be an area where students are oriented toward the teacher and any visual displays. Perhaps this seems painfully obvious, but we have seen many teachers talking to groups, half of whom had their backs to the teacher, or showing slides that many students had to turn around to see. Not only does this not make for good instruction, it creates opportunities for inappropriate behavior. Small groups require a table and chairs or a large enough floor area for all to sit comfortably. A kidney-shaped table is excellent because it enables the teacher to be close to all students at once. Many teachers who use the floor for instruction mark individual spaces with tape and require students to stay within their squares. This minimizes pushing and squirming. Carpet squares can serve the same function.

It is also important that the classroom be attractive. Brightly colored bulletin board displays, plants, aquariums, and student projects all contribute to a friendly, welcoming atmosphere. Displays of charts, graphs, visual prompts, and goals send a message that this classroom is a place where serious business is conducted. One caution is that some students with severe disabilities, such as autism, may need a more

Classroom Set-Up
Pearson eText
Video Example 13.1
In this video, an educator works with a small group on a math activity. How is the environment arranged to promote attention to the task?

distraction-free educational environment to be able to focus on the educational materials (Smith, 2001), though this is not always needed (Geiger et al., 2012). In general, students should have work areas in which it is easy to ensure that the task to which they are supposed to pay attention is the most attention-getting item in sight.

When we begin to talk about the importance of neatness in the classroom, students who have visited our offices invariably giggle. We maintain, like Professor Grundy, that it is easier for aging college professors to adapt to working in cluttered surroundings than it is for most children and adolescents. A messy classroom may even be dangerous, especially for students with delays in mobility. It certainly contributes to inefficient instruction. A teacher who must search her desk, a bookcase, and two cabinets to find teaching materials hidden under piles of paper wastes valuable time. She also provides a poor model for students. Students whose desks are covered with extraneous items may find it impossible to attend to the task at hand. It is worth the sometimes Herculean effort to keep things neat.

The physical classroom itself can and will become a complex S^D for appropriate student behavior. It is important to be consistent about what behaviors are reinforced and about room arrangement. Allowing students who exhibit challenging behavior to play in the work area on a rainy day may result in a weakening of the stimulus control of that area. Suddenly changing the room arrangement may also create problems for these students.

Time Structure

When we say "It's time to ...," we're using stimulus control.

The time of day functions as an S^D for many human behaviors. At certain times, certain behaviors are reinforced. A predictable schedule for the classroom will maximize the controlling aspects of time. Posting of schedules for daily activities and individual tasks has shown great promise in improving learning and behavior in students with autism and other developmental disorders (Akers et al., 2018; Betz et al., 2008; Brodhead et al., 2018). Other time aspects should also be considered. For example, students may work more quickly and accurately when their performance is timed (Frankhauser et al., 2001; Lingo, 2014; Rhymer et al., 1998). Apparently, being timed is an S^D for working rapidly.

A simple, relatively inexpensive kitchen timer can be of enormous help in structuring classroom time. There are multiple additional types of timers, including digital timers, smart phone and tablet timers that can be audible or tactile, and visual timers in which students can see how much time is left by looking at a red panel reducing in size as it circles an analog-type clock. As you will see below, the old-fashioned timer may have some advantages over newer models, though both have their uses. Students may be assigned a timer during individual work periods and instructed to "beat the clock." The timer may also be used to delineate segments of the class day. Students may be taught that when the timer is ticking, no talking or moving around is allowed. The ticking thus becomes an S^D for working independently and quietly. The ring becomes an S^D for stopping work and waiting for further instructions for beginning another activity. Teachers who have no assistant, and who work with small groups in the classroom, may teach students that a person who is not in the group receiving instruction may not talk to the teacher except in case of dire emergency (the fire is out of control, or there is more than a quart of blood on the floor). It appears that the S^D, "No talking to the teacher while the timer is set," is prompted by the ticking sound. People of all ages and ability levels can be taught to attend to a timer. As a matter of fact, my timer was ticking as I wrote this—it is an S^D for writing as well as an S^Δ for interruptions by colleagues, who, by the way, were much harder to train than preschool children. The ring is a conditioned reinforcer—coffee-break time.

When multiple timers are needed, digital timers are more handy. They can be used simultaneously with individual students, small groups, and the entire class. One caution with using smart phone timers and leaving them out in the classroom is there is no telling what students might do while the teacher is not looking.

Before leaving the topic of time, we must address the issue of maximizing it. As mentioned in Chapter 2, providing unengaging activities that simply aim for students to "be still, be quiet, be docile" (Winett & Winkler, 1972, p. 499) must be avoided. Teachers must also refrain from engaging in activities that benefit only them, such as chatting with each other or doing paperwork. In contract, particularly for at-risk students or those with disabilities, there is no time to waste (Heward, 2003). Every effort must be made to keep every student actively learning for as much of the school day as possible. We know a first-grade teacher who requires her students to give the answer to an addition or subtraction fact on a flash card to gain admittance to the restroom during the traditional routine of lining up in the hall for the morning break. We think this is perhaps a trifle extreme, but we applaud the determination to use every available minute to teach.

Instructional Structure

Good instructional structure begins with planning, and planning begins with goals and objectives. Chapter 3 describes at great length the process of deriving and writing appropriate goals and objectives. Once long- and short-term objectives have been established for a class or written on an IEP for a student with disabilities, daily objectives can be written. We do not agree with the statement that for an individual with disabilities the IEP is the lesson plan. Teachers must plan daily objectives that lead to accomplishing established goals and activities that help students master those objectives. A minimal lesson plan must include, in addition to the objective(s), a statement of what the teacher will do, what students will do, what materials will be required, and how mastery of the objective(s) will be assessed. If there is more than one teacher, the plan should also state who will be responsible for delivering instruction. If, as we suggested earlier, the classroom has a written daily and weekly schedule, lesson-plan forms can be duplicated and daily activities written quickly and efficiently. Previous chapters detail research-based ways to design verbal and visual stimuli, to use prompts effectively, and to reinforce student responses. These methods should be the basis of daily lessons. We remind you again that applied behavior analysis is a teaching method, not just a way to reduce challenging behaviors. In addition to ensuring that instruction is goal oriented and efficient, a written daily plan is a prompt for most teachers to "get on with it." It makes it much more difficult to decide just to extend the free-play period until lunch and forget about math for today.

The way instruction is delivered is also important. If the teacher does not show much interest and has low energy, the students will probably act similarly. It may be difficult to seem enthusiastic when teaching the concept "bigger" for the hundredth time, but it is absolutely necessary. Instruction that moves along briskly is much more likely to occasion student response than instruction that is delivered at a lethargic pace. All teaching must include providing time for student responses. Talking is not teaching; the teacher must continually seek responses from students that indicate they are learning. Asking students if they understand something, by the way, is a poor indication of their learning. Many students think they understand something when they don't; many will nod their heads enthusiastically simply so instruction will stop. Rather than simply explaining what "bigger" means, the effective teacher repeatedly asks students to tell which one is bigger, show which one is bigger, find a bigger one, draw a bigger one, build a bigger one. The teacher will also positively reinforce correct responses and correct those that are wrong.

The teaching materials used with students also generate responses. The teacher hopes these responses will be in the form of correct oral and written answers. For many students with learning disabilities and challenging behavior, however, traditional

Transitions
Pearson eText
Video Example 13.2
In this video, an educator reviews a reading activity with the students and signals a transition to the next activity. What are all the transition strategies you notice in her classroom?

Stimulus control can work against teachers.

Active Student Responding
Pearson eText
Video Example 13.3
In this video, an educator sets expectations for math board work. How does this teacher assess student learning on an ongoing basis during board work?

materials such as textbooks, workbooks, and worksheets may be S^Ds for inappropriate behaviors. It is often best to teach using multiple modalities, or Universal Design for Learning (Ok et al., 2017). This means using some materials that require auditory input, such as listening; visual input, such as looking at diagrams; tactile input, such as writing and typing; and kinesthetic input, such as moving around the classroom to engage with materials. A great deal of creativity is required to provide some students with assignments that cause appropriate responding. It is well worth being creative—a group of students doing long division as fast as they can is bound to be less disruptive than a group doing nothing.

Verbal Structure

All classrooms have rules. Whether or not expectations for student behavior are made explicit, they exist. Wise teachers share their expectations for classroom behavior with students—it is difficult for students to follow rules if they don't know what the rules are. Many students follow rules; for them, rules have become S^Ds for compliance (because of their history of reinforcement). The students whose behavior upsets the teacher are those who do not follow the rules, who are disruptive, or who fail to complete assigned tasks. For such students, merely specifying what is expected has little effect on behavior; for them, complying with rules is not under stimulus control. These students must be taught to follow rules. Adherence to the following rules about rules will facilitate this process:

1. Be specific about what is expected (specificity).
2. Make as few rules as possible (economy).
3. Be explicit about the relationship between rules and consequences (consequences).

Specificity

Effective rules describe observable behavior. An unequivocal decision can be made about whether or not an effective rule has been followed. Some teachers, in an effort to anticipate every situation, make rules that are so vague they have minimal utility. It can be difficult to decide whether a student has been a good citizen, has respected others' rights, or has done unto others as he would have others do unto him. Following such rules is also difficult—what does a good citizen do? What are others' rights? Had I not better do unto him before he does unto me? Teachers must decide what behaviors are important in their classrooms and describe these behaviors in a set of rules. If being a good citizen means "complete assignments" or "keep hands to yourself," those should be the rules. In general, it is preferable to specify which behaviors are desired rather than which are forbidden. "Keep hands to yourself" is a reasonable substitute for "don't hit people." However, "keep your saliva to yourself" lacks the impact and pellucid clarity of "don't spit." Sometimes it's all right to tell students what not to do.

Economy

It's also hard (even for the teacher) to remember all those rules.

Making too many rules is inefficient. Teachers who make 88 rules in an effort to anticipate every possible situation may find that students are challenged to find the 89th inappropriate behavior—"But there's no rule against it." This is the primary disadvantage of allowing students to make the rules. They always seem to want to make dozens (and to invoke the death penalty for noncompliance).

Sometimes, unnecessary rules can even give students ideas. If on the first day of school a teacher announces to his seventh graders, "Do not bring straws back from the cafeteria. I will not have students in my classroom dampening the ends of the paper covers and blowing them upward so they stick to the ceiling," he can expect them to do just that. They might never have thought of it themselves. For this reason, rules about hitting (especially about hitting the teacher) and other drastic forms of misbehavior should not be made unless there is incontrovertible evidence that they are necessary.

Furthermore, enforcing unnecessary rules is time consuming. It would be interesting to collect data on the amount of time spent dealing with the "problem" of chewing gum in the average classroom. Many of us have heard (or participated in) interchanges like this:

Teacher: "Are you chewing gum?"
Student: (swallowing rapidly) "Who me?"

Or

Teacher: "Are you chewing gum?"
Student: "No, Ms. Franklin."
Teacher: "Open your mouth. Let me see! You are chewing gum! Spit it out this minute! I want to see it in the trash can!"

Many students find exchanges like this reinforcing. They chew gum to avoid or escape instruction and to have their teacher's undivided attention for a few minutes. Classroom rules, therefore, should concentrate on behaviors necessary for efficient instruction. Making rules into effective S^Ds is often quite difficult. Why do it unless the rule is necessary?

It is usually necessary to teach students rules just as we teach them other things. If one of the rules is "raise your hand before you speak," the teacher may model appropriate hand raising, ask students to model and discriminate correct and incorrect examples, and be sure that students understand the usually unstated (because it makes the rule cumbersome) but necessary behaviors of refraining from waving the hand frantically or making repeated grunting noises and of waiting for the teacher to see and respond to the raised hand before asking or answering a question or offering a comment. Practice sessions with lots of laughter (students love to model incorrect examples), praise, and other reinforcement will help students learn the rule.

Consequences

For students whose behavior is not under the control of rules, systematic efforts must be made to establish a relationship between following rules and positive reinforcement or punishment. Prompts may be needed. The teacher may

1. Post the rules on a bulletin board in either written or pictorial form, thus providing a visual prompt.
2. State the rules at the beginning of each class period or ask a student to read them, thus providing a verbal prompt.
3. Draw attention to a student who is following rules, thus providing a model.
4. Less frequently, point out to a student that she is not following a rule and remind her what is expected.

When the rules have been learned and are in force, the teacher must continue to provide consistent reinforcement for following them. Systematic efforts like these to bring rule following under stimulus control will succeed even if students do not comply with rules in other settings either at school or at home. This teacher and this classroom will become S^Ds for following rules.

Rules and Procedures

Wong and Wong (2009) distinguish between rules and procedures. Rules tell students how they should behave; procedures tell them how things are done in the classroom. The more procedures become automatic, the more smoothly the classroom will run. Procedures should include, but not be limited to, such things as entering and leaving, passing out

Using Rules
Pearson eText
Video Example 13.4
In this video, an educator reviews the classroom rules with her students before an activity. Notice that her rules are focused on high priority behaviors, stated specifically, and followed by matched consequences.

materials, turning in completed work, sharpening pencils, and so on and on and on. It is well worth taking the time at the beginning of the school year to teach each procedure as it is needed. One of us taught next door to a third-grade teacher who spent the first 3 weeks of school doing nothing but teaching procedures. They lined up, they sat down, they lined up, they sat down; they didn't go anywhere. They handed out and passed in papers over and over; they didn't write anything. She even had a procedure for a designated student to answer the intercom when the teacher was out of the room (a frequent occurrence). Certainly one student replying, "She stepped out of the room for a moment; may I give her a message?" was more impressive than a chorus of voices shouting, "Haven't seen her this morning; have you tried the lounge?" This teacher perhaps overdid practicing procedures, but her classroom certainly moved smoothly, even in her absence.

Teacher Characteristics

Learning Outcome 13.3   Describe several characteristics of effective teachers.

Almost everyone—certainly, almost everyone who wants to be a teacher—remembers a special teacher. When we ask our students to tell us what made the teacher so special, they talk about warmth, caring, personal interest, a sense of humor, sensitivity, and many other similar characteristics. Being applied behavior analysts, of course, we are not satisfied with such vague descriptions. When we pinpointed them, we found that what those teachers did was to make themselves conditioned positive reinforcers. By delivering large amounts of positive reinforcement, usually social, they acquired reinforcing characteristics by just being around. Many uninformed people believe that teachers who systematically use applied behavior analysis procedures must be cold, mechanical, and impersonal. In fact, the opposite is true.

All classrooms provide consequences for behavior. There are some in which virtually all students are motivated to work hard in order to learn and to earn good grades. In such classrooms, good instruction and an occasional word of praise or gentle admonition are the only management techniques necessary. In other environments, students may have had so little experience with success and so much reinforcement for inappropriate behavior that no instruction is possible unless their behavior can be brought under control. Virtually all such students will respond positively to one of the token systems described in Chapter 8; a few may make it necessary to use procedures to decrease behavior. In yet other classrooms, students respond best to a combination of primary and social reinforcement, again with occasional procedures to decrease inappropriate behaviors. The teacher who is familiar with the tools of applied behavior analysis is equipped to design an appropriate management system for any setting.

Association with Positive Reinforcement
Pearson eText
Video Example 13.5
In this video, an educator sets expectations for a vocabulary task and assists students with the task. How does the teacher use positive reinforcement while maintaining high expectations?

A Look into Learning Environments

Learning Outcome 13.4   Label principles of applied behavior analysis operating in hypothetical classroom environments.

Now we will visit several teachers, all applied behavior analysts, teaching in several rather different settings. We will look at everything from their room arrangement to their daily schedules to see how they implemented the principles they have read about and observed.

Remember Miss Harper?

Miss Harper's second student teaching placement is in an integrated preschool setting. Since she is seeking a minor in early childhood special education, Professor Grundy feels that this will be perfect for her. Miss Harper is not so sure. She has been informed that about one-fourth of her prospective students are "developmentally delayed," and she knows that could mean almost anything.

Miss Harper tentatively approaches the classroom for her first day in this placement. As she walks through the open door into a large, airy room, she is struck by the appearance of the classroom. There are a few tables with tiny little chairs, but most of the room is divided into larger areas containing various collections of what she characterizes as toys—blocks, both sand and water tables with buckets and other utensils, colorful construction materials, dolls and furniture, and a miniature collection of kitchen and other household furniture. She also observes easels and paints, displays of children's art, and modeling clay, along with numerous riding toys, smaller toy vehicles, and what appears to be a huge number of very young children. As she attempts to identify those "developmentally delayed" ones, she is approached by a smiling young woman wearing cropped pants and tennis shoes, who Miss Harper assumes must be an assistant.

"Miss Harper?" she inquires, "I'm Amy Somerville, the lead teacher. Welcome to our class." She looks dubiously at Miss Harper's tailored suit, mid-heel pumps, and wary expression, but continues. "Come on over and meet the other teachers; we're really looking forward to working with you."

"Michael," she states firmly to a tot in a tiny electric wheelchair speeding perilously close to Miss Harper's pumps, "look where you're going, kiddo."

As they make their way through the mass of children, Miss Harper spots two children with Down syndrome and two more with leg braces. They appear to be engaged in playing with other children. As they approach the other teachers, Miss Amy asks, "What's your first name, Miss Harper? We're very informal here."

"Michelle," gasps Miss Harper as she is introduced to four other adults. No distinction is made as to status, but Barry, Lisa, Bonnie, and Lucille apparently have responsibility with Miss Amy for the 25 (could there really only be 25?) 3- and 4-year-olds in the classroom.

Lisa takes charge of Miss Harper, "We've already done circle this morning and most of the children are getting ready to work in the centers." Her pitying look at Miss Harper's outfit is undisguised. "Perhaps you'd like to just observe for a while." She guides Miss Harper to an adult-sized chair at a work table and hurries away to take a shovel away from a child at the sand table.

"Sand," she states firmly, "is for building, not throwing." She sinks to the floor at the sand table and begins asking the children about their activities. She encourages the children to work together and praises a student who gets a dump truck in order to move the sand more efficiently. Meanwhile, Miss Bonnie gathers three children and settles them at one of the tiny tables. She pulls objects from a box and asks the students to identify them, tell what color they are, and answer other questions about them. A young man whom Miss Harper recognizes as a fellow university student arrives to work with one of the children with autism who is receiving intensive one-on-one instruction for part of the time he is at school.

Positive social reinforcement.

As Miss Harper watches the activities in the room, a pattern begins to emerge. In addition to the direct instruction activities, she sees many small groups of children who are playing—working, she remembers—at the various centers. She decides to watch one center for a while to zero in on what's going on. She picks the block center. Four children are building a series of structures and chattering about their activities. One child sits by himself. Barry is seated on the floor nearby.

"Mr. Barry," insists one of the children, "Charlie's hogging the big blocks." Indeed, Charlie appears to be simply collecting the largest blocks and keeping himself between them and the other children.

"Maybe you should ask him to share, Dejohn," suggests Barry.

"No way," states Dejohn, "he'll hit me." Miss Harper begins to suspect that Charlie, too, may be "developmentally delayed."

"Charlie," suggests Barry quietly, "I think Dejohn doesn't know how hard we've been working on sharing. Remember, you earn computer time. Go on," he adds more loudly, "Dejohn, ask—you remember how."

"Charlie," says Dejohn, "we need big blocks. Come help us." With a glance at Barry, Charlie pushes several blocks from his hoard toward Dejohn and moves slightly toward the group. Barry quickly hands Charlie a token, which he slips into his pocket. "Good job, Charlie; you too, Dejohn."

Miss Harper turns her attention to the area where students are playing—working, working—with water. Both Miss Lisa and Miss Lucille are there with six children. One of them is Maria, a child with Down syndrome. The children are pouring water from smaller into larger containers, and yes, from larger into smaller containers. Miss Harper admires both the ingenious design of the table and the presence of two adults. Both adults converse with all the children. She notices that Maria answers with monosyllables when a teacher asks a question but does not initiate interaction. The other students talk among themselves but ignore Maria. Miss Harper begins, however, to pick up a pattern. Casually, Miss Lucille suggests, "Melanie, ask Maria to hand you that yellow cup, please. Good job saying thank you, Melanie."

A few minutes later, Miss Bonnie says, "Kyung, would you ask Maria if she would like to be a clean-up helper? You can be the leader." Miss Harper is impressed that the teachers are encouraging the typical students to interact with their peers with disabilities. She realizes that a setting using developmentally appropriate practices can adapt those practices to a wide variety of developmental levels, even those considered "delayed."

By the end of the day Miss Harper, having observed indoor work, outdoor work, lunchroom work, and quiet-time work, is convinced this is exactly the right placement for her. She leaves the preschool headed for the mall. She needs cropped pants and a pair of tennis shoes. What else would Miss Michelle wear?

Ms. Mitchell's Self-Contained Class

Ms. Mitchell teaches eight 6- to 9-year-olds. All have severe developmental disabilities. Three students use wheelchairs; one student has braces and crutches. Some of the students have no verbal skills; others can talk fairly well. Ms. Mitchell shares a two-room suite with a resource teacher. She has a full-time assistant, Ms. Post, and works with a speech and language therapist, a physical therapist, and an occupational therapist, all of whom work in several schools. Her room is arranged so the students with wheelchairs and crutches can move about easily and safely. There is a table where all the children and several adults can sit, areas where students can sit or lie on the floor, and a number of adapted seating and standing devices designed for specific children. There is also a screened area where students' clothing can be changed when necessary.

Ms. Mitchell's daily and weekly schedules are quite complex. She must arrange the schedules to take maximum advantage of the professional and paraprofessional help available and to see that all students have opportunities to be with their nondisabled and less disabled peers. Perhaps the best way to show how Ms. Mitchell puts it all together in her classroom is to spend an entire day with her class.

All Ms. Mitchell's students ride buses to school. Either she or Ms. Post, her assistant, meets each bus to help the driver get students off and to help the students get to the classroom. Several student volunteers from general education classrooms also meet their "buddies" and provide assistance. As little assistance as necessary is provided; indeed, the teachers have recently started just shadowing Malcolm as he makes his own way to the classroom. Because the buses arrive at considerable intervals, there is plenty of time to spend with individual students as they arrive in the classroom. Part of what makes Ms. Mitchell's planning so complex is that in getting coats and boots off and hung up, she must constantly remember that, for example, Malcolm is working on colors, Trish is working on counting objects, and Steven is working on responding to his name. As they arrive in the classroom, each student is prompted as necessary to go to his or her own coat hook. Students' names and pictures are posted by each hook.

> Bringing responses under stimulus control.

"Take off your coat, Trish. That's good, Malcolm, you took off your coat. Now hang it up. Good, Malcolm. Take off your coat, Trish." Ms. Mitchell puts her hand over Trish's and helps her through the unbuttoning process. "How many buttons, Trish? Let's count. One, two, three; three buttons. Take off your coat." As Trish begins to comply, Ms. Mitchell says, "Is your shirt red, Malcolm?" Malcolm nods. "Speak up, Malcolm, say 'yes.' Good, Malcolm. Good girl, Trish, you took off your coat. How many coats this morning? Good job, Trish, three coats. Steven!" As Steven turns his head, he is rewarded with a tickle and "Good, Steven, let's go to the circle."

Ms. Mitchell likes to start the day with a variation of "show and tell" as in general education primary classes. The speech and language therapist is here on Monday mornings, so today she leads the session, asking each student to respond verbally or with a communication device.

"Tell me something you did yesterday. Malcolm, what did you do yesterday? Did you watch TV? Tell me, 'I watched TV.' Good, Malcolm. Hannah, did you watch TV? Good, Hannah (when Hannah points to the TV on her communication board). What did you watch, Trish? Sponge Bob Square Pants? I watched that, too." Ms. Mitchell moves among the children, prompting responses and patting students who respond on the shoulder. Steven, who has the fewest language skills, responds to "TV" by laughing. Ms. Post, who is standing behind him, provides another tickle and says, "Do you like TV, Steven?" He giggles again.

After the circle activity, it is time for Malcolm to change to go to PE with the second grade. Ms. Post works on his dressing skills, helping him take off his red shirt and put on his blue shorts, while Ms. Mitchell and the speech and language therapist engage the other students in rearranging and putting things on and under the bookshelves, asking Trish to count the books, and occasionally attracting Steven's attention.

A second grader comes to get Malcolm. Ms. Mitchell and Ms. Post work intensively with individuals and small groups on various skills while other students work by themselves for short periods. When Malcolm returns about 45 minutes later, he tells Ms. Mitchell all about kickball (it was a red ball) while he changes into his regular clothes. Several of the children help Ms. Post prepare the morning snack. Malcolm gets the cups and hands the red one, the yellow one, and the blue one to Ms. Post. Trish counts two cookies for each student. After the snack has been cleaned up (surely, by now you can guess who washes the red cup and who counts the cups to be sure they were all washed), six of the children and Ms. Post join the resource class for a math activity, and Ms. Mitchell, Hannah, and Trish put on coats and go for a walk. Most of Hannah's neighbors walk to school, and Ms. Mitchell's goal is for Hannah to learn to cross the streets safely so she can join them. Trish lives too far away to walk, but is also ready to learn the skills. Ms. Mitchell talks with the girls as they walk, identifying things they see and asking them to do the same. She asks Trish to count several things during the walk. They walk to Hannah's house and back, looking both ways even after the light is green.

Several of the students eat lunch with general education classes, each with a lunch buddy to be sure that all goes well. Ms. Post takes several others, who still need a little more help and supervision, to the cafeteria as a group. Ms. Mitchell helps Steven in the classroom; he becomes very excited and displays some self-injurious behavior if he has to cope with the cafeteria. Ms. Mitchell plans to start taking him by himself in a few weeks.

After lunch, as in most primary classrooms, there is a quiet story and music listening time. Ms. Post and Ms. Mitchell each take charge of half the time so the other can eat lunch peacefully in the teacher's lounge. Ms. Mitchell times her lunch so she can eat with a friend and, for a change, have somebody tell her that she's doing a good job.

After the quiet time, Malcolm goes to the resource room for reading readiness activities. Ms. Post, Ms. Mitchell, and the physical therapist help the others change for PE. The physical therapist has helped develop a plan for gross motor activities for each

Barry prompts Dejohn, then Charlie.

student and also helps implement it. By the time the children have finished PE, it's time to start getting ready for the buses.

Ms. Mitchell used to be frustrated at the amount of time she spent in her classroom on routines, until she realized how much she could teach during those routines.

Ms. Washington's Resource Room

Ms. Washington is a resource and consulting teacher in a large, suburban elementary school. She works with about 30 fourth- and fifth-grade students who have learning disabilities or mild intellectual disabilities or whose behavior problems have earned them the label "seriously emotionally disturbed." Being a behaviorist, she doesn't worry too much about their disturbed emotions but concentrates on their academic and social behavior. All Ms. Washington's students spend at least half their day in a general education classroom. Some are with her for as much as 3 hours every day; others come only when they encounter a problem in the general education classroom. Ms. Washington is responsible, with a multidisciplinary team, for developing an IEP for each of her students and for coordinating the implementation of that IEP with general education classroom teachers. She has a half-time assistant who comes in the afternoons.

It usually takes Ms. Washington several weeks to get her weekly and daily schedule coordinated. She has to work around art, music, physical education, and lunch schedules for many classes; she must also be sure that her students do not, for example, miss math, which they're good at, to come to her for reading, which they're not good at, meanwhile sitting in a reading class in which they're totally lost. If that sounds very confusing, think how Ms. Washington feels. She does not try to schedule her students by grade level or type of disability but tries to schedule students who are working at about the same level in a subject area at the same time. She often has several subclasses in her room at a given time, for example, five students working on reading and one needing help with math. She does what all teachers do: she provides independent work for some students while she works with others. She schedules her largest groups and her most difficult students in the afternoon when the assistant will be available to monitor and help with independent work. This year she has two boys who spend all morning with her; she is responsible for their instruction in reading, math, and social studies. She has scheduled an additional five students for each hour of the morning, thus having seven students in her room at any given time. Three students spend 2 hours each afternoon, and Ms. Washington schedules five others during each of those 2 hours. She eats lunch from 11:30 a.m. to noon and keeps the hour from noon to 1:00 p.m. for observations and conferences. She has found that many working parents prefer to have meetings during the lunch hour. She requires students to be in their seats at their scheduled time and provides a small clock face with the time they need to leave the general education class for those students who need a prompt.

Ms. Washington uses a formal token system in her classroom. Each student has a point card and earns points for being on time, completing assignments, and behaving appropriately. Many students also bring less elaborate point cards from their general education teachers and earn additional points for having behaved appropriately in the general education classroom. She provides what her students call the "store" on Fridays; students may trade filled cards for food items, school supplies, and small toys. Ms. Washington, like many teachers, buys the items for the store herself. She maintains that it is cheaper than the psychiatric treatment that she would require without the token system. She also has a time-out area where disruptive students can be separated from the group.

All instruction in Ms. Washington's classroom is individualized. Contrary to what some teachers apparently believe, this means neither that all instruction is one-on-one nor that each student has his own personal packet of worksheets that he works on without interaction with the teacher. It means that each student's lesson for each day is designed to help her master the goals and objectives written in her IEP. Some children may have the same goals; they can often receive instruction as a group. Ms. Washington posts the daily schedule with what each child will be doing on a bulletin board that is convenient to her and her assistant.

Ms. Washington has arranged her room so that she has two teaching and work areas as far apart as possible. Most of the students sit at tables instead of desks. She provides separate desks for a few students to prevent them from bothering other students. Two of her students do some of their work at a study carrel that she has created with a bookcase.

We will visit Ms. Washington first thing Monday morning. At 8:30 a.m. on the dot, having said the Pledge of Allegiance and paid for lunch in the general education classroom, Alvin and Tyrone, the two children who stay all morning, along with Melanie, Michael, Donna, Charlie, and Harold, have picked up their point cards and are sitting in their assigned seats. Ms. Washington greets them only after they are seated.

"Good morning, Alvin; it's good to see your smile on this rainy Monday. You're right on time. You've already earned 10 points for that and 2 bonus ones for getting started on your order task." Each student's place has a simple paper-and-pencil task that reinforces following instructions. Each student is greeted and given points.
Tokens are always paired with praise.

As the students finish their order tasks (usually in less than 5 minutes), Ms. Washington puts a large A on each one, gives more points, and continues: "Alvin, we're going to be doing reading first. While I get the others started, you get three red books and bring them here." She gets four of the students started on a written reading comprehension activity based on a story they read yesterday, reminds them that they can raise their red (cardboard) flag if they need help, and sits down at the table with Alvin, Tyrone, and Harold.

"Alvin, thank you for bringing our books. You did a great job—no talking and fooling around on the way. That's worth another 3 bonus points." After a brisk 10-minute drill during which the students respond by chorally identifying words and sounds, Ms. Washington says, "Now I'm going to put the title of the story we're going to read today on the board. I'll bet somebody can read it easily because it has a lot of the clusters we've been working on." She prints the title "The Fantastic Voyage" on the board and, sure enough, all three students are eager to read it.
Praise is always specific.

"Marvin, you try." Marvin reads the title as "The Fantastic Voyeur." Suppressing a giggle, Ms. Washington prompts, "What sound do the letters *a-g-e* make? Right! Now try it. Great! Harold, what does *fantastic* mean? It's a word we might use about science fiction. Right! It means strange or hard to believe. Very good!"

Ms. Washington continues to present vocabulary words, prompting correct responses and heavily reinforcing them. She avoids getting sidetracked or slowing down, but keeps the group on task and her pace brisk. She starts the group silently reading the first paragraph and goes to check the students working independently. No one has raised a flag, but Melanie has not started. She is staring out the window.

"Melanie, take your work into the carrel, please. It will be easier for you to concentrate. I expect that work to be finished before it's time for you to read."

Ms. Washington's reading lesson is finished in about 20 minutes. She gives the boys an assignment and points for paying attention and participating. She then checks the work of other students, gives more points, and asks Charlie to get the blue books for his group. She determines that Melanie (who is a group unto herself) is working and spends about 2 minutes going over her work while Charlie distributes the blue books. She also gives Melanie fewer points than she could have earned "because you had a little trouble getting started today." The reading lesson has the same format as the first group's. As the group starts to review vocabulary, Alvin, who should be working independently, leans over and says something to Tyrone, who tries to ignore him.
Designing a token system so that partial credit can be earned is always a good idea.

Teachers need positive reinforcement too.

Student Specific Reinforcement Systems
Pearson eText
Video Example 13.6
In this video, a student with moderate-to-severe disabilities is working his teacher in a one-on-one setting. What accommodations are made to tailor the reinforcement system to his specific needs?

Positive reinforcement in action.

"Excuse me for interrupting our lesson, group. Alvin, you need to do your own work and leave Tyrone alone, please."

When this group is finished, Ms. Washington spends 10 uninterrupted minutes with Melanie, who is still having trouble with the short vowel sounds. She is frustrated that she has so little time to spend with each child, but she tries very hard to make the independent work meaningful and to make every minute of instruction count. She spends the last 5 minutes of the hour helping each student total his or her points and decide what kind of day he or she had. She dismisses the students and reminds them pleasantly that their teachers expect them back right on time.

Ms. Washington repeats the cycle four more times. During the afternoon, with the help of her assistant, she is able to give her undivided attention to each instructional group. For that reason, she tries to schedule most of the children with the most serious learning delays and all of the children with serious challenging behavior in the afternoon.

Who Needs ABA?

Ms. Samples is a 30-year veteran fifth-grade teacher at the elementary school where Ms. Washington teaches students with mild disabilities. She is somewhat of a legend—never sends children to the office and only reluctantly sends them to the resource room. At the beginning of the year she listened doubtfully to Ms. Washington's explanation of her token system.

"Good heavens," she declared, "you young teachers with your newfangled notions. All those points and charts. Coddling them with bribes. I've been tough as nails for 30 years and that's what works for me."

Mr. Jackson, the principal, is somewhat in awe of Ms. Samples. Her tough talk worries him, but the children seem happy and parents clamor to get their children in her class. In spite of the fact that she ridicules each successive wave of reform in curriculum and methodology, her students do well on standardized tests and are well prepared for sixth grade. Mr. Jackson generally leaves Ms. Samples alone and guiltily tends to assign her more than her share of children with learning delays and challenging behaviors. When he does observe in her classroom, he sees a variety of activities. Ms. Samples appears to use frequent episodes of rather intense direct instruction with either the whole class or some part of it. During these episodes, the students have many opportunities to respond individually and chorally. Although this kind of instruction, which Mr. Jackson himself thinks is rather old-fashioned, does not coincide with the activities recommended by the local curriculum development council, he sometimes wonders if other classes would do better on standardized tests of achievement if they had some of it. Ms. Samples sometimes groups students to complete tasks, and her students often work with manipulatives and do projects. Tyrone, Harold, and Melanie are all members of her class, along with several other children who attend the resource class.

Ms. Samples accosted Ms. Washington in the teacher's lounge one Monday morning. "Listen," she said, "I really need to keep all the kids all this week. I've got important stuff to teach and if they miss parts of it they'll get behind." Ms. Washington, having recently attended a seminar on inclusion, agreed to this temporary arrangement. She asked with some trepidation if she could observe how her children functioned under this arrangement.

"Come any time," said Ms. Samples. "I've got nothing to hide. Just don't expect to see any of your individualized education or whatever it is ... not any of your foolish ABA either."

Ms. Washington rearranged her schedule to free up a full hour Friday afternoon. She approached the door of Ms. Samples's class, firmly closed as usual, and quietly entered. To her immense surprise, the children were not seated quietly at their desks watching

Ms. Samples at the board. She did not, in fact, see Ms. Samples right away because the teacher was sitting on the floor surrounded by a group of children engaged in attaching curtain hooks to a 6-foot length of burlap with brightly colored pieces of felt glued to it. Other groups of children were occupied framing printed documents and arguing about the distance between cup hooks on a long piece of wood. Desks and tables were pushed aside or arranged in clusters, with several children working on other apparently nonacademic tasks. Ms. Washington sat down at an empty desk and tried to make some sense of the seemingly chaotic activity. Tyrone approached her and asked what she was doing. When she stated that she had wanted to see him and the others working in their "other" classroom, he gloated, "Oh, we haven't done any work all week. We all worked hard for the last 6 weeks and brought the class report card average up a whole letter grade, so we've just been making our tapestry about the American Revolution." Tyrone explained that he had been on the team that researched the battle of Bunker Hill and decided what scene to cut from felt and glue on the wall hanging.

"It was fun," he stated. "Amanda helped with the hard words, and I even got to measure the felt."

Ms. Washington immediately realized that Ms. Samples's teaching methods, whatever her statements about newfangled notions, were right up to date. When Tyrone went back to his group, she examined the classroom carefully. One bulletin board was labeled CLASSROOM POLICIES. Children's work was posted on another. She asked a student about it and was told that it wasn't really work, just copies of the best short reports about the Revolution that were being framed to accompany the mural.

"It's awesome to have your work on that board," she said. "It has to be, like, totally perfect. I rewrote mine three times and got help from my spelling partner before it was good enough." She proudly pointed out her essay. Ms. Washington was interested to see Melanie's essay, right next to it, much shorter, but neatly written and bearing the same big red A+. The heading attributed the essay to Melanie, as told to Lee Anne.

Ms. Samples had gotten up from the floor. "Thanks, guys," she said to two boys who had each given her a hand, "it's nice to know that you apply our class policy on helping others to me, too." She began to move around the room.

"Melanie," she asked, "have you finished cutting the mats? Remember, your group depends on you. Mike, watch Harold carefully—he's really an expert framer." Harold grinned hugely. A stranger to Ms. Washington muttered "That special ed kid is an expert?" to a friend, who snickered. Ms. Samples took each boy's arm, marched them to an unoccupied area of the room and quietly, but with steel in her voice, reminded them that another class policy was respect for others and that each of them was to copy that policy from the board and write an essay on how it makes others feel when you call them names.

Suddenly there was a commotion at one end of the room. Tyrone pushed a chair over and cocked his fist at another student. Ms. Samples had both his arms by the elbow before he could carry out the act.

"Tyrone, that is totally unacceptable. Hitting is not the solution to any problem. You will have to sit out for 15 minutes." Tyrone sullenly but obediently went to a chair behind a file cabinet and sat down. Ms. Washington noticed that while Tyrone was "sitting out," Ms. Samples spoke with the other boy, reminding him that Tyrone was sometimes volatile and that the kind of teasing other children take in stride was apt to make him blow.

Ms. Samples rang a bell on her desk. There was instant silence and all eyes turned to her.

"We have only 30 minutes left, boys and girls," she said to accompaniment of groans, which she ignored, "We'll have to finish up next week. Let's clean up now so our room will be a pleasure to enter on Monday. Think how proud we're all going to be when the students, teachers, and parents see our tapestry in the cafeteria. I can't wait, and I'll bet you can't either."

> Sometimes punishment is necessary.

As the students began very efficiently to put away supplies and restore order to the room, Ms. Washington reflected that for a real tough teacher who didn't believe in ABA, Ms. Samples certainly seemed to understand clearly the benefits of applying learning principles. She also decided to talk with her about placing some of her students with mild disabilities in her class on a full-time basis.

A Schoolwide Positive Behavior Support System

Laura Grishom started her career as a resource teacher for students with learning and behavior difficulties in a large urban middle school. In the last few years, the faculty and school administration, with enthusiastic agreement from the majority of the students' families, have embraced a schoolwide positive behavior support program designed to prevent the majority of the problems, both academic and social, that typically plague schools like theirs. Miss Grishom now serves as the facilitator of the schoolwide Positive Behavior Support Team responsible for implementing strategies for primary, secondary, and tertiary measures for problem prevention (Sugai & Horner, 2020). Primary strategies, which are effective for the majority of students, include making, teaching, and reinforcing consistent rules throughout the school, motivating students to succeed academically by providing appropriate curriculum and instruction, and reinforcing academic success in ways meaningful to students. Ms. Grishom and her team work with all faculty members to assist them in implementing these strategies.

Secondary strategies may be necessary for students with a history of either or both academic difficulties and behavior issues. Ms. Grishom's team has implemented several programs for the approximately 15% of students whose behavior warrants more intensive intervention. Based on functional assessment, some students receive social skills or anger management training in small groups facilitated by the guidance counselors; others participate in a check-in/check-out program (Boden et al., 2018; Drevon et al., 2019) requiring them to check in with a designated faculty member each morning, pick up a point card to use throughout the day, and check out and receive feedback at the end of the school day.

> FBA is discussed in Chapter 7.

It took Ms. Grishom and the school administrators a long time and a lot of meetings to get the entire faculty committed to the new approach to preventing rather than punishing disruptive behavior, but most teachers and other staff members are impressed with the results. A few students, however, remain a challenge. The behavior of these few students, less than 5% of the student body, requires more intensive intervention. One of these students is Les, whose fighting, bullying, disruptive outbursts, open defiance, and lack of response to primary and secondary prevention strategies has even some of the teachers most supportive of the new system muttering about detention, expulsion, alternative schools, and incarceration. Ms. Grishom and her team prepared to implement a tertiary intervention for Les. After a thorough FBA, it was determined that Les's behavior was reinforced by peer attention and that his inability to complete tasks requiring even minimal reading skills exacerbated his tendency to act out. His behavior appeared to be worse when he got insufficient sleep, as reported by his mother, and when he spent hours after school interacting with older peers while his parents were at work. The team designed a wraparound intervention (Eber et al., 2011) for Les, involving his family, who agreed to monitor and reinforce his going to bed at a reasonable hour; the local boys' and girls' club, the staff of which provided transportation and supervision after school; and the school itself, which offered additional support for both developing reading skills and compensating for their lack in content subjects. Although Les continued to present more problems than most other students, he and the other students receiving tertiary intervention responded positively and most were able to be maintained in their home school environment.

Mr. Boyd's Math Classes

Mr. Boyd teaches math in a large urban high school. He has a homeroom, three sections of ninth-grade arithmetic, and two sections of tenth-grade consumer math. Most of his students score below grade level on achievement tests, and each of his sections contains several students who have been classified as having special education needs. His class sizes range from 22 to 25. At the beginning of the year Mr. Boyd, using the diagnostic tests provided with the textbooks issued to the students, divided each class into four teams. He composed teams carefully so that each has a mixture of more and less competent students. One year he tried forming teams each week based on the past week's performance but found that to be a logistical nightmare. He now keeps the teams intact for a 6-week grading period. Each team has a captain, who is in charge of overall management, and an accountant, who is in charge of record keeping. These jobs rotate weekly. Each team is allowed to choose a name.

Mr. Boyd follows the same weekly schedule as much as possible because he has found that things run more smoothly when he does. When the schedule will not be followed, he tries to let the students know in advance. On Mondays and Wednesdays he presents new concepts and teaches new skills using large-group direct instruction. Tuesdays and Thursdays are team days. The students work together on assignments, helping one another as necessary. Mr. Boyd circulates, being sure that peer tutors are providing correct information and working with individuals and small groups when necessary. Fridays are test and reward days. Students receive grades for individual work but all activities also earn points for their team. Teams receive points when members are present and on time, have necessary materials, complete homework and class assignments, perform well on tests and other activities, and behave appropriately. Teams lose points when members are disruptive or noncompliant. Expectations are explained at the beginning of the school year and each student has a copy of the class rules and procedures in a required notebook. Every team can be a winner every week if enough points are earned. Each team's scores are posted on a bulletin board and the team with the highest score is named Team of the Week. Mr. Boyd was afraid that high school students might find this system too childish, but the students seem to enjoy it. There is a good bit of friendly competition and lots of encouragement to bring supplies, be on time, behave appropriately, and learn the material. Let's look at a typical Monday in Mr. Boyd's first-period arithmetic class.

| Stimulus control.

Mr. Boyd stands in the doorway as students enter. He greets each one by name, with a positive comment about appearance, or at least with a smile and eye contact. Because many of his students are athletes, he attends many games and keeps track of all of them. He often offers a word of congratulations or commiseration. He also remembers birthdays and writes them on his lesson plans so he can acknowledge them—quietly, of course, because he knows adolescents are easily embarrassed. This greeting routine also allows him to determine if any students are angry or upset.

| Public or effusive praise can function as a punisher for many adolescent students.

As students enter the room they go immediately to their assigned seats, which are arranged in rows so that all can see the whiteboard. There are several review problems on the board and all students except the accountants begin work immediately. The accountants, who are excused from the review activity (they get plenty of math practice keeping up with all those points), move down their team's row with a clipboard and a data sheet on which they record whether students have supplies. Mr. Boyd ignores team members' surreptitiously lending one another supplies; that's what teamwork is all about.

As soon as the bell rings, Mr. Boyd takes roll by referring to his seating chart. Each team captain also notes absences; captains are encouraged to find out why their team members are not at school. Although teams are not penalized for excused absences, a member who is not present can't earn bonus points. Within 5 minutes, the students have completed the review activity. Team members check one another's work, and the papers are passed to the front and collected.

> Task analysis is discussed in Chapter 10.

Mr. Boyd begins the lesson on equivalent fractions by donning a pizza deliverer's hat and asking how many students would like to order a pizza. All raise their hands eagerly, and Mr. Boyd passes out photocopies of a pizza he has drawn and cut into pieces. There is some good-natured muttering about the inedibility of this pizza and the pitifulness of Mr. Boyd's drawing, a standing joke.

Mr. Boyd raises his hand in his established signal for quiet and the students stop talking. He asks, "How many pieces do you have? Marvin? Sara? Hey, that's not fair, Marvin has eight pieces and Sara only has four! Marvin, you have to give Sara some of yours." When Marvin protests that Sara's pieces are bigger than his, Mr. Boyd is well launched into his lesson. He uses larger cardboard pizzas to illustrate that 1/2, 2/4, and 4/8 all represent the same amount of pizza.

"What about 500,000/1,000,000?" he asks, writing it on the board. Marvin quips, "You're going to have to eat that pizza with a spoon." There is general laughter. Mr. Boyd laughs, too, but soon raises his hand again. All students become quiet except two who are repeating the joke. Mr. Boyd says matter-of-factly, "Rappers just lost 2 points," and continues his lesson. The other members of the team glare at the malefactors and the room is again quiet.

Mr. Boyd models the procedure for determining equivalency, brings his student to the board to work problems, and assigns a short written lesson to be sure students understand the concept and can do the computation. He moves constantly about the room as students work independently, providing frequent positive comments, pointing out errors, and reteaching when necessary. He notes students who are having difficulty to be sure that they are assigned a peer tutor tomorrow.

Ten minutes before the end of the period, Mr. Boyd has students exchange papers again and goes over the correct answers. He reminds them not to panic if they're having trouble because they will get help tomorrow. He announces the number of points earned by each team and congratulates them. When the bell rings, Mr. Boyd dismisses the class and gets ready to do it all again with the next one.

On Tuesday, the first-period class rearranges the room into clusters of desks for each team. The procedure for doing this quickly and quietly was taught at the beginning of the year. Mr. Boyd gives each team captain the team's papers from yesterday, and the captains themselves work out how to ensure that each team member masters the material. Some captains assign individual tutors; some assign several students to one tutor; one looks at her team's papers and tells Mr. Boyd that they all need help. He makes sure all the teams are functioning efficiently and sits down to work with the "needy team." He reminds himself to distribute the members of this team differently during the next grading period. The two strongest members of the original team have moved and their replacements are weak. The in-class assignment for today will earn a grade for each student as well as points for the team.

After working with the weak group for several minutes, he tells them to continue working on the assignment and monitors the class to be sure that team members are working together but not doing one another's work. He answers questions, makes suggestions to tutors, and provides an enrichment activity for bonus points to one team whose members have all completed the assignment correctly. Several times the "busy hum" of the classroom approaches a roar. Mr. Boyd raises his hand and, because all of the students are not facing him, snaps his fingers twice. Team members shush one another and the noise never becomes a serious problem.

Ten minutes before the end of the period, Mr. Boyd asks the class to turn around and look at him. He collects the papers of students who are finished, reminds those who are not finished that their work must be turned in tomorrow, and gives a short homework assignment. He announces points earned for appropriate behavior, reminds the students that he will announce points for the in-class assignment when it has been graded, and allows the students to begin their homework assignment. The chairs remain as they are until sixth period, when that class rearranges them in rows.

Mr. Boyd at one time thought it might be more efficient to do 2 days of group work in a row to avoid all the furniture moving, but was quickly informed by the building engineer that it is impossible to clean any room whose desks are not in rows.

Ms. Michaels Has It in the Bag

Ms. Michaels teaches a group of students with moderate to severe disabilities. Her students range in age from 17 through 20. She shares responsibility for 24 students with another licensed teacher and two paraprofessionals. Her job has changed dramatically over the years. She started her career in a residential school and is now working with a similar population of students located at a public suburban high school. Her students spend a great deal of time outside of school learning skills they will need as adults.

Today she plans to take three of her students into the community for several hours. This requires a great deal of advance planning. She and her colleagues determine that the other teacher and one assistant will work on domestic skills, simulated shopping skills, and prevocational skills, with most of the students remaining at school. The classroom contains a fully equipped kitchen and laundry room, and the students will prepare lunch for themselves, wash and fold towels from the school gym, and prepare brochures from a local health club for mailing. In return, the health club has agreed to allow class members to use the facility. The classroom also has an area that can simulate a grocery, drug, or convenience store so that students can practice shopping using lists or picture cues. Four highly verbal students will accompany the assistant to the resource room, where the teacher is working on appropriate social skills on the job. They will eat lunch with some of the resource students and return to their classroom for the shopping simulation.

The students who are to be in the community will work at a job site for an hour, eat lunch at a cafeteria, and shop for clothing at a local discount department store. The students accompanying Ms. Michaels today are Sam, 17 years old with good verbal skills and excellent behavior; Kimberly, 18, who uses a communication device and behaves well unless frustrated or confused; and Ricardo, 18, who has some verbal skills but is prone to violent outbursts.

Ms. Michaels first checks to see that all three students are present and feeling well, then spends some time previewing the trip, using pictures. Sam and Kimberly are old hands at the grocery store, where they are learning job skills. They have also eaten at the cafeteria and shopped at the department store several times. Ricardo has less experience at the grocery store but has eaten and been shopping alone with a teacher. This will be his first group experience at these sites. Ms. Michaels has specific objectives for each student at each site. After the preview, which serves as a language lesson, Ms. Michaels checks to see that everyone has their identification, that everyone has used the restroom, that Kimberly's device has been programmed correctly for the various activities, and that she, herself, has everything she needs. Everyone makes fun of the large satchel she carries into the community, but she has learned to be prepared. She picks up the bag, as she calls it, as she leaves the room.

The bus stop is right outside the school. While waiting for the bus, each student counts out the correct change from his or her coin purse—they've been riding the bus since elementary school. The bus is right on time and the students put their coins in the container and greet the bus driver. Ricardo begins humming with excitement but that subsides immediately when Kimberly touches him on the shoulder and shakes her head. Ms. Michaels decides that Ricardo is going to need support today from the token system that they are trying to phase out. She pulls some chips from her bag and puts them in her pocket. She will give them throughout the trip on a random interval schedule contingent on good behavior. Ricardo is familiar with the tokens, their value, and the expected behaviors, so no explanation will be required. Ricardo can keep the chips in his pocket until they return to school. Ms. Michaels will try to keep the process as unobtrusive as possible.

After an uneventful ride—Sam takes charge of watching for the approach of the right stop and pulling on the cord—the students and Ms. Michaels exit at the stop near the supermarket. Sam and Kimberly immediately go to the time clock, followed by Ricardo after a reminder from Ms. Michaels. All three don red aprons with nametags. Kimberly makes her way independently to the deli, greets Ms. Phelps, her supervisor, with a smile, and is greeted in return. Today she will be filling containers with the various dips and spreads made in the deli. Ms. Phelps puts a poster from Ms. Michaels's bag showing pictures of each step of the task on the wall over the work area. She has asked for extras of the various posters Kimberly and the other students use. She believes they will help many of her nondisabled employees. Ms. Phelps gives Kimberly instructions, watches her go through this new task several times as she would with any employee, and shows her where she can get more containers from the storeroom if she runs out. She has agreed to keep track of the number of times Kimberly either gets new materials or asks for assistance (her communication device will audibly say "I need help, please," when she pushes the right button) rather than whining or shouting in frustration.

Ms. Michaels accompanies Sam and Ricardo to the check-out area, where they will be bagging groceries. Sam will also accompany customers to their cars and unload groceries. On his next visit he will begin learning to stock shelves and replenish the produce counters. This particular chain of grocery stores has an excellent history of hiring persons with disabilities, and Sam will have a summer job this year with the possibility of permanent employment when he finishes school. He greets his friend Stan, an older individual with intellectual disabilities, who is employed full-time at the store. They chat as they bag groceries quickly and efficiently. At one point they become excited about an upcoming sports event and are reminded by the checkout clerk to "Keep it down, guys." They comply immediately.

Ms. Michaels meanwhile works directly with Ricardo and the assistant manager who trains the bag persons. At a training station near the break room where all new employees are trained, they work on correctly loading sacks and being careful with fragile items. The students all take a break and get a soft drink from the machine in the break room. They interact with other employees, disabled and nondisabled, and groan like the others when the break is over. Sam and Kimberly can read the passage of 15 minutes on the clock. Ricardo carries a small timer that he is learning to set for various spans of time. Ms. Michaels observes and records on a small clipboard from her bag the number of times Sam appropriately interacts with a coworker, her main objective for him on this part of the trip.

After about an hour the students remove their aprons and clock out. Calling and waving their farewells, they leave the supermarket. The cafeteria is within walking distance, and Ms. Michaels has planned the excursion so that the hour is early enough that the restaurant will not be crowded. Sam asks for what he wants; Kimberly points. Ms. Michaels stays close to Ricardo, who is showing signs of agitation. Recognizing a potential crisis, Ms. Michaels decides to abandon education for expedience and begins positively reinforcing any semblance of OK behavior. She pulls from her bag Ricardo's list (made during the rehearsal this morning of what he wants for lunch). "Ricardo," she says cheerfully, "I like the way you're walking." She pops a token in his pocket.

"Fish," mutters Ricardo as she orders for him.

"Good talking quietly, Ricardo," she says quickly, popping another token. Ricardo begins to appear less agitated.

"Would you like to order your tea? Tell the lady 'I want tea, please.'" Ricardo complies.

"Good ordering, Ricardo," she says, hoping the danger of Ricardo's blowing it has passed. "Can you carry your tray?" Ricardo picks up the tray and follows Sam. Ms. Michaels picks up his check—she isn't about to remind him at this point—along with hers. She is disappointed because she had planned to collect data on his independent accomplishment of getting through the line, a task she has, of course, analyzed.

Ms. Michaels has done a very quick functional analysis, discussed in Chapter 7.

The students make it to an empty table without mishap and unload their trays. Ricardo suddenly announces loudly that he has to "GO." Ms. Michaels reminds him to announce that quietly in the future and directs him to the men's room. (She feels that she knows the location of every public restroom in the city.) She also reminds herself that she and her colleagues need to work on getting Ricardo to communicate his needs before they become urgent and thus cause him to become agitated.

After a lunch spent discussing the upcoming shopping trip, the students prepare to pay for their meals. Each reads the number on the bottom of the ticket and gets out one more dollar. They hand their tickets and the money to the clerk and hold out their hands for change. Ms. Michaels jots down that Sam, for the first time, responds, "Thanks, you too," to the clerk, who encouraged him to "Have a nice day." She is really pleased with Sam's social skills.

After another bus ride, they arrive at the department store. All three students need to buy sweats to wear to the health club they will begin using next week. The unisex sweats are in large bins. Kimberly finds the "M" bin, Sam finds the "L" bin, and Ms. Michaels helps Ricardo find the "S" bin. He wants red sweats but sees only black in his bin. He begins to shout and wave his arms. Ms. Michaels hands the bag to Kimberly, instructs Sam and Kimberly to "Come with me, please," and (thankful that Ricardo is an "S") hustles him into the gardening equipment area at the back of the store, which she knows from previous trips will be virtually unpopulated. She tells Ricardo "Let's calm down," while placing him in a safe hold of his arms to ensure safety. An elderly lady, looking horrified, says, "Young lady, you're abusing that poor, afflicted child. I'm going to report this." Ms. Michaels says through her teeth, "Kimberly, give the lady a blue card, please." Kimberly reaches into a side pocket and hands the woman an official-looking card explaining Ms. Michaels's qualifications and position and the purpose for her students' presence in the community. The card invites anyone who has concerns to call Ms. Michaels's supervisor and provides the telephone number. Ricardo, meanwhile, calms down and apparently no one else has noticed the episode. They return to the shopping floor, pick out the sweats (the red are in the other "S" bin), check the label for the correct letter, pay for them, and exit.

Ms. Michaels is delighted that she had earlier decided to put off until later in the week her students' prewashing the sweats at a local group home while they worked on kitchen cleaning. Breathing a sigh of relief, she arrives with her charges at the bus stop. Her sense of relief begins to wane when several minutes pass without the bus's arrival. Even Sam begins to shift restlessly on the bench and demand, "Where's the bus?" Ms. Michaels reaches into her bag and offers each student a choice of a magazine or a handheld video game. They sit quietly for the remaining 20 minutes of their wait.

Summary

In this chapter we have described how teachers implement the principles and procedures of applied behavior analysis in actual teaching environments. We have discussed the importance of structure, planning, consistency, and consequences. We have described the operation of several hypothetical learning environments. Although none of these will be exactly like yours, we believe that visiting them will help you put it all together.

Discussion Idea

For each of the classroom scenarios presented, we have provided a few marginal notes pointing out behavioral principles in use. There are literally dozens of others that you and your colleagues can find. See how many you can identify in each anecdote.

Glossary

AB design   A format for graphing single-subject data that allows for monitoring behavior change. The AB design has two phases: baseline (A) and treatment (B). This design cannot demonstrate a functional relation between dependent and independent variables because it does not include a replication of the effect of the independent variable. Single-subject experimental designs, which allow for a determination of functional relations, are extensions of this foundational design.

ABAB design   An extension of the AB design in which the independent variable is withdrawn and then reapplied. This reversal design can demonstrate a functional relation between dependent and independent variables.

accountability   In education, the assessment of students' progress on a regular basis and the publication of this assessment, as well as goals, objectives, and procedures, to parents, school administrators, and other parties with a right to the information.

acquisition   The basic level of student response competence. It implies the student's ability to perform a newly learned response to some criterion of accuracy.

alternating treatments design   A single-subject experimental design that allows comparison of the effectiveness of two or more treatments. It differs from other single-subject designs in that treatments (sometimes including baseline) are alternated randomly rather than presented sequentially (also known as multi-element design).

antecedent stimulus   A stimulus that precedes a behavior. This stimulus may or may not serve as discriminative for a specific behavior.

applied behavior analysis   Systematic application of behavioral principles to change socially significant behavior to a meaningful degree. Research tools enable users of these principles to verify functional relations between interventions and behaviors.

aversive stimulus   A stimulus that decreases the rate or probability of a behavior when presented as a consequence; as such, it is a type of punisher. Alternatively, an aversive stimulus may increase the rate or probability of a behavior when removed as a consequence; as such, it is a negative reinforcer.

backup reinforcer   An object or event received in exchange for a specific number of tokens, points, etc.

bar graph   A graph that employs vertical bars rather than horizontal lines to indicate levels of performance (also called a histogram).

baseline data   Data points that reflect an operant level of the target behavior. Operant level is the natural occurrence of the behavior before intervention. Baseline data serve a purpose similar to that of a pretest, to provide a level of behavior against which the results of an intervention procedure can be compared.

behavior   Any observable and measurable act of an individual (also called a response).

behavioral objective   A statement that communicates a proposed change in behavior. A behavioral objective must include statements concerning the learner, the behavior, the conditions under which the behavior will be performed, and the criteria for evaluation.

chaining   An instructional procedure that reinforces individual responses in sequence, forming a complex behavior.

changing criterion design   A single-subject experimental design that involves successively changing the criterion for reinforcement. The criterion is systematically increased or decreased in a stepwise manner.

concept   A set of characteristics shared by all members of a set and only the members of that set.

conditioned aversive stimulus   A stimulus that has acquired secondary aversive qualities through pairing with an unconditioned aversive stimulus, such as pain or discomfort.

conditioned reinforcer   A stimulus that has acquired a reinforcing function through pairing with an unconditioned or natural reinforcer; includes most social, activity, and generalized reinforcers (see *secondary reinforcers*).

conditions   Naturally existing or teacher-created circumstances under which a behavior is to be performed.

consequence   A stimulus presented after and contingent on a particular response.

contingent observation   A procedure that requires a student to watch other students without participating.

contracting   Placing contingencies for reinforcement (if ..., then ... statements) into a written document. This creates a permanent product that can be referred to by teacher and student.

dependent variable   The behavior to be changed through intervention.

deprivation state   A condition in which the student has not had access to a potential reinforcer.

determinism   A philosophical belief that events, including human behavior, follow certain fixed patterns.

differential reinforcement of alternative behavior (DRA)   Reinforcing an appropriate or expected behavior and withholding reinforcement (extinction) for a challenging behavior.

differential reinforcement of incompatible behavior (DRI)   Reinforcing a response that is topographically incompatible with a challenging behavior and withholding reinforcement (extinction) for the challenging behavior.

differential reinforcement of lower rates of behavior (DRL)   Delivering reinforcement when the number of responses in a specified period of time is less than or equal to a prescribed limit. This maintains a behavior at a predetermined rate, lower than at its baseline or naturally occurring frequency.

differential reinforcement of other behaviors (DRO)   Delivering reinforcement when the target behavior is not emitted for a specified period of time. Reinforcement is contingent on the nonoccurrence of a behavior.

discrete behaviors   Behaviors with a clearly discriminable beginning and ending.

discriminative stimulus (S^D)   A stimulus in the presence of which a certain behavior has previously been reinforced; therefore, the stimulus evokes this behavior.

duration recording   Recording the amount of time between the initiation of a response and its conclusion; an observational recording procedure.

educational goals   Statements providing the framework for planning an academic year or an entire unit of learning. They set the estimated parameters of anticipated academic and social development for which educators are responsible (also called long-term objectives).

errorless learning An instructional procedure that arranges S^Ds and prompts to evoke only correct responses.

event recording Recording a tally or frequency count of behavior as it occurs within an observation period; an observational recording procedure.

evoke See *occasion*.

exclusion time-out A time-out procedure that removes the student from the instructional setting as the means of denying access to reinforcement.

extinction Withholding reinforcement for a previously reinforced behavior and observing a reduction in the occurrence of the behavior.

fading The gradual removal of prompts to allow the S^D to occasion a response independently.

fixed-interval schedule (FI) See *interval schedules*.

fixed-ratio schedule (FR) See *ratio schedules*.

fluency The second level (after acquisition) of student competence. Fluency describes the rate at which students accurately perform a response (also known as accuracy + speed).

frequency The number of times a behavior occurs during an observation period.

functional analysis A method of testing the reinforcement for a given behavior. Usually conducted to test a hypothesized function of a challenging behavior by exposing the challenging behavior to potentially reinforcing consequences, such as attention and escape, and observing the condition in which the behavior occurs the most (usually in a multi-element design).

functional behavior assessment Gathering information to form a hypothesis regarding variables occasioning and maintaining a challenging behavior. May be done by interview, checklist, or direct observation (also known as a functional assessment).

functional relation A demonstration that a measure of a dependent variable, or behavior, systematically changes in the desired direction as a result of the introduction and manipulation of an independent variable, or intervention. This is accomplished using a single-subject design.

generalization Expansion of a student's performance beyond those conditions set for initial acquisition. Stimulus generalization refers to performance under conditions—that is, cues, materials, trainers, and environments—other than those present during acquisition. Maintenance refers to continued performance of learned behavior after an intervention has ended. Response generalization refers to a person emitting behaviors similar to those directly trained.

generalized conditioned reinforcer A reinforcer associated with a variety of primary or other conditioned reinforcers; may simply be called *generalized reinforcer*.

goal setting A process through which students, in collaboration with teachers or other adults, are encouraged to participate in choosing goals they wish to achieve.

group designs Experimental investigations comparing groups of individuals exposed to different conditions.

humane Marked by consideration for others. In education, providing a safe, comfortable environment, treating all individuals with respect, and providing effective interventions.

independent variable The treatment or intervention that the experimenter manipulates to change a behavior, or dependent variable.

individualized education program (IEP) A written educational plan developed for every school-aged student eligible for special education services.

informed consent A legal term meaning that the parents (or surrogates) and the student, if appropriate, have been fully informed, in their native language or other mode of communication, of all information relevant to the activity for which consent is sought and have agreed to the activity.

initial behavior A behavior that a student can perform that is different than, but resembles, the terminal behavior (the ultimate goal of the intervention; used with shaping).

intermediate behavior Behaviors that represent successive approximations toward the terminal behavior (used with shaping).

intermittent schedules Schedules in which reinforcement follows some, but not all, responses or follows when a period of appropriate behavior has elapsed. These schedules include ratio, interval, and response-duration schedules.

interval recording An observational recording system in which an observation period is divided into a number of short intervals. The observer counts the number of intervals when the behavior occurs and reports a percentage out of the total intervals.

interval schedules Schedules for the delivery of reinforcers contingent on the occurrence of a behavior following a specified period or interval of time. In a fixed-interval (FI) schedule, the interval of time is standard. For example, FI5 would reinforce the first occurrence of behavior following each 5-minute interval during the observation period. In a variable-interval (VI) schedule, the interval of time varies. For example, VI5 would reinforce the first response that occurs after intervals averaging 5 minutes.

intervention Any change in a person's environment that is designed to change that person's behavior.

iterative Repeated utilization and analysis of procedures to provide presumption of efficacy and allow for ongoing modifications of technique.

lag schedule of reinforcement A reinforcement schedule designed to encourage variability of responding. A response is reinforced under a lag schedule if it differs from a specified number of previous responses.

latency recording Recording the amount of time between a stimulus, such as an S^D, and the initiation of a response.

lawful behavior Behavior that can be predicted by knowledge of antecedent events and a history of reinforcement.

limited hold (LH) A procedure used with interval schedules of reinforcement that restricts the time during which the reinforcer is available.

maintenance The performance of a response over time, even after an intervention has ended. See *generalization*.

modeling Demonstrating a desired behavior in order to prompt an imitative response.

motivating operation An antecedent condition that changes the value of a stimulus as a reinforcer and changes the frequency of behavior that has produced that stimulus in the past.

multiple baseline design A single-subject experimental design in which a treatment is replicated across (1) two or more students, (2) two or more behaviors, or (3) two or more settings. Functional relations may be demonstrated as changes in the dependent variables occur with the systematic and sequenced introduction of the independent variable.

multiple probe technique An alternative to continuous measurement during extended multiple baselines. Rather than record the student's responses during each session, the researcher takes occasional, scheduled measures to verify that the student's behavior has not changed before intervention.

multiple treatments design A single-subject experimental design that involves successively changing the conditions for response performance to evaluate comparative effects. When implemented as an ABC design, this design does not demonstrate a functional relation between variables. When implemented as an ABAC, ABACAB, or related arrangement, a functional relation may be demonstrated.

negative reinforcement The contingent removal of an aversive stimulus immediately following a response. Negative reinforcement increases the future rate or probability of the response.

noncontingent reinforcement (NCR) The delivery of reinforcers at predetermined intervals regardless of student behavior.

nonexclusion time-out A time-out procedure wherein the student is not removed from the instructional setting in which reinforcers are being dispensed. The teacher denies access to reinforcement and manipulates the environment to signal a period of time during which access is denied.

observational recording systems Methods of data collection used to record aspects of behavior while they actually occur (event recording, interval recording, duration recording, and latency recording).

occasion An antecedent event is said to "occasion" a response when the response occurs reliably in its presence.

operational definition Providing concrete examples of a target behavior. This minimizes disagreements among observers as to the behavior's occurrence.

overcorrection A procedure used to reduce the occurrence of an inappropriate behavior. The student is taught the appropriate behavior through an exaggeration of experience. There are two forms of overcorrection. In restitutional overcorrection, the student must restore or correct an environment he or she has disturbed to its condition before the disturbance. The student must then improve it beyond its original condition, thereby overcorrecting the environment. In positive-practice overcorrection, the student, having behaved inappropriately, is required to engage in exaggerated practice of appropriate behaviors.

overlearning Providing students with more practice than is required for initial mastery.

pairing Simultaneous presentation of a reinforcer and a neutral stimulus to condition the neutral stimulus as a secondary reinforcer.

permanent product recording Recording tangible items or environmental effects that result from a behavior, for example, written academic work.

pinpointing Specifying in measurable, observable terms a behavior targeted for change.

positive reinforcement The contingent presentation of a stimulus immediately following a response, which increases the future rate or probability of the response. Written as S^{R+}.

positive reinforcer A stimulus that when presented immediately after a response increases the future rate or probability of that response.

preference assessment A procedure used to determine the items a student engages with or consumes most often and subsequently using those items as positive reinforcers. The multiple preference assessment methods involve exposing a student to one or more items and observing which items the student selects most often or engages with for the longest duration.

Premack principle A principle stating that any high-probability activity may serve as a positive reinforcer for any low-probability activity (also called activity reinforcement).

primary reinforcers Stimuli (such as food) that may have biological importance to an individual; such stimuli are innately motivating (also called unlearned or unconditioned reinforcers).

probes Collection of data at scheduled intervals rather than continuously.

prompt An added stimulus that increases the probability that the S^D will occasion the desired response (also known as supplementary antecedent stimulus).

punisher A stimulus presented immediately after a behavior that decreases the future rate or probability of the behavior.

punishment The contingent presentation of a stimulus immediately following a response, which decreases the future rate or probability of the response.

ratio schedules Schedules for the delivery of reinforcers contingent on the number of responses. In a fixed-ratio (FR) schedule, the number of responses required for reinforcement is held constant. For example, FR5 would reinforce every fifth response. In a variable-ratio (VR) schedule, the number of responses required for reinforcement varies. For example, VR5 would reinforce on the average of every fifth response.

ratio strain A disruption of response performance that occurs when the schedule of reinforcement has been thinned too quickly. The ratio between responding and reinforcement is too great to maintain a desired rate of responding.

reliability The consistency of data collection reports among independent observers. Interobserver agreement is determined by the formula: Agreements ÷ (Agreements + Disagreements) × 100 = % of agreement

repeated measures A requirement of single-subject research designs in that numerous measures of a student's behavior are taken in each condition rather than a single measure such as a test or survey.

response-cost Reducing challenging behavior through withdrawal of specific amounts of reinforcer contingent upon the behavior's occurrence.

response-duration schedules Schedules for the delivery of reinforcers contingent on how long a student engages in a continuous behavior. In a fixed-response-duration (FRD) schedule, the duration of the behavior required for reinforcement is held constant. For example, FRD10 minutes would deliver reinforcement following each 10 minutes of behavior. In a variable-response-duration (VRD) schedule, the amount of time required for reinforcement varies. For example, VRD10 minutes would deliver reinforcement following an average of 10 minutes of behavior.

response generalization The emission of behaviors different than, but functionally similar to, the behaviors exposed to an intervention. See *generalization*.

reversal design A single-subject experimental design that, after showing an behavioral improvement from baseline to an intervention, removes the intervention condition for a series of sessions, and then reinstates the intervention condition to verify the existence of a functional relation. This design has four phases: baseline, imposition of treatment, removal of treatment (also known as return to baseline), and reimposition of treatment (also called ABAB design).

satiation A condition that occurs when there is no longer a state of deprivation.

schedules of reinforcement The patterns of timing for delivery of reinforcers (see *intermittent schedules, interval schedules, ratio schedules,* and *response-duration schedules*).

S-delta (S^Δ) A stimulus in the presence of which a certain behavior has not been reinforced; therefore, this stimulus does not evoke this behavior.

secondary reinforcers Stimuli that are initially neutral but acquire reinforcing qualities through pairing with a primary reinforcer or another secondary reinforcer (also called *conditioned reinforcers*).

self-instruction The process by which a student provides verbal prompts to himself or herself in order to direct or maintain a particular behavior.

self-monitoring Data collection on one's own behavior (also called self-observation, self-evaluation, or self-recording).

self-punishment Self-administration of punishing consequences contingent on behavior.

self-reinforcement (self-punishment) Administering consequences to oneself. Students may be taught to select reinforcers (or punishers), determine criteria for their delivery, and deliver the consequences to themselves.

setting events Circumstances in an individual's life, ranging from cultural influences to an uncomfortable environment, that temporarily alter the power of reinforcers.

shaping Teaching new behaviors through differential reinforcement of successive approximations to a specified target behavior.

simultaneous prompting Providing an immediate, controlling prompt that ensures a correct response.

single-subject designs Experimental investigations in which each individual serves as his or her own control. (See *AB design, alternating treatments design, multiple treatments design, changing criterion design, multiple baseline design*, and *reversal design*.)

social reinforcers A category of secondary reinforcers that includes facial expressions, proximity, contact, privileges, words, and phrases.

social validity The extent to which members of persons community regard the importance of behavior changes; the acceptability of procedures to consumers.

stimulus class See *concept*.

stimulus control When, due to a history of reinforcement, one stimulus (the S^D) evokes a certain behavior, and another stimulus (S^Δ) does not evoke that behavior.

stimulus equivalence Stimuli are equivalent when they are interchangeable and occasion the same response.

stimulus generalization See *generalization*.

stimulus overselectivity A tendency to attend to only one or a few aspects of a stimulus rather than all aspects of the stimulus.

stimulus prompt An alteration of a stimulus to increase the probability of correct responding; often used in errorless learning procedures.

task analysis The process of breaking down a complex behavior into its component parts.

terminal behavior The ultimate goal of an intervention (used with shaping).

thinning Gradually making reinforcement available less often or contingent on greater amounts of responses.

time-out Reducing inappropriate behavior by denying the student access, for a fixed period of time, to the opportunity to receive reinforcement.

time-out ribbon A ribbon worn by students, the removal of which indicates that the opportunity for reinforcement has been temporarily lost.

time sampling An observational recording system in which an observation period is divided into equal intervals; an interval is counted in calculating the percentage of intervals with the target behavior if the target behavior is observed at the moment the interval ends.

trend A description of data represented on a graph. An ascending or descending trend is defined as three data points in a single direction.

trial A discrete opportunity for occurrence of a behavior. A trial is operationally defined by its three behavioral components: an antecedent stimulus, a response, and a consequating stimulus. The delivery of the antecedent stimulus marks the beginning of the trial, and the delivery of the consequating stimulus signifies the termination of the trial.

trial-by-trial recording Recording the level of performance for every trial in a teaching session, such as by writing a + or −; common in discrete trial teaching.

unconditioned aversive stimulus A stimulus that results in physical pain or discomfort to an individual (also called unlearned aversive stimulus).

variable Attributes unique to an individual involved in a study or to conditions associated with the environment in a study.

variable-interval (VI) schedule See *interval schedules*.

variable-response-duration (VRD) schedule See *response-duration schedules*.

video modeling Showing a video demonstrating a certain skill so that the student subsequently emits that behavior.

video prompting Teaching a behavior chain by showing a video of each behavior in the chain so that the student emits the behavior and then views a video of the next behavior.

***x*-axis** The horizontal axis of a graph. The time dimension (sessions) is represented along the *x*-axis, also referred to as the abscissa.

***y*-axis** The vertical axis of a graph. The amount or level of the target behavior is represented along the *y*-axis, also referred to as the ordinate.

References

Achenbach, T. H., & Lewis, M. (1971). A proposed model for clinical research and its application to encopresis and enuresis. *Journal of American Academy of Child Psychiatry, 10,* 535–554.

Ackerlund Brandt, J. A., Weinkauf, S., Zeug, N., & Klatt, K. P. (2016). An evaluation of constant time delay and simultaneous prompting procedures in skill acquisition for young children with autism. *Education and Training in Autism and Developmental Disabilities, 51*(1), 55–66.

Ackerman, J. M. (1972). *Operant conditioning techniques for the classroom teacher.* Scott, Foresman & Co.

Adamo, E. K., Wu, J., Wolery, M., Hemmeter, M. L., Ledford, J. R., & Barton, E. E. (2015). Using video modeling, prompting, and behavior-specific praise to increase moderate-to-vigorous physical activity for young children with Down syndrome. *Journal of Early Intervention, 37*(4), 270–285. https://doi.org/10.1177/1053815115620211

Adams, C., & Kelley, M. (1992). Managing sibling aggression: Overcorrection as an alternative to time-out. *Behavior Therapy, 23,* 707–717.

Adams, G., & Engelmann, S. (1996). *Research on direct instruction: 25 years beyond Distar.* Seattle, WA: Educational Achievement Systems.

Adams, N., Martin, R., & Popelka, G. (1971). The influence of time-out on stutterers and their dysfluency. *Behavior Therapy, 2,* 334–339.

Agran, M., Jackson, L., Kurth, J. A., Ryndak, D., Burnette, K., Jameson, M., et al. (2020). Why aren't students with severe disabilities being placed in general education classrooms: Examining the relations among classroom placement, learner outcomes, and other factors. *Research and Practice for Persons with Severe Disabilities, 45*(1), 4–13.

Aiken, J. M., & Salzberg, C. L. (1984). The effects of a sensory extinction procedure on stereotypic sounds of two autistic children. *Journal of Autism and Developmental Disorders, 14,* 291–299.

Akers, J. S., Higbee, T. S., Gerencser, K. R., & Pellegrino, A. J. (2018). An evaluation of group activity schedules to promote social play in children with autism. *Journal of Applied Behavior Analysis, 51*(3), 553–570. https://doi.org/10.1002/jaba.474

Akmanoglu, N., Yanardag, M., & Batu, E. S. (2014). Comparing video modeling and graduated guidance together and video modeling alone for teaching role playing skills to children with autism. *Education and Training in Autism and Developmental Disabilities, 49*(1), 17–31.

Ala'i-Rosales, S., Cihon, J. H., Currier, T. D. R., Ferguson, J. L., Leaf, J. B., Leaf, R., et al. (2019). The Big Four: Functional assessment research informs preventative behavior analysis. *Behavior Analysis in Practice, 12*(1), 222–234. https://doi.org/10.1007/s40617-018-00291-9

Alber, S., & Heward, W. (2000). Teaching students to recruit positive attention: A review and recommendations. *Journal of Behavioral Education, 10,* 177–204.

Albers, C. A., & Hoffman, A. (2012). Using flashcard drill methods and self-graphing procedures to improve the reading performance of English language learners. *Journal of Applied School Psychology, 28*(4), 367–388. https://doi.org/10.1080/15377903.2012.731365

Alberto, P., Heflin, J., & Andrews, D. (2002). Use of the time-out ribbon procedure during community-based instruction. *Journal of Autism and Developmental Disorders, 26,* 297–311.

Alberto, P., Troutman, A., & Briggs, T. (1983). The use of negative reinforcement to condition a response in a deaf-blind student. *Education of the Visually Handicapped, 15,* 43–50.

Alberto, P. A., Sharpton, W., & Goldstein, D. (1979). *Project Bridge: Integration of severely retarded students on regular education campuses.* Atlanta: Georgia State University.

Alberto, P. A., Sharpton, W. R., Briggs, A., & Stright, M. H. (1986). Facilitating task acquisition through the use of a self-operated auditory prompting system. *Journal of the Association for Persons with Severe Handicaps, 11,* 85–91.

Algozzine, B., Morsbach Sweeney, H., Choi, J. H., Horner, R., Sailor, W., McCart, A. B., et al. (2017). Development and preliminary technical adequacy of the schoolwide integrated framework for transformation fidelity of implementation tool. *Journal of Psychoeducational Assessment, 35*(3), 302–322. https://doi.org/10.1177/0734282915626303

Aljadeff-Abergel, E., Schenk, Y., Walmsley, C., Peterson, S. M., Frieder, J. E., & Acker, N. (2015). The effectiveness of self-management interventions for children with autism—A literature review. *Research in Autism Spectrum Disorders, 18,* 34–50. https://doi.org/10.1016/j.rasd.2015.07.001

Almeida, D. A., Allen, R., Maguire, R. W., & Maguire, K. (2018). Identifying community-based reinforcers of adults with autism and related disabilities. *Journal of Behavioral Education, 27*(3), 375–394. https://doi.org/10.1007/s10864-018-9295-x

Alnemary, F., Wallace, M., Alnemary, F., Gharapetian, L., & Yassine, J. (2017). Application of a pyramidal training model on the implementation of trial-based functional analysis: A partial replication. *Behavior Analysis in Practice, 10*(3), 301–306. https://doi.org/10.1007/s40617-016-0159-3

Alquraini, T., & Gut, D. (2012). Critical components of successful inclusion of students with severe disabilities: Literature review. *International Journal of Special Education, 27*(1), 42–59.

American Psychiatric Association. (2000). *Diagnostic and statistical manual of mental disorders* (4th ed., text revision; DSM-IV). Washington, DC: Author.

Anderson, C. M., Rodriguez, B. J., & Campbell, A. (2015). Functional behavior assessment in schools: Current status and future directions. *Journal of Behavioral Education, 24*(3), 338–371. https://doi.org/10.1007/s10864-015-9226-z

Anderson, D. H., Trinh, S. M., Caldarella, P., Hansen, B. D., & Richardson, M. J. (2018). Increasing positive playground interaction for kindergarten students at risk for emotional and behavioral disorders. *Early Childhood Education Journal, 46*(5), 487–496. https://doi.org/10.1007/s10643-017-0878-2

Anderson, J., & Le, D. D. (2011). Abatement of intractable vocal stereotypy using an overcorrection procedure. *Behavioral Interventions, 26*(2), 134–146. https://doi.org/10.1002/bin.326

Anderson-Inman, L., Walker, H. M., & Purcell, J. (1984). Promoting the transfer of skills across settings: Trans-environmental programming for handicapped students in the mainstream. In W. Heward, T. E. Heron, D. S. Hill, & J. Trap-Porter (eds.), *Focus on behavior analysis in education.* Columbus, OH: Merrill.

Andreou, T. E., McIntosh, K., Ross, S. W., & Kahn, J. D. (2015). Critical incidents in sustaining school-wide positive behavioral interventions and supports. *The Journal of Special Education, 49*(3), 157–167. https://doi.org/10.1177/0022466914554298

Andrews, W., Houchins, D., & Varjas, K. (2017). Student-directed check-in/check-out for students in alternative education settings. *TEACHING Exceptional Children, 49*(6), 380–390.

Apolito, P., & Sulzer-Azaroff, B. (1981). Lemon-juice therapy: The control of chronic vomiting in a twelve-year-old profoundly retarded female. *Education and Treatment of Children, 4,* 339–347.

Ardoin, S. P., Williams, J. C., Klubnik, C., & McCall, M. (2009). Three versus six rereadings of practice passages. *Journal of Applied Behavior Analysis, 42,* 375–380.

Argott, P. J., Townsend, D. B., & Poulson, C. L. (2017). Acquisition and generalization of complex empathetic responses among children with autism. *Behavior Analysis in Practice, 10*(2), 107–117. https://doi.org/10.1007/s40617-016-0171-7

Arhar, J., Holly, J., & Kasten, W. (2001). *Action research for teachers.* Upper Saddle River, NJ: Merrill/Pearson Education.

Arndorfer, R., Miltenberger, R., Woster, S., Rortvedt, A., & Gaffaney, T. (1994). Home-based descriptive and experimental analysis of problem behaviors in children. *Topics in Early Childhood Special Education, 14*(1), 64–87.

Artman, K., Wolery, M., & Yoder, P. (2012). Embracing our visual inspection and analysis tradition: Graphing interobserver agreement data. *Remedial and Special Education, 33*(2), 71–77. https://doi.org/10.1177/0741932510381653

Aspiranti, K. B., Bebech, A., Ruffo, B., & Skinner, C. H. (2019). Classroom management in self-contained classrooms for children with autism: Extending research on the color wheel system. *Behavior Analysis in Practice, 12*(1), 143–153. https://doi.org/10.1007/s40617-018-0264-6

Aspiranti, K. B., Skinner, C. H., McCleary, D. F., & Cihak, D. F. (2011). Using taped-problems and rewards to increase addition-fact fluency in a first grade general education classroom. *Behavior Analysis in Practice, 4*(2), 25–33.

Athens, E. S., & Vollmer, T. R. (2010). An investigation of differential reinforcement of alternative behavior without extinction. *Journal of Applied Behavior Analysis, 43*(4), 569–589. https://doi.org/10.1901/jaba.2010.43-569

Athens, E. S., Vollmer, T. R., & Pipkin, C. C. S. P. (2007). Shaping academic task engagement with percentile schedules. *Journal of Applied Behavior Analysis, 40*(3), 475–488. https://doi.org/10.1901/jaba.2007.40-475

Austin, J., Hackett, S., Gravina, N., & Lebbon, A. (2006). The effects of prompting and feedback on drivers' stopping at stop signs. *Journal of Applied Behavior Analysis, 39,* 117–121.

Austin, J. L., & Bevan, D. (2011). Using differential reinforcement of low rates to reduce children's requests for teacher attention. *Journal of Applied Behavior Analysis, 44*(3), 451–461. https://doi.org/10.1901/jaba.2011.44-451

Austin, J. L., Groves, E. A., Reynish, L. C., & Francis, L. L. (2015). Validating trial-based functional analyses in mainstream primary school classrooms. *Journal of Applied Behavior Analysis, 48*(2), 274–288. https://doi.org/10.1002/jaba.208

Axe, J. B., & Laprime, A. P. (2017). The effects of contingent pairing on establishing praise as a reinforcer with children with autism. *Journal of Developmental and Physical Disabilities, 29*(2), 325–340. https://doi.org/10.1007/s10882-016-9526-9

Axelrod, S. (1987). Functional and structural analyses of behavior: Approaches leading to reduced use of punishment procedures? *Research in Developmental Disabilities, 8,* 165–178.

Axelrod, S. (1996). What's wrong with behavior analysis? *Journal of Behavioral Education, 6,* 247–256.

Axelrod, S., Moyer, L., & Berry, B. (1990). Why teachers do not use behavior modification procedures. *Journal of Educational and Psychological Consultation, 1*(4), 310–320.

Ayllon, T., & Kelly, K. (1974). Reinstating verbal behavior in a functionally mute retardate. *Professional Psychology, 5,* 385–393.

Ayllon, T., Kuhlman, C., & Warzak, W. J. (1983). Programming resource room generalization using Lucky Charms. *Child and Behavior Therapy, 4,* 61–67.

Ayllon, T., Layman, D., & Kandel, H. J. (1975). A behavioral-educational alternative to drug control of hyperactive children. *Journal of Applied Behavior Analysis, 8,* 137–146.

Ayllon, T., & Milan, M. (1979). *Correctional rehabilitation and management: A psychological approach.* New York: Wiley.

Ayllon, T. A. (1963). Intensive treatment of psychotic behavior by stimulus satiation and food reinforcement. *Behavior Research and Therapy, 1,* 53–61.

Ayllon, T. A., & Michael, J. (1959). The psychiatric nurse as a behavior engineer. *Journal of the Experimental Analysis of Behavior, 2,* 323–334.

Azrin, N. H. (1960). Effects of punishment intensity during variable-interval reinforcement. *Journal of the Experimental Analysis of Behavior, 3,* 128–142.

Azrin, N. H., & Foxx, R. M. (1971). A rapid method of toilet training the institutionalized retarded. *Journal of Applied Behavior Analysis, 4,* 89–99.

Azrin, N. H., Hake, D. G., Holz, W. C., & Hutchinson, R. R. (1965). Motivational aspects of escape from punishment. *Journal of the Experimental Analysis of Behavior, 8,* 31–44.

Azrin, N. H., & Holz, W. C. (1966). Punishment. In W. A. Honig (ed.), *Operant behavior: Areas of research and application* (pp. 380–447). New York: Appleton-Century-Crofts.

Azrin, N. H., Holz, W. C., & Hake, D. F. (1963). Fixed-ratio punishment. *Journal of the Experimental Analysis of Behavior, 6,* 141–148.

Azrin, N. H., Hutchinson, R. R., & Hake, D. J. (1966). Extinction-induced aggression. *Journal of the Experimental Analysis of Behavior, 9,* 191–204.

Azrin, N. H., Sneed, T. J., & Foxx, R. M. (1973). Drybed: A rapid method of eliminating bedwetting (enuresis) of the retarded. *Behavior Research and Therapy, 11,* 427–434.

Azrin, N. H., Vinas, V., & Ehle, C. T. (2007). Physical activity as reinforcement for classroom calmness of ADHD children: A preliminary study. *Child & Family Behavior Therapy, 29*(2), 1–8. https://doi.org/10.1300/J019v29n02_01

Azrin, N. H., & Wesolowski, M. D. (1974). Theft reversal: An overcorrection procedure for eliminating stealing by retarded persons. *Journal of Applied Behavior Analysis, 7,* 577–581.

Azrin, N. H., & Wesolowski, M. D. (1975). The use of positive practice to eliminate persistent floor sprawling by profoundly retarded persons. *Behavior Therapy, 6,* 627–631.

Bachmeyer, M. H., Kirkwood, C. A., Criscito, A. B., Mauzy, C. R., & Berth, D. P. (2019). A comparison of functional analysis methods of inappropriate mealtime behavior. *Journal of Applied Behavior Analysis, 52*(3), 603–621. https://doi.org/10.1002/jaba.556

Bachmeyer, M. H., Piazza, C. C., Fredrick, L. D., Reed, G. K., Rivas, K. D., & Kadey, H. J. (2009). Functional analysis and treatment of multiply controlled inappropriate mealtime behavior. *Journal of Applied Behavior Analysis, 42*(3), 641–658. https://doi.org/10.1901/jaba.2009.42-641

Badgett, N., & Falcomata, T. S. (2015). A comparison of methodologies of brief functional analysis. *Developmental Neurorehabilitation, 18*(4), 224–233. https://doi.org/10.3109/17518423.2013.792298

Baer, A. M., Rowbury, T., & Baer, D. M. (1973). The development of instructional control over classroom activities of deviant preschool children. *Journal of Applied Behavior Analysis, 6,* 289–298.

Baer, D. M. (1971). Behavior modification: You shouldn't. In E. A. Ramp & B. L. Hopkins (eds.), *A new direction for education: Behavior analysis* (vol. 1). Lawrence: University of Kansas Support and Development Center for Follow Through.

Baer, D. M. (1999). *How to plan for generalization.* Austin, TX: Pro-Ed.

Baer, D. M., & Wolf, M. M. (1968). The reinforcement contingency in preschool and remedial education. In R. D. Hess & R. M. Bear (eds.), *Early education: Current theory, research, and action.* Chicago: Aldine.

Baer, D. M., & Wolf, M. M. (1970). The entry into natural communities of reinforcement. In R. Ulrich, T. Stachnik, &

J. Mabry (eds.), *Control of human behavior* (vol. 2). Glenview, IL: Scott, Foresman.

Baer, D. M., Wolf, M. M., & Risley, T. R. (1968). Some current dimensions of applied behavior analysis. *Journal of Applied Behavior Analysis, 1*, 91–97.

Baer, D. M., Wolf, M. M., & Risley, T. R. (1987). Some still-current dimensions of applied behavior analysis. *Journal of Applied Behavior Analysis, 20*, 313–327.

Bailey, D. B., Wolery, M., & Sugai, G. M. (1988). *Effective teaching: Principles and procedures of applied behavior analysis with exceptional children*. Boston: Allyn & Bacon.

Bailey, J., & Burch, M. (2016). *Ethics for behavior analysts*. New York: Routledge.

Bailey, S., Pokrzywinski, J., & Bryant, L. (1983). Using water mist to reduce self-injurious and stereotypic behavior. *Applied Research in Mental Retardation, 4*, 229–241.

Balka, K. E., Hausman, N. L., Schaller, E., & Kahng, S. (2016). Discriminated functional communication for attention: Evaluating fixed and varied durations of reinforcer availability. *Behavioral Interventions, 31*(2), 210–218. https://doi.org/10.1002/bin.1440

Balsam, P. D., & Bondy, A. S. (1983). The negative side effects of reward. *Journal of Applied Behavior Analysis, 16*, 283–296.

Balson, P. M. (1973). Case study: Encopresis: A case with symptom substitution. *Behavior Therapy, 4*, 134–136.

Bancroft, S. L., Weiss, J. S., Libby, M. E., & Ahearn, W. H. (2011). A comparison of procedural variations in teaching behavior chains: Manual guidance, trainer completion, and no completion of untrained steps. *Journal of Applied Behavior Analysis, 44*(3), 559–569. https://doi.org/10.1901/jaba.2011.44-559

Banda, D. R., McAfee, J. K., & Hart, S. L. (2012). Decreasing self-injurious behavior and fading self-restraint in a student with autism and Tourette syndrome. *Behavioral Interventions, 27*(3), 164–174. https://doi.org/10.1002/bin.1344

Banda, D. R., & Sokolosky, S. (2012). Effectiveness of noncontingent attention to decrease attention-maintained disruptive behaviors in the general education classroom. *Child & Family Behavior Therapy, 34*(2), 130–140. https://doi.org/10.1080/07317107.2012.684646

Bandura, A. (1965). Influence of models' reinforcement contingencies on the acquisition of imitative responses. *Journal of Personality and Social Psychology, 1*, 589–595.

Bandura, A. (1969). *Principles of behavior modification*. New York: Holt, Rinehart & Winston.

Bandura, A. (1975). The ethics and social purposes of behavior modification. In C. M. Franks & G. T. Wilson (eds.), *Annual review of behavior therapy, theory & practice* (vol. 3, pp. 13–20). New York: Brunner/Mazel.

Bandura, A. (1977). *Social learning theory*. Upper Saddle River, NJ: Prentice-Hall.

Bannerman, D. J., Sheldon, J. B., Sherman, J. A., & Harchik, A. E. (1990). Balancing the right to habilitation with the right to personal liberties: The rights of people with developmental disabilities to eat too many doughnuts and take a nap. *Journal of Applied Behavior Analysis, 23*, 79–89.

Barber, M., Cartledge, G., Council, M., III, Konrad, M., Gardner, R., & Telesman, A. O. (2018). The effects of computer-assisted culturally relevant repeated readings on English learners' fluency and comprehension. *Learning Disabilities: A Contemporary Journal, 16*(2), 205–229.

Barbera, M. L., & Kubina, R. M., Jr. (2005). Using transfer procedures to teach tacts to a child with autism. *Analysis of Verbal Behavior, 21*, 155–161. https://doi.org/10.1007/BF03393017

Barbetta, P. (1990). GOALS: A group-oriented adapted levels systems for children with behavior disorders. *Academic Therapy, 25*, 645–656.

Barczak, M. A. (2019). Simulated and community-based instruction: Teaching students with intellectual and developmental disabilities to make financial transactions. *TEACHING Exceptional Children, 51*(4), 313–321.

Barkley, R., Copeland, A., & Sivage, C. (1980). A self-control classroom for hyperactive children. *Journal of Autism and Developmental Disorders, 10*, 75–89.

Barlow, D., & Hayes, S. (1979). Alternating treatments design: One strategy for comparing the effects of two treatments in a single subject. *Journal of Applied Behavior Analysis, 12*, 199–210.

Barlow, D., & Hersen, M. (1984). *Single case experimental designs: Strategies for studying behavior change*. New York: Pergamon Press.

Barrett, C. A., Stevenson, N. A., & Burns, M. K. (2020). Relationship between disability category, time spent in general education and academic achievement. *Educational Studies, 46*(4), 497–512.

Barrish, H. H., Saunders, M., & Wolf, M. M. (1969). Good behavior game: Effects of individual contingencies for group consequences on disruptive behavior in a classroom. *Journal of Applied Behavior Analysis, 2*(2), 119–124. https://doi.org/10.1901/jaba.1969.2-119

Barton, L., Brulle, A., & Repp, A. C. (1987). Effects of differential scheduling of time-out to reduce maladaptive responding. *Exceptional Children, 53*, 351–356.

Bateman, B., & Linden, M. A. (1998). *Better IEPs* (3rd ed.). Longmont, CO: Sopris West.

Baumeister, R. F., Vohs, K. D., & Tice, D. M. (2007). The strength model of self-control. *Current Directions in Psychological Science, 16*(6), 351–355. https://doi.org/10.1111/j.1467-8721.2007.00534.x

Bayley, N. (2005). *Bayley Scales of Infant and Toddler Development* (3rd ed.). Upper Saddle River, NJ: Pearson.

Beaulieu, L., & Hanley, G. P. (2014). Effects of a classwide teacher-implemented program to promote preschooler compliance. *Journal of Applied Behavior Analysis, 47*(3), 594–599. https://doi.org/10.1002/jaba.138

Beaver, B. N., Reeve, S. A., Reeve, K. F., & DeBar, R. M. (2017). Self-reinforcement compared to teacher-delivered reinforcement during activity schedules on the iPod touch. *Education and Training in Autism and Developmental Disabilities, 52*(4), 393–404.

Becker, J., Turner, S., & Sajwaj, T. (1978). Multiple behavioral effects of the use of lemon juice with a ruminating toddler-age child. *Behavior Modification, 2*, 267–278.

Becker, W. C., & Engelmann, S. E. (1978). Systems for basic instruction: Theory and applications. In A. Catania & T. Brigham (eds.), *Handbook of applied behavior analysis: Social and instructional processes* (pp. 57–92). Chicago: Science Research Associates.

Becker, W. C., Engelmann, S., & Thomas, D. R. (1975a). *Teaching 1: Classroom management*. Chicago: Science Research Associates.

Becker, W. C., Engelmann, S., & Thomas, D. R. (1975b). *Teaching 2: Cognitive learning and instruction*. Chicago: Science Research Associates.

Beckman, A., Mason, B. A., Wills, H. P., Garrison-Kane, L., & Huffman, J. (2019). Improving behavioral and academic outcomes for students with autism spectrum disorder: Testing an app-based self-monitoring intervention. *Education & Treatment of Children, 42*(2), 225–244. https://doi.org/10.1353/etc.2019.0011

Becraft, J. L., Borrero, J. C., Mendres-Smith, A. E., & Castillo, M. I. (2017). Decreasing excessive bids for attention in a simulated early education classroom. *Journal of Behavioral Education, 26*(4), 371–393. https://doi.org/10.1007/s10864-017-9275-6

Becraft, J. L., & Rolider, N. U. (2015). Reinforcer variation in a token economy. *Behavioral Interventions, 30*(2), 157–165. https://doi.org/10.1002/bin.1401

Bedesem, P. L. (2012). Using cell phone technology for self-monitoring procedures in inclusive settings. *Journal of Special Education Technology, 27*(4), 33–46.

Beeks, A., & Graves, S., Jr. (2016). The effects of the mystery motivator intervention in an urban classroom. *School Psychology Forum, 10*(2), 142–156.

Bekker, M. J., Cumming, T. D., Osborne, N. K. P., Bruining, A. M., McClean, J. M., & Leland, L. S., Jr. (2010). Encouraging electricity savings in a university residential hall through a combination of feedback, visual prompts, and incentives. *Journal of Applied Behavior Analysis, 43*, 327–331.

Belisle, J., Stanley, C. R., Alholail, A. M., Galliford, M. E., & Dixon, M. R. (2019). Abstraction of tactile properties by individuals with autism and down syndrome using a picture-based communication system. *Journal of Applied Behavior Analysis, 52*(2), 467–475. https://doi.org/10.1002/jaba.526

Bellini, S., & Akullian, J. (2007). A meta-analysis of video modeling and video self-modeling interventions for children and adolescents with autism spectrum disorders. *Exceptional Children, 73*, 264–287.

Bennett, K., & Cavanaugh, R. A. (1998). Effects of immediate self-correction, delayed self-correction, and no correction on the acquisition and maintenance of multiplication facts by a fourth-grade student with learning disabilities. *Journal of Applied Behavior Analysis, 31*, 303–306.

Benoit, R. B., & Mayer, G. R. (1974). Extinction: Guidelines for its selection and use. *The Personnel and Guidance Journal, 52*, 290–295.

Berkeley, S., & Larsen, A. (2018). Fostering self-regulation of students with learning disabilities: Insights from 30 years of reading comprehension intervention research. *Learning Disabilities Research & Practice, 33*(2), 75–86. https://doi.org/10.1111/ldrp.12165

Berry, H. K. (1969). Phenylketonuria: Diagnosis, treatment and long-term management. In G. Farrell (ed.), *Congenital mental retardation*. Austin: University of Texas Press.

Bettenhausen, S. (1998). Make proactive modifications to your classroom. *Intervention in School and Clinic, 33*, 182–183.

Betz, A., Higbee, T. S., & Reagon, K. A. (2008). Using joint activity schedules to promote peer engagement in preschoolers with autism. *Journal of Applied Behavior Analysis, 41*(2), 237–241. https://doi.org/10.1901/jaba.2008.41-237

Betz, A. M., Fisher, W. W., Roane, H. S., Mintz, J. C., & Owen, T. M. (2013). A component analysis of schedule thinning during functional communication training. *Journal of Applied Behavior Analysis, 46*(1), 219–241. https://doi.org/10.1002/jaba.23

Bicard, D. F., Horan, J., Plank, E., & Covington, T. (2009). May I take a message? Using general case programming to teach students with disabilities to take and give phone messages. *Preventing School Failure, 54*, 179–189.

Bijou, S. W., Peterson, R. F., & Ault, M. H. (1968). A method to integrate descriptive and experimental field studies at the level of data and empirical concepts. *Journal of Applied Behavior Analysis, 1*, 175–191.

Binder, C., & Watkins, C. L. (2013). Precision teaching and direct instruction: Measurably superior instructional technology in schools. *Performance Improvement Quarterly, 26*(2), 73–115. https://doi.org/10.1002/piq.21145

Birnbrauer, J. S., Bijou, S. W., Wolf, M. M., & Kidder, J. D. (1965). Programmed instruction in the classroom. In L. P. Ullmann & L. Krasner (eds.), *Case studies in behavior modification*. New York: Holt, Rinehart & Winston.

Bishop, S. K., Moore, J. W., Dart, E. H., Radley, K., Brewer, R., Barker, L. K., ... & Toche, C. (2020). Further investigation of increasing vocalizations of children with autism with a speech-generating device. *Journal of Applied Behavior Analysis, 53*(1), 475–483.

Blair, B. J., Weiss, J. S., & Ahearn, W. H. (2018). A comparison of task analysis training procedures. *Education & Treatment of Children, 41*(3), 357–369. https://doi.org/10.1353/etc.2018.0019

Bloom, B. S. (ed.). (1956). *Taxonomy of educational objectives handbook I: Cognitive domain*. New York: David McKay.

Bloom, S. E., Clark, D. R., Boyle, M. A., & Clay, C. J. (2018). Effects of delaying demands on noncompliance and escape-maintained problem behavior. *Behavioral Interventions, 33*(4), 352–363. https://doi.org/10.1002/bin.1530

Bloomfield, B. S., Fischer, A. J., Clark, R. R., & Dove, M. B. (2019). Treatment of food selectivity in a child with avoidant/restrictive food intake disorder through parent teleconsultation. *Behavior Analysis in Practice, 12*(1), 33–43. https://doi.org/10.1007/s40617-018-0251-y

Blume, F., Göllner, R., Moeller, K., Dresler, T., Ehlis, A.-C., & Gawrilow, C. (2019). Do students learn better when seated close to the teacher? A virtual classroom study considering individual levels of inattention and hyperactivity-impulsivity. *Learning and Instruction, 61*, 138–147. https://doi.org/10.1016/j.learninstruc.2018.10.004

Boden, L. J., Jolivette, K., & Alberto, P. A. (2018). The effects of check-in, check-up, check-out for students with moderate intellectual disability during on- and off-site vocational training. *Journal of Classroom Interaction, 53*(1), 4–21.

Bohanon, H., Fenning, P., Hicks, K., Weber, S., Thier, K., Aikins, B., et al. (2012). A case example of the implementation of schoolwide positive behavior support in a high school setting using change point test analysis. *Preventing School Failure, 56*(2), 91–103.

Bollman, J. R., & Davis. P. K. (2009). Teaching women with intellectual disabilities to identify and report inappropriate staff-to-resident interactions. *Journal of Applied Behavior Analysis, 42*, 813–817.

Bonner, A. C., & Borrero, J. C. (2018). Differential reinforcement of low rate schedules reduce severe problem behavior. *Behavior Modification, 42*(5), 747–764. https://doi.org/10.1177/0145445517731723

Bornstein, P. H. (1985). Self-instructional training: A commentary and state-of-the-art. *Journal of Applied Behavior Analysis, 18*, 69–72.

Bornstein, P. H., & Quevillon, R. P. (1976). The effects of a self-instructional package on overactive preschool boys. *Journal of Applied Behavior Analysis, 9*, 179–188.

Borrero, C. S., Joseph Schlereth, G., Rubio, E. K., & Taylor, T. (2013). A comparison of two physical guidance procedures in the treatment of pediatric food refusal. *Behavioral Interventions, 28*(4), 261–280.

Borrero, C. S. W., England, J. D., Sarcia, B., & Woods, J. N. (2016). A comparison of descriptive and functional analyses of inappropriate mealtime behavior. *Behavior Analysis in Practice, 9*(4), 364–379. https://doi.org/10.1007/s40617-016-0149-5

Boswell, M. A., Knight, V., & Spriggs, A. D. (2013). Self-monitoring of on-task behaviors using the MotivAider® by a middle school student with a moderate intellectual disability. *Rural Special Education Quarterly, 32*(2), 23–30.

Bouck, E. C., Park, J., Levy, K., Cwiakala, K., & Whorley, A. (2020). App-based manipulatives and explicit instruction to support division with remainders. *Exceptionality, 28*(1), 45–59.

Bouck, E. C., Satsangi, R., & Bartlett, W. (2017). Supporting grocery shopping for students with intellectual disability: A preliminary study. *Disability and Rehabilitation: Assistive Technology, 12*(6), 605–613. https://doi.org/10.1080/17483107.2016.1201152

Bouck, E. C., Savage, M., Meyer, N. K., Taber-Doughty, T., & Hunley, M. (2014). High-tech or low-tech? Comparing self-monitoring systems to increase task independence for students with autism. *Focus on Autism and Other Developmental Disabilities, 29*(3), 156–167. https://doi.org/10.1177/1088357614528797

Bowman-Perrott, L., Burke, M. D., de Marin, S., Zhang, N., & Davis, H. (2015). A meta-analysis of single-case research on behavior contracts: Effects on behavioral and academic outcomes among children and youth. *Behavior Modification, 39*(2), 247–269. https://doi.org/10.1177/0145445514551383

Bowman-Perrott, L., Burke, M. D., Zaini, S., Zhang, N., & Vannest, K. (2016). Promoting positive behavior using the good behavior game: A meta-analysis of single-case research. *Journal of Positive Behavior Interventions, 18*(3), 180–190. https://doi.org/10.1177/1098300715592355

Boyle, J. R. (2013). Strategic note-taking for inclusive middle school science classrooms. *Remedial and Special Education, 34*(2), 78–90. https://doi.org/10.1177/0741932511410862

Bradley, R., Danielson, L., & Doolittle, J. (2007). Responsiveness to intervention: 1997 to 2007. *Teaching Exceptional Children, 19*, 8–12.

Bradshaw, C. A., & Reed, P. (2012). Relationship between contingency awareness and human performance on random ratio and random interval schedules. *Learning and Motivation, 43*(1–2), 55–65. https://doi.org/10.1016/j.lmot.2011.11.002

Brand, D., Henley, A. J., DiGennaro Reed, F. D., Gray, E., & Crabbs, B. (2019). A review of published studies involving parametric manipulations of treatment integrity. *Journal of Behavioral Education, 28*(1), 1–26. https://doi.org/10.1007/s10864-018-09311-8

Briesch, A. M., Daniels, B., & Beneville, M. (2019). Unpacking the term "self-management": Understanding intervention applications within the school-based literature. *Journal of Behavioral Education, 28*(1), 54–77. https://doi.org/10.1007/s10864-018-9303-1

Brigance, A. (1999). *Brigance diagnostic inventory of basic skills* (Revised). Billerica, MA: Curriculum Associates.

Briggs, A., Alberto, P. A., Berlin, K., McKinley, C., Sharpton, W. R., & Ritts, C. (1990). Generalized use of a self-operated audio prompt system. *Education and Training in Mental Retardation, 25*, 381–389.

Briggs, A. M., Dozier, C. L., Lessor, A. N., Kamana, B. U., & Jess, R. L. (2019). Further investigation of differential reinforcement of alternative behavior without extinction for escape-maintained destructive behavior. *Journal of Applied Behavior Analysis, 52*(4), 956–973.

Briggs, A. M., Fisher, W. W., Greer, B. D., & Kimball, R. T. (2018). Prevalence of resurgence of destructive behavior when thinning reinforcement schedules during functional communication training. *Journal of Applied Behavior Analysis, 51*(3), 620–633. https://doi.org/10.1002/jaba.472

Brock, M. E., Biggs, E. E., Carter, E. W., Cattey, G. N., & Raley, K. S. (2016). Implementation and generalization of peer support arrangements for students with severe disabilities in inclusive classrooms. *The Journal of Special Education, 49*(4), 221–232. https://doi.org/10.1177/0022466915594368

Brock, M. E., Cannella-Malone, H. I., Seaman, R. L., Andzik, N. R., Schaefer, J. M., Page, E. J., et al. (2017). Findings across practitioner training studies in special education: A comprehensive review and meta-analysis. *Exceptional Children, 84*(1), 7–26.

Brock, M. E., & Carter, E. W. (2016). Efficacy of teachers training paraprofessionals to implement peer support arrangements. *Exceptional Children, 82*(3), 354–371.

Brodhead, M. T., Abston, G. W., Mates, M., & Abel, E. A. (2017). Further refinement of video-based brief multiple-stimulus without replacement preference assessments. *Journal of Applied Behavior Analysis, 50*(1), 170–175. https://doi.org/10.1002/jaba.358

Brodhead, M. T., Courtney, W. T., & Thaxton, J. R. (2018). Using activity schedules to promote varied application use in children with autism. *Journal of Applied Behavior Analysis, 51*(1), 80–86. https://doi.org/10.1002/jaba.435

Brodhead, M. T., Kim, S. Y., Rispoli, M. J., Sipila, E. S., & Bak, M. Y. S. (2019). A pilot evaluation of a treatment package to teach social conversation via video-chat. *Journal of Autism and Developmental Disorders, 49*(8), 3316–3327. https://doi.org/10.1007/s10803-019-04055-4

Brooks, A., Todd, A., Tofflemoyer, S., & Horner, R. (2003). Use of functional assessment and a self-management system to increase academic engagement and work completion. *Journal of Positive Behavior Interventions, 5*, 144–152.

Bross, L. A., Common, E. A., Oakes, W. P., Lane, K. L., Menzies, H. M., & Ennis, R. P. (2018). High-probability request sequence: An effective, efficient low-intensity strategy to support student success. *Beyond Behavior, 27*(3), 140–145. https://doi.org/10.1177/1074295618798615

Browder, D. M., & Shapiro, E. S. (1985). Applications of self-management to individuals with severe handicaps: A review. *Journal of the Association for Persons with Severe Handicaps, 10*, 200–208.

Browning, E. R. (1983). A memory pacer for improving stimulus generalization. *Journal of Autism and Developmental Disorders, 13*, 427–432.

Bruhn, A. L., Vogelgesang, K., Fernando, J., & Lugo, W. (2016). Using data to individualize a multicomponent, technology-based self-monitoring intervention. *Journal of Special Education Technology, 31*(2), 64–76.

Bruhn, A. L., Wehby, J. H., & Hasselbring, T. S. (2020). Data-based decision making for social behavior: Setting a research agenda. *Journal of Positive Behavior Interventions, 22*(2), 116–126.

Bruhn, A. L., Woods-Groves, S., Fernando, J., Choi, T., & Troughton, L. (2017). Evaluating technology-based self-monitoring as a tier 2 intervention across middle school settings. *Behavioral Disorders, 42*(3), 119–131.

Bruinsma, Y., Minjarez, M. B., Schreibman, L., & Stahmer, A. C. (2020). *Naturalistic developmental behavioral interventions for autism spectrum disorder* (Y. Bruinsma, M. B. Minjarez, L. Schreibman, & A. C. Stahmer (eds.)). Paul H. Brookes Publishing Co.

Bruner, J. S. (1960). *The process of education*. Cambridge, MA: Harvard University Press.

Bruni, T. P., Drevon, D., Hixson, M., Wyse, R., Corcoran, S., & Fursa, S. (2017). The effect of functional behavior assessment on school-based interventions: A meta-analysis of single-case research. *Psychology in the Schools, 54*(4), 351–369. https://doi.org/10.1002/pits.22007

Bryant, L. E., & Budd, K. S. (1982). Self-instructional training to increase independent work performance in preschoolers. *Journal of Applied Behavior Analysis, 15*, 259–271.

Buchard, J. D., & Harig, P. T. (1976). Behavior modification and juvenile delinquency. In H. Leitenberg (ed.), *Handbook of behavior modification and behavior therapy*. Upper Saddle River, NJ: Prentice Hall.

Bulla, A. J., & Frieder, J. E. (2018). Self-management as a class-wide intervention: An evaluation of the "Self & Match" system embedded within a dependent group contingency. *Psychology in the Schools, 55*(3), 305–322. https://doi.org/10.1002/pits.22109

Bunch-Crump, K. R., & Lo, Y. (2017). An investigation of multitiered behavioral interventions on disruptive behavior and academic engagement of elementary students. *Journal of Positive Behavior Interventions, 19*(4), 216–227. https://doi.org/10.1177/1098300717696939

Burchard, J. D., & Barrera, F. (1972). An analysis of time-out and response cost in a programmed environment. *Journal of Applied Behavior Analysis, 5*, 271–282.

Burckley, E., Tincani, M., & Fisher, A. G. (2015). An iPad™-based picture and video activity schedule increases community shopping skills of a young adult with autism spectrum disorder and intellectual disability. *Developmental Neurorehabilitation, 18*(2), 131–136. https://doi.org/10.3109/17518423.2014.945045

Burgio, L. D., Whitman, T. L., & Johnson, M. R. (1980). A self-instructional package for increasing attending behavior in educable mentally retarded children. *Journal of Applied Behavior Analysis, 13*, 443–459.

Burke, J. D., & Romano-Verthelyi, A. M. (2018). Oppositional defiant disorder. In M. M. Martel (ed.), *Developmental pathways to disruptive, impulse-control, and conduct disorders* (pp. 21–52). Elsevier Academic Press. https://doi.org/10.1016/B978-0-12-811323-3.00002-X

Burns, M. K., Ysseldyke, J., Nelson, P. M., & Kanive, R. (2015). Number of repetitions required to retain single-digit multiplication math facts for elementary students. *School Psychology Quarterly*, 30(3), 398–405. https://doi.org/10.1037/spq0000097

Burt, J. L., & Pennington, R. C. (2017). A teacher's guide to using extinction in school settings. *Intervention in School and Clinic*, 53(2), 107–113.

Burt, J. L., & Whitney, T. (2018). From resource room to the real world: Facilitating generalization of intervention outcomes. *TEACHING Exceptional Children*, 50(6), 364–372.

Buzhardt, J., Greenwood, C. R., Walker, D., Jia, F., Schnitz, A. G., Higgins, S., et al. (2018). Web-based support for data-based decision making: Effect of intervention implementation on infant–toddler communication. *Journal of Early Intervention*, 40(3), 246–267.

Byra, K. L., White, S., Temple, M., & Cameron, M. J. (2018). An approach to cleanliness training to support bathroom hygiene among children with autism spectrum disorder. *Behavior Analysis in Practice*, 11(2), 139–143. https://doi.org/10.1007/s40617-017-0205-9

Byrne, G. (1989). We have met the enemy and it is us! *Science*, 243, 32.

Call, N. A., Trosclair-Lasserre, N. M., Findley, A. J., Reavis, A. R., & Shillingsburg, M. A. (2012). Correspondence between single versus daily preference assessment outcomes and reinforcer efficacy under progressive-ratio schedules. *Journal of Applied Behavior Analysis*, 45(4), 763–777.

Call, N. A., Wacker, D. P., Ringdahl, J. E., & Boelter, E. W. (2005). Combined antecedent variables as motivating operations within functional analyses. *Journal of Applied Behavior Analysis*, 38, 385–389.

Call, N. A., Zangrillo, A. N., Delfs, C. H., & Findley, A. J. (2013). A comparison of brief functional analyses with and without consequences. *Behavioral Interventions*, 28(1), 22–39. https://doi.org/10.1002/bin.1353

Callicott, K. J., & Park, H. (2003). Effects of self-talk on academic engagement and academic responding. *Behavioral Disorders*, 29, 48–64.

Cameron, J. (2005). The detrimental effect of reward hypothesis: Persistence of a view in the face of disconfirming evidence. In W. L. Heward et al. (Eds.), Focus on behavior analysis in education: Achievements, challenges, and opportunities (pp. 304-315). Upper Saddle River: Prentice Hall.

Cameron, J., Banko, K. M., & Pierce, W. D. (2001). Pervasive negative effects of rewards on intrinsic motivation: The myth continues. *The Behavior Analyst*, 24, 1–44.

Cameron, J., & Pierce, W. D. (1994). Reinforcement, reward, and intrinsic motivation: A meta-analysis. *Review of Educational Research*, 64, 363–423.

Camp, E. M., Iwata, B. A., Hammond, J. L., & Bloom, S. E. (2009). Antecedent versus consequent events as predictors of problem behavior. *Journal of Applied Behavior Analysis*, 42(2), 469–483. https://doi.org/10.1901/jaba.2009.42–469

Campbell, A., & Anderson, C. M. (2011). Check-in/check-out: A systematic evaluation and component analysis. *Journal of Applied Behavior Analysis*, 44(2), 315–326. https://doi.org/10.1901/jaba.2011.44–315

Campbell, C. R., & Stremel-Campbell, K. (1982). Programming "loose training" as a strategy to facilitate language generalization. *Journal of Applied Behavior Analysis*, 15, 295–305.

Cannella, M. H. I., Sabielny, L. M., & Tullis, C. A. (2015). Using eye gaze to identify reinforcers for individuals with severe multiple disabilities. *Journal of Applied Behavior Analysis*, 48(3), 680–684. https://doi.org/10.1002/jaba.231

Cannon, J., Easterbrooks, S., & Fredrick, L. (2010). Vocabulary acquisition through books in ASL. *Communication Disorders Quarterly*, 31, 96–112.

Capriotti, M. R., Brandt, B. C., Rickftts, E. J., Espii, F. M., & Woods, D. W. (2012). Comparing the effects of differential reinforcement of other behavior and response-cost contingencies on tics in youth with Tourette syndrome. *Journal of Applied Behavior Analysis*, 45(2), 251–263. https://doi.org/10.1901/jaba.2012.45–251

Capshew, J. H. (1993, Fall). Engineering behavior: Project Pigeon, World War II, and the conditioning of B. F. Skinner. *Technology & Culture*, 34(4), 835–857.

Carbone, V. J., Morgenstern, B., Zecchin-Tirri, G., & Kolberg, L. (2010). The role of the reflexive-conditioned motivating operation (CMO-R) during discrete trial instruction of children with autism. *Focus on Autism and Other Developmental Disabilities*, 25(2), 110–124. https://doi.org/10.1177/1088357610364393

Carbone, V. J., O'Brien, L., Sweeney-Kerwin, E. J., & Albert, K. M. (2013). Teaching eye contact to children with autism: A conceptual analysis and single case study. *Education & Treatment of Children*, 36(2), 139–159. https://doi.org/10.1353/etc.2013.0013

Carbone, V. J., Sweeney-Kerwin, E. J., Attanasio, V., & Kasper, T. (2010). Increasing the vocal responses of children with autism and developmental disabilities using manual sign mand training and prompt delay. *Journal of Applied Behavior Analysis*, 43(4), 705–709. https://doi.org/10.1901/jaba.2010.43–705

Cardoso-Martins, C., Gonçalves, D. T., & de Magalhães, C. G. (2013). What are the mechanisms behind exceptional word reading ability in hyperlexia?: Evidence from a 4-year-old hyperlexic boy's invented spellings. *Journal of Autism and Developmental Disorders*, 43(12), 3001–3003. https://doi.org/10.1007/s10803-013-1857-0

Carey, R., & Bucher, B. (1983). Positive practice overcorrection: The effects of duration of positive practice on acquisition and response duration. *Journal of Applied Behavior Analysis*, 16, 101–109.

Cariveau, T., & Kodak, T. (2017). Programming a randomized dependent group contingency and common stimuli to promote durable behavior change. *Journal of Applied Behavior Analysis*, 50(1), 121–133. https://doi.org/10.1002/jaba.352

Carlile, K. A., DeBar, R. M., Reeve, S. A., Reeve, K. F., & Meyer, L. S. (2018). Teaching help-seeking when lost to individuals with autism spectrum disorder. *Journal of Applied Behavior Analysis*, 51(2), 191–206. https://doi.org/10.1002/jaba.447

Carnett, A., Raulston, T., Lang, R., Tostanoski, A., Lee, A., Sigafoos, J., et al. (2014). Effects of a perseverative interest-based token economy on challenging and on-task behavior in a child with autism. *Journal of Behavioral Education*, 23(3), 368–377. https://doi.org/10.1007/s10864-014-9195-7

Carp, C. L., Peterson, S. P., Arkel, A. J., Petursdottir, A. I., & Ingvarsson, E. T. (2012). A further evaluation of picture prompts during auditory-visual conditional discrimination training. *Journal of Applied Behavior Analysis*, 45(4), 737–751.

Carpenter, S., & McKee-Higgins, E. (1996). Behavior management in inclusive classrooms. *Remedial and Special Education*, 17, 196–203.

Carr, E., & Durand, M. (1985). Reducing behavior problems through functional communication training. *Journal of Applied Behavior Analysis*, 18, 111–126.

Carr, E., & Newsom, C. (1985). Demand-related tantrums: Conceptualization and treatment. *Behavior Modification*, 9, 403–426.

Carr, E. G. (1996). The transfiguration of behavior analysis: Strategies for survival. *Journal of Behavioral Education*, 6, 263–270.

Carr, E. G., Horner, R. H., Turnbull, A. P., Marquis, J. G., McLaughlin, D. M., McAtee, M. L., et al. (1999). *Positive behavior support as an approach for dealing with problem behavior in people with developmental disabilities: A research synthesis.* Washington, DC: AAMR.

Carr, E. G., Smith, C. E., Giacin, T. A., Whelan, B. M., & Pancari, J. (2003). Menstrual discomfort as a biological setting event for severe problem behavior: Assessment and intervention. *American Journal on Mental Retardation, 108*, 117–133.

Carr, J. E., & Briggs, A. M. (2010). Strategies for making regular contact with the scholarly literature. *Behavior Analysis in Practice, 3*(2), 13–18.

Carr, M. E. (2016). Self-management of challenging behaviours associated with autism spectrum disorder: A meta-analysis. *Australian Psychologist, 51*(4), 316–333. https://doi.org/10.1111/ap.12227

Carter, E. W., Asmus, J., Moss, C. K., Biggs, E. E., Bolt, D. M., Born, T. L., et al. (2016). Randomized evaluation of peer support arrangements to support the inclusion of high school students with severe disabilities. *Exceptional Children, 82*(2), 209–233.

Carter, M., & Kemp, C. R. (1996). Strategies for task analysis in special education. *Educational Psychology, 16*, 155–171.

Carter, S., & Wheeler, J. (2007). Functional analysis and reduction of inappropriate spitting. *Education and Training in Developmental Disabilities, 42*, 59–64.

Carter, S. L., & Wheeler, J. J. (2019). *The social validity manual: Subjective evaluation of interventions.* (2nd ed.). London: Elsevier Academic Press.

Case, L. P., Harris, K. R., & Graham, S. (1992). Improving the mathematical problem-solving skills of students with learning disabilities. *Journal of Special Education, 26*(1), 1–19.

Casey, S., & Merical, C. (2006). The use of functional communication training without additional treatment procedures in an inclusive school setting. *Behavioral Disorders, 32*, 46–54.

Cashwell, T., Skinner, C., & Smith, E. (2001). Increasing second-grade students' reports of peers' prosocial behaviors via direct instruction, group reinforcement, and progress feedback: A replication and extension. *Education and Treatment of Children, 24*, 161–175.

Castillo, M. I., Clark, D. R., Schaller, E. A., Donaldson, J. M., DeLeon, I. G., & Kahng, S. (2018). Descriptive assessment of problem behavior during transitions of children with intellectual and developmental disabilities. *Journal of Applied Behavior Analysis, 51*(1), 99–117. https://doi.org/10.1002/jaba.430

Cazzell, S., Skinner, C. H., Ciancio, D., Aspiranti, K., Watson, T., Taylor, K., et al. (2017). Evaluating a computer flash-card sight-word recognition intervention with self-determined response intervals in elementary students with intellectual disability. *School Psychology Quarterly, 32*(3), 367–378. https://doi.org/10.1037/spq0000172

Cengher, M., Budd, A., Farrell, N., & Fienup, D. M. (2018). A review of prompt-fading procedures: Implications for effective and efficient skill acquisition. *Journal of Developmental and Physical Disabilities, 30*(2), 155–173. https://doi.org/10.1007/s10882-017-9575-8

Chadwick, B. A., & Day, R. C. (1971). Systematic reinforcement: Academic performance of underachieving students. *Journal of Applied Behavior Analysis, 4*, 311–319.

Chan, P. E. (2016). Controlling setting events in the classroom. *Preventing School Failure, 60*(2), 87–93. https://doi.org/10.1080/1045988X.2015.1007441

Chappell, N., Graff, R. B., Libby, M. E., & Ahearn, W. H. (2009). Further evaluation of the effects of motivating operations on preference assessment outcomes. *Research in Autism Spectrum Disorders, 3*(3), 660–669. https://doi.org/10.1016/j.rasd.2009.01.002

Charlop-Christy, M. H., Carpenter, M., Le, L., LeBlanc, L. A., & Kellet, K. (2002). Using the picture exchange communication system (PECS) with children with autism: Assessment of PECS acquisition, speech, social-communicative behavior, and problem behavior. *Journal of Applied Behavior Analysis, 35*(3), 213–231. https://doi.org/10.1901/jaba.2002.35-213

Chasnoff, I. J., Wells, A. M., Telford, E., Schmidt, C., & Messer, G. (2010). Neurodevelopmental functioning in children with FAS, pFAS, and ARND. *Journal of Developmental and Behavioral Pediatrics, 31*, 192–201.

Cheney, T., & Stein, N. (1974). Fading procedures and oddity learning in kindergarten children. *Journal of Experimental Child Psychology, 17*, 313–321.

Chess, S., & Thomas A. (1984). *Origins and evolution of behavior disorders.* Cambridge, MA: Harvard University Press.

Chevalier, T. M., Parrila, R., Ritchie, K. C., & Deacon, S. H. (2017). The role of metacognitive reading strategies, metacognitive study and learning strategies, and behavioral study and learning strategies in predicting academic success in students with and without a history of reading difficulties. *Journal of Learning Disabilities, 50*(1), 34–48. https://doi.org/10.1177/0022219415588850

Chezan, L. C., Drasgow, E., & Marshall, K. J. (2012). A report on using general-case programming to teach collateral academic skills to a student in a postsecondary setting. *Focus on Autism and Other Developmental Disabilities, 27*(1), 22–30. https://doi.org/10.1177/1088357611428334

Chezan, L. C., Drasgow, E., Martin, C. A., & Halle, J. W. (2016). Negatively-reinforced mands: An examination of resurgence to existing mands in two children with autism and language delays. *Behavior Modification, 40*(6), 922–953. https://doi.org/10.1177/0145445516648664

Chezan, L. C., Wolfe, K., & Drasgow, E. (2018). A meta-analysis of functional communication training effects on problem behavior and alternative communicative responses. *Focus on Autism and Other Developmental Disabilities, 33*(4), 195–205. https://doi.org/10.1177/1088357617741294

Chiesa, M. (2003). Implications of determinism: Personal responsibility and the value of science. In K. A. Lattal & P. N. Chase (eds.), *Behavior theory and philosophy.* (pp. 243–258). New York: Kluwer Academic/Plenum Publishers. https://doi.org/10.1007/978-1-4757-4590-0_13

Chok, J. T. (2019). Creating functional analysis graphs using Microsoft Excel® 2016 for PCs. *Behavior Analysis in Practice, 12*(1), 265–292. https://doi.org/10.1007/s40617-018-0258-4

Chok, J. T., Shlesinger, A., Studer, L., & Bird, F. L. (2012). Description of a practitioner training program on functional analysis and treatment development. *Behavior Analysis in Practice, 5*(2), 25–36.

Chung, E. Y. (2019). Robotic intervention program for enhancement of social engagement among children with autism spectrum disorder. *Journal of Developmental and Physical Disabilities, 31*(4), 419–434. https://doi.org/10.1007/s10882-018-9651-8

Ciccone, F. J., Graff, R. B., & Ahearn, W. H. (2015). Increasing the efficiency of paired-stimulus preference assessments by identifying categories of preference. *Journal of Applied Behavior Analysis, 48*(1), 221–226. https://doi.org/10.1002/jaba.190

Cicero, F., & Pfadt, A. (2002). Investigation of a reinforcement-based toilet training procedure for children with autism. *Research in Developmental Disabilities, 23*, 319–331.

Cihak, D. F., Alberto, P. A., Kessler, K. B., & Taber, T. A. (2004). An investigation of instructional scheduling arrangements for community-based instruction. *Research in Developmental Disabilities, 25*, 67–88.

Cihak, D., & Alaimo, D. (2003). *Using personal digital assistants (PDA) for collecting observational data in the classroom.* (Bureau for Students with Multiple and Severe Disabilities Monograph.) Atlanta: Georgia State University,

Department of Educational Psychology and Special Education.

Cihak, D., Alberto, P., & Fredrick, L. (2007). Use of brief functional analysis and intervention evaluation in public settings. *Journal of Positive Behavior Interventions, 9*, 80–93.

Cihak, D., Alberto, P. A., Taber-Doughty, T., & Gama, R. I. (2006). A comparison of static picture prompting and video prompting simulation strategies using group instructional procedures. *Focus on Autism and Other Developmental Disabilities, 21*, 89–99.

Cihon, J. H., Ferguson, J. L., Milne, C. M., Leaf, J. B., McEachin, J., & Leaf, R. (2019). A preliminary evaluation of a token system with a flexible earning requirement. *Behavior Analysis in Practice, 12*(3), 548–556. https://doi.org/10.1007/s40617-018-00316-3

Cihon, T. M., White, R., Zimmerman, V. L., Gesick, J., Stordahl, S., & Eshleman, J. (2017). The effects of precision teaching with textual or tact relations on intraverbal relations. *Behavioral Development Bulletin, 22*(1), 129–146. https://doi.org/10.1037/bdb0000056

Cipani, E. (1995). Be aware of negative reinforcement. *Teaching Exceptional Children, 27*(4), 36–40.

Cirelli, C. A., Sidener, T. M., Reeve, K. F., & Reeve, S. A. (2016). Using activity schedules to increase on-task behavior in children at risk for attention-deficit/hyperactivity disorder. *Education & Treatment of Children, 39*(3), 283–300. https://doi.org/10.1353/etc.2016.0013

Clay, C. J., Clohisy, A. M., Ball, A. M., Haider, A. F., Schmitz, B. A., & Kahng, S. (2018). Further evaluation of presentation format of competing stimuli for treatment of automatically maintained challenging behavior. *Behavior Modification, 42*(3), 382–397. https://doi.org/10.1177/0145445517740322

Clayton, M., Helms, B., & Simpson, C. (2006). Active prompting to decrease cell phone use and increase seat belt use while driving. *Journal of Applied Behavior Analysis, 39*, 341–349.

Clayton, M. C., & Helms, B. P. (2009). Increasing seat belt use on a college campus: An evaluation of two prompting procedures. *Journal of Applied Behavior Analysis, 42*, 161–164.

Cocchiola, M. A., Jr., Martino, G. M., Dwyer, L. J., & Demezzo, K. (2012). Toilet training children with autism and developmental delays: An effective program for school settings. *Behavior Analysis in Practice, 5*(2), 60–64.

Codding, R. S., Livanis, A., Pace, G. M., & Vaca, L. (2008). Using performance feedback to improve treatment integrity of classwide behavior plans: An investigation of observer reactivity. *Journal of Applied Behavior Analysis, 41*(3), 417–422.

Coffey, A. L., Shawler, L. A., Jessel, J., Nye, M. L., Bain, T. A., & Dorsey, M. F. (2020). Interview-informed synthesized contingency analysis (IISCA): Novel interpretations and future directions. *Behavior Analysis in Practice, 13*(1), 217–225. https://doi.org/10.1007/s40617-019-00348-3

Cohen-Almeida, D., Graff, R., & Ahearn, W. (2000). A comparison of verbal and tangible stimulus preference assessments. *Journal of Applied Behavior Analysis, 33*, 329–334.

Cole v. Greenfield-Central Community Schools, 667 F. Supp. 56 (S.D.Ind. 1986).

Cole, G., Montgomery, R., Wilson, K., & Milan, M. (2000). Parametric analysis of overcorrection duration effects. *Behavior Modification, 24*, 359–378.

Coleman, C., & Holmes, P. (1998). The use of noncontingent escape to reduce disruptive behaviors in children with speech delays. *Journal of Applied Behavior Analysis, 31*, 687–690.

Coleman, M. B., Hurley, K. J., & Cihak, D. F. (2012). Comparing teacher-directed and computer-assisted constant time delay for teaching functional sight words to students with moderate intellectual disability. *Education and Training in Autism and Developmental Disabilities, 47*(3), 280–292.

Coleman, P., & Blampied, N. M. (1977). Effects of self-monitoring, token reinforcement and different back-up reinforcers on the classroom behaviour of retardates. *Exceptional Child, 24*(2), 95–107. https://doi.org/10.1080/0156655770240207

Coleman-Martin, M., Heller, K., Cihak, D., & Irvine, K. (2005). Using computer-assisted instruction and the nonverbal reading approach to teach word identification. *Focus on Autism and Other Developmental Disabilities, 20*, 80–90.

Collins, B. C., Terrell, M., & Test, D. W. (2017). Using a simultaneous prompting procedure to embed core content when teaching a potential employment skill. *Career Development and Transition for Exceptional Individuals, 40*(1), 36–44. https://doi.org/10.1177/2165143416680347

Collins, S., Higbee, T. S., & Salzberg, C. L. (2009). The effects of video modeling on staff implementation of a problem-solving intervention with adults with developmental disabilities. *Journal of Applied Behavior Analysis, 42*, 849–854.

Common, E. A., & Lane, K. L. (2017). Social validity assessment. In J. K. Luiselli (ed.), *Applied behavior analysis advanced guidebook: A manual for professional practice*. (pp. 73–92). Elsevier Academic Press. https://doi.org/10.1016/B978-0-12-811122-2.00004-8

Conine, D. E., Vollmer, T. R., & Bolívar, H. A. (2020). Response to name in children with autism: Treatment, generalization, and maintenance. *Journal of Applied Behavior Analysis, 53*(2), 744–766. https://doi.org/10.1002/jaba.635

Conley, O., & Wolery, M. (1980). Treatment by overcorrection of self-injurious eye gouging in preschool blind children. *Journal of Behavior Therapy and Experimental Psychiatry, 11*, 121–125.

Connolly, A. (1998). *Key Math Diagnostic Arithmetic Test* (Revised). Circle Pines, MN: American Guidance Service.

Connolly, J. F. (2017). Seclusion of students with disabilities: An analysis of due process hearings. *Research and Practice for Persons with Severe Disabilities, 42*(4), 243–258.

Contreras, B. P., & Betz, A. M. (2016). Using lag schedules to strengthen the intraverbal repertoires of children with autism. *Journal of Applied Behavior Analysis, 49*(1), 3–16. https://doi.org/10.1002/jaba.271

Contrucci-Kuhn, S. A., Kuhn D. E., Lerman, D. C., Vorndran, C. M., & Addison, L. (2006). Analysis of factors that affect responding in a two-response chain in children with developmental disabilities. *Journal of Applied Behavior Analysis, 39*, 263–280.

Conyers, C., Miltenberger, R., Maki, A., Barenz, R., Jurgens, M., Sailer, A., et al. (2004). A comparison of response cost and differential reinforcement of other behavior to reduce disruptive behavior in a preschool classroom. *Journal of Applied Behavior Analysis, 37*, 411–415.

Cook, S. C., Rao, K., & Collins, L. (2017). Self-monitoring interventions for students with EBD: Applying UDL to a research-based practice. *Beyond Behavior, 26*(1), 19–27.

Coon, J. T., & Miguel, C. F. (2012). The role of increased exposure to transfer-of-stimulus-control procedures on the acquisition of intraverbal behavior. *Journal of Applied Behavior Analysis, 45*(4), 657–666.

Cooper, J. (1981). *Measuring behavior* (2nd ed.). Columbus, OH: Merrill.

Cooper, J. O., Heron, T. E., & Heward, W. L. (2020). *Applied behavior analysis* (3rd ed.). New York: Pearson.

Copeland, S. R., & Hughes, C. (2000). Acquisition of a picture prompt strategy to increase independent performance. *Education and Training in Mental Retardation and Developmental Disabilities, 35*, 294–305.

Coppage, S., & Meindl, J. N. (2017). Using video to bridge the gap between problem behavior and a delayed time-out procedure. *Behavior Analysis in Practice, 10*(3), 285–289. https://doi.org/10.1007/s40617-017-0197-5

Costenbader, V., & Reading-Brown, M. (1995). Isolation timeout used with students with emotional disturbance. *Exceptional Children, 61*(4), 353–363.

Cote, C., Thompson, R., Hanley, G., & McKerchar, P. (2007). Teacher report and direct assessment of preferences for identifying reinforcers for young children. *Journal of Applied Behavior Analysis, 40,* 157–166.

Cote, C., Thompson, R., & McKerchar, P. (2005). The effects of antecedent interventions and extinction on toddlers' compliance during transitions. *Journal of Applied Behavior Analysis, 38,* 235–238.

Coughlin, J., McCoy, K. M., Kenzer, A., Mathur, S. R., & Zucker, S. H. (2012). Effects of a self-monitoring strategy on independent work behavior of students with mild intellectual disability. *Education and Training in Autism and Developmental Disabilities, 47*(2), 154–164.

Council for Children with Behavioral Disorders. (2009). CCBD's position summary on the use of seclusion in school settings. *Behavioral Disorders, 34,* 235–247.

Council for Exceptional Children. (2005). CEC code of ethics for educators of persons with exceptionalities. Retrieved May 1, 2007, from http://www.cec.sped.org/Content/NavigationMenu/ProfessionalDevelopment/ProfessionalStandards/CEC.

Council for Exceptional Children. (2010). CEC ethical principles for special education professionals. Retrieved from http://www.cec.sped.org/Content/NavigationMenu/ProfessionalDevelopment/ProfessionalStandards/EthicsPracticeStandards/default.htm.

Courtemanche, A. B., Piersma, D. E., & Valdovinos, M. G. (2019). Evaluating the relationship between the rate and temporal distribution of self-injurious behavior. *Behavior Analysis: Research and Practice, 19*(1), 72–80. https://doi.org/10.1037/bar0000151

Cowdery, G., Iwata, B., & Pace, G. (1990). Effects and side effects of DRO as treatment of self-injurious behavior. *Journal of Applied Behavior Analysis, 23,* 497–506.

Cox, C. D., Cox, B. S., & Cox, D. J. (2005). Long-term benefits of prompts to use safety belts among drivers exiting senior communities. *Journal of Applied Behavior Analysis, 38,* 533–536.

Coy, J. N., & Kostewicz, D. E. (2018). Noncontingent reinforcement: Enriching the classroom environment to reduce problem behaviors. *TEACHING Exceptional Children, 50*(5), 301–309.

Craft, M. A., Alber, S. R., & Heward, W. L. (1998). Teaching elementary students with developmental disabilities to recruit teacher attention in a general education classroom: Effects on teacher praise and academic productivity. *Journal of Applied Behavior Analysis, 31,* 399–415.

Craig, A. R., & Shahan, T. A. (2018). Multiple schedules, off-baseline reinforcement shifts, and resistance to extinction. *Journal of the Experimental Analysis of Behavior, 109*(1), 148–163. https://doi.org/10.1002/jeab.300

Craighead, W. E., Kazdin, A. E., & Mahoney, M. J. (1976). *Behavior modification: Principles, issues, and applications.* Boston: Houghton Mifflin.

Critchfield, T. S., Doepke, K. J., Epting, L. K., Becirevic, A., Reed, D. D., Fienup, D. M., et al. (2017). Normative emotional responses to behavior analysis Jargon or how not to use words to win friends and influence people. *Behavior Analysis in Practice, 10*(2), 97–106. https://doi.org/10.1007/s40617-016-0161-9

Crone, D. A., Hawken, L. S., & Horner, R. H. (2015). *Building positive behavior support systems in schools: Functional behavioral assessment* (2nd ed.). New York: Guilford Press.

Cronin, K. A., & Cuvo, A. J. (1979). Teaching mending skills to mentally retarded adolescents. *Journal of Applied Behavior Analysis, 12,* 401–406.

Crossman, E. (1975). Communication. *Journal of Applied Behavior Analysis, 8,* 348.

Cullen, J. M., Alber-Morgan, S. R., Simmons-Reed, E. A., & Izzo, M. V. (2017). Effects of self-directed video prompting using iPads on the vocational task completion of young adults with intellectual and developmental disabilities. *Journal of Vocational Rehabilitation, 46*(3), 361–375. https://doi.org/10.3233/JVR-170873

Cumming, T. M., & O'Neill, S. C. (2019). Using data-based individualization to intensify behavioral interventions. *Intervention in School and Clinic, 54*(5), 280–285.

Cummings, C. (2000). *Winning strategies for classroom management.* Alexandria, VA: Association for Supervision and Curriculum Development.

Curiel, H., Curiel, E. S. L., Li, A., Deochand, N., & Poling, A. (2018). Examining a web-based procedure for assessing preference for videos. *Behavior Analysis in Practice, 11*(4), 406–410. https://doi.org/10.1007/s40617-018-0210-7

Curtis, K. S., Forck, K. L., Boyle, M. A., Fudge, B. M., Speake, H. N., & Pauls, B. P. (2020). Evaluation of a trial-based interview-informed synthesized contingency analysis. *Journal of Applied Behavior Analysis, 53*(2), 635–648. https://doi.org/10.1002/jaba.618

Dadson, S., & Horner, R. H. (1993). Manipulating setting events to decrease problem behaviors. *Teaching Exceptional Children, 24,* 53–55.

Da Fonte, M. A., Boesch, M. C., Edwards-Bowyer, M. E., Restrepo, M. W., Bennett, B. P., & Diamond, G. P. (2016). A three-step reinforcer identification framework: A step-by-step process. *Education & Treatment of Children, 39*(3), 389–409. https://doi.org/10.1353/etc.2016.0017

Daly, E. J., III, Wells, N. J., Swanger-Gagne, M. S., Carr, J. E., Kunz, G. M., & Taylor, A. M. (2009). Evaluation of the multiple-stimulus without replacement preference assessment method using activities as stimuli. *Journal of Applied Behavior Analysis, 42,* 563–574.

Daly, M., Jacob, S., King, D., & Cheramie, G. (1984). The accuracy of teacher predictions of student reward preferences. *Psychology in the Schools, 21,* 520–524.

Datchuk, S. M., Kubina, R. M., & Mason, L. H. (2015). Effects of sentence instruction and frequency building to a performance criterion on elementary-aged students with behavioral concerns and EBD. *Exceptionality, 23*(1), 34–53. https://doi.org/10.1080/09362835.2014.986604

Davis, C. A., Brady, M. P., Williams, R. E., & Burta, M. (1992). The effects of self-operated auditory prompting tapes on the performance fluency of persons with severe mental retardation. *Education and Training in Mental Retardation, 27,* 39–49.

Davis, T. N., Dacus, S., Strickland, E., Machalicek, W., & Coviello, L. (2013). Reduction of automatically maintained self-injurious behavior utilizing noncontingent matched stimuli. *Developmental Neurorehabilitation, 16*(3), 166–171. https://doi.org/10.3109/17518423.2013.766819

Davis, T. N., Weston, R., Hodges, A., Uptegrove, L., Williams, K., & Schieltz, K. M. (2018). Functional communication training and demand fading using concurrent schedules of reinforcement. *Journal of Behavioral Education, 27*(3), 343–357. https://doi.org/10.1007/s10864-017-9289-0

Davis-Temple, J., Jung, S., & Sainato, D. M. (2014). Teaching young children with special needs and their peers to play board games: Effects of a least to most prompting procedure to increase independent performance. *Behavior Analysis in Practice, 7*(1), 21–30. https://doi.org/10.1007/s40617-014-0001-8

DeCatanzaro, D., & Baldwin, G. (1978). Effective treatment of self-injurious behavior through a forced arm exercise. *Journal of Applied Behavior Analysis, 11,* 433–439.

Deci, E. L. (2016). Intrinsic motivation: The inherent tendency to be active. In R. J. Sternberg, S. T. Fiske, & D. J. Foss (eds.), *Scientists making a difference: One hundred eminent behavioral and brain scientists talk about their most important contributions.* (pp. 288–292). New York: Cambridge University Press.

Dehaven, E. D., Corley, M. J., Hofeling, D. V., & Garcia, E. (1982). Developing generative vocational behaviors in a business setting. *Analysis and Intervention in Developmental Disabilities, 2,* 345–356.

Deitz, S. M., & Repp, A. C. (1973). Decreasing classroom misbehavior through the use of DRL schedules of reinforcement. *Journal of Applied Behavior Analysis, 6*, 457–463.

DeLeon, I., & Iwata, B. (1996). Evaluation of a multiple-stimulus presentation format for assessing reinforcer preferences. *Journal of Applied Behavior Analysis, 29*, 519–533.

DeLeon, I., Fisher, W., Herman, K., & Crosland, K. (2000). Assessment of a response bias for aggression over functionally equivalent appropriate behavior. *Journal of Applied Behavior Analysis, 33*, 73–77.

Delprato, D. J. (2002). Countercontrol in behavior analysis. *The Behavior Analyst, 25*(2), 191–200. https://doi.org/10.1007/BF03392057

Denny, M. (1980). Reducing self-stimulatory behavior of mentally retarded persons by alternative positive practice. *American Journal of Mental Deficiency, 84*, 610–615.

Deno, S., & Jenkins, J. (1967). *Evaluating preplanned curriculum objectives*. Philadelphia: Research for Better Schools.

Deno, S. L., Reschly, A. L., Lembke, E. S., Magnusson, D., Callender, S. A., Windram, H., et al. (2009). Developing a school-wide progress-monitoring system. *Psychology in the Schools, 46*(1), 44–55.

Deochand, N., Costello, M. S., & Fuqua, R. W. (2015). Phase-change lines, scale breaks, and trend lines using Excel 2013. *Journal of Applied Behavior Analysis, 48*(2), 478–493. https://doi.org/10.1002/jaba.198

Deochand, N. (2017). Automating phase change lines and their labels using Microsoft Excel(R). *Behavior Analysis in Practice, 10*(3), 279–284. https://doi.org/10.1007/s40617-016-0169-1

DeQuinzio, J. A., Townsend, D. B., & Poulson, C. L. (2008). The effects of forward chaining and contingent social interaction on the acquisition of complex sharing responses by children with autism. *Research in Autism Spectrum Disorders, 2*(2), 264–275. https://doi.org/10.1016/j.rasd.2007.06.006

DeRosa, N. M., Roane, H. S., Bishop, J. R., & Silkowski, E. L. (2016). The combined effects of noncontingent reinforcement and punishment on the reduction of rumination. *Journal of Applied Behavior Analysis, 49*(3), 680–685. https://doi.org/10.1002/jaba.304

DeRosa, N. M., Roane, H. S., Wilson, J. L., Novak, M. D., & Silkowski, E. L. (2015). Effects of arm-splint rigidity on self-injury and adaptive behavior. *Journal of Applied Behavior Analysis, 48*(4), 860–864. https://doi.org/10.1002/jaba.250

Deshais, M. A., Fisher, A. B., & Kahng, S. (2018). A preliminary investigation of a randomized dependent group contingency for hallway transitions. *Education & Treatment of Children, 41*(1), 49–64. https://doi.org/10.1353/etc.2018.0002

Dewey, J. (1939). *Experience and education*. New York: Macmillan.

de Zubicaray, G., & Clair, A. (1998). An evaluation of differential reinforcement of other behavior, differential reinforcement of incompatible behavior, and restitution for the management of aggressive behaviors. *Behavioral Interventions, 13*(3), 157–168. https://doi.org/10.1002/(SICI)1099-078X(199808)13:3.0.CO;2-3

Dickens v. Johnson Country Board of Education, 661 F. Supp. 155 (E. D. Tenn. 1987).

Dixon, M., Jackson, J., Small, St., Horner-King, M., Lik, N., Garcia, Y., et al. (2009). Creating single-subject design graphs in Microsoft Excel. *Journal of Applied Behavior Analysis, 42*, 277–293.

Dixon, M. R., Stanley, C., Belisle, J., Galliford, M. E., Alholail, A., & Schmick, A. M. (2017). Establishing derived equivalence relations of basic geography skills in children with autism. *Analysis of Verbal Behavior, 33*(2), 290–295. https://doi.org/10.1007/s40616-017-0084-8

Doke, L., & Epstein, L. (1975). Oral overcorrection: Side effects and extended applications. *Journal of Experimental Child Psychology, 20*, 496–511.

Dollard, N., Christensen, L., Colucci, K., & Epanchin, B. (1996). Constructive classroom management. *Focus on Exceptional Children, 29*(2), 1–12.

Donaldson, J. M., Matter, A. L., & Wiskow, K. M. (2018). Feasibility of and teacher preference for student-led implementation of the good behavior game in early elementary classrooms. *Journal of Applied Behavior Analysis, 51*(1), 118–129. https://doi.org/10.1002/jaba.432

Donaldson, J. M., & Vollmer, T. R. (2012). A procedure for thinning the schedule of time-out. *Journal of Applied Behavior Analysis, 45*(3), 625–630. https://doi.org/10.1901/jaba.2012.45-625

Donaldson, J. M., Vollmer, T. R., Yakich, T. M., & Van Camp, C. (2013). Effects of a reduced time-out interval on compliance with the time-out instruction. *Journal of Applied Behavior Analysis, 46*(2), 369–378. https://doi.org/10.1002/jaba.40

Dorsey, M. F., Iwata, B. A., Ong, P., & McSween, T. E. (1980). Treatment of self-injurious behavior using a water mist: Initial response suppression and generalization. *Journal of Applied Behavior Analysis, 13*, 343–353.

Dougherty, S., Fowler, S., & Paine, S. (1985). The use of peer monitors to reduce negative interaction during recess. *Journal of Applied Behavior Analysis, 18*, 141–153.

Douglas, K. H., Ayres, K. M., & Langone, J. (2015). Comparing self-management strategies delivered via an iPhone to promote grocery shopping and literacy. *Education and Training in Autism and Developmental Disabilities, 50*(4), 446–465.

Dowdy, A., & Jacobs, K. W. (2019). An empirical evaluation of the disequilibrium model to increase independent seatwork for an individual diagnosed with autism. *Behavior Analysis in Practice, 12*(3), 617–621. https://doi.org/10.1007/s40617-018-00307-4

Dowdy, A., & Tincani, M. (2020). Assessment and treatment of high-risk challenging behavior of adolescents with autism in an aquatic setting. *Journal of Applied Behavior Analysis, 53*(1), 305–314. https://doi.org/10.1002/jaba.590

Dozier, C. L., Iwata, B. A., Thomason-Sassi, J., Worsdell, A. S., & Wilson, D. M. (2012). A comparison of two pairing procedures to establish praise as a reinforcer. *Journal of Applied Behavior Analysis, 45*(4), 721–735.

Dracobly, J. D., Dozier, C. L., Briggs, A. M., & Juanico, J. F. (2018). Reliability and validity of indirect assessment outcomes: Experts versus caregivers. *Learning and Motivation, 62*, 77–90. https://doi.org/10.1016/j.lmot.2017.02.007

Drevon, D. D., Hixson, M. D., Wyse, R. D., & Rigney, A. M. (2019). A meta-analytic review of the evidence for check-in check-out. *Psychology in the Schools, 56*(3), 393–412. https://doi.org/10.1002/pits.22195

Dube, W. V., Farber, R. S., Mueller, M. R., Grant, E., Lorin, L., & Deutsch, C. K. (2016). Stimulus overselectivity in autism, Down syndrome, and typical development. *American Journal on Intellectual and Developmental Disabilities, 121*(3), 219–235. https://doi.org/10.1352/1944-7558-121.3.219

Dubuque, E. M. (2015). Inserting phase change lines into Microsoft Excel® graphs. *Behavior Analysis in Practice, 8*(2), 207–211. https://doi.org/10.1007/s40617-015-0078-8

Duchaine, E. L., Jolivette, K., Fredrick, L. D., & Alberto, P. A. (2018). Increase engagement and achievement with response cards: Science and mathematics inclusion classes. *Learning Disabilities: A Contemporary Journal, 16*(2), 157–176.

Dudley, L. L., Axe, J. B., Allen, R. F., & Sweeney-Kerwin, E. J. (2019). Establishing praise as a conditioned reinforcer: Pairing with one versus multiple reinforcers. *Behavioral Interventions, 34*(4), 534–552. https://doi.org/10.1002/bin.1690

Dueñas, A. D., Plavnick, J. B., & Maher, C. E. (2019). Embedding tact instruction during play for preschool children with autism spectrum disorder. *Education & Treatment of Children, 42*(3), 361–384. https://doi.org/10.1353/etc.2019.0017

Dufek, S., & Schreibman, L. (2014). Natural environment training. In J. Tarbox, D. R. Dixon, P. Sturmey, & J. L. Matson (eds.), *Handbook of early intervention for autism spectrum disorders: Research, policy, and practice.* (pp. 325–344). Springer Science + Business Media. https://doi.org/10.1007/978-1-4939-0401-3_13

Dufour, M.-M., & Lanovaz, M. J. (2017). Comparing two methods to promote generalization of receptive identification in children with autism spectrum disorders. *Developmental Neurorehabilitation, 20*(8), 463–474. https://doi.org/10.1080/17518423.2016.1211191

Dufrene, B. A., Kazmerski, J. S., & Labrot, Z. (2017). The current status of indirect functional assessment instruments. *Psychology in the Schools, 54*(4), 331–350. https://doi.org/10.1002/pits.22006

Duker, P., & van Lent, C. (1991). Inducing variability in communicative gestures used by severely retarded individuals. *Journal of Applied Behavior Analysis, 24,* 379–386.

Dunlap, G. (2006). The applied behavior analytic heritage of PBS: A dynamic model of action-oriented research. *Journal of Positive Behavior Interventions, 8,* 58–60.

Dunlap, G., Carr, E. G., Horner, R. H., Koegel, R. L., Sailor, W., Clarke, S., et al. (2010). A descriptive, multiyear examination of positive behavior support. *Behavioral Disorders, 35*(4), 259–279.

Dunlap, G., & Kern, L. (1996). Modifying instructional activities to promote desirable behavior: A conceptual and practical framework. *School Psychology Quarterly, 11,* 297–312.

Dunlap, G., Koegel, R. L., Johnson, J., & O'Neill, R. E. (1987). Maintaining performance of autistic clients in community settings with delayed contingencies. *Journal of Applied Behavior Analysis, 20,* 185–191.

Dunlap, G., Strain, P., & Fox, L. (2012). Positive behavior support and young people with autism: Strategies of prevention and intervention. In B. Kelly & D. F. Perkins (eds.), *Handbook of implementation science for psychology in education* (pp. 247–263). New York: Cambridge University Press. https://doi.org/10.1017/CBO9781139013949.019

Dunlap, G., Strain, P. S., Lee, J. K., Joseph, J. D., Vatland, C., & Fox, L. (2017). *Prevent-teach-reinforce for families: A model of individualized positive behavior support for home and community.* Baltimore: Paul H Brookes Publishing.

Dunlap, K. (1928). A revision of the fundamental law of habit formation. *Science, 67,* 360–362.

Dunlap, K. (1930). Repetition in breaking of habits. *The Scientific Monthly, 30,* 66–70.

Dunlap, K. (1932). *Habits, their making and unmaking.* New York: Liverright.

Dupuis, D. L., Lerman, D. C., Tsami, L., & Shireman, M. L. (2015). Reduction of aggression evoked by sounds using noncontingent reinforcement and time-out. *Journal of Applied Behavior Analysis, 48*(3), 669–674. https://doi.org/10.1002/jaba.220

Durand, V. M. (1999). Functional communication training using assistive devices: Recruiting natural communities of reinforcement. *Journal of Applied Behavior Analysis, 32*(3), 247–267. https://doi.org/10.1901/jaba.1999.32-247

Durand, V. M., Berotti, D., & Weiner, J. (1993). Functional communication training: Factors affecting effectiveness, generalization, and maintenance. In J. Reichle & D. Wacker (eds.), *Communicative alternatives to challenging behavior: Integrating functional assessment and intervention strategies* (pp. 317–340). Baltimore: Paul Brookes.

Durand, V. M., & Crimmins, D. (1988). Identifying the variables maintaining self-injurious behavior. *Journal of Autism and Developmental Disorders, 18,* 99–117.

Durand, V. M., & Crimmins, D. (1992). *The Motivation Assessment Scale (MAS).* Topeka, KS: Monaco & Associates Inc.

Dutt, A. S., Berg, W. K., Wacker, D. P., Ringdahl, J. E., Yang, L.-Y., Vinquist, K. M., et al. (2014). The effects of skill training on preference for children with severe intellectual and physical disabilities. *Journal of Developmental and Physical Disabilities, 26*(5), 585–601. https://doi.org/10.1007/s10882-014-9383-3

Eber, L., Hyde, K., & Suter, J. C. (2011). Integrating wraparound into a schoolwide system of positive behavior supports. *Journal of Child and Family Studies, 20*(6), 782–790. https://doi.org/10.1007/s10826-010-9424-1

Ecott, C. L., & Critchfield, T. S. (2004). Noncontingent reinforcement, alternative reinforcement, and the matching law: A laboratory demonstration. *Journal of Applied Behavior Analysis, 37*(3), 249–265. https://doi.org/10.1901/jaba.2004.37-249

Edwards, C. K., Landa, R. K., Frampton, S. E., & Shillingsburg, M. A. (2018). Increasing functional leisure engagement for children with autism using backward chaining. *Behavior Modification, 42*(1), 9–33. https://doi.org/10.1177/0145445517699929

Edwards, N. M., & Lambros, K. M. (2018). Video self-modeling as a reading fluency intervention for dual language learners with disabilities. *Contemporary School Psychology, 22*(4), 468–478. https://doi.org/10.1007/s40688-018-0207-9

Embregts, P. J. C. M. (2000). Effectiveness of video feedback and self-management on appropriate social behavior of youth with mild mental retardation. *Research in Developmental Disabilities, 21,* 409–423.

Engelmann, S., & Carnine, D. (1982). *Theory of instruction: Principles and applications.* New York: Irvington.

Engelmann, S., & Colvin, G. (1983). *Generalized compliance training: A direct-instruction program for managing severe behavior problems.* Austin, TX: Pro-Ed.

Engelmann, S., Meyers, L., Carnine, L., Becker, W., Eisele, J., & Johnson, G. (1988). *Corrective reading: Decoding strategies.* Chicago: Science Research Associates.

English, C. L., & Anderson, C. M. (2006). Evaluation of the treatment utility of the analog functional analysis and the structured descriptive assessment. *Journal of Positive Behavior Interventions, 8*(4), 212–229. https://doi.org/10.1177/10983007060080040401

Ennis, R. P. (2018). Group contingencies to increase appropriate behaviors in the classroom: Tips for success. *Beyond Behavior, 27*(2), 82–89.

Ennis, R. P., & Jolivette, K. (2014). Using self-regulated strategy development for persuasive writing to increase the writing and self-efficacy skills of students with emotional and behavioral disorders in health class. *Behavioral Disorders, 40*(1), 26–36.

Ennis, R. P., Lane, K. L., & Flemming, S. C. (2020). Empowering teachers with low-intensity strategies: Supporting students at-risk for ebd with instructional choice during reading. *Exceptionality.* https://doi.org/10.1080/09362835.2020.1729766

Ennis, R. P., Lane, K. L., Oakes, W. P., & Flemming, S. C. (2020). Empowering teachers with low-intensity strategies to support instruction: Implementing across-activity choices during third-grade reading instruction. *Journal of Positive Behavior Interventions, 22*(2), 78–92.

Epstein, L. H., Doke, L. A., Sajwaj, T. E., Sorrell, S., & Rimmer, B. (1974). Generality and side effects of overcorrection. *Journal of Applied Behavior Analysis, 7,* 385–390.

Epstein, R. (1997). Skinner as self-manager. *Journal of Applied Behavior Analysis, 30,* 545–568.

Erickson, J., Derby, K. M., McLaughlin, T. F., & Fuehrer, K. (2015). An evaluation of Read Naturally® on increasing reading fluency for three primary students with learning disabilities. *Educational Research Quarterly, 39*(1), 3–20.

Espin, C. A., Wayman, M. M., Deno, S. L., McMaster, K. L., & de Rooij, M. (2017). Data-based decision-making: Developing a method for capturing teachers' understanding of CBM graphs. *Learning Disabilities Research & Practice, 32*(1), 8–21. https://doi.org/10.1111/ldrp.12123

Ezzeddine, E. W., DeBar, R. M., Reeve, S. A., & Townsend, D. B. (2020). Using video modeling to teach play comments to dyads with ASD. *Journal of Applied Behavior Analysis, 53*(2), 767–781. https://doi.org/10.1002/jaba.621

Fabry, B., Mayhew, G., & Hanson, A. (1984). Incidental teaching of mentally retarded students within a token system. *American Journal of Mental Deficiency, 89,* 29–36.

Fairbanks, S., Sugai, G., Guardino, D., & Lathrop, M. (2007). Response to intervention: Examining classroom behavior support in second grade. *Exceptional Children, 73,* 288–310.

Falcomata, T. S., & Gainey, S. (2014). An evaluation of noncontingent reinforcement for the treatment of challenging behavior with multiple functions. *Journal of Developmental and Physical Disabilities, 26*(3), 317–324. https://doi.org/10.1007/s10882-014-9366-4

Falcomata, T. S., Muething, C. S., Roberts, G. J., Hamrick, J., & Shpall, C. (2016). Further evaluation of latency-based brief functional analysis methods: An evaluation of treatment utility. *Developmental Neurorehabilitation, 19*(2), 88–94.

Falcomata, T., Roane, H., Hovanetz, A., Kettering, T., & Keeney, K. (2004). An evaluation of response cost in the treatment of inappropriate vocalizations maintained by automatic reinforcement. *Journal of Applied Behavior Analysis, 37,* 83–87.

Falcomata, T. S., & Wacker, D. P. (2013). On the use of strategies for programming generalization during functional communication training: A review of the literature. *Journal of Developmental and Physical Disabilities, 25*(1), 5–15. https://doi.org/10.1007/s10882-012-9311-3

Falcomata, T. S., Wacker, D. P., Ringdahl, J. E., Vinquist, K., & Dutt, A. (2013). An evaluation of generalization of mands during functional communication training. *Journal of Applied Behavior Analysis, 46*(2), 444–454. https://doi.org/10.1002/jaba.37

Falkenberg, C. A., & Barbetta, P. M. (2013). The effects of a self-monitoring package on homework completion and accuracy of students with disabilities in an inclusive general education classroom. *Journal of Behavioral Education, 22*(3), 190–210. https://doi.org/10.1007/s10864-013-9169-1

Falligant, J. M., Carver, A., Zarcone, J., & Schmidt, J. D. (2020). Assessment and treatment of public disrobing using noncontingent reinforcement and competing stimuli. *Behavior Analysis: Research and Practice.* https://doi.org/10.1037/bar0000179

Fallon, L. M., & Feinberg, A. B. (2017). Implementing a tier 2 behavioral intervention in a therapeutic alternative high school program. *Preventing School Failure, 61*(3), 189–197.

Faloon, B. J., & Rehfeldt, R. A. (2008). The role of overt and covert self-rules in establishing a daily living skill in adults with mild developmental disabilities. *Journal of Applied Behavior Analysis, 41,* 393–404.

Faraone, S. V., & Larsson, H. (2019). Genetics of attention deficit hyperactivity disorder. *Molecular Psychiatry, 24*(4), 562–575. https://doi.org/10.1038/s41380-018-0070-0

Farkas, M. S., Simonsen, B., Migdole, S., Donovan, M. E., Clemens, K., & Cicchese, V. (2012). Schoolwide positive behavior support in an alternative school setting: An evaluation of fidelity, outcomes, and social validity of tier 1 implementation. *Journal of Emotional and Behavioral Disorders, 20*(4), 275–288. https://doi.org/10.1177/1063426610389615

Farlow, L., & Snell, M. (1994). *Making the most of student performance data.* Washington, DC: American Association on Mental Retardation.

Favell, J. (1973). Reduction of stereotypes by reinforcement of toy play. *Mental Retardation, 11,* 21–23.

Fee, A., Schieber, E., Noble, N., & Valdovinos, M. G. (2016). Agreement between questions about behavior function, the motivation assessment scale, functional assessment interview, and brief functional analysis of children's challenging behaviors. *Behavior Analysis: Research and Practice, 16*(2), 94–102. https://doi.org/10.1037/bar0000040

Fee, V., Matson, J., & Manikam, R. (1990). A control group outcome study of a nonexclusionary time-out package to improve social skills with preschoolers. *Exceptionality, 1,* 107–121.

Felixbrod, J. J., & O'Leary, K. D. (1974). Self-determination of academic standards by children: Toward freedom from external control. *Journal of Educational Psychology, 66,* 845–850.

Feng, H., Chou, W.-C., & Lee, G. T. (2017). Effects of tact prompts on acquisition and maintenance of divergent intraverbal responses by a child with autism. *Focus on Autism and Other Developmental Disabilities, 32*(2), 133–141. https://doi.org/10.1177/1088357615610540

Ferguson, J. L., Milne, C. M., Cihon, J. H., Dotson, A., Leaf, J. B., McEachin, J., et al. (2020). An evaluation of estimation data collection to trial-by trial data collection during discrete trial teaching. *Behavioral Interventions, 35*(1), 178–191. https://doi.org/10.1002/bin.1705

Ferman, D. M., Reeve, K. F., Vladescu, J. C., Albright, L. K., Jennings, A. M., & Domanski, C. (2020). Comparing stimulus equivalence-based instruction to a video lecture to increase religious literacy in middle-school children. *Behavior Analysis in Practice, 13*(2), 360–374. https://doi.org/10.1007/s40617-019-00355-4

Ferron, J., Goldstein, H., Olszewski, A., & Rohrer, L. (2020). Indexing effects in single-case experimental designs by estimating the percent of goal obtained. *Evidence-Based Communication Assessment and Intervention, 14*(1–2), 6–27.

Ferster, C. B., Culbertson, S., & Boren, M. C. P. (1975). *Behavior principles* (2nd ed.). Upper Saddle River, NJ: Prentice Hall.

Ferster, C. B., & Skinner, B. F. (1957). *Schedules of reinforcement.* New York: Appleton-Century-Crofts.

Fetherston, A. M., & Sturmey, P. (2014). The effects of behavioral skills training on instructor and learner behavior across responses and skill sets. *Research in Developmental Disabilities, 35*(2), 541–562. https://doi.org/10.1016/j.ridd.2013.11.006

Feuerborn, L. L., Tyre, A. D., & King, J. P. (2015). The staff perceptions of behavior and discipline survey: A tool to help achieve systemic change through schoolwide positive behavior support. *Journal of Positive Behavior Interventions, 17*(2), 116–126. https://doi.org/10.1177/1098300714556675

Fewell, R. M., Romani, P. W., Wacker, D. P., Lindgren, S. D., Kopelman, T. G., & Waldron, D. B. (2016). Relations between consumption of functional and arbitrary reinforcers during functional communication training. *Journal of Developmental and Physical Disabilities, 28*(2), 237–253. https://doi.org/10.1007/s10882-015-9463-z

Fienup, D. M., Shelvin, K. H., & Doepke, K. (2013). Increasing recall of information of children diagnosed with Asperger's Syndrome: Utilization of visual strategies. *Research in Autism Spectrum Disorders, 7*(12), 1647–1652. https://doi.org/10.1016/j.rasd.2013.09.015

Filderman, M. J., Austin, C. R., & Toste, J. R. (2019). Data-based decision making for struggling readers in the secondary grades. *Intervention in School and Clinic, 55*(1), 3–12.

Finn, L., Ramasamy, R., Dukes, C., & Scott, J. (2015). Using WatchMinder to increase the on-task behavior of students with autism spectrum disorder. *Journal of Autism and Developmental Disorders, 45*(5), 1408–1418. https://doi.org/10.1007/s10803-014-2300-x

Fisher, W., Piazza, C., Bowman, L., Hagopian, L., Owens, J., & Slevin, I. (1992). A comparison of two approaches for identifying reinforcers for persons with severe and profound disabilities. *Journal of Applied Behavior Analysis, 25,* 491–498.

Fisher, W., Thompson, R., Piazza, C., Crosland, K., & Gotjen, D. (1997). On the relative reinforcing effects of choice and differential consequences. *Journal of Applied Behavior Analysis, 30,* 423–438.

Fisher, W. W., Greer, B. D., Fuhrman, A. M., Saini, V., & Simmons, C. A. (2018). Minimizing resurgence of destructive behavior using behavioral momentum theory. *Journal of Applied Behavior Analysis*, 51(4), 831–853. https://doi.org/10.1002/jaba.499

Fisher, W. W., Greer, B. D., Querim, A. C., & DeRosa, N. (2014). Decreasing excessive functional communication responses while treating destructive behavior using response restriction. *Research in Developmental Disabilities*, 35(11), 2614–2623. https://doi.org/10.1016/j.ridd.2014.06.024

Fishley, K. M., Konrad, M., & Hessler, T. (2017). GO FASTER: Building morpheme fluency. *Intervention in School and Clinic*, 53(2), 94–98.

Fiske, K., & Delmolino, L. (2012). Use of discontinuous methods of data collection in behavioral intervention: Guidelines for practitioners. *Behavior Analysis in Practice*, 5(2), 77–81.

Fiske, K. E., Isenhower, R. W., Bamond, M. J., Delmolino, L., Sloman, K. N., & LaRue, R. H. (2015). Assessing the value of token reinforcement for individuals with Autism. *Journal of Applied Behavior Analysis*, 48(2), 448–453. https://doi.org/10.1002/jaba.207

Flanagan, T. F., & DeBar, R. M. (2018). Trial-based functional analyses with a student identified with an emotional and behavioral disorder. *Behavioral Disorders*, 43(4), 423–435. https://doi.org/10.1177/0198742917719231

Flanagan, T. F., DeBar, R. M., Sidener, T. M., Kisamore, A. N., Reeve, K. F., & Reeve, S. A. (2019). Teacher-implemented trial-based functional analyses with students with emotional/behavioral disorders. *Journal of Developmental and Physical Disabilities*. https://doi.org/10.1007/s10882-019-09700-5

Floress, M. T., Zoder-Martell, K., & Schaub, R. (2017). Social skills plus relaxation training with a child with ASD in the schools. *Research in Developmental Disabilities*, 71, 200–213. https://doi.org/10.1016/j.ridd.2017.10.012

Flynn, S. D., & Lo, Y. (2016). Teacher implementation of trial-based functional analysis and differential reinforcement of alternative behavior for students with challenging behavior. *Journal of Behavioral Education*, 25(1), 1–31. https://doi.org/10.1007/s10864-015-9231-2

Fong, E. H., Catagnus, R. M., Brodhead, M. T., Quigley, S., & Field, S. (2016). Developing the cultural awareness skills of behavior analysts. *Behavior Analysis in Practice*, 9(1), 84–94. https://doi.org/10.1007/s40617-016-0111-6

Fong, E. H., Ficklin, S., & Lee, H. Y. (2017). Increasing cultural understanding and diversity in applied behavior analysis. *Behavior Analysis: Research and Practice*, 17(2), 103–113. https://doi.org/10.1037/bar0000076

Fonger, A. M., & Malott, R. W. (2019). Using shaping to teach eye contact to children with autism spectrum disorder. *Behavior Analysis in Practice*, 12(1), 216–221. https://doi.org/10.1007/s40617-018-0245-9

Fosnot, C. (1996). Constructivism: A psychological theory of learning. In C. Fosnot (ed.), *Constructivism: Theory, perspectives, and practice* (pp. 8–33). New York: Teachers College Press.

Fosnot, C. T., & Perry, R. S. (2005). In C. T. Fosnot (ed.), *Constructivism: Theory, perspectives, and practice*, 3–38.

Fowler, S. A., & Baer, D. M. (1981). "Do I have to be good all day?": The timing of delayed reinforcement as a factor in generalization. *Journal of Applied Behavior Analysis*, 14, 13–24.

Foxx, R., & Shapiro, S. (1978). The timeout ribbon: A nonexclusionary timeout procedure. *Journal of Applied Behavior Analysis*, 11, 125–136.

Foxx, R. M., & Azrin, N. H. (1972). Restitution: A method of eliminating aggressive-disruptive behavior of retarded and brain-damaged patients. *Behavior Research and Therapy*, 10, 15–27.

Foxx, R. M., & Azrin, N. H. (1973a). The elimination of autistic self-stimulatory behavior by overcorrection. *Journal of Applied Behavior Analysis*, 6, 1–14.

Foxx, R. M., & Azrin, N. H. (1973b). *Toilet training the retarded: A rapid program for day and nighttime independent toileting*. Champaign, IL: Research Press.

Foxx, R. M., McMorrow, M. J., & Mennemeier, M. (1984). Teaching social/vocational skills to retarded adults with a modified table game: An analysis of generalization. *Journal of Applied Behavior Analysis*, 17, 343–352.

Fradenburg, L., Harrison, R., & Baer, D. (1995). The effect of some environmental factors on inter-observer agreement. *Research in Developmental Disabilities*, 16(6), 425–437.

Fragale, C., Rojeski, L., O'Reilly, M., & Gevarter, C. (2016). Evaluation of functional communication training as a satiation procedure to reduce challenging behavior in instructional environments for children with autism. *International Journal of Developmental Disabilities*, 62(3), 139–146. https://doi.org/10.1080/20473869.2016.1183957

France, K., & Hudson, S. (1990). Behavior management of infant sleep disturbance. *Journal of Applied Behavior Analysis*, 23, 91–98.

Frankhauser, M. A., Tso, M. E., & Martella, R. C. (2001). A comparison of curriculum-specified reading checkout timings and daily 1-minute timings on student performance in reading mastery. *Journal of Direct Instruction*, 1(2), 85–96.

Freeland, J. T., & Noell, G. H. (2002). Programming for maintenance: An investigation of delayed intermittent reinforcement and common stimuli to create indiscriminable contingencies. *Journal of Behavioral Education*, 11(1), 5–18.

Freeman, J., Kern, L., Gambino, A. J., Lombardi, A., & Kowitt, J. (2019). Assessing the relationship between the positive behavior interventions and supports framework and student outcomes in high schools. *Journal of At-Risk Issues*, 22(2), 1–11.

Freeman, J., Simonsen, B., McCoach, D. B., Sugai, G., Lombardi, A., & Horner, R. (2016). Relationship between school-wide positive behavior interventions and supports and academic, attendance, and behavior outcomes in high schools. *Journal of Positive Behavior Interventions*, 18(1), 41–51. https://doi.org/10.1177/1098300715580992

Freeman, R., Lohrmann, S., Irvin, L. K., Kincaid, D., Vossler, V., & Ferro, J. (2009). Systems change and the complementary roles of in-service and preservice training in schoolwide positive behavior support. In W. Sailor, G. Dunlop, G. Sugai, & R. Horner (eds.), *Handbook of positive behavior support*. (pp. 603–629). Springer Publishing Company. https://doi.org/10.1007/978-0-387-09632-2_25

Friman, P., & Poling, A. (1995). Making life easier with effort: Basic findings and applied research on response effort. *Journal of Applied Behavior Analysis*, 28, 583–590.

Fritz, J. N., Iwata, B. A., Rolider, N. U., Camp, E. M., & Neidert, P. L. (2012). Analysis of self-recording in self-management interventions for stereotypy. *Journal of Applied Behavior Analysis*, 45(1), 55–68. https://doi.org/10.1901/jaba.2012.45-55

Fritz, J. N., Jackson, L. M., Stiefler, N. A., Wimberly, B. S., & Richardson, A. R. (2017). Noncontingent reinforcement without extinction plus differential reinforcement of alternative behavior during treatment of problem behavior. *Journal of Applied Behavior Analysis*, 50(3), 590–599. https://doi.org/10.1002/jaba.395

Fryxell, D., & Kennedy, C. H. (1995). Placement along the continuum of services and its impact on students' social relationships. *Journal of the Association for Persons with Severe Handicaps*, 20, 259–269.

Fuchs, D., Fuchs, L. S., & Vaughn, S. (2014). What is intensive instruction and why is it important? *TEACHING Exceptional Children*, 46(4), 13–18.

Fuchs, L. S. (2017). Curriculum-based measurement as the emerging alternative: Three decades later. *Learning Disabilities Research & Practice*, 32(1), 5–7. https://doi.org/10.1111/ldrp.12127

Fuchs, L. S., Fuchs, D., Compton, D. L., Wehby, J., Schumacher, R. F., Gersten, R., et al. (2015). Inclusion versus specialized intervention for very-low-performing students: What does "access" mean in an era of academic challenge? *Exceptional Children*, 81(2), 134–157.

Fuhrman, A. M., Greer, B. D., Zangrillo, A. N., & Fisher, W. W. (2018). Evaluating competing activities to enhance functional communication training during reinforcement schedule thinning. *Journal of Applied Behavior Analysis*, 51(4), 931–942.

Fuller, T. C., & Dubuque, E. M. (2019). Integrating phase change lines and labels into graphs in Microsoft Excel®. *Behavior Analysis in Practice*, 12(1), 293–299. https://doi.org/10.1007/s40617-018-0248-6

Gage, N. A., Sugai, G., Lewis, T. J., & Brzozowy, S. (2015). Academic achievement and school-wide positive behavior supports. *Journal of Disability Policy Studies*, 25(4), 199–209. https://doi.org/10.1177/1044207313505647

Gagnon, D. J., Mattingly, M. J., & Connelly, V. J. (2017). The restraint and seclusion of students with a disability: Examining trends in US school districts and their policy implications. *Journal of Disability Policy Studies*, 28(2), 66–76. https://doi.org/10.1177/1044207317710697

Gaisford, K. L., & Malott, R. L. (2010). The acquisition of generalized matching in children with developmental delays. *The Behavior Analyst Today*, 11, 85–94.

Galiatsatos, G. T., & Graff, R. B. (2003). Combining descriptive and functional analyses to assess and treat screaming. *Behavioral Interventions*, 18(2), 123–138. https://doi.org/10.1002/bin.133

Garcia, A. E., Reeve, S. A., Brothers, K. J., & Reeve, K. F. (2014). Using audio script fading and multiple-exemplar training to increase vocal interactions in children with autism. *Journal of Applied Behavior Analysis*, 47(2), 325–343. https://doi.org/10.1002/jaba.125

Garcia, D., Dukes, C., Brady, M. P., Scott, J., & Wilson, C. L. (2016). Using modeling and rehearsal to teach fire safety to children with autism. *Journal of Applied Behavior Analysis*, 49(3), 699–704. https://doi.org/10.1002/jaba.331

García-Zambrano, S., Rehfeldt, R. A., Hertel, I. P., & Boehmert, R. (2019). Effects of deictic framing and defusion on the development of self-as-context in individuals with disabilities. *Journal of Contextual Behavioral Science*, 12, 55–58. https://doi.org/10.1016/j.jcbs.2019.01.007

Gardner, A. W., Wacker, D. P., & Boelter, E. W. (2009). An evaluation of the interaction between quality of attention and negative reinforcement with children who display escape-maintained problem behavior. *Journal of Applied Behavior Analysis*, 42(2), 343–348. https://doi.org/10.1901/jaba.2009.42-343

Gardner, S. J., & Wolfe, P. S. (2015). Teaching students with developmental disabilities daily living skills using point-of-view modeling plus video prompting with error correction. *Focus on Autism and Other Developmental Disabilities*, 30(4), 195–207. https://doi.org/10.1177/1088357614547810

Gast, D., & Wolery, M. (1987). Severe maladaptive behaviors. In M. E. Snell (ed.), *Systematic instruction of people with severe handicaps* (3rd ed.). Columbus, OH: Merrill.

Gaylord-Ross, R. J., & Holvoet, J. (1985). *Strategies for educating students with severe handicaps*. Boston: Little, Brown.

Gehrman, C., Wilder, D. A., Forton, A. P., & Albert, K. (2017). Comparing resetting to non-resetting DRO procedures to reduce stereotypy in a child with autism. *Behavioral Interventions*, 32(3), 242–247. https://doi.org/10.1002/bin.1486

Geiger, K. B., Carr, J. E., LeBlanc, L. A., Hanney, N. M., Polick, A. S., & Heinicke, M. R. (2012). Teaching receptive discriminations to children with autism: A comparison of traditional and embedded discrete trial training. *Behavior Analysis in Practice*, 5(2), 49–59.

Gerow, S., Davis, T., Radhakrishnan, S., Gregori, E., & Rivera, G. (2018). Functional communication training: The strength of evidence across disabilities. *Exceptional Children*, 85(1), 86–103.

Gerow, S., Radhakrishnan, S., Davis, T. N., Hodges, A., & Feind, A. (2020). A comparison of demand fading and a dense schedule of reinforcement during functional communication training. *Behavior Analysis in Practice*, 13(1), 90–103. https://doi.org/10.1007/s40617-019-00403-z

Gesell, A., & Ilg, F. L. (1943). *Infant and child in the culture of today*. New York: Harper.

Ghaemmaghami, M., Hanley, G. P., Jessel, J., & Landa, R. (2018). Shaping complex functional communication responses. *Journal of Applied Behavior Analysis*, 51(3), 502–520. https://doi.org/10.1002/jaba.468

Giangreco, M. F. (2020). "How can a student with severe disabilities be in a fifth-grade class when he can't do fifth-grade level work?" Misapplying the least restrictive environment. *Research and Practice for Persons with Severe Disabilities*, 45(1), 23–27.

Gibbs, A. R., Tullis, C. A., Thomas, R., & Elkins, B. (2018). The effects of noncontingent music and response interruption and redirection on vocal stereotypy. *Journal of Applied Behavior Analysis*, 51(4), 899–914. https://doi.org/10.1002/jaba.485

Gil, V., Bennett, K. D., & Barbetta, P. M. (2019). Teaching young adults with intellectual disability grocery shopping skills in a community setting using least-to-most prompting. *Behavior Analysis in Practice*, 12(3), 649–653. https://doi.org/10.1007/s40617-019-00340-x

Gilbert, G. (1975). Extinction procedures: Proceed with caution. *Mental Retardation*, 13, 25–29.

Gilberts, G., Agran, M., Hughes, C., & Wehmeyer, M. (2001). The effects of peer delivered self-monitoring strategies on the participation of students with severe disabilities in general education classrooms. *JASH*, 26, 25–36.

Gilley, C., & Ringdahl, J. E. (2014). The effects of item preference and token reinforcement on sharing behavior exhibited by children with autism spectrum disorder. *Research in Autism Spectrum Disorders*, 8(11), 1425–1433. https://doi.org/10.1016/j.rasd.2014.07.010

Gillis, J. M., & Carr, J. E. (2014). Keeping current with the applied behavior-analytic literature in developmental disabilities: Noteworthy articles for the practicing behavior analyst. *Behavior Analysis in Practice*, 7(1), 10–14. https://doi.org/10.1007/s40617-014-0002-7

Giunta, F. T., Reeve, S. A., DeBar, R. M., Vladescu, J. C., & Reeve, K. F. (2016). Comparing continuous and discontinuous data collection during discrete trial teaching of tacting by children with autism. *Behavioral Interventions*, 31(4), 311–331. https://doi.org/10.1002/bin.1446

Glover, P., McLaughlin, T., Derby, K. M., & Gower, J. (2010). Using a direct instruction flashcard system with two students with learning disabilities. *Electronic Journal of Research in Educational Psychology*, 8(2), 457–472.

Goh, A. E., & Bambara, L. M. (2013). Video self-modeling: A job skills intervention with individuals with intellectual disability in employment settings. *Education and Training in Autism and Developmental Disabilities*, 48(1), 103–119.

Goldiamond, I. (1975). Toward a constructional approach to social problems: Ethical and constitutional issues raised by applied behavior analysis. In C. M. Franks & G. T. Wilson (eds.), *Annual review of behavior therapy, theory & practice* (vol. 3, pp. 21–63). New York: Brunner/Mazel.

Goldstein, K. (1939). *The organism*. New York: American Book.

Gomes, S. R., Reeve, S. A., Brothers, K. J., Reeve, K. F., & Sidener, T. M. (2020). Establishing a generalized repertoire of initiating bids for joint attention in children with autism. *Behavior Modification*, 44(3), 394–428. https://doi.org/10.1177/0145445518822499

Gongola, L. C., & Daddario, R. (2010). A practitioner's guide to implementing a differential reinforcement of other behaviors procedure. *TEACHING Exceptional Children, 42*(6), 14–20.

Gonzalez, M. L., Taylor, T., Borrero, C. S. W., & Sangkavasi, E. (2013). An individualized levels system to increase independent mealtime behavior in children with food refusal. *Behavioral Interventions, 28*(2), 143–157. https://doi.org/10.1002/bin.1358

Goodnight, C. I., Whitley, K. G., & Brophy-Dick, A. A. (2019). Effects of response cards on fourth-grade students' participation and disruptive behavior during language arts lessons in an inclusive elementary classroom. *Journal of Behavioral Education*. https://doi.org/10.1007/s10864-019-09357-2

Graber, A., & Graber, J. E. (2018). The unique challenge of articulating the behavior analysts' ethical obligations and the case of punishment. *Behavior Analysis in Practice*. https://doi.org/10.1007/s40617-018-00310-9

Graham, S., & Harris, K. R. (2005). *Writing better: Effective strategies for teaching students with learning difficulties*. Baltimore: Brookes.

Graham, S., Hebert, M., & Harris, K. R. (2015). Formative assessment and writing: A meta-analysis. *The Elementary School Journal, 115*(4), 523–547. https://doi.org/10.1086/681947

Green, C., Middleton, S., & Reid, D. (2000). Embedded evaluation of preferences sampled from person-centered plans for people with profound multiple disabilities. *Journal of Applied Behavior Analysis, 33*, 639–642.

Green, C., Reid, D., White, L., Halford, R., Brittain, D., & Gardner, S. (1988). Identifying reinforcers for persons with profound handicaps: Staff opinion vs. systematic assessment of preferences. *Journal of Applied Behavior Analysis, 21*, 31–43.

Greer, B. D., Neidert, P. L., & Dozier, C. L. (2016). A component analysis of toilet-training procedures recommended for young children. *Journal of Applied Behavior Analysis, 49*(1), 69–84. https://doi.org/10.1002/jaba.275

Greer, B. D., Neidert, P. L., Dozier, C. L., Payne, S. W., Zonneveld, K. L. M., & Harper, A. M. (2013). Functional analysis and treatment of problem behavior in early education classrooms. *Journal of Applied Behavior Analysis, 46*(1), 289–295. https://doi.org/10.1002/jaba.10

Grieco, J. C., Bahr, R. H., Schoenberg, M. R., Conover, L., Mackie, L. N., & Weeber, E. J. (2018). Quantitative measurement of communication ability in children with Angelman syndrome. *Journal of Applied Research in Intellectual Disabilities, 31*(1), e49–e58. https://doi.org/10.1111/jar.12305

Griffin, M. M., & Copeland, S. R. (2018). Effects of a self-management intervention to improve behaviors of a child with fetal alcohol spectrum disorder. *Education and Training in Autism and Developmental Disabilities, 53*(4), 405–414.

Griffith, K. R., Price, J. N., & Penrod, B. (2020). The effects of a self-instruction package and group training on trial-based functional analysis administration. *Behavior Analysis in Practice, 13*(1), 63–80. https://doi.org/10.1007/s40617-019-00388-9

Grob, C. M., Lerman, D. C., Langlinais, C. A., & Villante, N. K. (2019). Assessing and teaching job-related social skills to adults with autism spectrum disorder. *Journal of Applied Behavior Analysis, 52*(1), 150–172. https://doi.org/10.1002/jaba.503

Gronlund, N. (1985). *Stating objectives for classroom instruction*. New York: Macmillan.

Grossi, T., & Heward, W. (1998). Using self-evaluation to improve the work productivity of trainees in community-based restaurant training program. *Education and Training in Mental Retardation and Developmental Disabilities, 33*(3), 248–263.

Groves, E. A., & Austin, J. L. (2017). An evaluation of interdependent and independent group contingencies during the good behavior game. *Journal of Applied Behavior Analysis, 50*(3), 552–566. https://doi.org/10.1002/jaba.393

Groves, E. A., & Austin, J. L. (2019). Does the good behavior game evoke negative peer pressure? Analyses in primary and secondary classrooms. *Journal of Applied Behavior Analysis, 52*(1), 3–16. https://doi.org/10.1002/jaba.513

Grow, L. L., Kelley, M. E., Roane, H. S., & Shillingsburg, M. A. (2008). Utility of extinction-induced response variability for the selection of mands. *Journal of Applied Behavior Analysis, 41*(1), 15–24. https://doi.org/10.1901/jaba.2008.41–15

Guertin, E. L., Vause, T., Jaksic, H., Frijters, J. C., & Feldman, M. (2019). Treating obsessive compulsive behavior and enhancing peer engagement in a preschooler with intellectual disability. *Behavioral Interventions, 34*(1), 19–29. https://doi.org/10.1002/bin.1646

Gunby, K. V., Carr, J. E., & LeBlanc, L. A. (2010). Teaching abduction-prevention skills to children with autism. *Journal of Applied Behavior Analysis, 43*, 107–112.

Guralnick, M. J., Neville, B., Hammond, M. A., & Connor, R. T. (2008). Continuity and change from full-inclusion early childhood programs through the early elementary period. *Journal of Early Intervention, 30*(3), 237–250. https://doi.org/10.1177/1053815108317962

Gureasko-Moore, S., DuPaul, G. J., & White, G. P. (2006). The effects of self-management in general education classrooms on the organizational skills of adolescents with ADHD. *Behavior Modification, 30*, 159–183.

Gushanas, C. M., & Thompson, J. L. (2019). Effect of self-monitoring on personal hygiene among individuals with developmental disabilities attending postsecondary education. *Career Development and Transition for Exceptional Individuals, 42*(4), 203–213.

Guzman, G., Goldberg, T. S., & Swanson, H. L. (2018). A meta-analysis of self-monitoring on reading performance of K–12 students. *School Psychology Quarterly, 33*(1), 160–168. https://doi.org/10.1037/spq0000199

Haas, L. B., Stickney, E. M., & Ysseldyke, J. E. (2016). Using growth norms to set instructional goals for struggling students. *Journal of Applied School Psychology, 32*(1), 82–99. https://doi.org/10.1080/15377903.2015.1121195

Haberman, M. (1995). *Star teachers of children in poverty*. West Lafayette, IN: Kappa Delta Pi.

Hagopian, L. P., Rush, K. S., Richman, D. M., Kurtz, P. F., Contrucci, S. A., & Crosland, K. (2002). The development and application of individualized levels systems for the treatment of severe problem behavior. *Behavior Therapy, 33*(1), 65–86. https://doi.org/10.1016/S0005-7894(02)80006-5

Hall, R. V., & Fox, R. G. (1977). Changing-criterion designs: An applied behavior analysis procedure. In B. C. Etzel, J. M. LeBlanc, & D. M. Baer (eds.), *New developments in behavioral research: Theory, method and application*. Hillsdale, NJ: Lawrence Erlbaum Associates, Inc., Publishers (in honor of Sidney W. Bijou).

Hammerschmidt-Snidarich, S. M., McComas, J. J., & Simonson, G. R. (2019). Individualized goal setting during repeated reading: Improving growth with struggling readers using data based instructional decisions. *Preventing School Failure, 63*(4), 334–344.

Hanley, G., Iwata, B., & Roscoe, E. (2006). Some determinants of change in preference over time. *Journal of Applied Behavior Analysis, 39*, 189–202.

Hanley, G., Piazza, C., Fisher, W., & Eidolons, J. (1997). Stimulus control and resistance to extinction in attention-maintained SIB. *Research in Developmental Disabilities, 18*, 251–260.

Hanley, G., Piazza, C., Keeney, K., Blackeley-Smith, A., & Worsdell, A. (1998). Effects of wrist weights on self-injurious and adaptive behaviors. *Journal of Applied Behavior Analysis, 31*, 307–310.

Hanley, G. P. (2010). Toward effective and preferred programming: A case for the objective measurement of social validity with recipients of behavior-change programs. *Behavior Analysis in Practice*, 3(1), 13–21.

Hanley, G. P., Jin, C. S., Vanselow, N. R., & Hanratty, L. A. (2014). Producing meaningful improvements in problem behavior of children with autism via synthesized analyses and treatments. *Journal of Applied Behavior Analysis*, 47(1), 16–36. https://doi.org/10.1002/jaba.106

Hansen, B. D., Sabey, C. V., Rich, M., Marr, D., Robins, N., & Barnett, S. (2019). Latency-based functional analysis in schools: Correspondence and differences across environments. *Behavioral Interventions*, 34(3), 366–376. https://doi.org/10.1002/bin.1674

Hansen, B. D., & Wills, H. P. (2014). The effects of goal setting, contingent reward, and instruction on writing skills. *Journal of Applied Behavior Analysis*, 47(1), 171–175. https://doi.org/10.1002/jaba.92

Haq, S. S., & Aranki, J. (2019). Comparison of traditional and embedded DTT on problem behavior and responding to instructional targets. *Behavior Analysis in Practice*, 12(2), 396–400. https://doi.org/10.1007/s40617-018-00324-3

Haring, N. G., & Liberty, K. A. (1990). Matching strategies with performance in facilitating generalization. *Focus on Exceptional Children*, 22(8), 1–16.

Harjusola-Webb, S. M., & Robbins, S. H. (2012). The effects of teacher-implemented naturalistic intervention on the communication of preschoolers with autism. *Topics in Early Childhood Special Education*, 32(2), 99–110. https://doi.org/10.1177/0271121410397060

Harmon, S., Street, M., Bateman, D., & Yell, M. L. (2020). Developing present levels of academic achievement and functional performance statements for IEPs. *TEACHING Exceptional Children*, 52(5), 320–332.

Harn, B., Basaraba, D., Chard, D., & Fritz, R. (2015). The impact of schoolwide prevention efforts: Lessons learned from implementing independent academic and behavior support systems. *Learning Disabilities: A Contemporary Journal*, 13(1), 3–20.

Harris, F. R., Johnston, M. K., Kelley, C. S., & Wolf, M. M. (1964). Effects of social reinforcement on repressed crawling of a nursery school child. *Journal of Educational Psychology*, 55, 34–41.

Harris, G. M., Little, S. G., & Akin-Little, A. (2017). Video self-modelling as an intervention for remediating dysgraphia in children with autism spectrum disorders. *Australian Journal of Learning Difficulties*, 22(2), 153–170.

Harris, J. (1996). Physical restraint procedures for managing challenging behaviours presented by mentally retarded adults and children. *Research in Developmental Disabilities*, 17(2), 99–134.

Hartmann, D. P., & Hall, R. V. (1976). The changing criterion design. *Journal of Applied Behavior Analysis*, 9, 527–532.

Hay, D., Murray, P., Cecire, S., & Nash, A. (1985). Social learning and social behavior in early life. *Child Development*, 56, 43–57.

Hay, L., Nelson, R., & Hay, W. (1977). Some methodological problems in the use of teachers as observers. *Journal of Applied Behavior Analysis*, 10, 345–348.

Hay, L., Nelson, R., & Hay, W. (1980). Methodological problems in the use of participant observers. *Journal of Applied Behavior Analysis*, 13, 501–504.

Hayes, S. C., Rosenfarb, I., Wulfert, E., Munt, E. D., Korn, Z., & Zettle, R. D. (1985). Self-reinforcement effects: An artifact of social standard setting? *Journal of Applied Behavior Analysis*, 18, 201–214.

Hayes v. Unified School District No. 377, 877 F. 2d 809 (10th Cir. 1989).

Heal, N. A., & Hanley, G. P. (2011). Embedded prompting may function as embedded punishment: Detection of unexpected behavioral processes within a typical preschool teaching strategy. *Journal of Applied Behavior Analysis*, 44(1), 127–131. https://doi.org/10.1901/jaba.2011.44-127

Healy, O., Lydon, S., Brady, T., Rispoli, M., Holloway, J., Neely, L., et al. (2019). The use of differential reinforcement of other behaviours to establish inhibitory stimulus control for the management of vocal stereotypy in children with autism. *Developmental Neurorehabilitation*, 22(3), 192–202. https://doi.org/10.1080/17518423.2018.1523246

Hedges, L. V., Pustejovsky, J. E., & Shadish, W. R. (2012). A standardized mean difference effect size for single case designs. *Research Synthesis Methods*, 3(3), 224–239. https://doi.org/10.1002/jrsm.1052

Hedquist, C. B., & Roscoe, E. M. (2020). A comparison of differential reinforcement procedures for treating automatically reinforced behavior. *Journal of Applied Behavior Analysis*, 53(1), 284–295. https://doi.org/10.1002/jaba.561

Heffernan, L., & Lyons, D. (2016). Differential reinforcement of other behaviour for the reduction of severe nail biting. *Behavior Analysis in Practice*, 9(3), 253–256. https://doi.org/10.1007/s40617-016-0106-3

Heldt, J., & Schlinger, H. D., Jr. (2012). Increased variability in tacting under a Lag 3 schedule of reinforcement. *Analysis of Verbal Behavior*, 28, 131–136. https://doi.org/10.1007/BF03393114

Herman, C., Healy, O., & Lydon, S. (2018). An interview-informed synthesized contingency analysis to inform the treatment of challenging behavior in a young child with autism. *Developmental Neurorehabilitation*, 21(3), 202–207. https://doi.org/10.1080/17518423.2018.1437839

Herrnstein, B. J., & Loveland, D. H. (1964). Complex visual concept in the pigeon. *Science*, 146, 549–550.

Herscovitch, B., Roscoe, E. M., Libby, M. E., Bourret, J. C., & Ahearn, W. H. (2009). A procedure for identifying precursors to problem behavior. *Journal of Applied Behavior Analysis*, 42(3), 697–702. https://doi.org/10.1901/jaba.2009.42-697

Heward, W. L. (2003). Ten faulty notions about teaching and learning that hinder the effectiveness of special education. *The Journal of Special Education*, 36, 186–205.

Heyvaert, M., Saenen, L., Maes, B., & Onghena, P. (2015). Systematic review of restraint interventions for challenging behaviour among persons with intellectual disabilities: Focus on experiences. *Journal of Applied Research in Intellectual Disabilities*, 28(2), 61–80. https://doi.org/10.1111/jar.12095

Higa, W. R., Tharpe, R. G., & Calkins, R. P. (1978). Developmental verbal control of behavior: Implications for self-instructional training. *Journal of Experimental Child Psychology*, 26, 489–497.

Higbee, T., Carr, J., & Harrison, C. (1999). The effects of pictorial versus tangible stimuli in stimulus-preference assessments. *Research in Developmental Disabilities*, 20, 63–72.

Hill, W. F. (1963). *Learning: A survey of psychological interpretations*. San Francisco: Chandler.

Hill, W. F. (1970). *Psychology: Principles and problems*. Philadelphia: Lippincott.

Hine, J. F., Ardoin, S. P., & Foster, T. E. (2015). Decreasing transition times in elementary school classrooms: Using computer-assisted instruction to automate intervention components. *Journal of Applied Behavior Analysis*, 48(3), 495–510. https://doi.org/10.1002/jaba.233

Hirst, E. S. J., Lockenour, F. M., & Allen, J. L. (2019). Decreasing toe walking with differential reinforcement of other behavior, verbal rules, and feedback. *Education & Treatment of Children*, 42(2), 185–199. https://doi.org/10.1353/etc.2019.0009

Hodges, A. C., Wilder, D. A., & Ertel, H. (2018). The use of a multiple schedule to decrease toe walking in a child with autism. *Behavioral Interventions*, 33(4), 440–447. https://doi.org/10.1002/bin.1528

Hogan, A., Knez, N., & Kahng, S. (2015). Evaluating the use of behavioral skills training to improve school staffs' implementation of behavior intervention plans. *Journal* of *Behavioral Education*, 24(2), 242–254. https://doi.org/10.1007/s10864-014-9213-9

Holden, C. (1973). Psychosurgery: Legitimate therapy or laundered lobotomy? *Science*, 173, 1104–1112.

Holifield, C., Goodman, J., Hazelkorn, M., & Heflin, L. J. (2010). Using self-monitoring to increase attending to task and academic accuracy in children with autism. *Focus on Autism and Other Developmental Disabilities*, 25(4), 230–238. https://doi.org/10.1177/1088357610380137

Holland, J. G., & Skinner, B. F. (1961). *The analysis of behavior*. New York: McGraw-Hill.

Holmes, G., Cautela, J., Simpson, M., Motes, P., & Gold, J. (1998). Factor structure of the school reinforcement survey schedule: School is more than grades. *Journal of Behavioral Education*, 8, 131–140.

Holyfield, C. (2019). Preliminary investigation of the effects of a prelinguistic AAC intervention on social gaze behaviors from school-age children with multiple disabilities. *AAC: Augmentative and Alternative Communication*, 35(4), 285–298. https://doi.org/10.1080/07434618.2019.1704866

Homlitas, C., Rosales, R., & Candel, L. (2014). A further evaluation of behavioral skills training for implementation of the picture exchange communication system. *Journal of Applied Behavior Analysis*, 47(1), 198–203. https://doi.org/10.1002/jaba.99

Homme, L., Csanyi, A., Gonzales, M., & Rechs, J. (1970). *How to use contingency contracting in the classroom*. Champaign, IL: Research Press.

Honig v. Doe, 56 S. Ct. 27 1988.

Hood, S. A., Luczynski, K. C., & Mitteer, D. R. (2017). Toward meaningful outcomes in teaching conversation and greeting skills with individuals with autism spectrum disorder. *Journal of Applied Behavior Analysis*, 50(3), 459–486. https://doi.org/10.1002/jaba.388

Hood, S. A., Rodriguez, N. M., Luczynski, K. C., & Fisher, W. W. (2019). Evaluating the effects of physical reactions on aggression via concurrent-operant analyses. *Journal of Applied Behavior Analysis*, 52(3), 642–651. https://doi.org/10.1002/jaba.555

Horcones, C. L. (1992). Natural reinforcements: A way to improve education. *Journal of Applied Behavior Analysis*, 25, 71–75.

Horner, R., & Day, H. (1991). The effects or response efficiency on functionally equivalent competing behaviors. *Journal of Applied Behavior Analysis*, 24, 719–732.

Horner, R., Sprague, J., O'Brien, M., & Heathfield, L. (1990). The role of response efficiency in the reduction of problem behaviors through functional equivalence training: A case study. *Journal of the Association for Persons with Severe Handicaps*, 15, 91–97.

Horner, R., Sugai, G., & Anderson, C. (2010). Examining the evidence base for school-wide positive behavior support. *Focus on Exceptional Children*, 42, 1–14.

Horner, R. D., & Baer, D. M. (1978). Multiple-probe technique: A variation on the multiple baseline. *Journal of Applied Behavior Analysis*, 11, 189–196.

Horner, R. H., & Budd, C. M. (1985). Acquisition of manual sign use: Collateral reduction of maladaptive behavior, and factors limiting generalization. *Education and Training of the Mentally Retarded*, 20, 39–47.

Horner, R. H., Eberhard, J. M., & Sheehan, M. R. (1986). Teaching generalized table bussing: The importance of negative teaching examples. *Behavior Modification*, 10, 457–471.

Horner, R. H., Jones, D., & Williams, J. A. (1985). A functional approach to teaching generalized street crossing. *Journal of the Association for Persons with Severe Handicaps*, 13, 71–78.

Horner, R. H., Williams, J. A., & Steveley, J. D. (1987). Acquisition of generalized telephone use by students with moderate and severe mental retardation. *Research in Developmental Disabilities*, 8(2), 229–247.

Horrocks, E., & Higbee, T. (2008). An evaluation of a stimulus preference assessment of auditory stimuli for adolescents with developmental disabilities. *Research in Developmental Disabilities*, 29, 11–20.

Hudson, M. E. (2019). Using iPad-delivered instruction and self-monitoring to improve the early literacy skills of middle school nonreaders with developmental disabilities. *International Journal of Special Education*, 34(1), 182–196.

Hudson, M. E., Browder, D. M., & Jimenez, B. A. (2014). Effects of a peer-delivered system of least prompts intervention and adapted science read-alouds on listening comprehension for participants with moderate intellectual disability. *Education and Training in Autism and Developmental Disabilities*, 49(1), 60–77.

Hudson, T. M., Hinkson-Lee, K., & Collins, B. (2013). Teaching paragraph composition to students with emotional/behavioral disorders using the simultaneous prompting procedure. *Journal of Behavioral Education*, 22(2), 139–156. https://doi.org/10.1007/s10864-012-9167-8

Hughes, C., Rung, L. L., Wehmeyer, M. L., Agran, M., Copeland, S. R., & Hwang, B. (2000). Self-prompted communication book use to increase social interaction among high school students. *Journal of the Association for Persons with Severe Handicaps*, 25, 153–166.

Hughes, E. M. (2019). Point of view video modeling to teach simplifying fractions to middle school students with mathematical learning disabilities. *Learning Disabilities: A Contemporary Journal*, 17(1), 41–58.

Hughes, M. A., Alberto, P., & Fredrick, L. (2006). Self-operated auditory prompting systems as a function-based intervention in public community settings. *Journal of Positive Behavior Interventions*, 8, 230–243.

Huguenin, N. (1993). Reducing chronic noncompliance in an individual with severe mental retardation to facilitate community integration. *Mental Retardation*, 31, 332–339.

Huguenin, N., & Mulick, J. (1981). Nonexclusionary timeout: Maintenance of appropriate behavior across settings. *Applied Research in Mental Retardation*, 2, 55–67.

Hundert, J., Rowe, S., & Harrison, E. (2014). The combined effects of social script training and peer buddies on generalized peer interaction of children with ASD in inclusive classrooms. *Focus on Autism and Other Developmental Disabilities*, 29(4), 206–215. https://doi.org/10.1177/1088357614522288

Hunter, M. (1984). Knowing, teaching, and supervising. In P. Hosford (ed.), *Using what we know about teaching*. Alexandria, VA: Association for Supervision and Curriculum Development.

Hunter, W. C., Barton-Arwood, S., Jasper, A., Murley, R., & Clements, T. (2017). Utilizing the PPET mnemonic to guide classroom-level PBIS for students with or at risk for EBD across classroom settings. *Beyond Behavior*, 26(2), 81–88.

Hyatt, K. J., & Filler, J. W. (2016). Developing IEPs: The complete guide to educationally meaningful individualized educational programs for students with disabilities.

Iannaccone, J. A., Hagopian, L. P., Javed, N., Borrero, J. C., & Zarcone, J. R. (2020). Rules and statements of reinforcer loss in differential reinforcement of other behavior. *Behavior Analysis in Practice*, 13(1), 81–89. https://doi.org/10.1007/s40617-019-00352-7

Inglesfield, E., & Crisp, A. (1985). Teaching dressing skills to the severely mentally handicapped: A comparison of intensive and non-intensive strategies. *British Journal of Mental Subnormality*, 31, 46–53.

Ingvarsson, E. T., & Le, D. D. (2011). Further evaluation of prompting tactics for establishing intraverbal responding in children with autism. *Analysis of Verbal Behavior*, 27, 75–93. https://doi.org/10.1007/BF03393093

Iovannone, R., Anderson, C., & Scott, T. (2017). Understanding setting events: What they are and how to identify them. *Beyond Behavior, 26*(3), 105–112. https://doi.org/10.1177/1074295617729795

Irvin, D. S., Thompson, T. J., Turner, W. D., & Williams, D. E. (1998). Utilizing increased response effort to reduce chronic hand mouthing. *Journal of Applied Behavior Analysis, 31,* 375–385.

Ivy, J. W., Meindl, J. N., Overley, E., & Robson, K. M. (2017). Token economy: A systematic review of procedural descriptions. *Behavior Modification, 41*(5), 708–737. https://doi.org/10.1177/0145445517699559

Ivy, J. W., Neef, N. A., Meindl, J. N., & Miller, N. (2016). A preliminary examination of motivating operation and reinforcer class interaction. *Behavioral Interventions, 31*(2), 180–194. https://doi.org/10.1002/bin.1436

Ivy, J. W., Payne, J., & Neef, N. A. (2019). Increasing across-session variability of leisure activity selection for children with autism. *Behavior Analysis: Research and Practice, 19*(3), 261–272. https://doi.org/10.1037/bar0000132

Ivy, S. E., Hatton, D. D., & Wehby, J. H. (2018). Using graduated guidance to teach spoon use to children with severe multiple disabilities including visual impairment. *Research and Practice for Persons with Severe Disabilities, 43*(4), 252–268.

Iwata, B., & Bailey, J. S. (1974). Reward versus cost token systems: An analysis of the effects on students and teacher. *Journal of Applied Behavior Analysis, 7,* 567–576.

Iwata, B., & DeLeon, I. (1996). *The Functional Analysis Screening Tool.* Gainesville, FL: University of Florida, Florida Center on Self-Injury.

Iwata, B. A., Dorsey, M. F., Slifer, K. J., Bauman, K. E., & Richman, G. S. (1982). Toward a functional analysis of self-injury. *Analysis & Intervention in Developmental Disabilities, 2*(1), 3–20. https://doi.org/10.1016/0270-4684(82)90003-9

Iwata, B. A., Dorsey, M. F., Slifer, K. J., Bauman, K. E., & Richman, G. S. (1994). Toward a functional analysis of self-injury. *Journal of Applied Behavior Analysis, 27*(2), 197–209. https://doi.org/10.1901/jaba.1994.27-197

Iwata, B., Pace, G., Dorsey, M., Zarcone, J., Vollmer, T., Smith, R., et al. (1994). The functions of self-injurious behavior: An experimental epidemiological analysis. *Journal of Applied Behavior Analysis, 27,* 215–240.

Iwata, B., Pace, G., Kalsher, M., Cowdery, G., & Cataldo, M. (1990). Experimental analysis and extinction of self-injurious escape behavior. *Journal of Applied Behavior Analysis, 23,* 11–27.

Jacob, S., Decker, D. M., & Lugg, E. T. (2016). *Ethics and law for school psychologists.* Hoboken, NJ: John Wiley & Sons.

Jenkins, J. R., Schiller, E., Blackorby, J., Thayer, S. K., & Tilly, W. D. (2013). Responsiveness to intervention in reading: Architecture and practices. *Learning Disability Quarterly, 36*(1), 36–46. https://doi.org/10.1177/0731948712464963

Jeong, Y., & Copeland, S. R. (2020). Comparing functional behavior assessment-based interventions and non-functional behavior assessment-based interventions: A systematic review of outcomes and methodological quality of studies. *Journal of Behavioral Education, 29*(1), 1–41. https://doi.org/10.1007/s10864-019-09355-4

Jerome, J., Frantino, E. P., & Sturmey, P. (2007). The effects of errorless learning and backward chaining on the acquisition of Internet skills in adults with developmental disabilities. *Journal of Applied Behavior Analysis, 40,* 185–189.

Jessel, J., Hausman, N. L., Schmidt, J. D., Darnell, L. C., & Kahng, S. (2014). The development of false-positive outcomes during functional analyses of problem behavior. *Behavioral Interventions, 29*(1), 50–61. https://doi.org/10.1002/bin.1375

Jessel, J., & Ingvarsson, E. T. (2016). Recent advances in applied research on DRO procedures. *Journal of Applied Behavior Analysis, 49*(4), 991–995. https://doi.org/10.1002/jaba.323

Jessel, J., Ingvarsson, E. T., Metras, R., Kirk, H., & Whipple, R. (2018). Achieving socially significant reductions in problem behavior following the interview-informed synthesized contingency analysis: A summary of 25 outpatient applications. *Journal of Applied Behavior Analysis, 51*(1), 130–157. https://doi.org/10.1002/jaba.436

Jessel, J., Ingvarsson, E. T., Whipple, R., & Kirk, H. (2017). Increasing on-task behavior of an adolescent with autism using momentary differential reinforcement. *Behavioral Interventions, 32*(3), 248–254. https://doi.org/10.1002/bin.1480

Jimenez, B. A., Lo, Y., & Saunders, A. F. (2014). The additive effects of scripted lessons plus guided notes on science quiz scores of students with intellectual disability and autism. *The Journal of Special Education, 47*(4), 231–244. https://doi.org/10.1177/0022466912437937

Jones, J., Lerman, D. C., & Lechago, S. (2014). Assessing stimulus control and promoting generalization via video modeling when teaching social responses to children with autism. *Journal of Applied Behavior Analysis, 47*(1), 37–50. https://doi.org/10.1002/jaba.81

Jones, M. C. (1924). A laboratory study of fear: The case of Peter. *The Pedagogical Seminary and Journal of Genetic Psychology, 31,* 308–315.

Joseph, L. M., & Eveleigh, E. L. (2011). A Review of the effects of self-monitoring on reading performance of students with disabilities. *Journal of Special Education, 45,* 143–153.

Journal of Applied Behavior Analysis. (1977). 10, Society for the Experimental Analysis of Behavior.

Journal of Applied Behavior Analysis. (2000). 33, Society for the Experimental Analysis of Behavior.

Journal of Applied Behavior Analysis. (2000). 33(3), 399.

Journal of Applied Behavior Analysis. (2004). 37, 469–480.

Journal of Applied Behavior Analysis. (2006). 39, Society for the Experimental Analysis of Behavior.

Journal of Teacher Education. (1986). 37. Thousand Oaks, CA: Sage.

Jowett Hirst, E. S., Dozier, C. L., & Payne, S. W. (2016). Efficacy of and preference for reinforcement and response cost in token economies. *Journal of Applied Behavior Analysis, 49*(2), 329–345. https://doi.org/10.1002/jaba.294

Jung, S., & Sainato, D. M. (2015). Teaching games to young children with autism spectrum disorder using special interests and video modelling. *Journal of Intellectual and Developmental Disability, 40*(2), 198–212. https://doi.org/10.3109/13668250.2015.1027674

Kahng, S. W., & Iwata, B. (1998). Computerized systems for collecting real-time observational data. *Journal of Applied Behavior Analysis, 31*(2), 253–261.

Kahng, S. W., Iwata, B., Fischer, S., Page, T., Treadwell, K., Williams, D., et al. (1998). Temporal distributions of problem behavior based on scatter plot analysis. *Journal of Applied Behavior Analysis, 31,* 593–604.

Kamps, D., Heitzman-Powell, L., Rosenberg, N., Mason, R., Schwartz, I., & Romine, R. S. (2016). Effects of reading mastery as a small group intervention for young children with ASD. *Journal of Developmental and Physical Disabilities, 28*(5), 703–722. https://doi.org/10.1007/s10882-016-9503-3

Kamps, D., Wendland, M., & Culpepper, M. (2006). Active teacher participation in functional behavior assessment for students with emotional and behavioral disorders risks in general education classrooms. *Behavioral Disorders, 31*(2), 128–146. https://doi.org/10.1177/019874290603100203

Karsten, A. M., Carr, J. E., & Lepper, T. L. (2011). Description of a practitioner model for identifying preferred stimuli with individuals with autism spectrum disorders. *Behavior Modification, 35*(4), 347–369. https://doi.org/10.1177/0145445511405184

Kartal, M. S., & Ozkan, S. Y. (2015). Effects of class-wide self-monitoring on on-task behaviors of preschoolers with developmental disabilities. *Education and Training in Autism and Developmental Disabilities, 50*(4), 418–432.

Kauchak, D. P., & Eggen, P. D. (1998). *Learning and teaching.* Boston: Allyn & Bacon.

Kauffman, J. M., Travers, J. C., & Badar, J. (2020). Why some students with severe disabilities are not placed in general education. *Research and Practice for Persons with Severe Disabilities, 45*(1), 28–33.

Kaufman, A., & Kaufman, N. (2007). *Kaufman Assessment Battery for Children, second edition (KABC-II)*. Upper Saddle River, NJ: Pearson Education.

Kautz, M. E., DeBar, R. M., Vladescu, J. C., & Graff, R. B. (2018). A further evaluation of choice of task sequence. *The Journal of Special Education, 52*(1), 16–28. https://doi.org/10.1177/0022466917735655

Kayser, J. E., Billingsley, F. F., & Neel, R. S. (1986). A comparison of in context and traditional instructional approaches: Total task single trial vs. backward chaining multiple trial. *Journal of the Association for Persons with Severe Handicaps, 11*, 28–38.

Kazbour, R. R., & Bailey, J. S. (2010). An analysis of a contingency program on designated drivers at a college bar. *Journal of Applied Behavior Analysis, 43*, 273–277.

Kazdin, A. E. (1976). Statistical analyses for single-case experimental designs. In M. Hersen & D. Barlow (eds.), *Single-case experimental designs: Strategies for studying behavior change* (pp. 265–316). New York: Pergamon Press.

Kazdin, A. E. (1977a). Artifact, bias, and complexity of assessment: The ABCs of reliability. *Journal of Applied Behavior Analysis, 10*, 141–150.

Kazdin, A. E. (1977b). Assessing the clinical or applied importance of behavior change through social validation. *Behavior Modification, 1*, 427–451.

Kazdin, A. E. (1977c). *The token economy: A review and evaluation*. New York: Plenum Press.

Kazdin, A. E. (1982). *Single-case research designs*. New York: Oxford University Press.

Kazdin, A. E. (2000). *Behavior modification in applied settings*. Belmont, CA: Wadsworth.

Kazdin, A. E. (2001). *Behavior modification in applied settings* (6th ed.). Belmont, CA: Wadsworth.

Kazdin, A. E. (2011). *Single-case research designs* (2nd ed.). New York: Oxford.

Kazdin, A. E., & Bootzin, R. R. (1972). The token economy: An evaluative review. *Journal of Applied Behavior Analysis, 5*, 343–372.

Kazdin, A. E., & Polster, R. (1973). Intermittent token reinforcement and response maintenance in extinction. *Behavior Therapy, 4*, 386–391.

Keeling, K., Myles, B., Gagnon, E., & Simpson, R. (2003). Using the power card strategy to teach sportsmanship skills to a child with autism. *Focus on Autism and Other Developmental Disabilities, 18*, 105–111.

Kellems, R. O., & Edwards, S. (2016). Using video modeling and video prompting to teach core academic content to students with learning disabilities. *Preventing School Failure, 60*(3), 207–214.

Kelley, K. R., Test, D. W., & Cooke, N. L. (2013). Effects of picture prompts delivered by a video iPod on pedestrian navigation. *Exceptional Children, 79*(4), 459–474.

Kelley, M. E., Shillingsburg, M. A., & Bowen, C. N. (2016). Stability of daily preference across multiple individuals. *Journal of Applied Behavior Analysis, 49*(2), 394–398. https://doi.org/10.1002/jaba.288

Kennedy, C. (2005). *Single-case designs for educational research*. Boston: Allyn & Bacon.

Kennedy, C. H. (2002). The maintenance of behavior change as an indicator of social validity. *Behavior Modification, 26*(5), 594–604. https://doi.org/10.1177/014544502236652

Kern, L., Dunlap, G., Clarke, S., & Childs, K. (1994). Student-assisted functional assessment interview. *Diagnostique, 19*, 29–39.

Kern, L., Koegel, R., & Dunlap, G. (1984). The influence of vigorous versus mild exercise on autistic stereotyped behaviors. *Journal of Autism and Developmental Disorders, 14*, 57–67.

Kerth, D. M., Progar, P. R., & Morales, S. (2009). The effects of non-contingent self-restraint on self-injury. *Journal of Applied Research in Intellectual Disabilities, 22*(2), 187–193. https://doi.org/10.1111/j.1468-3148.2008.00487.x

Kettering, T. L., Fisher, W. W., Kelley, M. E., & LaRue, R. H. (2018). Sound attenuation and preferred music in the treatment of problem behavior maintained by escape from noise. *Journal of Applied Behavior Analysis, 51*(3), 687–693. https://doi.org/10.1002/jaba.475

Kettering, T. L., Neef, N. A., Kelley, M. E., & Heward, W. L. (2018). A comparison of procedures for unpairing conditioned reflexive motivating operations. *Journal of the Experimental Analysis of Behavior, 109*(2), 422–432. https://doi.org/10.1002/jeab.321

Kimball, J. W., Kinney, E. M., Taylor, B. A., & Stromer, R. (2003). Lights, camera, action: Using engaging computer-cued activity schedules. *Teaching Exceptional Children, 36*, 40–45.

Kincaid, M., & Weisberg, P. (1978). Alphabet letters as tokens: Training preschool children in letter recognition and labeling during a token exchange period. *Journal of Applied Behavior Analysis, 11*, 199.

King, A., Gravina, N., & Sleiman, A. (2018). Observing the observer. *Journal of Organizational Behavior Management, 38*(4), 306–323. https://doi.org/10.1080/01608061.2018.1514346

King, B., Radley, K. C., Jenson, W. R., Clark, E., & O'Neill, R. E. (2014). Utilization of video modeling combined with self-monitoring to increase rates of on-task behavior. *Behavioral Interventions, 29*(2), 125–144. https://doi.org/10.1002/bin.1379

King-Sears, M. E. (1999). Teacher and researcher co-design self-management content for an inclusive setting: Research training, intervention, and generalization effects on student performance. *Education and Training in Mental Retardation and Developmental Disabilities, 34*, 134–156.

King-Sears, M. E. (2008). Using teacher and researcher data to evaluate the effects of self-management in an inclusive classroom. *Preventing School Failure, 52*(4), 25–36.

Kirby, K. C., & Bickel, W. K. (1988). Toward an explicit analysis of generalization: A stimulus control interpretation. *The Behavior Analyst, 11*, 115–129.

Kirkpatrick, M., Akers, J., & Rivera, G. (2019). Use of behavioral skills training with teachers: A systematic review. *Journal of Behavioral Education, 28*(3), 344–361. https://doi.org/10.1007/s10864-019-09322-z

Kitchener, R. F. (1980). Ethical relativism and behavior therapy. *Journal of Consulting and Clinical Psychology, 48*, 1–7.

Kleeberger, V., & Mirenda, P. (2010). Teaching generalized imitation skills to a preschooler with autism using video modeling. *Journal of Positive Behavior Interventions, 12*(2), 116–127.

Knight, V. F., Kuntz, E. M., & Brown, M. (2018). Paraprofessional-delivered video prompting to teach academics to students with severe disabilities in inclusive settings. *Journal of Autism and Developmental Disorders, 48*(6), 2203–2216. https://doi.org/10.1007/s10803-018-3476-2

Kodak, T., Bergmann, S., LeBlanc, B., Harman, M. J., & Ayazi, M. (2018). Examination of the effects of auditory and textual stimuli on response accuracy and latency during a math task and tangram puzzle. *Analysis of Verbal Behavior, 34*(1–2), 24–43. https://doi.org/10.1007/s40616-018-0098-x

Kodak, T., Fisher, W. W., Paden, A., & Dickes, N. (2013). Evaluation of the utility of a discrete-trial functional analysis in early intervention classrooms. *Journal of Applied Behavior Analysis, 46*(1), 301–306. https://doi.org/10.1002/jaba.2

Koegel, L. K., Park, M. N., & Koegel, R. L. (2014). Using self-management to improve the reciprocal social conversation of children with autism spectrum disorder. *Journal of Autism and Developmental Disorders, 44*(5), 1055–1063. https://doi.org/10.1007/s10803-013-1956-y

Koegel, R. L., & Koegel, L. K. (1984). *Programming rapid generalization of speech gains through self-monitoring procedures.*

Koegel, R. L., & Rincover, A. (1974). Treatment of psychotic children in a classroom environment: I. Learning in a large group. *Journal of Applied Behavior Analysis, 7,* 45–59.

Koehler-Platten, K., Grow, L. L., Schulze, K. A., & Bertone, T. (2013). Using a lag reinforcement schedule to increase phonemic variability in children with autism spectrum disorders. *Analysis of Verbal Behavior, 29,* 71–83. https://doi.org/10.1007/BF03393125

Kohlberg, L., Yaeger, J., & Hjertholm, E. (1968). Private speech: Four studies and a review of theories. *Child Development, 39,* 691–736.

Kohler, F., Strain, P., Hoyson, M., Davis, L., Donina, W., & Rapp, N. (1995). Using a group-oriented contingency to increase social interactions between children with autism and their peers. *Behavior Modification, 19*(1), 10–32.

Kohn, A. (1993). *Punished by rewards.* Boston: Houghton Mifflin.

Kohn, A. (2001). Five reasons to stop saying "Good Job." *Young Children, 56,* 24–28.

Kohn, A. (2006). *Beyond discipline: From compliance to community.* Alexandria, VA: Association for Supervision and Curriculum Development.

Kohn, A. (2018). *Punished by rewards: The trouble with gold stars, incentive plans, A's, praise, and other bribes, 25th ed.* Houghton Mifflin Harcourt.

Kolbenschlag, C. M., & Wunderlich, K. L. (2019). The effects of self-monitoring on on-task behaviors in individuals with autism spectrum disorders. *Journal of Behavioral Education.* https://doi.org/10.1007/s10864-019-09352-7

Konrad, M., Keesey, S., Ressa, V. A., Alexeeff, M., Chan, P. E., & Peters, M. T. (2014). Setting clear learning targets to guide instruction for all students. *Intervention in School and Clinic, 50*(2), 76–85.

Konrad, M., Trela, K., & Test, D. (2006). Using IEP goals and objectives to teach paragraph writing to high school students with physical and cognitive disabilities. *Education and Training in Developmental Disabilities, 41,* 111–124.

Kostewicz, D. E. (2010). A review of timeout ribbons. *The Behavior Analyst Today, 11*(2), 95–104. https://doi.org/10.1037/h0100693

Kostewicz, D. E., King, S. A., Datchuk, S. M., Brennan, K. M., & Casey, S. D. (2016). Data collection and measurement assessment in behavioral research: 1958–2013. *Behavior Analysis: Research and Practice, 16*(1), 19–33. https://doi.org/10.1037/bar0000031

Kostewicz, D. E., Kubina, R. M., Jr., & Brennan, K. M. (2020). Improving spelling for at-risk kindergartners through element skill frequency building. *Behavioral Interventions, 35*(1), 131–144. https://doi.org/10.1002/bin.1701

Kourassanis, J., Jones, E. A., & Fienup, D. M. (2015). Peer-video modeling: Teaching chained social game behaviors to children with ASD. *Journal of Developmental and Physical Disabilities, 27*(1), 25–36. https://doi.org/10.1007/s10882-014-9399-8

Kourea, L., Gibson, L., & Werunga, R. (2018). Culturally responsive reading instruction for students with learning disabilities. *Intervention in School and Clinic, 53*(3), 153–162.

Kourea, L., Konrad, M., & Kazolia, T. (2019). Effects of a guided-notes intervention program on the quiz and note-taking Greek history performance of high school students with learning difficulties in Cyprus. *Education & Treatment of Children, 42*(1), 47–71. https://doi.org/10.1353/etc.2019.0003

Kowalewicz, E. A., & Coffee, G. (2014). Mystery Motivator: A Tier 1 classroom behavioral intervention. *School Psychology Quarterly, 29*(2), 138–156. https://doi.org/10.1037/spq0000030.supp (Supplemental)

Kranak, M. P., Alber-Morgan, S. R., & Sawyer, M. R. (2017). A parametric analysis of specific praise rates on the on-task behavior of elementary students with autism. *Education and Training in Autism and Developmental Disabilities, 52*(4), 453–464.

Krantz, P. J., & McClannahan, L. E. (1993). Teaching children with autism to initiate to peers: Effects of a script-fading procedure. *Journal of Applied Behavior Analysis, 26,* 121–132.

Krantz, P. J., & McClannahan, L. E. (1998). Social interaction skills for children with autism: A script-fading procedure for beginning readers. *Journal of Applied Behavior Analysis, 31,* 191–202.

Krasner, L. (1976). Behavioral modification: Ethical issues and future trends. In H. Leitenberg (ed.), *Handbook of behavior modification and behavior therapy* (pp. 627–649). Upper Saddle River, NJ: Prentice-Hall.

Kratochwill, T., Hitchcock, J., Horner, R., Levin, J., Odom, S., Rindskopf, D., et al. (2010). *Single-case designs technical documentation.* Retrieved from What Works Clearinghouse at http://ies.ed.gov/ncee/wwc/pdf/wwc_scd.pdf.

Kratochwill, T. R., Hitchcock, J. H., Horner, R. H., Levin, J. R., Odom, S. L., Rindskopf, D. M., et al. (2013). Single-case intervention research design standards. *Remedial and Special Education, 34*(1), 26–38. https://doi.org/10.1177/0741932512452794

Kressler, B., Chapman, L. A., Kunkel, A., & Hovey, K. A. (2020). Culturally responsive data-based decision making in high school settings. *Intervention in School and Clinic, 55*(4), 214–220.

Krombach, T., & Miltenberger, R. (2020). The effects of stability ball seating on the behavior of children with autism during instructional activities. *Journal of Autism and Developmental Disorders, 50*(2), 551–559. https://doi.org/10.1007/s10803-019-04283-8

Kruger, A. M., Strong, W., Daly, E. J., III, O'Connor, M., Sommerhalder, M. S., Holtz, J., et al. (2016). Setting the stage for academic success through antecedent intervention. *Psychology in the Schools, 53*(1), 24–38. https://doi.org/10.1002/pits.21886

Kuhn, D., DeLeon, I., Fisher, W., & Wilke, A. (1999). Clarifying an ambiguous functional analysis with matched and mismatched extinction procedures. *Journal of Applied Behavior Analysis, 32,* 99–102.

Kuhn, S., Lerman, D., Vorndran, C., & Addison, L. (2006). Analysis of factors that affect responding in a two-response chain in children with developmental disabilities. *Journal of Applied Behavior Analysis, 39,* 263–280.

Kunnavatana, S. S., Bloom, S. E., Samaha, A. L., Slocum, T. A., & Clay, C. J. (2018). Manipulating parameters of reinforcement to reduce problem behavior without extinction. *Journal of Applied Behavior Analysis, 51*(2), 283–302. https://doi.org/10.1002/jaba.443

Lagomarcino, T. R., Hughes, C., & Rusch, F. R. (1989). Utilizing self-management to teach independence on the job. *Education and Training of the Mentally Retarded, 24*(2), 139–148.

Lai, M.-C., Chiang, M.-S., Shih, C.-T., & Shih, C.-H. (2018). Applying a vibration reminder to ameliorate the hyperactive behavior of students with Attention Deficit Hyperactivity Disorder in class. *Journal of Developmental and Physical Disabilities, 30*(6), 835–844. https://doi.org/10.1007/s10882-018-9623-z

Lalli, J., Livezey, K., & Kates, K. (1996). Functional analysis and treatment of eye poking with response blocking. *Journal of Applied Behavior Analysis, 29,* 129–132.

Lalli, J., Zanolli, K., & Wohn, T. (1994). Using extinction to promote response variability in toy play. *Journal of Applied Behavior Analysis, 27,* 735–736.

Lambert, J. M., Bloom, S. E., & Irvin, J. (2012). Trial-based functional analysis and functional communication training in an early childhood setting. *Journal of Applied Behavior Analysis, 45*(3), 579–584. https://doi.org/10.1901/jaba.2012.45-579

Lambert, J. M., Lloyd, B. P., Staubitz, J. L., Weaver, E. S., & Jennings, C. M. (2014). Effect of an automated training presentation on pre-service behavior analysts' implementation of trial-based functional analysis. *Journal of Behavioral Education, 23*(3), 344–367. https://doi.org/10.1007/s10864-014-9197-5

Lambert, J. M., Lopano, S. E., Noel, C. R., & Ritchie, M. N. (2017). Teacher-conducted, latency-based functional analysis as basis for individualized levels system in a classroom setting. *Behavior Analysis in Practice, 10*(4), 422–426. https://doi.org/10.1007/s40617-017-0200-1

Lambert, J. M., Parikh, N., Stankiewicz, K. C., Houchins-Juarez, N. J., Morales, V. A., Sweeney, E. M., et al. (2019). Decreasing food stealing of child with Prader-Willi syndrome through function-based differential reinforcement. *Journal of Autism and Developmental Disorders, 49*(2), 721–728. https://doi.org/10.1007/s10803-018-3747-y

Lambert, N., Nihira, K., & Leland, H. (1993). *AAMR Adaptive Behavior Scales: School edition* (2nd ed.). Austin, TX: Pro-Ed.

Lancioni, G., O'Reilly, M., & Emerson, E. (1996). A review of choice research with people with severe and profound developmental disabilities. *Research in Developmental Disabilities, 17*(5), 391–411.

Lancioni, G. E., & O'Reilly, M. F. (2001). Self-management of instruction cues for occupation: Review of studies with people with severe and profound developmental disabilities. *Research in Developmental Disabilities, 22*, 41–65.

Lancioni, G. E., Singh, N. N., O'Reilly, M. F., Sigafoos, J., Alberti, G., Perilli, V., et al. (2014). Microswitch-aided programs to support physical exercise or adequate ambulation in persons with multiple disabilities. *Research in Developmental Disabilities, 35*(9), 2190–2198. https://doi.org/10.1016/j.ridd.2014.05.015

Lancioni, G. E., Singh, N. N., O'Reilly, M. F., Sigafoos, J., Buonocunto, F., D'Amico, F., et al. (2015). Extending the assessment of technology-aided programs to support leisure and communication in people with acquired brain injury and extensive multiple disabilities. *Perceptual and Motor Skills, 121*(2), 621–634. https://doi.org/10.2466/15.PMS.121c19x1

Lancioni, G. E., Singh, N. N., O'Reilly, M. F., Sigafoos, J., Green, V., Oliva, D., et al. (2011). Microswitch and keyboard-emulator technology to facilitate the writing performance of persons with extensive motor disabilities. *Research in Developmental Disabilities, 32*(2), 576–582. https://doi.org/10.1016/j.ridd.2010.12.017

Lancioni, G. E., Singh, N. N., O'Reilly, M. F., Sigafoos, J., Oliva, D., Smaldone, A., et al. (2010). Promoting ambulation responses among children with multiple disabilities through walkers and microswitches with contingent stimuli. *Research in Developmental Disabilities, 31*(3), 811–816. https://doi.org/10.1016/j.ridd.2010.02.006

Lane, J. D., Gast, D. L., Ledford, J. R., & Shepley, C. (2017). Increasing social behaviors in young children with social-communication delays in a group arrangement in preschool. *Education & Treatment of Children, 40*(2), 115–144. https://doi.org/10.1353/etc.2017.0007

Lane, J. D., Ledford, J. R., Shepley, C., Mataras, T. K., Ayres, K. M., & Davis, A. B. (2016). A brief coaching intervention for teaching naturalistic strategies to parents. *Journal of Early Intervention, 38*(3), 135–150. https://doi.org/10.1177/1053815116663178

Lane, K. L., Oakes, W. P., Menzies, H. M., Oyer, J., & Jenkins, A. (2013). Working within the context of three-tiered models of prevention: Using schoolwide data to identify high school students for targeted supports. *Journal of Applied School Psychology, 29*(2), 203–229. https://doi.org/10.1080/15377903.2013.778773

Lang, R., Machalicek, W., Rispoli, M., O'Reilly, M., Sigafoos, J., Lancioni, G., et al. (2014). Play skills taught via behavioral intervention generalize, maintain, and persist in the absence of socially mediated reinforcement in children with autism. *Research in Autism Spectrum Disorders, 8*(7), 860–872. https://doi.org/10.1016/j.rasd.2014.04.007

Lang, R., van der Werff, M., Verbeek, K., Didden, R., Davenport, K., Moore, M., et al. (2014). Comparison of high and low preferred topographies of contingent attention during discrete trial training. *Research in Autism Spectrum Disorders, 8*(10), 1279–1286. https://doi.org/10.1016/j.rasd.2014.06.012

Langthorne, P., McGill, P., & Oliver, C. (2014). The motivating operation and negatively reinforced problem behavior: A systematic review. *Behavior Modification, 38*(1), 107–159. https://doi.org/10.1177/0145445513509649

Lanovaz, M. J., Turgeon, S., Cardinal, P., & Wheatley, T. L. (2019). Using single-case designs in practical settings: Is within-subject replication always necessary? *Perspectives on Behavior Science, 42*(1), 153–162. https://doi.org/10.1007/s40614-018-0138-9

Laprime, A. P., & Dittrich, G. A. (2014). An evaluation of a treatment package consisting of discrimination training and differential reinforcement with response cost and a social story on vocal stereotypy for a preschooler with autism in a preschool classroom. *Education & Treatment of Children, 37*(3), 407–430. https://doi.org/10.1353/etc.2014.0028

Laraway, S., Snycerski, S., Olson, R., Becker, B., & Poling, A. (2014). The motivating operations concept: Current status and critical response. *The Psychological Record, 64*(3), 601–623. https://doi.org/10.1007/s40732-014-0080-5

LaRue, R. H., Stewart, V., Piazza, C. C., Volkert, V. M., Patel, M. R., & Zeleny, J. (2011). Escape as reinforcement and escape extinction in the treatment of feeding problems. *Journal of Applied Behavior Analysis, 44*(4), 719–735. https://doi.org/10.1901/jaba.2011.44-719

Lassman, K., Jolivette, K., & Wehby, J. (1999). Using collaborative behavioral contracting. *Teaching Exceptional Children, 31*, 12–18.

Lastrapes, R. E., Fritz, J. N., & Casper-Teague, L. (2018). Effects of the teacher versus students game on teacher praise and student behavior. *Journal of Behavioral Education, 27*(4), 419–434. https://doi.org/10.1007/s10864-018-9306-y

Lattal, K., & Neef, N. (1996). Recent reinforcement-schedule research and applied behavior analysis. *Journal of Applied Behavior Analysis, 29*, 213–230.

Lavay, B., Sakai, J., Ortiz, C., & Roth, K. (2015). Tablet technology to monitor physical education IEP goals and benchmarks. *Journal of Physical Education, Recreation & Dance, 86*(6), 16–23.

Layng, T. V. J. (2019). Tutorial: Understanding concepts: Implications for behavior analysts and educators. *Perspectives on Behavior Science, 42*(2), 345–363. https://doi.org/10.1007/s40614-018-00188-6

Leaf, J. A., Leaf, J. B., Milne, C., Townley-Cochran, D., Oppenheim-Leaf, M. L., Cihon, J. H., et al. (2016). The effects of the cool versus not cool procedure to teach social game play to individuals diagnosed with autism spectrum disorder. *Behavior Analysis in Practice, 9*(1), 34–49. https://doi.org/10.1007/s40617-016-0112-5

Leaf, J. B., Cihon, J. H., Alcalay, A., Mitchell, E., Townley, C. D., Miller, K., et al. (2017). Instructive feedback embedded within group instruction for children diagnosed with autism spectrum disorder. *Journal of Applied Behavior Analysis, 50*(2), 304–316. https://doi.org/10.1002/jaba.375

Leaf, J. B., Townley, C. D., Mitchell, E., Milne, C., Alcalay, A., Leaf, J., et al. (2016). Evaluation of multiple-alternative prompts during tact training. *Journal of Applied Behavior Analysis, 49*(2), 399–404. https://doi.org/10.1002/jaba.289

Leatherby, J., Gast, D., Wolery, M., & Collins, B. (1992). Assessment of reinforcer preference in multi-handicapped students. *Journal of Developmental and Physical Disabilities, 4*(1), 15–36.

LeBlanc, L., & Matson, J. (1995). A social skills training program for preschoolers with developmental delays. *Behavior Modification, 19*(2), 234–246.

LeBlanc, L. A., Lund, C., Kooken, C., Lund, J. B., & Fisher, W. W. (2020). Procedures and accuracy of discontinuous measurement of problem behavior in common practice of applied behavior analysis. *Behavior Analysis in Practice, 13*(2), 411–420. https://doi.org/10.1007/s40617-019-00361-6

LeBlanc, L. A., Sump, L. A., Leaf, J. B., & Cihon, J. (2020). The effects of standard and enhanced data sheets and brief video training on implementation of conditional discrimination training. *Behavior Analysis in Practice, 13*(1), 53–62. https://doi.org/10.1007/s40617-019-00338-5

Ledford, J. R., Ayres, K. M., Lane, J. D., & Lam, M. F. (2015). Identifying issues and concerns with the use of interval-based systems in single case research using a pilot simulation study. *The Journal of Special Education, 49*(2), 104–117. https://doi.org/10.1177/0022466915568975

Ledford, J. R., Barton, E. E., Rigor, M. N., Stankiewicz, K. C., Chazin, K. T., Harbin, E. R., et al. (2019). Functional analysis and treatment of pica on a preschool playground. *Behavior Analysis in Practice, 12*(1), 176–181. https://doi.org/10.1007/s40617-018-00283-9

Ledford, J. R., & Gast, D. L. (eds.). (2009). *Single subject research methodology in behavioral sciences: Applications in special education and behavioral sciences*. New York: Routledge.

Lee, C. Y. Q., Anderson, A., & Moore, D. W. (2014). Using video modeling to toilet train a child with autism. *Journal of Developmental and Physical Disabilities, 26*(2), 123–134. https://doi.org/10.1007/s10882-013-9348-y

Lee, D., & Belfiore, P. (1997). Enhancing classroom performance: A review of reinforcement schedules. *Journal of Behavioral Education, 7*(2), 205–217.

Lee, G. T., Chen, J., Xu, S., Feng, H., & Guo, Z. (2018). Effects of self-monitoring intervention on independent completion of a daily living skill for children with autism spectrum disorders in China. *Child & Family Behavior Therapy, 40*(2), 148–165. https://doi.org/10.1080/07317107.2018.1477352

Lee, G. T., & Singer-Dudek, J. (2012). Effects of fluency versus accuracy training on endurance and retention of assembly tasks by four adolescents with developmental disabilities. *Journal of Behavioral Education, 21*(1), 1–17. https://doi.org/10.1007/s10864-011-9142-9

Lee, R., & Sturmey, P. (2014). The effects of script-fading and a lag-1 schedule on varied social responding in children with autism. *Research in Autism Spectrum Disorders, 8*(4), 440–448. https://doi.org/10.1016/j.rasd.2014.01.003

Legge, D. B., DeBar, R. M., & Alber-Morgan, S. R. (2010). The effects of self-monitoring with a MotivAider® on the on-task behavior of fifth and sixth graders with autism and other disabilities. *Journal of Behavior Assessment and Intervention in Children, 1*(1), 43–52. https://doi.org/10.1037/h0100359

LeGray, M. W., Dufrene, B. A., Sterling-Turner, H., Joe Olmi, D., & Bellone, K. (2010). A comparison of function-based differential reinforcement interventions for children engaging in disruptive classroom behavior. *Journal of Behavioral Education, 19*(3), 185–204. https://doi.org/10.1007/s10864-010-9109-2

LeGray, M. W., Dufrene, B. A., Mercer, S., Olmi, D. J., & Sterling, H. (2013). Differential reinforcement of alternative behavior in center-based classrooms: Evaluation of pre-teaching the alternative behavior. *Journal of Behavioral Education, 22*(2), 85–102. https://doi.org/10.1007/s10864-013-9170-8

LeJeune, L. M., Lambert, J. M., Lemons, C. J., Mottern, R. E., & Wisniewski, B. T. (2019). Teacher-conducted trial-based functional analysis and treatment of multiply controlled challenging behavior. *Behavior Analysis: Research and Practice, 19*(3), 241–246. https://doi.org/10.1037/bar0000128

Leko, M. M. (2014). The value of qualitative methods in social validity research. *Remedial and Special Education, 35*(5), 275–286. https://doi.org/10.1177/0741932514524002

Lennox, D., Miltenberger, R., & Donnelly, D. (1987). Response interruption and DRL for the reduction of rapid eating. *Journal of Applied Behavior Analysis, 20*, 279–284.

Lenz, M., Singh, N., & Hewett, A. (1991). Overcorrection as an academic remediation procedure. *Behavior Modification, 15*, 64–73.

Leon, Y., Hausman, N. L., Kahng, S. W., & Becraft, J. L. (2010). Further examination of discriminated functional communication. *Journal of Applied Behavior Analysis, 43*, 525–530.

Lerman, D., & Iwata, B. (1996). Developing a technology for the use of operant extinction in clinical settings: An examination of basic and applied research. *Journal of Applied Behavior Analysis, 29*, 345–382.

Lerman, D., Iwata, B., & Wallace, M. (1999). Side effects of extinction: Prevalence of bursting and aggression during the treatment of self-injurious behavior. *Journal of Applied Behavior Analysis, 32*, 1–8.

Lerman, D., Kelley, M., Van Camp, C., & Roane, H. (1999). Effects of reinforcement magnitude on spontaneous recovery. *Journal of Applied Behavior Analysis, 32*, 197–200.

Lerman, D. C., Iwata, B. A., Shore, B. A., & DeLeon, I. G. (1997). Effects of intermittent punishment on self-injurious behavior: An evaluation of schedule thinning. *Journal of Applied Behavior Analysis, 30*(2), 187–201. https://doi.org/10.1901/jaba.1997.30-187

Lerman, D. C., Tetreault, A., Hovanetz, A., Bellaci, E., Miller, J., Karp, H., et al. (2010). Applying signal-detection theory to the study of observer accuracy and bias in behavioral assessment. *Journal of Applied Behavior Analysis, 43*(2), 195–213. https://doi.org/10.1901/jaba.2010.43-195

Levingston, H. B., Neef, N. A., & Cihon, T. M. (2009). The effects of teaching precurrent behaviors on children's solution of multiplication and division word problems. *Journal of Applied Behavior Analysis, 42*, 361–367.

Lewis, T., Scott, T., & Sugai, G. (1994). The problem behavior questionnaire: A teacher-based instrument to develop functional hypotheses of problem behavior in general education classrooms. *Diagnostique, 19*(2–3), 103–115.

Lewis, T. J., Jones, S. E. L., Horner, R. H., & Sugai, G. (2010). School-wide positive behavior support and students with emotional/behavioral disorders: Implications for prevention, identification and intervention. *Exceptionality, 18*(2), 82–93. https://doi.org/10.1080/09362831003673168

Li, Y.-F., Chen, H., Zhang, D., & Gilson, C. B. (2019). Effects of a self-monitoring strategy to increase classroom task completion for high school students with moderate intellectual disability. *Education and Training in Autism and Developmental Disabilities, 54*(3), 263–273.

Libby, M. E., Weiss, J. S., Bancroft, S., & Ahearn, W. H. (2008). A comparison of most-to-least and least-to-most prompting on the acquisition of solitary play skills. *Behavior Analysis in Practice, 1*(1), 37–43.

Liberman, R. P., Teigen, J., Patterson, R., & Baker, V. (1973). Reducing delusional speech in chronic, paranoid schizophrenics. *Journal of Applied Behavior Analysis, 6*, 57–64.

Lieberman, R. G., Yoder, P. J., Reichow, B., & Wolery, M. (2010). Visual analysis of multiple baseline across participants graphs when change is delayed. *School Psychology Quarterly, 25*(1), 28–44. https://doi.org/10.1037/a0018600

Lim, L., Browder, D., & Sigafoos, J. (1998). The role of response effort and motion study in functionally equivalent task designs and alternatives. *Journal of Behavioral Education, 8*, 81–102.

Lindström, E. R., Gesel, S. A., & Lemons, C. J. (2019). Data-based individualization in reading: Tips for successful implementation. *Intervention in School and Clinic, 55*(2), 113–119.

Lindstrom, J. H. (2019). Dyslexia in the schools: Assessment and identification. *TEACHING Exceptional Children, 51*(3), 189–200.

Lingo, A. S. (2014). Tutoring middle school students with disabilities by high school students: Effects on oral reading fluency. *Education & Treatment of Children, 37*(1), 53–75. https://doi.org/10.1353/etc.2014.0005

Litow, L., & Pumroy, D. K. (1975). A brief review of classroom group-oriented contingencies. *Journal of Applied Behavior Analysis, 8,* 341–347.

Little, S. G., Akin-Little, A., & O'Neill, K. (2015). Group contingency interventions with children—1980–2010: A meta-analysis. *Behavior Modification, 39*(2), 322–341. https://doi.org/10.1177/0145445514554393

Liu, Y., Moore, D. W., & Anderson, A. (2015). Improving social skills in a child with autism spectrum disorder through self-management training. *Behaviour Change, 32*(4), 273–284. https://doi.org/10.1017/bec.2015.14

Livi, J., & Ford, A. (1985). Skill transfer from a domestic training site to the actual homes of three moderately handicapped students. *Education and Training of the Mentally Retarded, 20,* 69–82.

Livingston, C. E., & Graff, R. B. (2018). Further evaluation of the use of preference categories to identify novel reinforcers: A systematic replication. *Behavioral Interventions, 33*(2), 173–184.

Lloyd, B. P., Weaver, E. S., & Staubitz, J. L. (2016). A review of functional analysis methods conducted in public school classroom settings. *Journal of Behavioral Education, 25*(3), 324–356. https://doi.org/10.1007/s10864-015-9243-y

Lloyd, J., Bateman, D., Landrum, T., & Hallahan, D. (1989). Self-recording of attention versus productivity. *Journal of Applied Behavior Analysis, 22,* 315–323.

Lo, Y., Algozzine, B., Algozzine, K., Horner, R., & Sugai, G. (2010). Schoolwide positive behavior support. In *Preventing problem behaviors: Schoolwide programs and classroom practices* (2nd ed., pp. 33–51). Thousand Oaks, CA: Corwin Press.

Looney, K., DeQuinzio, J. A., & Taylor, B. A. (2018). Using self-monitoring and differential reinforcement of low rates of behavior to decrease repetitive behaviors: A case study. *Behavioral Interventions, 33*(3), 251–259. https://doi.org/10.1002/bin.1517

Lopez, A. R., & Wiskow, K. M. (2020). Teaching children with autism to initiate social interactions using textual prompts delivered via Apple Watches®. *Behavior Analysis in Practice, 13*(3), 641–647. https://doi.org/10.1007/s40617-019-00385-y

Lorah, E. R., Karnes, A., & Speight, D. R. (2015). The acquisition of intraverbal responding using a speech generating device in school aged children with autism. *Journal of Developmental and Physical Disabilities, 27*(4), 557–568. https://doi.org/10.1007/s10882-015-9436-2

Losinski, M., Maag, J. W., Katsiyannis, A., & Ryan, J. B. (2015). The use of structural behavioral assessment to develop interventions for secondary students exhibiting challenging behaviors. *Education & Treatment of Children, 38*(2), 149–174. https://doi.org/10.1353/etc.2015.0006

Lovaas, O. I. (1987). Behavioral treatment and normal educational and intellectual functioning in young autistic children. *Journal of Consulting and Clinical Psychology, 55*(1), 3–9. https://doi.org/10.1037/0022-006X.55.1.3

Lovaas, O. I. (2003). *Teaching individuals with developmental delays: Basic intervention techniques.* Austin, TX: PRO-ED.

Lovaas, O. I., Schreibman, L., Koegel, R. L., & Rhen, R. (1971). Selective responding by autistic children to multiple sensory input. *Journal of Abnormal Psychology, 77,* 211–222.

Lovaas, O. I., & Simmons, J. Q. (1969). Manipulation of self-destruction in three retarded children. *Journal of Applied Behavior Analysis, 2,* 143–157.

Lovelace, T. S., Gibson, L., & Tabb, J. (2013). Response to intervention techniques and students with learning disabilities.In J. P. Bakken, F. E. Obiakor, & A. F. Rotatori (Eds.), *Learning Disabilities: Practice Concerns And Students With LD.* Bingley, UK: Emerald Group Publishing Limited.

Lovitt, T. C. (1973). Self-management projects with children with behavioral disabilities. *Journal of Learning Disabilities, 6,* 138–154.

Luce, S. C., Delquadri, J., & Hall, R. V. (1980). Contingent exercise: A mild but powerful procedure for suppressing inappropriate verbal and aggressive behavior. *Journal of Applied Behavior Analysis, 13*(4), 583–594. https://doi.org/10.1901/jaba.1980.13-583

Luczynski, K. C., & Hanley, G. P. (2009). Do children prefer contingencies? An evaluation of the efficacy of and preference for contingent versus noncontingent social reinforcement during play. *Journal of Applied Behavior Analysis, 42*(3), 511–525. https://doi.org/10.1901/jaba.2009.42–511

Luczynski, K. C., & Hanley, G. P. (2013). Prevention of problem behavior by teaching functional communication and self-control skills to preschoolers. *Journal of Applied Behavior Analysis, 46*(2), 355–368. https://doi.org/10.1002/jaba.44

Lugo, A. M., King, M. L., Lamphere, J. C., & McArdle, P. E. (2017). Developing procedures to improve therapist–child rapport in early intervention. *Behavior Analysis in Practice, 10*(4), 395–401. https://doi.org/10.1007/s40617-016-0165-5

Luiselli, J. (1996). Multicomponent intervention for challenging behaviors of a child with pervasive developmental disorder in a public school setting. *Journal of Developmental and Physical Disabilities, 8*(3), 211–219.

Luiselli, J., & Rice, D. (1983). Brief positive practice with a handicapped child: An assessment of suppressive and re-educative effects. *Education and Treatment of Children, 6,* 241–250.

Luiselli, J. K., & Cameron, M. J. (1998). *Antecedent control: Innovative approaches to behavioral support.* Baltimore: Paul H. Brookes.

Luiselli, J. K., & Sobezenski, T. (2017). Escape-motivated bathroom visits: Effects of activity scheduling, cuing, and duration-fading in an adult with intellectual disability. *Clinical Case Studies, 16*(5), 417–426. https://doi.org/10.1177/1534650117718630

Luiselli, J. K., Sperry, J. M., & Draper, C. (2015). Social validity assessment of physical restraint intervention by care providers of adults with intellectual and developmental disabilities. *Behavior Analysis in Practice, 8*(2), 170–175. https://doi.org/10.1007/s40617-015-0082-z

Maas, A. P. H. M., Didden, R., Bouts, L., Smits, M. G., & Curfs, L. M. G. (2009). Scatter plot analysis of excessive daytime sleepiness and severe disruptive behavior in adults with Prader-Willi syndrome: A pilot study. *Research in Developmental Disabilities, 30*(3), 529–537. https://doi.org/10.1016/j.ridd.2008.08.001

Mabee, W. (1988). The effects of academic positive practice on cursive letter writing. *Education and Treatment of Children, 11,* 143–148.

MacAulay, D. J. (1990). Classroom environment: A literature review. *Educational Psychology, 10,* 239–253.

MacDonald, J. M., Ahearn, W. H., Parry-Cruwys, D., Bancroft, S., & Dube, W. V. (2013). Persistence during extinction: Examining the effects of continuous and intermittent reinforcement on problem behavior. *Journal of Applied Behavior Analysis, 46*(1), 333–338. https://doi.org/10.1002/jaba.3

MacDonald, R., Parry-Cruwys, D., Dupere, S., & Ahearn, W. (2014). Assessing progress and outcome of early intensive behavioral intervention for toddlers with autism. *Research in Developmental Disabilities, 35*(12), 3632–3644. https://doi.org/10.1016/j.ridd.2014.08.036

Mace, F. C., Pratt, J., Prager, K., & Pritchard, D. (2011). An evaluation of three methods of saying "No" to avoid an escalating response class hierarchy. *Journal of Applied Behavior Analysis, 44,* 83–94.

MacNaul, H. L., & Neely, L. C. (2018). Systematic review of differential reinforcement of alternative behavior without extinction for individuals with autism. *Behavior Modification, 42*(3), 398–421. https://doi.org/10.1177/0145445517740321

Maher, G. (1989). Punch out: A behavior management technique. *Teaching Exceptional Children, 21,* 74.

Mahoney, M. J. (1974). *Cognition and behavior modification.* Cambridge, MA: Ballinger.

Maïano, C., Aimé, A., Salvas, M.-C., Morin, A. J. S., & Normand, C. L. (2016). Prevalence and correlates of bullying perpetration and victimization among school-aged youth with intellectual disabilities: A systematic review. *Research in Developmental Disabilities, 49–50,* 181–195. https://doi.org/10.1016/j.ridd.2015.11.015

Malik, S., Khan, Y. S., Sahl, R., Elzamzamy, K., & Nazeer, A. (2019). Genetics of autism spectrum disorder: An update. *Psychiatric Annals, 49*(3), 109–114. https://doi.org/10.3928/00485713-20190212-01

Manolov, R. (2018). Linear trend in single-case visual and quantitative analyses. *Behavior Modification, 42*(5), 684–706. https://doi.org/10.1177/0145445517726301

March, R., Horner, R., Lewis-Palmer, T., Brown, D., Crone, D., Todd, A., et al. (2000). *Functional Assessment Checklist: Teachers and Staff (FACTS).* Eugene, OR: Educational and Community Supports.

Marchand-Martella, N., Martella, R., Bettis, D., & Blakely, M. (2004). Project PALS: A description of a high school-based tutorial program using corrective reading and peer-delivered instruction. *Reading and Writing Quarterly, 20*(2), 179–201.

Marchetti, A. G., McCartney, J. R., Drain, S., Hooper, M., & Dix, J. (1983). Pedestrian skills training for mentally retarded adults: Comparison of training in two settings. *Mental Retardation, 21,* 107–110.

Marholin, D., & Gray, D. (1976). Effects of group response-cost procedures on cash shortages in a small business. *Journal of Applied Behavior Analysis, 9,* 25–30.

Markelz, A. M., & Taylor, J. C. (2016). Effects of teacher praise on attending behaviors and academic achievement of students with emotional and behavioral disabilities. *Journal of Special Education Apprenticeship, 5*(1).

Marshall, H. (1965). The effect of punishment on children. A review of the literature and a suggested hypothesis. *Journal of Genetic Psychology, 106,* 23–33.

Martens, B., Muir, K., & Meller, P. (1988). Rewards common to the classroom setting: A comparison of regular and self-contained room student ratings. *Behavior Disorders, 13,* 169–174.

Martens, B. K., Baxter, E. L., McComas, J. J., Sallade, S. J., Kester, J. S., Caamano, M., et al. (2019). Agreement between structured descriptive assessments and functional analyses conducted over a telehealth system. *Behavior Analysis: Research and Practice, 19*(4), 343–356. https://doi.org/10.1037/bar0000153

Martens, B. K., Gertz, L. E., de Lacy Werder, C. S., & Rymanowski, J. L. (2010). Agreement between descriptive and experimental analyses of behavior under naturalistic test conditions. *Journal of Behavioral Education, 19*(3), 205–221. https://doi.org/10.1007/s10864-010-9110-9

Martin, R. (1975). *Legal challenges to behavior modification: Trends in schools, corrections, and mental health.* Champaign, IL: Research Press.

Mason, B. (1974). Brain surgery to control behavior. *Ebony, 28*(4), 46.

Mason, L. H., Kubina, R. M., Jr., & Hoover, T. (2013). Effects of quick writing instruction for high school students with emotional disturbances. *Journal of Emotional and Behavioral Disorders, 21*(3), 163–175. https://doi.org/10.1177/1063426611410429

Mason, L. L., Davis, D., & Andrews, A. (2015). Token reinforcement of verbal responses controlled by temporally removed verbal stimuli. *Analysis of Verbal Behavior, 31*(1), 145–152. https://doi.org/10.1007/s40616-015-0032-4

Mason, L. L., Rivera, C. J., Spencer, T. D., O'Keeffe, B. V., Petersen, D. B., & Slocum, T. A. (2016). A preliminary investigation of visual goal markers to prompt fluent oral reading. *Psychology in the Schools, 53*(1), 58–72. https://doi.org/10.1002/pits.21888

Mason, S., McGee, G., Farmer-Dougan, V., & Risley, T. (1989). A practical strategy for ongoing reinforcer assessment. *Journal of Applied Behavior Analysis, 22,* 171–179.

Mastropieri, M., Jenne, T., & Scruggs, T. (1988). A level system for managing problem behaviors in a high school resource program. *Behavioral Disorders, 13,* 202–208.

Mastropieri, M. A., & Scruggs, T. E. (1984). Generalization: Five effective strategies. *Academic Therapy, 19,* 427–431.

Mather, N., & Woodcock, R. (2001). *Woodcock Johnson III Tests of Achievement.* Hasca, IL: Riverside.

Matson, J., & Keyes, J. (1988). Contingent reinforcement and contingent restraint to treat severe aggression and self-injury in mentally retarded and autistic adults. *Journal of the Multihandicapped Person, 1,* 141–148.

Matson, J., & Stephens, R. (1977). Overcorrection of aggressive behavior in a chronic psychiatric patient. *Behavior Modification, 1,* 559–564.

Matson, J., & Vollmer, T. (1995). *User's guide: Questions about behavior function (QABF).* Baton Rouge, LA: Scientific Publishers.

Matter, A. L., & Zarcone, J. R. (2017). A comparison of existing and novel communication responses used during functional communication training. *Behavioral Interventions, 32*(3), 217–224. https://doi.org/10.1002/bin.1481

Maxfield, T. C., Miltenberger, R. G., & Novotny, M. A. (2019). Evaluating small-scale simulation for training firearm safety skills. *Journal of Applied Behavior Analysis, 52*(2), 491–498.

May, M. E., Sheng, Y., Chitiyo, M., Brandt, R. C., & Howe, A. P. (2014). Internal consistency and inter-rater reliability of the Questions About Behavioral Function (QABF) rating scale when used by teachers and paraprofessionals. *Education & Treatment of Children, 37*(2), 347–364. https://doi.org/10.1353/etc.2014.0013

Mayhew, G., & Harris, F. (1979). Decreasing self-injurious behavior: Punishment with citric acid and reinforcement of alternative behaviors. *Behavior Modification, 3,* 322–336.

Mazaleski, J., Iwata, B., Rodgers, T., Vollmer, T., & Zarcone, J. (1994). Protective equipment as treatment for stereotypic hand mouthing: Sensory extinction or punishment effects? *Journal of Applied Behavior Analysis, 27,* 345–355.

Mazzocco, M. M. M., Quintero, A. I., Murphy, M. M., & McCloskey, M. (2016). Genetic syndromes as model pathways to mathematical learning difficulties: Fragile X, Turner, and 22q deletion syndromes. In D. B. Berch, D. C. Geary, & K. Mann Koepke (eds.), *Development of mathematical cognition: Neural substrates and genetic influences* (vol. 2, pp. 325–357). Elsevier Academic Press. https://doi.org/10.1016/B978-0-12-801871-2.00012-5

Mazzotti, V. L., Test, D. W., & Wood, C. L. (2013). Effects of multimedia goal-setting instruction on students' knowledge of the self-determined learning model of instruction and disruptive behavior. *Journal of Positive Behavior Interventions, 15*(2), 90–102. https://doi.org/10.1177/1098300712440452

McAdam, D. B., Klatt, K. P., Koffarnus, M., Dicesare, A., Solberg, K., Welch, C., et al. (2005). The effects of establishing operations on preferences for tangible items. *Journal of Applied Behavior Analysis, 38*(1), 107–110. https://doi.org/10.1901/jaba.2005.112-03

McConnell, J. V. (1970). Stimulus/response: Criminals can be brain-washed now. *Psychology Today, 3,* 14–18, 74.

McCord, B. E., Ringdahl, J. E., Meindl, J. N., & Wallace, L. A. (2019). Using data-driven processes to clarify behavioral function: A case example. *Behavior Analysis: Research and Practice, 19*(4), 357–372. https://doi.org/10.1037/bar0000156

McDaniel, S. C., & Bruhn, A. L. (2016). Using a changing-criterion design to evaluate the effects of check-in/check-out with goal modification. *Journal of Positive Behavior Interventions, 18*(4), 197–208. https://doi.org/10.1177/1098300715588263

McDaniel, S. C., Kim, S., & Guyotte, K. W. (2017). Perceptions of implementing positive behavior interventions and supports in high-need school contexts through the voice of local stakeholders. *Journal of At-Risk Issues, 20*(2), 35–44.

McDonald, M. E., Reeve, S. A., & Sparacio, E. J. (2014). Using a tactile prompt to increase instructor delivery of behavior-specific praise and token reinforcement and their collateral effects on stereotypic behavior in students with autism spectrum disorders. *Behavioral Development Bulletin, 19*(1), 40–43. https://doi.org/10.1037/h0100573

McDonnell, A., & Sturmey, P. (2000). The social validation of three physical restraint procedures: A comparison of young people and professional groups. *Research in Developmental Disabilities, 21*, 85–92.

McDougall, D., Heine, R. C., Wiley, L. A., Sheehey, M. D., Sakanashi, K. K., Cook, B. G., et al. (2017). Meta-analysis of behavioral self-management techniques used by students with disabilities in inclusive settings. *Behavioral Interventions, 32*(4), 399–417. https://doi.org/10.1002/bin.1491

McDougall, D., Morrison, C., & Awana, B. (2012). Students with disabilities use tactile cued self-monitoring to improve academic productivity during independent tasks. *Journal of Instructional Psychology, 39*(2), 119–130.

McIntosh, K., Borgmeier, C., Anderson, C., Horner, R., Rodriguez, B., & Tobin, T. (2008). Technical adequacy of the Functional Assessment Checklist: Teachers and Staff (FACTS) FBA interview measure. *Journal of Positive Behavior Intervention, 10*, 33–45.

McIntosh, K., Massar, M. M., Algozzine, R. F., George, H. P., Horner, R. H., Lewis, T. J., et al. (2017). Technical adequacy of the SWPBIS tiered fidelity inventory. *Journal of Positive Behavior Interventions, 19*(1), 3–13. https://doi.org/10.1177/1098300716637193

McIntosh, K., Mercer, S. H., Hume, A. E., Frank, J. L., Turri, M. G., & Mathews, S. (2013). Factors related to sustained implementation of schoolwide positive behavior support. *Exceptional Children, 79*(3), 293–311.

McKay, J. A., Weiss, J. S., Dickson, C. A., & Ahearn, W. H. (2014). Comparison of prompting hierarchies on the acquisition of leisure and vocational skills. *Behavior Analysis in Practice, 7*(2), 91–102. https://doi.org/10.1007/s40617-014-0022-3

McKeegan, G., Estill, K., & Campbell, B. (1984). Use of nonseclusionary time-out for the elimination of stereotypic behavior. *Journal of Behavior Therapy and Experimental Psychiatry, 15*, 261–264.

Mckenzie, S. D., Smith, R. G., Simmons, J. N., & Soderlund, M. J. (2008). Using a stimulus correlated with reprimands to suppress automatically maintained eye poking. *Journal of Applied Behavior Analysis, 41*(2), 255–259. https://doi.org/10.1901/jaba.2008.41-255

McNamara, K., & Cividini, M. C. (2019). Further evaluation of treatments for vocal stereotypy: Response interruption and redirection and response cost. *Behavioral Interventions, 34*(2), 181–197. https://doi.org/10.1002/bin.1657

McNiff, M. T., Maag, J. W., & Peterson, R. L. (2019). Group video self-modeling to improve the classroom transition speeds for elementary students. *Journal of Positive Behavior Interventions, 21*(2), 117–127. https://doi.org/10.1177/1098300718796788

McSweeny, A. J. (1978). Effects of response cost on the behavior of a million persons: Charging for directory assistance in Cincinnati. *Journal of Applied Behavior Analysis, 11*, 47–51.

Mechling, L., Gast, D., & Cronin, B. (2006). The effects of presenting high-preference items, paired with choice, via computer-based video programming on task completion of students with autism. *Focus on Autism and Developmental Disabilities, 21*, 7–13.

Mechling, L. C., Ayres, K. M., Foster, A. L., & Bryant, K. J. (2015). Evaluation of generalized performance across materials when using video technology by students with autism spectrum disorder and moderate intellectual disability. *Focus on Autism and Other Developmental Disabilities, 30*(4), 208–221. https://doi.org/10.1177/1088357614528795

Meichenbaum, D. H. (1977). *Cognitive-behavior modification: An integrative approach.* New York: Plenum Press.

Meichenbaum, D. H., & Goodman, J. (1971). Training impulsive children to talk to themselves: A means of developing self-control. *Journal of Abnormal Psychology, 77*, 115–126.

Mellard, D. F., McKnight, M., & Woods, K. (2009). Response to intervention screening and progress-monitoring practices in 41 local schools. *Learning Disabilities Research & Practice, 24*(4), 186–195. https://doi.org/10.1111/j.1540-5826.2009.00292.x

Mesmer, E. M., Duhon, G. J., & Dodson, K. G. (2007). The effects of programming common stimuli for enhancing stimulus generalization of academic behavior. *Journal of Applied Behavior Analysis, 40*(3), 553–557.

Michael, J. & Miguel, C. F. (2020). Motivating operations. In J. O. Cooper, T. E. Heron, & W. L. Heward (eds.), *Applied behavior analysis* (3rd ed., pp. 372–394). New York: Pearson.

Milata, E. M., Reeve, S. A., Reeve, K. F., & Dickson, C. A. (2020). A blueprint for general-case procedures illustrated by teaching adolescents with autism spectrum disorder to use a chip-debit card. *Behavioral Interventions, 35*(3), 346–371. https://doi.org/10.1002/bin.1719

Miles, N. I., & Wilder, D. A. (2009). The effects of behavioral skills training on caregiver implementation of guided compliance. *Journal of Applied Behavior Analysis, 42*, 405–410.

Miller, B., & Taber-Doughty, T. (2014). Self-monitoring checklists for inquiry problem-solving: Functional problem-solving methods for students with intellectual disability. *Education and Training in Autism and Developmental Disabilities, 49*(4), 555–567.

Miller, J. R., Lerman, D. C., & Fritz, J. N. (2010). An experimental analysis of negative reinforcement contingencies for adult-delivered reprimands. *Journal of Applied Behavior Analysis, 43*(4), 769–773. https://doi.org/10.1901/jaba.2010.43-769

Miltenberger, R., Rapp, J., & Long, E. (1999). A low-tech method for conducting real-time recording. *Journal of Applied Behavior Analysis, 32*(1), 119–120.

Miltenberger, R. G., Roberts, J. A., Ellingson, S., Galensky, T., Rapp, J. T., Long, E. S., et al. (1999). Training and generalization of sexual abuse prevention skills for women with retardation. *Journal of Applied Behavior Analysis, 32*, 385–388.

Mishel, W., & Patterson, C. J. (1976). Substantive and structural elements of effective plans for self-control. *Journal of Personality and Social Psychology, 34*, 942–950.

Mitchell, B. S., Hatton, H., & Lewis, T. J. (2018). An examination of the evidence-base of school-wide positive behavior interventions and supports through two quality appraisal processes. *Journal of Positive Behavior Interventions, 20*(4), 239–250. https://doi.org/10.1177/1098300718768217

Mitchell, B. S., Lewis, T. J., & Stormont, M. (2020). A daily check-in/check-out intervention for students with internalizing concerns. *Journal of Behavioral Education.* https://doi.org/10.1007/s10864-020-09365-7

Mitchell, R. J., Schuster, J. W., Collins, B. C., & Gassaway, L. J. (2000). Teaching vocational skills with a faded auditory prompting system. *Education and Training in Mental Retardation and Developmental Disabilities, 35,* 415–427.

Mitteer, D. R., Fisher, W. W., Briggs, A. M., Greer, B. D., & Hardee, A. M. (2019). Evaluation of an omnibus mand in the treatment of multiply controlled destructive behavior. *Behavioral Development, 24*(2), 74–88. https://doi.org/10.1037/bdb0000088

Mitteer, D. R., Romani, P. W., Greer, B. D., & Fisher, W. W. (2015). Assessment and treatment of pica and destruction of holiday decorations. *Journal of Applied Behavior Analysis, 48*(4), 912–917. https://doi.org/10.1002/jaba.255

Mohammadzaheri, F., Koegel, L. K., Rezaei, M., & Bakhshi, E. (2015). A randomized clinical trial comparison between Pivotal Response Treatment (PRT) and adult-driven applied behavior analysis (ABA) intervention on disruptive behaviors in public school children with autism. *Journal of Autism and Developmental Disorders, 45*(9), 2899–2907. https://doi.org/10.1007/s10803-015-2451-4

Moher, C. A., Gould, D. D., Hegg, E., & Mahoney, A. M. (2008). Non-generalized and generalized conditioned reinforcers: Establishment and validation. *Behavioral Interventions, 23*(1), 13–38. https://doi.org/10.1002/bin.253

Molgaard, K. (2001). *Count It* V 2.7 Manual. Retrieved August 18, 2002, from http://palmguy.surfhere.net.

Moore, D. W., Anderson, A., Glassenbury, M., Lang, R., & Didden, R. (2013). Increasing on-task behavior in students in a regular classroom: Effectiveness of a self-management procedure using a tactile prompt. *Journal of Behavioral Education, 22*(4), 302–311. https://doi.org/10.1007/s10864-013-9180-6

Moore, J. W., Fisher, W. W., & Pennington, A. (2004). Systematic application and removal of protective equipment in the assessment of multiple topographies of self-injury. *Journal of Applied Behavior Analysis, 37*(1), 73.

Moore, T. C., Robinson, C. C., Coleman, M. B., Cihak, D. F., & Park, Y. (2016). Noncontingent reinforcement to improve classroom behavior of a student with developmental disability. *Behavior Modification, 40*(4), 640–657. https://doi.org/10.1177/0145445516629937

Morales v. Turman, 1974, 383 F. Supp. 53 (E.D. TX.).

Morgan, A. C., Wilder, D. A., Podlesnik, C. A., & Kelley, M. E. (2017). Evaluation of an arm-splint belt to reduce self-injury. *Behavioral Interventions, 32*(3), 255–261. https://doi.org/10.1002/bin.1469

Morgan, R. L., & Horrocks, E. L. (2011). Correspondence between video-based preference assessment and subsequent community job performance. *Education and Training in Autism and Developmental Disabilities, 46*(1), 52–61.

Morgenstern, B. D., Causin, K. G., & Weinlein, J. L. (2019). Teaching pronouns to individuals with autism. *Behavioral Interventions, 34*(4), 525–533. https://doi.org/10.1002/bin.1685

Morris, R. (1976). *Behavior modification with children.* Cambridge, MA: Winthrop Publications.

Morse, T. E., & Schuster, J. W. (2004). Simultaneous prompting: A review of the literature. *Education and Training in Developmental Disabilities, 39,* 153–168.

Morton, W. L., Heward, W. L., & Alber, S. R. (1998). When to self-correct: A comparison of two procedures on spelling performance. *Journal of Behavioral Education, 8,* 321–335.

Mowrer, D., & Conley, D. (1987). Effect of peer administered consequences upon articulatory responses of speech defective children. *Journal of Communication Disorders, 20,* 319–326.

Moyer, J. R., & Dardig, J. C. (1978). Practical task analysis for educators. *Teaching Exceptional Children, 11,* 16–18.

Mueller, M. M., & Palkovic, C. M. (2007). Errorless learning: Review and practical application for teaching children with pervasive developmental disorders. *Psychology in the Schools, 44*(7), 691–700. https://doi.org/10.1002/pits.20258

Muething, C. S., Call, N. A., Mevers, J. L., Zangrillo, A. N., Clark, S. B., & Reavis, A. R. (2017). Correspondence between the results of functional analyses and brief functional analyses. *Developmental Neurorehabilitation, 20*(8), 549–559. https://doi.org/10.1080/17518423.2017.1338776

Muething, C. S., Falcomata, T. S., Ferguson, R., Swinnea, S., & Shpall, C. (2018). An evaluation of delay to reinforcement and mand variability during functional communication training. *Journal of Applied Behavior Analysis, 51*(2), 263–275. https://doi.org/10.1002/jaba.441

Munk, D. D., & Repp, A. C. (1994). The relationship between instructional variables and problem behavior: A review. *Exceptional Children, 60,* 390–401.

Musti-Rao, S., Lo, Y., & Plati, E. (2015). Using an iPad® app to improve sight word reading fluency for at-risk first graders. *Remedial and Special Education, 36*(3), 154–166. https://doi.org/10.1177/0741932514541485

Neely, L., Davis, H., Davis, J., & Rispoli, M. (2015). Review of reliability and treatment integrity trends in autism-focused research. *Research in Autism Spectrum Disorders, 9,* 1–12. https://doi.org/10.1016/j.rasd.2014.09.011

Neisworth, J., Hunt, F., Gallop, H., & Nadle, R. (1985). Reinforcer displacement: A preliminary study of the clinical application of CRF/EXT effect. *Behavior Modification, 9,* 103–115.

Nelson, M. A., Caldarella, P., Hansen, B. D., Graham, M. A., Williams, L., & Wills, H. P. (2018). Improving student behavior in art classrooms: An exploratory study of CW-FIT Tier 1. *Journal of Positive Behavior Interventions, 20*(4), 227–238.

Nese, R. N. T., Horner, R. H., Dickey, C. R., Stiller, B., & Tomlanovich, A. (2014). Decreasing bullying behaviors in middle school: Expect Respect. *School Psychology Quarterly, 29*(3), 272–286. https://doi.org/10.1037/spq0000070

Neuringer, A. (2004). Reinforced variability in animals and people: Implications for adaptive action. *American Psychologist, 59*(9), 891–906. https://doi.org/10.1037/0003-066X.59.9.891

Nevin, J. A., & Grace, R. C. (2000). Behavioral momentum and the Law of Effect. *Behavioral and Brain Sciences, 23*(1), 73–130. https://doi.org/10.1017/S0140525X00002405

Newcomb, E. T., Wright, J. A., & Camblin, J. G. (2019). Assessment and treatment of aggressive behavior maintained by access to physical attention. *Behavior Analysis: Research and Practice, 19*(3), 222–231. https://doi.org/10.1037/bar0000136

Newman, B., Buffington, D. M., & Hemmes, N. S. (1996). External and self-reinforcement used to increase the appropriate conversation of autistic teenagers. *Education and Training in Mental Retardation and Developmental Disorders, 31,* 304–309.

Newman, B., Reinecke, D. R., & Kurtz, A. L. (1996). Why be moral: Humanist and behavioral perspectives. *The Behavior Analyst, 19,* 273–280.

Nichols, P. (1992). The curriculum of control: Twelve reasons for it, some arguments against it. *Beyond Behavior, 3,* 5–11.

Noel, C. R., & Rubow, C. C. (2018). Using noncontingent reinforcement to reduce perseverative speech and increase engagement during social skills instruction. *Education & Treatment of Children, 41*(2), 157–167. https://doi.org/10.1353/etc.2018.0006

Nolan, J. D., & Filter, K. J. (2012). A function-based classroom behavior intervention using non-contingent reinforcement plus response cost. *Education & Treatment of Children, 35*(3), 419–430. https://doi.org/10.1353/etc.2012.0017

Nolan, J. D., Houlihan, D., Wanzek, M., & Jenson, W. R. (2014). The Good Behavior Game: A classroom-behavior intervention effective across cultures. *School Psychology International, 35*(2), 191–205. https://doi.org/10.1177/0143034312471473

Northup, J. (2000). Further evaluation of the accuracy of reinforcer surveys: A systematic replication. *Journal of Applied Behavior Analysis, 33*, 335–338.

Northup, J., George, T., Jones, K., Broussard, C., & Vollmer, T. (1996). A comparison of reinforcer assessment methods: The utility of verbal and pictorial choice procedures. *Journal of Applied Behavior Analysis, 29*, 201–212.

Nosik, M. R., & Carr, J. E. (2015). On the distinction between the motivating operation and setting event concepts. *The Behavior Analyst, 38*(2), 219–223. https://doi.org/10.1007/s40614-015-0042-5

Nuernberger, J. E., Vargo, K. K., & Ringdahl, J. E. (2013). An application of differential reinforcement of other behavior and self-monitoring to address repetitive behavior. *Journal of Developmental and Physical Disabilities, 25*(1), 105–117. https://doi.org/10.1007/s10882-012-9309-x

Oakes, W. P., Lane, K. L., & Hirsch, S. E. (2018). Functional assessment-based interventions: Focusing on the environment and considering function. *Preventing School Failure, 62*(1), 25–36.

Obiakor, F. E., Harris, M., Mutua, K., Rotatori, A., & Algozzine, B. (2012). Making inclusion work in general education classrooms. *Education & Treatment of Children, 35*(3), 477–490. https://doi.org/10.1353/etc.2012.0020

O'Connor, M. A., & Daly, E. J., III. (2018). Selecting effective intervention strategies for escape-maintained academic-performance problems: Consider giving 'em a break! *Journal of School Psychology, 66*, 41–53. https://doi.org/10.1016/j.jsp.2017.09.003

Odom, S., & Strain, P. (1986). A comparison of peer-initiation and teacher-antecedent interventions for promoting reciprocal social interaction of autistic preschoolers. *Journal of Applied Behavior Analysis, 19*, 59–71.

O'Donnell J. (2001). The discriminative stimulus for punishment or SDp. *The Behavior Analyst, 24*, 261–262.

O'Handley, R. D., Radley, K. C., & Cavell, H. J. (2016). Utilization of superheroes social skills to reduce disruptive and aggressive behavior. *Preventing School Failure, 60*(2), 124–132.

O'Hara, M., & Hall, L. J. (2014). Increasing engagement of students with autism at recess through structured work systems. *Education and Training in Autism and Developmental Disabilities, 49*(4), 568–575.

Ok, M. W., Rao, K., Bryant, B. R., & McDougall, D. (2017). Universal design for learning in pre-K to grade 12 classrooms: A systematic review of research. *Exceptionality, 25*(2), 116–138. https://doi.org/10.1080/09362835.2016.1196450

O'Leary, K. D. (1972). The assessment of psychopathology in children. In H. C. Quay & J. S. Werry (eds.), *Psychopathological disorders of childhood* (pp. 234–272). New York: Wiley.

O'Leary, K. D., Becker, W. C., Evans, M. B., & Saudargas, R. A. (1969). A token reinforcement program in a public school: A replication and systematic analysis. *Journal of Applied Behavior Analysis, 2*, 3–13.

O'Leary, K. D., Kaufman, K., Kass, R., & Drabman, R. (1970). The effects of loud and soft reprimands on the behavior of disruptive students. *Exceptional Children, 37*, 145–155.

Oliveira, C., Font-Roura, J., Dalmau, M., & Giné, C. (2018). Teaching a phonological awareness skill with the time-delay system in a mainstream setting: A single-subject research study. *Reading & Writing Quarterly: Overcoming Learning Difficulties, 34*(5), 396–408. https://doi.org/10.1080/10573569.2018.1463188

Ollendick, T., & Matson, J. (1976). An initial investigation into the parameters of overcorrection. *Psychological Reports, 39*, 1139–1142.

O'Neill, R., Horner, R., Albin, R., Sprague, J., Storey, K., & Newton, J. S. (1997). *Functional assessment and program development for problem behavior* (2nd ed.). Pacific Grove, CA: Brooks/Cole Publishing Co.

O'Reilly, M. F., Lancioni, G. E., & Kierans, I. (2000). Teaching leisure social skills to adults with moderate mental retardation: An analysis of acquisition, generalization, and maintenance. *Education and Training in Mental Retardation and Developmental Disabilities, 35*(3), 250–258.

Oropeza, M. E., Fritz, J. N., Nissen, M. A., Terrell, A. S., & Phillips, L. A. (2018). Effects of therapist-worn protective equipment during functional analysis of aggression. *Journal of Applied Behavior Analysis, 51*(3), 681–686. https://doi.org/10.1002/jaba.457

Ottenbacher, K. (1993). Interrater agreement of visual analysis in single-subject decisions: Quantitative review and analysis. *American Journal on Mental Retardation, 98*, 135–142.

Ottenbacher, K. J. (2016). Republication of "when is a picture worth a thousand p values? A comparison of visual and quantitative methods to analyze single subject data." *The Journal of Special Education, 50*(3), 133–140. https://doi.org/10.1177/0022466916668503

Pace, G., Ivancic, M., Edwards, G., Iwata, B., & Page, T. (1985). Assessment of stimulus preference and reinforcer value with profoundly retarded individuals. *Journal of Applied Behavior Analysis, 18*, 249–255.

Paclawskyj, T., Matson, J., Rush, K., Smalls, Y., & Vollmer, T. (2000). Questions about behavioral function (QABF): A behavioral checklist for functional assessment of aberrant behavior. *Research in Developmental Disabilities, 21*, 223–229.

Panyan, M. C., & Hall, R. V. (1978). Effects of serial versus concurrent task sequencing on acquisition, maintenance, and generalization. *Journal of Applied Behavior Analysis, 11*, 67–74.

Panyan, M. P. (1980). *How to use shaping*. Lawrence, KS: H&H Enterprises.

Park, E.-Y., & Blair, K.-S. C. (2019). Social validity assessment in behavior interventions for young children: A systematic review. *Topics in Early Childhood Special Education, 39*(3), 156–169.

Park, G., Collins, B. C., & Lo, Y. (2020). Teaching a physical activity to students with mild to moderate intellectual disability using a peer-delivered simultaneous prompting procedure: A single-case experimental design study. *Journal of Behavioral Education*. https://doi.org/10.1007/s10864-020-09373-7

Pastrana, S. J., Frewing, T. M., Grow, L. L., Nosik, M. R., Turner, M., & Carr, J. E. (2018). Frequently assigned readings in behavior analysis graduate training programs. *Behavior Analysis in Practice, 11*(3), 267–273. https://doi.org/10.1007/s40617-016-0137-9

Patterson, E. T., Panyan, M. C., Wyatt, S., & Morales, E. (1974, September). Forward vs. backward chaining in the teaching of vocational skills to the mentally retarded: An empirical analysis. Paper presented at the 82nd Annual Meeting of the American Psychological Association, New Orleans.

Patterson, G. R. (1965). An application of conditioning techniques to the control of a hyperactive child. In L. P. Ullmann & L. Krasner (eds.), *Case studies in behavior modification* (pp. 370–375). New York: Holt, Rinehart & Winston.

Pence, S. T., St. Peter, C. C., & Giles, A. F. (2014). Teacher acquisition of functional analysis methods using pyramidal training. *Journal of Behavioral Education, 23*(1), 132–149. https://doi.org/10.1007/s10864-013-9182-4

Pennington, R., Courtade, G., Jones Ault, M., & Delano, M. (2016). Five essential features of quality educational programs for students with moderate and severe intellectual disability: A guide for administrators. *Education and Training in Autism and Developmental Disabilities, 51*(3), 294–306.

Pennington, R., & Koehler, M. (2017). Effects of modeling, story templates, and self-graphing in the use of story elements by students with moderate intellectual disability. *Education and Training in Autism and Developmental Disabilities, 52*(3), 280–290.

Perle, J. G. (2016). Teacher-Provided Positive Attending to Improve Student Behavior. *TEACHING Exceptional Children, 48*(5), 250–257.

Perrin, C. J., Perrin, S. H., Hill, E. A., & DiNovi, K. (2008). Brief functional analysis and treatment of elopement in preschoolers with autism. *Behavioral Interventions, 23*(2), 87–98. https://doi.org/10.1002/bin.256

Peters, L. C., & Thompson, R. H. (2013). Some indirect effects of positive practice overcorrection. *Journal of Applied Behavior Analysis, 46*(3), 613–625. https://doi.org/10.1002/jaba.63

Peters, R., & Davies, K. (1981). Effects of self-instructional training on cognitive impulsivity of mentally retarded adolescents. *American Journal of Mental Deficiency, 85,* 377–382.

Peterson, C., Lerman, D. C., & Nissen, M. A. (2016). Reinforcer choice as an antecedent versus consequence. *Journal of Applied Behavior Analysis, 49*(2), 286–293. https://doi.org/10.1002/jaba.284

Peterson, S. M., Eldridge, R. R., Rios, D., & Schenk, Y. A. (2019). Ethical challenges encountered in delivering behavior analytic services through teleconsultation. *Behavior Analysis: Research and Practice, 19*(2), 190–201. https://doi.org/10.1037/bar0000111

Peterson, S. P., Rodriguez, N. M., & Pawich, T. L. (2019). Effects of modeling rote versus varied responses on response variability and skill acquisition during discrete-trial instruction. *Journal of Applied Behavior Analysis, 52*(2), 370–385. https://doi.org/10.1002/jaba.528

Petrill, S. A. (2014). Behavioral genetics, learning abilities, and disabilities. In H. L. Swanson, K. R. Harris, & S. Graham (eds.), *Handbook of learning disabilities* (2nd ed). (pp. 293–306). New York: The Guilford Press.

Petrongolo, M., DuBard, M., & Luiselli, J. K. (2015). Effects of an idiosyncratic stimulus on functional analysis of vocal stereotypy in two settings. *Developmental Neurorehabilitation, 18*(3), 209–212. https://doi.org/10.3109/17518423.2013.869271

Phillips, C. L., Iannaccone, J. A., Rooker, G. W., & Hagopian, L. P. (2017). Noncontingent reinforcement for the treatment of severe problem behavior: An analysis of 27 consecutive applications. *Journal of Applied Behavior Analysis, 50*(2), 357–376. https://doi.org/10.1002/jaba.376

Phillips, E. L., Phillips, E. A., Fixsen, D. L., & Wolf, M. M. (1971). Achievement place: Modification of the behaviors of predelinquent boys within a token economy. *Journal of Applied Behavior Analysis, 4,* 45–59.

Phillips, N., Amos, T., Kuo, C., Hoare, J., Ipser, J., Thomas, K. G., & Stein, D. J. (2016). HIV-associated cognitive impairment in perinatally infected children: a meta-analysis. Pediatrics, 138(5).

Piaget, J., & Inhelder, B. (1969). *The psychology of the child*. New York: Basic Books.

Piazza, C. C., Hanley, G. P., & Fisher, W. W. (1996). Functional analysis and treatment of cigarette pica. *Journal of Applied Behavior Analysis, 29,* 437–450.

Pierce, K. I., & Schreibman, L. (1994). Teaching daily living skills to children with autism in unsupervised settings through pictorial self-management. *Journal of Applied Behavior Analysis, 27,* 471–481.

Pierce, W. D., & Cameron, J. (2002). A summary of the effects of reward contingencies on interest and performance. *The Behavior Analyst Today, 3*(2), 221–228. https://doi.org/10.1037/h0099969

Pigott, H. E., Fantuzzo, J., & Clement, P. (1986). The effects of reciprocal peer tutoring and group contingencies on the academic performance of elementary school children. *Journal of Applied Behavior Analysis, 19,* 93–98.

Pinkelman, S. E., & Horner, R. H. (2017). Improving implementation of function-based interventions: Self-monitoring, data collection, and data review. *Journal of Positive Behavior Interventions, 19*(4), 228–238. https://doi.org/10.1177/1098300716683634

Pinkston, E. M., Reese, N. M., LeBlanc, J. M., & Baer, D. M. (1973). Independent control of a preschool child's aggression and peer interaction by contingent teacher attention. *Journal of Applied Behavior Analysis, 6,* 115–124.

Podlesnik, C. A., Miranda, D. L., Jonas Chan, C. K., Bland, V. J., & Bai, J. Y. H. (2017). Generalization of the disruptive effects of alternative stimuli when combined with target stimuli in extinction. *Journal of the Experimental Analysis of Behavior, 108*(2), 255–268. https://doi.org/10.1002/jeab.272

Polick, A. S., Carr, J. E., & Hanney, N. M. (2012). A comparison of general and descriptive praise in teaching intraverbal behavior to children with autism. *Journal of Applied Behavior Analysis, 45*(3), 593–599. https://doi.org/10.1901/jaba.2012.45-593

Poling, A., & Byrne, T. (1996). Reactions to Reese: Lord, let us laud and lament. *The Behavior Analyst, 19,* 79–82.

Poling, A., Methot, L., & LeSage, M. (1994). *Fundamentals of behavior analytic research*. New York: Plenum Press.

Poling, A., & Normand, M. (1999). Noncontingent reinforcement: An inappropriate description of time-based schedules that reduce behavior. *Journal of Applied Behavior Analysis, 32,* 237–238.

Polloway, E., & Polloway, C. (1979). Auctions: Vitalizing the token economy. *Journal for Special Educators, 15,* 121–123.

Popham, M., Counts, J., Ryan, J. B., & Katsiyannis, A. (2018). A systematic review of self-regulation strategies to improve academic outcomes of students with EBD. *Journal of Research in Special Educational Needs, 18*(4), 239–253. https://doi.org/10.1111/1471-3802.12408

Popovic, S. C., Starr, E. M., & Koegel, L. K. (2020). Teaching initiated question asking to children with autism spectrum disorder through a short-term parent-mediated program. *Journal of Autism and Developmental Disorders, 50*(10), 3728–3738. https://doi.org/10.1007/s10803-020-04426-2

Porter, A., & Sy, J. R. (2020). Assessment and treatment of self-control with aversive events. *Journal of Applied Behavior Analysis, 53*(1), 508–521. https://doi.org/10.1002/jaba.604

Powell, M. B., & Gadke, D. L. (2018). Improving oral reading fluency in middle-school students: A comparison of repeated reading and listening passage preview. *Psychology in the Schools, 55*(10), 1274–1286. https://doi.org/10.1002/pits.22184

Powers, K. V., Roane, H. S., & Kelley, M. E. (2007). Treatment of self-restraint associated with the application of protective equipment. *Journal of Applied Behavior Analysis, 40*(3), 577–581. https://doi.org/10.1901/jaba.2007.40-577

Preis, J. (2006). The effect of picture communication symbols on the verbal comprehension of commands by young children with autism. *Focus on Autism and Other Developmental Disabilities, 21,* 194–210.

Premack, D. (1959). Toward empirical behavior laws: I. Positive reinforcement. *Psychological Review, 66,* 219–233.

Prykanowski, D. A., Martinez, J. R., Reichow, B., Conroy, M. A., & Huang, K. (2018). Brief report: Measurement of young children's engagement and problem behavior in early childhood settings. *Behavioral Disorders, 44*(1), 53–62. https://doi.org/10.1177/0198742918779793

Pugach, M. C., & Warger, C. L. (1996). *Curriculum trends, special education, and reform: Refocusing the conversation*. New York: Teacher's College Press.

Purrazzella, K., & Mechling, L. C. (2013). Evaluation of manual spelling, observational and incidental learning using computer-based instruction with a tablet PC, large screen projection, and a forward chaining procedure. *Education and Training in Autism and Developmental Disabilities, 48*(2), 218–235.

Quigley, J., Griffith, A. K., & Kates-McElrath, K. (2018). A comparison of modeling, prompting, and a multi-component intervention for teaching play skills to children with developmental disabilities. *Behavior Analysis in Practice, 11*(4), 315–326. https://doi.org/10.1007/s40617-018-0225-0

Rachman, S. (1963). Spontaneous remission and latent learning. *Behavior Research and Therapy, 1*, 3–15.

Radley, K. C., Dart, E. H., Battaglia, A. A., & Blake Ford, W. (2019). A comparison of two procedures for assessing preference in a classroom setting. *Behavior Analysis in Practice, 12*(1), 95–104. https://doi.org/10.1007/s40617-018-0244-x

Radley, K. C., Moore, J. W., Dart, E. H., Ford, W. B., & Helbig, K. A. (2019). The effects of lag schedules of reinforcement on social skill accuracy and variability. *Focus on Autism and Other Developmental Disabilities, 34*(2), 67–80.

Radstaake, M., Didden, R., Bolio, M., Lang, R., Lancioni, G. E., & Curfs, L. M. G. (2011). Functional assessment and behavioral treatment of skin picking in a teenage girl with Prader-Willi Syndrome. *Clinical Case Studies, 10*(1), 67–78. https://doi.org/10.1177/1534650110395013

Radstaake, M., Didden, R., Lang, R., O'Reilly, M., Sigafoos, J., Lancioni, G. E., et al. (2013). Functional analysis and functional communication training in the classroom for three children with Angelman syndrome. *Journal of Developmental and Physical Disabilities, 25*(1), 49–63. https://doi.org/10.1007/s10882-012-9302-4

Rafferty, L. A. (2012). Self-monitoring during whole group reading instruction: Effects among students with emotional and behavioral disabilities during summer school intervention sessions. *Emotional & Behavioural Difficulties, 17*(2), 157–173. https://doi.org/10.1080/13632752.2012.672866

Rahn, N. L., Coogle, C. G., & Ottley, J. R. (2019). Early childhood special education teachers' use of embedded learning opportunities within classroom routines and activities. *Infants & Young Children, 32*(1), 3–19. https://doi.org/10.1097/IYC.0000000000000132

Ramirez, H., Cengher, M., & Fienup, D. M. (2014). The effects of simultaneous prompting on the acquisition of calculating elapsed time in children with autism. *Journal of Developmental and Physical Disabilities, 26*(6), 763–774. https://doi.org/10.1007/s10882-014-9394-0

Ramsey, M. L., Jolivette, K., Kennedy, C., Fredrick, L. D., & Williams, C. D. (2017). Functionally-indicated choice-making interventions to address academic and social behaviors of adolescent students with emotional/behavioral disorders (E/BD) in a residential facility. *Journal of Classroom Interaction, 52*(2), 45–66.

Randall, K. R., Lambert, J. M., Matthews, M. P., & Houchins-Juarez, N. J. (2018). Individualized levels system and systematic stimulus pairing to reduce multiply controlled aggression of a child with autism spectrum disorder. *Behavior Modification, 42*(3), 422–440. https://doi.org/10.1177/0145445517741473

Rapp, J. T., Colby-Dirksen, A. M., Michalski, D. N., Carroll, R. A., & Lindenberg, A. M. (2008). Detecting changes in simulated events using partial-interval recording and momentary time sampling. *Behavioral Interventions, 23*(4), 237–269. https://doi.org/10.1002/bin.269

Rapp, J. T., Vollmer, T. R., St. Peter, C., Dozier, C. L., & Cotnoir, N. M. (2004). Analysis of response allocation in individuals with multiple forms of stereotyped behavior. *Journal of Applied Behavior Analysis, 37*(4), 481–501. https://doi.org/10.1901/jaba.2004.37-481

Rapport, M. D., Murphy, H. A., & Bailey, J. S. (1982). Ritalin vs response cost in the control of hyperactive children: A within-subject comparison. *Journal of Applied Behavior Analysis, 15*, 205–216.

Raschke, D. (1981). Designing reinforcement surveys: Let the student choose the reward. *Teaching Exceptional Children, 14*, 92–96.

Rathel, J. M., Drasgow, E., Brown, W. H., & Marshall, K. J. (2014). Increasing induction-level teachers' positive-to-negative communication ratio and use of behavior-specific praise through e-mailed performance feedback and its effect on students' task engagement. *Journal of Positive Behavior Interventions, 16*(4), 219–233. https://doi.org/10.1177/1098300713492856

Reed, D. K., & Lynn, D. (2016). The effects of an inference-making strategy taught with and without goal setting. *Learning Disability Quarterly, 39*(3), 133–145. https://doi.org/10.1177/0731948715615557

Reed, H., Thomas, E., Sprague, J., & Horner, R. (1997). The student guided functional assessment interview: An analysis of student and teacher agreement. *Journal of Behavioral Education, 7*(1), 33–45.

Reeves, L. M., Umbreit, J., Ferro, J. B., & Liaupsin, C. J. (2013). Function-based intervention to support the inclusion of students with autism. *Education and Training in Autism and Developmental Disabilities, 48*(3), 379–391.

Reid, D. H. (2017). Competency-based staff training. In J. K. Luiselli (ed.), *Applied behavior analysis advanced guidebook: A manual for professional practice.* (pp. 21–40). London: Elsevier Academic Press. https://doi.org/10.1016/B978-0-12-811122-2.00002-4

Reid, D. H., Parsons, M. B., & Lattimore, L. P. (2010). Designing and evaluating assessment-based interventions to reduce stereotypy among adults with autism in a community job. *Behavior Analysis in Practice, 3*(2), 27–36.

Reitman, D., & Drabman, R. (1999). Multifaceted uses of a simple time-out record in the treatment of a noncompliant 8-year-old boy. *Education and Treatment of Children, 22*, 136–145.

Repp, A. (1983). *Teaching the mentally retarded.* Upper Saddle River, NJ: Prentice Hall.

Reynolds, G. S. (1961). Behavioral contrast. *Journal of the Experimental Analysis of Behavior, 4*, 57–71.

Rhymer, K. N., Skinner, C. H., Henington, C., D'Reaux, R. A., & Sims, S. (1998). Effects of explicit timing on mathematics problem completion rates in African-American third-grade elementary students. *Journal of Applied Behavior Analysis, 31*(4), 673–677. https://doi.org/10.1901/jaba.1998.31-673

Richards, C., Davies, L., & Oliver, C. (2017). Predictors of self-injurious behavior and self-restraint in autism spectrum disorder: Towards a hypothesis of impaired behavioral control. *Journal of Autism and Developmental Disorders, 47*(3), 701–713. https://doi.org/10.1007/s10803-016-3000-5

Richman, D., Berg, W., Wacker, D., Stephens, T., Rankin, B., & Kilroy, J. (1997). Using pretreatment and posttreatment assessments to enhance and evaluate existing treatment packages. *Journal of Applied Behavior Analysis, 30*, 709–712.

Richman, D., Wacker, D., Asmus, J., Casey, S., & Andelman, M. (1999). Further analysis of problem behavior in response class hierarchies. *Journal of Applied Behavior Analysis, 32*, 269–283.

Richman, D., Wacker, D., & Winborn, L. (2000). Response efficiency during functional communication training: Effects of effort on response allocation. *Journal of Applied Behavior Analysis, 34*, 73–76.

Richman, G. S., Reiss, M. L., Bauman, K. E., & Bailey, J. S. (1984). Teaching menstrual care to mentally retarded women: Acquisition, generalization, and maintenance. *Journal of Applied Behavior Analysis, 17*, 441–451.

Riley-Tillman, T. C., Burns, M. K., & Kilgus, S. P. (2020). *Evaluating educational interventions: Single-case design for measuring response to intervention* (2nd ed.). The Guilford practical intervention in the schools series. New York: Guilford Press.

Rincover, A. (1981). *How to use sensory extinction.* Lawrence, KS: H&H Enterprises.

Rincover, A., & Devany, J. (1982). The application of sensory extinction procedures to self-injury. *Analysis and Intervention in Developmental Disabilities, 2*, 67–81.

Rincover, A., & Koegel, R. L. (1975). Setting generality and stimulus control in autistic children. *Journal of Applied Behavior Analysis, 8*, 235–246.

Rios, D., Schenk, Y. A., Eldridge, R. R., & Peterson, S. M. (2020). The effects of remote behavioral skills training on conducting functional analyses. *Journal of Behavioral Education*. https://doi.org/10.1007/s10864-020-09385-3

Risley, T. R. (1975). Certify procedures not people. In W. S. Wood (ed.), *Issues in evaluating behavior modification* (pp. 159–181). Champaign, IL: Research Press.

Rispoli, M., Neely, L., Healy, O., & Gregori, E. (2016). Training public school special educators to implement two functional analysis models. *Journal of Behavioral Education*, 25(3), 249–274. https://doi.org/10.1007/s10864-016-9247-2

Rispoli, M. J., Davis, H. S., Goodwyn, F. D., & Camargo, S. (2013). The use of trial-based functional analysis in public school classrooms for two students with developmental disabilities. *Journal of Positive Behavior Interventions*, 15(3), 180–189. https://doi.org/10.1177/1098300712457420

Ritschl, C., Mongrella, J., & Presbie, R. (1972). Group time-out from rock and roll music and out-of-seat behavior of handicapped children while riding a school bus. *Psychological Reports*, 31, 967–973.

Ritter, W. A., Barnard-Brak, L., Richman, D. M., & Grubb, L. M. (2018). The influence of function, topography, and setting on noncontingent reinforcement effect sizes for reduction in problem behavior: A meta-analysis of single-case experimental design data. *Journal of Behavioral Education*, 27(1), 1–22. https://doi.org/10.1007/s10864-017-9277-4

Roane, H. S., & DeRosa, N. M. (2014). Reduction of emergent dropping behavior during treatment of elopement. *Journal of Applied Behavior Analysis*, 47(3), 633–638. https://doi.org/10.1002/jaba.136

Roane, H. S., Vollmer, T. R., Ringdahl, J. E., & Marcus, B. A. (1998). Evaluation of a brief stimulus preference assessment. *Journal of Applied Behavior Analysis*, 31(4), 605–620. https://doi.org/10.1901/jaba.1998.31-605

Roberts, G. J., Mize, M., Reutebuch, C. K., Falcomata, T., Capin, P., & Steelman, B. L. (2019). Effects of a self-management with peer training intervention on academic engagement for high school students with autism spectrum disorder. *Journal of Behavioral Education*, 28(4), 456–478.

Roberts, M. (1988). Enforcing chair timeouts with room time-outs. *Behavior Modification*, 12, 353–370.

Roberts, R. N., Nelson, R. O., & Olson, T. W. (1987). Self-instruction: An analysis of the differential effects of instruction and reinforcement. *Journal of Applied Behavior Analysis*, 20, 235–242.

Robison, M. A., Mann, T. B., & Ingvarsson, E. T. (2020). Life skills instruction for children with developmental disabilities. *Journal of Applied Behavior Analysis*, 53(1), 431–448. https://doi.org/10.1002/jaba.602

Roche, L., Carnett, A., Sigafoos, J., Stevens, M., O'Reilly, M. F., Lancioni, G. E., et al. (2019). Using a textual prompt to teach multiword requesting to two children with autism spectrum disorder. *Behavior Modification*, 43(6), 819–840. https://doi.org/10.1177/0145445519850745

Rodriguez, P. P., & Gutierrez, A. (2017). A comparison of two procedures to condition social stimuli to function as reinforcers for children with autism. *Behavioral Development Bulletin*, 22(1), 159–172. https://doi.org/10.1037/bdb0000059

Rogers, C. R., & Skinner, B. F. (1956). Some issues concerning the control of human behavior: A symposium. *Science*, 124, 1057–1066.

Rollings, J., Baumeister, A., & Baumeister, A. (1977). The use of overcorrection procedures to eliminate the stereotyped behaviors of retarded individuals: An analysis of collateral behaviors and generalization of suppressive effects. *Behavior Modification*, 1, 29–46.

Romani, P. W., Alcorn, A. S., & Linares, J. (2018). Improving accuracy of data collection on a psychiatric unit for children diagnosed with intellectual and developmental disabilities. *Behavior Analysis in Practice*, 11(4), 307–314. https://doi.org/10.1007/s40617-018-00305-6

Romani, P. W., Alcorn, A. S., Miller, J. R., & Clark, G. (2017). Preference assessment for dimensions of reinforcement to inform token economies targeting problem behavior. *Journal of Behavioral Education*, 26(3), 221–237. https://doi.org/10.1007/s10864-017-9270-y

Romani, P. W., Donaldson, A. M., Ager, A. J., Peaslee, J. E., Garden, S. M., & Ariefdjohan, M. (2019). Assessment and treatment of aggression during public outings. *Education & Treatment of Children*, 42(3), 345–360. https://doi.org/10.1353/etc.2019.0016

Roncati, A. L., Souza, A. C., & Miguel, C. F. (2019). Exposure to a specific prompt topography predicts its relative efficiency when teaching intraverbal behavior to children with autism spectrum disorder. *Journal of Applied Behavior Analysis*, 52(3), 739–745. https://doi.org/10.1002/jaba.568

Rooker, G. W., Iwata, B. A., Harper, J. M., Fahmie, T. A., & Camp, E. M. (2011). False-positive tangible outcomes of functional analyses. *Journal of Applied Behavior Analysis*, 44(4), 737–745. https://doi.org/10.1901/jaba.2011.44-737

Rooker, G. W., & Roscoe, E. M. (2005). Functional analysis of self-injurious behavior and its relation to self-restraint. *Journal of Applied Behavior Analysis*, 38(4), 537–542. https://doi.org/10.1901/jaba.2005.12-05

Rosa, K. A. D., Fellman, D., DeBiase, C., DeQuinzio, J. A., & Taylor, B. A. (2015). The effects of using a conditioned stimulus to cue DRO schedules. *Behavioral Interventions*, 30(3), 219–230. https://doi.org/10.1002/bin.1409

Rosales, R., Worsdell, A., & Trahan, M. (2010). Comparison of methods for varying item presentation during noncontingent reinforcement. *Research in Autism Spectrum Disorders*, 4(3), 367–376. https://doi.org/10.1016/j.rasd.2009.10.004

Roscoe, E. M., Iwata, B. A., & Zhou, L. (2013). Assessment and treatment of chronic hand mouthing. *Journal of Applied Behavior Analysis*, 46(1), 181–198. https://doi.org/10.1002/jaba.14

Rosenbloom, R., Wills, H. P., Mason, R., Huffman, J. M., & Mason, B. A. (2019). The effects of a technology-based self-monitoring intervention on on-task, disruptive, and task-completion behaviors for adolescents with autism. *Journal of Autism and Developmental Disorders*, 49(12), 5047–5062. https://doi.org/10.1007/s10803-019-04209-4

Rothstein, L. F. (1990). *Special education law*. New York: Longman.

Rouse, C. A., Alber, M. S. R., Cullen, J. M., & Sawyer, M. (2014). Using prompt fading to teach self-questioning to fifth graders with LD: Effects on reading comprehension. *Learning Disabilities Research & Practice*, 29(3), 117–125. https://doi.org/10.1111/ldrp.12036

Rouse, C. A., Everhart-Sherwood, J. M., & Alber-Morgan, S. R. (2014). Effects of self-monitoring and recruiting teacher attention on pre-vocational skills. *Education and Training in Autism and Developmental Disabilities*, 49(2), 313–327.

Rowling, J. K. (1998). *Harry Potter and the chamber of secrets*. New York: Scholastic Press.

Rozenblat, E., Reeve, K. F., Townsend, D. B., Reeve, S. A., & DeBar, R. M. (2019). Teaching joint attention skills to adolescents and young adults with autism using multiple exemplars and script-fading procedures. *Behavioral Interventions*, 34(4), 504–524. https://doi.org/10.1002/bin.1682

Rubio, E. K., Pichardo, D., & Borrero, C. S. W. (2018). Using backward chaining and a physical guidance delay to teach self-feeding. *Behavioral Interventions*, 33(1), 87–92. https://doi.org/10.1002/bin.1504

Rubio, E. K., Volkert, V. M., Farling, H., & Sharp, W. G. (2020). Evaluation of a finger prompt variation in the treatment of pediatric feeding disorders. *Journal of Applied Behavior Analysis, 53*(2), 956–972.

Rubow, C. C., Noel, C. R., & Wehby, J. H. (2019). Effects of noncontingent attention on the behavior of students with emotional/behavioral disorders and staff in alternative settings. *Education & Treatment of Children, 42*(2), 201–223. https://doi.org/10.1353/etc.2019.0010

Rubow, C. C., Vollmer, T. R., & Joslyn, P. R. (2018). Effects of the good behavior game on student and teacher behavior in an alternative school. *Journal of Applied Behavior Analysis, 51*(2), 382–392. https://doi.org/10.1002/jaba.455

Rusch, F., & Close, D. (1976). Overcorrection: A procedural evaluation. *AAESPH Review, 1*, 32–45.

Rusch, F., Connis, R., & Sowers, J. (1978). The modification and maintenance of time spent attending to task using social reinforcement, token reinforcement and response cost in an applied restaurant setting. *Journal of Special Education Technology, 2*, 18–26.

Russa, M. B., Matthews, A. L., & Owen-DeSchryver, J. S. (2015). Expanding supports to improve the lives of families of children with autism spectrum disorder. *Journal of Positive Behavior Interventions, 17*(2), 95–104. https://doi.org/10.1177/1098300714532134

Russell, D., Ingvarsson, E. T., Haggar, J. L., & Jessel, J. (2018). Using progressive ratio schedules to evaluate tokens as generalized conditioned reinforcers. *Journal of Applied Behavior Analysis, 51*(1), 40–52. https://doi.org/10.1002/jaba.424

Russo, S. R., Tincani, M., & Axelrod, S. (2014). Evaluating open-ended parent reports and direct preference assessments to identify reinforcers for young children with autism. *Child & Family Behavior Therapy, 36*(2), 107–120. https://doi.org/10.1080/07317107.2014.910732

Ryan, J. B., Peterson, R. L., & Rozalski, M. (2007). State policies concerning the use of seclusion timeout in schools. *Education & Treatment of Children, 30*, 215–239.

Sabielny, L. M., & Cannella-Malone, H. I. (2014). Comparison of prompting strategies on the acquisition of daily living skills. *Education and Training in Autism and Developmental Disabilities, 49*(1), 145–152.

Sainato, D. M., Jung, S., Salmon, M. D., & Axe, J. B. (2008). Classroom influences on young children's emerging social competence. In W. H. Brown, S. L. Odom, & S. R. McConnell (eds.), *Social competence of young children: Risk, disability, and intervention* (pp. 99–116). Baltimore: Paul H. Brookes Publishing.

Saini, V., Greer, B. D., & Fisher, W. W. (2015). Clarifying inconclusive functional analysis results: Assessment and treatment of automatically reinforced aggression. *Journal of Applied Behavior Analysis, 48*(2), 315–330. https://doi.org/10.1002/jaba.203

Salend, S., & Gordon, B. (1987). A group-oriented time-out ribbon procedure. *Behavioral Disorders, 12*, 131–137.

Salend, S., & Kovalich, B. (1981). A group response cost system mediated by free tokens. *American Journal of Mental Deficiency, 86*, 184–187.

Salend, S., & Maragulia, D. (1983). The time-out ribbon: A procedure for the least restrictive environment. *Journal for Special Educators, 20*, 9–15.

Salend, S., & Meddaugh, D. (1985). Using a peer-mediated extinction procedure to decrease obscene language. *The Pointer, 30*, 8–11.

Salvatore, J. E., & Dick, D. M. (2018). Genetic influences on conduct disorder. *Neuroscience and Biobehavioral Reviews, 91*, 91–101. https://doi.org/10.1016/j.neubiorev.2016.06.034

Sanford, A. K., & Horner, R. H. (2013). Effects of matching instruction difficulty to reading level for students with escape-maintained problem behavior. *Journal of Positive Behavior Interventions, 15*(2), 79–89. https://doi.org/10.1177/1098300712449868

Sani-Bozkurt, S., & Ozen, A. (2015). Effectiveness and efficiency of peer and adult models used in video modeling in teaching pretend play skills to children with autism spectrum disorder. *Education and Training in Autism and Developmental Disabilities, 50*(1), 71–83.

Satsangi, R., Hammer, R., & Hogan, C. D. (2019). Video modeling and explicit instruction: A comparison of strategies for teaching mathematics to students with learning disabilities. *Learning Disabilities Research & Practice, 34*(1), 35–46. https://doi.org/10.1111/ldrp.12189

Saunders, A. F., Browder, D. M., & Root, J. R. (2017). Teaching mathematics and science to students with intellectual disability. In M. L. Wehmeyer & K. A. Shogren (eds.), *Handbook of research-based practices for educating students with intellectual disability* (pp. 343–364). New York: Routledge/Taylor & Francis Group.

Saunders, A. F., Spooner, F., & Ley Davis, L. (2018). Using video prompting to teach mathematical problem solving of real-world video-simulation problems. *Remedial and Special Education, 39*(1), 53–64.

Saunders, R., & Koplik, K. (1975). A multi-purpose data sheet for recording and graphing in the classroom. *AAESPH Review, 1*, 1.

Sautter, R. A., LeBlanc, L. A., & Gillett, J. N. (2008). Using free operant preference assessments to select toys for free play between children with autism and siblings. *Research in Autism Spectrum Disorders, 2*(1), 17–27. https://doi.org/10.1016/j.rasd.2007.02.001

Sawyer, M. R., Andzik, N. R., Kranak, M. P., Willke, C. P., Curiel, E. S. L., Hensley, L. E., et al. (2017). Improving pre-service teachers' performance skills through behavioral skills training. *Behavior Analysis in Practice, 10*(3), 296–300. https://doi.org/10.1007/s40617-017-0198-4

Scalzo, R., Henry, K., Davis, T. N., Amos, K., Zoch, T., Turchan, S., et al. (2015). Evaluation of interventions to reduce multiply controlled vocal stereotypy. *Behavior Modification, 39*(4), 496–509. https://doi.org/10.1177/0145445515573986

Schanding, G. T., Jr., Tingstrom, D. H., & Sterling-Turner, H. E. (2009). Evaluation of stimulus preference assessment methods with general education students. *Psychology in the Schools, 46*(2), 89–99. https://doi.org/10.1002/pits.20356

Schardt, A. A., Miller, F. G., & Bedesem, P. L. (2019). The effects of Cellf-Monitoring on students' academic engagement: A technology-based self-monitoring intervention. *Journal of Positive Behavior Interventions, 21*(1), 42–49. https://doi.org/10.1177/1098300718773462

Scheithauer, M., O'Connor, J., & Toby, L. M. (2015). Assessment of self-restraint using a functional analysis of self-injury. *Journal of Applied Behavior Analysis, 48*(4), 907–911. https://doi.org/10.1002/jaba.230

Scheithauer, M. C., Lomas Mevers, J. E., Call, N. A., & Shrewsbury, A. N. (2017). Using a test for multiply-maintained self injury to develop function-based treatments. *Journal of Developmental and Physical Disabilities, 29*(3), 443–460. https://doi.org/10.1007/s10882-017-9535-3

Schieltz, K. M., Wacker, D. P., Suess, A. N., Graber, J. E., Lustig, N. H., & Detrick, J. (2019). Evaluating the effects of positive reinforcement, instructional strategies, and negative reinforcement on problem behavior and academic performance: An experimental analysis. *Journal of Developmental and Physical Disabilities*. https://doi.org/10.1007/s10882-019-09696-y

Schiff, R., Nuri Ben-Shushan, Y., & Ben-Artzi, E. (2017). Metacognitive strategies: A foundation for early word spelling and reading in kindergartners with SLI. *Journal of Learning Disabilities, 50*(2), 143–157. https://doi.org/10.1177/0022219415589847

Schilling, D., & Cuvo, A. (1983). The effects of a contingency-based lottery on the behavior of a special education class. *Education and Training of the Mentally Retarded, 18*, 52–58.

Schlichenmeyer, K. J., Dube, W. V., & Vargas, I. M. (2015). Stimulus fading and response elaboration in differential reinforcement for alternative behavior. *Behavioral Interventions*, 30(1), 51–64. https://doi.org/10.1002/bin.1402

Schlinger, H. D., Jr. (2017). The importance of analysis in applied behavior analysis. *Behavior Analysis: Research and Practice*, 17(4), 334–346. https://doi.org/10.1037/bar0000080

Schloss, P., & Smith, M. (1987). Guidelines for ethical use of manual restraint in public school settings for behaviorally disordered students. *Behavioral Disorders*, 12, 207–213.

Schnaitter, R. (1999). Some criticisms of behaviorism. In B. A. Thyer (ed.), *The philosophical legacy of behaviorism*. Dordrecht, The Netherlands: Kluwer Academic Publishers.

Schoen, S., & Nolen, J. (2004). Decreasing acting-out behavior and increasing learning. *Teaching Exceptional Children*, 37, 26–29.

Schopler, E., Van Bourgondien, M., Wellman, G., & Love, S. (2010). *Childhood Autism Rating Scale* (2nd ed.). Upper Saddle River, NJ: Pearson.

Schrauben, K. S., & Dean, A. J. (2019). Cover-Copy-Compare for multiplication with students with emotional and behavioral disorders: A brief report. *Behavioral Disorders*, 45(1), 22–28. https://doi.org/10.1177/0198742918808484

Schreibman, L. (1975). Effects of within-stimulus and extra-stimulus prompting on discrimination learning in autistic children. *Journal of Applied Behavior Analysis*, 8, 91–112.

Schroeder, G. L., & Baer, D. M. (1972). Effects of concurrent and serial training on generalized vocal imitation in retarded children. *Development Psychology*, 6, 293–301.

Schroeder, S. R., & MacLean, W. (1987). If it isn't one thing, it's another: Experimental analysis of covariation in behavior management data of severely disturbed retarded persons. In S. Landesman & P. Vietze (eds.), *Living environments and mental retardation* (pp. 315–338). Washington, DC: AAMD Monograph.

Schroeder, S. R., Oldenquist, A., & Rohahn, J. (1990). A conceptual framework for judging the humaneness and effectiveness of behavioral treatment. In A. C. Repp & N. N. Singh (eds.), *Perspectives on the use of nonaversive and aversive interventions for persons with developmental disabilities*. New York: Sycamore.

Schultz, D. P. (1969). *A history of modern psychology*. New York: Academy Press.

Schumaker, J. B., Hovell, M. F., & Sherman, J. A. (1977). An analysis of daily report cards and parent-managed privileges in the improvement of adolescents' classroom performance. *Journal of Applied Behavior Analysis*, 10, 449–464.

Schwarz, M. L., & Hawkins, R. P. (1970). Application of delayed reinforcement procedures to the behavior of an elementary school child. *Journal of Applied Behavior Analysis*, 3, 85–96.

Sciuchetti, M. B. (2017). Addressing inequity in special education: An integrated framework for culturally responsive social emotional practice. *Psychology in the Schools*, 54(10), 1245–1251. https://doi.org/10.1002/pits.22073

Scott, T. M., & Alter, P. J. (2017). Examining the case for functional behavior assessment as an evidence-based practice for students with emotional and behavioral disorders in general education classrooms. *Preventing School Failure*, 61(1), 80–93.

Scott, T. M., & Cooper, J. (2013). Tertiary-tier PBIS in alternative, residential, and correctional school settings: Considering intensity in the delivery of evidence-based practice. *Education & Treatment of Children*, 36(3), 101–119. https://doi.org/10.1353/etc.2013.0029

Scott, T. M., & Cooper, J. T. (2017). Functional behavior assessment and function-based intervention planning: Considering the simple logic of the process. *Beyond Behavior*, 26(3), 101–104.

Scott-Goodwin, A. C., Puerto, M., & Moreno, I. (2016). Toxic effects of prenatal exposure to alcohol, tobacco and other drugs. *Reproductive Toxicology*, 61, 120–130.

Seaman-Tullis, R. L., Cannella-Malone, H. I., & Brock, M. E. (2019). Training a paraprofessional to implement video prompting with error correction to teach a vocational skill. *Focus on Autism and Other Developmental Disabilities*, 34(2), 107–117.

Seaver, J. L., & Bourret, J. C. (2014). An evaluation of response prompts for teaching behavior chains. *Journal of Applied Behavior Analysis*, 47(4), 777–792. https://doi.org/10.1002/jaba.159

Sedlak, R. A., Doyle, M., & Schloss, P. (1982). Video games: A training and generalization demonstration with severely retarded adolescents. *Education and Training for the Mentally Retarded*, 17, 332–336.

Sellers, T. P., Kelley, K., Higbee, T. S., & Wolfe, K. (2016). Effects of simultaneous script training on use of varied mand frames by preschoolers with autism. *Analysis of Verbal Behavior*, 32(1), 15–26. https://doi.org/10.1007/s40616-015-0049-8

Seward, J., Schuster, J. W., Ault, M. J., Collins, B. C., & Hall, M. (2014). Comparing simultaneous prompting and constant time delay to teach leisure skills to students with moderate intellectual disability. *Education and Training in Autism and Developmental Disabilities*, 49(3), 381–395.

Shabani, D. B., Katz, R. C., Wilder, D. A., Beauchamp, K., Taylor, C. R., & Fischer, K. J. (2002). Increasing social initiations in children with autism: Effects of a tactile prompt. *Journal of Applied Behavior Analysis*, 35, 79–83.

Shafer, M. S., Inge, K. J., & Hill, J. (1986). Acquisition, generalization, and maintenance of automated banking skills. *Education and Training of the Mentally Retarded*, 21, 265–272.

Sheehey, P. H., Wells, J. C., & Rowe, M. (2017). Effects of self-monitoring on math competency of an elementary student with cerebral palsy in an inclusive classroom. *Preventing School Failure*, 61(3), 211–219.

Shepley, S. B., Spriggs, A. D., Samudre, M. D., & Sartini, E. C. (2019). Initiation and generalization of self-instructed video activity schedules for elementary students with intellectual disability. *The Journal of Special Education*, 53(1), 51–62. https://doi.org/10.1177/0022466918800797

Shillingsburg, M. A., Gayman, C. M., & Walton, W. (2016). Using textual prompts to teach mands for information using "who?" *Analysis of Verbal Behavior*, 32(1), 1–14. https://doi.org/10.1007/s40616-016-0053-7

Shogren, K. A., & Wehmeyer, M. L. (2017). Goal setting and attainment. In M. L. Wehmeyer, K. A. Shogren, T. D. Little, & S. J. Lopez (eds.), *Development of self-determination through the life-course* (pp. 237–250). Springer Science + Business Media. https://doi.org/10.1007/978-94-024-1042-6_18

Shrestha, A., Anderson, A., & Moore, D. W. (2013). Using point-of-view video modeling and forward chaining to teach a functional self-help skill to a child with autism. *Journal of Behavioral Education*, 22(2), 157–167. https://doi.org/10.1007/s10864-012-9165-x

Shumate, E. D., & Wills, H. P. (2010). Classroom-based functional analysis and intervention for disruptive and off-task behaviors. *Education & Treatment of Children*, 33(1), 23–48. https://doi.org/10.1353/etc.0.0088

Sidman, M. (1960). *Tactics of scientific research: Evaluating experimental data in psychology*. Boston: Authors Cooperative.

Siegel, G. M., Lenske, J., & Broen, P. (1969). Suppression of normal speech disfluencies through response cost. *Journal of Applied Behavior Analysis*, 2, 265–276.

Silbaugh, B. C., & Falcomata, T. S. (2017). Translational evaluation of a lag schedule and variability in food consumed by a boy with autism and food selectivity. *Developmental Neurorehabilitation*, 20(5), 309–312. https://doi.org/10.3109/17518423.2016.1146364

Silbaugh, B. C., & Falcomata, T. S. (2019). Effects of a lag schedule with progressive time delay on sign mand variability in a boy with autism. *Behavior Analysis in Practice, 12*(1), 124–132. https://doi.org/10.1007/s40617-018-00273-x

Singh, N. (1987). Overcorrection of oral reading errors. *Behavior Modification, 11*, 165–181.

Singh, N., Dawson, M., & Manning, P. (1981). Effects of spaced responding DRL on the stereotyped behavior of profoundly retarded persons. *Journal of Applied Behavior Analysis, 14*, 521–526.

Singh, N. N., Lancioni, G. E., Myers, R. E., Karazsia, B. T., Courtney, T. M., & Nugent, K. (2017). A mindfulness-based intervention for self-management of verbal and physical aggression by adolescents with Prader–Willi syndrome. *Developmental Neurorehabilitation, 20*(5), 253–260. https://doi.org/10.3109/17518423.2016.1141436

Skerbetz, M. D., & Kostewicz, D. E. (2015). Consequence choice and students with emotional and behavioral disabilities: Effects on academic engagement. *Exceptionality, 23*(1), 14–33. https://doi.org/10.1080/09362835.2014.986603

Skinner, B. F. (1953). *Science and human behavior*. New York: Macmillan.

Skinner, B. F. (1957). *Verbal behavior*. New York: Appleton-Century-Crofts.

Skinner, B. F. (1963). Operant behavior. *American Psychologist, 18*, 503–515.

Skinner, B. F. (1968). *The technology of teaching*. New York: Appleton-Century-Crofts.

Skinner, B. F. (1969). Communication. *Journal of Applied Behavior Analysis, 2*, 247.

Skinner, B. F. (1971). *Beyond freedom and dignity*. New York: Knopf.

Skinner, B. F., & Vaughan, M. E. (1983). *Enjoy old age: A program of self-management*. New York: Warner Books.

Slavin, R. E. (1991, February). Group rewards make groupwork work: A response to Kohn. *Educational Leadership*, 89–91.

Sleeper, J. D., LeBlanc, L. A., Mueller, J., Valentino, A. L., Fazzio, D., & Raetz, P. B. (2017). The effects of electronic data collection on the percentage of current clinician graphs and organizational return on investment. *Journal of Organizational Behavior Management, 37*(1), 83–95. https://doi.org/10.1080/01608061.2016.1267065

Slocum, S. K., Grauerholz, F. E., Peters, K. P., & Vollmer, T. R. (2018). A multicomponent approach to thinning reinforcer delivery during noncontingent reinforcement schedules. *Journal of Applied Behavior Analysis, 51*(1), 61–69. https://doi.org/10.1002/jaba.427

Slocum, S. K., Vollmer, T. R., & Donaldson, J. M. (2019). Effects of delayed time-out on problem behavior of preschool children. *Journal of Applied Behavior Analysis, 52*(4), 994–1004. https://doi.org/10.1002/jaba.640

Smith, D. (1979). The improvement of children's oral reading through the use of teacher modeling. *Journal of Learning Disabilities, 12*, 172–175.

Smith, K. A., Shepley, S. B., Alexander, J. L., & Ayres, K. M. (2015). The independent use of self-instructions for the acquisition of untrained multi-step tasks for individuals with an intellectual disability: A review of the literature. *Research in Developmental Disabilities, 40*, 19–30. https://doi.org/10.1016/j.ridd.2015.01.010

Smith, K. A., Ayres, K. A., Alexander, J., Ledford, J. R., Shepley, C., & Shepley, S. B. (2016). Initiation and generalization of self-instructional skills in adolescents with autism and intellectual disability. *Journal of Autism and Developmental Disorders, 46*(4), 1196–1209. https://doi.org/10.1007/s10803-015-2654-8

Smith, L. M., LaGasse, L. L., Derauf, C., Grant, P., Rizwan, S., et al. (2006). The infant development, environment, and lifestyle study: Effects of prenatal methamphetamine exposure, polydrug exposure, and poverty on intrauterine growth. *Pediatrics, 118*, 1149–1156.

Smith, R., Iwata, B., & Shore, B. (1995). Effects of subject versus experimenter-selected reinforcers on the behavior of individuals with profound developmental disabilities. *Journal of Applied Behavior Analysis, 28*, 61–71.

Smith, R., Russo, L., & Le, D. (1999). Distinguishing between extinction and punishment effects of response blocking: A replication. *Journal of Applied Behavior Analysis, 32*(3), 367–370.

Smith, S., & Farrell, D. (1993). Level system use in special education: Classroom intervention with prima facie appeal. *Behavioral Disorders, 18*(4), 251–264.

Smith, S. C., & Higbee, T. S. (2020). Effects of behavioral skills training on teachers conducting the recess-to-classroom transition. *Journal of Behavioral Education*. https://doi.org/10.1007/s10864-020-09395-1

Smith, T. (2001). Discrete trial training in the treatment of autism. *Focus on Autism and Other Developmental Disabilities, 16*(2), 86–92. https://doi.org/10.1177/108835760101600204

Snell, M., & Loyd, B. (1991). A study of effects of trend, variability, frequency, and form of data on teachers' judgments about progress and their decisions about program change. *Research in Developmental Disabilities, 12*, 41–62.

Snodgrass, M. R., Chung, M. Y., Meadan, H., & Halle, J. W. (2018). Social validity in single-case research: A systematic literature review of prevalence and application. *Research in Developmental Disabilities, 74*, 160–173. https://doi.org/10.1016/j.ridd.2018.01.007

Sobsey, D. (1990). Modifying the behavior of behavior modifiers. In A. Repp & N. Singh (eds.), *Perspectives on the use of nonaversive and aversive interventions for persons with developmental disabilities* (pp. 421–433). Sycamore, IL: Sycamore Publishing.

Solomon, R. W., & Wahler, R. G. (1973). Peer reinforcement control of classroom problem behavior. *Journal of Applied Behavior Analysis, 6*, 49–56.

Soukup, J. H., Wehmeyer, M. L., Bashinski, S. M., & Bovaird, J. A. (2007). Classroom variables and access to the general curriculum for students with disabilities. *Exceptional Children, 74*(1), 101–120. https://doi.org/10.1177/001440290707400106

Sparrow, S., Cicchetti, O., & Balla, D. (2007). *Vineland Adaptive Behavior Scales, second edition (Vineland-II)*. Upper Saddle River, NJ: Merrill/Pearson Education.

Spitz, D., & Spitz, W. (1990). Killer pop machines. *Journal of Forensic Science, 35*, 490–492.

Spooner, F. (1981). An operant analysis of the effects of backward chaining and total task presentation. *Dissertation Abstracts International, 41*, 3992A [University Microfilms No. 8105615].

Spooner, F., Kemp-Inman, A., Ahlgrim-Delzell, L., Wood, L., & Ley Davis, L. (2015). Generalization of literacy skills through portable technology for students with severe disabilities. *Research and Practice for Persons with Severe Disabilities, 40*(1), 52–70.

Spooner, F., & Spooner, D. (1983). Variability: An aid in the assessment of training procedures. *Journal of Precision Teaching, 4*(1), 5–13.

Spooner, F., & Spooner, D. (1984). A review of chaining techniques: Implications for future research and practice. *Education and Training of the Mentally Retarded, 19*, 114–124.

Sprague, J. R., & Horner, R. H. (1984). The effects of single instance, multiple instance, and general case training on generalized vending machine use by moderately and severely handicapped students. *Journal of Applied Behavior Analysis, 17*(2), 273–278. https://doi.org/10.1901/jaba.1984.17-273

Sprague, J., Jolivette, K., Boden, L. J., & Wang, E. (2020). Implementing facility-wide positive behavior interventions and supports in secure juvenile correction settings: Results of an evaluation study. *Remedial and Special Education, 41*(2), 70–79.

Staats, A. W., & Staats, C. K. (1963). *Complex human behavior*. New York: Holt, Rinehart & Winston.

Stafford, A., Alberto, P., Fredrick, L., Heflin, J., & Heller, K. (2002). Preference variability and the instruction of choice making with students with severe intellectual disabilities. *Education and Training in Mental Retardation and Developmental Disabilities, 37*, 70–88.

Stahmer, A. C., & Carter, C. (2005). An empirical examination of toddler development in inclusive childcare. *Early Child Development and Care, 175*(4), 321–333. https://doi.org/10.1080/0300443042000266231

Stainback, S., & Stainback, W. (1984). Broadening the research perspective in special education. *Exceptional Children, 50*, 400–408.

Stainback, W., Payne, J., Stainback, S., & Payne, R. (1973). *Establishing a token economy in the classroom*. Columbus, OH: Merrill.

Stainback, W., Stainback, S., & Strathe, M. (1983). Generalization of positive social behavior by severely handicapped students: A review and analysis of research. *Education and Training of the Mentally Retarded, 18*, 293–299.

Stainton, T., & Clare, I. C. H. (2012). Human rights and intellectual disabilities: An emergent theoretical paradigm? *Journal of Intellectual Disability Research, 56*(11), 1011–1013. https://doi.org/10.1111/jir.12001

Steed, S. E., & Lutzker, J. R. (1997). Using picture prompts to teach an adult with developmental disabilities to independently complete vocational tasks. *Journal of Developmental and Physical Disabilities, 9*, 117–133.

Steege, M., & Northup, J. (1998). Functional analysis of problem behavior: A practical approach for school psychologists. *Proven Practice, 1*, 4–12.

Steege, M. W., Pratt, J. L., Wickerd, G., Guare, R., & Watson, T. S. (2019). *Conducting school-based functional behavioral assessments: A practitioner's guide* (3rd ed.). The Guilford Practical Intervention in the Schools Series. New York: Guilford Press.

Stephens, T. M. (1976). *Directive teaching of children with learning and behavioral handicaps*. Columbus, OH: Merrill.

Steuart, W. (1993). Effectiveness of arousal and arousal plus overcorrection to reduce nocturnal bruxism. *Journal of Behavior Therapy & Experimental Psychiatry, 24*, 181–185.

Stevens, K. B., & Schuster, J. W. (1987). Effects of a constant time delay procedure on the written spelling performance of a learning disabled student. *Learning Disability Quarterly, 10*, 9–16.

Stevenson, J., & Clayton, F. (1970). A response duration schedule: Effects of training, extinction, and deprivation. *Journal of the Experimental Analysis of Behavior, 13*, 359–367.

Stewart, C., & Singh, N. (1986). Overcorrection of spelling deficits in mentally retarded persons. *Behavior Modification, 10*, 355–365.

Stewart, S. C., & Evans, W. H. (1997). Setting the stage for success: Assessing the instructional environment. *Preventing School Failure, 41*(2), 53–56.

Stocco, C. S., Thompson, R. H., Hart, J. M., & Soriano, H. L. (2017). Improving the interview skills of college students using behavioral skills training. *Journal of Applied Behavior Analysis, 50*(3), 495–510. https://doi.org/10.1002/jaba.385

Stocker, J. D., Jr., & Kubina, R. M., Jr. (2017). Impact of cover, copy, and compare on fluency outcomes for students with disabilities and math deficits: A review of the literature. *Preventing School Failure, 61*(1), 56–68.

Stoiber, K. C., & Gettinger, M. (2011). Functional assessment and positive support strategies for promoting resilience: Effects on teachers and high-risk children. *Psychology in the Schools, 48*(7), 686–706. https://doi.org/10.1002/pits.20587

Stokes, J. V., Cameron, M. J., Dorsey, M. F., & Fleming, E. (2004). Task analysis, correspondence training, and general case instruction for teaching personal hygiene skills. *Behavioral Interventions, 19*(2), 121–135. https://doi.org/10.1002/bin.153

Stokes, T. F., & Baer, D. M. (1976). Preschool peers as mutual generalization-facilitating agents. *Behavior Therapy, 7*(4), 549–556. https://doi.org/10.1016/S0005-7894(76)80177-3

Stokes, T. F., & Baer, D. M. (1977). An implicit technology of generalization. *Journal of Applied Behavior Analysis, 10*, 349–367.

Stokes, T. F., Baer, D. M., & Jackson, R. L. (1974). Programming the generalization of a greeting response in four retarded children. *Journal of Applied Behavior Analysis, 7*, 599–610.

Stolz, S. B. (1977). Why no guidelines for behavior modification? *Journal of Applied Behavior Analysis, 10*, 541–547.

Stormont, M., & Reinke, W. M. (2013). Implementing Tier 2 social behavioral interventions: Current issues, challenges, and promising approaches. *Journal of Applied School Psychology, 29*(2), 121–125. https://doi.org/10.1080/15377903.2013.778769

Stotz, K. E., Itoi, M., Konrad, M., & Alber-Morgan, S. R. (2008). Effects of self-graphing on written expression of fourth grade students with high-incidence disabilities. *Journal of Behavioral Education, 17*(2), 172–186. https://doi.org/10.1007/s10864-007-9055-9

Strauss, A. A., & Lehtinen, L. E. (1947). *Psychopathology and education of the brain-injured child*. New York: Grune & Stratton.

Streifel, S., & Wetherby, B. (1973). Instruction-following behavior of a retarded child and its controlling stimuli. *Journal of Applied Behavior Analysis, 6*, 663–670.

Strickland-Cohen, M. K., Kennedy, P. C., Berg, T. A., Bateman, L. J., & Horner, R. H. (2016). Building school district capacity to conduct functional behavioral assessment. *Journal of Emotional and Behavioral Disorders, 24*(4), 235–246.

Stringer, E. T. (2014). *Action research* (4th ed.). Los Angeles, CA: Sage.

Stringfield, S. G., Luscre, D., & Gast, D. L. (2011). Effects of a Story Map on accelerated reader postreading test scores in students with high-functioning autism. *Focus on Autism and Other Developmental Disabilities, 26*(4), 218–229. https://doi.org/10.1177/1088357611423543

Strohmeier, C., Mulé, C., & Luiselli, J. K. (2014). Social validity assessment of training methods to improve treatment integrity of special education service providers. *Behavior Analysis in Practice, 7*(1), 15–20. https://doi.org/10.1007/s40617-014-0004-5

Strohmeier, C., Pace, G. M., & Luiselli, J. K. (2014). Brief (test-control) functional analysis and treatment evaluation of aggressive behavior evoked by divided attention. *Behavioral Interventions, 29*(4), 331–338. https://doi.org/10.1002/bin.1394

Sugai, G., & Horner, R. H. (2020). Sustaining and scaling positive behavioral interventions and supports: Implementation drivers, outcomes, and considerations. *Exceptional Children, 86*(2), 120–136.

Sullivan, W. E., & Roane, H. S. (2018). Incorporating choice in differential reinforcement of other behavior arrangements. *Behavioral Development, 23*(2), 130–137. https://doi.org/10.1037/bdb0000079

Sulzer-Azaroff, B., & Mayer, G. R. (1986). *Achieving educational excellence*. New York: Holt, Rinehart & Winston.

Sulzer-Azaroff, B., Thaw, J., & Thomas, C. (1975). Behavioral competencies for the evaluation of behavior modifiers. In W. S. Wood (ed.), *Issues in evaluating behavior modification* (pp. 47–98). Champaign, IL: Research Press.

Summers, J., Rincover, A., & Feldman, M. (1993). Comparison of extra- and within-stimulus prompting to teach prepositional discriminations to preschool children with developmental disabilities. *Journal of Behavioral Education, 3*(3), 287–298.

Sumner, J., Meuser, S., Hsu, L., & Morales, R. (1974). Overcorrection treatment of radical reduction of aggressive-disruptive behavior in institutionalized mental patients. *Psychological Reports, 35,* 655–662.

Sundberg, M. L. (2008). *VB-MAPP: Verbal behavior milestones assessment and placement program.* Concord, CA: AVB Press.

Sundberg, M. L., & Partington, J. W. (1999). The need for both discrete trial and natural environment language training for children with autism. In P. M. Ghezzi, W. L. Williams, & J. E. Carr (eds.), *Autism: Behavior analytic perspectives* (pp. 139–156). Reno, NV: Context Press.

Susa, C., & Schlinger, H. D., Jr. (2012). Using a lag schedule to increase variability of verbal responding in an individual with autism. *Analysis of Verbal Behavior, 28,* 125–130. https://doi.org/10.1007/BF03393113

Sutherland, K., Wehby, J., & Copeland, S. (2000). Effect of varying rates of behavior-specific praise on the on-task behavior of students with EBD. *Journal of Emotional and Behavioral Disorders, 8,* 2–8.

Swain, R., Lane, J. D., & Gast, D. L. (2015). Comparison of constant time delay and simultaneous prompting procedures: Teaching functional sight words to students with intellectual disabilities and autism spectrum disorder. *Journal of Behavioral Education, 24*(2), 210–229. https://doi.org/10.1007/s10864-014-9209-5

Swain-Bradway, J., Pinkney, C., & Flannery, K. B. (2015). Implementing schoolwide positive behavior interventions and supports in high schools: Contextual factors and stages of implementation. *TEACHING Exceptional Children, 47*(5), 245–255.

Swanson, L. (1981). Self-monitoring effects on concurrently reinforced reading behavior of a learning disabled child. *Child Study Journal, 10*(4), 225–232.

Sweeney, W. J., Salva, E., Cooper, J. O., & Talbert-Johnson, C. (1993). Using self-evaluation to improve difficult-to-read handwriting of secondary students. *Journal of Behavioral Education, 3,* 427–443.

Swerdan, M. G., & Rosales, R. (2017). Comparison of prompting techniques to teach children with autism to ask questions in the context of a conversation. *Focus on Autism and Other Developmental Disabilities, 32*(2), 93–101. https://doi.org/10.1177/1088357615610111

Szalwinski, J., Thomason, S. J. L., Moore, E., & McConnell, K. (2019). Effects of decreasing intersession interval duration on graduated exposure treatment during simulated routine dental care. *Journal of Applied Behavior Analysis, 52*(4), 944–955. https://doi.org/10.1002/jaba.642

Szmacinski, N. J., DeBar, R. M., Sidener, T. M., & Sidener, D. W. (2018). Fading an auditory model by volume to teach mands to children with autism spectrum disorder. *Journal of Developmental and Physical Disabilities, 30*(5), 653–668. https://doi.org/10.1007/s10882-018-9610-4

Taber, K. S. (2019). Constructivism in education: Interpretations and criticisms from science education. In Information Resources Management Association (Ed.), *Early childhood development: Concepts, methodologies, tools, and applications* (pp. 312–342). Hershey, Pennsylvania: IGI Global.

Taber, T. A., Alberto, P. A., & Fredrick, L. D. (1998). Use of self-operated auditory prompts by workers with moderate mental retardation to transition independently through vocational tasks. *Research in Developmental Disabilities, 19,* 127–145.

Taber, T. A., Alberto, P. A., Seltzer, A., Hughes, M., & O'Neill, R. (2003). Obtaining assistance when lost in the community using cell phones. *Research and Practice for Persons with Severe Disabilities, 28*(3), 105–116. https://doi.org/10.2511/rpsd.28.3.105

Tapp, J., Wehby, J., & Ellis, D. (1995). A multi-option observation system for experimental studies: MOOSES. *Behavior Research Methods, Instruments, & Computers, 27,* 25–31.

Tarbox, J., Wilke, A. E., Findel-Pyles, R. S., Bergstrom, R. M., & Granpeesheh, D. (2010). A comparison of electronic to traditional pen-and-paper data collection in discrete trial training for children with autism. *Research in Autism Spectrum Disorders, 4*(1), 65–75. https://doi.org/10.1016/j.rasd.2009.07.008

Taylor, B. A., Hughes, C. A., Richard, E., Hoch, H., & Coello, A. R. (2004). Teaching teenagers with autism to seek assistance when lost. *Journal of Applied Behavior Analysis, 37,* 79–82.

Taylor, B. R., & Levin, L. (1998). Teaching a student with autism to make verbal initiations: Effects of a tactile prompt. *Journal of Applied Behavior Analysis, 31,* 651–654.

Tekin-Iftar, E., Olcay-Gul, S., & Collins, B. C. (2019). Descriptive analysis and meta analysis of studies investigating the effectiveness of simultaneous prompting procedure. *Exceptional Children, 85*(3), 309–328.

Tereshko, L., & Sottolano, D. (2017). The effects of an escape extinction procedure using protective equipment on self-injurious behavior. *Behavioral Interventions, 32*(2), 152–159. https://doi.org/10.1002/bin.1475

Terrace, H. S. (1966). Stimulus control. In W. K. Honig (ed.), *Operant behavior: Areas of research and application.* New York: Appleton–Century–Crofts.

Test, D. W., & Spooner, F. (1996). *Community-based instructional support.* Washington, DC: American Association on Mental Retardation.

Therrien, M. C. S., & Light, J. C. (2018). Promoting peer interaction for preschool children with complex communication needs and autism spectrum disorder. *American Journal of Speech-Language Pathology, 27*(1), 207–221. https://doi.org/10.1044/2017_AJSLP-17-0104

Thiemann-Bourque, K., Feldmiller, S., Hoffman, L., & Johner, S. (2018). Incorporating a peer-mediated approach into speech-generating device intervention: Effects on communication of preschoolers with autism spectrum disorder. *Journal of Speech, Language, and Hearing Research, 61*(8), 2045–2061. https://doi.org/10.1044/2018_JSLHR-L-17-0424

Thomas, E. M., DeBar, R. M., Vladescu, J. C., & Townsend, D. B. (2020). A comparison of video modeling and video prompting by adolescents with ASD. *Behavior Analysis in Practice, 13*(1), 40–52. https://doi.org/10.1007/s40617-019-00402-0

Thomas, J. D., Presland, I. E., Grant, M. D., & Glynn, T. L. (1978). Natural rates of teacher approval and disapproval in grade-7 classrooms. *Journal of Applied Behavior Analysis, 11,* 91–94.

Thomason-Sassi, J. L., Iwata, B. A., & Fritz, J. N. (2013). Therapist and setting influences on functional analysis outcomes. *Journal of Applied Behavior Analysis, 46*(1), 79–87. https://doi.org/10.1002/jaba.28

Thompson, J. L., Plavnick, J. B., & Skibbe, L. E. (2019). Eye-tracking analysis of attention to an electronic storybook for minimally verbal children with autism spectrum disorder. *The Journal of Special Education, 53*(1), 41–50. https://doi.org/10.1177/0022466918796504

Thompson, R. H., Fisher, W. W., & Contrucci, S. A. (1998). Evaluating the reinforcing effects of choice in comparison to reinforcement rate. *Research in Developmental Disabilities, 19*(2), 181–187. https://doi.org/10.1016/S0891-4222(97)00050-4

Thompson, R. H., & Iwata, B. A. (2007). A comparison of outcomes from descriptive and functional analyses of problem behavior. *Journal of Applied Behavior Analysis, 40*(2), 333–338. https://doi.org/10.1901/jaba.2007.56-06

Thomson, K. M., Czarnecki, D., Martin, T. L., Yu, C. T., & Martin, G. L. (2007). Predicting optimal preference assessment methods for individuals with developmental disabilities. *Education and Training in Developmental Disabilities, 42*(1), 107–114.

Thorndike, E. L. (1905). *The elements of psychology.* New York: Seiler.

Thorndike, E. L. (1931). *Human learning*. New York: Appleton-Century-Crofts.

Tiger, J. H., Fisher, W. W., Toussaint, K. A., & Kodak, T. (2009). Progressing from initially ambiguous functional analyses: Three case examples. *Research in Developmental Disabilities, 30*(5), 910–926. https://doi.org/10.1016/j.ridd.2009.01.005

Tiger, J. H., Hanley, G. P., & Bessette, K. K. (2006). Incorporating descriptive assessment results into the design of a functional analysis: A case example involving a preschooler's hand mouthing. *Education & Treatment of Children, 29*(1), 107–124.

Tiger, J. H., Wierzba, B. C., Fisher, W. W., & Benitez, B. B. (2017). Developing and demonstrating inhibitory stimulus control over repetitive behavior. *Behavioral Interventions, 32*(2), 160–174. https://doi.org/10.1002/bin.1472

Tolman, E. C. (1932). *Purposive behavior in animals and men*. New York: Appleton-Century-Crofts.

Torelli, J. N., Lambert, J. M., Da Fonte, M. A., Denham, K. N., Jedrzynski, T. M., & Houchins-Juarez, N. J. (2016). Assessing acquisition of and preference for mand topographies during functional communication training. *Behavior Analysis in Practice, 9*(2), 165–168. https://doi.org/10.1007/s40617-015-0083-y

Touchette, P., MacDonald, R., & Langer, S. (1985). A scatter plot for identifying stimulus control of problem behavior. *Journal of Applied Behavior Analysis, 18*, 343–351.

Toussaint, K. A., Kodak, T., & Vladescu, J. C. (2016). An evaluation of choice on instructional efficacy and individual preferences among children with autism. *Journal of Applied Behavior Analysis, 49*(1), 170–175. https://doi.org/10.1002/jaba.263

Toussaint, K. A., Scheithauer, M. C., Tiger, J. H., & Saunders, K. J. (2017). Teaching identity matching of braille characters to beginning braille readers. *Journal of Applied Behavior Analysis, 50*(2), 278–289. https://doi.org/10.1002/jaba.382

Toussaint, K. A., & Tiger, J. H. (2012). Reducing covert self-injurious behavior maintained by automatic reinforcement through a variable momentary DRO procedure. *Journal of Applied Behavior Analysis, 45*(1), 179–184. https://doi.org/10.1901/jaba.2012.45-179

Trant, L. (1977). Pictorial token card (communication). *Journal of Applied Behavior Analysis, 10*, 548.

Trask-Tyler, S. A., Grossi, T. A., & Heward, W. L. (1994). Teaching young adults with developmental disabilities and visual impairments to use tape-recorded recipes: Acquisition, generalization, and maintenance of cooking skills. *Journal of Behavioral Education, 4*, 283–311.

Traub, M. R., & Vollmer, T. R. (2019). Response latency as a measure of behavior in the assessment of elopement. *Journal of Applied Behavior Analysis, 52*(2), 422–438. https://doi.org/10.1002/jaba.541

Travers, J. C. (2017). Evaluating claims to avoid pseudoscientific and unproven practices in special education. *Intervention in School and Clinic, 52*(4), 195–203.

Trevino-Maack, S. I., Kamps, D., & Wills, H. (2015). A group contingency plus self-management intervention targeting at-risk secondary students' class-work and active engagement. *Remedial and Special Education, 36*(6), 347–360. https://doi.org/10.1177/0741932514561865

Trussell, R. P., Chen, H. J., Lewis, T. J., & Luna, N. E. (2018). Reducing escape-maintained behavior through the application of classroom-wide practices and individually designed interventions. *Education & Treatment of Children, 41*(8), 507–531. https://doi.org/10.1353/etc.2018.0027

Tsami, L., & Lerman, D. C. (2020). Transfer of treatment effects from combined to isolated conditions during functional communication training for multiply controlled problem behavior. *Journal of Applied Behavior Analysis, 53*(2), 649–664. https://doi.org/10.1002/jaba.629

Tsiouri, I., & Greer, R. D. (2007). The role of different social reinforcement contingencies in inducing echoic tacts through motor imitation responding in children with severe language delays. *Journal of Early and Intensive Behavior Intervention, 4*(4), 629–647. https://doi.org/10.1037/h0100397

Tullis, C. A., Frampton, S. E., Delfs, C. H., Greene, K., & Reed, S. (2019). The effects of instructive feedback and stimulus equivalence procedures on group instructional outcomes. *Journal of Behavioral Education*. https://doi.org/10.1007/s10864-019-09349-2

Turnbull, H. R., Wilcox, B., Stowe, M., & Turnbull, A. (2001). IDEA requirements for use of PBS. *Journal of Positive Behavior Interventions, 3*, 11–18.

Turnbull, R. (2017). Education, ethical communities, and personal dignity. *Intellectual and Developmental Disabilities, 55*(2), 110–111. https://doi.org/10.1352/1934-9556-55.2.110

Turner, J., Rafferty, L. A., Sullivan, R., & Blake, A. (2017). Action research of an error self-correction intervention: Examining the effects on the spelling accuracy behaviors of fifth-grade students identified as at-risk. *Preventing School Failure, 61*(2), 146–154.

Twyman, J., Johnson, H., Buie, J., & Nelson, C. M. (1994). The use of a warning procedure to signal a more intrusive timeout contingency. *Behavioral Disorders, 19*(4), 243–253.

Tzanakaki, P., Grindle, C. F., Dungait, S., Hulson-Jones, A., Saville, M., Hughes, J. C., et al. (2014). Use of a tactile prompt to increase social initiations in children with autism. *Research in Autism Spectrum Disorders, 8*(6), 726–736. https://doi.org/10.1016/j.rasd.2014.03.016

Umbreit, J., Ferro, J., Liaupsin, C., & Lane, K. (2007). *Functional behavioral assessment and function-based intervention*. Upper Saddle River, NJ: Merrill/Pearson Education.

Valentino, A. L., LeBlanc, L. A., Veazey, S. E., Weaver, L. A., & Raetz, P. B. (2019). Using a prerequisite skills assessment to identify optimal modalities for mand training. *Behavior Analysis in Practice, 12*(1), 22–32. https://doi.org/10.1007/s40617-018-0256-6

Van Camp, C., Lerman, D., Kelley, M., Contrucci, S., & Vorndran, C. (2000). Variable-time reinforcement schedules in the treatment of socially maintained problem behavior. *Journal of Applied Behavior Analysis, 33*, 545–557.

van den Berg, Y. H. M., & Stoltz, S. (2018). Enhancing social inclusion of children with externalizing problems through classroom seating arrangements: A randomized controlled trial. *Journal of Emotional and Behavioral Disorders, 26*(1), 31–41. https://doi.org/10.1177/1063426617740561

van den Pol, R. A., Iwata, B. A., Ivancic, M. T., Page, T. J., Need, N. A., & Whitely, F. P. (1981). Teaching the handicapped to eat in public places: Acquisition, generalization and maintenance of restaurant skills. *Journal of Applied Behavior Analysis, 14*, 61–69.

van der Burg, J. J. W., Sohier, J., & Jongerius, P. H. (2018). Generalization and maintenance of a self-management program for drooling in children with neurodevelopmental disabilities: A second case series. *Developmental Neurorehabilitation, 21*(1), 13–22. https://doi.org/10.1080/17518423.2016.1232763

van der Meer, L., Achmadi, D., Cooijmans, M., Didden, R., Lancioni, G. E., O'Reilly, M. F., et al. (2015). An iPad-based intervention for teaching picture and word matching to a student with ASD and severe communication impairment. *Journal of Developmental and Physical Disabilities, 27*(1), 67–78. https://doi.org/10.1007/s10882-014-9401-5

Van Houten, R. (1993). The use of wrist weights to reduce self-injury maintained by sensory reinforcement. *Journal of Applied Behavior Analysis, 26*, 197–203.

Van Houten, R., Axelrod, S., Bailey, J. S., Favell, J. E., Foxx, R. M., Iwata, B. A., et al. (1988). The right to effective behavioral treatment. *The Behavior Analyst, 11*, 111–114.

Van Houten, R., Nau, P., Mackenzie-Keating, S., Sameoto, D., & Colavecchia, B. (1982). An analysis of some variables influencing the effectiveness of reprimands. *Journal of Applied Behavior Analysis, 15*, 65–83.

Van Houten, R., & Retting, R. A. (2001). Increasing motorist compliance and caution at stop signs. *Journal of Applied Behavior Analysis, 34*, 185–193.

Van Laarhoven, T., Kraus, E., Karpman, K., Nizzi, R., & Valentino, J. (2010). A comparison of picture and video prompts to teach daily living skills to individuals with autism. *Focus on Autism and Other Developmental Disabilities, 25*(4), 195–208. https://doi.org/10.1177/1088357610380412

Van Laarhoven, T., & Van Laarhoven-Myers, T. (2006). Comparison of three video-based instructional procedures for teaching daily living skills to persons with developmental disabilities. *Education and Training in Developmental Disabilities, 41*, 365–381.

Van Laarhoven, T., Winiarski, L., Blood, E., & Chan, J. M. (2012). Maintaining vocational skills of individuals with autism and developmental disabilities through video modeling. *Education and Training in Autism and Developmental Disabilities, 47*(4), 447–461.

Van Laarhoven, T., Zurita, L. M., Johnson, J. W., Grider, K. M., & Grider, K. L. (2009). A comparison of self, other, and subjective video models for teaching daily living skills to individuals with developmental disabilities. *Education and Training in Developmental Disabilities, 44*, 509–522.

Vanselow, N. R., & Bourret, J. C. (2012). Online interactive tutorials for creating graphs with Excel 2007 or 2010. *Behavior Analysis in Practice, 5*(1), 40–46.

Varsamis, P., & Agaliotis, I. (2011). Profiles of self-concept, goal orientation, and self-regulation in students with physical, intellectual, and multiple disabilities: Implications for instructional support. *Research in Developmental Disabilities, 32*(5), 1548–1555. https://doi.org/10.1016/j.ridd.2011.01.054

Vedora, J., & Barry, T. (2016). The use of picture prompts and prompt delay to teach receptive labeling. *Journal of Applied Behavior Analysis, 49*(4), 960–964. https://doi.org/10.1002/jaba.336

Vegas, K., Jenson, W., & Kircher, J. (2007). A single-subject meta-analysis of the effectiveness of time-out in reducing disruptive classroom behavior. *Behavioral Disorders, 32*, 109–121.

Verriden, A. L., & Roscoe, E. M. (2016). A comparison of preference-assessment methods. *Journal of Applied Behavior Analysis, 49*(2), 265–285. https://doi.org/10.1002/jaba.302

Verriden, A. L., & Roscoe, E. M. (2019). An evaluation of a punisher assessment for decreasing automatically reinforced problem behavior. *Journal of Applied Behavior Analysis, 52*(1), 205–226. https://doi.org/10.1002/jaba.509

Verschuur, R., Didden, R., van der Meer, L., Achmadi, D., Kagohara, D., Green, V. A., et al. (2011). Investigating the validity of a structured interview protocol for assessing the preferences of children with autism spectrum disorders. *Developmental Neurorehabilitation, 14*(6), 366–371. https://doi.org/10.3109/17518423.2011.606509

Vieillevoye, S., & Nader-Grosbois, N. (2008). Self-regulation during pretend play in children with intellectual disability and in normally developing children. *Research in Developmental Disabilities, 29*(3), 256–272. https://doi.org/10.1016/j.ridd.2007.05.003

Vollmer, T. (1999). Noncontingent reinforcement: Some additional comments. *Journal of Applied Behavior Analysis, 32*, 239–240.

Vollmer, T., Ringdahl, J., Roane, H., & Marcus, B. (1997). Negative side effects of noncontingent reinforcement. *Journal of Applied Behavior Analysis, 30*, 161–164.

Vollmer, T. R., Hagopian, L. P., Bailey, J. S., Dorsey, M. F., Hanley, G. P., Lennox, D., et al. (2011). The Association for Behavior Analysis International position statement on restraint and seclusion. *The Behavior Analyst, 34*(1), 103–110. https://doi.org/10.1007/BF03392238

Vollmer, T. R., Sloman, K. N., & Pipkin, C. S. P. (2008). Practical implications of data reliability and treatment integrity monitoring. *Behavior Analysis in Practice, 1*(2), 4–11.

Voltz, D. L. (2003). Personalized contextual instruction. *Preventing School Failure, 47*, 138–143.

Vorndran, C. M., Pace, G. M., Luiselli, J. K., Flaherty, J., Christian, L., & Kleinmann, A. (2008). Functional analysis and treatment of chronic hair pulling in a child with Cri du Chat Syndrome: Effects on co-occurring thumb sucking. *Behavior Analysis in Practice, 1*(1), 10–15.

Voulgarakis, H., & Forte, S. (2015). Escape extinction and negative reinforcement in the treatment of pediatric feeding disorders: A single case analysis. *Behavior Analysis in Practice, 8*(2), 212–214. https://doi.org/10.1007/s40617-015-0086-8

Wacker, D., Berg, W., Wiggins, B., Muldoon, M., & Cavanaugh, J. (1985). Evaluation of reinforcer preferences for profoundly handicapped students. *Journal of Applied Behavior Analysis, 18*, 173–178.

Wadsworth, J. P., Hansen, B. D., & Wills, S. B. (2015). Increasing compliance in students with intellectual disabilities using functional behavioral assessment and self-monitoring. *Remedial and Special Education, 36*(4), 195–207. https://doi.org/10.1177/0741932514554102

Wahl, E., Hawkins, R. O., Haydon, T., Marsicano, R., & Morrison, J. Q. (2016). Comparing versions of the good behavior game: Can a positive spin enhance effectiveness? *Behavior Modification, 40*(4), 493–517. https://doi.org/10.1177/0145445516644220

Walker, H. M., & Buckley, N. K. (1972). Programming generalization and maintenance of treatment effects across time and across settings. *Journal of Applied Behavior Analysis, 5*, 209–224.

Walker, H. M., Mattsen, R. H., & Buckley, N. K. (1971). The functional analysis of behavior within an experimental class setting. In W. C. Becker (ed.), *An empirical basis for change in education*. Chicago: Science Research Associates.

Walker, V. L., Chung, Y.-C., & Bonnet, L. K. (2018). Function-based intervention in inclusive school settings: A meta-analysis. *Journal of Positive Behavior Interventions, 20*(4), 203–216. https://doi.org/10.1177/1098300717718350

Walker, V. L., Lyon, K. J., Loman, S. L., & Sennott, S. (2018). A systematic review of functional communication training (FCT) interventions involving augmentative and alternative communication in school settings. *AAC: Augmentative and Alternative Communication, 34*(2), 118–129. https://doi.org/10.1080/07434618.2018.1461240

Wallace, A. M., Bechtel, D. R., Heatter, S., & Barry, L. M. (2016). A comparison of prompting strategies to teach intraverbals to an adolescent with Down syndrome. *Analysis of Verbal Behavior, 32*(2), 225–232. https://doi.org/10.1007/s40616-016-0058-2

Wallace, I. (1977). Self-control techniques of famous novelists. (Introduction by J. J. Pear.) *Journal of Applied Behavior Analysis, 10*, 515–525.

Walls, R. T., Zane, T., & Ellis, W. D. (1981). Forward chaining, backward chaining, and whole task methods for training assembly tasks. *Behavior Modification, 5*, 61–74.

Ward, K. D., & Shukla Mehta, S. (2019). The use of a stimulus control transfer procedure to teach motivation-controlled mands to children with autism. *Focus on Autism and Other Developmental Disabilities, 34*(4), 215–225.

Ward, R. D., & Higbee, T. S. (2008). Noncontingent reinforcement as treatment for tub-standing in a toddler.

Wasano, L. C., Borrero, J. C., & Kohn, C. S. (2009). Brief Report: A comparison of indirect versus experimental strategies for the assessment of pica. *Journal of Autism and Developmental Disorders, 39*(11), 1582–1586.

Wasik, B. A., & Hindman, A. H. (2018). Why wait? The importance of wait time in developing young students' language and vocabulary skills. *Reading Teacher, 72*(3), 369–378.

Wathen, S. N., & Podlesnik, C. A. (2018). Laboratory models of treatment relapse and mitigation techniques. *Behavior Analysis: Research and Practice, 18*(4), 362–387. https://doi.org/10.1037/bar0000119

Watkins, N., & Rapp, J. T. (2014). Environmental enrichment and response cost: Immediate and subsequent effects on stereotypy. *Journal of Applied Behavior Analysis, 47*(1), 186–191. https://doi.org/10.1002/jaba.97

Watras, J. (1986). Will teaching applied ethics improve schools of education? *Journal of Teacher Education, 37,* 13–16.

Watson, J. B. (1914). *Behavior: An introduction to comparative psychology.* New York: Holt, Rinehart & Winston.

Watson, J. B. (1919). *Psychology from the standpoint of a behaviorist.* Philadelphia: Lippincott.

Watson, J. B. (1925). *Behaviorism.* New York: Norton.

Watson, J. B., & Raynor, R. (1920). Conditioned emotional reactions. *Journal of Experimental Psychology, 3,* 1–4.

Watson, L. S. (1967). Application of operant conditioning techniques to institutionalized severely and profoundly retarded children. *Mental Retardation Abstracts, 4,* 1–18.

Waugh, R. E., Alberto, P. A., & Fredrick, L. D. (2010). Effects of error correction during assessment probes on the acquisition of sight words for students with moderate intellectual disabilities. *Research in Developmental Disabilities, 32,* 1, 47–57.

Waugh, R. E., Alberto, P. A., & Fredrick, L. D. (2011). Simultaneous prompting: An instructional strategy for skill acquisition. *Education and Training in Autism and Developmental Disabilities, 46*(4), 528–543.

Wechsler, D. (2003). *The Wechsler Intelligence Scale for Children–IV.* San Antonio, TX: The Psychological Corporation.

Weeden, M., Wills, H. P., Kottwitz, E., & Kamps, D. (2016). The effects of a class-wide behavior intervention for students with emotional and behavioral disorders. *Behavioral Disorders, 42*(1), 285–293.

Wells, J. C., Sheehey, P. H., & Sheehey, M. (2017). Using self-monitoring of performance with self-graphing to increase academic productivity in math. *Beyond Behavior, 26*(2), 57–65.

Welsh, F., Najdowski, A. C., Strauss, D., Gallegos, L., & Fullen, J. A. (2019). Teaching a perspective-taking component skill to children with autism in the natural environment. *Journal of Applied Behavior Analysis, 52*(2), 439–450. https://doi.org/10.1002/jaba.523

Werry, J. S. (1986). Organic factors in childhood psychopathology. In H. G. Quay & J. S. Werry (eds.), *Psychopathological disorders of childhood* (3rd ed.). New York: Wiley.

Weston, R., Hodges, A., & Davis, T. N. (2018). Differential reinforcement of other behaviors to treat challenging behaviors among children with autism: A systematic and quality review. *Behavior Modification, 42*(4), 584–609. https://doi.org/10.1177/0145445517743487

Wheatley, R. K., West, R. P., Charlton, C. T., Sanders, R. B., Smith, T. G., & Taylor, M. J. (2009). Improving behavior through differential reinforcement: A praise note system for elementary school students. *Education & Treatment of Children, 32*(4), 551–571. https://doi.org/10.1353/etc.0.0071

White, A., & Bailey, J. (1990). Reducing disruptive behaviors of elementary physical education students with sit and watch. *Journal of Applied Behavior Analysis, 23,* 353–359.

White, M. A. (1975). Natural rates of teacher approval and disapproval in the classroom. *Journal of Applied Behavior Analysis, 8,* 367–372.

White, M. W., Houchins, D. E., Viel-Ruma, K. A., & Dever, B. V. (2014). Effects of direct instruction plus procedural facilitation on the expository writing of adolescents with emotional and behavioral disabilities in residential schools. *Education & Treatment of Children, 37*(4), 567–588. https://doi.org/10.1353/etc.2014.0035

White, O., & Liberty, K. (1976). Evaluation and measurement. In N. G. Haring & R. L. Schielfelbusch (eds.), *Teaching special children* (pp. 31–71). New York: McGraw-Hill.

White, O. R. (1977). Behaviorism in special education: An arena for debate. In R. D. Kneedler & S. G. Tarber (eds.), *Changing perspectives in special education.* Columbus, OH: Merrill.

Whiting, S. W., & Dixon, M. R. (2012). Creating an iPhone application for collecting continuous ABC data. *Journal of Applied Behavior Analysis, 45*(3), 643–656. https://doi.org/10.1901/jaba.2012.45-643

Whittington, J. R., Simmons, P. M., Phillips, A. M., Gammill, S. K., Cen, R., Magann, E. F., et al. (2018). The use of electronic cigarettes in pregnancy: A review of the literature. *Obstetrical & gynecological survey, 73*(9), 544–549.

Wichnick, G. A. M., Vener, S. M., & Poulson, C. L. (2019). Script fading for children with autism: Generalization of social initiation skills from school to home. *Journal of Applied Behavior Analysis, 52*(2), 451–466. https://doi.org/10.1002/jaba.534

Wicker, T. (1974, February 8). A bad idea persists. *The New York Times,* p. 31.

Wilder, D. A., & Neve, D. (2018). Assessment and treatment of rumination in a young man with autism. *Behavioral Interventions, 33*(3), 297–305. https://doi.org/10.1002/bin.1633

Wilder, D. A., Schadler, J., Higbee, T. S., Haymes, L. K., Bajagic, V., & Register, M. (2008). Identification of olfactory stimuli as reinforcers in individuals with autism: A preliminary investigation. *Behavioral Interventions, 23*(2), 97–103. https://doi.org/10.1002/bin.257

Wilkinson, G. (2006). *Wide Range Achievement Test 4.* Los Angeles, CA: Western Psychological Services.

Wills, H., Kamps, D., Fleming, K., & Hansen, B. (2016). Student and teacher outcomes of the class-wide function-related intervention team efficacy trial. *Exceptional Children, 83*(1), 58–76.

Wills, H. P., & Mason, B. A. (2014). Implementation of a self-monitoring application to improve on-task behavior: A high-school pilot study. *Journal of Behavioral Education, 23*(4), 421–434. https://doi.org/10.1007/s10864-014-9204-x

Wilson, R., Majsterek, D., & Simmons, D. (1996). The effects of computer-assisted versus teacher-directed instruction on the multiplication performance of elementary students with learning disabilities. *Journal of Learning Disabilities, 29*(4), 382–390.

Winborn-Kemmerer, L., Wacker, D., Harding, J., Boelter, E., Berg, W., & Lee, J. (2010). Analysis of mand selection across different stimulus conditions. *Education and Treatment of Children, 33,* 49–64.

Winett, R. A., & Winkler, R. C. (1972). Current behavior modification in the classroom: Be still, be quiet, be docile. *Journal of Applied Behavior Analysis, 5,* 499–504.

Winsler, A. (2009). Still talking to ourselves after all these years: A review of current research on private speech. In A. Winsler, C. Fernyhough, & I. Montero (eds.), *Private speech, executive functioning, and the development of verbal self-regulation* (pp. 3–41). Cambridge University Press. https://doi.org/10.1017/CBO9780511581533.003

Wiskow, K. M., Donaldson, J. M., & Matter, A. L. (2017). An evaluation of generalization of compliance across response types. *Behavior Analysis: Research and Practice, 17*(4), 402–420. https://doi.org/10.1037/bar0000087

Wiskow, K. M., Matter, A. L., & Donaldson, J. M. (2018). An evaluation of lag schedules and prompting methods to increase variability of naming category items in children with autism spectrum disorder. *Analysis of Verbal Behavior, 34*(1–2), 100–123. https://doi.org/10.1007/s40616-018-0102-5

Witts, B. N., Brodhead, M. T., Adlington, L. C., & Barron, D. K. (2020). Behavior analysts accept gifts during practice: So now what? *Behavior Analysis: Research and Practice, 20*(3), 196–202. https://doi.org/10.1037/bar0000117

Wolery, M., & Gast, D. L. (1984). Effective and efficient procedures for the transfer of stimulus control. *Topics in Early Childhood Special Education, 4*, 52–77.

Wolf, M. (1978). Social validity: The case for subjective measurement or how applied behavior analysis is finding its heart. *Journal of Applied Behavior Analysis, 11*, 203–214.

Wolfe, K., Barton, E. E., & Meadan, H. (2019). Systematic protocols for the visual analysis of single-case research data. *Behavior Analysis in Practice, 12*(2), 491–502. https://doi.org/10.1007/s40617-019-00336-7

Wolfe, K., Kunnavatana, S. S., & Shoemaker, A. M. (2018). An investigation of a video-based preference assessment of social interactions. *Behavior Modification, 42*(5), 729–746. https://doi.org/10.1177/0145445517731062

Wong, H. K., & Wong, R. T. (2009). *The first days of school: How to be an effective teacher*. Mountain View, CA: Harry K. Wong Publications, Inc.

Wood, L., Browder, D. M., & Flynn, L. (2015). Teaching students with intellectual disability to use a self-questioning strategy to comprehend social studies text for an inclusive setting. *Research and Practice for Persons with Severe Disabilities, 40*(4), 275–293.

Woodbury, S. M., & Scherer, S. W. (2018). Progress in the genetics of autism spectrum disorder. *Developmental Medicine & Child Neurology, 60*(5), 445–451. https://doi.org/10.1111/dmcn.13717

Woods, T. S. (1987). Programming common antecedents: A practical strategy for enhancing the generality of learning. *Behavioural Psychotherapy, 15*, 158–180.

Wright, C., & Vollmer, T. (2002). Evaluation of a treatment package to reduce rapid eating. *Journal of Applied Behavior Analysis, 35*, 89–93.

Wright, H. (1960). Observational study. In P. H. Mussen (ed.), *Handbook of research methods in child development*. New York: Wiley.

Wright-Gallo, G. L., Higbee, T. S., Reagon, K. A., & Davey, B. J. (2006). Classroom-based functional analysis and intervention for students with emotional/behavioral disorders. *Education & Treatment of Children, 29*(3), 421–436.

Wu, P.-F., Wheaton, J. E., & Cannella-Malone, H. I. (2016). Effects of video prompting and activity schedules on the acquisition of independent living skills of students who are deaf and have developmental disabilities. *Education and Training in Autism and Developmental Disabilities, 51*(4), 366–378.

Wunderlich, K. L., & Vollmer, T. R. (2017). Effects of serial and concurrent training on receptive identification tasks: A systematic replication. *Journal of Applied Behavior Analysis, 50*(3), 641–652. https://doi.org/10.1002/jaba.401

Wunderlich, K. L., Vollmer, T. R., Donaldson, J. M., & Phillips, C. L. (2014). Effects of serial and concurrent training on acquisition and generalization. *Journal of Applied Behavior Analysis, 47*(4), 723–737. https://doi.org/10.1002/jaba.154

Wyatt v. Stickney, 344 F. Supp. 373, 344 F. Supp. 387 (M. D. Ala. 1972) affirmed sub nom.

Xu, S., Wang, J., Lee, G. T., & Luke, N. (2017). Using self-monitoring with guided goal setting to increase academic engagement for a student with autism in an inclusive classroom in China. *The Journal of Special Education, 51*(2), 106–114. https://doi.org/10.1177/0022466916679980

Yates, A. J. (1970). *Behavior therapy*. New York: Wiley.

Yorlets, C. B., Maguire, R. W., King, C. M., & Breault, M. (2018). Acquisition of complex conditional discriminations in a child with autism spectrum disorder. *The Psychological Record, 68*(2), 219–229. https://doi.org/10.1007/s40732-018-0283-2

Young, M. E. (2018). A place for statistics in behavior analysis. *Behavior Analysis: Research and Practice, 18*(2), 193–202. https://doi.org/10.1037/bar0000099

Zangrillo, A. N., Fisher, W. W., Greer, B. D., Owen, T. M., & DeSouza, A. A. (2016). Treatment of escape-maintained challenging behavior using chained schedules: An evaluation of the effects of thinning positive plus negative reinforcement during functional communication training. *International Journal of Developmental Disabilities, 62*(3), 147–156. https://doi.org/10.1080/20473869.2016.1176308

Zarcone, J., Iwata, B., Mazaleski, J., & Smith, R. (1994). Momentum and extinction effects on self-injurious escape behavior and noncompliance. *Journal of Applied Behavior Analysis, 27*, 649–658.

Zarcone, J., Rodgers, T., Iwata, B., Rourke, D., & Dorsey, M. (1991). Reliability analysis of the Motivational Assessment Scale: A failure to replicate. *Research in Developmental Disabilities, 12*, 349–360.

Zhou, L., Goff, G., & Iwata, B. (2000). Effects of increased response effort on self-injury and object manipulation as competing responses. *Journal of Applied Behavior Analysis, 33*, 29–40.

Zigmond, N., Kloo, A., & Volonino, V. (2009). What, where, and how? Special education in the climate of full inclusion. *Exceptionality, 17*(4), 189–204. https://doi.org/10.1080/09362830903231986

Zirkel, P. A. (2017). An update of judicial rulings specific to FBAs or BIPs under the IDEA and corollary state laws. *The Journal of Special Education, 51*(1), 50–56. https://doi.org/10.1177/0022466917693386

Zirpoli, T. J., & Melloy, K. J. (1993). *Behavior management: Applications for teachers and parents*. New York: Macmillan.

Name Index

A
Abel, E. A., 208
Abston, G. W., 208
Achenbach, T. H., 7
Ackerman, J. M., 338
Adamo, E. K., 227
Adams, C., 285
Adams, N., 275
Addison, L., 265, 316
Agaliotis, I., 351
Agran, M., 35, 226
Ahearn, W. H., 82, 206, 208, 210, 270, 302, 308, 317
Aiken, J. M., 270
Akers, J. S., 370
Akin-Little, A., 231, 301
Akmanoglu, N., 305
Akullian, J., 299
Ala'i-Rosales, S., 252
Alaimo, D., 95
Alber-Morgan, S. R., 47, 81, 226, 301
Alber, M., 304
Alber, S. A., 335
Albers, C. A., 227
Albers, S., 281, 335, 358
Albert, K. M., 126, 257
Alberto, P. A., 81, 87, 185, 186, 210, 218, 246, 274–275, 296, 299, 307, 317, 327
Albright, L. K., 295
Alcorn, A. S., 98, 217
Algozzine, B., 200
Alholail, A. M., 294
Aljadef-Abergel, E., 364
Allen, R., 215
Almeida, D. A., 215
Alnemary, F., 186
Alquraini, T., 35
Anderson-Inman, L., 332
Anderson, A., 301, 303, 311
Anderson, C. M., 166, 183, 200, 218
Anderson, D. H., 81
Anderson, J., 285–286
Andreou, T. E., 199
Andrews, A., 217
Andrews, D., 274–275, 296
Andrews, T. E., 219
Apolito, P., 279
Aranki, J., 340
Ardoin, S. P., 92
Argott, P. J., 74
Arhar, J., 159
Arkel, A. J., 297
Arndorfer, R., 265
Artman, K., 98
Aspiranti, K. B., 81, 139
Athens, E. S., 91
Attanasio, V., 213
Ault, M. H., 69
Ault, M. J., 307
Austin, C. R., 94, 157
Austin, J., 300
Austin, J. L., 185, 233, 235–236, 254
Axe, J. B., 212, 215, 241, 335
Axelrod, S., 22–25, 179, 206
Ayazi, M., 92
Ayllon, T. A., 18, 23, 223, 304, 334, 342–343
Ayres, K. M., 81, 297, 301
Azrin, N. H., 215, 223, 266, 272, 277, 282, 284–285, 305, 333–334

B
Bachmeyer, M. H., 265
Badgett, N., 186
Baer, A. M., 276
Baer, D. M., 14, 18–19, 27, 35, 98, 142, 154, 199, 265, 276, 326, 329, 334, 340, 341, 343, 345, 357
Bailey, D. B., 12–13, 272, 291
Bailey, J. S., 23, 26, 275, 300, 343
Bailey, S., 279
Baker, V., 269
Bakshi, E., 248
Baldwin, G., 280
Balla, D., 44
Balsam, P. D., 24, 214, 235
Bambara, L. M., 301
Bancroft, S. L., 270, 308, 317
Banda, D. R., 280
Bandura, A., 25, 268, 278, 282, 300
Banko, K. M., 24
Bannerman, D. J., 32
Barber, M., 74
Barbera, M. L., 310
Barbetta, P. M., 72, 224, 308, 355
Barkley, R., 361
Barlow, D., 48, 123–124, 143–144
Barnard-Brak, L., 263
Barrera, F., 273
Barrett, C. A., 35
Barrish, H. H., 233, 236
Barry, L. M., 298
Barry, T., 297
Bartlett, W., 297
Barton, E. E., 157
Barton, L., 275
Bateman, D., 61, 90
Battaglia, A. A., 208
Batu, E. S., 305
Bauman, K. E., 166, 184, 252, 268, 343
Baumeister, A., 286
Baumeister, R. F., 348
Bayley, N., 44
Beaulieu, L., 139
Beaver, B. N., 81, 359
Bebech, A., 81
Bechtel, D. R., 298
Becker, J., 279
Becker, W. C., 223, 294, 296, 315, 320, 336, 339
Beckman, A., 355, 364
Becraft, J. L., 218, 254
Bedesem, P. L., 366
Beeks, A., 342
Bekker, M. J., 300
Belfiore, P., 239
Belisle, J., 294
Bellini, S., 299
Ben-Artzi, E., 351
Beneville, M., 349–350
Benitez, B. B., 92
Bennett, K. D., 308, 358
Benoit, R. B., 269

Berg, W., 208
Bergmann, S., 92
Bergstrom, R. M., 77
Berkely, S., 351
Berry, B., 22–23
Berry, H. K., 5
Bessette, K. K., 183
Bettenhausen, S., 369
Bettis, D., 94
Betz, A. M., 240, 370
Bevan, D., 254
Bicard, D. F., 337
Bickel, W. K., 342
Biggs, E. E., 300
Bijou, S. W., 18, 69
Binder, C., 56
Birnbrauer, J. S., 18
Bishop, J. R., 74, 280
Blackeley-Smith, A., 269
Blackorby, J., 61
Blair, B. J., 302
Blair, K.-S. C., 27
Blake Ford, W., 208
Blakely, M., 94
Blampied, N. M., 355
Blood, E., 301
Bloom, B. S., 57–59
Bloom, S. E., 260, 261
Bloomfield, B. S., 74
Blume, F., 369
Boden, L. J., 81, 218, 382
Boehmert, R., 74
Boelter, E. W., 245
Bohanon, H., 200
Bolivar, H. A., 56
Bondy, A. S., 24, 214, 235
Bonner, A. C., 254
Bootzin, R. R., 217
Boren, M. C. P., 14, 294
Bornstein, P. H., 361, 363
Borrero, C. S. W., 224, 310, 315
Borrero, J. C., 158, 254
Boswell, M. A., 303, 355, 364
Bouck, E. C., 91, 297, 355–356
Bouck, F. C., 138
Bourret, J. C., 119, 302
Bowen, C. N., 210
Bowman-Perrott, L., 228, 233
Boyle, J. R., 72
Bradley, R., 19
Bradshaw, C. A., 242
Brady, M. P., 296–297, 302
Brand, D., 27
Brandt, B. C., 257, 307
Brandt, J. A., 306
Breault, M., 305
Brennan, K., 74, 99
Briesch, A. M., 349–351, 356
Briggs, A. M., 34, 266
Briggs, T., 246, 296
Brittain, D., 206
Brock, M. E., 35, 300, 301
Brodhead, M. T., 91, 206, 208, 333, 370
Broen, P., 273
Brooks, A., 47
Brophy-Dick, A. A., 130
Bross, L. A., 296
Brothers, K. J., 72, 299
Broussard, C., 206
Browder, B. M., 361

Browder, D. M., 261, 308
Brown, M., 301
Brown, W. H., 227
Browning, E. R., 332
Bruhn, A. L., 134, 157, 355
Bruinsma, Y., 340
Brulle, A., 275
Bruner, Jerome, 8–9
Bryant, K. J., 301
Bryant, L. E., 279, 361
Bucher, B., 286
Buckley, N. K., 342
Budd, A., 295, 303
Budd, K. S., 344, 361
Buffington, D. M., 364
Buie, J., 275
Bulla, A. J., 297
Bunch-Crump, K. R., 198, 367
Burch, M., 26
Burchard, J. D., 273
Burgio, J. D., 361
Burgio, L. D., 361
Burke, J. D., 3
Burke, M. D., 228, 233
Burns, M. K., 56, 148
Burt, J. L., 264, 327
Burta, M., 296–297
Buzhardt, J., 157
Byra, K. L., 343
Byrne, G., 267

C

Calderella, P., 81
Calkins, R. P., 363
Call, N. A., 186, 269, 321
Callicott, K. J., 361
Cameron, J., 24
Cameron, M. J., 291
Camp, E. M., 171
Campbell, A., 166, 218
Campbell, B., 274
Campbell, C. R., 340
Cannella-Malone, M. H. I., 207–208, 301, 302
Cannon, J., 74
Capriotti, M. R., 257
Capshew, J. H., 18
Carbone, V. J., 126, 172, 213, 245–247
Cardoso-Martins, C., 299
Carey, R., 286
Cariveau, T., 233, 342
Carlile, K., 344
Carmine, D., 9
Carnett, A., 218
Carnine, D., 294, 336
Carp, C. L., 297
Carpenter, S., 218, 235
Carr, E. G., 24, 34, 168, 197–198, 208, 245, 260–261, 263, 265, 291, 364
Carr, J. E., 172, 206, 208, 227
Carroll, R. A., 81
Carter, C., 35
Carter, E. W., 35, 300
Carter, M., 47
Carter, S., 27
Carver, A., 92
Case, L., 361
Casey, S. D., 99, 189
Cashwell, T., 235
Casper-Teague, L., 226, 233
Castillo, M. I., 171, 254

Cataldo, M., 265
Cattey, G. N., 300
Causin, K. G., 306
Cautela, J., 206
Cavanaugh, J., 208
Cavanaugh, R. A., 358
Cavell, H. J., 150
Cazzell, S., 74
Cecire, S., 302
Cengher, M., 295, 303, 307
Chan, J., 301
Chan, P. E., 12
Chang, M.-S., 91
Chapman, L. A., 157
Chappell, N., 210
Charlop-Christy, M. H., 34
Chasnoff, J. J., 4
Cheney, T., 309
Cheramie, G., 206
Chess, S., 5
Chevalier, T. M., 351
Chezan, L. C., 168, 247, 337
Chiesa, M., 25
Childs, K., 175
Chok, J. T., 119, 186
Chou, W.-C., 298
Christensen, L., 25
Christian, L., 81
Chung, E. Y., 91
Chung, M. Y., 154
Cicchetti, O., 44
Ciccone, F. J., 208
Cicero, F., 214
Cihak, D. F., 95, 139, 150, 186, 262–264, 299, 306, 327
Cihon, J. H., 74, 77, 218
Cipani, E., 246
Cirelli, C. A., 47
Cividini, M. C., 272
Clair, A., 259
Clare, I. C. H., 32
Clark, A. J., 74
Clark, G., 217
Clarke, S., 175
Clay, C. J., 260
Clayton, F., 237
Clayton, M., 300
Clement, P., 235
Close, D., 284–285
Cocchiola, M. A., 333
Codding, R. S., 98
Coello, A., 303
Coffee, G., 215
Coffey, A. L., 175
Cohen-Almeida, D., 206
Colavecchia, B., 281
Colby-Dirksen, A. M., 81
Cole, G., 286
Coleman-Martin, M., 150
Coleman, M. B., 262–264, 306
Coleman, P., 355
Collins, B. C., 94, 208, 296, 307
Colucci, K., 25
Colvin, G., 336
Common, E. A., 27
Conine, D. E., 56
Conley, D., 272
Conley, O., 286
Connelly, V. J., 281
Connis, R., 272
Connolly, A., 44

Connolly, J. F., 24
Conroy, M., 72, 81
Contreras, B. P., 240
Contrucci, S. A., 185, 212
Conyers, C., 272
Cook, S., 355
Cooke, N. L., 297
Coon, J. T., 298
Cooper, J. O., 64, 90, 97, 128, 133, 135, 143, 147, 154–155, 158, 280, 328, 358
Cooper, J. T., 252
Copeland, A., 361
Copeland, S. R., 166, 168, 227, 297, 364
Coppage, S., 276
Corley, M. J., 344
Costello, M. S., 119
Costenbader, V., 276
Cote, C., 206, 265
Coughlin, J., 365–367
Council for Children with Behavior Disorders, 34
Council for Exceptional Children, 26
Counts, J., 351
Courtemanche, A. B., 74
Coviello, L., 147
Covington, T., 337
Cowdery, G., 257, 265
Cox, B. S., 300
Cox, C. D., 300
Cox, D. J., 300
Coy, A. R., 262
Craft, M. A., 335
Craig, A. R., 265
Craighead, W. E., 25
Crimmins, D., 176
Crisp, A., 340
Critchfield, T. S., 263
Crone, D. A., 198
Cronin, B., 214
Cronin, K. A., 227
Crosland, K., 261
Csanyi, A., 228–230
Culbertson, S., 14, 294
Cullen, J. M., 301, 304
Cummings, C., 369
Curiel, E. S., 207
Curiel, H., 207
Curtis, K. S., 74
Cuvo, A. J., 222, 227
Cwiakala, K., 138
Czarnecki, D., 207

D

Da Fonte, M., 208
Dacus, S., 147
Daddario, R., 256
Dadson, S., 291
Dalmau, M., 306
Daly, E. J., 208, 245
Daly, M., 206
Daniels, B., 349–351
Danielson, L., 19
Dardig, J. C., 311
Dart, E. H., 208
Datchuk, S. M., 74, 99
Davies, K., 361–362
Davies, L., 280
Davis-Temple, J., 308
Davis, C. A., 246–247, 296–297
Davis, D., 217

Davis, H., 97, 228, 233
Davis, J., 97
Davis, T. N., 147, 168, 255, 260
Dawson, M., 253
Day, .H., 261
de Magalhães, C. G., 299
De Marin, S., 228, 233
de Zubicaray, G., 259
Dean, A. J., 74
DeBar, R. M., 47, 81, 94, 177, 297, 299, 301
DeCatanzaro, D., 280
Deci, E. L., 24
Dehaven, E. D., 344
Deitz, S. M., 253, 258–259
DeLeon, I., 208, 261, 270, 282
DeLeon, J., 176
Delfs, C. H., 295
Delmolino, L., 81
Delprato, D., 282
Delquadri, J., 280
Denny, M., 285
Deno, S. L., 48, 64, 157
Deochand, N., 119, 207
DeQuinzio, J. A., 254, 310
Derby, K. M., 74
DeRosa, N. M., 257, 280
Deshais, M.A., 234
DeSouza, A. A., 245, 261
Devany, J., 269–270, 295
Dever, B. V., 72
Dewey, John, 349
Dick, D. M., 3
Dickson, C. A., 302, 336
Didden, R., 303
Dittrich, G. A., 272
Dix, J., 343
Dixon, M. R., 95, 119, 237
Doepke, K., 297
Doke, L. A., 285
Dollard, N., 25
Domanski, C., 295
Donaldson, J. M., 233, 260, 274
Donnelly, D., 254, 259
Doolittle, J., 19
Dorsey, M., 166, 177, 184, 252, 268, 279
Dougherty, S., 272
Douglas, K. H., 364
Dove, M., 74
Dowdy, A., 91–92
Doyle, M., 343
Dozier, C. L., 215, 217, 241, 272
Drabman, R., 276, 281
Dracobly, J. D., 175, 177
Drain, S., 343
Draper, C., 280
Drasgow, E., 168, 227, 247, 332
Drevon, D. D., 218, 382
Dube, W. V., 270, 294
Dubuque, E. M., 119
Duchaine, E. L., 35
Dudley, L. L., 335
Dueñas, A. D., 72
Dufek, S., 340
Dufour, M.-M., 340
Dufrene, B. A., 177
Dukes, C., 227, 302
Dunlap, G., 175, 197, 198, 280, 305, 341
DuPaul, G. J., 352
Dupere, S., 82
Dupuis, D. L., 274
Durand M., 168, 245, 261
Durand, V. M., 176, 214, 248
Dutt, A. S., 208

E

Easterbrooks, S., 74
Eberhard, J. M., 337
Ecott, C. L., 263
Edwards, C. K., 317
Edwards, G., 207
Edwards, N. M., 301
Edwards, S., 301
Eggen, P. D., 306
Ehle, C. T., 215
Elkins, B., 81, 91
Ellingson, S., 269–270
Ellis, D., 95
Embregts, P. J., 358
Emerson, E., 214
Engelmann, S., 9, 23, 294, 315, 336, 339
English, C. L., 183
Ennis, R. P., 233, 352, 366–367
Epanchin, B., 25
Epstein, L. H., 285
Epstein, R., 351
Ericksoln, J., 74
Ertel, H., 281, 282
Espii, F. M., 257
Espin, C. A., 157
Estill, K., 274
Evans, M. B., 223
Evans, W. H., 369
Eveleigh, E. L., 355
Ezzeddine, E. W., 301

F

Fabry, B., 223
Fairbanks, S., 47
Falcomata, T. S., 186, 272, 338, 346
Falkenberg, C. A., 72, 355
Falligant, J. M., 92
Fallon, L. M., 198
Faloon, B. J., 361
Fantuzzo, J., 235
Faraone, S. V., 3
Farkas, M. S., 198
Farlow, L., 94
Farmer-Dougan, V., 210
Farrell, D., 224
Farrell, N., 295, 303
Fee, A., 177, 274
Fee, S., 274
Feinberg, A. B., 198
Feldman, M., 91, 214
Feldmiller, S., 74
Felixbrod, J., 359
Feng, H., 298
Ferguson, J. L., 77
Ferman, D. M., 295
Ferron, J., 157, 179
Ferster, C. B., 14, 237, 270, 294, 314
Feuerborn, L. L., 199
Fienup, D. M., 295, 297, 301, 303, 307
Filderman, M. J., 94, 157
Filler, J. W., 60
Filter, K. J., 272
Findel-Pyles, R. S., 77
Findley, A. J., 210
Finn, L., 227

Fischer, A., 74
Fisher, A. B., 234
Fisher, W. W., 48, 85, 92, 207, 212, 240, 245, 261, 266, 268, 269, 270, 280
Fishley, K. M., 23
Fiske, K., 81
Fiske, W. W., 217
Fixsen, D. L., 341
Flaherty, J., 81
Flannagan, T. F., 177, 185
Floress, M. T., 74
Fong, E. H., 13, 27
Fonger, A. M., 91, 322
Font-Roura, J., 306
Ford, A., 343
Forte, S., 265
Forton, A. P., 257
Fosnot, C. T., 9
Foster, A. L., 301
Foster, T. E., 92
Fowler, S. A., 341
Fox, R. G., 133
Foxx, R. M., 155, 274–275, 284–285, 305, 333, 343
Fradenburg, L., 98
Frampton, S. E., 295, 317
France, K., 265
Francis, L. L., 185
Frankhauser, M. A., 370
Franklin, Benjamin, 16
Frantino, E. P., 315
Fredrick, L. D., 74, 185, 186, 210, 215, 296, 307
Freeland, J. T., 241
Freeman, J., 199–200
Freud, Sigmund, 6
Frieder, J. E., 297
Frijters, J. C., 91
Fritz, J. N., 186, 226, 233, 262–263, 281, 357, 364
Fryxell, D., 35
Fuchs, D., 61
Fuchs, L. S., 35, 61, 64
Fuehrer, K., 74
Fuhrman, A. M., 48, 240
Fuller, T. C., 119
Fuqua, R. W., 119
Furhman, A. M., 268

G

Gadke, D. L., 148
Gaffaney, T., 265
Gage, N. A., 200
Gagnon, D. J., 281
Gagnon, E., 91
Galiatsos, G. T., 183
Galliford, M. E., 294
Gallop, H., 270
Gama, R. I., 299
García-Zambrano, S., 74
Garcia, A. E., 72, 299
Garcia, D., 302
Garcia, E., 344
Gardner, A. W., 245
Gardner, S. J., 206, 301
Gassaway, J., 296
Gast, D. L., 72, 97, 102, 139, 143, 147, 154–155, 157, 158, 208, 214, 251, 295, 297
Gaylord-Ross, R. J., 317
Gayman, C. M., 299
Gehrman, C., 257
Geiger, K. B., 370
George, T., 206

Gerow, S., 168, 260
Gesel, S. A., 99
Gesell, A., 6
Gettinger, M., 198
Ghaemmaghami, M., 322
Giacin, T. A., 291
Giangreco, E. M., 35
Gibbs, A. R., 81, 91
Gil, V., 308
Gilbert, G., 226, 265
Gillett, J. N., 207
Gilley, C., 217
Gillis, J. M., 34
Giné, C., 306
Giunta, F. T., 94
Glassenbury, M., 303
Glover, McLaughlin, Derby, & Gower, 74
Glynn, T. L., 281
Goff, G., 269
Goh, A. E., 245, 301
Gold, J., 206
Goldiamond, I., 23
Goldstein, D., 87
Goldstein, H., 157
Goldstein, K., 4
Gomes, S., 338
Gonçalves, D. T, 299
Gongola, L. C., 256
Gonzales, M., 228–230
Gonzalez, M. L., 224
Goodman, J., 361–362
Goodnight, C. I., 130
Gordon, B., 274
Gould, D. D., 215
Graber, A., 280
Graber, J. E., 280
Grace, R. C., 270
Graff, R. B., 183, 206, 208, 210
Graham, S., 64, 361, 362
Grandpeesheh, D., 77
Grant, M. D., 281
Grauerholz, F. E., 262
Graves, S. Jr., 342
Gravina, N., 98, 300
Gray, D., 272
Green, C., 207
Greene, K., 295
Greenwood, C. R., 157
Greer, B. D., 48, 185, 226, 240, 245, 261, 266, 268, 269, 280
Gregori, E., 260
Grider, K., 299
Grider, K. L., 299
Grieco, J. C., 72
Griffin, M. M., 364
Griffith, A. K., 302
Griffith, K. R., 186
Grob, C. M., 338
Gronlund, N., 57–58
Grossi, T. A., 72, 91, 327, 332, 352
Groves, E. A., 185, 233, 235–236
Grow, L. L., 265
Grubb, L. M., 263
Guardino, G., 47
Guertin, E. L., 91
Guralnick, M. J., 32
Gureasko-Moore, S., 352
Gushanas, C. M., 364
Gut, D., 35
Gutierrez, A., 241
Guzman, G., 355, 367

H

Haberman, M., 22–23
Hackett, S., 300
Haggar, J. L., 217
Hagopian, L. P., 224, 262
Hake, W. C., 282
Halford, R., 206
Hall, L. J., 305
Hall, M., 307
Hall, R. V., 133, 135, 280, 340
Hallahan, D., 90
Halle, J. W., 154, 247, 332
Hammer, R., 301
Hammerschmidt-Snidarich, S. M., 157
Hanley, G. P., 27, 34, 139, 154, 175, 183, 184, 206, 210, 260, 268–269, 309, 322
Hanney, N. M., 227
Hanratty, L. A., 268
Hansen, B. D., 72, 81, 92, 185–186
Haq, S. S., 340
Harchik, A. E., 32
Haring, N. G., 156, 327
Harjusola-Webb, S. M., 340
Harman, M. J., 92
Harris, F. R., 14, 279
Harris, G. M., 301
Harris, J., 280
Harris, K. R., 64, 361, 362
Harrison, C., 206
Harrison, E., 81
Harrison, R., 98
Hart, S. L., 280
Hartmann, D. P., 133, 135
Hasselbring, T. S., 157
Hatton, D. D., 305
Hawkins, R. O., 233
Hawkins, R. P., 341
Hay, D., 302
Hay, L., 98
Hay, W., 98
Haydon, T., 233
Hayes, S. C., 144, 295, 359
Heal, N. A., 309
Healy, O., 257
Heathfield, L., 261
Heatter, S., 298
Hedges, L. V., 157
Heffernan, L., 257
Heflin, J., 210, 274–275
Hegg, E., 215
Heldt, J., 346
Heller, K., 150, 210
Helms, B., 300
Hemingway, Ernest, 350
Hemmes, N. S., 364
Hensen, M., 48, 123–124
Herbert, M., 64
Herman, K., 261
Heron, T. E., 64, 97, 133, 143, 154, 280
Herrnstein, B. J., 294
Herscovitch, B., 177
Hersen, M., 143
Hertel, I. P., 74
Heward, W. L., 34, 64, 72, 91, 97, 143, 154, 245, 280–281, 327, 335, 352, 358, 371
Hewett, A., 285
Heyvaert, M., 157
Higa, W. R., 363
Higbee, T. S., 184, 206, 208, 299
Higgins, S., 258, 274
Hill, J., 333
Hindman, A. H., 306
Hine, J. F., 92
Hinkson-Lee, K., 307
Hixson, M. D., 218
Hjertholm, E., 350
Hoch, H., 303
Hodges, A. C., 255, 281, 282
Hofeling, D. V., 344
Hoffman, A., 227
Hoffman, L., 74
Hogan, C. D., 301
Holden, C., 23
Holifield, C., 355
Holmes, G., 206
Holvoet, J., 317
Holyfield, C., 74
Holz, W. C., 272, 282
Homme, L., 228–230
Hood, S. A., 48, 334
Hooper, M., 343
Hoover, T., 72
Horan, J., 337
Horner, R. D., 47, 142, 175, 198, 200, 214, 261, 336–337, 343–344, 382
Horner, R. H., 139, 245, 291
Horocones, C. L., 333
Horrocks, E. L., 207, 208
Houchins, D., 219
Houchins, D. E., 72
Houlihan, D., 233
Hovanetz, A., 272
Hovell, M. F., 223
Hovey, K. A., 157
Hsu, L., 285
Huang, K., 72, 81
Hudson, M. E., 307–308, 355
Hudson, S., 265
Hughes, C. A., 226, 297, 303, 361
Hughes, M. A., 185, 301, 317
Huguenin, N., 274
Hundert, J., 81
Hunt, F., 270
Hunter, M., 302
Hurley, K. J., 306
Hutchinson, R. R., 282
Hyatt, K. J., 60

I

Iannaccone, J. A., 262
Ilg, F. L., 6
Inge, K. J., 333
Inglesfield E., 340
Ingvarsson, E. T., 47, 217, 257, 299
Inhelder, B., 7
Iovanonne, R., 12
Irvin, D. S., 269
Irvin, J., 261
Irvine, K., 150
Ivancic, M., 207
Ivy, J. W., 81, 215, 218, 221, 305, 345
Iwata, B., 94, 166, 176, 177, 183, 184, 186–189, 208, 210, 214, 215, 241, 245, 247, 257, 261, 265–266, 268–270, 272, 279–280, 282, 363
Izzo, M.V., 301

J

Jackson, L. M., 262
Jackson, R. L., 329
Jacob, S., 206
Jacobs, K. W., 91

Jaksic, H., 91
Jenkins, J. R., 48, 61
Jennings, A. M., 295
Jenson, W. R., 233, 276
Jeong, Y., 166, 168
Jerome, J., 315
Jessel, J., 47, 175, 186, 217, 257, 322
Jimenez, B. A., 72, 308
Jin, C. S., 268
Johner, S., 74
Johnson, H., 275
Johnson, J. W., 299, 341
Johnson, M. R., 361
Johnston, M. K., 14
Jolivette, K., 81, 215, 218, 228, 367
Jones, E. A., 301
Jones, J., 301
Jones, K., 206
Jones, M. C., 17
Joseph, L. M., 355
Joslyn, P. R., 226, 233
Jowett Hirst, E. S., 217, 272
Jung, J., 308
Jung, S., 301

K

Kahng, S. W., 94, 179, 234, 261
Kalsher, M., 265
Kamps, D., 23, 226
Kandel, H. J., 23
Kanive, R., 56
Karnes, A., 302
Karpman, K., 297
Karsten, A. M., 208
Kartal, M. S., 364
Kasper, T., 213
Kass, R., 281
Kates-McElrath, K., 302
Kates, K., 270
Katsiyannis, A., 72, 351
Kauchak, D. P., 306
Kauffmann, J. M., 32
Kaufman, A., 44
Kaufman, K., 281
Kaufman, N., 44
Kautz, M. E., 32
Kazbour, R. R., 300
Kazdin, A. E., 12, 25, 98, 102, 122–123, 133, 143, 147, 154–155, 157, 158, 163, 172, 175, 215, 217, 223, 230–231, 291, 329, 331, 334, 341, 349
Kazolia, T., 72
Keeling, K., 91
Keeney, K., 269, 272
Kellems, R. O., 301
Kelley, C. S., 14
Kelley, K. R., 297, 299
Kelley, M. E., 185, 210, 245, 265, 268, 272, 280, 285
Kelly, K., 342
Kemp, C. R., 47
Kennedy, C. H., 27, 35, 119, 154–155, 158, 215
Kern, L., 175, 177, 280, 305
Kerth, D. M., 280
Kessler, K. B., 327
Kettering, T., 245, 272
Keyes, J., 280
Kidder, J. D., 18
Kierans, I., 233
Kilgus, S. P., 148
Kimball, J. W., 297
Kimball, R. T., 266

Kincaid, M., 223
King-Sears, M. E., 359, 364
King, A., 98
King, B., 355
King, C. M., 305
King, D., 206
King, M. L., 215
King, S. A., 99
Kinney, E. M., 297
Kirby, K. C., 342
Kircher, J., 276
Kirk, H., 47
Kitchener, R. F., 26
Klatt, K. P., 306
Kleeberger, V., 299
Kleinmann, A., 81
Knight, V., 303
Knight, V. F., 301
Kodak, T., 185, 212, 233, 342
Koegel, L. K., 74, 248, 355
Koegel, R. L., 280, 294, 329, 341, 343, 355, 364
Koehler-Platten, K., 346
Koehler, M., 227, 358
Kohlberg, L., 350
Kohler, F., 235
Kohn, A., 22–24
Kolbenschlag, C. M., 355–356
Kolberg, L., 245–246
Konrad, M., 72
Kooken, C., 85
Koplik, K., 80
Kostewicz, D. E., 32, 74, 99, 262
Kottwitz, E., 226
Kourassanis, J., 301
Kourea, L., 23, 72
Kovalich, B., 272
Kowalewicz, E. A., 215
Kranak, M. P., 47, 81, 226
Krantz, P. J., 299
Krasner, L., 278
Kratochwill, T., 155
Kraus, E., 297
Kressler, B., 157
Krombach, T., 91
Kruger, A., 215
Kubina, R. M., 72, 74, 310, 367
Kuhlman, C., 343
Kuhn, D., 270
Kuhn, S., 265, 316
Kunkel, A., 157
Kunnavatana, S. S., 207, 260
Kuntz, E. M., 301
Kurtz, A. L., 25

L

Lagomarcino, T. R., 361
Lai, M.-C., 91
Lalli, J., 270
Lam, M. F., 81
Lambert, J. M., 92, 185–186, 224, 261
Lambros, K. M., 301
Lamphere, J. C., 215
Lancioni, G. E., 74, 214, 265, 297, 333
Landa, R. K., 317, 322
Landrum, T., 90
Lane, J. D., 81, 340, 352
Lane, K. L., 27, 139, 179
Lang, R., 208, 303, 346
Langer, S., 177, 179
Langthorne, P., 245

Lanovaz, M. J., 158–159, 340
Laprime, A. P., 212, 215, 241, 272, 335
Laraway, S., 172
Larsen, A., 350
Larsson, H., 3
LaRue, R. H., 265
Lassman, K., 228
Lastrapes, R. E., 226, 233
Lathrop, M., 47
Lavay, B., 77
Layman, D., 23
Layng, T. V. J., 294
Le, D., 270, 285–286, 299
Leaf, J. A., 138–139, 304
Leaf, J. B., 77
Leatherby, J., 208
Lebbon, A., 300
LeBlanc, B., 92
LeBlanc, J. M., 265
LeBlanc, L. A., 74, 77, 85, 207, 276
Lechago, S., 301
Ledford, J. R., 81, 139, 143, 147, 154–155, 158, 185
Lee, C. Y. Q., 301
Lee, D., 239
Lee, G. T., 72, 298, 364
Lee, R., 265
Legge, D. B., 364
Lehtinen, L. E., 4
LeJeune, L. M., 92
Leko, M. M., 27
Lemons, C. J., 92, 99
Lennox, D., 254
Lenske, J., 273
Lenz, M., 285
Lepper, T. L., 208
Lerman, D. C., 99, 168, 185, 215, 265, 266, 268, 274, 281, 282, 301, 316
LeSage, M., 157
Levin, L., 303
Levy, K., 138
Lewis, M., 7
Lewis, T. J., 91, 176, 198, 200
Ley, Davis, 301
Li, A., 207
Li, Y.-F., 355, 364
Liauspin, C., 179
Libby, M. E., 210, 308, 317
Liberman, R. P., 269
Liberty, K. A., 155, 327
Lieberman, R. G., 157
Light, J. C., 74, 139
Lim, L., 261
Linares, J., 98
Lindenberg, A. M., 81
Lindstrom, E. R., 61, 99
Lingo, A. S., 370
Litow, L., 232–233
Little, S. G., 231, 301
Liu, Y., 364
Livanis, A., 98
Livezey, K., 270
Livi, J., 343
Livingston, C. E., 210
Lloyd, B. P., 185, 318
Lloyd, J., 90
Lo, Y., 72, 74, 94, 198, 366
Loman, S. L., 168
Lomas Meyers, J. E., 269
Long, E., 82
Looney, K., 254, 364
Lopano, S. E., 185, 224

Lopez, A. R., 74, 299
Lorah, E. R., 302
Losinski, M., 72
Lovaas, O. L., 265–266, 294, 339
Love, S., 44
Lovelace, T. S., 35
Loveland, D. H., 294
Lovitt, T. C., 349
Luce, S. C., 280
Luczynski, K. C., 34, 48, 260
Lugo, A. M., 215
Luiselli, J. K., 34, 81, 91, 184, 276, 280, 285, 291
Lund, C., 85
Lund, J. B., 85
Luscre, D., 72
Lutzker, J. R., 296, 363
Lynn, D., 352–353
Lyon, K. J., 168
Lyons, D., 257

M

Maag, J. W., 72, 301
Maas, A. P., 177
Mabee, W., 285
MacAulay, D. J., 369
MacDonald, J. M., 82, 270
MacDonald, R., 177, 179
Mace, F. C., 281
Machalicek, W., 147
Mackenzie-Keating, S., 281
MacNaul, H. L., 258
Maes, B., 157
Maguire, K., 215
Maguire, R. W., 215, 305
Maher, C. E., 72
Maher, G., 218
Mahoney, A. M., 215
Mahoney, M. J., 14, 25
Maïano, C., 32
Malik, S., 3
Malott, R. W., 34, 91, 300, 304, 321–322
Manikam, R., 274
Manning, P., 253
Manolov, R., 155
Maragulia, D., 274
March, R., 175
Marchand-Martella, N., 94, 139
Marchetti, A. G., 343
Marcus, B. A.k, 207
Marholin, D., 272
Mariscano, R., 233
Marketz & Taylor, 227
Marshall, H., 278, 357
Marshall, K. J., 227
Martella, R., 94, 139
Martens, B., 171, 183, 235
Martin, C. A., 247
Martin, R., 30, 275
Martin, T. L., 207
Martinez, J. R., 72, 81
Mason, B. A., 366
Mason, L. H., 74
Mason, L. L., 23, 72, 74, 210, 217
Mastropieri, M. A., 224
Mates, M., 208
Mather, N., 44
Matson, J., 274, 276, 280, 285, 286
Matter, A. L., 233, 260
Mattingly, M. J., 281

Maxfield, T. C., 343
May, M. E., 177
Mayer, G. R., 269, 301
Mayhew, G., 223, 279
Mazaleski, J., 189, 265, 269
Mazzocco, M. M. M., 3
Mazzotti, V. L., 41, 352
McAdam, D. B., 210
McAfee, J. K., 280
McArdle, P. E., 215
McCartney, J. R., 343
McClannahan, L. E., 299
McCleary, D. F., 139
McCoach, D. B., 200
McComas, J. J., 157
McConnell, J. V., 23
McCord, B. E., 48
McDaniel, S. C., 134, 200
McDonald, M. E., 299
McDougall, D., 297, 355–356, 365
McGee, G., 210
McGill, P., 245
McIntosh, K., 175, 198, 200
McKay, J. A., 302
McKee-Higgins, E., 235
McKeegan, G., 274
McKenzie, S. D., 338
McKerchar, P., 206, 265
McKnight, M., 94
McLaughlin, T. F., 74, 258
McMorrow, M. J., 343
McNamara, K., 272
McNiff, T., 301
McSween, T. E., 279
McSweeny, A. J., 272
Meadan, H., 154, 157
Mechling, L. C., 214, 301, 316
Meddaugh, D., 265
Meichenbaum, D. H., 361–362
Meindl, J. N., 48, 215, 218, 221, 276
Mellard, D. F., 94
Meller, P., 235
Mendes-Smith, A. E., 254
Mennemeier, M., 343
Merical, C., 189
Mesmer, E. M., 344
Messer, G., 4
Methot, L., 157
Meuser, S., 285
Michael, J., 12, 18, 172
Michalski, D. N., 81
Middleton, S., 207
Miguel, C. F., 12, 172, 298
Milan, M., 286
Milata, E. M., 336, 340
Miller, J. R., 217, 281
Miller, N., 215, 218, 221
Miller, B., 355, 364
Miltenberger, R., 91, 254, 265, 269–270
Miltenberger, R. G., 82, 344
Mirenda, P., 299
Mishel, W., 363
Mitchell, B. S., 91
Mitchell, R. J., 296
Mitteer, D. R., 280
Mohammadzaheri, F., 248
Moher, C. A., 215
Molgaard, K., 95
Mongrella, J., 274
Montgomery, R., 286

Moore, D. W., 301, 303, 310, 311
Moore, T. C., 262–264, 270
Morales, E., 316
Morales, R., 285
Morales, S., 280
Morgan, A. C., 280
Morgan, R. L., 207
Morgenstern, B. D., 245–246, 306
Morris, R., 48
Morrison, J. Q., 233
Morse, T. E., 307, 310
Morton, W. L., 358
Motes, P., 206
Mottern, R. E., 92
Mowrer, D., 272
Moyer, J. R., 311
Moyer, L., 22–23
Mueller, M. M., 304–305
Mueuthing, C. S., 168, 186
Muir, K., 235
Muldoon, M., 208
Mulick, J., 274
Munk, D. D., 305
Murphy, H. A., 23
Murray, P., 302
Musti-Rao, S., 74
Myles, B., 91

N

Nader-Grosbois, N., 351
Nadle, R., 270
Nash, A., 302
Nau, P., 281
Neef, N. A., 81, 215, 245
Neely, L., 97
Neely, L. C., 258
Neisworth, J., 270
Nelson, C. M., 275
Nelson, M. A., 226
Nelson, P. M., 56
Nelson, R., 98
Nelson, R. O., 363
Nese, R. N., 200
Neuringer, A., 240
Neve, D., 74, 281–282
Nevin, J. A., 270
Newman, B., 25, 364
Newsom, C., 265
Nichols, P., 25
Nissen, M. A., 215
Nizzi, R., 297
Noel, C. R., 185, 224, 262–263
Noell, G. H., 241
Nolan, J. D., 233, 272
Nolen, J., 125, 159–160
Normand, M., 157, 262
Northrup, J., 206
Nosik, M., 172
Novak, M. D., 280
Nuernberger, J. E., 256–257
Nuri Ben-Shushan, Y., 351

O

O'Brien, L., 126
O'Brien, M., 261
O'Connor, J., 280
O'Connor, M. E., 245
O'Donnell, J., 292
O'Handley, R. D., 150

O'Hara, M., 305
O'Leary, K. D., 30, 223, 281, 359
O'Neill, K., 231
O'Neill, R., 175, 179, 261, 317, 341
O'Reilly, M. F., 214, 265, 297, 333
Oakes, W. P., 198
Obiakor, F. E., 35
Odom, S., 218
Ok, M., 372
Olcay-Gul, S., 307
Oldenquist, A., 32
Oliveira, C., 306
Oliver, C., 245, 280
Ollendick, T., 285
Olson, T. W., 363
Olszewski, A., 157
Ong, P., 279
Onghena, P., 157
Ortiz, C., 77
Ottenbacher, K. J., 155
Overley, E., 218, 221
Owen, T. M., 245, 261
Ozen, A., 301
Ozkan, S. Y., 364

P

Pace, G., 81, 207–208
Pace, G. M., 98, 184, 257, 265, 280
Page, T., 207
Palkovic, C. M., 304–305
Pancari, J., 291
Panyan, M. C., 316, 340
Park, E-Y., 27
Park, G., 94
Park, H., 361
Park, J., 138
Park, Y., 262–264
Parry-Cruwys, D., 82, 270
Patterson, C. J., 363
Patterson, E. T., 316
Patterson, G. R., 269
Patterson, R., 269
Pavlov, Ivan, 16–17
Pawich, T. L., 301
Payne, J., 81, 221
Payne, R., 221
Payne, S. W., 217, 272
Pence, S. T., 186
Pennington, A., 270
Pennington, R. C., 32, 227, 264, 358
Perle, J. G., 227
Perrin, C. K., 186
Perry, R. S., 9
Peters, K. P., 262
Peters, L. C., 285–286
Peters, R., 361–362
Peterson, C., 215
Peterson, R. F., 69
Peterson, R. L., 34, 301
Peterson, S. M., 30
Peterson, S. P., 297, 301
Petrill, S. A., 3
Petrongolo, M., 186
Petursdottir, A. L., 297
Pfadt, A., 214
Phillips, C. L., 4, 262–263
Phillips, E. A., 341
Phillips, E. L., 341
Piaget, Jean, 7–8

Piazza, C. C., 269
Piazza. C. C., 338
Pichardo, D., 310, 315
Pierce, K. I., 363
Pierce, W. D., 24
Piersma, D. E., 74
Pigott, H. E., 235
Pinkelman, S. E., 139
Pinkston, E. M., 265, 269
Pipkin, C. C. S. P., 91, 97
Plank, E., 337
Plati, E., 74
Plavnick, J. B., 72, 91
Podlesnik, C. A., 268, 280, 338
Pokrzywinski, J., 279
Polick, A. S., 227
Poling, A., 157, 207, 261–262
Polloway, C., 222
Polloway, E., 222
Polster, R., 223, 341
Pope, Alexander, 2
Popelka, G., 275
Popham, M., 351
Popovic, S. C., 74
Porter, A., 92
Poulson, C. L., 74, 299, 310
Powers, K. V., 280
Prager, K., 281
Pratt, J., 281
Preis, J., 214
Premack, David, 210
Presbie, R., 274
Presland, I. E., 281
Pritchard, D., 281
Progar, P. R., 280
Prykanowski, D. A., 72, 81
Pugach, M., 22
Pumroy, D. K., 232–233
Purcell, J., 332
Purrazzella, K., 316
Pustejovsky, J. E., 157

Q

Quevillon, R. P., 361
Quigley, J., 302

R

Radhakrishnan, S., 168, 260
Radley, K. C., 150, 208, 345
Radstaake, M., 245, 259
Rafferty, L. A., 303
Ramasamy, R., 133, 227
Ramirez, H., 307
Ramsey, M. L., 215
Randall, K. R., 224
Rapp, J. T., 81, 82, 272
Rapport, M. D., 23
Raschke, D., 210
Rathel, J. M., 227
Raynor, R., 17
Reading-Brown, M., 276
Reavis, A., 210
Rechs, J., 228–230
Reed, D. K., 352–353
Reed, H., 175
Reed, P., 242
Reed, S., 295
Reese, N. M., 265
Reeve, K. F., 47, 72, 81, 94, 295, 299, 336

Reeve, S. A., 47, 72, 81, 94, 299, 301, 336
Reeves, L. M., 35
Rehfeldt, R. A., 74, 361
Reichow, B., 72, 81, 157
Reid, D. H., 206, 207
Reinecke, D. R., 25, 357
Reinke, W. M., 198
Reiss, M. I., 343
Reitman, D., 276
Repp, A. C., 123, 183, 253, 257, 258–259, 275, 286, 305
Retting, R., 300
Reynish, L. C., 185
Reynolds, G. S., 255
Rezae, M., 248
Rhen, R., 294
Rhymer, K. N., 370
Rice, D., 285
Richard, E., 303
Richards, C., 133, 135, 158, 280
Richardson, A. R., 262, 297
Richardson, M. J., 81, 297
Richie, M. N., 185
Richman, D. M., 183, 263
Richman, G. S., 166, 184, 252, 268, 343
Ricketts, E. J., 257
Rigney, A. M., 218
Riley-Tillman, T. C., 148
Rimmer, B., 285
Rincover, A, 214, 269–270, 329, 341, 343
Ringdahl, J. E., 48, 207, 217, 256–257, 263
Rios, D., 186
Risley, T. R., 14, 18–19, 24, 27, 154, 199, 210, 326
Rispoli, M. J., 97, 185–186
Ritschl, C., 274
Ritter, W. A., 263
Rivera, G., 260
Roane, H. S., 207, 257–259, 263, 265, 268, 272, 280
Roberts, M., 276, 364
Roberts, R. N., 363
Robinson, C. C., 262–264
Robison, M. A., 34
Roche, L., 299
Rodgers, T., 177, 269
Rodriguez, B. J., 166
Rodriguez, N. M., 48, 301
Rodriguez, P. P., 241
Rogers, C. R., 25
Rohahn, J., 32
Rohrer, L., 157
Rolider, N. U., 218
Rollings, J., 286
Romani, P. W., 98, 217, 280
Romano-Verthelyi, A. M., 3
Roncati, A. L., 298
Rooker, G. W., 186, 262, 280
Rortvelt, A., 265
Rosales, R., 299
Roscoe, E. M., 207, 210, 278, 280
Rosenbloom, R., 355–356
Roth, K., 77
Rothstein, L. F., 30
Rourke, D., 177
Rouse, C. A., 304, 355, 364
Rowbury, T., 276
Rowe, M., 227
Rowe, S., 81
Rowling, J. K., 350
Rozalski, M., 34
Rozenblat, E., 299
Rubio, E. K., 310, 315

Rubow, C. C., 226, 233, 262–263
Ruffo, B., 81
Rusch, F. R., 272, 284–285, 361
Russa, M. B., 198
Russell, Bertrand, 18
Russell, D., 217
Russo, L., 270
Russo, S. R., 206
Ryan, J. B., 34, 72, 351

S
Sabielny, L. M., 207–208, 302
Saenen, L., 157
Sainato, D. M., 301, 308, 369
Saini, V., 268, 269
Sajwaj, T., 279, 285
Sakai, J., 77
Salend, S., 265, 272, 274
Salva, E., 358
Salvatore, J. E., 3
Salzberg, C. L., 270
Samaha, A. L., 260
Sameoto, D., 281
Sanford, A. K., 245
Sangkavasi, E., 224
Sani-Bozkurt, S., 301
Satsangi, R., 297, 301
Saudargas, R. A., 223
Saunders, A. F., 30, 72, 301
Saunders, K., 305
Saunders, M., 233, 236
Saunders, R., 80
Sautter, R. A., 207
Savage, M., 91
Sawyer, M. R., 47, 81, 226, 304
Schanding, G. T., 210
Schardt, A. A., 355
Schaub, R., 74
Scheithauer, M. C., 269, 280, 305
Scherer, S. W., 3
Schieltz, K. M., 72, 81
Schiff, R., 351
Schiller, E., 61
Schilling, D., 222
Schlinger, H. D. Jr., 39, 346
Schloss, P., 280, 343
Schmidt, C., 4
Schmidt, J. D., 92
Schnaitter, R., 22
Schoen, S., 125, 159–160
Schopler, E., 44
Schrauben, K. S., 74
Schreibman, L., 294, 309, 340, 363
Schroeder, G. L., 340
Schroeder, S. R., 32
Schultz, D. P., 7
Schumaker, J. B., 223
Schuster, J. W., 296, 306, 307, 310
Schwarz, M. L., 341
Sciuchetti, M. B., 13
Scott-Goodwin, A. C., 4
Scott, J., 227, 302
Scott, T. M., 176, 252
Scruggs, T. E., 47, 224
Seaman-Tullis, R. L., 301
Seaver, J. L., 302
Sedlack, R. A., 343
Sellers, T. P., 299
Seltzer, A., 317

Sennott, S., 168
Seward, J., 307
Shabani, D. B., 303
Shadish, W. R., 157
Shafer, M. S., 333
Shahan, T. A., 265
Shapiro, E. S., 361
Shapiro, S., 155, 274–275
Sharpton, W., 87, 296
Sheehan, M. R., 337
Sheehey, M., 227
Sheehey, P. H., 227
Sheehey, S. B., 364
Sheldon, J. B., 32
Shelvin, K. H., 297
Shepley, C., 139
Shepley, S. B., 361
Sherman, J. A., 32, 223
Shih, C-H., 91
Shih, C-T., 91
Shillingsburg, M. A., 210, 265, 299, 317
Shireman, M. L., 274
Shoemaker, A. M., 207
Shogren, K. A., 352
Shore, B. A., 214, 245, 282
Shrestha, A., 311
Shrewsbury, A. N., 269
Shukla-Mehta, S., 72, 74
Shumate, E. D., 260
Sidener, D., 297
Sidener, T. M., 47, 297
Sidman, M., 122–123
Siegel, G. M., 273
Sigafoos, J., 261
Silbaugh, B. C., 346
Silkowski, E. L., 280
Simmons-Reed, E. A., 301
Simmons, C. A., 268
Simmons, J. Q., 265–266
Simonsen, B., 200
Simonson, G. R., 157
Simpson, C., 300
Simpson, M., 206
Simpson, R., 91
Singer-Dudek, J., 72
Singh, N., 253, 285, 364
Sivage, C., 361
Skerbetz, M. D., 32
Skibbe, L. E., 91
Skinner, B. F., 7, 14, 18, 23, 25–26, 56, 237–239, 265, 268, 270, 351
Skinner, C. H., 81, 139, 235
Sleeper, J. D., 95
Sleiman, A., 98
Slifer, K. J., 166, 184, 252, 268
Slocum, S. K., 262–263
Slocum, T. A., 260
Sloman, K. N., 97
Smith, C. E., 291
Smith, D., 148
Smith, E., 235
Smith, K. A., 361, 363
Smith, M., 280
Smith, R., 189, 214, 245, 265, 270
Smith, S., 224
Sneed, T. J., 333
Snell, M., 94, 318
Snodgrass, M. R., 27, 154
Sobezenski, T., 91
Solomon, R. W., 269
Sorrell, S., 285

Sottolano, D., 246, 265
Soukup, J. H., 369
Souza, A. C., 298
Sowers, J., 272
Sparacio, E. J., 299
Sparrow, S., 44
Speight, D. R., 302
Sperry, J. M., 280
Spitz, D., 267
Spitz, W., 267
Spooner, D., 305, 317
Spooner, F., 301, 305, 317, 331
Sprague, J. R., 175, 199, 214, 261, 336
Spriggs, A. D., 297, 303
Staats, A. W., 314
Staats, C. K., 314
Stafford, A., 210
Stahmer, A. C., 35
Stainback, S., 27, 221
Stainback, W., 27, 221, 343
Stainton, T., 32
Stanley, C. R., 294
Starr, E. M., 74
Staubitz, J. L., 185
Steed, E., 296, 363
Stein, N., 309
Stephens, R., 286
Stephens, T. M., 339
Sterling-Turner, H. E., 210
Steuart, W., 285
Stevens, K. B., 306
Stevenson, J., 237
Stewart, C., 285
Stewart, S. C., 369
Stiefler, N. A., 262
Stocker, J. D. Jr., 367
Stoiber, K. C., 198
Stokes, J. V., 337, 343, 345
Stokes, T. F., 248, 329–336
Stoltz, S., 369
Stolz, S. B., 24
Stormer, R., 297
Stormont, M., 91, 198
Stotz, K. E., 358
Stowe, M., 173
Strain, P., 218
Straithe, M., 343
Strauss, A. A., 4
Streifel, S., 302
Stremel-Campbell, K., 340
Strickland, E., 147
Stright, M. H., 296
Stringer, E. T., 159
Stringfield, S. G., 72
Strohmeier, C., 27, 184
Sturmey, P., 265, 315
Sugai, G. M., 12–13, 47, 176, 198, 200, 291, 382
Sullivan, W. E., 257–259
Sulzer-Azaroff, B., 26–27, 269, 279, 301, 404
Summers, J., 214
Sumner, J., 285
Sump, L. A., 77
Sundberg, M. L., 339
Susa, C., 346
Sutherland, K., 90, 227
Swain-Bradway, J., 200
Swanson, L., 355
Sweeney-Kerwin, E. J., 126, 213
Sweeney, W. J., 358
Swerdan, M. G., 299

Sy, J. R., 92
Szmacinski, N. J., 297

T

Taber-Doughty, T., 91, 299, 355, 364
Taber, T. A., 9, 296, 317, 327
Talbert-Johnson, C., 358
Tapp, J., 95
Tarbox, J., 77
Taylor, B. A., 133, 254, 297, 303
Taylor, B. R., 303
Taylor, T., 224
Teigen, J., 269
Tekin-Iftar, E., 307
Telford, E., 4
Tereshko, L., 246, 265
Terrace, H. S., 305
Terrell, M., 307
Test, D. W., 41, 72, 297, 307
Tharpe, R. G., 363
Thaw, J., 26–27
Thayer, S. K., 61
Therrien, M. C. S., 74, 139
Thiemann-Bourque, K., 74
Thomas, A., 5
Thomas, C., 26–27
Thomas, D. R., 294, 315, 339
Thomas, E., 175, 214
Thomas, E. M., 47
Thomas, J. D., 281
Thomas, R., 81, 91
Thomason-Sassi, J. L., 186, 215, 241
Thompson, J. L., 91, 364
Thompson, R., 206, 265
Thompson, R. H., 183, 212, 285–286
Thompson, T. J., 269
Thomson, K. M., 207
Thorndike, Edward, 17
Tice, D. M., 348
Tiger, J. H., 92, 183, 256, 305
Tilly, W. D., 61
Tincani, M., 92, 150, 206
Tingstrom, D. H., 210
Toby, L. M., 280
Todd, A., 47
Tofflemoyer, S., 47
Tolman, E. C., 18
Torelli, J. N., 48
Toste, J. R., 94, 157
Touchette, P., 177, 179
Toussaint, K. A., 212, 256, 305
Townsend, D. B., 47, 74, 299, 301, 310
Trant, L., 218
Trask-Tyler, S. A., 327, 332, 344
Traub, M. R., 92
Travers, J. C., 34
Trela, K., 72
Trevino-Maack, S. I., 367
Trinh, S. M., 81
Troclair-Lasserre, N. M., 210
Trollope, Anthony, 350
Troutman, A., 246
Trussell, R. P., 177
Tsami, L., 168, 274
Tsiouri, I., 226
Tullis, C. A., 81, 91, 207–208, 295
Turnbull, A., 173
Turnbull, H. R., 173
Turnbull, R., 32

Turner, J., 358
Turner, S., 279
Turner, W. D., 269
Twyman, J., 275
Tzanakaki, P., 303

U

Umbreit, J., 179

V

Vaca, L., 98
Valdovinos, M. G., 74
Valentino, A. L., 74, 265
Valentino, J., 297
Van Bourgondien, M., 44
Van Camp, C., 185, 268, 274
van den Berg, Y. H. M., 369
van den Pol, R. A., 343
van der Burg, J. J., 364
Van Houten, R., 28–31, 33–34, 269, 281, 300
Van Laarhoven-Myers, T., 299
Van Laarhoven, T., 297, 299, 301
Vannest, K., 233
Vanselow, N. R., 119, 268
Vargo, K. K., 256–257
Varjas, K., 219
Varsamis, P., 351
Vaughan, M. E., 351
Vaughn, S., 61
Vause, T., 91
Veazey, S. E., 74
Vedora, J., 297
Vegas, K., 276
Vener, S. M., 299
Verriden, A. L., 207, 278
Verschuur, R., 206
Viel-Ruma, K. A., 72
Viellevoye, S., 351
Vinas, V., 215
Vladescu, J. C., 47, 94, 212, 295
Vohs, K. D., 348
Vollmer, T. R., 34, 48, 56, 91, 92, 97, 186–189, 206, 207, 226, 233, 254, 262, 263, 269, 274, 276, 278, 280–281, 283
Voltz, D. L., 13
Vorndran, C. M., 81, 185, 265, 316
Voulgarakis, H., 265

W

Wacker, D. P., 208, 245, 261, 338
Wadsworth, J. P., 355, 364
Wahl, E., 233
Wahler, R. G., 269
Walker, D., 157
Walker, H. M., 168, 332, 342
Wallace, A. M., 298
Wallace, Irving, 350
Wallace, L. A., 48
Wallace, M., 266
Walton, W., 299
Wanzek, M., 233
Ward, K. D., 72, 74
Ward, R. D., 184
Warger, L. C., 22
Warzak, W. J., 343
Wasano, L. C., 177
Wasik, B. A., 306
Wathen, S. N., 268
Watkins, C. L., 56

Watkins, N., 272
Watras, J., 26
Watson, John, 17, 266
Waugh, R. F., 307
Wayman, M. M., 157
Weaver, E. S., 185
Weaver, L. A., 74
Weeden, M., 226, 352
Wehby, J. H., 90, 95, 157, 177, 179, 227, 228, 305
Wehmeyer, M. L., 226, 352
Weinlein, J. L., 306
Weisberg, P., 223
Weiss, J. S., 302, 308, 317
Wellman, G., 44
Wells, A. M., 4
Wells, J. C., 227, 355
Welsh, F., 338
Werry, J. S., 5
Wertheimer, Max, 8–9
Wesolowski, M. D., 284–285
Weston, R., 255
Wetherby, B., 302
Wheatley, K. K., 259
Wheaton, J. E., 301
Wheeler, J., 27
Whelan, B. M., 291
Whipple, R., 47
White, A., 275
White, G. P., 352
White, L., 206
White, M. A., 281
White, M. W., 72
White, O., 155–156
Whiting, S. W., 95
Whitley, K. G., 130
Whitman, T. L., 361
Whitney, T., 327
Whittington, J. R., 4
Whorley, A., 138
Wichnick, G. A. M., 299, 338
Wicker, T., 23
Wierzba, B. C., 92
Wiggins, B., 208
Wilcox, B., 173
Wilder, D. A., 74, 214, 257, 280, 281–282
Wilke, A., 270
Wilke, A. E., 77
Wilkinson, G., 44
Williams, C. D., 215
Williams, D. A., 337
Williams, D. E., 269
Williams, R. E., 296–297
Wills, H. P., 72, 226, 260, 367
Wilson, C. L., 302
Wilson, D. M., 215, 241
Wilson, J. L., 280
Wilson, K., 286

Wimberly, B. S., 262
Winborn-Kemmerer, L., 48
Winborn, L., 261
Winette, R. A., 29–30, 371
Winiarski, L., 301
Winkauf, S., 306
Winkler, R. C., 29–30, 371
Winsler, A., 350
Wiskow, K. M., 74, 233, 260, 299, 346
Wisniewski, B. T., 92
Wolery, M., 12–13, 98, 157, 208, 251, 286, 291, 295
Wolf, M. M., 14, 18–19, 27, 154, 199, 233, 236, 326, 329, 334, 341
Wolfe, K., 157, 168, 207, 299
Wolfe, P. S., 301
Wong, H. K., 373
Wong, R. T., 373
Wood, C. L., 41
Woodbury, S. M., 3
Woodcock, R., 44
Woods, D. W., 256
Woods, K., 94
Woods, T. S., 343
Worsdell, A. S., 215, 241, 269
Woster, S., 265
Wright, C., 254
Wright, H., 68
Wu, P.-F., 301
Wunderlich, K. L., 340, 355–356
Wyatt, S., 316
Wyse, R. D., 218

X
Xu, S., 352, 355, 364

Y
Yaeger, J., 350
Yakich, T. M., 274
Yanardag, M., 305
Yell, M. L., 60
Yoder, P., 98, 157
Yorlets, C. B., 305
Young, M. E., 158
Ysseldyke, J., 56
Yu, C. T., 207

Z
Zaini, S., 233
Zangrillo, A. N., 48, 240, 245, 261
Zarcone, J., 92, 177, 189, 260, 265, 269
Zecchin-Tirri, C., 245–246
Zeug, N., 306
Zhang, N., 228, 233
Zhou, L., 269
Zigmond, N., 32
Zoder-Martell, K., 74
Zurita, L. M., 299

Subject Index

A

AB design, 125–127, 159–160
ABAB design (reversal design), 127–133, 150, 159–160, 326
ABACAB design, 149–150
ABAC design, 149–150
A-B-C descriptive analysis, 177–182
ABC design, 148–149, 153, 160
Abscissa, 102–104
Accidental (adventitious) reinforcement, 263
Accountability, 35–38, 66
Acquisition, 50
Action research, single-subject designs and, 159–160
Action verbs, 47–48
Activities, multiple, 337–339
Activity reinforcers, 215–217
Adaptive behavior, 44
Adaptive Behavior Scale, 44
ADD (attention deficit disorder), 4, 23
ADHD (attention deficit hyperactivity disorder), 4
Aggression, 48
    extinction-induced, 266–267
Alone condition, 184–185
Alternating treatments design, 143–147
Anal (expulsive and retentive) state, 6
Anecdotal reports, 68–71, 177
Antecedent conditions, 290–291
Antecedent control, 12–13
Antecedent influences on behavior, 290–291
Antecedent stimulus, 12, 80
    conditions of intervention and, 49–50
Application, 59
Applied behavior analysis
    accountability and, 35–38
    biophysical explanations, 2–3
    competence in, 28–29
    concerns about, 22–26
    design categories, 120–121
    ethical use of, 26–35
    historical development, 2
    interventions and, 18
    theory *vs.* recipes, 38–39
    treatment effectiveness, 34–35
Ascending baseline, 124
Assessment, behavioral, 30–31. *See also* functional assessment
    informant assessment, 174–175
    preference assessments, 206
Assimilation, 7
Associationism, 17
At-risk students, 367
Attention
    behavior to escape from, 168
    behavior to gain, 166–167
    condition, 184
    controlling, 266
Attention-deficit disorder (ADD), 4, 23
Attention-deficit hyperactivity disorder (ADHD), 4
Autism, 4, 44
Automatic reinforcement, 242–247
Aversive procedures, 24, 34–35
Aversive stimuli
    disadvantages, 282–283
    presentation, 277–283
    types of, 279–282
    unconditioned, 279
Axes, 102–104

B

Backup reinforcers, 218, 221–225
Backward chaining, 315–316
Bar graphs, 115–117
Baseline data, 113–114
    single-subject designs, 122–124
Bayley Scales for Infant Development, 44
Behavior
    antecedent influences on, 290–291
    assessment, 30–31
    complex behaviors, 310–318
    dimensions of, 64–68
    functions of, 164–170
    multiple baseline design across, 136–143
    operational definition of, 47–48
    procedural alternatives for reducing, 251–252
    reinforcement and, 11
Behavioral chain, 313–318
Behavioral explanations, 10–15
Behavioral interview, 175
Behavioral objectives
    components, 46–51
    defined, 41
    educational goals, 44–46
    format, 52–53
    IEP and, 60–62
    purpose, 41–43
    scope of, 54–60
Behavioral strategies, 31
Behavior Analyst Certification Board (BACB), 26, 28–29, 33
Behavior analysts, 31–33
Behavior change, data collection during, 93–95
Behavior-change programs, 31
Behaviorism, historical development of, 15–19, 22–24
Behavior modification, 22–23
Behavior rating scales, 175–177
Behavior reduction, procedural alternatives, 252–253
Behavior-specific praise, 227
Behavior support plan (BSP) 170–200
    brief functional analysis, 186–200
    functional behavior assessment and, 173–184
    sample plan, 188–195
Behavior Tracker Pro, 95
Biochemical explanations, 3–5
Biophysical explanations, 2–3, 5
Brain damage, biochemical abnormalities and, 4–5
Brief functional analysis (BFA), 186–200
    components, 196
Brigance Comprehensive Inventory of Basic Skills II, 44
Burst of behavior, 266

C

Chaining, 313–318
Changing criterion design, 131–136
Check In/Check Out (CICO) system, 134, 218–219
Childhood Autism Rating Scale, 44
Childmind.org, 22
Classical conditioning, 17, 19

Classroom
   instructional structure, 371–372
   physical arrangement, 369–370
   positive behavior support in, 199
   rules, 373–374
   time structure, 370–371
   verbal structure, 372
Clinical criterion, single-subject designs, 154
Coded data sheets
   legends, 88
   tracks, 90
Coercion, 25
Cognitive development theory, 7–8
Cognitive explanations, 8–10
Cognitive training strategies, 350
Common stimuli, 342–344
Communication, behavior and, 164–170
Competence in treatment, 28–29
Complex behaviors, 310–318
Complexity, data collection, 98–99
Comprehension, 57
Concept formation, 294
Concrete operations stage, 7
Conditioned aversive stimuli, 281
Conditioned stimulus (CS), 17
Conditions, graphing, 113–114
Condition statement formats, 50
Confounding variable, single-subject designs, 120
Consent, 30
Consequences. *See also* reinforcement
   behavior reduction, 252–253
   contingent presentation of, 204–205
   learning and, 373
   reinforcement and, 11
   rules and, 373–374
Consequent stimulus, 80
Constructivism, 9–19
Contigent removal, 204
Contingencies
   aversive stimuli, 279–280
   group contingencies, 231–236
   indiscriminate, 341–342
   limited hold (LH) contingency, 239
   maintaining, 332–333
   negative reinforcement, 243
   self-reinforcement, 359–360
Contingent observation, 275
Contingent presentation, 204–205
Contingent reinforcer, 211
Continuous schedule of reinforcement (CRF), 236–242
Contracting, 228–231
Count It software, 95
Criterion statement, 50
Cued self-monitoring, 354–357
Cumulative graphs, 114–115

D

Data collection
   anecdotal reports, 68–71
   duration recording, 91–92
   functional behavior assessment, 182–185
   graphs (*See* graphs)
   interobserver agreement, 98–99
   interval recording, 81–83
   observational recording systems, 73–90
   permanent product recording, 71–72
   rationale, 64
   reliability, 96–97
   student groups, 90
   systems, 64–68, 96
   technology, 94–95
   time samplling, 81, 84–86
   variations on, 86–90
Data path, 104
Data point, 103–104
Delayed reaction, 265
Demand condition, 184
Dependent group-oriented contingency systems, 233
Dependent variable, 122
   alternating treatments design, 144
   single-subject designs, 120
Deprivation state, 212–213
Descending baseline, 124
Descriptive assessment, 177
Descriptive function, baseline data, 122–123
Desirable stimuli, removal of, 271–273
Determinism, 25–26
Developmental explanations, 6–8
Difference, 336
"The Difference Between Operant and Classical Conditioning" (video), 17
Differential reinforcement, 291–324
   antecedent influences, 290–291
   complex behaviors, 310–318
   discrimination principles, 292–295
   fading, 303–310
   modeling, 300–302
   physical guidance, 302–303, 369–370
   shaping, 318, 320–324
   stimulus control and, 292
Differential reinforcement of alternative behavior (DRA), 258–261
Differential reinforcement of incompatible behavior (DRI), 259–261
Differential reinforcement of lower rates of behavior (DRL), 253–255
Differential reinforcement of other behaviors (DRO), 255–260
Direct observation strategies, 177
Disabilities
   biochemical abnormalities and, 3–4
   self-management for learners with, 364–367
   therapeutic environment, 31–32
Discomfort, behavior to escape from, 169
Discovery learning, 8–9
Discrete behaviors, 74, 79
Discrimination, principles of, 292–295
   training, 293–295
Discriminative stimulus, 292
Distributed practice, 56
Duration data, graph of, 108–109, 112
Duration of behavior, 66
Duration recording, 73, 91–92

E

Economy, in stimulus control, 372–373
Educational achievement, 44
Educational goals, 44–46
Education for All Handicapped Children Act of 1975, 60–62
Effectiveness, 34–35, 308–310
   reinforcers, 206–208
Effect size, graph analysis, 157
Environment
   behavior and, 11–15
   determinism and, 25–26
   learning, 374–389
Equilibration, 7
Errorless learning, 304
Escape, negative reinforcement, 245–246
Ethical Code (BACB), 28
Ethical use of applied behavior analysis, 26–35
Ethics in single-subject designs, 158–159
Evaluation, 59
   ethical guidelines for, 31

Event recording, 73–80
  graphing of data, 105–106
Evidence-based treatment, 34
Evocation of response, 292
Exclusion time-out, 275–277
Executive Council of the Association for Behavior Analysis (ABA), 28
Exemplars, 336–339
Expectancy, data collection, 99
Experimental control, single-subject designs, 124
Explanations, behavioral, 10–15
  biochemical, 3–5
  biophysical, 2–3
  cognitive, 8–10
  developmental, 6–8
  usefulness of, 2–3, 5, 7–10, 14–15
Explanatory fictions, 15
Extinction, 11–12, 264–270
  resistance to, 265
  sensory, 269–270

F

Fading, 303–310
  assistance, 148–149, 153, 160
  prompts, effectiveness, 308–309
Fixation, 6
Fixed-interval scallop, 239
Fixed-interval schedule, 238–239
Fixed-ratio schedule, 237–238
Fixed-response-duration schedule, 239–240
Fixed time schedule, 263
Fluency of performance, 55
Force of behavior, 66
Formal operations stage, 7
Forward chaining, 316–317
Fractionation, alternating treatments design, 144
Free operant preference assessment, 207
Free will, 25
Frequency, of behavior, 65, 75
Full inclusion, 32, 34–35
Full-session DRL and DRO, 253–254
Functional analysis, 172
  brief analysis, 186–200
  settings for conducting, 185–186
Functional Analysis Screening Tool (FAST), 176
Functional Assessment Checklist: Teachers and Staff (FACTS), 175
Functional assessment interview (FAI), 175
Functional behavior assessment (FBA), 172–200
  A-B-C descriptive analysis, 177–182
  anecdotal reports, 177
  behavioral interview, 175
  behavior rating scales, 175–177
  data collecting, 182–185
  direct observation strategies, 177
  informant assessment, 174–175
  scatter plot analysis, 177–179
  strategies, 173–174
Functional communication training (FCT), 260–261
Functional relationship
  multiple baseline design, 137–138
  single-subject designs, 120
Functional skills programs, 33–34

G

General case programming, 336–337
Generalization, 56–57
  behavior change, 326–329
  defined, 327–328
  mediation and training, 345–346
  programming for, 329–346
  response, 329
  stimulus generalization, 328
Generalized conditioned reinforcers, 217–218
Generalized imitation response, 268–269
Generalized reinforcement, extinction, 269
Genetics, behavior and, 3
Gestalt theory, 8–9
Goals, 44–46
  self-management and, 350–353
Good Behavior Game, 233–236
Graduated guidance, 305, 309
Graphs, 101–117
  AB design, 125
  additional conventions, 113–114
  alternating treatments design, 144–149
  bar graphs, 115–117
  changing criterion design, 133–135
  cumulative graphs, 114–115
  data transfer, 104–113
  multiple baseline design across, 137–141
  multiple treatments design, 150–153
  purpose of, 101–102
  reversal design, 129–130
  simple line graph, 102–104
  single-subject designs, 155–158
  visual analysis, 155–158
Group contingencies, 231–236, 342
Group data collection, 90
Group designs, 120–121

H

Heredity, behavior and, 3
Hints, as verbal prompts, 296
Histograms, 115–117
Humane goals, 26
Humors theory, historical development of behavior analysis and, 2–3
Hyperactivity, 4

I

Imitation, reinforcement and, 268–269
Immediate positive reinforcement, 205
Immediate reinforcer, 211
Incidental teaching, 317–320
Inclusion, 32, 34–35
Independent group-oriented contingency systems, 233
Independent variable
  alternating treatments design, 144
  single-subject designs, 120
Indiscriminable contingencies, 341–342
Individual education plan (IEP), 44
  behavioral objectives, 60–62
  behavioral objectives in, 43
  functional behavior assessment and, 173–174
Individualized contingencies, 231
Individuals
  multiple baseline design across, 136–143
  positive behavior support for, 197–199
Individuals with Disabilities Education Improvement Act (IDEA), 60–61, 170–171
Informant assessment, 174–175
Informed consent, 30
Initial behavior, 321
Instruction
  data collection during, 93
  self-instruction, 360–363
  as verbal prompt, 296
Instructional packages, ABC design, 148

Instructional structure, 371–372
Instructional target, 48
Interactions, behavior to escape from, 168
Interdependent group-oriented contingency systems, 233
Intermediate behaviors, 321
Intermittent reinforcement, 341–342
   schedule, 238–240, 270
Internal pain, behavior to escape from, 169
Interobserver agreement, data collection, 98–99
Interresponse-time DRL, 253
Interval DRL, 253–254
Intervalminder, 95
Interval recording, 73, 81–83
   graphing of data, 108–109
Interval schedules, 237–239
Intervention
   based on function, 197
   conditions of, 49–50
   graphing, 113–114
   measures, 124
Intrinsic motivation, 24–25
ISBO (Is the Berhavior Specific and Objective) questions, 48
Iterative process, 163

J

Journal of Applied Behavior Analysis, 18–19, 29–30
Journal of Teacher Education, 26

K

Kaufman Assessment Battery for Children, 44
Key Math-3 Diagnostic Assessment, 44
Knowledge, 57

L

Lag schedule of reinforcement, 240, 345
Latency of behavior, 66
   graphing of data, 108, 113
   recording, 73, 92–93
Lawful behavior, 25
Law of Effect, 17
Law of Exercise, 17
Learner, identification of, 46
Learning
   behavior and, 11–15
   environment for, 374–389
   hierarchical levels of, 57–60
   learner with limitations, levels for, 59–60
   principles, 13–14
Least restrictive environment, 31
Least-to-most prompting, 307–309
Legends, coded data sheets, 88
Limited generalizability of extinction, 269
Limited hold (LH) contingency, 239
Limited learners, learning levels for, 59–60
Line graphs, 102–104
Locus of behavior, 66–67
Loose training, 339–340

M

Maintenance, 56, 328–329
Massed practice, 56
Metacognitive training strategies, 350
Minimoose software, 95
Modeling, 13, 300–302
Momentary DRO, 255–260
Mooses software, 95
Most-to-least prompts, 303–305, 309
MotivAiderTM, 256

Motivating operations, 12, 172–173
Motivation
   learning and, 9
   positive reinforcement and, 24–25
Motivation Assessment Scale (MAS), 176
Multiple baseline design, 136–143
Multiple baseline design across behavior, 136–143
Multiple baseline design across individuals, 136–143
Multiple baseline design across settings, 136–143
Multiple probe technique, 142
Multiple stimulus without replacement preference assessment, 208
Multiple treatments design, 147–154
Music, learning and, 13
Mystery Motor intervention, 342

N

Naturalistic training, 339–340
Natural reinforcement, 247–248
Negative reinforcement, 11, 242–247
   inadvertent use, 243–245
   instruction, 246–247
Noncontingent reinforcement (NCR), 261–264
Non-cued self-monitoring, 354–357
Nonexclusion time-out, 274–275
Nonintensive training, 339
Nonoccurrence reliability, 97
Non-specific behavior praise, 227

O

Observation, behavioral theory, 14
Observational recording systems, 73–90
Observer drift, 98
Occasioning of response, 292
Occurrence reliability, 97
Off-task behavior, 83
On-task behavior, 47–48, 90
Operant conditioning, 17–18
Operational definition of behavior, 47–48
Oral (dependent and aggressive) state, 6
Ordinate, 102–104
Outcome recording, 73
Overcorrection, 284–286
Overlearning, 56

P

Paired stimulus preference assessment, 207–208
Pairing, 214–215
Parallel procedures, single-subject designs, 160
Parsimony, 5
Partial-interval recording, 82
Peer mediation, group contingencies and, 235–236
Performance
   changing criterion design, 131–136
   criteria, 50–51
   self-management and, 364
Permanent product recording, 71–72
   graphing of data, 104–105
Personal welfare services, 29–30
Phallic (gender awareness) stge, 6
Phenylketonuria (PKU) testing, 5
Physical guidance, 302–303, 369–370
Physical health, behavior and, 44
Pinpointing behavior, 43
Play condition, 185
Positive attending, 226
Positive behavior support (PBS), 197–198, 382
Positive-practice overcorrection, 284–286

Positive reinforcement, 11, 225–228
    defined, 205
    hyperactivity and, 23–25
    inappropriate behavior and, 168
    time-out from, 274
Positive reinforcer, 205
Praise Note, 259
Predictive utility
    baseline data, 123
    behavioral explanations, 15
    reversal design, 128
Preference assessments, 206–208
Preference Inventory Checklist, 209
Premack principle, 210, 215–217
Preoperational stage, 7
Presentation, single-item presentation, 207
Primary reinforcers, 211–214
Probes
    data collection, 93
    simultaneous prompting, 307
Problem Behavior Questionnaire (PBQ), 176
Procedural integrity, 27–28
Procedures, 373–374
Progress, behavioral objectives and, 423
"Project Pigeon," 18
Prompts, 293, 295–300
    effectiveness, 309–310
    fading, 303–310
    hints, 296
    instructions, 296
    least-to-most, 307–309
    most-to-least, 303–305, 309
    rules as, 295
    self-operated prompts, 296–297
    simultaneous procedures, 307
    stimulus prompts, 304
    tactile, 303
    verbal prompts, 295–297
    visual, 297–300
Psychoanalytic theory, 6
Psychological antecedents, 16–17
Punisher, 11–12, 271
Punishment, 11–12, 271
    removal of desirable stimuli, 271–277
    self-punishment, 350–351, 360

Q

Quantifiable data, behavioral theory, 14
Quarter-intersect method, graph analysis, 155–156
Questions About Behavioral Function (QABF), 176–177

R

Rate data
    graph of, 105–108
    increased extinction, 266
Rate of behavior, 65
Ratio of reinforcement, 236–237
Ratio schedules, 237–238
Ratio strain, 242
Reactivity, data collection, 98
Recovery, spontaneous, 268
Reinforcement. *See also* negative and positive reinforcement
    behavior support plan, 171–173
    contingency, 171–173
    defined, 203–204
    natural, 247–248
    noncontingent reinforcement, 261–264
    by others, 268–269
    schedules, 236–242, 270
    self-reinforcement, 350–351, 359–360
    summary of procedures, 262
    thinning schedules, 240–242
Reinforcers
    activity, 215–217
    administrative variants in, 231–242
    backup, 218, 221–225
    categories and examples, 204–205
    contingent reinforcers, 211
    effective, 206–208
    generalized conditioned reinforcers, 217
    immediate, 211
    individualization, 206
    menu, 207
    positive, 205
    primary, 211–214
    secondary, 214–215
    social, 225–225
    tangible, 215
    token, 217–225
    types of, 211–227
Relevance of Behavior Rule, 334
Reliability, data collection, 96–97
Repeated measures, single-subject designs, 122
Replication of effect
    reversal design, 128
Research designs, 124
    changing criterion design, 133–135
    reversal design, 130–131
Resistance to extinction, 265
Respondent conditioning, 16–17
Response, occasion or evoking of, 292
Response competence hierarchy, 55–57
Response-cost procedures, 271–273
Response-duration schedule, 237, 239–240
Responsibility to Clients (BACB), 29
Responsiveness to Intervention (RTI), 19, 61–62, 148
Restitutional overcorrection, 284
Reversal design, 127–133
Round-robin data collection format, 90
Rules, 373–374
    as verbal prompts, 295

S

Sameness, 336
Satiation, 212–213
Scale break, 102
Scatter plot analysis, 177–179
Schedules of reinforcement, 236–242
School Classroom Observation and Analysis (SCOA), 95
School psychology, 44
School Reinforcement Survey Schedule, 206
Schoolwide positive behavior support, 200
S-deltas, 292
Seclusionary intervention, 34–35
    time-out, 276–277
Secondary reinforcers, 214–215
Self-evaluation, 357–358
Self-graphing, 358
Self-instruction, 350–351, 360–363
Self-management, 348–350
    as common experience, 350–351
    learners with disabilities, 364–367
    special populations, 364–367
Self-monitoring, 350–351, 354–357
Self-operated verbal prompts, 296–297
Self-punishment, 350–351, 360
Self-reinforcement, 350–351, 359–360
Sensory extinction, 269–270

Sensory-motor stage, 7
Sensory stimulation, challenging behavior to gain, 168
Sequential modification, 332–333
Setting events, 12, 172, 291
Settings
    multiple baseline design across, 136–143
    multiple settings, 337–339
Shaping, 13–14, 290, 318, 320–324
Short-term exclusion, 34
Simple discrimination, 293–294
Simultaneous prompting, 307
Single-item presentation, 207
Single-subject designs, 118–160
    AB design, 125–127
    action research, 159–160
    alternating treatments, 143–147
    baseline measures, 122–124
    categories, 120–121
    changing criterion design, 131–136
    components, 122–124
    ethics, 158–159
    evaluation, 154–159
    experimental control, 124
    functional relationships, 120
    intervention measurements, 124
    multiple baseline design, 136–143
    multiple treatments design, 147–154
    parallels and contributions, 160
    reversal design, 127–133
    summary, 153–154, 163
    variables and functional relations, 120
Skills acquisition, 364
Social reinforcers, 225–225
Social validity, 27, 154
Space-responding DRL, 253
Specificity, 372
Spontaneous recovery, 268
Stability, baseline data, 123
Standardized contingencies, 231
Stimulus class, 328
    common stimuli, 342–344
Stimulus control, 12, 368–374
    differential reinforcement, 292
    discriminative stimulus, 292
    shaping and, 290
Stimulus equivalence, 294–295
Stimulus generalization, 328
Stimulus overactivity, 294
Stimulus prompts, 304
Student-Assisted Functional Assessment Interview, 175
Student Guided Functional Assessment Interview, 175
Synthesis, 59

T

Tactile prompts, 303
Tangibles
    behavior to gain, 167–168
    condition, 184
    reinforcers, 215
Target behavior
    statement of, 46–48
    task analysis, 310–312
Task analysis, 310–313
Tasks, behavior to escape from, 168–169
Teachers
    characteristics, 374
    ethical guidelines for, 33
    multiple, 337–339
Teaching chains, 317–320
Teaching designs, 124
    AB design, 125–127
Technology, data collection, 94–95
Terminal behavior, 321
Theory, basic properties of, 2
Therapeutic environment, 31–32
Therapeutic services, 44
Thinning schedules of reinforcement, 240–242
Time delay, 305–307, 309
Time graphs, 105, 107–108
Time-out procedures, 24, 274–277
Time-out ribbon, 274–275
Time sampling, 73, 81, 84–86
    graphing of data, 109–111
Time structure, 370–371
Token reinforcers, 217–225, 272
Topography of behavior, 66
Total task presentation, 317
Train and hope, 331
Training for generalization, 345–346
Transenvironmental programming, 332
Trapping, 334
Trend, baseline data, 124
Trial-by-trial recording, 77, 80

U

Unconditioned stimulus (US), 17
    aversive stimuli, 279
Universal Design for Learning, 372

V

Variable-interval schedule, 239
Variable-ratio schedule, 238
Variable-response-duration schedule, 240
Variables
    functional behavior assessment, 184–185
    single-subject designs, 120
Variable time schedule, 263
Verbal prompts, 295–296
Verbal reprimands, 281
Verbs, observability classification of, 48
Verifiability
    behavioral explanations, 14–15
    of prediction, reversal design, 128
Video modeling, 301
Video prompting, 301
Vineland Adaptive Behavior Scales, 44
Vineland III, 44
Visual analysis, single-subject graphs, 155–158
Visual prompts, 297–300

W

Wechsler Intelligence Scale for Children-V, 44
Whole-interval DRO, 255–260
Whole-interval recording, 82
Wide Range Achievement Test-Revision 5, 44
Woodcock-Johnson® IV Tests of Achievement, 44

X

X-axis, 102–104

Y

Y-axis, 102–104